Y0-BPT-977

Maybe the best rail travel guide you'll ever buy. Jay Brunhouse's paperback is crammed with tips on railroad travel from Ireland to the Ukraine, along with sample timetables, maps, fares, railpass information, route descriptions, and anecdotes. Brunhouse also provides transit and excursion advice for major cities. Don't wait—read it now, before you start planning your trip.
Goeurope.guide@miningco.com

You need a European relative who knows it all and has a few weeks to spare, or better yet, a comprehensive guidebook. Jay Brunhouse's book has everything you need—itinerary suggestions, train and line descriptions, and tips for greater efficiency and economy.
Amazon.com

I cannot imagine any serious European rail traveler being without this book.
Larry Townsend, *Chicago Tribune*

Few books better prepare the train traveler for the pleasures and surprises that await them on the other side of the Atlantic. . . . This is an indispensable guide for first-timers as well as for those who have been there and done that.
Jill Rigby, *Toronto Sun*

Anyone planning a train odyssey in Europe should put the purchase of this book at the top of the list of things to do.
Vincent Randazzo, *New Orleans Times-Picayune*

Written in a witty, supportive tone.
Book News

This is an exuberant invitation to enjoy rail travel all over Western Europe and Britain. Humor contributes to making this a highly readable book.
Robert Scott Milne, *Travelwriter Marketletter*

The book is more than a routine compilation of routes and hundreds of timetables. Brunhouse reveals historical and cultural aspects of the destinations in a readable and entertaining text.
Dallas Morning News

This up-to-the-minute manual sorts out all the details on European rail travel for those who have never used the system. It also brings up to date those people who have traveled Eurail in the past but not in the past couple of years.
Jackie Peterson, *Sacramento Union*

Brunhouse's carefully planned rail adventures take the intrepid voyager from the Arctic Circle in Sweden to the sun-baked beaches of Greece.
Paige Palmer, *World Travel Update*
J. L. Wittmayer, *Valley Magazine*

The definitive effort on traveling by rail through Europe.
Marcia Levin, *The Hallandale Digest*

Inexperienced and experienced travelers alike will benefit from timely advice and numerous tips on touring Europe by train. Recommended.
Library Journal

Brunhouse has written the ideal book for visitors to Europe who want to see plenty of countryside, like to meet people, enjoy comfortable traveling and relish good food on the journey: in other words, like to travel by train.
Marlow Rayner, *HolidayMaker*

If roaming around Europe is on your travel horizon, the train's the answer. And Jay Brunhouse's book gives you all the information.
Philip Sousa, *San Diego Union*

Best Book on Europe train travel.
Jens Jurgen, *Arthur Frommer's Budget Travel*

With this book and a Eurailpass in hand, Europe is your oyster. Guides the traveler through the intricacies of European train travel as smoothly as the Spanish Talgo trains ride the tracks. This book can serve as a valuable resource for the arm-chair traveler and a necessity for the traveler on the scene.
Gay Nagle Myers, *Travel Weekly*

An excellent guide to train travel in Europe.
Eric Lindberg, *Salt Lake Tribune*

Brunhouse has lots of information about the ins and outs of Western and Eastern European trains. Packed with helpful tips on how to save money on tickets, navigating your way through the various train stations and finding hotel accommodations. It includes some easy-to-read rail schedules.
Book Passage Magazine

Brunhouse offers current information about rail passes, travel essentials for trains, and how to avoid problems. Learn which trains travel where and how to find them. Now, go out there and make the most of your trip to Europe. We think you can! **Stacy Myers, *Hemispheres***

What Brunhouse doesn't know about European trains is not worth knowing.
Contra Costa Times

Brunhouse tells us how to get the most enjoyment out of exploring Europe in his book. The paperback is an excellent guide to the joys of inexpensive European train travel. **Bob Young, Sr., *Glendale News-Press***

Brunhouse offers a plethora of information on the most scenic trains in every Eurailpass nation, as well as in-depth general tips on arranging an itinerary, including numerous sample itineraries.
Peter Hamm, *Travel Agent Magazine*

For train enthusiasts and . . . an excellent book within its specific interests.
International Travel News

Traveling *the* Eurail Express

*T*raveling *the* Eurail Express

6th Edition

Jay Brunhouse

PELICAN PUBLISHING COMPANY
Gretna 2004

Maps by Brian Clarke and Jay Brunhouse
Flap maps courtesy Eurail Group GIE (www.eurail.com)
Cisalpino map courtesy Rail Europe

Information in this guidebook is based on authoritative data available at the time of printing. Prices and hours of operation of businesses listed are subject to change without notice. Readers are asked to take this into account when consulting this guide.

Printed in the United States of America

Published by Pelican Publishing Company, Inc.
1000 Burmaster Street, Gretna, Louisiana 70053

Contents

Preface

Train travel in Europe is catering to your needs. The railroads want to get you from place to place as fast, as comfortably, and as conveniently as possible lest other passengers defect to auto and air. Europeans drive their cars to points less than an hour away and fly to points more than four hours away. It is in the one- to four-hour trip range that railroads shine.

The new high speed doesn't peril the traditional scenic routes that delight visitors. These routes have been protected. Government and local authorities underwrite their costs on the grounds that they attract tourists and/or provide service for the communities. These routes remain to charm you.

Throughout all of Western Europe, trains are convenient, comfortable, and economical highways of travel, free of gridlock. Europeans prefer them and, once aboard, you learn why. They give you the opportunity to dart from one city center to another. With insight, you see and enjoy Europe's beautiful rivers, lakes, Alps, seasides and hillside chateaux from panoramic windows. Travelers on Europe's trains save money, learn from Europeans in congenial, give-and-take surroundings, explore corners of Europe where scenery dazzles their eyes, eat and sleep well and soundly, and arrive fully ready to go. They enjoy more than just a trip. They create a memory.

This book tips travelers on Europe's trains about how to get from here to there in the most efficient, convenient, comfortable, and fastest ways while saving money in the act. Pleasure-lovers discover thrilling scenery and wild and secret corners aboard exciting, offbeat trains—comfortable and dazzling—for little money, little hassle, and maximum delight.

Trains steal into hidden corners uncorrupted by automobile exhaust. Those who have traveled in the past are thrilled to discover European trains' time-warp speed, efficient infrastructure, and old-fashioned ambience.

Traveling the Eurail Express gives insight into the art of moving yourself here and there free of stress. Train travelers have perfected this art to its finest form. Take your pencil in hand. This guide tells you how to use Europe's trains and how to discover Europe from Wales to Russia. Highlight the information you'll use and put this book in your travel bag.

New from scratch and remodeled stations, subway links, and airport connections make trains easier to use. You use architecturally stunning new stations, like Lisbon's Oriente, Berlin's Lehrter, and Liege's Guillemins as well as the three new state-of-the-art stations on the route of the TGV Mediterranean: Avignon TGV, Aix-en-Provence TGV, and Valence TGV. In addition, you appreciate the convenience of innovative new stations like Frankfurt International Airport's high-speed *Fernbahnhof* and those remodeled so thoroughly that they look like new, including Zurich, Leipzig, Nuremburg, Bremen, Mainz, and Graz main train stations. You use escalators and ramps instead of steps, read electronic and digital signboards, and use tourist offices located in the stations to help you see the city and book hotels for you. And of course, you can wear mouse ears to the Disneyland Paris TGV station.

Narrow-gauge, cogwheel trains take you to the North Face of the Eiger; lonely lines reach the Midnight Sun at the most northerly station of Western Europe; rickety trams teeter along the cliffs of the Isle of Man, through the feudal highlands of Sardinia, and down Alpine ridges to the French Riviera.

You find that Europe's trains give you more time to enjoy yourself, smoother and more social travel, flexible and simple planning, and—with one of the new crop of cheap rail passes—your best value in Europe.

Acknowledgments

Thank you to those who helped me gather and confirm information, making this edition current and complete. Thank you Veronique Amato, David Boyce, Dave Beal, Helga Brenner-Khan, Eric Buhlmann, Orla Carey, Cece Drummond, Maebeth Fenton, Cyril Ferris, Nils Flo, Hugo Furrer, Guirec Grand-Clement, Lisa Brainin Greenberg, Pat Gudel, Bruce C. Haxthausen, Jean Heger, Christof Heller, Robert Jenkins, Helmut Klee, Andy Lazarus, Chris Lazarus, Benson Leung, Erika Lieben, Alexander Loidl, Joe Lustenberger, Gerhard Markus, Dominique Martin, Silvia Mayr-Pranzeneder, Evelyne Mock, Jan Nijboer, Armond Noble, Louise O'Brien, Liliane Opsomer, Sigrid Pichler, Jim Prchlik, Alan F. Reekie, Richard Rheindorf, Ingrid Rowe, Jim Rowe, Nathan Sawyer, Dag Scher, Kirsten Schmidt, Jayne Shackleford, Cynthia Smith, Malcolm Smith, Sandra Tharas, Patricia Titley, Robert Titley, Richard Tretten, Elke van Dommelen, Pilar Vico, and Alan C. Wissenberg. I also thank Rail Europe for the Eurail Flexipasses that allowed me to write and update this edition. Flowery bouquets to expert editor Nina Kooij.

Introduction

There is feeling and thrill in traveling Europe's trains. Eurostar under the English Channel, across the Oresund Fixed Link to Sweden, TGVs, ICEs and gracefully tilting Pendolinos ignite travelers' sense of imagination with their thundering "whooshes," space-age speed, and sci-fi interiors. At the beginning of each chapter, read the Savvy Traveling tips about how to get from here to there in the most efficient and economical ways. The first chapter helps you plan and takes you to Europe, well coached, with the right rail pass in your hand. You are guided aboard your train, to your destination, and back onto your train again so carefully a first-time traveler will have no worries. It steers veteran travelers toward overlooked scenery and wild and secret corners aboard exciting trains—the most comfortable and the most dazzling—for little money, little hassle, and maximum delight. You choose the scenic trains to enjoy. It makes traveling Europe's trains a snap.

You won't have to wave your passports at border guards or be disturbed during the night for passport checks when traveling between countries participating in the Schengen agreement. These include Austria, Italy, France, Germany, Spain, Portugal and the Benelux countries. Switzerland has not participated—no surprise.

Experienced travelers know all national train systems have their quirks and secrets. Chapters revealing the fascination and operation of traveling through the Eurotunnel by train, taking you aboard Europe's trains from Dublin to Moscow, through the Alps, and from the Midnight Sun to the Mediterranean beaches show you how to use trains to your advantage. Trips taking you everywhere a train ticket goes—West Europe, Britain, and East Europe, too—are described in careful detail to simplify your traveling and your planning so you return home happy, filled with memories, and still with money in your bank.

Timetables follow each trip to give you the latest schedules. Remember that summer and winter timetables change yearly. Times are shown using the same twenty-four-hour clock you see in Europe. Major cities and connections are capitalized, and indications in a time column show you when the train does not stop at that station. Notes indicate special restrictions and tell you what you will find aboard your train. Here is your first tip: when you can punch up a twenty-four-hour clock on your digital watch, use this mode when reading timetables.

Other travel books tell you where to stay and what to see. This one tells you how. It gives you tips to make your travel time exciting, social, and offbeat—every moment a pleasure.

For simplicity, this book has dropped all the umlauts, accents, and other pronunciation marks you see as you travel. The Thomas Cook European timetable retains all local spellings.

Will you have language troubles in Western Europe? None. Most of the words you need to know to travel by train are obvious. Pictographs (illustrated in the free rail pass reference materials you send for) are used throughout Europe—and you won't need them in Britain. You have found already most of the important word translations in this book.

City names are generally the same as in English. Just a few baffle: Copenhagen is Kobenhavn; Florence is Firenze; Venice is Venezia in Italian, Venedig in German; Antwerp is Anvers in French, Antwerpen in Dutch; Geneva is Geneve in French, Genf in German; Munich is Munchen in German, Monaco in Italian (the state of Monaco is Monte Carlo to the Europeans); Vienna is Wien; Helsinki is Helsingfors in Swedish; Athens is Athinai; Prague is Praha; Warsaw is Warszawa; Moscow is Moskva; the Danube is the Donau; Hauptbahnhof is German for main train station and Bahnhof refers to any train station.

It's advisable always to travel as though you were trekking through

New York's Times Square, but it is never so dangerous. Except for areas of high drug activity and unemployment, such as in Eastern Europe, most travelers report smooth and safe travel. Paranoia is not worth your mental effort, but caution is. (One publicized incident where travelers on a night train were reputedly gassed and robbed sounds as likely as flying saucers.) Carry little cash, preferably in a hanging pouch, rely on ATMs, and keep separate a photocopy of your passport and credit cards.

Savvy Traveling on the Trains of Europe

Arranging Your Itinerary

*Study guidebooks—Milk tourist offices—Get free train informa-
tion—Use the Web—Plot your train travel strategies craftily—Let
travel agents fill in the blanks*

Study Guidebooks

You can gather all your general and specific information about
packing, hotel and hostel accommodations, air transportation, food,
shopping, and sightseeing from guidebooks in your library and book-
shops. Tailored for train travelers with flexibility are the *Let's Go*
guides, edited by the Harvard Student Agencies (St. Martin's Press,
175 Fifth Avenue, New York, NY 10010). Pelican also has a complete
line of destination guides that you should consult (Pelican Publishing
Company, P.O. Box 3110, Gretna, LA 70054-3110).

Milk Tourist Offices

After you have a general idea of your plans, check the Internet and
contact the national tourist office of every country you think you
might possibly visit. Their addresses and Web sites are in Appendix A.

Don't simply ask for "information" or you will receive broad-brush brochures with pretty pictures. Ask specifically for details about your special interests, e.g., discount programs for hotels, subway savings and maps, castles to see, scenic bicycle routes, city "keys" or discount programs for museum admissions and city tours, regional maps and sightseeing in specific cities and areas.

Get Free Train Information

Even when you are not considering buying a Eurail product, its distributors provide you with excellent, free information (see below, and Appendix A for addresses). Ask for all the following:

• The Eurail/InterRail eighty-nine-page timetable (with map) for the best European InterCity trains.

• "Eurail Traveler's Guide" and large-scale Eurail Map. The foldout Eurail train map of Europe will be indispensable in planning your trip and the Traveler's Guide tips you to the basics and bonuses.

• "Europe on Track" (from Rail Europe, *www.raileurope.com*), "Europe Rail" (from DER Tours, *www.dertravel.com*), "Discover Europe by Train" (from CIT Tours, *www.cit-tours.com*), "Britain Secrets" and the excellent "Best of Britain by BritRail" (from BritRail, *www.BritRail.net* or *www.britainsecrets.com*), giving you Eurail and other rail-pass prices and rules.

• Free area maps from Rail Europe covering Spain/Portugal, Central Europe, and/or Italy.

Rail Europe has a fast and convenient tool for you to obtain train schedules and prices between city pairs by fax-back. Dial either 1-888-382-7245 or 1-800-EUROSTAR and select from a menu of four options: information on rail passes, hotels, air, and rental cars; information on specific countries; information on train fares and schedules between more than 3,000 European cities; or a brochure. When you enter on your telephone keypad your arrival and departure cities you receive fare and schedule information for train travel between them, and when you then enter your fax number, almost immediately your fax machine receives the printout, which you can use for your planning.

Use the Web

The Web is overflowing with travel information. Almost every railroad company has a Web page. To save cataloging the many sites, you can access the GermanRail site at *www.bahn.de* and then click on "virtual railways" for links to most sites. A search engine will quickly locate country, regional, and city tourist-office Web sites. Specific Web sites are identified in the text.

MERITS (Multiple European Integrated Timetable Storage) was officially launched on December 3, 2002. The database was developed to centralize timetable data on both national and international trains (approximately 180,000 trains of thirty-two European railroads). You can access MERITS through *www.bahn.de* and many of the national railroads Web sites. Simply enter "from" and "to" and choose your date and time of departure or arrival. By clicking "earlier" or "later" you can scan the offerings. Do not worry about other details, which are only used for pricing information.

EU-Spirit (*www.vbb-fahrinfo.de*) is a European travel information system offering calculation of door-to-door travel itineraries between European cities or regional areas. It is not a travel planner in itself. It will give you your total plan from street address to street address. It works for addresses in Denmark, Germany, Italy, Sweden, and Austria.

Also check to see whether the reference desk of your public library has a copy of the Thomas Cook European Timetable, which is updated monthly. Should your library fail you, look for it in bookstores specializing in travel literature. If there is no travel bookstore near you, order the timetable from Forsyth Travel Library (1-800-FORSYTH). June and subsequent summer issues have the complete summer timetables.

The European railroads have agreed to synchronize their timetable changes to mid-December, but there will be significant midyear revisions as new services come online or are delayed. The complete timetables are generally too bulky to carry around. In some countries they run into many volumes. Agents in the train information offices will check their computers for you, but most railroads also publish pocket-sized timetables for their most heavily traveled routes and place on racks leaflets listing connections between popular city pairs or regions. These are available, free for the asking, in the information offices of the railroads (not the tourist offices) in train stations.

Plot Your Train Travel Strategies Craftily

Consider several travel strategies depending on where you decide to go and what you want to do. Travelers covering long distances prefer the circular trip plan. Start and end your train travel at your airline's

European gateway and cover your stops with a circular plan that brings you back to your gateway city. (You can sometimes arrange an "open-jaw" airline ticket that allows you to return from a different city than the one in which you arrived.) When you want to see Europe extensively, you can see more using this plan.

You have best results when you plan at least one overnight following your arrival at your airline gateway city to allow for jet lag and familiarization, and at least two when you return there. This gives you flexibility to change your plans or cope with any unexpected delays during your trip.

Before you leave home, make a working itinerary. Using your timetables, select the best trains as given chapter by chapter. Outline your day, city, and train connections. Carefully note the days of the week because some trains do not run on weekends or local holidays.

Make your itinerary loose enough so you can vary it depending on circumstances. Keep backup and alternative plans in the back of your mind. You can usually count on reliable train connections, but strikes and natural disasters such as floods and washouts can (and do) devastate split-second plans.

Some travelers save money by alternating nights in hotels and aboard trains. They travel on an overnight train, check into their hotel in the morning, shower, etc., do their sightseeing in the afternoon, and see the city by night. On the following day, they check out of their hotel, leave their luggage with the concierge, top off their daylight sightseeing, dine, pick up their luggage, and leave on the late-evening overnight train for their next destination. This plan works either with a consecutive-day rail pass or a flexible rail pass allowing you to validate a single box for overnight trains departing after 7 P.M. (see below).

The second strategy involves locating in one city and taking day trips to nearby places of interest. This fits well with a flexible rail pass because you can conserve your day boxes for long distances. You double your time on the train and return to your bed at the mercy of the train schedule, but you won't waste time packing, unpacking, and checking in and out of hotels. When you want to see an area intensively, this is the plan you follow.

Let Travel Agents Fill in the Blanks

The right travel agent will save you a lot of time and effort and surprise you with good advice. Their computers handle rail passes. Let them buy for you your Eurail, regional, and national rail-pass products, hotel packages, and airline tickets. They also can make reservations (up to two months in advance) for seats, overnight sleeping cars, and couchettes in the trains. Make your sleeping reservations at the same time you buy your rail pass, as soon as you can, to avoid electronic glitches. You must pay a service charge for seat reservations, making them more expensive than when you make them in Europe, so unless it is essential to secure them early, which is particularly important when you plan travel before holidays such as Easter, you are generally wiser to wait until you arrive in Europe and visit your first train station to make reservations.

In conjunction with rail passes, Rail Europe and Destination Europe Resources offer "Go as you please" hotel voucher plans for use throughout Europe (see "Locating a hotel room," below) and Hilton International Hotels offer discounts.

It's not worth agents' time to write your letters for inexpensive hotels or pensions, and you are better off handling this yourself before you leave or, even easier, arranging accommodations at the tourist office when you get there. Most travelers like to have a confirmed place to stay for the day they arrive and then make their subsequent arrangements as they travel along.

Choosing the Right Pass

Eurail products—Pass protection—Eurail Selectpass—Eurail Flexipass—National and regional rail passes—European East Pass—Rail/Drive passes

Eurail Products

The national train companies of seventeen countries—Austria, Belgium, Denmark, Finland, France, Germany, Greece, Hungary, Republic of Ireland, Italy, Luxembourg, the Netherlands, Norway, Portugal, Spain, Sweden, and Switzerland—belong to the Eurail system and honor Eurail products to give you free passage over their networks, although some trains may require a surcharge.

For those with wide-ranging travel plans, a Eurailpass is your best bet. It continues to be the favorite of youth/student travelers. Eurailpasses let you make a grand tour of seventeen Western European countries without ticketing every leg. You can use your additional days to enjoy some of the bonuses free with Eurail products, such as the Rhine River cruise.

You can choose consecutive-day Eurailpasses for fifteen or twenty-one days or one, two, or three months. Treat it like a cow. Milk it every day. Eurailpass gives you free the kinds of things you would want to do even if you had no other reason to buy the pass itself. Read how best to use them in each section of this book.

It is true that when you pay for all your transportation in one lump sum, Eurail products seem like a lot of money, but nothing approaches their value when you take total advantage of them.

• They are convenient. By buying rail passes before leaving home, you avoid standing in lines at counters you sometimes can't find to purchase tickets or surcharge coupons in unfamiliar currencies from foreign agents who often do not speak English (this problem is acute in Eastern Europe). This frees you to board almost any train you choose, thus making it easier for you to travel on impulse, especially on the more popular lines with trains departing hourly.

• They are easy to use. You don't have to sort through stapled and loose tickets and coupons to show the conductor. Just flash your pass.

• You can change your mind. When an acquaintance convinces you to go to Rome instead of Vienna, just board the next train. When it's flooding in Venice, get off the train in sunny Salzburg.

• They are cheap when the dollar is weak vs. the euro. You pay in low-inflation dollars. Fixed prices reflect last year's exchange rate and protect you from creeping dollar devaluation.

• You pay at home and know in advance to the cent exactly how much your transportation will cost. When crises rack the European currency markets, you are secure in having locked in dollar prices before departure. If the dollar sags, wheezes, or does a loop the loop, you have no worry.

• Free train travel information gives you a planning edge. Maps and pocket timetables guide you through Europe.

Eurail products cover fast-train surcharges with only a few exceptions. You sit in first-class sections of the best trains of Europe without having to go to the trouble and expense of buying a supplement coupon. Further, you have access to the handful of elite trains that are limited to buyers of first-class tickets only, such as the panoramic dome cars of the Swiss railroads.

Your travel agent provides your Eurailpass with the line blank where your passport number is to be entered. Before you board your first train, you must have staff at the train station (any train station in Europe) validate the pass by entering your passport number and hand-stamping it or validating it with the agent's validator. Agents in some countries have been instructed to ask you when you will begin your travel in order to keep you from wasting days and will refuse to validate your pass in advance so you will have to wait in line again, carrying your luggage, when you depart. This is silly especially when you have bought a flexipass allowing a small number of travel days within a generous time and thus will lose no travel days by not traveling immediately after validation. *Tip:* When asked, always tell the agent, "Today."

When traveling, you should keep your passport handy so the conductor can check it against the passport number on the rail pass. In practice this happens very rarely, except where forgeries have been found. Arrests have been made in Hungary.

The Eurail Executive Committee authorizes four European railroads to distribute Eurailpasses in North America: French, Swiss, German, and Italian. These are represented by Rail Europe (FrenchRail owns the majority interest, SwissRail the minority), Destination Europe Resources (originally owned by GermanRail), and CIT Tours (Italian Railroads). In addition, in 2003, Eurail designated ACP Marketing, based in Canada, as Worldwide Sales Agent. Each of the companies also market national and regional passes associated with their interests including a stable of passes for travel in Eastern European countries.

Buy your pass through your travel agent or directly through the distributors. Their addresses are listed in Appendix A.

Travelers planning to visit Europe in the spring (through June) can compound their savings by buying at the last tick of the old year's clock, when rail pass prices may increase. When you buy before the turn of the calendar, you have six months to validate your rail pass in Europe before boarding your first train. This makes it particularly convenient for travelers planning to use passes valid for longer periods of time, such as one or two months, because you can validate your pass before your deadline in June, and travel during the summer at the previous year's prices (which were set even the year before that).

Eurail products are most easily purchased from your nearby travel agent at home. But—contrary to popular notion—permanent residents of North and South America, Australia, New Zealand, most of

Africa, and Asia excluding the C.I.S. who have been in Europe less than six months may also purchase them in Britain and the Eurail countries at any of the Eurail Aid offices listed in Appendix B. In addition to being less available in Europe, they are sold at a 10 percent premium over the price you pay at home and you must pay in local currencies. This latter restriction is less onerous than you would think because most Eurail Aid offices accept MasterCard and Visa. The price is pegged to the U.S. dollar price plus 10 percent, so no matter whether the dollar is weak or strong relative to the currency of the country where you make your purchase, you will always pay 10 percent more than at home.

When you start your trip between 7 P.M. and midnight, date the box with the following day so your validation continues until the following midnight. Some travelers ride overnight and use up only one validation date while avoiding the cost of lodging.

Traveling on one of the overnight international sea crossings covered by Eurailpass uses up only one validation date because you enter either the date of departure or the next day's date to take advantage of connecting trains at both ends.

Eurail gives a 15 percent discount for groups of two or more travelers traveling together on a first-class consecutive or flexipass basis. The problem is traveling together. Your group can't break up and go traveling off in separate directions and still qualify for the discount. However, children aged four to eleven pay only half price but count fully as part of your group. When you tailor your traveling to these restrictions, you qualify for the good deal.

When you are younger than twenty-six on your first day of travel, you qualify for a 30 percent discount for a second-class Youthpass. You save money of course, and you find it easier to meet Europeans of your same age, who almost always will be traveling at the lower fares. Second-class travel is more crowded, more social, and every bit as scenic as first-class travel.

Rail passes do not cover Eurostar trains from London to Paris or Brussels, but those with Eurail products valid in France or Benelux—BritRail, France Railpass, two-country France Railpasses, or Benelux Tourrail—receive discounts up to 50 percent.

The blemish on rail passes is that holders are required to pay supplemental charges on many of the most scenic and fastest trains. The list of these is long, but the most blatant examples include Thalys,

AVE, and Eurostar Italia. Deluxe overnight trains always include sleeping supplements. Reservations, even when required, are included in the ticket price only when a supplement payment is required.

BritRail, Eastern European countries (except Hungary), and some private lines are not affiliated with the Eurail system. If you enter a Eurail country from a non-Eurail country, the conductor on the train is responsible for validating your rail pass. The passes do not cover reservation fees, special business train supplements for meals or deluxe seats, the Flam line supplement (see "Scandinavia" chapter), and charges for sleeping accommodations on trains or aboard ships.

Eurail Youthpasses give you the same benefits and bonuses as first-class Eurailpasses, except that you must pay to upgrade to first-class-only trains and express steamers on the Rhine River. You would only ride these anyway when you travel with parents or older adults (especially when they need you to qualify for a Eurail Saverpass) or when you want extra comfort and greater flexibility with a full-fare Eurail product.

Pass Protection

The European Railroads' policy is that no pass is refundable or replaceable if lost or stolen, but North American distributors have come up with plans that protect you against this. If you sign up for their plan, at a cost of $14 per pass, they will compensate you for the unused portion of a lost or stolen pass. To qualify for reimbursement, you need to file a police report, and then you must purchase a replacement rail pass or rail ticket and complete your train travel. You will be reimbursed for the unused value of the pass. The procedure and conditions for obtaining a reimbursement are listed in a flyer that you receive with your pass.

BritRail Passes are never refunded or replaced. Refunds are limited to completely unused, unvalidated passes returned within six months to one year of date of issue and subject to cancellation charges of 15 percent.

Eurail Selectpass

The radical Eurail Selectpass, first offered to travelers on January 1, 2001, and expanded in 2003, turned upside down traditional rail-pass buying and the travel habits that had gone with it. For shorter and more geographically limited European travel, the Eurail Selectpass allows you to travel among any three, four, or five adjoining Eurailpass countries (seventeen in total, plus Romania in 2004, making eighteen), whether they are adjoined by land or water. You select the countries you know you will visit. Examples include Germany-France-Ireland, Germany-Denmark-Finland, Switzerland-Italy-Greece, and, because Benelux is counted as one country for Selectpass purposes, Netherlands-Belgium-Luxembourg-Germany-Austria. Monaco is counted with France and Liechtenstein merges with Switzerland. Norway and Finland are not considered adjoining, which will surely surprise the Nordic border customs officials.

The Eurail Selectpass is available only as a flexipass for five, six, eight, and ten days within two months so a Selectpass is more economical for you if you only plan to travel in three, four, or five countries.

Flexipasses are do-it-yourself passes. Your airline-style pass includes spaces to date in ink on the days you travel. Enter the date when you decide to board the train—or aboard the train quickly when the conductor ("controlleur") starts to pass through—but enter it carefully with the correct date because the conductor is not allowed to accept cross-outs and you will waste a date. Then you travel that entire day as much as you want until midnight.

When you choose a Eurail flexi product or national flexipass that you can use at your discretion, it makes sense to conserve the days for long-haul travel and buy local tickets for inexpensive, short excursions. *Tip:* Buy a flexipass valid for the number of days you will be making long, expensive trips. Any trip that costs under $40, ticket on the spot, point to point.

The Eurail Selectpass is available as a Saverpass for two to five persons traveling together at all times, which gives a 15 percent discount. A Eurail Youth Selectpass is available to persons ages twelve to twenty-five for a discount of 30 percent, traveling second class.

Eurail Flexipass

Travelers do best buying consecutive first-class Eurailpasses when traveling extensively across Europe, but those visiting only a few international destinations save money buying Eurail Flexipasses or Eurail Youth Flexipasses. These provide travel for the specific number of days required and allow a reasonable time in which to use them. Their advantage over a Eurail Selectpass is that you can buy them for longer durations and use them in as many of the seventeen Eurail countries as you please.

There was a time when European trains were blooming with flower children holding Eurailpasses and knocking about carefree from Narvik to Naples. Those days are long gone. Modern rail-pass purchasers are known to be more likely to stop longer at a single destination.

Eurail Flexipasses gives you new options in planning. You stay as long as you want in one place without squandering money you invest in a pass. Concentrate your time in fewer locations and range less far afield with your travel adventures. Break your train traveling to rent a car, spend some time with relatives in the old country, sunbathe on a Greek isle, ski in Switzerland, or even take time to visit England or Eastern European countries that don't honor Eurail products.

The Eurail Flexipass is available as a Saverpass for two to five persons traveling together at all times, which gives a 15 percent discount. A Eurail Youth Flexipass is available to perons ages twelve to twenty-five for a discount of 30 percent, traveling second class.

National and Regional Rail Passes

So many American travelers use Eurail products on long European express trains that conductors' eyes sometimes blur checking the passes. When a conductor sees you flashing the colorful rail pass of his homeland, he knows you have an interest in his country. He adjusts his eyeglasses, smiles, and mentally snaps to attention.

Most national railroads of Europe have their own all-purpose rail passes valid for unlimited travel within their borders. Some are good deals you buy in advance in U.S. dollars. The most popular ways to save money—and have lots of fun—are the best-selling passes of Britain, Finland, France, Germany, Italy, the Netherlands, Norway, Spain, Sweden, Switzerland, and the Eastern countries. Regional passes for Scandinavia, Iberia, Benelux, Britain + Ireland, European East (Austria, Hungary, Poland, the Czech Republic, and Slovakia), two-country France Railpasses, and Balkan Railpass combine travel on several networks and extend the coverage you receive with a Eurail product.

Such passes save you money in several ways. You pay less per day, adults can travel second class at lower prices, you take juniors with you and pay as little as half for their tickets (free with a Swiss Pass), and sometimes you receive useful side benefits that are more generous than Eurail bonuses.

National rail passes and regional rail passes do not let you travel across unlimited national boundaries like the continent-wide Eurail products, but when you plan to travel in a single country or region these passes will save you money compared to a Eurailpass. Residents have their own promotional pass programs for which you are ineligible.

Travelers buying a single-country or regional pass use the same reasoning to decide whether to buy consecutive-day or flexible rail passes when both are available. When you want to travel extensively, you choose consecutive rail passes. When you want to travel selectively, you take Flexipasses. You get even more value from Youth Flexipasses when you combine them with inexpensive second-class national and regional passes according to your travel plans.

European East Pass

A European East Pass is a crutch to get you around Eastern Europe without complications. You feel free to travel as you please over the national railroads of Austria, the Czech Republic, Hungary, Poland, and Slovakia without ticketing. It is available for five to ten days in one month in first or second class. Travelers under twenty-six now save 30 percent over the cost of the five-country pass. Children four to eleven pay half the adult fare; those under four travel free. After you purchase your pass, you have six months to validate it at *any* train station in Europe, not necessarily in Eastern Europe.

You travel as you wish aboard good international EuroCity (EC) trains and crack InterCity (IC) trains between all major cities. Regional and local trains complete the five extensive national networks. None of the countries requires visas for Americans, but Canadians need a visa for the Czech Republic.

Reservations are required on many of the better trains, but when you carry a first-class rail pass, you will find the first-class sections relatively empty, compared with the often-crowded second-class sections. Travelers who enjoy leaning out windows and cursing air-conditioning will love these trains. The windows can be lowered after you locate the push button in the stainless-steel grip at the top.

The Puchberg am Schneeberg-Hochschneeberg rack railroad gives a 10 percent discount to European East Pass holders. The ships of Wurm & Kock give a 50 percent reduction for trips on the Danube between Linz and Passau and the ships of the DDSG Blue Danube Line allow a 20 percent discount on trips between Melk, Krems, and

Vienna. You also receive a reduced price to rent bicycles at over forty train stations in Austria.

Rail/Drive Passes

When you want to combine local driving with train travel, look to the Rail/Drive passes available in Britain, France, Germany, Iberia, Italy, and Scandinavia and to Eurail products. A Rail/Drive pass can be an ideal marriage, but leave the driving to your spouse.

Some of your friends report good results driving through Europe in rented cars. They argue fiercely with others who advocate train travel. Both cite the relative convenience, cost, and ability to learn about and appreciate Europe while traveling by their favorite means.

Rental-auto advocates insist that you can visit villages not served by trains and thus take advantage of cheaper lodging; that you can drive to the front door of your destination and make detours on a whim.

The most common reason that you hear for not traveling by train is that train travel doesn't let you see the countryside or reach remote areas. Renting a car, just like at home, seems to be a solution, but Europe is different than home. Visiting Europe gives you the additional, and better, viable option of traveling by train—an option you don't have at home.

Annually, you see four times as many fatal accidents on European roads as on North American ones. Your chance of having an accident in Europe is 125 times greater on a highway than on a train. Each year, nearly 60,000 people are killed on the roads in western Europe, but the railroads have managed to improve their safety record, year in and year out. Twenty years ago there was 1.0 passenger fatality per billion train passenger miles, but today this figure has fallen to 0.3. Renting a car means cursing gridlock, fighting congestion, and watching the road ahead. Is this why you visit Europe? The cost can also be higher than expected, considering the high cost of gasoline, taxes of 6 to 33 percent, and highway and bridge tolls.

Local trains carry visitors to remote towns just as easily as rental cars. Unlike the train system in North America, the European rail system not only spreads out like a series of high-speed connecting webs between major cities, but connecting local trains take you from the closest hub to the tiniest village. When you visit friends, they expect to meet you in front of the station. Otherwise use the taxi, streetcar, or subway in front of the station.

Everyone who has traveled by train will tell you that you get on and off easily. With a train, you don't isolate yourself, you get the feeling of the country, you learn information you can use, and you gain insights from the Europeans you meet in your train compartment. You cut the red tape, insurance headaches, and difficulties of picking up and returning cars. You see more than when you are behind a wheel cursing crazy drivers or buried in a road map sorting out lines that don't seem to exist. You don't have to stuff the back seats of small automobiles with your luggage or worry about it or the car getting ripped off. You don't suffer the quirks of foreign automobiles or strange, and sometimes dangerous, obscure rules of the road. You don't have to search out parking places, figure out the parking fee system, and walk even greater distances through pedestrian malls from a parking place than from the train station.

Whether Rail/Drive passes will save you money depends on your travel plans. When you drive the cars here and there along your route you save considerably over expensive one-day car rentals. But when you break your travels and drive a car from one location for an extended time, a weekly rate may save you money.

Rail passes give you the freedom to travel easily over long distances. Your car gives you local transportation, delivers you to doorsteps of relatives, and takes you to special, secluded hideaways.

Rail/Drive Avis and Hertz plans in connection with national rail passes work similarly. The car-rental companies have locations throughout Europe (and on the Greek islands), many in or near train stations. On average their European fleets are less than six months old and English-speaking personnel are on call twenty-four hours a day.

Hertz offers a special plan to Eurail holders who are twenty-six years and older. The rate includes unlimited mileage, collision damage waiver, and local taxes. You can reserve through a Hertz reservation center in Europe or directly in Europe at the nearest Hertz office.

Boarding Your Train

Using subway and rapid-transit services—Finding your departure platform—Locating your proper carriage—Dining on wheels

Using Subway and Rapid-Transit Services

All of Europe's major cities have either a subway or a rapid-transit connection to their principal train stations—and usually both.

Subways save you steps by bringing you directly into the platform areas in many stations ("Bahnhof," "Estacion," "Gare," "Pu," "Stazione"). Rapid-transit trains, which in all cases you ride free with a Eurail product except for Paris's RER rapid-transit electric trains not connecting with an airport, sometimes let you off on platforms parallel to the one from which you leave.

Almost all major cities have two or more train stations. Be absolutely certain you go to the correct one. You don't want to carry your luggage into Paris's Gare d'Austerlitz only to find out your train is boarding at the Gare de Lyon.

Finding Your Departure Platform

When you arrive, especially when you are in a hurry, immediately look for departure information. This could be in the form of numeric signs, clacking digital signs, huge electronic displays, or old-fashioned, yellow posters—"Abfahrt," "Avgaende," "Avgang," "Depart," "Lahtevat," "Partenze," "Salida," "Vertrek" (not the white ones, nor the ones printed in red in the Netherlands; those are for train arrivals). They confirm your departure time and tell you the number of the departure platform or track ("Arden," "Bahnsteig," "Binario," "Gleis," "Linho," "Plattaforma," "Quai," "Raide," "Spar," "Spoor," "Spor," "Via," "Voie").

Locating Your Proper Carriage

While you are walking to your platform, look for posters (sometimes on blue paper) or glassed-in bulletin boards ("Composition des Trains," "Composizione Principali Treni," "Indulo Vonatok," "Kaukojunien Vaunujarjestys," "Nemzetzoki Vonatok Osszeallitasa," "Placement des Voitures," "Stand van de Rijtvtgen," "Var i Taget gar Vagnen," "Vognanviser," "Vognenes Placering i Perron Afsnit," "Wagenstandanzeiger") with color-coded cutouts of lined-up locomotives and train carriages (couchettes, dining, first and second class, etc.). You may see these anywhere but most often right in the center of the departure platform when you get there. It is easiest to pick out your train by its departure time.

On these posters you identify the carriage in which you have a reservation by its destination and carriage number. Often, vertical lines or strings are superimposed to form a grid. A "sector" ("repere," "secteur," "Sektor," "vagnlage") letter (*A, B, C,* etc.) indicates where your carriage now stands or will stand when it arrives. These letters are prominently hung above the proper platform locations. Walk to the stopping sector for your carriage to avoid having to rush down the platform when your long train pulls in and makes ready to depart. When you have no reservation and are traveling by rail pass—and don't care which carriage you board—still determine where the carriage you prefer to your specific destination comes to a stop.

While you are looking at the train makeup, look to see whether your train is carrying a buffet or restaurant car and where it is located relative to your carriage.

In Swiss stations, in addition to composition boards, the digital departure signs above the platforms give you the entire train make-up at the bottom: an arrow indicates the direction the train travels, a "1" indicates each first-class carriage, a knife-and-fork dining symbol indicates the restaurant car, and a "2" indicates each second-class carriage. Below this shorthand is a note telling at which sector the car for children will arrive. (These carriages are marked with a teddy bear and a "Kinderwagen" sign.) Zurich Hauptbahnhof's digital signs contain lists of destinations, type of train, departure time, and digits showing how the carriages stand in sectors *A, B,* and *C.*

A yellow stripe above the carriage windows (blue dashes on some Dutch trains) indicates first class although most high-speed trains have abandoned this convention in favor of using more distinguished liveries. When your train slows to a stop, you should be standing beside your carriage, but be sure to check that your destination matches the signboard fixed to the outside of the carriage (some new trains have LED displays on the outside showing destinations and times of arrival). Another signboard is usually posted in the vestibule. French TGV, Thalys, Spanish AVE, and German ICE trains have LED displays in the vestibule showing their destination, train number, and carriage number, so it is difficult to go wrong.

When you are carrying heavy luggage, leave it in the space usually provided at the entryways of salon carriages, but guard it carefully at station stops. When it is light, hoist it onto the overhead rack above your seat or slide it into a space between back-to-back seats.

When you sit in a compartment, you have overhead privileges. Etiquette requires that you pile your suitcases in the space in the overhead rack directly above your seat and not distribute them randomly. This makes it easy to see that your seat is occupied even when you leave it for a moment.

With a reservation, you have an assigned seat. Without one, you must be careful not to sit in one already reserved. These are marked electronically or with paper or plastic strips (usually yellow) inserted in seat backs or on hallway doors. On the other hand, when there is no slip or it says "non reserve" or "nicht reserviert," it is available. When the seat is reserved from Hamburg to Cologne, for example, you are welcome to sit in it between Frankfurt and Basel.

In a compartment, try to sit next to the window facing forward. In a salon car, you can appreciate the scenery better by sitting next to a window at the back of the carriage.

Dining on Wheels

Europe's newest and fastest trains generally position dining cars in the center of the trains, effectively separating first- and second-class carriages. The dining spaces are divided functionally into two sections. The half facing the first-class carriages has tables set with white table-cloths, a complete menu, and waiters standing ready. The adjacent half facing the second-class carriages has a bistro, pub, or cafeteria selling snacks and refreshments or (in Britain) a takeaway counter. Dining cars vary from train to train depending on the market served and customs of the country. You are guaranteed meal service on all international trains, except Thalys on weekends, including Eurostar Italia, EuroCity, most InterCity trains, and all the new night trains, e.g., Tren Hotel, InterCity Night, and CityNightLine.

You find exemplary dining cars on the best EuroCity trains, Switzerland's Glacier Expresses, Germany's ICE 1 trains, and Cisalpino and InterCity trains in Germany, Austria, Italy, and Switzerland. Waiters bring meals to your seat on Eurostar, British InterCities, French TGVs, Spanish Talgos, Norwegian Agendas, Swedish X 2000s, and Finnish InterCities. Wheeled refreshment trolleys (called "mini-bars") overflowing with local specialties, sandwiches, pastries, and refreshments clatter through the aisles on most long-distance trains.

As you would expect, prices are higher aboard trains than in stations and higher in stations than in local supermarkets. Large train stations have some sort of travelers' provisions, supermarket, or grocery store you should visit. One of the more important things to buy for long trips is a liter or two-liter plastic bottle of mineral water with a twist-on cap. Some travelers bring canteens with them. A Swiss army knife with a bottle opener and corkscrew is even handier.

Arriving in Your City

Luggage carts—Changing your money—Locating a hotel room—
Reserving your train connection—Getting to your hotel

When you arrive in a new city, get money, a hotel, and your onward reservation before leaving the station. Public transportation to your hotel is usually a snap.

Luggage carts

Luggage carts are usually available on the platform, and sometimes free for you to use, but in most large stations they are linked together so that to release one you must have a coin of the proper denomination. These annoying mechanisms refund your coin when you lock up your cart. Using the cart costs you nothing, but it means you must have a correct coin when you arrive and must return the cart to a stand.

Big spenders will be pleased to hear that porter services are making a comeback. You can find them in just a few of the largest stations such as Paris Nord, in Italy, and main train stations in Germany. They are not cheap.

When you leave your train you often pass into an underground passageway. The direction toward platform one leads you to the main hall. Here you usually find a change bank, ATMs, a train information office, and—in most countries—a tourist office nearby.

Changing Your Money

The very first thing to do upon arrival is to change for local currency. ATMs are your best bet for favorable exchange rates and they are open after the banks close. Every traveler will benefit from carrying a bank credit card or ATM card for withdrawals or instant cash. These friendly devices will accept your Visa or MasterCard or "Plus" or "Cirrus" network ATM card, depending on whether the machine's bank is affiliated with your home bank. It helps to carry two cards from different banks to increase your chances that one will be accepted. Some machines will read your card as being issued in the United States and automatically give you directions in English. Some call you by name and then refuse the card you carry. Most require you to press the "English" button. Often there are also change machines with directions in English that change currencies twenty-four hours a day. You simply insert banknotes from any hard-currency country and receive bills in the local currency. Beware of any change office that is not a bank. You can expect poorer rates and/or a heavy service charge no matter what the large posters claim. Avoid getting caught with very high denomination coins by changing them into paper before you leave. Spend the lower-denomination coins for provisions.

The euro (€) is the official currency of twelve European countries—Austria, Belgium, Finland, France, Germany, Greece, Ireland, Italy, Luxembourg, the Netherlands, Portugal, and Spain. Every euro coin carries a common European face. On the reverse, each member state has decorated the coins with its own motifs. No matter which motif is on the coins, they can be used anywhere inside the twelve member states. For example, a French citizen will be able to buy a Bratwurst in Berlin using a euro coin carrying the imprint of the king of Spain. Thus, the coins attract the attention of collectors. A Greek or Finnish €1 coin in Amsterdam would be more in demand than a German €1 coin. The euro banknotes are identical, regardless of the country they are issued in, and differ according to denomination in size and color.

Locating a Hotel Room

Your second order of business is locating a room for the night. Some tourists scrupulously follow hotel recommendations in travel guides, but the rule is simple: the more you pay the more you get, and vice versa. Competing hotels on the same block with equal amenities charge virtually the same. In fact, ones recommended in best-selling guides may be able to charge slightly more because of their popularity with guidebook-reading disciples. *Tip:* Beware of hotels that guidebooks describe as "clean." When authors say nothing more positive, look elsewhere.

It's often worth a few minutes after your arrival just to go outside the train station and look around. Frequently you see an attractive or suitable hotel nearby. There are sparkling hotels in Paris's Gare de l'Est and Gare de Lyon. There are hotels right in Madrid's Chamartin and Barcelona's Sants train stations. Glasgow's two stations have hotels in the station. In Cologne and Zurich, you will see clusters of hotels outside the back entrances. GermanRail has an affiliated string of InterCityHotels that you can book right at GermanRail reservation counters. Most of them are located adjacent to the train stations. Find them in Augsburg, Berlin Ostbahnhof, Frankfurt/Main, Hamburg, Magdeburg, Nuremburg, Stuttgart, and Ulm. The InterCityHotel in Munich is not affiliated.

In many large train stations there are two information offices—one operated by the railroads ("Auskunft," "Information," "Inlichtingen," "Neuvonta," "Oplysninger," "Reise Zentrum," "Renseignements," "Travel Centre") and one by the city tourist office. The personnel in the train information office usually will politely refuse to answer your questions about hotel rooms. Those in the city tourist office send you across the station for train information.

You often find the city tourist office ("Bureau de Turisme," "Tourist Information Centre," "Turismo," "Syndicat d'Initiative," "Verkehrsverein," "Verkehrsburo," "VVV") by looking for the information sign: "i." You may see it adjacent to the train information office, a few doors down the street from the exit of the train station, across the street, in a kiosk in the plaza in front of the train station, or nearby, but indicated by an arrow. When the city tourist office does not have a location at the train station, often a commercial, profit-making organization performs the function of finding you a room. In many Swiss and German train stations you find electronic consoles with photos of hotels, their prices, indications of whether they are filled, a city map showing you their locations, and—in Switzerland—automatic, free telephone connections with their room clerks to make reservations.

The best time to arrive at the tourist office for a hotel booking is about 10 A.M. When you arrive at popular or convention destinations late in the afternoon or in the evening, you will find it very difficult or impossible to find a good room unless you have made a reservation in advance. You may have to reboard a train just to find a soft place to sleep.

At the tourist office counter, specify how much you want to pay and the area you want to stay in. Staying near the train station is often convenient, but sometimes an off-color neighborhood is also nearby. The tourist office personnel advise you. You are usually charged a nominal service fee. Sometimes you must also leave a reasonable deposit, which is later deducted from your hotel bill, and are told to check into your assigned hotel within a specified period of time. This time is negotiable when you have errands to accomplish first.

This plan usually gets you a suitable hotel, but in some cities you can't find a tourist office. In any event, you lose time you would rather be spending seeing your new destination.

Rail Europe offers hotel vouchers. Hotels can be either reserved in advance or through toll-free telephone numbers as you go. Sofitel Hotels are usually well-located, modernistic, gleaming business hotels. Mercure offers Spartan, budget rooms in brand-new, efficient settings, sometimes near train stations. Best Western has 1,000 hotels throughout Europe. SRS properties tend to be upscale and located in downtown locations.

Prepurchased vouchers let independent travelers do the following:

• budget exactly how much they are spending in U.S. dollars before they leave,

• know beforehand where they are going to stay so that they won't have to rush to locate a hotel before sunset,

• eliminate time wasted standing in line at the tourist office or otherwise locating a hotel, and

• retain their flexibility.

You already have heard how well rail passes work. You will be delighted to find that vouchers also work marvelously well for train travelers in hotels geared more for independent travelers than business travelers. Careful analysis of the hotel rack rates compared with the price of vouchers shows that vouchers come out price winners, but not by much.

Hotel ratings are of little or no use to independent travelers. Obviously, ratings by an official or quasi-official organization cannot take into account subjective factors such as friendliness, hospitality, and coziness, where smaller hotels excel. Facilities such as a gymnasium or health club may be important to a traveler tired from business negotiations and earn a five-star rating. Independent travelers want to see the sights instead of spending their time within four walls.

During the summer, many of the larger hotel chains try to fill their rooms when business travel slackens by offering discounts. A little Web research can save you up to 50 percent. During July and August, and on weekends only throughout the rest of the year, from Belfast to Bucharest, Hilton International gives 30 to 40 percent off to holders of Eurailpasses. Quote code RR.

Reserving Your Train Connection

Before you leave the train station, go back to make your reservation for your next train. Rail-pass holders do not pay fast-train surcharges but must pay for seat reservations where required. A reservation will cost you several dollars, and if you change your plans you will have to throw it away, but it will save you time and reassure you to make it now.

Reservations are one of the most arbitrary factors in train travel. Each country has its own rules. Modern trends in European train travel seem to be copied from airline experience: speed, at-seat meal service, and, unfortunately, also complicated reservation requirements. High-speed trains, which were on the drawing boards a few years ago, generally demand a reservation.

Which trains require reservations? While you are in the train station, look at the electronic bulletin boards and the yellow departure sheets. The national timetables and the Thomas Cook European Timetable are otherwise your definitive sources. As a reasonable rule of thumb, here is an outline:

In every Western European country, the highest-speed and premium trains require reservations. Obligatory reservations are shown in the timetables by an R surrounded by a box.

On some trains you can make reservations that are not obligatory but recommended. These are shown by a white-on-black R, or (in Italy) *PG*. For your own peace of mind, reserve seats on EuroCity (EC), British IC, and international express trains during busy travel seasons on Fridays, Sundays, and local holidays. Even domestic trains can be fully booked on holidays and especially before Easter. Couchettes and sleeping compartments always require reservations. Regional and local trains are not reservable.

You can make prior reservations up to two months in advance through a travel agent in North America, but it is generally easier and less expensive to make them after you arrive in Europe, at any large train station. Generally you can ask for a seat by a window or next to a corridor, smoking or nonsmoking, but you cannot reserve specific seats.

• In France, seat reservations are available for a small fee on most long-distance trains and are obligatory for all TGV trains within France and Thalys. You can book them as late as the same day you depart. Look for the reservations window marked "Jour." Reservations at the ticket window or on the touch-screen reservation installations allow you to specify smoking or nonsmoking, window or corridor, direction of travel on some TGV Southeast trains, and upstairs or downstairs on TGV Duplex trains.

• Benelux is a reservation-free zone, but even here reservations are required for international Thalys trains.

• In Germany, only the Metropolitan and ICE Sprinter trains require reservations, but all ICEs are reservable and those buying point-to-point tickets receive a reservation included in the price. Board any GermanRail train without a reservation, but be sure not to sit in a seat reserved for someone else.

• In Switzerland, reservations are not required on most trains, except that they are compulsory on the Golden Pass Panoramic, Glacier, William Tell, and some Bernina Express trains. The ETR 470 Cisalpino tilting trains also require reservations when you travel to Italy. You encounter two reservations systems in Switzerland. With EPR you can only choose smoking/nonsmoking and window/corridor; with Resarail you can choose the exact seat.

Seat reservations may be made on all Swiss EC and IC trains. On EC trains between Switzerland and Austria, Italy, and the Netherlands, the Swiss Railroads runs a number of first-class-only observation cars. When you travel first class on these routes, be sure to use these trains and reserve seats in the Panoramawagen.

• In Austria, seat reservations are not required, but you may make them on all EC, National EC, IC, and Fast (D) trains. You may ask for a compartment carriage or one with open seating.

• In Italy, seat reservations are compulsory on all Eurostar Italia/Pendolino trains. Check the timetables. Reservation requirements are strictly enforced in Italy. If you board and find an unreserved seat in a train requiring reservations, the conductor will charge you for the seat, plus a penalty! It is only possible to reserve either a corridor or a window seat, smoking or nonsmoking.

• The Spanish Railroads' (RENFE) long-distance trains can be very crowded at peak hours. Reservations are compulsory. AVEs and Talgo 200 trains using Spain's high-speed corridor fall into a special category. They are not covered by rail passes without payment of a substantial supplement. The special fare structure depends on the class of travel and the time of day. Reservations are included in the supplement. The Spanish computer system automatically allocates smoking/nonsmoking seats.

• In Portugal, seat reservations are compulsory on international, IC, and Alfa Pendular trains. You may make them on InterRegional (IR) trains.

• In Britain, you can reserve seats in advance on all InterCity trains (except Gatwick Express) and on certain Regional Railways and

Network SouthEast trains. It is essential for you to reserve on certain services at peak periods (Friday afternoon/evening, bank holiday, and Christmas periods) and to and from Scotland. You can normally reserve from about two months in advance up to about two hours before departure (for early-morning trains, up to the previous evening). Reservations are obligatory on trains marked in the timetable with a white *R* in a black box. Those marked with an *R* in a white box are often crowded, and reservations are recommended.

• Reservations are not required in either the Republic of Ireland or in Northern Ireland except for the deluxe Gold service between Dublin and Cork.

• All Nordic countries burden their prestige trains with mandatory reservations requirements.

• In Denmark, only trains to Germany and X 2000 trains to Sweden require a reservation.

• Norwegian Railroads (NSB) requires reservations on their Signatur tilting trains (their fastest trains on long routes). If you board without a reservation, the conductor will collect the fee. NSB also requires reservations on their Agenda trains to and from Oslo. Their cost depends on destination and class of service booked.

• In Sweden, you need reservations on all X 2000, IR, and IC trains except on local segments of less than 100 miles. Travelers north to Kiruna/Narvik require a seat, couchette, or sleeping reservation as far as Kiruna. Be sure to reserve trains running above the Arctic Circle far in advance. You can choose your seat window/corridor, facing forward/backward, when you book at a Swedish booking office

• Finland requires that you reserve on IC, S 220 Pendolino, and trains indicated in the timetable. Finnish Railroads has pictures and diagrams of all its coaches both in stations and on its Web site.

Not all booking agents can or want to be bothered speaking or misunderstanding English. You save yourself many headaches by giving to the reservations agent a piece of paper showing your date of travel (numerals for the day, month, and year, in that order), the time you want to leave (using the twenty-four-hour clock), departure city with arrow pointing to destination city, and whether you prefer a smoking or a nonsmoking ("Nicht Raucher," "Niet rokers," "Non-fumar," "Non-fumeurs," "Non fumatori") compartment or section.

Smoking is prohibited on many local and regional trains, but most long-distance trains (which will require reservations) such as

FrenchRail's TGVs (excepting TGV Atlantique, which is nonsmoking), GermanRail's ICEs, and Swedish X 2000s have placed single, separate carriages or compartments front and rear, for first- and second-class smoking passengers respectively, so that nonsmoking passengers will not have to walk through smoke-filled areas to and from the dining or bistro car located in the center of the train.

Present your reservations request simultaneously with your Eurail product and—if you wish—your bank credit card. (To conserve cash, consider using your bank credit cards to make as many Europe-wide advance reservations as possible.) Present all three at once. In many countries there is a minimum credit-card charge.

In larger stations in Germany and in Stockholm's Central station, you find computerized timetable information machines, which print out train connections. You can take the printouts to the reservations counter to show exactly on which train you wish to reserve a seat or couchette.

Usually reservations counters are separated into domestic ("Binnenland, "Inland," "Inrikes," "Interieur," "Paikkalippuja") and international ("Ausland," "Buitenland," "Matkapalvelu," "Utrikes") reservations. Make sure you don't stand in a long line at the wrong counter.

Getting to Your Hotel

Rapid-transit trains and/or subways serve many large train stations. There are almost always discounts available on the subways ("Metro," "Metron/Metroon," "Metropolitano," "Underground," "U-Bahn," "T-Bana") including multiple-ride, magnetically encoded tickets, strip-tickets, and passes for a day, a week, or longer.

Rapid-transit (except Paris's RERs) but not subway trains are covered by your rail pass. In the Munich Hauptbahnhof you find parallel "S-Bahn" and "U-Bahn" lines. Rail passes cover only the former.

International

Savvy Traveling on International Trains

Eurostar under the English Channel—London to Paris in two hours, thirty-five minutes—Le Shuttle—taking your car along—Thalys—red and rapid—Brussels-France TGV—Cisalpino Italy-Switzerland-Germany—ICE International—Artesia takes you between France and Italy—Switzerland-Paris on Lyria—Linx between Norway and Sweden—EuroCity—the European standard

Eurostar Under the English Channel

Eurostar is the brand name of your train. Marketing consultants devised a stylized logo with three wavy strokes to represent the British, French, and Belgian railroads working together and a gold star to indicate the future. Twentieth century's most dramatic train is waiting for you in London's Waterloo International terminal.

The already warmed-up supertrain is ready to take you through the Channel Tunnel and, at 186 mph, over FrenchRail's TGV Nord Europe and Belgian high-speed lines to Paris or Brussels.

Eurostar has a full range of fares, first and second class, some with

advance-purchase and exchange restrictions. The lowest prices on a limited number of seats go to those who book early and those who travel off peak Mondays-Thursdays. Once the lowest-price seats are sold, you receive the next-lower price. There are multiple tiers, depending on class of service and type of ticket. Seniors (over sixty) and youths (under twenty-six) may purchase inexpensive fares without compulsory overnight stays. "First Class" seats you in first-class reclining seats and gives you a meal at your seat and a complimentary newspaper. "Standard Class" provides seats in second-class carriages and allows you to walk to the bar car to purchase food.

Those with a Eurail product or BritRail Pass receive a 30 to 35 percent discount when buying first- or second-class Eurostar tickets. Those with second-class Eurail Youthpasses qualify for the discount even when buying first-class Eurostar tickets. You must validate your pass before your trip on Eurostar. When you have a France Railpass you receive the same discount on Eurostar tickets between France and England. Purchasers of Benelux Tourrail rail passes receive the same discount between Brussels and England. Seniors receive 27 percent off.

Past, Present, and Future

July 29, 1987—Anglo French Fixed Link Treaty signed by Prime Minister Margaret Thatcher and President Francois Mitterand.

1988—Tunnel boring started from English and French coasts.

October 30, 1990—Pilot bore established contact between tunnels from Britain and France.

December 1, 1990—Service tunnels connected.

May 17, 1993—Waterloo International terminal completed.

May 24, 1993—First running of TGV-R over TGV Nord Europe high-speed line.

June 20, 1993—First Eurostar train transported through tunnel for intensive trials and testing.

September 24, 1993—First scheduled TGV-R services on the Nord Europe high-speed line between Paris and Calais, via Lille Flandres station.

March 7, 1994—First running of freight trains through the Channel Tunnel.

May 6, 1994—Official inauguration of the Channel Tunnel by French president Mitterand and Queen Elizabeth, who traveled through it one direction aboard Eurostar and the opposite by car-carrying train.

May 19, 1994—First scheduled operation of truck-carrying trains through the Channel Tunnel.

May 29, 1994—TGV interconnection between TGV Nord Europe and TGV Southeast opened. Disneyland Paris TGV station opened.

November 13, 1994—Paris Charles de Gaulle Airport TGV station opened.

November 14, 1994—Commercial Eurostar train service inaugurated.

December 22, 1994—Scheduled public operation of "Le Shuttle" double-decked, auto-carrying trains.

January 23, 1995—Calais Frethun Station opened to Eurostar traffic.

May 23, 1995—One-millionth passenger traveled on Eurostar.

January 8, 1996—Ashford International Station opened.

June 2, 1996—Opening of the first segment of high-speed line between Lille and Brussels cut travel time between London and Brussels (with stop in Lille) to three hours, twelve minutes; Thalys trains linked Amsterdam and Paris via Brussels in four hours, forty-six minutes.

June 2, 1996—Opening of Jonction Sud allowed direct connections for Eurostar passengers at Lille TGV station to Brittany and the south-west of France.

December 14, 1997—King Albert II and the president of France opened the Belgian high-speed line to link the 186-mph TGV Nord French line to the Belgian capital, cutting journey time between London and Brussels to two hours, forty-five minutes.

October 5, 1998—Construction contracts signed for the Channel Tunnel Rail Link (CTRL). Construction began on CTRL Section One from the tunnel to Fawkham Junction.

December 16, 2002—High-speed line between Brussels and Liege opened to cut travel time to Cologne and Frankfurt.

January 2003—Civil engineering work completed on CTRL Section One.

September 28, 2003—Eurostar commenced service on the CTRL Section One, cutting travel time between London and Paris to two hours, thirty-five minutes; London and Brussels to two hours, twenty minutes.

2005—Tunnel beneath Antwerp will be completed to allow running through Antwerp Central Station.

2005—Upgraded Brussels-Antwerp line will be opened, reducing travel time between London and Amsterdam by seven minutes.

2006—High-speed line between Liege and Welkenraedt will be opened, reducing travel time between London and Cologne by twelve minutes, to three hours, fifty-one minutes.

2006—High-speed line will open from Brussels via Antwerp and Rotterdam to Amsterdam, cutting travel time between London and Amsterdam by fifty-six minutes, to four hours, forty-seven minutes.

2007 (Christmas '06?)—CTRL Section Two through Kent will open from the tunnel to the new St. Pancras Station, cutting travel time between London and Paris to two hours, fifteen minutes; two hours flat to Brussels.

London to Paris in Two Hours, Thirty-five Minutes

Time Zero—Waterloo International

Scripted bilingual announcements are made at 15, eight, and three minutes before departure. English is used first when in England, and French is first in France.

When your yellow-and-white train purrs out of London's Waterloo International station, you feel as though you are embarking on a momentous trip instead of a quick dash to Paris.

You venture where no passenger had gone before. You glide at 100 mph through a $15 billion undersea tunnel beneath the expanse of water that separated Britain from the European continent since the Pleistocene or Ice Age.

In several competitions, two travelers left a common location (usually a hotel) in London (or Paris) at the same time. One traveled to Paris (or London) via Eurostar; one by scheduled airline.

Usually the one traveling by Eurostar arrived at the common destination in downtown Paris (or London) only a few minutes earlier than his partner who had traveled via Heathrow and Paris Charles de Gaulle airports. With the 20 minutes time savings introduced in 2003, the Eurostar passenger should arriver comfortably earlier than his counterpart. Further, Eurostar is on time, or within 15 minutes, 87 percent of the time, compared with 70 percent for the airlines.

So, the time differential is not significant. What the competing travelers did with their time is more important. The air passenger had about 60 minutes in the air to do his or her work, relax with friends, or skim a good book. The Eurostar traveler had up to three hours. When the racers arrived at their destination, it is safe to say that one was groggy. The other was relaxed and ready to go. No wonder Eurostar holds a market share of 65 percent Paris-London and 46 percent Brussels-London.

First class is configured 2+1, but even the passengers seated 2+2 in the second-class carriages feel the freedom of the train despite fewer empty seats. The train's seats are like an airplane's except that they face in two directions, forward and back, so the train won't have to turn around at the end of its run. But passengers feel as though they have more room, even in second class. It is no illusion. If they had a tape measure they would find their second-class seats are on a 33.3-inch pitch. Airlines' B-767s' seven-across seats from London to Paris are configured 2-3-2 with a 32-inch pitch. Your first-class seat has a 36.4-inch pitch, giving you all the legroom you deserve.

Eurostar trains had been in service since 1994, so by 2003 Eurostar decided to restyle the entire concept of Eurostar travel. Management recognized that restyling had to include check-in areas, business lounges, train interiors, and staff uniforms. Eurostar chose renowned French designer Philippe Starck to create a new travel concept under the banner "New Eurostar."

Philippe Starck redecorated the business lounges in London, Paris, and Brussels terminuses with new furniture and cabinetry designed by Starck, including "egg chairs" in warm colors, marble bar tables, high aluminum stools, and remarkable newspaper holders with a touch of British humor.

Starck's new second-class interiors feature yellow- and gray-striped 2+2 seating. His first class has 2+1 solid gray seats with wings to fold out to cradle your head. The revelation is the new premium-class carriage next to the bar car. It has very large, towering seats that Starck thinks are "better than a private jet." The new bar car features wood veneer, jump seats, and a curious transparent table lit from below. The train crews' new uniforms complement the "New Eurostar" concept.

Friendly hosts help you run the magnetic stripe on the back of your Eurostar ticket through the automatic entry gate. Then you pass through a metal detector and the X-ray unit and pass French and British passport controls before you enter the waiting areas. Guards allow passengers onto the platform only 20 minutes before departure. Check-in time is 30 minutes before departure.

The departure lounge has a west wall of glass, so you see the trains through the west sidewall. On the north side, the wall of glass gives you a view of the train shed and platforms of the domestic concourse. You find electronic signboards, an information counter, telephones, shops, a cafeteria, and a bar. There are separate departure lounges for holders of first- and second-class tickets and an exclusive full-service lounge for First Premium ticket purchasers. An information system directed you to the escalator or ramp nearest your seat on Eurostar.

On signal, you board your Eurostar at one of Waterloo International's five platforms, and your quarter-mile-long train rumbles over a familiar path out of Waterloo. Eurostar is sluggish over the British third-rail network, but comes alive once it hits the overhead catenary wire.

Eurostar enters Section One of the CTRL (Channel Tunnel Rail Link) at Fawkham Junction and you immediately feel the acceleration and smoother ride. This is the first new mainline in Britain in over 100 years and the first to be built for 186 mph. In fact, Eurostar set a new British high-speed record of 208 mph over this line on July 30, 2003. A large part of CTRL runs alongside highways, so you can judge your speed against the automobile traffic.

The ride quality throughout the train is truly amazing. At 186 mph it seems like 120 mph (except when passing another Eurostar). Before you reached the high-speed line, 90 mph seemed like 40. One traveler did a coin test of Eurostar's ride. He balanced a pound sterling coin on its edge atop his Eurostar's fold-down table. The coin nestled, most stable, in a groove in the table and remained upright. Try that on a standard British train and you will be chasing your money faster than inflation.

A number of landmarked buildings located along the new route have been relocated, including a medieval barn that was moved from Charing Heath and an 11th-century half-timbered house at Mersham that was moved 180 feet in one piece.

While, as a first-class passenger, you approach the tunnel, a steward serves you a generous meal at your seat that is included in the ticket price. You receive breakfast before 10:30 A.M., lunch until 2:00 P.M., *collation* until 5:00 P.M., and dinner after that. In second class you can visit one of the two bar-buffet carriages or wait at your seat for the mobile trolley service. British and euro currencies are accepted. All products are the same regardless of where you boarded.

0:40 Hour—Ashford

After nearly 50 miles on CTRL Section One, you approach Ashford International Station, 13 miles from the tunnel entrance. It was officially opened on Monday, January 8, 1996. The station cost about $150 million, including platforms, tracks, and signaling, as well as a domestic ticket office. The parking lot has space for 2,000 cars and opens up a large swath of the southeast for park-and-ride passengers.

The Ashford International Station is on two levels with the ground floor consisting of immigration and arrivals halls, ticket office, and entrance concourse. The upper level has a departure lounge for 800 travelers, shops, a cafe, and security control. Flows of arriving and departing international travelers are separated by an underpass and footbridge connecting the station building and international platforms. Frequent trains from many parts of Kent and East Sussex serve the domestic platform at Ashford, north of the Eurostar platforms but linked to them by an underpass.

0:50 Hour—Enter the Channel Tunnel

At Cheriton you slow for the "UK Terminal," where you glimpse the car park, tollbooths (payment by cash, credit card, or prepaid ticket), frontier offices, and a food and shopping center resembling a highway service stop. Cars, buses, and trucks are moving up and down the eight loading and unloading platforms (each 0.6 mile long) for loading onto and off of Le Shuttle.

Eurostar enters the tunnel complex without stopping. Running down the one in 90 gradient, you have no trouble reaching 100 mph in a very short time. You hear a kind of humming—a slight increase in sound level. The windows are pitch black, and all you see for the next 25 or so minutes is a procession of green lights flying past every four seconds. The Channel Tunnel is the longest undersea tunnel ever built, but your Eurostar crossing itself is a short part of your journey. Passengers timing the passage report differences of 27 minutes (69 mph) to 23.5 minutes (80 mph).

For enthusiasts who wish to time their run, from Waterloo station it is 58.1 miles to Ashford, England; 71.3 miles to the north (English) portal; 102.7 to the south (French) portal; 104.7 to Calais; 168.1 to Lille; and 307.7 to Paris.

The Channel Tunnel consists of three separate tunnels. The two train tunnels are known as Running Tunnel North (RTN) and Running Tunnel South (RTS). Between them, and linked to them, is the Service Tunnel (ST). Each of these tunnels is just over 31 miles long. To prevent rabid foxes and rats from racing through the tunnel and infecting England, electrical barriers on the floor stun wayward animals so that they can be repatriated.

You exit near Calais at "Terminal France," the Coquelles complex's loading point (La Cite de l'Europe), which is similar to the British one, but more than four times larger. The unloading of the automobiles reminds you that the French and English normally drive on different sides of the road and you wonder how easily British visitors will adapt—a frightening thought—to the French style of right-hand-side, aggressive driving.

1:13 Hours—Calais-Frethun

Don't forget to adjust your watch for the one-hour time change. Several Paris-bound Eurostar trains call at FrenchRail's first station, Calais-Frethun, two miles after you leave the Channel Tunnel. Passengers from London are allowed to disembark, but passengers coming from Paris are not, on the theory that terrorists might leave a bomb on Eurostar before it enters the Channel Tunnel.

From here you follow the lines of TGV Nord Europe to Paris and Eurostar accelerates effortlessly to 186 mph. Drivers are required to tell the train captain when the train reaches that speed so that he may announce it to the passengers. Sometimes drivers never need to reach 186 mph, but they exaggerate so that you can go home with a smile on your face and tell your friends.

You have a chance to look at your 20-carriage-long (1,291 feet) train. You think of Eurostar as a train. It is also a computer network on wheels. Each carriage has its own computer; the power cars have 11 at each end. Each computer interacts and exchanges information. The 18-carriage train is divided into two mirror-image segments, each with three first-class carriages, five second-class carriages, and a bar car (plus a power car for each segment). This feature allows the train to be separated for removal from the tunnel, if necessary, and also allows the train to split for eventual destinations beyond London or Paris.

Each first-class car seats 39; each second-class car seats 60. A fully loaded train carries 210 first-class and 584 second-class passengers.

Your Eurostar train was fabricated under contract to a consortium that has since changed composition several times. The original British share of the contract was 46.67 percent, which is equivalent to 16 of the 38 basic trainsets, with 18 for FrenchRail and four for the Belgian Railroads. Eurostar's 38 trains are interchangeable, but the trainsets are separately owned, maintained, and berthed. You can tell who owns a particular Eurostar trainset and where it is based by the first two numerals of the four-digit identification numbers stenciled on the power cars. Those 16 beginning with "30" are owned by Eurostar UK and based at North Pole International. Belgian Railroads' four, the "31" series, are based at Forest Midi, Brussels. FrenchRail's 18 trainsets are the "32" series at Le Landy, Paris.

1:40 Hours—Lille

Your Eurostar slows at the Eurostar station named Lille Europe. It stops only if it is bound for Brussels. Aboard your Paris-bound Eurostar, you see Lille Europe only as a long tunnel while you travel over the central tracks bypassing the four platform lines.

Lille Europe TGV station not only is used by Eurostar trains between Brussels and London, but it anchors TGV trains to Paris and Brussels-France TGV trains (see below) running along the TGV Paris bypass corridor to the Southeast and Atlantic networks.

For those passengers changing trains in Gare Lille Europe, the station introduced departure boards show you the *acces* (access) letter, *A* to *L*, for your train. When you find your platform you are directed by video screen to your boarding sector depending on the carriage ("voiture") number shown on your reservation coupon.

Gare Lille Europe is massive. Escalators zigzag between levels and *acces* areas. The connecting Lille Metro station adds to the bustle. The enormous oval building is called the "Lille Grand Palais." It is Lille's exhibition hall. On your left is the soaring business center complex "EuraLille," which consists of geometric high-rise offices; a four-star, 200-bedroom hotel; and businesses including the World Trade Center Tower, the Credit Lyonnais Tower, and the Hotel and Office Tower.

Lille Europe station is located on the edge of the city's center but only a quarter-mile from the existing classical dead-end terminal, which was renamed Lille Flandres to prevent confusion. Lille Flandres was France's busiest outside Paris. You can count on a five-minute walk between Lille Europe and Lille Flandres stations unless you hold any SNCF (FrenchRail) ticket involving a transfer between the two stations. It is valid for one free trip on the VAL metro.

1:42 Hours—Fretin Triangle

About seven miles out of Lille Europe station, Eurostars to Paris and Brussels diverge. They each take the appropriate side of the triangular junction near Fretin to join the main Brussels-Paris high-speed line. You may see a red Amsterdam-Brussels-Paris Thalys train curving around the opposite arc.

South of the Fretin triangle, Eurostars for Paris pass through the former coal-mining country. Now that the pits have closed, all is lush and green—a paradise for cattle.

2:01 Hours—Arras Cutoff

About three miles south from the point where you see Arras on the west, you pass the junction of the spur to Arras. This spur is bypassed by Eurostar but allows use of the high-speed track for 186-mph TGV service between Paris and Arras.

2:09 Hours—TGV Haute Picardie Station

The small Picardy TGV station was the last detail of the TGV Nord Europe to be settled. It is located at a road crossing near the super-highway between Amiens and St. Quentin. Part of the reason for the delay in this choice was civil disobedience by supporters of an alternate route for the high-speed line to the Channel Tunnel via Amiens, the capital of Picardy. This second line has been promised "when the line via Lille is saturated." This may be a long way off.

You notice Eurostar coasting now, and realize that it is slowing to rejoin conventional tracks at Gonesse, 9.8 miles north of the rejuvenated Paris Gare du Nord. As Eurostar enters Paris you see a nice view of Sacre Coeur, high atop its hill, dominating the skyline.

2:35 hours—Paris Gare du Nord

At Paris's Gare du Nord, you arrive on a dedicated track, formerly number three, now the "Quai du Talent," celebrating leading French and English film, music, sports, and media personalities. In the station you find one of the most amazing things of your entire trip: signs in the English language! The entire station was remodeled for the arrival of Eurostar and TGV Nord Europe trains. The departure lounge opened May 12, 1998, and accommodates 1,000 travelers. For First Premium passengers, the Salon Eurostar provides newspapers, beverages, phones, copiers, and Internet access, as well as direct access to the train through a passageway. You would know the station is old only because the 1865-69 facade and clock have been preserved.

An airy and spacious addition was completed in 2002 to give you convenient access by escalator to and from Paris's metro and RER trains (see "Getting around Paris" in the "France" chapter).

Departing taxis are lined up outside on the level below your arrival. Porters meet the trains. Use the elevators for luggage carts; otherwise you can ride the down escalator. Mainline and international ticketing and reservation services are grouped in an office ("Espace Grandes Lignes") across the arriving taxi right-of-way to the west of the building next to track number one. Several fast-food franchises are across the street. You find ATMs, and the tourist office (open daily, 8 A.M. to 9 P.M.) will make hotel reservations for you.

Brussels—All Change for Amsterdam or Cologne/Frankfurt

There are no direct day services between London and the Netherlands or Germany, but you make connections from Eurostar at Brussels' South station to Thalys trains headed for Amsterdam or Cologne (see Thalys section below) or ICE 3 trains to Frankfurt (Main) (see ICE International section below). When Eurostar passengers connect to Thalys trains in Brussels, they don't need to pay the Thalys surcharge, so it is convenient for them to use Thalys without extra charge to Rotterdam, The Hague, Amsterdam Schiphol Airport, and Amsterdam Central Station. The additional fare to the Netherlands is the same wherever you travel, making Eurostar's fares to the Netherlands among the best Eurostar bargains. The cost per mile from London to Rotterdam is lower than that to Paris, even lower to Amsterdam, and dirt cheap when you change trains and continue without extra cost to the northern city of Groningen.

Changing between Eurostar and conventional trains at Brussels' South station is very easy. You don't have to change train stations. The permanent, airport-style, dedicated high-speed train terminal, which is located on the west side of Brussels' South station at street level below the platforms off to the right (as you depart) at the Rue de France end of the concourse, includes an enclosed departure area, bar, shops, and toilet facilities.

Passengers coming from the Netherlands changing at Brussels South station are subject to the required security check before boarding Eurostar trains for London. Modern escalators and elevators have been installed. Rolling beltways simplify baggage movement. Luggage lockers, 370 of them, accept British one-pound coins as well as euros.

Le Shuttle—Taking Your Car Along

Le Shuttle is the rail service that allows passengers to travel with their vehicles through the Channel Tunnel. When service started on December 22, 1994, reservations were required and trains ran hourly. Now Le Shuttle is operated as a true shuttle: turn-up-and-go with trains departing every 20 minutes around the clock. It's a free-flow system, with no reservations. Passengers show up and wait their turn to cross.

All types of vehicles make the undersea crossing, including cars, vans, trucks, motor coaches, motorcycles, and bicycles. Le Shuttle offers a Short Break fare, which is a round-trip ticket that requires a return within five days.

Hertz, Le Shuttle's preferred car rental supplier, offers a plan called Le Swap where you rent a left- or right-hand-drive car and exchange it at the Hertz office at the entrance/exit to the Channel Tunnel for another with the steering wheel on the opposite side. For example, you might rent a left-hand-drive car in London, drive through Britain, ending in Folkestone, take your car on the train though the tunnel, swap it for a right-hand-drive car at the Hertz office at Coquelles and continue driving through France. Rates include the transportation through the tunnel.

The Le Shuttle consortium bought 126 single-deck vehicles for carrying trucks and buses, 126 double-deck ("tourist") vehicles for carrying automobiles, 33 loaders, and 38 locomotives. Since 1999 the Channel Tunnel has more than doubled its train fleet. It has a freight shuttle fleet of 16 of the most powerful locos in the world. The shuttle trains are arranged into two separate segments that are coupled together to form a 2,600-foot-long, 30-vehicle train capable of carrying about 120 automobiles and 12 buses per shuttle train. Each completely enclosed, two-level tourist vehicle has room for five average-size family cars per deck. The completely enclosed, single-deck shuttles carry one bus or four or five cars. Semi-open shuttles carry trucks. Shuttles measure 85.3 feet long. Their 18.4-foot height is sufficient to transport 13.8-foot-high buses and their internal width of 12.3 feet leaves room for walking on both sides.

The Channel Tunnel opened two new tracks and platforms in Cheriton, England, and Coquelles, France, in 2002, thanks to the strong growth of truck as well as automobile and bus traffic.

Although the tunnel infrastructure has been designed for a possible maximum speed of 125 mph, the Channel Tunnel's shuttles run at a maximum speed of 80.8 mph so that it takes 35 minutes for the Channel Tunnel shuttle to deliver cars and passengers from platform to platform (and only eight minutes to load or unload).

The Channel Tunnel's revenue comes from two sources: its own dedicated shuttle trains ferrying cars, coaches, trucks, and passengers between Cheriton and Coquelles and from tolls paid by European Passenger Services for the passage of Eurostar.

Thalys—Red and Rapid

You gotta love a train whose name means exactly nothing. Thalys is not the goddess of transportation. The train's operating company, owned 70 percent by SNCF and 30 percent by SNCB, hired a consulting firm to create a distinctive name that would be acceptable to both the French- and Dutch-speaking regions of Belgium and one they could trademark to avoid the cross-channel Eurostar's embarrassment over the appearance of Italian State Railroads' Eurostar Italia, Eurostar-named pubs, kiosks, shops, and restaurants, and general rip-offs. The contractors field-tested names that both Dutch- and French-speaking passengers could pronounce easily. A committee selected the name Thalys. They didn't check with English speakers. Say "ta-LEES."

Thalys (*www.Thalys.com*) is a network of high-speed TGV trains. It connects Paris six times daily via Brussels, Liege, and Aachen with Cologne Hbf and Cologne's Deutz Station, where you may change to the high-speed ICE trains to Frankfurt Airport, but allow seven minutes to change between the upper and lower levels at Deutz. Thalys services six to eight times daily take you between Paris and Amsterdam Central Station via Brussels, Antwerp, Rotterdam, The Hague, and Amsterdam Schiphol Airport. There are five daily trains between

Brussels and Paris Charles de Gaulle Airport. On weekends these also call at Disneyland Paris. Two trains a day connect Paris with Bruges and Ostend, and once a day, airline passengers from Chicago ride Thalys from Brussels Zaventem Airport to Paris Gare du Nord. All this amounts to half-hourly services between Paris and Brussels, one of the most frequent international connections in Europe.

Once a day Thalys runs from Amsterdam to Marseille via Avignon during the summer and you can ride Ski Thalys from Rotterdam to Bourg St. Maurice during the winter.

Thalys uses two different types of power cars but the carriages are all the same (similar to TGV-Rs) for all routes, except for adaptation of the bar/buffet carriages. The power car of the PBKA Thalys—Paris-Brussels-Koln (Cologne)-Amsterdam—has a rounded, red nose and one big square windshield, with the driver positioned in the middle as with Eurostar. The PBKA was built especially to run into Germany using 15,000 volts A.C. In Belgium, it works with 3,000 volts D.C., in the Netherlands with 1,500 volts D.C., and on the high-speed lines in France it Belgium, it uses 25,000 volts A.C. The PBKA was the first train that could handle four different voltages.

The power car of the PBA Thalys (Paris-Brussels-Amsterdam) has a sharklike snout, identical to a TGV-R, and two smaller, square windshields. This Thalys runs in France, Belgium (except Liege), and the Netherlands but not in Germany, because it is not suitable for the German voltage.

Both PBA and PBKA consist of eight passenger carriages with one power car at each end, seat 377 passengers (120 in first class, 257 in second), and reach 186 mph on the high-speed lines.

Thalys service personnel are employees of the Thalys operating company, not the national railroads. They welcome you at the doors and stamp your ticket as you board. There are no passport checks or customs inspections between any of these Schengen Treaty signatory countries.

Reservations and payment of a supplement are obligatory to ride a Thalys. Discounts are given to rail-pass holders. Even when you hold a valid rail pass you are required to pay a variable supplement in the range of $25 for first class and $13 for second class (which include reservations), but it depends on your class of travel, itinerary, and type of rail pass.

The supplement covers the cost of the meal, which is served only on

weekdays. On weekends, no meal is served, and you do not pay the supplement.

Amsterdam-Brussels-Paris

When your Thalys train glides into boarding position at Amsterdam's 19th-century, neorenaissance Central train station, you see it is massive and bold. It is basically a French TGV-R train painted Thalys red—which is the same shade as the Belgian Railroads' Bordeaux red—and gray, which is universal.

When you board you find that the Thalys's first-class interiors feature orange-red seats arranged 2+1. They recline electrically with a touch of the control. The finish is gray, with gray carpeting. Unfortunate decorations rise above the tables in first class like hooded cobras ready to strike. These ill-conceived fixtures are lights, but are usually switched off.

Second class is decorated similarly, even with gray carpeting, which is unusually ritzy for second class, and the narrower seats are arranged 2+2. Between first- and second-class sections, most of one carriage is devoted to a bar arranged similarly to FrenchRail's TGV-Rs. In the vestibules you can read routing and train numbers on the LCD display screens. One carriage has a conference room at the end.

The train manager greets you in Dutch, French, and English. "The doors will be closing in a few minutes." They do, and off you go without further warning—on the dot.

You reach the Amsterdam Schiphol Airport stop almost before you get settled. You zoom underground, with lights zipping by you like lasers in a special-effects space movie. Schiphol train station has modern digital signs, marble flooring, a moving walkway going up, and abundant, conventional luggage carts (because walkways are used instead of escalators, special luggage carts are not needed). Luckily, there are large luggage spaces at the ends of the carriages to accommodate the air travelers boarding here. NS and SNCF have an agreement with KLM for the sale of combined tickets covering KLM flights and journeys by Thalys on the Amsterdam-Paris route. On the Amsterdam-Antwerp-Brussels route, passengers are free to choose between air and Thalys for the same price. They simply exchange their flight ticket for a Thalys ticket and reservation at the airport or at Antwerp Berchem station.

A hostess pushes a refreshment trolley down the aisle and offers you free coffee and orange juice. Refreshments in the Netherlands plus the weekday snack served between Brussels and Paris are included in the Thalys supplement you paid. Catering is by Agape, part of Italy's largest rail catering company.

You next stop is the Netherlands' seat of parliament, The Hague. Do not confuse the HS station with The Hague's Central Station. HS was built by the Hollandsche Yzeren Spoorweg railroad, was damaged by fire in 1989, and had new fittings installed, arches replaced, and the whole refined to achieve a well-functioning station completed in 1993. The original red-brick Romanesque facades were braced and preserved and the yellow-stained windows retained. In 1996, escalators to the platforms were installed.

At Rotterdam's Central Station, more passengers board but no one gets off. Amsterdam-Rotterdam passengers will have taken a Dutch InterCity train. Passengers boarding here hurry up the stairs from Rotterdam's Metro station. The streetcar and bus circle is on the plaza in front. (Your national strip-tickets are valid.) The bank and train information office ("NS Inlichtingen Bureau") can be found in the entrance hall.

Rotterdam Central is a bright, airy station. Buses to North Sea ferries depart from the side door. City information (VVV) and train information share a yellow kiosk in the main hall. Cut flowers usually sold in Dutch stations brightly overflow an entire corner of the main hall.

Out of Rotterdam CS your Thalys passes the Rotterdam Blaak station opened by Her Majesty the Queen Beatrix on September 15, 1993, wearing an NS-blue-and-yellow dress. Then you enter the 1.74-mile Willemspoor Tunnel under the Meuse River that replaced the Meuse Bridge, part of which has been preserved as a monument to Rotterdam's World War II survivors. The tunnel consists of eight parts, each weighing 25,000 tons. At its lowest point you are 50 feet below the water level. Your ride is smooth. TGVs are the smoothest-riding high-speed trains in Europe.

No sooner do you cross the Belgian border than you are slowing slightly through brown brick villages and traversing stations of the greater Antwerp local network. Past Antwerpen Dam halt you speed past the automobiles on the major motorways, and the train supervisor announced "Antwerp Berchem," where you arrive at freshly paved platform number one.

Approaching Brussels, you pass through Schaerbeck station into the tunnel connecting Brussels' three main train stations. Surfacing at Brussels Kappelbrucke station you coast into Brussels South (*Midi/Zuid*) platform number five for a five-minute break. The platform is located in the nicely tiled annex and looks spiffy compared to the older, run-down, local-train platforms awaiting similar treatment. Up and down escalators take you to the station hall and the Eurostar trains standing nearby, on platforms number one and two, which are separated by a cyclone fence.

Eurostar passengers are able to use Thalys trains to and from the Netherlands without paying the Thalys supplement. Further, their additional fare is not based on the distance they travel, which means that they can reach distant Groningen for the same price as Amsterdam or Rotterdam.

A French-speaking announcer greets the new arrivals on Thalys. He struggles through the Dutch greeting but relaxes speaking English.

On December 14, 1997, King Albert II and the president of France opened the Belgian high-speed line that links into the 186 mph TGV Nord French line. You can feel your train accelerate. A Thalys TGV on routine test set a new Belgian speed record on April 10, 1996, by reaching 167 mph on this stretch.

Lunch served at your seat is very skimpy. A hearty eater will need to supplement the meal with food from the bar car, but you can choose a beverage and it is followed by coffee or tea.

Running west across a plain in a shallow cutting designed to minimize the impact on the environment, your Thalys curves through one of the rounding sides of the Fretin triangle, about seven miles down from Lille Europe train station to the west and about 134 miles north of Paris. This marks your entrance to the TGV Nord-Europe line and the 186-mph speed limit.

The scenery along the high-speed line is almost nonexistent. You speed south through fields of grain and leafy, green vegetables that you can't make out. You are traveling so fast they appear a blur. You can't pick out the names of the towns or the TGV station you pass, although you know it is little-used TGV Picardy.

Somewhere along here is where a French TGV-R, very much like your Thalys, fell into a World War I tunnel at 183 mph on December 21, 1993. The train remained upright and traveled 7,447 feet before coming to rest. Tunnels that the armies had burrowed under no man's land in order to lay mines beneath enemy trenches had undermined this unmapped area. After the accident, the TGV line was rigorously inspected for additional subsidence and liquid concrete inserted at suspicious locations.

Finally your driver cuts power and you coast into the dedicated pair of tracks at Paris's Gare du Nord (see "Paris train stations" and "Getting around Paris").

Paris-Brussels-Cologne

Your four-voltage Thalys commenced service on September 29, 1997. From Cologne it undergoes a transformation on its way to Brussels and Paris. Riders board in Cologne Hauptbahnhof or Cologne-Deutz, having changed from trains from Dusseldorf, the Ruhr, Hamburg, Berlin, or the 2002 high-speed line from Frankfurt/Main. Passing through Aachen, Thalys feels and sounds like a German train. German is the language of choice. Past Liege's glistening 2002 Guillemins Station you accelerate over the 2002 high-speed line to the outskirts of Brussels.

When Thalys arrives in Brussels Midi/Zuid station, there is a complete change of crew and language. The Germans hurry to other appointments, possibly to the Eurostar to London on the next track, and new passengers board. Your Thalys becomes a French train on its 186-mph way to Paris's Gare du Nord.

Brussels-France TGV

The Brussels-France TGV is similar to Thalys, but its network differs from Thalys because Thalys bypasses Lille, while Brussels-France TGVs bypass downtown Paris's Gare du Nord to avoid a need to change trains. Aboard a Brussels-France TGV you can travel at 186 mph from Brussels to Paris Charles de Gaulle Airport, Disneyland Paris, and Lyon and over the TGV Med high-speed line to Avignon, Marseille, Nice, and Perpignan on the Spanish border. The Paris Bypass takes you along the TGV Atlantique route to Bordeaux.

Brussels-France TGVs are multivoltage TGV-R ("R" for *reseau,* or "network") trains, which were first introduced in 1993 for running at 186 mph on the TGV Nord line. They are well suited for long-distance service because of their heavy-duty engines and electric braking. The 377-seat trains (120 seats in first class) are pressure sealed to avoid discomforting passengers in tunnels.

No meals are included in the TGV ticket, but you may special order at-seat meals in advance or visit the TGV buffet car. Many like the pizza.

Cisalpino Italy-Switzerland-Germany

When you board in Lugano, Cisalpino's first stop in Switzerland (say Chees-alpino, like an Italian), for the over-and-through-the-Alps south-north trip across Switzerland, you may be especially curious to see what would happen when the conductor finds that you have boarded without a reservation and have only your Eurailpass in hand.

Regular passengers know that reservations certainly are required for riding Cisalpino trains in Italy, but it was your understanding that reservations are not required for riding Cisalpino within Switzerland or Germany. However, you never can be sure that it also would be the conductor's understanding.

You soon find out. You had no difficulty choosing a seat without a yellow reservation card attached. The Swiss conductor approaches your seat, looking very official in his full dark blue uniform with kepi and ticket punch, and asks routinely, "Do you have a reservation?"

"No."

"No? No? Where did you board?"

"Lugano."

The conductor raises his eyebrows. He is not pleased. He looks at you as if you are stealing from his piggy bank. He frowns, skeptically. "If you got on in Italy you must have a reservation."

You shrug your shoulders.

He examines your Eurailpass very carefully and holds it up to the light, maybe looking for an Italian conductor's punch hole.

Your rail pass completely covered your trip. No reservation fee. No supplement.

The surprising blue-and-white ETR 470 Pendolino train is the sparkling, 1996 creation of Cisalpino (CIS), the operating company held equally by the Swiss Federal Railroads and the Italian State Railroads, which financed the $20 million fleet of tilting trains.

Derived from Italy's ETR 460 Pendolino (see "Italy" chapter), but capable of running also on the Swiss electrical power supplies, the dual-voltage 470s are equally as powerful in either country, but Cisalpino ETR 470 trains are geared lower than ETR 460s so that they reach a maximum speed of 125 mph rather than the 460's 155 mph, a trade-off necessary to give them higher traction for better climbing power over Swiss mountain routes. Remember how your automobile climbs hills better in low gear than in high.

When they began operation on June 2, 1996, between Geneva and Milano, they had the honor of becoming the world's first international tilting trains. On September 29, 1996, nine-carriage, first- and second-class Cisalpino trains augmented the Cisalpino network by carrying passengers over the Basel-Bern-Brig-Milan and Zurich-Lugano-Milan routes with nine, 475-passenger ETR 470 Fiat trainsets.

Cisalpino added service to Stuttgart in autumn 1997, just as soon as Fiat could modify nine trainsets (at a cost of $5.5 million). Cisalpino considered this an efficient deployment of its high-priced equipment because the line between Zurich and Stuttgart is so highly curved that the tilting trains very effectively reduce travel time. It shares this running with the tilting German ICE T trainsets (see "ICE Generation").

Now, you ride CIS Geneva-Lausanne-Brig-Milan-Venice, Basel-Bern-Brig-Milan, Stuttgart-Zurich-Lugano-Milan, and Zurich-Lugano-Milan-Florence.

Whoa! What's happening?

Some passengers don't realize they have boarded a tilting train when they take their seats aboard the high-speed Cisalpino.

It comes as a surprise, then, but they know it well and good when their smart-looking, white-and-royal-blue train serpentines upward from their station, ducking and diving round curves. You feel Cisalpino's tilting right from the start of your trip. Few stretches of railroad line are straight in Switzerland.

Tilting trains perform beautifully on *C* curves, as in Italy. It's another matter when they execute *S* curves on the Lotschberg and Gotthard routes through Switzerland.

Tilting is the now-well-developed system of rounding curves 20 percent faster without upsetting passengers and thus decreasing overall travel time. Sensors in Cisalpino's leading vehicle send messages to the Fiat tilt system, which tilts the carriages one after another per software instructions.

Tilting works so well on curving older tracks that it eliminates the need to build expensive new high-speed lines. There is not a European railroad network that does not have plans for tilt in its future.

On Italian routes, curve radii exceed 1,600 feet and intermediate straight stretches separate consecutive curves. Tilting trains have time to return to vertical before they attack a second curve, but Switzerland's Alpine Gotthard and Lotschberg lines are lined with curves as tight as 820 to 1,000 feet, often one following another. Tracks verge on sheer drops and you burst through a whole series of short tunnels, some of which open straight onto perilous viaducts. By the time the back carriages of your train are starting to tilt for a left-hand curve, the front carriages and tilt sensor are already entering a right-hand curve, and at times it seems as though your train is tilting left at the front while your rear section is still tilting right. At one curve you look down on the receding valley floor; at the next, up at 8,000-foot Alpine summits.

It is not advisable to walk along the train.

The nine-carriage Cisalpino trains offer 475 seats (153 first class, 322 second class). The $20 million trains are air-conditioned and air-tight in order to make travel through tunnels more comfortable. The interiors, designed by the Turin designer Giugiaro, sport seats separated by tables. Interiors are subdued, gray blue in first class, sea green in second. Earphone jacks for taped music are installed beside every seat. Long windows are equipped with sunscreens that you control electrically, but this is the downside of the Cisalpino, the shape of the windows. They are long but horizontal. They limit your vertical vision so severely you cannot see conveniently some of the mountain crests, which is a shame when traveling in a country as scenic as Switzerland.

The tilt system is located entirely beneath the carriages instead of taking up passenger space. Full pressure sealing lets you pass through the many tunnels traversed by CIS at full speed without popping your ears.

Italian designers know how to do bar/restaurants right. They have provided only 25 seats for you in their intimate bar/restaurant car but positioned their dining space beneath a low, intimate, light-studded ceiling, to make it the most beautiful restaurant area on the rails.

The restaurant seems to want to grab at passers-through by their elbows: "Come. Sit down; join us for a meal." The brilliant, low-backed, bright-blue, velour-covered seats are arranged around varnished, real-wood tables. An authentic Italian coffee machine dominates the bar.

The adjacent bar for takeaway food, next to the second-class carriages, is nearly as elegant.

Cisalpino accepts customary tickets, rail passes, and half-fare cards. Seat reservations are obligatory within Italy and include a supplement of about $8. In first class, you receive a welcome drink, and newspapers are available.

ICE International

Thirteen ICE 3s, designated ICE 3M, trains are equipped with multivoltage power equipment to allow them to range internationally throughout Europe. ICE 3M debuted on November 5, 2000, when DB's multivoltage, third-generation InterCity Express Train, dubbed "ICE International," began to take travelers between Amsterdam and Cologne every two hours. Combined German and Dutch teams staff the trains.

On December 16, 2002, when the new high-speed line between Cologne and Frankfurt went full service, the Amsterdam ICE 3Ms were extended to run to Frankfurt and Frankfurt Airport at 186 mph and, at the same time, three daily ICE 3Ms were introduced between Brussels and Frankfurt/Frankfurt Airport.

The Amsterdam trains serve Duivendrecht, Utrecht Centraal, Arnhem, Oberhausen, Duisburg, and Dusseldorf as well as Cologne Hbf, Frankfurt/Main International Airport and Frankfurt Hbf, taking three hours, 56 minutes. The Brussels trains depart from Brussels South Station and serve Liege and Aachen as well as Cologne Hbf, Frankfurt Airport, and Frankfurt Hbf, taking three hours, 45 minutes.

Artesia Takes You Between France and Italy

SNCF and Italy's railroads formed a unique collaboration in 1996 to cut travel time between the two countries by providing high-speed joint service between France and Italy, with each country's prestige trains running with new multivoltage locomotives into its neighbor's stations. Seat reservations are compulsory, and rail passes are honored.

Artesia (*www.Artesia-geie.com*) is the marketing name for the 1998 mini-network of high-speed trains connecting Milano, Italy, and Paris, France, in less than seven hours.

Artesia is one of the enterprises of Grande Lignes International (GLI), the division of FrenchRail (SNCF) that has fingers in almost everything including Eurostar. In the case of Artesia, GLI cooperates with the Italian State Railroads (FS).

On the Paris-Milan route, you ride FrenchRail's TGV-R (Reseau) trains like those that first ran on the TGV Nord line, but they are specially equipped to run on both 3 kV dc and 1.5 kV dc. Similarly, FS's ETR 500 power car, with the FS logo on the front, can handle both Italian and French power supplies so that you don't have to wait for a change of locomotives at the border.

Your starting point, Milano Centrale, is the grand station of Europe. Allow yourself time to look around (see "Islands of Order" in the Italy chapter). Your Artesia calls first in Torino's (Turin) Porta Susa train station, where a wave of new passengers boards.

From Turin your Artesia takes you below wine terraces that zigzag precariously up mountainsides so steep and so difficult to harvest that you marvel at the vines' clinging tenacity. At Chiomonte, you see the Italian Alps looming high to the south. To the north the pines lining the mountain crests give the serrated summits a fuzzy, tentative profile.

The mountainside houses look as if they were snatched from Switzerland on a quiet day. Their aged wooden beams blend with white plaster and irregular windows, balconies, and dark tile roofs.

Soon, you realize you are riding a true mountain railroad. The Alps here are formidable, but Artesia trains trace their twisting ways through the towering mountains between France and Italy with all possible speed and good comfort. Wildly racing brooks, elevated motorways running next to your route, and camping sites crowded with camper vehicles bearing license plates from faraway countries mark your route.

Past Oulx-Cesana your Artesia begins to run in and out of tunnels. Alps to 11,500 feet tower high above with faces so chiseled and broken and made barren by landslides and erosion that your Artesia seems a tiny toy below these giants.

After a quick stop in the white plaster Bardonecchia station, which has a remarkable roof of a brown stone hewn like slate, you pass in and out of so many tunnels that every time you emerge from a tunnel, the new view seems more magnificent than the last.

Through the Tunnel de Frejus, you arrive at Modane, the border town in the Rhone-Alpes region of France, and your Artesia train changes from 3,000 volts dc to 1,500 volts dc. The historical 8.5-mile rail tunnel was ordered by the Sardinian monarch in 1872 to unite those parts of his domain lying to either side of the Alpine divide.

From the station, Modane with its steeply spired church on the Frejus Valley floor appears very small. On the crests above you see the crenellated walls of a medieval fortress.

Leaving Modane, you pass into still another tunnel, but now your Artesia always heads down, down 18 minutes along the long valley of the River Arc to St-Jean-de-Marienne at the division between the north and south French Alps.

In Modane and St-Jean-de-Marienne, industry is more important than agriculture. You see metalworking and electrochemical plants, but you also admire the rows of green grapevines haphazardly planted on startling white soil and the castles perched high on the mountainside.

The valley city of Chambery on the River Isere lies below high Chartreuse and Bauges Savoy Alps. Slices of the mountain look as though they were cleaved with a chainsaw.

From 1232 until 1562, Chambery was the capital city of Savoy at the strategic crossroads of the ancient trade to Italy. It will surely remind you of a quaint Italian city with its rosy facades, wrought-iron balconies, and grand arcades. The Sainte-Chapelle part of Chambery's Chateau of the Dukes of Savoy was built by Amadeus VIII to house the Holy Shroud. When Savoy became part of France in 1860, Italians removed the shroud to Torino, where it is now known as the Turin Shroud.

In Chambery you can change for trains in every direction. Chambery's tidy station is a major rail hub. Artesia's Milan-Paris TGVs take you from here via Dijon's Ville station over high-speed tracks. The departures board also shows connections to Annecy, Geneva, Marseille, and Lyon.

Artesia Service
Paris-Milan

EC9251	EC9255				EC9252	EC9258
Manzoni	Dumas				Dumas	Manzoni
0804	1104	dep	PARIS (Lyon)	arr	1611	2251
1059	1359	dep	Chambery	dep	1312	1957
1142	I	dep	St-Jean-de-Maurienne	dep	1229	I
1208	1508	dep	Modane	dep	1202	1849
1227	1527	dep	Bardonecchia	dep	1141	1827
1237	1537	dep	Oulx	dep	1131	1816
1327	1627	dep	TURIN (Porta Susa)	dep	1043	1726
1406	1706	dep	Vercelli	dep	1000	1644
1422	1722	dep	Novara	dep	0946	1629
1455	1755	arr	MILAN (Centrale)	dep	0915	1600

Switzerland-Paris on Lyria

"What is this? Everybody knows that from Zurich you go through Basel to get to Paris. We've done it for years. Why would anyone go through Neuchatel?"

The *Neue Zurcher Zeitung,* Zurich's preeminent newspaper, sharply criticized the new Swiss Railroads' timetable when it was issued.

For years the only rational way between Paris and Zurich was via Basel. Suddenly, with the advent of high-speed French TGVs, you were able to use the high-speed line from Paris's Lyon station to Frasne and then branch through Neuchatel to Bern. This route offers wonderful scenery of the Jura mountains, castles, distant Alps, and Lake Neuchatel.

It took many years of negotiations before Zurich was at last granted a no-change TGV connection with Paris's Gare de Lyon to join the Paris-Lausanne Lyria high-speed services that had been running almost since the advent of the first high-speed TGV line.

Lyria has dedicated a fleet of nine silver-and-blue "Renovation 1" three-voltage trains for these services to give passengers in second class more legroom, with a resulting loss of seating capacity. Each train now has carriages with an interior design containing only 110, more spacious seats in first class and 240 in second and an extended bar area. There are 220-volt sockets in first class for computers, luggage racks in the middle of the carriages, and both forward- and rear-facing seats.

When making your required reservation, you are now able to specify in which direction you prefer to sit.

In addition to the year-round Zurich and Lausanne trains, Lyria operates winter sports trains branded "TGV des Neiges" and a summer connection, "TGV Valais," continuing past Lausanne to Montreux, Sion, Sierre, Visp (for connections to Zermatt), and Brig.

		Lyria Weekday Service Paris-Zurich		
1544	dep.	Zurich (Hbf)	arr.	1346
1701	dep.	Bern	dep.	1223
1737	dep.	Neuchatel	dep.	1152
1822	dep.	Pontarlier	dep.	1108
1842	dep.	Frasne	dep.	1051
1914	dep.	Mouchard	dep.	1013
1938	dep.	Dole (Ville)	dep.	0951
2010	dep.	Dijon (Ville)	dep.	0924
2147	arr.	Paris (Lyon)	dep.	0744

Linx between Norway and Sweden

Linx AB is the name of the joint venture set up by Swedish and Norwegian railroads in 2001 to improve cross-border services. It has a staff of 170 in its Gothenburg headquarters. You ride upgraded X2000 trains in startling blue Linx livery from Stockholm to Copenhagen and to Oslo and Gothenburg three times a day on weekdays and twice a day on weekends. Linx initially reduced travel times from more than six hours between Oslo and Stockholm to four hours, 50 minutes. Because of improvements to the track and scheduling, this journey improved to four hours, 30 minutes (four hours Oslo-Gothenburg). Further track improvements will eventually reduce the time to only three hours.

Linx is a premier train, and as such, special fares apply, but youths and holders of Eurail products and ScanRail Passes receive special fares. Children under 16 travel free when accompanied by an adult.

The interior rebuilding includes a curvy bar counter in a buffet car and Internet/movie screens at every seat. Linx first-class passengers have a complimentary meal served at their seats, complimentary coffee/tea, aerial boosters for clear wireless communications, electrical outlets for laptops, and special lounges at each city station. Passengers in both first and second class have access to the buffet car for snacks and beverages. All Linx trains are nonsmoking.

EuroCity—The European Standard

For international travel, EuroCity (EC) trains are the workhorses. About 160 EC trains of European standard connect 200 European cities directly. They promise you multilingual personnel to help you on the departure platform and serve you on the train; dining cars, cafeterias, or at least a refreshments trolley; usually a free timetable at your seat; minimal wasted time (less than three minutes) at intermediate stops and border crossings; modern carriages; and speeds up to 167 mph (57 mph minimum). Rail-pass holders don't pay the EC surcharge. For your own peace of mind, you can reserve seats on ECs during busy travel seasons.

International Night Trains

Savvy train lodging—Euronight-European quality trains— Elipsos France-Spain—CityNightLine from Berlin, Amsterdam, Hamburg, Vienna, and Zurich—Artesia de Nuit—GermanRail International

Savvy Train Lodging

One of the great pleasures of train travel in Europe is waking up in a brand-new city, yawning, stretching, and peeking expectantly out of the train window at bright, quaint, and surprising surroundings that promise fresh new adventures. Feeling vigorous and eager after a good night's sleep, you feel charged to conquer exciting new worlds.

Travelers often choose overnight trains through Europe to save their travel time, see more during the day, and cut down on hotel expenses.

Overnight trains are time and cost effective, but night trains do not let you view the scenery and give you time to relish the last stay and prepare for the next. If you can appreciate a kaleidoscope of impressions racing through your brain as you travel from place to place, overnight trains are your dish.

Throw out your preconceived ideas about overnight train travel.

The generation of high-tech, high-convenience, tilting, and double-decked sleeper trains known collectively as hotel trains now provides pampered service or even economic seats on Europe's most popular overnight routes. Tren Hotel (operated by Elipsos Internacional) and CityNightLine (based in Switzerland) are fresh air. These trains have nudged aside the familiar, older generation of overnight trains that have long carried seemingly endless strings of sit-up carriages, sleeping carriages, sleeperettes, and couchettes throughout Western Europe.

The hotel trains are targeted primarily to business travelers by traveling along the most appealing business routes, but they provide space for budget travelers using rail passes in sleeperette seats and innovative couchette bunks costing $20 to $40. Visitors still rely on their old favorite overnight trains to take them to vacation destinations.

Even on holiday routes, vacationers can board trains with fully equipped sleeping carriages ("Bedplaats," "Bedrijtuig," "Makuu-vannu," "Place-Lits," "Schlafwagen," "Sovvagn," "Sovewagn," "Voiture-Lits") that were designed for demanding business travelers. Traditional couchettes ("Cabina de literas," "Cuccetta," "Ligplaats," Ligrijtuig," "Liegeplatz," "Voiture-couchettes") and reclining seats (sleeperettes) give you your best value for your money. Couchettes traditionally are mini-dormitories with four or six bunks attached to the walls of the compartments. Their popularity with travelers and European families is well deserved.

Sleeping compartments are more private and more expensive. Top of the line is the "Single" (S), available in first class. This is a twin-bedded first-class compartment with only the lower bunk used. A first-class "Special" (Sp) is a smaller one-bed-only compartment. The larger first-class compartment is also available as a "Double" (D), with the top bed folded down. When one travels on a second-class ticket, the Sp compartments are called "Tourist 2" (T2) with two beds, either one above the other or two upper beds, across from each other, and "Tourist 3" (T3), with three beds in a tier, one above the other.

Nordic and British railroads offer only sleeping-car accommodations instead of couchette accommodations, but the three-berth sleeping compartments in Nordic countries cost about the same as couchettes farther south. British sleeping-car prices are substantially higher but still save you money compared to hotel prices.

Travelers who don't want to pay for either a couchette or sleeping compartment still sleep very well by riding one of the older trains whose seats recline partially or collapse together by pulling forward at the bottoms, but the number of these trains is declining. When you ride one, it takes no practice to make three beds side by side by pulling forward at the bottoms. This is so practical the whole passenger list does it, but it's a nuisance when the claustrophobic person nearest the window crawls over two sleeping people to get off the train at 3:30 A.M.

Wise overnight travelers sit nearest the corridor so they can step out to visit the washrooms or snack bar, or even get off to buy a sandwich from a platform vendor during a lingering, middle-of-the-night stop. Overnight trains are usually in no hurry.

When there are only two riding in a compartment overnight, it is more comfortable to fold up the armrests, stretch full length along the seats, use a parka or even unsnap the padded headrests for pillows, and sleep soundly until morning. However, when the train is crowded and the compartments filled, no one can stretch out. Travelers spend the night uncomfortably avoiding their companions' space. It's not pleasant trying to sleep on crowded trains; a couchette is a better bet.

Food may or may not be available on overnight trains, and if it is, it is expensive, so take aboard water and whatever refreshments you require. A good rule of thumb: travelers staying in five-star hotels should book a sleeping compartment; those staying in two- and three-star hotels should book a couchette; those staying in youth hostels make do in folded-together seats. Use the Thomas Cook European Timetable or the free Eurail pocket timetable to block out your overnight travels and apportion your travel time so you still have time to enjoy the cities you are visiting.

Traditional couchettes

All the various sleeping-car configurations are not always on a given train or even in every country. Even international couchettes can be a surprise. A couchette originating in Zurich, Switzerland, for Amsterdam, the Netherlands, runs mostly through Germany but may use an Italian Railroads' carriage staffed with a Danish porter.

You sleep two to a side in first-class couchettes and three to a side in second-class couchettes. The lodging cost is the same in both classes. The difference is the train fare. You receive more room in first class because you pay more for your ticket (or pass).

When you board carriages fitted with traditional couchettes, depending on the time of night, the standard bench seats usually have already been converted into bunks. Otherwise, passengers agree when it is time to convert them. All Europeans know how. Bright and (too) early in the morning, train employees clear the bedding and reconvert the couchettes to regular seating for daylight arrival.

Porters leave plastic-wrapped packages containing blankets, sheet bags, and a pillow for every bunk. The sheet bags, sometimes made of a soft, porous, synthetic fiber—they are disposable—are partially fitted like bottom sheets to keep them from slipping, but there is no way to tuck in the blanket. It is always a tug of war between you and gravity to keep the blanket from dropping to the floor. Sleepers stretch out quite comfortably, but undressing is discretionary in mixed company as there is no gender distinction when assigning bunks.

There is a surprising difference in comfort between four-person, air-conditioned, first-class couchettes and six-person, second-class ones (which may or may not be air-conditioned). The extra space created by removing two bunks and two people is astonishing, but only French and Italian trains offer first-class couchettes and then only on domestic trips. When day compartments are not crowded, many travelers find it more comfortable to sleep in an air-conditioned first-class sit-up compartment than a second-class, six-passenger, natural-ventilation couchette.

Sometimes couchette porters (who hold the passports to show at frontier crossings so sleepers need not be disturbed) often have a case or two of cold beer and soft drinks they are happy to sell when the journey begins. Many make their private compartments available for a pickup party of talkative international travelers. Couchettes can be reserved and paid for up to two months in advance through a travel agent in America, but it is easier and less expensive to reserve them in Europe at any large train station. All Western railroads but Portugal's and Greece's have connected, computerized reservations systems, but the Nordic system interfaces only with the German one. When couchettes are not completely sold in advance, you usually see a railroad agent selling couchettes at a portable reservations counter set up next to the train to accommodate last-minute arrivals.

When making a couchette reservation, specify which level bunk you prefer. Some travelers prefer top bunks because they are most private and give them space for their carry-ons. A ladder is provided to reach the higher bunks. Some prefer bottom bunks because they are most convenient. You find storage space beneath the bottom bunk and next to the top bunk. No one prefers middle bunks.

Euronight—European Quality Trains

The glamorous Wagons-Lits sleeping-car system is a thing of the past, although you occasionally see a sleeping carriage still carrying an old Wagons-Lits logo. These have more or less been replaced by nationally owned trains running international routes. The 1993 train classification Euronight (EN) is applied to international night trains of high standard. Euronight trains are available for boarding in the starting train station a half-hour before departure and do not stop anywhere between midnight and 5 A.M. Porters speak at least one foreign language (usually English). Men and women have separate wash and WC facilities.

Euronight trains consist exclusively of sleeping carriages, couchettes, and in some cases reclining-seat sleeperette cars. Sleeping car and some couchette passengers receive breakfast packs and other travel accessories without extra charge, depending on the amount they have paid for their berths. Second-class passengers receive mineral water before retiring and a basic Continental breakfast. Couchette as well as sleeper customers receive a towel, soap, and a cup of drinking water. First-class passengers are greeted with a glass of champagne, Kir, or other alcoholic beverage as well as mineral water, a basket of fruit, a morning newspaper, and a more elaborate breakfast including muesli, cheese, etc. Disposable razors and toothbrushes are available from the conductor, who accepts credit cards for the purchase of extra drinks or snacks.

The Austrian EN Wiener Walzer takes you from Budapest to Zurich via the Austrian capital. The EN Spree-Donau Kurier from Berlin via Leipzig, and Passau, to Vienna (Wbf.) carries blue and white Austrian sleeping carriages that were rebuilt in 2000 with 11 triple-berth compartments and 2001 couchette carriages. The EN Hans Christian Andersen takes you from Copenhagen and splits for three destinations: Bonn, Stuttgart, or Innsbruck via Munich. Good EN trains also include the EN San Marco between Vienna and Venice; the EN Gottardo linking Lugano and Zurich with Florence and Rome; the EN Zurichsee connecting Basel via Zurich and Graz; the EN Remus between Vienna and Rome; the EN Capri between Munich, Rome, and Naples; the EN West-Kurier between Vienna and Bregenz; and the EN Kalman Imre Munich-Vienna-Budapest. They all carry one- and two-bedded sleeping compartments and four- and six-bunk couchette compartments.

German ENs include the Donauwalzer between Brussels and Vienna/Munich via Cologne, Koblenz, and Nuremberg; the EN Jan Kiepura, running Cologne-Dortmund-Hanover-Frankfurt/Oder-Warsaw; and the EN Hans Albers between Hamburg and Vienna via Hanover, Fulda, Nuremberg, and Linz; as well as the Paris-Frankfurt overnight with connections for Darmstadt, Heidelberg, and Karlsruhe.

The EN Berlin Night Express is a train of another color inside and out because it is a joint operation of the private company GVG and the Swedish State Railways. The EN train with Swedish sleeping carriages runs along the route Berlin-Malmo-Copenhagen-Gothenburg-Stockholm nightly over the Oresund Fixed Link.

Elipsos France-Spain

Elipsos Internacional is a limited company owned 50-50 by the French and Spanish railroads. Between Spain and France, you travel on its fleet of overnight Trens Hotel (TH). Low-slung, tilting, Talgo Pendular trains (see "Iberia" chapter) fitted with two- and four-person rooms take you in comfort on international trunk routes between Spain and France and through France to Italy, Switzerland, and even Germany. The services have proved so popular that Elipsos added 20 new Talgo carriages 2003.

Additional Trens Hotel run between Madrid and Lisbon as well as within Spain on the Barcelona-Madrid-Seville/Malaga route. Their Gran Clase compartments even have a shower stall.

Trens Hotel are priced using a "Global" chart in which special prices are applied in regard to the category of class, the passenger type, the length of stay, and the purchase, refund, and exchange conditions. It excludes the normal use of rail passes, but rail-pass holders receive a discount, which varies between 30 and 50 percent depending on class of accommodation. The global prices include the night accommodation and a complimentary breakfast served in the dining car for those booked in single or double accommodation (even rail-pass holders). You may make your reservations in the U.S. or in Europe, but travelers report that agents in cities not served by Trens Hotel are not familiar with booking procedures.

The TH Pablo (Pau) Casals from Barcelona (Sants) to Geneva, Lausanne, Bern, and Zurich (Hauptbahnhof); the EN Lusitania between Madrid (Chamartin) and Lisbon (Santa Apolonia); and the Antonio Machado between Barcelona (Sants) and Seville/Malaga carry "Gran Clase" sleeping carriages, which can be used for single or double occupancy and contain private toilets and showers. Four-berth compartments on these trains are known as Turista class. You can also choose to ride in sleeperette seats to economize.

The EC Joan Miro between Paris (Austerlitz) and Barcelona (Sants), the EC Francisco de Goya between Paris (Austerlitz) and Madrid (Chamartin), the EC Salvador Dali between Barcelona (Sants) and Milan (Centrale), and the 2002 Talgo from Barcelona to Frankfurt/Main, Germany (taking 15 hours) with service to Strasbourg, France, complete your choice of upscale Talgo Pendular Trens Hotel traveling north from Spain.

Trens Hotel feature numerous people-friendly touches. Compartments are not roomy, but designers exploited every inch of space. You have a full-length mirror and a stepladder that drops out of the wall, providing easy access to the top bunks. You sleep under bright plaid blankets on comfy mattresses that make for a good night's sleep. You lock your compartment with a security key card, and the Talgo's platform-level floor makes it easy to move your luggage on and off.

A Spartan breakfast is included and is served in the dining car, which features white tablecloths, silverware, and good service.

The Salvador Dali and Pau Casals also carry carriages with second-class sleeperette seats costing about $40, while the Lusitania also carries carriages with first-class seats costing $11 and second-class seats for $8, but these receive no breakfast.

CityNightLine from Berlin, Amsterdam, Hamburg, Vienna, and Zurich

The giant yellow letters on the $2.6 million, dark-blue, double-decked carriages shout "CityNightLine," the marketing name of

CityNightLine CNL AG (*www.CityNightLine.ch*), wholly owned by GermanRail. CNL's fleet consists of high-quality, double-decked overnight hotel train carriages, single-level sleeperette carriages, and couchette carriages.

The Donaukurier CNL train takes you overnight between Vienna's Westbahnhof and Cologne/Dortmund, serving also Frankfurt/Main and Salzburg. Ride the CNL Komet between Zurich and Hamburg with service to Hanover, Dortmund, Freiburg, and Basel, and the CNL train named Berliner between Berlin's Zoo station and Zurich, stopping at Frankfurt/Main, Freiburg, and Basel. A portion of this train is split at Halle to serve Dresden via Leipzig instead of Berlin, and this portion is known as the CNL Semper. CityNightLine Pegasus runs from Amsterdam to Basel and Zurich and CityNightLine Pollux from Amsterdam to Munich and Garmisch-Partenkirchen (on winter Fridays only). The CNL Sirius connects Zurich and Dortmund via Cologne and Dusseldorf and continues to the North Sea on weekends but does not carry sleeperette reclining chairs.

CNL's air-conditioned trains give you three choices, all with breakfast included. When you choose "Deluxe" category *A*, you ride on the upper deck so that the additional panoramic windows expose the skyline; also, you have one or two wide beds, plus your own stall shower and private WC.

At 11.4 feet long, the Deluxe compartments are twice the length of the "Economy" compartments so that you can use a table and two armchairs. First-class rail-pass holders pay about 64 percent for a Deluxe accommodation.

When you choose lower-cost, "Economy" category *B* compartments, you have one or two beds—one above the other—and a washbasin. Stewards can connect two "B2" cabins together for four-person, family travel ("B4"). Rail-pass holders and second-class, youth rail-pass holders pay about 64 percent.

"Budget" category *C* passengers sleep in reclining, giant-sized seats designed to give you a feeling of seclusion by incorporating a canopy containing a personal reading lamp. Deposit your backpack and luggage in the storage space above you or between the seats. Your small Continental breakfast is served on the fold-down table at your seat by a host. Rail-pass holders, first or second class, pay $80, which is about 64 percent of the normal fare.

Refurbished couchettes owned by GermanRail carry the same dark-blue livery as other CNL stock and carry CNL logos, but you will also spot the GermanRail DB insignia. The air-conditioned compartments have either four or six berths each. Couchette passengers with rail passes pay about 64 percent for either four- or six-person accommodations.

Until midnight, you can party in CNL's nearly carriage length "Thousand-Stars Bar" beneath a lighting panel made possible by the use of fiber-optic cabling. Or you can dine in the small, white-table-cloth restaurant area of the lounge car designed by GermanRail's supplier of Bistro Cafes. Nearby you can patronize the souvenir shop and/or use the reception desk with telephone and fax connections.

Artesia de Nuit

Artesia's scenic daylight trains through the Alps are a delight, but if you need to save time and hotel expense, in 1999, SNCF and FS branded the extensive system of four Paris-Italy overnight trains with the Artesia mini-network label, taking into its fleet the famous name trains from Paris: the Stendhal to Milano, the Palatino to Roma, the Rialto to Venezia (Venice), and the Galilei to Firenza (Florence), which depart nightly from Paris's Bercy Station (see "Getting around Paris") between 6 and 10:30 P.M. for arrivals between 8:18 and 10:42 A.M. and serve also Turin, Dijon, and Bologna.

Artesia de Nuit includes an upmarket hotel carriage, known as "Excelsior," introduced on September 26, 1999. The refurbished coaches were completely gutted and interiors that were designed by Giugiaro were installed at a cost of $1.5 million. Each Excelsior carriage has seven "classic" compartments for two, as well as one "matrimonial" compartment with a couch that makes into a double bed. Every compartment has its own shower and toilet, plus enough room for one child to join the couple. Every carriage has a small reception desk where you can take your own room key. The manager can lock doors centrally and observe corridors with closed-circuit television.

All have first-class two- or three-person sleeping compartments and four- or six-person second-class couchettes. On the routes Paris-Florence-Rome and Paris-Venice, you have a choice of menus in the on-board restaurant. Wagons-Lits supply on-board services.

Artesia de Nuit uses global pricing, but rail passes are accepted for travel, plus of course you must pay for sleeping accommodations. First-class sleeping-car passengers can avail themselves of the Club Eurostar lounges in the major Italian train stations.

GermanRail International

In addition to the domestic night trains (NZ) described in the "Germany" chapter, GermanRail operates night trains between Amsterdam and Berlin, Paris and Berlin, Paris and Hamburg, and Bonn and Prague. These carry conventional five- or six-person couchettes, three-person sleeping carriages, compartments seating six, and bistro service. The Paris-Hamburg services are the first to use 2003 sleeping carriages with improved suspension and a compartment with shower and toilet. You can take your bicycle, except to Paris.

France

Savvy Traveling on the Trains of France

Paris train stations—Getting around Paris—Airport trains—Versailles—Disneyland Paris—Overnight trains—Rail-pass travel

More than two million passengers and 400,000 tons of freight are conveyed daily over the 21,100 miles of line operated by the French National Railroads ("Societe Nationale des Chemins de Fer Francais," or SNCF, *www.sncf.fr*). If they were put together to form a single train, the 15,300 passenger coaches and 153,000 wagons of the fleet would form a train almost 4,000 miles long and stretch from Paris to New York.

France is known for comfortable, convenient, and the world's fastest trains. Its "Train a Grande Vitesse" (TGV, *www.tgv.com*) put train travel back on the map of France. When the TGV Southeast went into service in 1981, it was the first new line to open since 1928. Originally a technical solution to the problem of saturation on the Paris-Lyon route, the TGV became a way of life. Taking two and a quarter hours to cover the 260 miles from city center to city center, it became easy for visitors to make a one-day round-trip excursion—no trek out to the airport, no delayed flights, no horror on the busiest toll highway in France. TGV ridership on the Paris-Lyon line started at 6.4 million a year. It now surpasses 21 million.

TGV Atlantique is the world's speed record holder at 320 mph, but the point is that TGV trains are a joy to ride, and well-planned station modifications make them easy to use. There are six TGV networks: TGV Southeast, Rhone-Alps (the Lyon bypass), TGV Atlantique, TGV Nord, the Paris bypass opened in 1996, and TGV Mediterranee opened on June 10, 2001. Construction of TGV East is under way for 2006 opening.

Eurostar cross-channel services described earlier in part use the lines of the 186-mph TGV Nord Europe system. They are also used for travel to and from Brussels and serve 16 French cities using Brussels-France TGV-R (*R* for "reseau," or "network") trains (sometimes supplemented by surplus French Eurostar trains).

The third-generation TGV-R trains, inaugurated on May 24, 1993, are a refinement of the TGV-A (Atlantique) trains (see below). They are blue and silver and look at a glance like TGV-As, but they are slightly roomier—each carriage has one row of seats less—and have been shortened by dropping the carriages fitted with "Club Atlantique" semi-compartments and shrinking the buffet-bar to only two-thirds of a carriage. The shortening permits them to cross the TGV Interconnection (serving Paris Charles de Gaulle Airport and Disneyland Paris) and run on the TGV Southeast network, where the platforms are shorter. They are also pressure sealed (like German ICE trains) to allow running through tunnels without popping passengers' ears.

TGV-R power cars also incorporate a more powerful transformer and motors of higher capacity than TGV-A power cars. The profiles of the power cars make them look like sharks with backpacks. These changes allow their high-speed running on the steeper stretches of the TGV Mediteranee line south of Valence and have been incorporated in the TGV Duplex trains.

TGV Southeast's extensive network stretches from Paris's Gare de Lyon terminus throughout 50 cities in southeastern France to the Italian border. TGV Southeast trains take you directly to five cities in Switzerland, two in Italy, French ski country, and the Riviera. TGV Southeast's 1981 carriages have been refitted on a program known as "Renovation 2," which pushed speed up to 186 mph, increased seat spacing so capacity fell from 384 to 345 passengers, and repainted to match the rest of SNCF's TGV fleet.

TGV Atlantique trains take you at 186 mph from Paris's Gare Montparnasse terminus to Brittany; the Atlantique/Aquitaine branch takes you through Bordeaux to the Spanish border. Taking the afternoon Atlantique/Aquitaine to Irun shaves three hours off your travel time to Portugal. You change at Irun onto the Portuguese Sud Express, which continues overnight to Lisbon/Porto.

Running first on the TGV Southeast network and later on the TGV Mediterranee line, SNCF introduced its towering blue-and-silver Duplex TGVs on December 19, 1996. Paris managers argued among themselves whether to call their new train a "double-decker," which sounds like a Dagwood sandwich/Vegas card-dealing policy, or "bilevel," which sounds like a house in the suburbs.

They compromised on the French "Duplex," which suggests to French thinking an apartment boasting a lively reception area (the train's upper deck) plus a private and calmer area on a different level (lower deck).

Lively or not, FrenchRail's new high-speed TGV Duplex train between Paris and Lyon, Marseille, and Montpellier as well as Nice-Marseille-Lille solved the more pressing problem of saturation. The TGV line was a victim of its own success—too many passengers, not enough space.

Engineers relied on the successful power equipment of earlier TGVs but rearranged the drivers' compartments with the driver positioned in the center like Eurostar's. With no sacrifice of speed, they configured their trains to carry 545 passengers in three first-class carriages, four second-class carriages, and bar car. This is 45 percent more than a single-decked TGV unit.

You find ample space to set your luggage beside the larger-than-usual doors and face a circular flight of stairs. Bold, striped fabrics and basic colors attract you to the seats in the upper and lower decks. Your leg space is comfortable; seat pitch is 36.2 inches vs. 33.5 inches in the second-generation TGV. Everyone, even those in second class, can recline his or her seat.

"Personally, I'd rather ride on a Duplex carriage that is 60 percent full than a standard carriage that is packed," said a spokesman.

Headspace is so generous on the livelier upper level that you never consider that designing it might have been a problem. It is airy and not the least claustrophobic. From the upper windows you have good views and you can really see how high you are. "Cool," said one traveler, peeking at an older TGV passing below.

Head clearance is less on the calmer lower level, where it is better to read a book or take a quick nap. The two smoking rooms (one each in first and second class) are on the lower levels only.

The stairway is wide and so convenient that some passengers prefer to sit on the carpeted stairs than in their seats. Nevertheless, trudging up the stairs to the upper level is a nuisance for those with children and luggage.

Regardless of how safe it is to sit upstairs and to leave your luggage below, travelers feel more comfortable with their luggage nearby. They don't want to leave it out of sight. Getting small children up and down the stairs is sometimes a struggle.

Another drawback of a Duplex design is that there is only one corridor through the train, and to the bar car, and it is on the upper level. Passengers sitting downstairs must climb the curved staircases to walk through the train.

When you get to the bar car you probably won't realize that its floor level is lower than in the carriages with seats. It was designed to give you more height to stand—a nod to taller passengers. You can sit only at supremely uncomfortable stools at Formica-topped, sculpted places facing the windows, but the windows are larger than in the rest of the train and give you a better view of the passing scenery.

Tip: Avoid the upstairs WCs. They are so tiny that one can hardly avoid inadvertently stepping on the floor button that releases a torrent of water into the washbasin and splashes the occupant. The downstairs WCs are, by comparison, mansions.

With the opening of the Paris TGV bypass on May 29, 1996, through Massy TGV station, 18 miles from the center of Paris in the southern suburbs, Brussels-France TGVs have access to the TGV Atlantique line and you can make high-speed TGV connections from one area of France to another without having to go into Paris and transfer to a second train station. You also don't have to transfer between stations in Paris to travel from London or northern France to western or southwestern France by using Eurostar's stop at Lille Europ station. Instead of three hours and 30 minutes, the trip between Lille and Le Mans takes two hours and 30 minutes; between Tours and Arras only two hours and 20 minutes, rather than three hours. Similarly, the last link in the Paris bypass reduces your travel time between the southeast or west of France and Normandy. Traveling from Lyon to Le Mans takes you three hours and five minutes (previously four hours); from Lyon to Rouen, three hours and 35 minutes (previously four hours and 30 minutes).

Massy TGV station is served by RER (rapid-transit) line *B* and provides you with an interchange with RER line *C* at the adjacent Massy-Palaiseau station, so that you may board or leave the TGV network without traveling into downtown Paris.

The 186-mph TGV Mediterranee opened on June 10, 2001, from Valence, the terminus of the TGV Southeast network, to Marseille on the Mediterranean Sea, with a branch to Nimes, which will be extended to the Spanish border. One year after its opening, the proportion of traffic between Paris and Marseille had shifted from 60 percent air to 60 percent TGV.

Aboard TGV Med you visit hospitable cities like Aix-en-Provence (two hours, 54 minutes from Paris), Avignon (two hours, 37 minutes), Marseille (three hours flat), Nimes (two hours, 52 minutes), and Arles (three hours, 30 minutes), and return to Paris on the same day using only a single day box on a France Railpass or flexible Eurail product valid in France.

Avignon's 2001 TGV station is not connected to the existing network and it is nearly two miles from or to the downtown Avignon Ville train station, in front of the city walls, but free SNCF shuttle buses connect the two.

The TGV line at the point of the new Avignon TGV station is on an embankment about 20 feet above ground, so architects designed the station below the tracks to create an unusual arrangement. Visitors access the tracks by means of a ramp, escalator, or panoramic elevator. The station is supposed to look like a capsized boat, but some maintain it looks more like a banana, a long baguette, or a stretched armadillo. One side is designed to shelter the blazing sun and the other side to resist the 150-mph Mistral winds. The flooring is iroco wood from Africa while the elevated platforms are made of Brazilian wood, which should resist wear from luggage wheels.

One of Cezanne's favorite subjects was Sainte-Victoire, the nearby limestone mountain range. Architects designed the roof of Avignon TGV to look like Sainte-Victoire, but in fact it looks more like an ocean swell.

Aix-en-Provence is easily accessible from Paris by using its $53 million 2001 TGV station, but the station lies so far from downtown Aix that it is misleading to think of it as a city station. It is eight miles southwest of Aix and only 12 miles from Marseille's city center, so that the station not only serves travelers to and from Aix and the satellite towns but also is a boon to travelers to and from the northern suburbs of Marseille who prefer to avoid gridlock auto traffic to downtown Marseille.

Aix TGV is not the usual glass-and-aluminum station. It is nearly all glass, with movable louvers made of iroco wood on the outside to control the sun's heating and give it an attractive look.

To accommodate the large increase in passengers traveling from Marseille for the three-hour run to Paris, architects enlarged the classic Marseille St. Charles station to double train arrivals and departures at peak hours. They doubled the station front and extended it to the university by means of a hall with transparent walls.

The Nimes train station has been completely renovated for the arrival of the TGV Med, making Nimes one hour closer to Paris than before. From Nimes the high-speed line will be extended to Montpellier and then to Perpignan to meet a new Spanish high-speed line to Barcelona.

In main train stations, pick up small, free pocket timetables ("Le Fiches Horaires") between 180 cities served by the main lines and free brochures ("Guides TGV") giving the timetables together with the price for TGV regions: Atlantique Ouest, Atlantique Sud-Ouest, Sud-Est, Mediterranee, Nord-Europe, and Province-Province. Similarly, there are brochures ("Guides") for popular routes. Even if your French is faulty, you can puzzle them out.

Tip: The SNCF English-language Internet site has a "Regions/Paris" option that leads to a clickable regional map of France. Clicking over a region brings up the relevant regional page not only with a journey planner but also *telechargement fiches horaires,* which when then clicked brings up a menu of all *fiches horaires* in the region and a clickable, printable set of timetables for your route of interest.

Eurostar takes you to London, Thalys takes you to Amsterdam and Brussels, multivoltage TGVs and Italian ETR 480 trains take you to Italy, and Lyria TGVs take you to Switzerland. EuroCity trains take you into all the other neighboring countries. (See "International" chapter.)

SNCF requires advance seat reservations on all TGVs. They are available up to 60 days in advance, but same-day reservations present no problem. Go to the reservations window marked "Jour." Specify first (with or without TGV at-seat meal service) or second class, smoking (if available) or nonsmoking, and aisle or window seat. TGV tickets are not based on distance of travel, but regional trains still maintain distance-related pricing. There are two price levels for second-class TGV tickets. The higher applies to the most-used peak services.

Finally, validate the tickets you buy in France in the orange, automatic ticket punchers ("composteur") at the entrances to platforms. These validate the tickets based on an honor system, as conductors do not always check the tickets on board, and are required for insurance reasons. When you travel on a rail pass purchased before you leave and use a reservation made in France, you only need punch your reservation coupon.

Bicycles are for rent at the Paris Gare de l'Est in front of track No. 12 and in front of Paris Gare Montparnasse near the merry-go-round. They are permitted on trains on weekdays between 9:30 A.M. and 4:30 P.M. and after 7 P.M. and without restriction on weekends, except on the Paris metro and on three stretches of RER line. Disassembled bicycles in transportation bags are permitted on Corail and TGV trains without additional charge.

France's regions almost ran out of lively colors for distinctive liveries and logos on their modern diesel or electrified railcars or trains comprising a network of practical, regional TER trains ("Trains Express Regionaux"). Largely unknown by foreigners, they provide you with local connections in 19 regions of France (all but the Ile de France, which has its own organization). TER timetables, which you can pick up free at the local stations, have been coordinated with the high-speed TGV lines, so that 20 percent of all long-distance travelers begin or finish their trips on the TER network.

TER trains are operated under agreements between SNCF and the respective regions. They are usually lighter than mainline trains and designed with commuter seating. You won't find them in timetables available in the United States, but their frequent departures will take you from city to city in the provinces, allowing you to visit by train cities off the beaten tourist paths. Be sure to pick up "Guide Regional des Transports" at regional SNCF stations.

Paris Train Stations

Base your travel in Paris, the hub of the French train system. Be sure to double-check from which train station your train departs. Each of Paris's six stations serves a sector of France and areas beyond. The stations are all terminuses, which means your train ends and does not continue through Paris. You must use suburban Paris stations to connect between lines.

You can say without exaggeration that all Paris main train stations are good and big. All but perhaps Austerlitz and Montparnasse give a grand feeling and a sense of nostalgia. They have complete facilities. Tourist information offices (open Mon.-Sat., 8 A.M. to 9 P.M., May-Oct.) will make hotel arrangements for you in the Paris Gare du Nord (also open Sun., 1 to 8 P.M.), Paris Gare d'Austerlitz (open to 3 P.M. only), Paris Gare de l'Est, Paris Gare de Lyon, and Paris Gare Montparnasse. Look for the frequent "Point Argent" kiosks, which are ATMs.

As you might guess, Paris's stations do not use the arrival and departure time sheets standard in most of Europe. In some cases departures are shown on green sheets (not yellow), but more often you are treated to large overhead electronic arrival and departure boards giving your departure time and track number. Unfortunately, the track number may be posted so close to departure time that you must rush to the platform.

All main stations have pushcarts for your luggage, but you must have a coin to unlock them (which is released when you return the cart), and the carts are usually hard to find.

Electronic lockers, which remain closed for 72 hours, operate as follows: put your bag(s) inside a locker with door ajar, close door, deposit coins, receive a sealed slip of paper with instructions in French and English. Inside is your "secret" code. When you are ready to leave, you punch in your secret numeric code and the door pops open.

Paris's Montparnasse station on five levels, all connected with escalators, is headquarters for your TGV service to Brittany, Bordeaux, Lourdes, and Spain via Hendaye. It's the newest and snazziest of Paris's stations. The present station was built from the ground up in 1989 for the Atlantique and Aquitaine 186-mph TGV trains. You rise on escalators from one of the Paris metro stations on the bottom level, through the second level, a commercial gallery, to the middle level, street level. You then pass the consigne level to finally reach the top, platform level, with tracks 1 to 24. Buffets, fast food, shops, and essential services such as reservations and ticketing are scattered according to destination. In the rear of the track level you find Vaugirard station, with tracks 25-28. Montparnasse is Paris's busiest station—and it can handle all traffic within its vast glass and precast concrete shell.

Across from the station you can easily visit the Tour ("tower") Montparnasse, which many Parisians criticize because it is the tallest skyscraper in Paris and too close, they feel, to the city center. It weighs 1.43 million tons, is 686 feet tall, and from the top you can see planes departing from both airports on opposite sides of Paris. The elevator to the Panoramic Tower lookout on the 59th floor takes 38 seconds. There is an entrance fee. At the open rooftop lookout, telescopes will show you all the detail of Paris. It is Paris's best panoramic viewing spot. On the 56th floor is the glassed-in, elegant "Ciel de Paris" restaurant. Also across the street to the side of the station is the luxurious, four-star Le Meridien Montparnasse Hotel (*www.lemeridien.com/france/paris/hotel_fr1610.shtml*), which is very convenient for travelers on the TGV Atlantique line.

The large area was created by demolishing smaller streets in Montparnasse (meaning "muses"), which was named for the hill. It used to be the artistic quarter of Paris, associated with such names as Edith Piaf, Ernest Hemingway, F. Scott Fitzgerald, James Joyce, and Oscar Wilde, who congregated in bars.

Trains from Paris's *Gare d'Austerlitz* also serve the south of France and Iberia but with deluxe Spanish Hotel trains. Austerlitz is the terminal for RER line *C* to Paris Orly Airport. It contains a tourist office counter and a separate desk for youth hostel information (Avis is in the same room). Included in its services are the Francisco de Goya and the Joan Miro.

Paris Gare du Nord is the terminus of the TGV Nord Europe network and the most user friendly of the Paris stations to make it as simple as possible for English-speaking visitors and arrivals on Eurostar.

The ground level is divided into three sections:

• a fenced-off security area for Eurostar arrivals and departures (with mezzanine departure lounge);

• mainline trains (Grande Lignes) such as Thalys to Amsterdam, TGV-Rs to Brussels and Lille, conventional trains, and overnight trains north; and

• regional trains (Banlieue) in a separate fenced-off area with turnstile entry.

On November 22, 2001, SNCF opened the new "Echanges" section with striking space and convenient escalators to the east of the main hall. The enlargement successfully mimics the architecture of the station and makes much easier changing between long-distance and metro/RER stations.

Below ground level are Paris metro stations on two lines, the RER stations for lines *B* and *D*, and a tunnel to Magenta RER station for line *E*. The line *B* station is your terminal for the RER line to Paris Charles de Gaulle Airport.

The exterior of the Gare du Nord has been cleaned and preserved. If you have a chance to go outside, do so. Stand back a little; the facade is considered one of the masterpieces of railroad architecture. The same architect who redesigned Paris's Place de la Concorde built it between 1861 and 1865. The facade has three arches. The nine statues represent the capitals and leading cities of Europe: Paris (in the middle), London, Vienna, Berlin, Cologne, Brussels, Warsaw, Amsterdam, and Frankfurt. The statues above the ground floor represent Lille and other cities of northern France.

Trains from Paris's tidy *Gare de l'Est* serve Strasbourg, Luxembourg, German points south, and German-speaking Switzerland through Basel. The reserved waiting room for Venice Simplon Orient Express passengers is located opposite track 2. There are many inexpensive hotels across the street. Via elevator, the three-star Paris-Est hotel occupies the second and third floors above one wing of the station. There is also a room of coin-operated no-key lockers.

Paris Gare de Lyon, the origin of the TGV Southeast network, takes you to Lyon, Provence, Marseille, and Switzerland. It was rebuilt top to bottom for the first TGV Southeast network in 1981. At that time the dowdy terminus was transformed into a sprawling, multilevel jumble of a megastation with more trains, more tracks, more platforms, and boarding areas. They preserved the classic clock tower and added TGV tracks and access to the RER rapid-transit network below. It features the Belle Epoque Le Train Bleu restaurant (open noon to 2:30 P.M. and 7 to 10:30 P.M.) dedicated in 1900 at the time of the World's Fair. The adjacent, modern, two-star, 315-room Hotel Paris-Lyon is convenient—and a good value—for overnighters just passing through Paris.

Paris *Gare Saint-Lazare* serves conventional trains to Normandy (including Dieppe harbor for ferries to Britain), Le Havre, and Cherbourg for ferry crossings to the Republic of Ireland. TGVs to

Normandy depart from Paris Gare du Nord. The attractive square in front of the station is the site of the tunnel to the Paris metro line known as "Meteor" and the RER station named Haussman, which dates from 2000.

Getting around Paris

The Paris metro system (*www.paris.org/metro*) is so good, it's contagious. You get around easily aboard the ever-increasing and more-useful Paris metro and RER (rapid-transit) systems. Opened by Pres. Jacques Chirac on October 15, 1998, the Paris metro's 14th cross-city line, known as Meteor, is driverless (it is controlled from a computer screen). The absence of a driver means that passengers can look ahead, into the tunnel. Transparent passenger doors on the platforms control access to the Meteor and safeguard against accidents. RER line *E*, known as EOLE ("Est-Ouest Liaison Express"), takes you into the outskirts with segments opened on July 14 and August 30, 1999.

It's a shame that Paris has perhaps the most convenient and efficient and surely the least expensive public transportation system of any capital, because it discourages you from walking and really seeing the city. Looking at the metro map makes distances seem longer than they are. It's just as easy to walk two or three stops as to take the metro because you don't have to wind your way through corridors and climb stairs. For longer distances, riding Paris metro's subway lines is a given. Even better, there's RER, a second, independent underground train system. Tickets on one are valid on the other within city limits. With two overlapping/complementary underground transportation systems available to you in Paris, it is natural to ask which is better. Plan to use both. RER rapid-transit trains are larger (some are double decked), less crowded, faster, and cleaner and make fewer stops. Their large stations are spacious with the latest in electronic signing and interconnect with the metro at key locations. RER trains are better than the metro trains, but there are far fewer stations and therefore less chance to use them.

Stop at the Paris Tourist Office at metro stop Charles de Gaulle Etoile (127, avenue des Champs-Elysees, open daily, 9 A.M. to 8 P.M.) for details on public transportation, system maps, and purchase of tourist tickets. Metro trains are not covered by Eurail products or France Railpass.

The Paris metro is usually the easiest and cheapest way to change between train stations. All Paris train stations are connected to the subway net with metro stations, but to connect between train stations you must usually change subway lines and this often requires considerable time and—if you are carrying luggage—effort. Here are the best ways:

• Paris-Nord to Paris-Lyon: Take RER line *D* south in the direction of Melun and Malesherbes. Get off at Paris-Lyon, the second stop.

• Paris-Lyon to Paris-Nord: Take RER line *D* north in the direction of Orry-la-Ville. Get off at Paris-Nord, the second stop.

• Paris-Nord or Paris-Est to Paris-Montparnasse: Take metro line No. 4 in the direction of Porte d'Orleans. Get off at Montparnasse-Bienvenue.

• Paris-Nord to Paris-Est: Walk (10 minutes). You can walk through a tunnel to Magenta RER station and then rise to street level to complete your exercise.

• Paris-Montparnasse to Paris-Nord or Paris-Est: Take metro line No. 4 in the direction of Porte de Clignancourt. Get off at station.

• Paris-Montparnasse to Paris-Lyon. Take metro line No. 6 in the direction of Montgallet. At Bercy (which you use for the Artesia de Nuit trains to/from Italy) change to line No. 14 in the direction of Madelaine.

• Paris-Lyon to Paris-Montparnasse. Take metro line No. 14 in the direction of Bibliotheque. At Bercy change to line No. 6 in the direction of Charles de Gaulle.

• Paris-Nord or Paris-Est to Paris-Austerlitz: Take metro line No. 5 in the direction of Place d'Italie. Get off at Paris Gare d'Austerlitz station.

• Paris-Est to Paris-Nord: Walk on surface streets to Magenta RER station, descend, and reach Paris-Nord through a tunnel.

• Paris-Austerlitz to Paris-Nord or Paris-Est: Take metro line No. 5 in the direction of Bobigny. Get off at station.

• Paris-Nord to Paris-Saint-Lazare: Take RER line *E* from Magenta RER station to Haussman RER station. Both RER stations are connected to their respective terminuses by tunnels.

• Paris-Est to Paris-Saint-Lazare: Take metro line No. 7 in the direction of Mairie d'Ivry. Get off at Opera. Opera metro station is connected by tunnel to Haussman RER station. Haussman is, in turn, connected to Paris-Saint-Lazare by tunnel. Don't get lost.

• Paris-Saint-Lazare to Paris-Nord: Use tunnel to Haussman RER station, get off at Magenta RER station, connect by tunnel to Paris-Nord.

• Paris-Saint-Lazare to Paris-Est: Walk via tunnel to Opera metro station. Board metro line No.7 in the direction of La Courneuve. Get off at Gare d'Est station.

You don't have to use stairs within Paris's train stations, but once you enter the metro system below, you encounter endless flights of stairs and long corridors in addition to escalators that usually work, but not always. The metro stations are not luggage friendly, especially when you try to pass items through the gates. *Tip:* Push or shove your baggage ahead of you when you insert your ticket into the gate-opening slot.

Riding Paris's 2,000 buses shows more of Paris and gives you a feeling for the relationships between major sights, but this is not as easy as it sounds because it requires a grasp of the surface streets, something riding the metro does not.

Each metro line takes its name from the end stops. For example, line 1 is called "La Defense/Chateau de Vincennes." When you take line 1 in the direction of La Defense you will travel west until you reach the end stop of the same name. Think in terms of directions. The orange signs in stations marked "Correspondence" mean you can change lines at that station to go in another direction. Just follow the signs. Trains run from 5:30 A.M. to about 12:30 A.M. During the night there are night buses.

RER crisscrosses Paris in the center and branches into the suburbs, to the airports, Versailles, and Disneyland Paris. There are five RER lines: *A, B, C, D,* and *E. A* and *B* are run jointly by RATP and SNCF, while *C, D,* and *E* are run by SNCF on its own. Line *A* shifts more than 50,000 passengers per hour per direction at the peak—and ridership continues to grow. B3 connects to Paris Charles de Gaulle Airport, C2 and B4 to Paris Orly Airport, C5 to Versailles, and A4 to Disneyland Paris. Metro tickets and passes are valid on RER within the city center.

The best way to ride the Paris metro is to use one of the metro passes designed for voters of the city rather than tourists. These are issued for calendar weeks beginning Monday (Coupon jaune—meaning "yellow") and for calendar months beginning on the first (Carte orange). There is also a pass valid for a year. Their disadvantage is that you need to supply a small passport-type photo (which the agent will affix). You may buy your photo at a quick-photo machine in Paris but will save aggravation by bringing it with you.

The average visitor, who doesn't stay long enough to take advantage of these passes, can best buy 10 tickets at once (called a "carnet") from a machine (press *E* for English) or an agent, or use two kinds of wallet-sized passes designed for tourists: the one-day "Formule Une" or the "Paris Visite," valid for either two, three, or five days. Neither the Formule Une nor the Paris Visite cards require a photo. The Paris Visite also gives significant discounts at many sites, including 20 percent off admission to the Cite des Sciences et de l'Industrie and 35 percent off Canauxama cruises on Canal St-Martin.

The prices for all the passes mentioned above provide unlimited second-class travel on the metro, RER, and buses in zones 1 and 2 (also zone 3 for the "Paris Visite"), which is all that the usual visitor uses, but for higher costs you can extend these passes to increased zones or first-class RER and include RER transportation to Versailles, Paris Charles de Gaulle Airport (zone 5), and Paris Orly Airport (zone 4). In most cases it is cheaper to buy tickets for these longer distances separately.

In addition consider the "Carte Musees et Monuments" available from the Paris Tourist Office and metro ticket counters. They are available for one, three, or five consecutive days in 65 Paris museums including the Louvre and Musee d'Orsay. The cost savings can be significant. Additionally, with such a card you don't have to stand in line—and the time you save may make it worthwhile to you. You go straight to the head of the line.

Airport Trains

There are two train stations located underground near Paris Charles de Gaulle Airport's terminal 2C (Air France's terminal). Free, yellow-striped, "ADP" shuttle buses circling the airport connect both of CDG's two terminals ("Aerogare") to them. The RER station takes you to Paris; the TGV station leads to Lyon, Bordeaux, Marseille, Nice, Lille, Poitiers, London, Brussels, and other cities without a time-consuming trip into Paris. Thirty-six high-speed TGVs, all covered by rail passes, serve the airport's TGV train station. You can board a TGV train at CDG and arrive in Lyon two hours later, in Bordeaux about four hours later, or in Lille, to connect with a Eurostar train to London, in less than an hour. In other words, if Pierre takes a TGV from Lille and Paul takes a cab from Paris, they just may arrive at CDG at the same time.

RER trains use the 1994 RER station. Prices vary with distance (not covered by rail passes), but when you purchase a single ticket you have access to more than a hundred RER stations in the Paris area. RER line

B3 trains depart every seven minutes, taking 30 minutes to Gare du Nord and then continuing to Chatelet-Les Halles, St-Michel-Notre-Dame, Luxembourg, and Denfert-Rochereau stations between 5:05 A.M. and 11:50 P.M. Eurail products cover only the segment between the airport and Gare-du-Nord.

The Air France bus (costing about the same as first-class rail) takes about an hour (barring gridlock on the motorway) from the Porte Maillot bus terminus near the Arc de Triomphe or Place Charles-de-Gaulle-Etoile (avenue Carot) with departures about every 12 minutes between 6 A.M. and 11 P.M. Roissybus, the transit authority's bus to the square in front of the Opera, where there is a metro stop, departs from Paris Charles de Gaulle Airport every 15 minutes from 5:45 A.M. to 8 P.M. and every 20 minutes from 8 P.M. to 11 P.M. It takes about 45 minutes, barring gridlock. A special KLM bus takes longer because the driver must wait for the last passenger off the plane to clear customs.

From Paris Orly Airport, board the Orly-Rail shuttle from Orly to the SNCF Orly-Rail station at Pont de Rungis station on RER line *C*. RER line *C* runs every 15 minutes to Austerlitz train station, St. Michel/Notre Dame, Musee d'Orsay, Invalides, Pont de l'Alma, and Eiffel Tower between 5:50 A.M. and 11:30 P.M. Eurail products cover only the segment between the airport and Gare d'Austerlitz.

The 1991 Orlyval automated, light-rail minimetro links Orly West and Orly South terminals with RER line *B* at Antony-Orly station in seven minutes, with connections every five to seven minutes to/from St. Michel/Notre Dame, Chatelet-Les Halles, Gare du Nord, and Paris Charles de Gaulle Airport stations. Your Orlyval ticket is also valid on metro and RER lines as needed to your destination.

Orlybus, the transit authority's bus, runs between Paris Orly Airport East terminal and Paris Orly Airport South to Denfert-Rochereau every 13 minutes (peak) and takes 30 minutes on average. At Denfert-Rochereau you find Paris metro lines No. 4 and No. 6. Orlybus service runs from 5:35 A.M. to 11 P.M. from Orly South. The Air France buses leave Paris Orly Airport every 12 minutes daily between 5:50 A.M. and 11 P.M. for Montparnasse. A second stop takes you to the Invalides air terminal. Allow 30 minutes.

Formula One and Paris Visite tickets (see above) are valid on Orlyval provided they include zones 1-5. They provide discounts on Orlybus and Roissybus as well.

Before returning to Paris Orly Airport on your RER *B* train, make sure that Antony-Orly station is illuminated on the station billboard. Sit toward the rear of the RER train to make changing to Orlyval easier. Similarly, when taking line *B* to Paris Charles de Gaulle Airport from one of the stations mentioned above, be sure the electronic sign or video monitor states "Roissy Rail," for this is just one of the two branches of the northbound RER, and you want to be on the correct train.

TGVs between FrenchRail's CDG airport train station and the train station at Lyon's airport, which has been renamed Saint-Exupery (formerly Satolas) for Antoine de Saint-Exupery, aviator and author of *The Little Prince,* whisk passengers hither and yon, but contrary to logic, TGV trains connect the Lyon airport train station to downtown Paris and the Paris airport train station to downtown Lyon. This is the kind of stuff that makes travelers scratch their heads and rail fans chortle.

Stunning is not too strong a word to describe the architecturally inspiring 1994 TGV train station at Lyon's airport. Dramatic fan-shaped arches of steel-supported glass soar like a bird with outstretched wings above a central overpass. A schematic electric signboard directs you to one of two gates leading to two island platforms, each served by four tracks. Your gate depends on your carriage number. Porte Rhone leads you to five sectors ("repere") and Porte Alpes leads you to four.

While air arrivals use RER rapid-transit trains from Paris Charles de Gaulle Airport to central Paris, bus is their connection from Saint-Exupery airport to central Lyon. Buses depart from Lyon's Perrache train station every 20 minutes from 5 A.M. to 9 P.M. (except Sat. 1 P.M. to Sun. 9 P.M. and French holidays, when they run every 30 minutes). The travel time is about 45 minutes, depending on highway traffic.

Versailles

There are three train routes from downtown Paris to Versailles, taking 20 to 30 minutes. Of these, RER line C5 route to Versailles Rive-Gauche station takes you closest to the chateau and is covered by a Eurail product, or you may prefer to take a train from Paris Gare Saint Lazare to Versailles Rive-Gauche or one of the hourly Transilien TER trains from Paris Gare Montparnasse to Versailles-Chantiers.

The 1991 opening of Massy TGV station gives you a fourth route to Versailles. TGV trains between Lyon and Rouen pass through Massy TGV in the southern outskirts of Paris (use RER lines *B* or *C*), taking 10 minutes from Massy-Palaiseau to Versailles.

Alternately you can take bus line 171 from above Trocadero metro station to the last stop. For the bus you need either three metro tickets, a Formule Une valid for zones 1-4, or a Paris Visite valid for zones 1-2-3-Airport.

The chateau is open Tuesday-Sunday 9:45 A.M. to 5 P.M.; the Grand Trianon, Tuesday-Sunday 9:45 A.M. to noon and 2 to 5 P.M.

Disneyland Paris

Paris RER line A4 takes you to the "Disneyland Paris" complex, which is situated 12.4 miles to the east of Paris. Good places to board include the Chatelet-Les Halles interconnect with RER lines *B* and *D*, Gare de Lyon, and Vincennes.

In 1994 Disneyland Paris took on a new life when long-distance TGVs began calling at the Marne-la-Vallee station on the Interconnection Link between the Southeast and Nord Europe TGV networks, so that now you can wear your mouse ears on the TGVs from Brussels, Lille, Lyon, and Dijon and nobody will think it is odd.

Overnight Trains

SNCF's overnight equipment is so good it is exported. You can hardly resist riding overnight on the long routes from Paris because with a first-class rail pass you pay no more to sleep in a domestic couchette with four bunks than second-class passengers pay for six-bunk couchettes.

"Service Nuit" trains are entirely composed of Corail couchette carriages and Corail reclining-seat carriages. In the center of each train, you find a staffed service coach with vending machines selling drinks and snacks. You check in before departure to ensure no unwelcome visitors are aboard. For security, trains do not stop between 12:30 and 5:30 A.M. Women may request same-sex couchettes positioned close to the conductor's compartment. Couchette passengers use a fixed duvet instead of blankets and a sheet sleeping bag and receive a welcome kit including a bottle of mineral water. Reservations are obligatory.

On Friday-Sunday evenings, SNCF supplement Service Nuit with overnight TGV trains, which do not necessarily run over high-speed lines to allow maintenance of the lines and to schedule arrivals and departures at a reasonable hour. Routes of the TGV overnight services include between Paris and Brest, Toulon/Nice, Montpellier/ Perpignan, and Hendaye/Tarbes as well as between Lyon and

Toulon/Nice. The Perpignan and Hendaye trains run daily during July and August.

Rail-Pass Travel

SNCF honors Eurail products, France Railpass, and cooperative passes with Italy, Spain, and Switzerland on all lines. In addition, you receive discounted fares on Eurostar to England and Artesia to Italy. The Chemins de Fer de la Provence (CP) gives holders 25 percent off (50 percent with a France Railpass), Chemins de Fer de la Corse on the island of Corsica gives 50 percent off, and the ferries between France and Corsica give a discount of 30 percent.

You receive free passage on RER line *B* between Paris Charles de Gaulle Airport and Gare du Nord and RER line *C* between Paris Orly Airport and Massy, Gare d'Austerlitz, Versailles-Rive-Gauche, and Versailles-Chantiers.

You receive 50 percent off on Sea France crossings between Calais and Dover and Irish Ferries that alternate sailings between Cherbourg and Rosslare and Roscoff and Rosslare, Ireland. There are limited winter services, and advance reservations are recommended.

The France 'n Spain Pass and the France 'n Switzerland Pass cover the respective national railroads of the two countries for any four days of unlimited travel. Additional days up to 10 may be added as needed. The pass is available for both first- and second-class travel and has different pricing schedules for adults, two or more traveling together, and youth. Children under four travel free and those between four and 11 pay half the adult fare. A complete list of bonuses is supplied with the pass.

Expressly excluded are Trens Hotel, the AVE high-speed trains, and Talgos operating on the high-speed line, and to ride these trains you will be required to pay hefty supplements. Supplements for your use of all other trains, including those normally requiring *A* supplements, are included, but not sleeping or eating surcharges. Neither FEVE nor the Al Andalus Expreso honor the pass.

The France 'n Italy Pass is a big advantage for travelers planning to visit both countries compared with buying separate national passes, especially for those planning fewer than eight combined travel days, and you won't have to validate both a France Railpass and an Italian Flexi Rail Card for the day or days you travel between France and Italy. You may choose between four to 10 travel days in two months, traveling either first or second class. Those under 26 receive a discount of about 20 percent for second-class travel. Groups traveling together pay 30 percent less for the additional travelers.

A France Railpass is as flexible as a Parisian tart's affections and as thrifty as a Gascon goatherd. With a four-day France Railpass, you can travel anywhere you choose on SNCF for a month for less than the round-trip fare on TGV between Paris and Lyon. Moreover, you can tailor your pass to your exact needs by buying the precise number of days you need (up to six extra days). All passes must be validated at any French train station (which may be done up to six months after issuance in the U.S.). Fast-train surcharges are covered but you must pay for the reservations that are required on all TGVs.

When you travel with a companion you can obtain a special price. Two persons together pay about three-quarters of what they would pay buying individual passes. Children four to 11 pay half the adult fare. Those under four ride free.

Enter your name and passport number and have it validated at an SNCF station (at an "Orientation" kiosk or ticket window), where the agent will enter the first and last day of validity. If the agent asks you when you will start travel, tell a fib. Tell him, "Today." You have one full month to travel. Otherwise the agent will demand that you come back and stand in line again on your first day of travel. Personally complete the day boxes in ink in numerical sequence on the days you travel. When you start your trip after 7 P.M., enter the next day's date and travel overnight using up only one validation day.

The France Rail'n Drive program allows you to combine the France Railpass with an Avis car rental. Avis has 520 locations throughout France including more than 200 in train stations. SNCF/Avis's basic one-month package gives you three days of unlimited train travel in France (plus the free airport transfer coupons and discounts) and two days of Avis car rental with unlimited mileage, VAT (value-added tax), and basic insurance included. (Gasoline is extra.) You can purchase extra days of train travel and auto rental. Third and fourth persons sharing the car need only buy a France Railpass.

Many French regions provide economical Regional Passes on week-ends in the summer months in second class on TER trains and buses, but not TGVs.

To sample France's rail speed and adventure to offbeat corners, travel on the 186-mph TGV Atlantique to Brittany, the TGV Genevois from Paris to Geneva, the Chemins de Fer de Provence from Nice to

Digne, and Metro Basque from Bayonne to St. Jean-Pied-de-Port described here.

TGV Atlantique
Into Brittany by 186-mph Supertrain

Blasting through Brittany at 186 mph, passengers use the white-striped, hinged vinyl tables separating their seats to write postcards as smoothly as if they were writing from their nearest library. You accept the well-known fact that TGV-A ("A" for "Atlantique") is fast. It comes as a surprise that TGV-A's innovative concept in pneumatic suspension makes its ride as calm as a Breton cow.

Atlantique is a victim of its own success. It moves so effortlessly, without shimmy or shake, that passengers can't appreciate that it holds the world's speed record of 320 mph set on May 18, 1990. Ten-carriage-long return trains take 2.9 seconds to flick past your window. Atlantique pulverizes rain into nuclei so microscopic that the 186-mph wind wipes them from the windows even before they wet it.

TGV-A impresses you with its substance and power. These trains differ from the other blue and silver streaks you see in France. They are longer and carry a full-length bar car and special club cars with small, four-person compartments down one side of the aisle with electronically controlled seats. Many travelers prefer this seating. Pairs occupying the facing seats along the window chat intimately. TGV-A is a no-smoking train and has "voiture silence" carriages where mobile phones are not used and are set to vibrate rather than ring.

Climb TGV-A's shiny aluminum steps from a platform on the top level of the five-level, bright glass, metal, and red granite Paris Montparnasse station, your high-rise "Ocean Gateway" to the Atlantique network. Your TGV-A takes you to Brittany along dedicated high-speed track that branches into three routes. The 386-mile North Brittany line takes you to Rennes, St. Brieuc, and Brest with a further branch from Rennes to the south coast of Brittany through Lorient to Quimper, Brittany's ceramic and pottery center. The 304-mile South Brittany line takes you to Nantes, St. Nazaire, and Le Croisic.

The southern fork of the high-speed stretch to St. Pierre des Corps opened in September 1990. It takes travelers via the TGV station in Vendome from Paris to Bordeaux in less than three hours, reaching the Spanish border in just over five hours.

TGV ATLANTIQUE

PARIS-MONTPARNASSE

HIGH-SPEED LINE

Brest

Rennes

Quimper

Le Mans

Vendome

Tours

St. Nazaire

Nantes

Poitiers

La Rochelle

- N -

Bordeaux

0   20   100
MILES

Bayonne

Hendaye

Lourdes

Your blue-and-silver Atlantique supertrain's livery was designed to reflect the sun, sea, and sand of Brittany and the Atlantic coast. It was so successful that the livery was then applied to SNCF's entire fleet of TGVs. Instead of yellow roofline striping to mark first-class sections, TGV-A's doors are color coded (ocean blue-green for second class, cherry red for first, and yellow for the bar), but you may not even notice this. It is easier for you to rely on the easy-to-see numerals indicating class of carriage.

Check your seat reservation coupon in the vestibule before making your way to your seat. Above the compartments' entrances, LCD signs blink destination, train number, and carriage number.

A horn sounds and TGV-A's doors slide shut. In an instant, you leave Paris so quickly that when you enter tunnels you feel depressurization of your carriage. In the tunnel you enter the new high-speed line. While your TGV is coasting, the DC pantograph goes down and the AC pantograph goes up for high-speed travel. Above, environmentalists have created playgrounds, open spaces, and a cycle path. In open space, you are already passing the outskirts of Paris along land lucky enough to have been already reserved for a railroad line. This land included a roadbed that had been nearly completed before work was abandoned in 1934—a highly prized right of way, which came close to accommodating a motorway 30 years after the railroad was abandoned. On return, when your ears pop, you know they are signaling your approach to Paris.

It doesn't take long for your TGV-A to run quickly up to speed: 186 mph like a stopwatch. Your speed is programmed by computer. In first class, passengers read newspapers and fashion magazines and pound laptop computers on the tabletops.

Outside, the land is flat, spotted with woods along the high-speed track, but: think frogs. You see some of the ponds where environmentalists spent years relocating endangered species away from the train route and protecting them from hungry herons.

When you leave the high-speed railbed, past Le Mans, your train takes on a new feel. You hear the familiar clickety-clack of standard rails and slow down enough to appreciate the Gothic spires marking every village. You see why Brittany is famous for its characteristic, small black-and-white prolific milk producers, "Pie Noire" cows, which sometimes mingle with brown "Salers" from Auvergne, in the mountains of France's Central Massif.

When you leave Angers' St. Laud train station (made attractive by tufa stone quarried in the Loire Valley), you see greenhouses, artichokes in the fields, and parasitic mistletoe richly infesting many of the trees. Brittany is the only region in France where mistletoe grows.

Soon you are running along the right bank of the Loire River, wide and quiet. Magnolia trees and camellia bushes were brought from the French settlements in Louisiana before the colony's sale to the United States in 1803.

You recognize Nantes from a distance by its tall buildings. Nantes train station has two accesses. The South access, added in 1989 with the introduction of TGVs, is modern and has all amenities, ramps instead of stairs, a small restaurant, and an elevator to the passageways below the tracks. The North access echoes from the 1960s but is well marked and easily accessible. The waiting room is called "Salon Jules Verne," named after a local boy made good.

The rafters of Nantes's St. Peter and Paul Cathedral, destroyed by a devastating fire in the 1970s, have been rebuilt. Beige tufa pillars soar higher than Westminster Abbey's to make this the brightest and warmest large cathedral in Europe.

In Nantes, among its many balconied mansions and its busy port, take time to visit Passage Pommeraye, an original three-level stepped galleria and the predecessor of today's malls. Completed in 1843, the ancient faces, mice, and snails carved in stair risers and cheerful sculptures scattered throughout lend a feeling of fun.

Nearby, visitors are lucky when they come across the delightfully decorated La Cigale (meaning "cicada") tearoom. Try a pastry and a cup of coffee (or dinner) just to enjoy the atmosphere. It first opened at 4, place Greslin (facing the Opera) in April 1895.

After your train's three-minute halt in Nantes, new passengers board to join your entrance to traditional Brittany, a rough and tumble land of Celts, bagpipes, and the Breton tongue. In Brittany's center you find evocative regions where followers of King Arthur come to see "The Land of the Round Table" and the enchanted Broceliande forest charred by fire in 1990 where the wizard Merlin met the fairy Viviane and love inflamed them both. (To make sure of keeping Merlin, Viviane enclosed him in a magic circle. It would have been easy for him to escape, but he joyfully accepted his romantic captivity forever.) You see Merlin's seat and Viviane's bed. From here Sir

Lancelot of the Lake set out for England and his seduction of Gweniviere, King Arthur's wife.

Past Nantes you run through fertile farming country where farmers harvest melons, cabbage, and onions. To the south tower the major harbor and industrial zone facilities of St. Nazaire on the Loire estuary.

St. Nazaire grew to a great shipbuilding center when, in 1856, large ships found it difficult to reach Nantes. During the Second World War St. Nazaire was a major German submarine base and the center of strategic fighting, blockades, bombardment, and, ultimately, massive destruction.

St. Nazaire train station is the final destination for many passengers. They carry their baggage up the apple-green stairwell.

Past St. Nazaire you enter the well-named Cote d'Amour. Even the sun gets brighter as you approach what many French vacationers to La Baule consider the finest beach in Europe—and they frolic here in July and August.

You stop at La Baule's Escourlac Breton-style station house on the northern tip of the diving, soling (the Olympic sport), and windsurfing resort, and then you cross the canal to Le Croisic peninsula, traveling close above the salt marshes that identify this region. Women scrape crystals off the surface of the salt flats to obtain the finest-quality white sea salt in Europe.

Sea birds watch your train riding bumpily onto a siding at Le Croisic's small station, the end of the line. Its continuation is blocked by Mont-Espirit, the curious 98-foot double-corkscrew mound, built from ships' ballast. From the summit you see the salt marshes to the east, the landmark belfry of Batz-sur-mer to the west, and the Atlantic Ocean in the distance.

Even while you are stepping down TGV-A's aluminum stairs, a cleaner is plugging in a vacuum cleaner to make your Atlantique spotless for its return trip.

Your TGV-A has a whole array of features for you to use throughout its 10 carriages, including telephone booths and a special diaper room in second class for parents with distressed babies. Probably your biggest surprise is that the mechanism adjusting seats in first class makes them rise or sink at the touch of a button just as in a luxury automobile.

Each first-class table has an individual light. Reading lights are behind the passengers, who control a fluorescent overhead lamp by button.

Walking through the carpeted first-class sections, you start behind a power car with the elevated nine-passenger, horseshoe-shaped "Le Salon" with video monitors and then cross the standard "La Coach," half with 2+1 seats facing forward, half with seats facing backward.

FrenchRail calls the next two cars "Club Cars." "Le Club Duo" pairs gray-and-white-striped plush seats facing one another beside the aisle across from "Le Club Quatre," four seats upholstered with black-and-white-striped plush within partially closed, tinted-glass minisalons.

Atlantique's social whole-carriage bar car provides passengers with staggered rows of vinyl-topped snack counters. Across its stainless-steel sales counter, service personnel wearing SNCF badges heat microwave sandwiches and sell magazines, candy, coffee, wine, and minibottles of liquor. Low vinyl counters at the windows are equipped with small swivel stools to give you a fine place to eat, drink, and watch the scenery flashing past. *Tip:* Be sure to drop in. It's a great place to hang out and socialize.

The crowd in second class is definitely younger. They are sleeping and listening to earphones. The equivalent of club in second class provides facing seats with partial tinted-glass partitions above the seats. Regular salons where half the seats face forward, half backward, have no need for these sound barriers.

Second class features rubber-mat flooring, fold-down footrests, rough-wearing fabric upholstery, and tables that fold down from seat backs. Only in the center, where passengers face one another, are there tables similar to those in first class. Up a few steps at the end brings you to "Le Kiosque," the second-class lounge arranged with two tables and second-class seats designated for single children.

Doubled TGV-A trains on the North Brittany line race from Paris's Montparnasse to Rennes, where its multilevel station is part of the district development plan that provided a shopping street above the tracks, a sweeping access hall to the platforms, elevators, and escalators. North of Rennes, visit one of the world's foremost pilgrim's shrines, Mont St. Michel. Villedieu-les-Poeles is your changing point to bus, taxi, or rented bicycle from trains from Paris or Rennes. Follow the crowds. Bypassing the train connection, tour buses (air-conditioning, video, toilet) of Les Courriers Bretons leave directly from Rennes.

At Rennes, your doubled TGV is divided. One section continues on the North Brittany line to Brest's Art Deco, end-of-the-line, centrally located train station, allowing you to make the 386-mile trip from Paris in about something over four hours (including stops). Brest's station offers a splendid view overlooking enormous shipyards from the train station terrace. Brest's bus station is located in front of the train station.

The second TGV travels from Rennes along the completely electrified southern Brittany coastline to Quimper, the prosperous city still distinctly Breton in character and full of intriguing churches (including the cathedral of St. Corentin, the city's patron saint).

You need reservations for all TGV Atlantique runs. In first class, you can reserve seats "Club Quatre" in the minisalons or beside the window "solo" for intimate conversations. A "couloir" is an aisle seat, and "compartiment" is compartment.

TGV Atlantique timetables are among the most complicated in Europe. You find different schedules for Fridays, Saturdays, Sundays, Mondays, and Tuesdays-Thursdays. Fares and supplements, which vary with times of day in addition to days of the week, make it necessary to plan in advance. Rail passes save you from this torture. Pick up a free pocket timetable or "Guide TGV Atlantique Ouest" and just tell the reservation agent approximately what time and on what day you want to leave. With the opening of the southern bypass of Paris in 1996, you can ride some trains from Brittany straight through to Paris Charles de Gaulle Airport via Massy TGV station.

TGV Genevois
Computer-Age Anachronism

The Genevois was one of the first group of TGV trains included in the select EuroCity network. It carries you on one of EC's most fascinating routes, linking Paris with Switzerland's cosmopolitan city through mountainous regions and past villages still anchored in the 19th century.

Until the TGV Atlantique's new railbed opened in fall 1989, your TGV Southeast train was the fastest in the world—but even if it were merely a speedy way of getting from one place to another, you would still find it fun, smooth, and exciting to ride. As it is, you get a scenic eyeful as well.

By using either the Paris metro's Gare de Lyon stop or RER station and climbing the escalator to ground level, you reach the station's TGV platform without ever seeing the light of morning. When you

TGV PARIS-GENEVA

Rhone River

LYON

Bellegarde

Bourg-en-Bresse

Macon

GENEVA

LAKE GENEVA

Le Creusot

-N-

0   20   50

MILES

PARIS

arrive at the platform, you step into the future. Purring, shark-snouted, Trains a Grande Vitesse surround you as far as you can see.

The TGVs are screamers. They sound as if they are growling as their engines warm for fast getaways. Speeding at 186 mph much of the way, your TGV Genevois cuts your travel time to Geneva by more than two hours, to just over three and a half hours. Introduction of TGVs butchered air service and delayed congestion of toll roads on this route. It provided excitement for your trip.

TGVs on the Southeast network are single, articulated units of eight air-conditioned cars with engines at both ends. Usually SNCF couples two units together to double the seating to 772 (222 in first class, 550 in second). Still, trains are totally filled on busy days. *Tip:* Book early for travel before holidays.

You purchase coffee, Parisian croissants, and reading materials in the bar car. In some carriages, you can order a Continental breakfast served on the tray in front of you.

The TGV Genevois, followed later in the day by five or six identical TGVs, depending on the day and date, whisks you away promptly at 7:10 A.M. It doesn't immediately leap forward. While toiling through the suburbs of Paris, it vibrates with restrained energy. If you feel some disappointment, it is because you don't feel a jolt when your Genevois enters the high-speed corridor and accelerates to 186 mph. There is no speedometer to fascinate you.

Past the suburbs of the capital, your high-speed trip to Macon is pastoral. You study spotted cows grazing in the fields and ponder the speed of the train. There are no highways paralleling the tracks so you can't accurately gauge your speed, but the buttercups beside the tracks become a mustard-colored blur and you hear no clickety-clack from segmented rails. You know you must be at maximum speed.

You branch from the TGV Southeast high-speed line at the modern Macon Loche TGV's stone stationhouse. The platforms are covered, but there are no luggage carts. The clickety-clack reminds you that you have returned to old-fashioned—and slower—railbeds.

Past the Bourg-en-Bresse station, two hours from Paris, you enter the Jura region of France. Green woods roll up the impressive heights above the train line. Old villages of monochrome stone houses center around churches that seem to belong on old sepia-tone postcards.

The passing scenery becomes so eye-catching that French travelers around you fold up the magazines that had interested them before and put away their attache cases and laptop computers.

Your attention focuses on the mountains taking shape in the distance. The French word "grandeur" says it all.

You can't escape the anachronism: speeding through ageless Jura Mountains and time-forgotten villages in a computer-age bullet.

You see individual farmers tending little fields. Tiny vineyards spot the hillsides. You notice details that date from quieter times: a river with lily pads, a fisherman in a leaky rowboat, old towns pressed defensively against high mountains, churches of stone, an outcropping with a statue of an unknown hero on its summit.

Finally your Genevois passes the first of many tunnels. You aren't in the tunnel long, but it breaks the scenery. You continue at a brisk pace—no longer at 186 mph, but still very fast.

You finally slow when a broad river, the Rhone, appears on your right. Battlements of once-powerful castles dot the mountainsides overlooking the Rhone. A modern bridge spans the chasm.

At Bellegarde-sur-Valserine, an industrial city at the meeting of the Valserine and Rhone rivers, the only thing level is the huge rail yard. The city trails down the hillside toward the Rhone.

Here you can change for the French Lake Geneva resort of Evian-les-Bains by connecting railcar. It stands across the platform below the patina eaves of the weathered train station. "Evian" mineral water is served aboard the TGV Genevois.

From Bellegarde, a long tunnel brings your TGV to a route that twists miraculously through mountain valleys on embankments braced by stone. Mountains tower around the train. You follow the Rhone River below.

Finally your train levels off. TGV chimes sound. Passengers take Swiss bank notes from envelopes and you approach Geneva's Cornavin station along a level route surrounded by endless vineyards.

You arrive at the French/International TGV terminal at Geneva's Cornavin station. Tracks ("Voie") 7 and 8 are separated from Swiss national train traffic by glass doors kept closed except at arrival and departure times. Border guards check your passport as you enter Switzerland. Ramps allow you to wheel your luggage cart to Geneva's Tourist Office, which occupies a gleaming suite in the train station.

When you leave Geneva through the SNCF terminal for France, don't arrive more than a half-hour before departure time. You must

linger in the modest waiting room until guards open the doors pneu-
matically.

Chemins de Fer de Provence
Scenic Gateway to the Riviera

You climb to your second summit at St. Andre-les-Alpes station over-
looking the stone houses of the village and prominent stone church.
A fine, long view of snow-covered Alps opens before you to the south.
Climbing higher, you see the weirdly scalloped shores of Le Verdon
Lake below to the west, with water so calm ducks scarcely bob on the
surface.

The little-known Chemins de Fer de Provence (CP) narrow-gauge
private railroad takes you 103 miles between Digne and Nice through
Cote d'Azur's 103-mile-long backdoor, a bright, crisp ride through the
backcountry of the Var department, through sunshine and mountain
air, gorges, pre-Alps, and river valleys. The *Train des Pignes* (named at
the time that the railroad's steam engines had to burn pinecones to
keep running) on *Ligne Digne* is a little trip, an off-the-beaten-track
secret. CP allows a 25 percent discount with your Eurail product and
gives you half off when you show your France Railpass. Those over 55
also receive 25 percent off and those four-12 get 50 percent off.

CP's blue-and-white diesel railcar is so intimate and open that you
look over the engineer's shoulder at the rails ahead while your train
skirts the edges of deep precipices and climbs steeply over the last
range of Alps between the French interior and the Mediterranean.

More rock canyons than you will find in any other part of France,
some as deep as 700 or 900 feet, mark your path. Your railcar teeters
precariously on mountain rims and rocks from side to side along a
roadbed that chatters your teeth. It is well known that this trip is wash-
board rough.

You travel down again, past level fields of wheat and mountainsides
covered with pine to the Asse River, where you cross into Barreme
(pop. 435).

Between Barreme and Digne-les-Bains, the capital of the high country in Provence, you roughly trace the route of former mule paths
Napoleon and his handful of supporters took returning from Elba in
1815. "The eagle will fly from steeple to steeple until he reaches the
towers of Notre Dame." Villages boast commemorative plaques and

CHEMINS de FER
de la PROVENCE

Bleone
DIGNE
Mezel-Chateauredon
L'Asse
Barreme
St. Andre
Le Verdon
Thorame-Haute
Le Fugeret
Annot
Le Coulomp
La Vaire
Le Var
Entrevaux
Puget-Theniers
Le Cians
Touet sur Var
Villars-Var
La Tinee
La Vesubie
La Vesubie
Colomars
Le Var
MEDITERRANEAN SEA
NICE

N

0   10   20
                MILES

monuments bear the flying-eagle symbol inspired by Napoleon's remark. A house near Barreme's town square carries the inscription that Napoleon slept there on March 3, 1815.

Nice, in the Riviera, attracts visitors like a sunny magnet. Holiday makers enjoy frolicking along the beaches and feeling the charm of the Riviera while sipping coffee on the busy, four-mile-long Promenade des Anglais that borders the Mediterranean and represents the heart of the delightful Queen of the Riviera. Monte Carlo, a destination Americans enjoy visiting for its casino and princely flavor, is 24 minutes away by train from SNCF's Nice Ville station. The Nice station is pleasant, although you may not agree if you arrive at a platform accessible only by climbing and descending flights of stairs. Visit the Nice Tourist Office outside, adjacent to the station, for hotel reservations and information. It is open 8 A.M. to 12:30 P.M. and 2 to 6 P.M., Monday to Saturday, during the summer.

When you enter the modern, but lightweight, three-track 1992 CP terminus at 4bis, Rue Alfred Bihet (Tel. 93-82-10-17), look behind you at CP's former Gare du Sud, which is listed as a historic monument. Sud was a superb four-track station, the oldest in Nice, built in 1892, and the Place de Gaulle outside was an enchantment with sidewalk fruit-and-fish markets and flower stalls and kiosks selling snack items ranging from excellent pizza to extraordinary, odd pastries. Now the station has been converted into the city hall.

CP's Nice station is about a 20-minute stroll from SNCF's Nice Ville station. In the CP station, ask for a map of your route to Digne at the ticket counter below the bright wall mural of the route.

The driver shifts your railcar's large diesel engine into low gear and accelerates sharply through Nice's city streets. You not only cross traffic intersections, but you have to stop for red lights when you meet them. You pass stop signals and cross boulevards bumper to bumper with automobiles before entering a black tunnel that takes you out of the city center.

You watch the surroundings through panoramic windows. The driver maneuvers jerkily. The orange seats and maroon leatherette headrests do not recline but are thickly padded. It is a very wide carriage for a narrow-gauge railcar. The rubber-mat floor still shows mop marks.

In 1994 floods closed the line at numerous points and washed out whole sections. Buses bypassing the destroyed sections were used for nearly two years and it wasn't until April 1996 that the CP railcars were able to run the entire length once more without interruption when the replacement Gueydan Bridge was opened. The French army carried out this last major piece of work. Total cost of repair was $6.6 million, of which the region paid $2.1 million.

Running rockily along the river Le Var, you begin to notice strange secluded hilltop chateaux. At St. Martin-du-Var station house, you see tulips and other flowers blooming under the trees in back.

You are traveling parallel to highway N202 on the east and the river on the west. Orient yourself by the names shown on road signs.

After stopping at La Vesubie-Plan-du-Var, you cross La Vesubie River on a gray steel-girder bridge to run counter to the racing river while the highway continues high on the mountainside. Alpine snows feed the Vesubie, a tributary of the Var. Its valley reaches up to your right through gorges cut into vertical walls, a popular area for French tourists. You are entering the mountains and it becomes more fun. A tunnel takes you to the left bank of the cottonwood-lined Var. As you pass, you see a woman cranking up the red-and-white highway barrier to let road traffic resume.

Past Touet-sur-Var station house and the Cians Bridge, a small road breaks away to your right for the Cians gorges, some of the finest in the Alps.

Puget-Theniers, the largest village along this route (pop. 2,000), is a southern town at the meeting of the Roudoule and Var rivers. You leave the Maritime Alps district and enter Alps de Haute Provence—at one and the same time the High Mountains and Provence.

You see high chateaux on the hillside before entering Entrevaux, a surprising fortified town (pop. 1,040) surmounted by its citadel. A short walk takes you to the west bank of the Var at the foot of a curious rocky spur.

When you leave Entrevaux, rocks take on strange, worn shapes. You first see distant snow at the time you enter your first snow tunnel. Streams in the Var Valley become wilder. Horses—grown mares and brownish-gray yearlings—romp in the fields.

You leave the Var to the east, flowing from the Daluis gorges, and continue up the Coulomp valley below landslide-scarred slopes to the Var's tributary, the Vaire, and then follow the Vaire Valley.

Rising above Annot's church steeple and red-tile roofs surmounting high facades in the medieval "old town," you gain your first true

Alpine sensation. The mountainside is terraced in rock. Above Le Fugeret, your railcar wanders freely, through tunnels and loops, to gain altitude. Snow remains on the ground until April.

Passengers peer from the windows and take an interest in the jagged rocks to the east and the curious birds flapping as you pass through a jagged gorge. Everything looks greener.

You cross the Vaire River and pass through a black tunnel onto a second bridge across the Verdon River, a tributary of the Durance, which forms magnificent gorges in the limestone of the Haute-Provence. The fresh pine-scented air has a mountainous feeling to it.

You reach the first summit of your mountain railroad. Thorame-Haute's mountain stone church looks handsome beside the flower-decorated station house.

Now you travel downhill through the upper valley of the Verdon in the same direction as the rushing river to the east. The hills are covered with trees of many different shades of green. You receive a hint of the Alps by forests of beech, pine, and larch. The crisp air and bright sky make this a summer tourist destination for the people of Provence.

Geologists recognize the name Barreme for the name "Barremian," given to part of the lower cretaceous layer.

Past Barreme, your railcar seems to be speeding downhill, but it can't be going too fast, because new Renaults on highway N85 outdistance you with little trouble. Children in the autos' backseats fan the air with their waving at you.

Past the stone Chaudon-Norante station house, you enter the pre-Alps of Digne, climbing through tunnels and along a creek to that capital of the Lavender Alps—a mountain city looking onto Alps nearby.

Lavender is characteristic of Haute-Provence. In the 1930s, farmers began cultivating plantations of this wild-growing mountain flower on higher slopes. Breathe deeply in July, when mauve flowers scent the air.

In Digne, a pleasant spa town, the CP and SNCF stations share the same building. The SNCF rails are still there, side by side with CP's, and although Digne has been abandoned by SNCF and you must take a bus, local authorities are determined to reopen the line to St. Auban and are trying to determine whether they should simply refurbish the existing standard-gauge line or, alternatively, lay a third rail on the standard-gauge track to allow CP to extend to St. Auban.

Until they do, your best connection to Paris, Lyon, or Marseille is via the two-hour bus ride from Digne bus station (a 10-minute walk) to

Aix-en-Provence TGV station, where you board a TGV on the TGV Med line. *Tip:* This is a good chance to enjoy Aix. Buses leave at 6:40 A.M., noon, and 5:50 P.M. Alternately, there are buses to Chateau-Arnoux-St. Auban for a local train to Marseille St. Charles station, and buses to Veynes-Devolay to for trains to Grenoble or Valence Ville TGV station, also on the TGV Med line. These leave at 9:15 A.M. (Valence) and 12:30 P.M. (Grenoble).

Chemins de Fer de Provence
Summer Service between Nice and Digne

0642	0900	1243	1700	dep.	NICE (CP)	arr.	1018	1349	1715	2035
0657	0915	1258	1717	dep.	Lingostiere	dep.	1004	1335	1659	2921
0705	0922	1306	1724	dep.	Colomars	dep.	0956	1327	1652	2014
0714	0931	1317	1732	dep.	St.-Martin-Var	dep.	0947	1318	1642	2005
0717	0934	1321	1736	dep.	Pont-Charles-Albert	dep.	0944	1314	1637	2002
0721	0939	1326	1740	dep.	La Vesubie	dep.	0940	1310	1633	1958
0737	0955	1342	1756	dep.	Malaussene	dep.	0921	1252	1615	1941
0742	1000	1347	1801	dep.	Villars-sur-Var	dep.	0917	1248	1611	1937
0752	1010	1357	1811	dep.	Touet-sur-Var	dep.	0907	1238	1601	1926
0804	1022	1410	1823	dep.	Puget-Theniers	dep.	0855	1226	1549	1914
0812	1030	1418	1831	dep.	Entrevaux	dep.	0847	1218	1541	1906
0828	1046	1434	1847	arr.	Annot	dep.	0830	1201	1524	1849
0832	1050	1449	1852	dep.	Annot	arr.	0823	1155	1521	1846
0838	1056	1446	1858	dep.	Le Fugeret	dep.	0817	1149	1515	1840
0843	1101	1451	1903	dep.	Meailles	dep.	0812	1144	151	1835
0853	1111	1502	1913	dep.	Thorame-Haute	dep.	0803	1135	1501	1826
0904	1123	1513	1924	dep.	Saint-Andre	dep.	0751	1124	1448	1815
0910	1129	1519	1930	dep.	Moriez	dep.	0745	1117	1442	1809
0920	1139	1529	1940	dep.	Barreme	dep.	0735	1107	1432	1759
0927	1146	1536	1947	dep.	Chaudon-Norante	dep.	0727	1059	1424	1751
0939	1158	1548	1959	dep.	Mezel	dep.	0715	1047	1412	1739
0953	1212	1602	2013	arr.	DIGNE	dep.	0700	1033	1358	1725

Metro Basque
Heart and Soul of Basque Country

Local Basque leaders call the railcar that takes you to the heart and soul of French Basque country "Metro Basque." It runs between Bayonne, the northern limit of the Basque coast in France, and St. Jean-Pied-de-Port, a different world, 31 miles, one hour, and 515 feet

METRO BASQUE

To Paris

BAY OF BISCAY

Biarritz

BAYONNE

Villefranque

St. Jean-de-Luz

Ustaritz

FRANCE

To San Sebastian

Itxassou

SPAIN

- N -

St. Martin-d'Arrossa

Eyharce

ST. JEAN-PIED-DE-PORT

0   5   10
MILES

above it. St. Jean-Pied-de-Port, as its name suggests, sits at the foot of the pass of Roncevalles in the Atlantic Pyrenees, the gateway to Spain only five miles above.

Breaking your journey here on a trip between Madrid and Paris is an adventure, a diversion, and a prerequisite when you are interested in Basque culture.

Many Americans of Basque descent return every two or three years to visit their relatives. St. Jean's busy season is July and August, when French, German, English, and American visitors (no one counts Spanish Basques, who are not considered tourists) swell the population of St. Jean's 3,000 permanent inhabitants to 12,000 to 15,000. You enjoy the many summer festivities such as jai alai (which is as important to the Basque as the church), folkloric dancing, and serenades by choral groups.

Many young Basques came to the New World because at home only the oldest sons inherit their parents' farms and properties. Without property, younger sons tended to immigrate to the New World to make their fame and fortune. Many did, and became prosperous. Because Paul Laxhault is of Basque origin, many Basques have a keen interest in American politics and a fondness for American visitors. Even now the population is not increasing.

Bayonne's station, where you begin your climb, is remodeled to accommodate TGVs from Paris. It is grand, distinguished by the preserved clock tower on the outside, and efficient inside. You snack in the adjacent modern buffet. Look for the departure times posted prominently above the information office and ticketing windows.

You see waiting on track No. 1 a pair of red-and-white railcars, which are part of the TER Aquitaine regional train system. The first-class section contains seats for nonsmokers and fewer, through an automatically opening glass door, for "fumeurs."

It's a comfortable, modern, pleasing train, no doubt completed by the same interior designers who won awards for the Corail trains.

Both cars have seats arranged like salons. First class has 2+2 maroon bucket-type seats facing each other. Second class, through another glass door that you open with a push on a lever (like Corail trains), is configured similarly with slightly less distance between brown leatherette seats. There is almost no difference between first and second class except for the blue carpeting in first and nonskid rubber flooring in second. Both are modern, spotless, and decorated with tidy, plaited curtains.

A few minutes late for departure, and concluding his gossip with the driver, the white-capped dispatcher waves his white-and-green paddle. The driver scampers aboard, closes the doors, and starts your electrified railcar on its single track away through a tunnel.

While your conductor checks the tickets and nods at your rail pass, you cross the Nive, a broad, brown river, and enter a second, long tunnel. Woods and fruit trees surround your line. Thorny berry thickets flourish on the slopes of the elevated railbed while you pass through flat farm country, with cornstalks thriving in the fields.

Your conductor announces your first stop, Ustaritz, on the speaker system. Ustaritz's station house is brown stucco with brown trim. All stations on this line are clearly marked even when the signs are covered with climbing, green vines.

You still travel on the level, running parallel to the slow-flowing Nive, to your second stop, Cambo-les-Bains, where white postwar homes are roofed with tiles.

Not all trains halt at the next stop, Itxassou, where villagers still don curious costumes and perform their annual, elaborate Corpus Christi procession.

Now you are beginning to climb modestly past whitewashed farmhouses with sagging tile roofs. Many Basques drive up the parallel two-lane blacktop highway, but still prefer the train occasionally to relish the scenery.

You feel the temperature cool when you slow for the station house serving St. Martin-d'Arrossa and the nearby villages of Eyharce and Osses. This is the junction of two rivers that form the now-raging Nive. You see large white Basque houses with cornerstones and brown or green shutters and trim. A few passengers change here for buses to Saint Etienne de Baigorny.

Finally you see black-faced sheep for the first time, happily munching the long green grass on the slopes. Some sheepherders own them; some rent. You see merinos with long, fine, silky wool, and the Basque sheep, manech, which are black and white with curved horns. But if you visit during the summer, you must go to the peaks of the Pyrenees to find them. The sheep are kept in the cities for six months until May 1, and then they spend six months in the high mountains.

On every side of the wide valley, trim Basque villages nestle amid manicured pastures. Each is centered on a church with a clock tower—the local custom is to toll the hour twice. Everything is green, casual, pastoral, and the epitome of quiet.

High above the ridges, hawks cry and immense golden vultures soar on the breeze, eyeing the flocks of long-wooled sheep below. Herds of sleek, blonde Basque cattle graze beside shaggy dark ponies called "pottoks," which are horses unchanged in appearance since they were portrayed on the walls of the Paleolithic limestone caves not far away.

At last you see St. Jean-Pied-de-Port, the former capital of Lower Navarre, built by Garcia Ximenes in 716. It became a French town as a result of the Treaty of the Pyrenees in 1659. Louis XIV had it fortified by Vauban and you can still see its ramparts, walls, and citadel dominating the town and the Pyrenees. When Wellington crossed the Pyrenees in 1813, he entered France via St. Jean-Pied-de-Port.

You are on the pilgrim's route through northern Spain to Santiago de Compostela. (Refer to this book's section on the Talgo Pendular to Santiago de Compostela.)

Bracken fern, green in spring, reddish brown in the fall, cover the steep slopes of the surrounding mountains, which dwarf the wooded hill above the town. Farmers scythe fern into tall, conical stacks for fodder or simply burn it, turning the air blue with pleasant-smelling smoke.

Disembark at St. Jean-Pied-de-Port and walk from the train station to the city center along streets clearly posted with signs. The Syndicat d'Initiative in the center (on the left as you approach) is located in a modern building.

Inspecting the seven Gothic gates in the wall that used to surround the whole town (which were formerly locked at night) gives you an excellent grasp of the complex angles and divisions of this curiously exciting village.

St. Jean consists of shops and stone houses, each with two or three apartments, scattered along cobblestone streets fronted with steps instead of sidewalks. The crosspieces over the doors proudly proclaim who built them and when. Like all Basque houses, town and country, these are sturdy, half-timbered with stone and whitewashed stucco facades. Green or red-brown shutters are obligatory, for they are the Basque colors, but "Basque red" comes in many shades these days, depending on where the owner buys his or her paint.

The citadel you see brooding over the rooftops is used as a high school in winter and a museum in summer. Sheep graze in its moat.

The church's clock tower set into the city wall contains a small room that served as the city hall in medieval times. From the gate in the base of the tower, you cross a graceful stone bridge arching over the Nive.

Monday is market day all year long, all day long, in St. Jean, as it has been for centuries. You can buy berets (black only) from traveling peddlers, rope-soled canvas Basque slippers, Citroen tractors, Apple computers, fresh-killed wild doves, and ripe cheeses. Two thousand lambs are bought here every Monday.

During the summer, trains climb from Bayonne at 9:03 A.M., 11:24 A.M., 3:04 P.M., 7:30 P.M., and 9:05 P.M. From St. Jean-Pied-de-Port, you can return at 7:10 A.M. (except Sun.), 10:20 A.M., 1:30 P.M., 4:17 P.M., and 6:50 P.M., although like most French timetables, services vary with day and date.

Britain and Ireland

Savvy Traveling on the Trains of Britain and Ireland

British trains—New Pendolino—Cross Country—White Rose between London and Leeds—Airport trains—Caledonian Sleeper—London train stations—The London Underground— Glasgow stations—Irish trains—CityGold between Dublin and Cork—Enterprise between Belfast and Dublin—Crossing the Channel by ship—Crossing the Irish Sea—Rail-pass travel in Britain—BritRail Pass + Ireland—Using Eurail product bonuses in Ireland

British Trains

Starting on May 20, 1996, with the Initial Public Offering (IPO) of the rail infrastructure in Britain, the British government privatized its former BritRail and created 25 train-operating companies (TOCs), including one to maintain and improve the infrastructure including train stations, and therefore the familiar "BritRail" ceased to exist.

Trips of any length at all mean you will use the services and see the strange logos and liveries of two or more companies. *Tip:* Do not be confused by what the logo on the side of your train says. They all accept BritRail Passes without question and they work together seamlessly so that you can book any train in Britain at any TOC's reservation counter and get information on every railroad in Britain there. Their Web sites are all linked to a common timetable, so you can find your timetable through any of the TOC's Web sites.

Coping with the different tariffs makes a BritRail Pass just as optimum in Britain as a Eurail product on the Continent, and fortunately, in 2000, the Association of Train Operating Companies began marketing passenger services as "National Rail," with an excellent Web site, *www.nationalrail.co.uk*, to make train travel as seamless as possible for the general public. Their "National Rail Guide" includes sections on how to get information, and explains their ticketing schemes and how to buy tickets and plan journeys. It includes a network map.

All InterCity trains carry first-class and standard-class (the British railroads call their second classes "standard class") carriages, but most of the local trains consist of standard-class carriages only. It is essential to reserve InterCity trains at peak periods (Fri. afternoon/evening, bank holiday periods) and to and from Scotland. You can normally reserve from about two months in advance up to about two hours before departure (for early-morning trains, up to the previous evening).

After a period of mutation, three TOCs emerged as the predominant companies:

• Virgin Trains, which manages two TOCs, the important West Coast Mainline and Cross Country Trains;

• Great North East Company (GNEC), which manages the crack East Coast Mainline; and

• ScotRail, the National Railroad of Scotland.

New Pendolino

The important, twisting West Coast Mainline line, which connects important cities such as Manchester and Birmingham with London and Scotland, was sadly neglected by former BritRail and used mostly aging Intercity 125 trains, which were also neglected.

In 2003, Virgin Trains progressively replaced the well-used trains with 110-mph Pendolinos built capable of tilting to 8 percent. They were built by Alstom (do not confuse these with Italian Pendolinos because they are larger and more comfortable), while leaving the timetable unchanged. The whole timetable will update with journey time reductions of 30 minutes or more when the West Coast Mainline's track improvements have been completed and the trains accelerate to 140 mph.

The Pendolino is a magnificent, substantial train even without the tilting mode that will be activated in September 2004. It introduced innovative features such as electronically displaying your name and seat number above your seat (provided you have a reservation). All seats have an audio jack and socket to recharge cell phones and laptops. (*Tip:* If your equipment has a U.S. plug, you will need to take an adapter.) A novelty is the "Shop," where you can browse for magazines, novelties, and CDs as well as food and refreshments in about one-third of one carriage. There are toilets in all carriages, including three for disabled use.

The Pendolinos run as eight-, nine-, and 10-carriage sets. First-class seats are spacious and comfortable, mixed airline-style seats arranged 2+1 and service tables. Second-class seats, arranged 2+2, are full of new features and the electronic seat-reservation displays.

Cross Country

Virgin Trains created a new regional InterCity network with new red-and-silver Voyager trains connecting over a hundred regional towns and cities with high-frequency, regular-interval timings. It is the only regional network in Europe that does not touch the country's largest city. (*Tip:* Ask the train captain for a "Windowgazer Guide," which highlights the interesting sights along your route.)

This is the first time that the Cross-Country network has ever had brand-new trains since the days of steam. The pleasant standard class has 2+2 red and dark blue seats with plugs for headphones, but the tilt-body profile limits the width of the seats to only 19 inches. Similar to the Pendolino, the trains feature an electronic reservations system and a "Shop."

Look for the 125-mph Voyagers and tilting Super Voyagers. The latter are named after international explorers and have a mechanism that allows an extra six-degree tilt, permitting them to lean around curves up to 20 percent faster, giving you a gentler ride. You will not see, only feel, the difference because they will be the same except for the undercarriage mechanisms (and Super Voyagers will have one additional carriage). However, the Super Voyagers will not benefit from the tilting until September 2004, when operation in tilt mode will commence.

White Rose between London and Leeds

Travelers have to admit that compared with some of the views they see through the window of a train, their approach to Leeds is not that arresting. But as your GNER (Great North Eastern Railway) White Rose Eurostar train approaches Leeds station, the familiar preamble to virtually any northern industrial city becomes more interesting.

In the midst of railroad cuttings and warehouses, passengers note an extraordinary tower. During West Yorkshire's heyday a Victorian industrialist modeled a factory chimney after Giotto's campanile for Florence Cathedral—in brick, not marble—and his industrial folly still stands.

GNER launched Britain's most prestigious train service from London Kings Cross on May 30, 2000, using Eurostar trains leased from Eurostar UK. Billed as "White Rose" service for the traditional emblem of Yorkshire, the Eurostar trains provide two million extra seats a year to reduce the overcrowding of GNER's route between London and Scotland. GNER operates the busiest mainline fleet in Europe and offers 125 services a day during the summer, including 26 to and from Leeds.

The trains, now sporting GNER's dark blue and red livery, were originally built in 1994-95 for Eurostar service to Paris but had not entered commercial service. The leased trains are integrated with GNER's timetable to provide 12 addition services each weekday although they run less frequently on weekends. Each of the 14-carriage trains can carry 558 passengers. Eurostar has two power cars, four first-class carriages, two cafe-bar coaches, and eight for second-class passengers, including a cellular-telephone-free carriage and a family carriage.

From what you hear about Leeds these days, it is, according to its champions, the new capital of England's revived and assertive North. Its magnetism is expected to increase now that business travelers commute to Leeds from London aboard GNER's White Rose in two hours, 10 minutes. But it comes as something of a disappointment to stroll down its main business streets. Buildings like the magnificent Town Hall and the Corn Exchange show an undeniable grandeur, but Leeds also has more than its fair share of bleak office blocks.

Leeds station, in the center of town, is a covered, efficient, medium-sized station with a GNER first-class lounge. The station's best feature, facing City Square, is the 1937 Queens Hotel with its Art-Deco Portland stone facade. On the concourse to your left when you arrive, you find telephones, luggage checking, ticketing, and train information. Arrows point to city information nearby outside.

Weekday White Rose Service

```
0805 0905 1305 1405 1505 1850 dep. LONDON        arr. 0833 1232 1428 1817 1925 2026
                                    (Kings Cross)
0850 0951 1350 1450 1550 1405 arr. Peter-        arr. 0737 1136 |    |    |    1930
                                    borough
 |    |   1412 1514 1612  |   dep. Grantham      dep. 0717 1116 1319 |    |    |
 |    |   1425 1527 1625 2006 arr. Newark        arr. 0702 1101 |    |    |    |
                                    North Gate
 |    |    |    |   1641  |   dep. Retford        dep. 0647 |    1253 |    1756 |
 |    |   1452 1553 1658  |   arr. Doncaster      dep. |    1036 1236 1636 1736 1836
0956 1056 1513 1612 1722 2046 arr. Wakefield     dep. 0619 1019 1219 1619 1719 1820
                                    Westgate
1014 1115 1531 1631 1740 2105 arr. LEEDS         dep. 0605 1005 1205 1605 1705 1805
```

Airport Trains

London's Gatwick and Heathrow airports take about the same time to reach from central London, but the cost of the least expensive ground transportation from London to Heathrow is about a quarter that of getting to Gatwick.

The January 19, 1998, Heathrow Express train speeds nonstop at 100 mph between London Heathrow Airport and Paddington Station, in central London, in 15 minutes, every 15 minutes. You board at two brand-new stations at the airport: Heathrow Central for terminals 1, 2, and 3, and a second at terminal 4, which adds five or six minutes to your travel time. The Heathrow Express is spiffy, but long, with first-class carriages at each end of the train. When you arrive at London Heathrow Airport holding a first-class BritRail Pass, have it validated at the ticketing office, and then proceed to the first-class carriage at the head of the train. The air-conditioned interiors are comfortable, with two-opposite-two seating in second class and one-opposite-two in first class, with generous legroom and abundant luggage and overhead space.

Incidentally, you can use the train, free, to transfer between terminal 4 and the other terminals.

Heathrow Express trains depart from Paddington Station, platforms 6 and 7, between 5:10 A.M. and 11:40 P.M. daily. Second class costs about $15 each way; first class costs about $30. BritRail Passes are accepted.

Paddington train station has 27 desks served by most airlines, including Air Canada, American Airlines, British Airways, Canadian Airlines, Qantas, and United Airlines. You can check in your luggage anytime on the day you fly, up to two hours before your flight time, collect your boarding card at Paddington, ride the Heathrow Express to your terminal, and go straight through passport control to your departure gate.

The Piccadilly Line on London's Underground serves London Heathrow Airport, and using it has the advantage that you can reach an Underground stop near your final destination either directly or by changing to another of London Underground's 11 lines. The downside is that it is slower, can be crowded, is not luggage friendly, and changing lines with luggage is a bother. Trains run every few minutes, from early morning until after midnight.

The Piccadilly Line has two stops at London Heathrow Airport: use the first stop for Heathrow terminus 4, the second for terminals 1, 2, and 3 (make sure you know which terminal your flight departs from). Allow at least 50 minutes between the airport and Piccadilly Circus; 58 minutes from Kings Cross/St. Pancras. When you must change from one subway line to another, your trip will take much, much longer, especially on Sundays when service is less frequent.

At London's Heathrow terminals 1, 2, and 3, you wheel your suitcases right up the gates of the Underground. Fare is about $5, which seems a lot for a subway ticket, but compared to airport transportation in other cities, it is cheap. Heathrow lies in London Underground's outer tariff zone, zone 6.

Arriving passengers should use the information desk as they leave the airport and enter the Underground station. Agents will give you directions to your destination, an Underground map, and sell you your ticket (which you will keep to exit the system).

Departing passengers with only hand luggage can check in with British Airways in Heathrow's Underground station and go straight to their departure lounge for their flight.

London Gatwick Airport has its own train station right in the heart of the airport with direct train services to many parts of England. To reach Gatwick from London, board the Gatwick Express (*www.gatwick-*

express.co.uk) at Victoria station's modern Rail/Air check-in facilities on platforms 13 and 14. This area is equipped with elevator, escalator, and special escalator-friendly luggage carts. British Airways maintains a passenger lounge above the platform.

The gray-and-white, red-striped, aging Gatwick Express train, specifically designed for air travelers, is being replaced by a red, yellow, and white "Darth Vader" eight-carriage electric railcar. You ride in carpeted, air-conditioned carriages, enter through wide doors, store your luggage on convenient shelves, and walk between compartments through automatically opening doors. You may telephone from the train and charge it to your credit card.

The Gatwick Express carries you nonstop at speeds up to 90 mph, cutting your travel time between Gatwick and Victoria station to 30 minutes. Quarter-hourly service runs from 5:50 A.M. from Victoria until 12:50 A.M. During the night, standard train service (taking 52 minutes) continues hourly. Second class costs about $18 one way; first class, about $28. BritRail Passes are accepted.

The Gatwick Express takes you to Victoria station. When you wish to go to other spots in London, or beyond, it may be more convenient to take Thameslink Rail (TR, *www.thameslink.co.uk*), which serves 11 stops from Gatwick as far as Bedford, and makes a stop at Kings Cross Thameslink train station, about 1,000 feet from the main Kings Cross train terminus, where you board the GNER trains to York and Scotland.

TR drops you about 10 minutes from London Gatwick Airport's South Terminal and 15 minutes from the North Terminal. Air arrivals follow the train symbols to the TR stations. TR tickets are available from the ticket desks in the North and South terminals between passport control and baggage reclaim, South Terminal arrivals hall, and opposite check-in zone H for London tickets only. Ask for Thameslink when buying your ticket. There are about four departures per hour, and the trip takes about 46 minutes between Gatwick and Kings Cross.

London Stansted Airport, 33 miles from London's Liverpool Street station, has its own train station right in the heart of the user-friendly, 1991 airport terminal building. It knocks spots off Heathrow for convenience. It is the only airport in Britain where you can wheel baggage carts right onto train station platforms. The shining Stansted Express operated by WAGN is a dedicated train with departures every 15 minutes between 8 A.M. and 4 P.M. on weekdays and half-hourly from 5 A.M. to 11 P.M. daily. It takes you to London's Liverpool Street station in 42 minutes, with an intermediate stop at Tottenham Hale that you can use to transfer to the Victoria Line of the London Underground for a direct route to the West End (Oxford Circus) as well as Euston and Victoria stations. First class gives you a free hot drink, newspaper, and laptop connection. BritRail Passes are accepted. Taxis are about five times more expensive and take longer. There is also hourly service to Cambridge and Peterborough continuing to Liverpool or Birmingham.

When Manchester Airport train station was opened in 1993, Manchester Piccadilly station express trains were extended to the airport, calling at Stalybridge and the airport-branch junction station, Heald Green. Manchester airport train station is right in the heart of the airport complex, linked to Terminal One by a covered escalator and Terminal Two by a 24-hour-a-day shuttle-bus service. There are up to six trains per hour (three trains per hour on Sun.; hourly during the night) between Manchester's Piccadilly station and Manchester Airport, taking 15 to 23 minutes, operated by electric railcars with blue Manchester Airport "air-express" regional railways logo. You find increased luggage space. There are regular through trains connecting the airport with Preston, Lancaster, Liverpool, Sheffield, Leeds, York, Glasgow, and Edinburgh. You have good mainline connections to London's Euston station.

Birmingham Airport is beside Birmingham International train station, which is served by direct trains to principal towns and cities. Frequent Tyne and Wear Metro service runs between Newcastle Central train station and Newcastle Airport, linking the north's Regional Railways and InterCity networks directly with the airport.

Southampton Parkway train station is adjacent to Southampton/Eastleigh Airport—a three-minute walk. Direct InterCity services link Southampton Parkway with Midlands, northwest and northeast England, and Scotland. London Luton Airport and Glasgow Airport still lack rail links, so you rely on frequent bus connections to the nearby cities.

Airlink buses offer frequent connections between Dublin Airport and the downtown Connolly train station.

Caledonian Sleeper

Scotrail has assumed control of Britain's Caledonian Sleeper train between London's Euston Station, North West England, and Scotland aboard refurbished Mark III carriages. First-class sleepers accommodate one passenger; second-class cabins accommodate two in an upper and a lower berth. Each cabin is equipped with blankets, cotton sheets, air-conditioning, bedside lighting, washbasin with electrical shaver outlet, and hand towel. All berths are nonsmoking.

There is also a nonsmoking carriage fitted with reclining seats, footrests, tray tables, individual reading lights, and access to buffet facilities. Advance reservations are compulsory.

Scotrail provides Caledonian Sleeper departures from London Euston at 11:55 P.M. for Edinburgh and Glasgow, and at 9:30 P.M. for Aberdeen, Fort William, and Inverness. Reservations are required. BritRail Passes cover the transportation, but you must pay supplements for the cabin facilities. A 10 percent discount is available on Caledonian Sleeper standard fares when traveling to or from Scotland with a Freedom of Scotland Travelpass (see below).

Travelers joining at the starting point of the train may occupy cabins one hour before departure time. At end stations, you may remain in your cabin until 8 A.M. Your porter asks you whether you wish to be awakened early for arrival or after sleeping late. He awakens first-class passengers by delivering a newspaper and complimentary orange juice, hot croissant, jelly, and coffee or English tea freshly loaded aboard en route. Second-class passengers receive cookies in lieu of croissants.

Special Caledonian Sleeper reception lounges are available for complimentary coffee or tea and cookies before boarding at London Euston (access via platform 16), Inverness (station concourse), Aberdeen (station concourse), Carlisle (in the Lakes Court Hotel), and Edinburgh Waverley (adjacent to platforms 11/14). At Glasgow Central, passengers can board the sleeper at 9:40 P.M., where the on-board lounge car will be open.

The on-board lounge service is provided primarily for first-class passengers although second-class passengers are welcome during slack periods. The lounges are first-class salon cars converted into pubs with bars, 26 lounge seats, and a public telephone. Located midtrain, this is where first-class passengers buy drinks, light meals, and snacks before turning in and after awakening.

London Train Stations

London has seven principal train stations. Most are terminuses of a particular line and dominated by a single TOC. Euston station is home for Virgin Trains and the terminus of the West Coast Mainline. Go to

Kings Cross station for GNER East Coast Mainline service. Waterloo International station is your gateway to Eurostar services to France and Brussels. Paddington station is the downtown terminus of the Heathrow Express train and Victoria station is the terminus of the Gatwick Express train and home of Connex South Eastern. St. Pancras station will be converted to the new terminus of Eurostar when the second phase of the CTRL is completed. Liverpool Street station leads to Southampton and Portsmouth Harbor for cruise ships and is the terminus of the express train to Stansted Airport. Charing Cross station is the terminus for Connex trains to Dover Priory and Ashford International.

All London's train stations are different but feature lots of shops, "Cash Point" ATMs, newsstands, separated ticketing rooms, hotel-reservations offices, and usually a pub and Burger King restaurant. They also have one or more large digital departure-time displays with hordes of passengers standing beneath them waiting for their train's platform number to be announced.

GNER's first-class lounge in Kings Cross station and the pleasant Virgin Trains first-class lounge on the mezzanine on the east side of Euston station are available to holders of first-class BritRail Passes. They are complete with office equipment, writing areas, deep-cushion chairs, sofas, and complimentary hot and cold soft drinks.

Several of the train stations are connected to hotels that provide convenient accommodations. Above Charing Cross station you find the traditional Thistle Charing Cross Hotel (*www.thistlehotels.com/charing cross*). There is an entrance to the Thistle Victoria Hotel (*www.thistlehotels.com/Victoria*) directly from Victoria station's platforms. In 2002, Hilton reopened (with 60 million pounds sterling) the historic Great Western Royal Hotel at Paddington station with escalator entrance from the platforms (*www.Hilton.com*). If you travel to Manchester on Virgin Trains' flagship service, the Malmaison Hotel (*www.malmaison.com*) is five minutes' walk from Manchester Piccadilly station.

The London Underground

London's train stations, and London Heathrow Airport too, are connected by London's busy subway system known as the Underground, or "Tube." When you buy individual tickets, remember to keep them to operate the automatic turnstiles when you exit.

It's convenient to buy day or longer-term London Travelcards for the Underground. They are reasonably priced. When you buy them by the day, no photograph is required. You can even buy them from the vending machines located in Underground stations for unlimited travel over a 650-square-mile area, but with a catch: you can't buy day Travelcards before 9:30 A.M., Mondays to Fridays. This is fine for late-rising visitors but makes them unsuitable for business travelers.

Travelcards are valid for unlimited travel by the Underground, Docklands Light Railway, and London-area trains and on most of London's buses (not the Airbus). For slightly less, you buy a Travelcard valid for a day only in central London, which is usually sufficient.

You can buy longer-term Travelcards for seven or more days for the exact number of days you require. Generally, when you will be traveling in London for four or more days, it is cheaper to buy a seven-day Travelcard than single one-day Travelcards. For these, in London you will need to obtain a free photocard, requiring a passport-type photograph either brought with you or bought from a machine. These make it economical to take buses for very short distances, transfer from bus to bus, and from Underground to bus and vice versa—which is a great travel advantage.

When you want the convenience of paying in dollars, the security of having a Travelcard voucher in hand before you leave, and the ability to exchange the voucher at London Heathrow Airport for your trip to central London, buy either an "All Zone" or "Central Zone" London Visitor Travelcard valid for three, four, or seven consecutive days of unlimited travel. Central Zone covers zones 1 and 2 of London's Underground. All Zone also includes transportation between Heathrow Airport and central London (but not on the Heathrow Express Train) and the Docklands Light Railway.

Glasgow Stations

Glasgow is not only a good jumping-off place for the West Highland line (see section following), it is an interesting city to visit in its own right. Rail fans should not miss visiting the Glasgow Museum of Transport (free admission and free guide service), which is one of the happy surprises of Scotland.

Glasgow has two stations. Both of them are very good, with adjacent hotel and all facilities. The Station Hotel is located right in Glasgow Central station, which is the terminus of the electrified trains to London on both the East Coast and West Coast mainlines and your jumping-off station for your trip through Burns country to Stranraer and Stena Line's HSS fast ferry service to Belfast, taking 90 minutes. This spacious and airy terminus is one of the best organized in Britain and certainly one of the most comfortable in all Europe. It dates from the 1870s, when a pioneering steel-trussed roof was built to shelter the platforms. Crossing the concourse, look out for "The Shell," a First World War collecting box and favorite meeting point.

Glasgow Queen Street station is the terminus for the diesel railcars on the West Highland line and the excellent Express Trains, which shuttle to and from Edinburgh on the hour and half-hour from both cities. The Copthorne Hotel fronts on George Square. It has its entrance a few feet from the Queen Street station exit.

There is a quarter-hourly shuttle bus between the two train stations, but if you are not burdened with luggage and the weather is good, it will be more pleasant and faster to walk the five blocks. For directions, look for Strathclyde Transport Central Area maps posted in both stations.

Irish Trains

With a Eurail product, it is not expensive to make Ireland your gateway to Europe because IrishRail (IR, *www.irishrail.ie*), which honors Eurail products, allows holders free use of their entire network, including DART (Dublin's state-of-the-art electric regional transportation system). Irish Ferries gives 50 percent off for passage from Rosslare, Ireland, to Cherbourg/Roscoff, France.

Irish trains run upon a nonstandard track gauge of five feet, three inches (1,600 mm). Clearly it was never considered that a link to the European mainland would ever take place. Still, IrishRail is the most convenient way to see the green countryside for rail-pass holders. The black-and-orange IR trains are mainly standard class and many are standard class only. Some trains also have "super standard" class available for a supplement of $5, or $8 if meal service is offered. "CityGold" Pullman-style service is also offered on certain Dublin-Cork services (see below).

Make Dublin your rail hub to reach all popular tourist centers. Dublin has three main train stations: Connolly, Pearse, and Heuston. Heuston and Connolly were redeveloped in 1998 to make these flagship stations the symbol of 21st-century train travel. New entrances and retail shops make the stations bright and convenient. Connolly and Pearse are connected by DART, which is free with your IrishRail or Eurail product. Hop on bus line No. 90 for express service between Heuston and Connolly stations.

Travel times are short on IrishRail's modern diesel trains. Train journeys never take more than four hours—which is about the time it takes you to get from Dublin in the east to Tralee in the southwest. On mainline service you relax in comfort and watch the green Irish countryside.

To see completely the Republic of Ireland, supplement your train travel with the red-and-yellow Irish Bus buses. They link every city and hamlet with mainline trains from stops usually in front of the train stations. Like IrishRail, Irish Bus is an arm of the national Irish Transport Company, "Coras Iompair Eireann" (CIE), and you receive a reduced price on a Bus Eireann Rover Ticket when you hold a rail pass.

CityGold between Dublin and Cork

IrishRail is proudest of its first-class-only "CityGold" service (*www.irishrail.ie/our_services/citygold.asp*). Holders of first-class Eurail products and BritRail Passes + Ireland are welcomed with Irish warmth. Those with second-class passes are treated equally royally after they pay a supplement of about $25, Dublin-Cork ($6.50 on Sun.). You join gregarious white-collar commuters with bulging briefcases who relax as they travel back and forth between Dublin and Cork in upgraded, first-class IC carriages attached to the front of IrishRail's best IC trains. You can identify the carriages by the CityGold logo.

CityGold passengers are greeted by a host and shown to their reserved seats in new, air-conditioned carriages. Seating is 2+1, divided by a table with an elaborate lighting console/telephone jack. Free earphones connect to a Blaupunkt console for popular or classical music or news. The highlight is the meal service served at your seat by a waiter with a sense of humor.

The meal is not free to rail-pass holders. Including Salmon Supreme, Linguine Primavera, Baked Limerick Ham, Platform Grill, or the Station Master Special (an Irish beefsteak with vegetables and farmhouse French fries), dinner runs $10-$20. Prices include taxes, tip, and coffee or tea. Credit cards are accepted.

CityGold leaves from Dublin's Heuston station. The locomotive at the head is shining in IrishRail's orange and black livery. Look to see if it is the "Abhainn na Sionainne" ("The River Shannon"), the first diesel locomotive given a name by IrishRail.

The River Shannon 201-class locomotive was shipped by air from London (Ontario) to Dublin airport aboard a Ukrainian Antonov 124-100 airplane. The 112-ton locomotive was the second-heaviest air cargo in history (the first was an electrical generator).

Traveling eastward into County Kildare you pass through deep-green pasturelands and past hedge-lined roads through Droichead Nuc (Newbridge) to Kildare city. The horses roaming the fields belong to the dozens of stud farms that make up the heart of Ireland's famous racing industry.

Turning southeast at Portarlington where the River Barrow divides the town into two counties (Laois and Offaly), you reach the county town of Portlaoise. Continuing into the natural charm of eastern Tipperary's landscape through Ballybrophy (where there are branch-line connections via Nenach to Limerick), Templemore, and Thurles, you halt in Limerick Junction so that, if you wish, you can change to or from the primary train to Limerick and Ennis, where the Irish government has spent $17 million to link most households and businesses to the Internet.

Your IC makes good time to Charleville (Rathluirc), the point where you enter County Cork. This northwest corner of County Cork is a region of stone, hills, and country estates of studding and riding stables set in parkland. You can make out the slopes of the Boggeragh mountains rising to the south.

Mallow, where the horse is king, is the center for processing sugar beets, fishing, hunting, and changing passengers to and from Killarney and Tralee.

Through the slopes of the Nagles mountains to the east, fertile land, and thickly wooded valleys, your IC reaches vine-covered, end-of-the-line Cork train station. Nearby Blarney Castle is a magnet for visitors to Ireland who hope to win the gift of eloquence by kissing the Blarney Stone. To kiss this rough limestone block, lie on your back and lean out over a sheer drop. Make sure a pair of strong hands holds your shins. The stone is scrubbed with disinfectant four times a day.

Although IR's locomotives are capable of higher speeds, and the Cork line has already received substantial investment to bring the maximum line speed up to 90 mph, IR is cautious about changing the timetables so as not to upset the routines of regular travelers. Currently the CityGold train takes you over the 165 miles in two hours, 30 minutes, making two stops and averaging 66 mph.

Enterprise between Belfast and Dublin

There was a good deal of speculation about the color of the Enterprise (*www.irishrail.ie/our_services/enterprise.asp*) cross-border express trains between Dublin and Belfast that began service late in 1996. Because it is a joint operation between North Ireland Railroads (NIR, *www.nirail-ways.co.uk*) and IrishRail, the color question was sensitive.

When the first of the 28 new carriages for the Dublin-Belfast service arrived from Zeebrugge at Dublin Port, reporters marveled at the handsome light-gray/dark-gray livery that didn't seem to antagonize anyone.

Eight daily departures (five on Sun.) take you between Dublin's Connolly station and Belfast's Central station over upgraded tracks in just over two hours. The trip exposes the essence of beautiful Ireland and contrasts Belfast, the capital of Northern Ireland, with its historic Troubles, and peaceful Dublin, the metropolis of the Republic of Ireland.

At Droghede you begin one of the most colorful stretches of train travel you will find in Europe.

The church tower of Droghede lies on your right. The brick and tile-roofed residential quarter is on your left. The river is wide and crammed with ships. The dockside is very quiet this day, a bank holiday. Orange-and-black "Arrow" IrishRail trains wait on adjoining platforms.

Passengers are mostly reading newspapers and dozing aboard your Enterprise train heading south, but some do business on their cellular telephones now that you have entered the Republic of Ireland from the north.

At Laytown station, where you do not stop, you meet the Irish Sea full on, as it stretches quietly toward Wales. A few large, white ships dot the horizon, and you wonder whether they are the ferries connecting Wales and Ireland. Seagulls perch on the brown sand and waves roll in quietly. On the side of a cliff dropping to the sea, there appears to be a military firing range. A golf course can't be far away.

In the distance, across the green waters, you make out the peninsula of Howth.

Beside the sea, hay is arranged in yellow bales and rolls and the sheep and cattle grazing on the green slopes are oblivious to the grand view. From your Enterprise train window, it is a glorious panorama as you race past a fishing village. This is one of the most scenic stretches you will find in Europe.

Finally your spectacle ends as you pass the prim and proper town-houses and windmills at Skerries, north of Howth, but still, before you arrive in Dublin's Connolly station, you see instances of dramatic beauty in the waters and green fields heading south, such as the massive shipping and fishing fleet and marina at Malahide (no stop) with the white fishing vessels lined up side by side.

It would be a sensitive issue in the pubs of Northern Ireland whether North Ireland trains (NIR has a 221-mile network) were included in the British section or the Irish section of this guidebook, but because the international train from Belfast runs to Dublin, and not to London, it makes more sense to include it in the Ireland section.

In Belfast (*www.gotoBelfast.com*), The Troubles is spelled with a capital *T* because it refers specifically to the Nationalist-Unionist fighting that hauled Belfast into newspaper headlines. But since the 1995 ceasefire, Belfast is booming. The city center is alive with new shops, pubs, restaurants, and discos, and because central Belfast is now an attractive place to live, both property prices and tourism have tripled.

The Troubles has the same historic fascination for visitors as the Berlin Wall had after the German *Wende*. Since the 1995 ceasefire, the number of hotel beds has quintupled. Residents of Belfast brag about living in a special city with two cultures—both British and Irish.

In today's much-changed atmosphere, Loyalist and Republican wall murals have become popular tourist attractions in West Belfast. These political paintings are among the few remaining symbols of The Troubles, while there are hundreds of buildings, such as opulent Georgian, Victorian, and Edwardian edifices around Donegall Square, that prove Belfast's industrial and cultural strength over the past 200 years, when Belfast claimed the world's largest weaving and tobacco factories, the most extensive ropeworks built, and the world's greatest shipyard.

If you choose to take a rail 'n drive pass or simply to rent an automobile, you can make a day excursion from Belfast to the mysterious and beautiful Giants Causeway (*www.giantscausewayofficialguide.com*), so named because when it was discovered it was believed to have been built prehistorically by giants. It is Ireland's number two visitor attraction (after the Book of Kells in Dublin) and a World Heritage Site of exceptional interest and universal value, accessible by the coast road via Larne.

Nearby the Giants Causeway, most everyone visits the Old Bushmills Distillery of Irish malt whiskey for the free tour and educational sampling.

IrishRail refers to the Enterprise trains as their "Eurostar," claiming that they were modeled on the cross-channel train, and pointing out that they connect two capital cities and were built by the French company, De Dietrich, which built the end passenger carriages for the TGV and Eurostar trains. Half are owned by IR; half by NIR. Like the Dublin-Cork service (above), the trains are pulled by new GM diesels, but in this case, half are owned by NIR. First-class carriages seat 47 travelers, sitting 2+1, separated by tables. You can use the radio/tape/CD unit. Meals are served at your seat in first class. Second-class passengers, seated 2+2, patronize the cafe/bar carriage, where they buy sandwiches and drinks to eat there or take to their seats.

Eurail products are valid only in the Republic of Ireland, and not in Northern Ireland (which also does not honor BritRail Passes), so Eurail holders will need to buy a ticket between Belfast and Dundalk, which costs exactly half of the Belfast-Dublin fare of about $50, first class, and $30, second class.

Crossing the Channel by Ship

In 2003, the Stena Line launched the new passenger and freight superferry *Stena Britannica* between Harwich International Port and Hoek van Holland, boosting passenger capacity by 50 percent.

The ships of the Stena Line (*www.stenaline.com*) were hit hard by competition from the Eurotunnel on its choice English Channel link, but the Gothenburg-based line, which took over Sealink British Ferries in 1990, operates more ships to more places from Britain than any other company. The Stena Line's 40-knot high-speed *Stena Discovery* catamaran between Harwich and Hoek van Holland gives a 30 percent reduction for holders of Eurail products.

Although designated boat trains have been eliminated, traditional surface crossings between London and Paris still exist in the form of SeaFrance ferries that offer a 50 percent reduction to holders of Eurail products on 10 daily sailings between Calais and Dover.

The company Speedferries operates cross-channel service between Folkestone and Boulogne, Belgium, with five roundtrips a day by catamaran.

DFDS Scandinavian Seaways offers 20-hour crossings between

Harwich, England, and Esbjerg, Denmark. Board the train from London's Liverpool station.

Crossing the Irish Sea

The Stena Line launched a new vessel, the *Stena Adventurer,* on the Irish Sea in the summer of 2003.

Crossing the Irish Sea for Dublin (*www.ukireland-fastlinks.com*)? Leave London's Euston station for Holyhead, where you board *Stena Lynx III* fast ferry service taking 99 minutes to Dun Laoghaire or the *Stena Explorer* high-speed catamaran HSS 1500. There you connect for a short trip to Dublin by bus or DART train (see section following). In addition, you may board five daily Irish Ferries. The cruise ferry takes three hours and 15 minutes, while *Dublin Swift* takes one hour and 49 minutes.

Visiting southern Ireland? Leave London's Paddington station on an InterCity train for Fishguard, where you board Stena's 19-knot multipurpose ferry, the *Stena Europe,* for Rosslare.

For Northern Ireland, take Scotrail from Glasgow to Stranraer. The Stena Line's *Stena Voyager* high-speed catamaran from Stranraer West Pier to Belfast Donegall Quay (covered by the BritRail Pass + Ireland, see below), with 40-knot crossings each way in summer, takes one and a half hours. The HSSs alternate with the Stena Line's *Caledonia,* departing every two to three hours, and take three hours for the crossing.

Rail-Pass Travel in Britain

Eurail products are not valid in Britain, but you can choose from such an array of tempting train values that your head begins to swim. Check the Web sites and write for the free color brochures from BritRail and Rail Europe (see Appendix A), take it slow, and find the right combination for you.

BritRail Passes are your basic go-everywhere, see-everything travel convenience. One of the beauties of the passes is precisely that they are valid throughout Britain. You have no concern about which train company you are traveling on. They are your ideal way to adventure in Britain by train. You travel free on every train in England, Scotland, and Wales (but not North Ireland), with the exception of Eurostar (where you receive a discount); Tyne and Wear Metro trains (Newcastle area); Glasgow Underground trains; London Regional Transport Underground trains; buses, ships, hovercraft, and jetfoils;

the narrow-gauge private railroads in Wales; the Isle of Man trains; and the steam locomotive in Scotland.

You can buy consecutive and flexipass first- and second-class passes. Second-class passes ("standard class") are sold for more than one-fourth off the prices of the first-class passes. Buy consecutive passes for four, eight, 15, or 22 days or one month.

The passes are especially attractive to those over 60 and those between 15 and 26. Seniors pay about 15 percent less for a first-class Senior Pass and youths pay about 46 percent less for a second-class Youth Pass. There are no first-class Youth Passes or second-class Senior Passes. When you buy an adult or Senior Pass, one accompanying child (age five to 15) gets a free pass of the same type and duration. *Tip:* Ask for the BritRail Family Pass when booking. Additional children purchase the appropriate pass at half the price of a regular adult pass. Children under five travel free.

BritRail Flexipasses allow you leisure time, like Eurail Flexipasses. You pay a premium of about 28 percent to be able to stretch your travel days over a two-month time period. This would give you a chance to settle in one spot or take excursions such as Eurostar to the Continent. BritRail Flexipasses are available for four, eight, and 15 days. Senior and Youth BritRail Passes are also available with the same Flexipass option.

Travel for any flexipass day ends at midnight, but you can continue past midnight to the destination or intermediate stops on trains that have commenced their journeys before midnight without using the following day's validation. For example, a pass whose day of use is May 14 may be used on a train departing at 11 P.M. that does not reach its destination until 8 A.M. on May 15, without writing in "May 15."

BritRail has a special deal called the *BritRail Party Pass* for groups of three or four, where the third and fourth passengers receive a 50 percent discount. It applies to first-class BritRail consecutive-day and flexipasses. Passengers must travel together at all times and passes must be of the same type and validity/duration.

You buy BritRail Passes on the Continent, in Germany and France, for example, and in the Republic of Ireland, but you pay in local currencies, so it is more convenient to buy them before leaving America.

The *BritRail Days Out of London* pass allows you to save big if you will be traveling solely in southeastern England. Network Southeast offers special flexipasses for the large swath surrounding London between

Exeter and Kings Lynn, which includes the famous Kent resorts and major port cities. You have access to beautiful countryside, the rolling South Downs, and some of the most fascinating cities in England, such as Oxford, Salisbury, Cambridge, and Brighton. You can visit East Anglia to the northeast, or go as far west as Exeter on the edge of Dartmoor. These make refreshing day trips from London.

Days Out of London passes are available for two or four travel days in eight, or seven days in 15. You have a choice of first- or second-class passes, but you will have to pay supplements to reach cities outside Network Southeast's service area such as Bath or use InterCity trains via Reading. Those five to 15 years old pay one-third or less, depending on the length of the pass's validity.

The *Freedom of Scotland Travelpass* gives you four days of travel within eight, or eight days of travel within 15. It is available only in "standard class." It is valid on all scheduled daytime passenger trains for journeys wholly within Scotland including GNER and Virgin trains to/from Carlisle and Berwick-upon-Tweed, but travelpass tickets cannot be used to travel before 9:15 A.M. on weekdays except between Glasgow-Oban/Fort William/Mallaig and Inverness-Kyle/Wick/Thurso.

The travelpass is also valid for Scottish Citylink bus travel, Stagecoach in Fife services, bus travel on the Isle of Mull with Bowmans Coaches (*bowmanscoaches.sagenet.co.uk*), Highland Country Buses, and First Edinburgh services to/from the Scottish borders. It is valid on all Caledonian MacBrayne (*www.calmac.co.uk*) scheduled ferry services within Scotland and gives a 30 percent discount on Northlink Ferries as well as discounts on Edinburgh Bus Tour and sightseeing tours in Glasgow, Inverness, Perth, and Stirling.

To gain the greatest benefit from your Freedom of Scotland Travelpass, timetables and a map are essential. These are included in the complimentary pack issued to all purchasers. The pack also contains a free "Scotland Discount" 40-page booklet and plastic countdown card valid in more than 400 stores and services where the Scottish Tourist Board has negotiated at least a 10 percent discount and a 10-50 percent discount in more than 200 restaurants, night spots, and sightseeing attractions.

In Scotland all trains are second class only, except for the InterCity trains running south to England and the blue-livery Express, which runs along the Glasgow-Edinburgh flagship route—and to Inverness and Aberdeen through Stirling, Perth, and Dundee. It is smooth-riding luxury for a two-car unit, with indirect lighting and storage space between seat backs.

The tourist routes are operated with lighter-weight Sprinter and Super Sprinter railcars, in bright liveries. These cars are sized and panoramic-designed for the scenic routes. They have, incidentally, the best-designed loos of any train running, but don't forget to push the "lock" button or the next customer will be as startled as you.

The Freedom of Scotland Travelpass sold in Britain is identical to the Freedom of Scotland Travelpass sold abroad, but it is priced in pounds sterling. Normally it is cheaper to buy a Freedom of Scotland Travelpass before you leave.

None of the passes or tickets is valid on special excursion trains, privately owned railroads, Fort William to Mallaig steam services, or the Strathclyde PTE Underground. You must pay supplements for seat reservations and sleeper accommodations.

The *BritRail England Flexipass,* introduced in 2004, is available for four, eight, or 15 days within two months at 80 percent of the cost of a full BritRail Flexipass. It is valid for train travel throughout England, to Berwick and Carlisle near the Scottish border, to Chester, Shrewsbury, and Hereford near the Welsh border, and on ferries between Harwich and Rotterdam.

The *BritRail Pass 'n Drive* plan combines a two-month BritRail Flexipass with three days' train travel and a Hertz rental automobile with unlimited mileage for two days within a month. For long hauls, you use the train, and for short hauls and exploring the countryside, you have a car from some 100 pickup stations at major train stations, at 11 airports, or 89 more at practically any place you might venture.

Before leaving home, you obtain your travel documents from your travel agent. Each car rental voucher is valid for 24 hours and includes unlimited mileage, so you keep the car for blocks of 24-hour periods. You pay no drop-off charge, so you can pick up a car in one station and drop it off in another. You may choose to use the vouchers individually or in multiples at locations along the way. You pay for the package in dollars and receive all instructions before you leave, making it very easy to use. Minimum age for rental is 25.

BritRail Pass + Ireland

The BritRail Pass + Ireland combines the Stena Line sea crossings with train travel in Britain, Northern Ireland, and the Republic of

Ireland. You combine visits to England, Scotland, and Wales with Dublin's pubs, museums, and cathedrals; or the scenic beauty of Cork with London's history; or Northern Ireland's mountains and glens with Scotland's remote Highlands.

You travel roundtrip on the Stena Line ships, HSS fast ferries, or catamarans across the Irish Sea between Dun Laoghaire and Holyhead, Fishguard and Rosslare, and Belfast and Stranraer. The flexipasses are sold only in the U.S. for any five or 10 days within one month.

You may buy Ireland Rail & Bus Cards through CIE in the U.S. (see Appendix A) or wait until arrival in the Republic of Ireland. (Passes that are valid in Northern Ireland also may be bought there, but you pay in the Irish Republic's currency.) Ireland Rail & Bus Cards give you four choices of travel throughout Ireland by either IrishRail or Irish Bus's network of frequent, modern coaches that covers the Republic via major highways between large centers, and via local roads between smaller towns and villages.

The Irish Explorer Pass (rail only) gives you unlimited travel in standard class on IR service throughout the Republic of Ireland, including DART and Suburban Rail services in Dublin. It is valid for five travel days' out of 15. When you add a bus option for 50 percent extra, your number of days increases to eight, and you can use also unlimited Irish Bus services and city bus services in Cork, Limerick, Galway, and Waterford.

The Irish Rover Pass is valid for train travel in both Northern Ireland and the Republic, and includes IrishRail, Northern Ireland Rail, DART, Suburban Rail services in Dublin, and suburban services in Northern Ireland.

The Emerald Card provides unlimited intercity and city travel through both the Republic of Ireland and Northern Ireland using the services of Irish Bus, IrishRail, Northern Ireland Rail, Ulsterbus, and city bus services in Dublin, Belfast, Cork, Limerick, Galway, and Waterford. You buy the flexipass for either eight days' travel in 15 or 15 days in 30. It is available in the U.S., the Irish Republic, and Northern Ireland. Children under 12 travel for half-fare.

The Freedom of Northern Ireland Ticket, costing about $50, allows seven days' unlimited travel on NIR and Ulsterbus (*www.ulsterbus. co.uk*). On Sundays you can take as many NIR train journeys as you wish for about $4.50. A family of four pays $11. Buy these offers in Northern Ireland.

Using Eurail Product Bonuses in Ireland

Eurail products give you a bonus that is essential for Eurail product purchasers. It allows you to connect with the trains on the Continent at half-price plus port taxes. Irish Ferries gives Eurail product holders 50 percent off and Irish hospitality on its Normandy sailing from the Irish port of Rosslare alternately to the French ports of Cherbourg and Roscoff. Irish Ferries' Rosslare-Cherbourg sailings (17 hours) take you twice weekly from early April to late September.

You will compare Irish Ferries' sailings with minicruises. You dine in a dining room or cafeteria, shop duty free, gamble, go to the movies, and socialize in the bar-lounge and disco. You must pay extra for cabin accommodations, but by the time your Eurail credit is deducted from the overall charge, your costs for these are quite reasonable. Advance reservation is compulsory if cabin accommodation is requested. For the months of July and August reservation is compulsory whether or not cabins are requested.

Britain and Ireland's great trains take you speeding from London to Edinburgh aboard InterCity supertrains, aboard Scotrail's scenic North Highland and West Highland lines, across the Isle of Man, along the coast of Wales and through slate-mining Welsh countryside, and on an electric odyssey along the Bay of Dublin.

Flying Scotsman
The Plum of Britain

Your Flying Scotsman train is six miles out of London's Kings Cross station accelerating past 100 mph when you see the light at the end of Wood Green tunnel. You feel the sensation of top speed and a kaleidoscope of impressions. At milepost 8, you are at 115 mph. Running level, Great North Eastern Railway's supertrain romps. Wooden picket fences divide green fields. The first 140-mph marker board zips past your window.

GNER's Pullman trains take you up the electrified East Coast line to Edinburgh from London in four hours, 22 minutes in stunning "Mark 4" passenger carriages behind Britain's powerful locomotives, Electra power units.

Great North Eastern Railway (GNER, *www.gner.co.uk*) is considered the winner of the plum of the train operating franchises, with Britain's best route and InterCity 225 trains. InterCity 225 is aptly named, because it can run at 225 kilometers an hour (140 mph) through rolling green British countryside.

GNER introduced a somber navy-blue livery, with gold GNER logos, a broad orange band in the middle of the body sides, and the legend "The Route of the Flying Scotsman." The head-turning Mark 4 carriages stand apart because their sleek walls cant aerodynamically inward. In addition to the Flying Scotsman train, GNER runs a stable of high-speed Pullman trains to Scotland. The Highland Chieftain leaves London's Kings Cross Station at 12 noon and Inverness at 7:55 A.M. Northern Lights departs London at 10:30 A.M. and Aberdeen at 9:55 A.M. The Scottish Pullman races from London at 8 A.M. and from Edinburgh at 5:50 A.M. The Tees-Tyne Pullman leaves at 5:50 P.M. from London and 6:30 A.M. from Newcastle.

Everywhere that Pullman's Electras with class 91 serial numbers stop, you see towheaded youngsters crowding platforms, pursuing their peculiarly British hobby: "train spotting." Everyone in Britain seems to be a "Griser," named after Sir Alfred Griser's steam engine. The instant that observers recognize a never-before-seen Electra coming into view, they add it to their lists by jotting into their copybooks its serial number, date, and where they spotted it.

When you press the push buttons to slide open the external doors and board, the first thing you observe is "Metro-Cammell" milled into the serrated aluminum steps. These Mark 4 carriages were the first to be designed and built outside former BritRail's workshops by competitive bidders.

Mark 4's spacious interiors surprise you with their radical departure from the standard look you expect from trains in Britain. Designers created a restful ambience with decorative shiny chrome-plate tubing, soothing gray fabrics, diffused ceiling lighting, indirect light spilling down the wall, pink linen gardenias and Dudson china set upon permanently anchored gray tabletops, and overlapping black-and-white box designs in the woven carpet. Staff looks efficient wearing company-issue red ties, gray vests, red-striped white shirts, and black skirts or trousers.

Variations in seating layout and full-height tinted glass screens disguise the length of the salon and create an intimate first-class interior. In the middle of the carriage, files of 1+2 seats change to 2+1, offsetting the aisle and creating an interesting focal point, or key.

Tip: For individuals or pairs, the roomiest seats are those facing pairs at the key: numbers 12F and 12B and 13F and 13B (*F* for front facing and *B* for back facing).

The gray plush seats recline a few inches with a tug on the black release. Put your soft-sided luggage in the overhead racks; store your hard suitcases and backpacks in the ample space near the entryways.

The bar/buffet (say "buffey") section is situated between first- and second-class sections. You find pay telephones in both.

GNER's first-class Pullman service gives you a choice of reservations either in a normal salon with at-seat meal service or in the dining room where, mornings, a complete English breakfast is served. Because of Pullman's departures timed for business travelers, few stops, high velocity, and two catering cars for meals, Pullman's passenger carriages are usually crammed with briefcases.

The decor in the second-class carriage is rosier, not gray. Travelers sit 2+2 throughout, which prevented designers from staggering the files. Decorators instead staggered tinted glass partitions and inserted occasional tables to achieve a social atmosphere with denser seating.

In second class, service personnel push snack trolleys through carpeted aisles (what a surprise to find rough-wearing synthetic tweed carpeting in second class!). Passengers use tables folding down from seat backs.

North of Stevenage, your Pullman settles into a steady 125-mph warm-up. It feels as if it wants to go faster as it skims quickly atop elevated trestles. You stop first at small, brick Peterborough station, already 76 miles up the line in 44 minutes (averaging 104 mph). On departure the conductor announces over the intercom, "We would like to welcome those passengers who have just set a train at Peterborough."

North of Peterborough, track and overhead wiring run arrow-straight to the perspective's vanishing point. Toward Grantham you glide through countryside populated by nibbling, black-faced sheep and snug, tile-roofed brick row houses nestled far away from motorways peppered with commerce. Above Grantham's Georgian houses, you see one of Britain's noblest church spires. This miracle of medieval achievement, built just before 1300, towers 300 feet with its sculptures intact.

Up the East Coast line, golden fields of rapeseed (Canola) grown for monounsaturated oil brighten one side and bored-looking, brown-and-white dairy cows opposite make a striking contrast to the occasional industrial site.

Past Newark, your train begins to feel as though it is hurrying. It rocks through a complex of curves. The driver is obviously pushing the limits of existing track. You worry that your coffee cup will bounce into your lap. "It's time to wake passengers getting off at Doncaster," the conductor jokes.

York, the best-preserved medieval city in Britain, provides your Pullman's second stop. In 1840, the city fathers knocked two holes in the city wall to provide access to their new train station. The present site was Europe's largest station when it was built in 1870-77. It still has the longest platform in England. The Royal York Hotel in the station was splendidly rejuvenated in 1991. Guy Fawkes, the folk hero who tried to blow up Parliament, came from York. Try to visit York's famous Railway Museum (open daily), which was recently expanded. It houses a history of the railroad.

Approaching Durham, 18 minutes after your stop in Darlington, you are treated to one of the most memorable views on your journey north as Durham Cathedral and Castle, jointly designated as a World Heritage Site, come into view.

After four hours, 22 minutes, you run through a cutting into Edinburgh's Waverley station (the conductor announces: "Weaverly"). From above, the cutting's banks look so similar to a river's that passers-by are astonished to see rails below.

Edinburgh's Waverley station, romantically named after the hero of Sir Walter Scott's novel, has a sensitive location between Princes Street and the Old Town and Castle. Its location places it amidst visible highlights of Scotland and below Edinburgh Castle. In front you see the memorial erected by the queen's own Cameron Highlanders to their comrades fallen in Egypt. It shows a Highlander in a kilt. The Gothic Sir Walter Scott Memorial is across the street.

Waverley is a rambling affair, with tracks on four sides of the covered middle area that is bisected by auto, bus, and taxi traffic. The area in front of the station contains an amazing multilevel atrium shopping center opened July 4, 1988, by Her Majesty the Queen. Up the escalators and past the modern sculptures, the Edinburgh Tourist Board's Information Center (open Mon.-Sat., 8 A.M. to 11 P.M.; Sun., from 9 A.M.) offers a hotel accommodations desk and an Internet cafe. The Information Center is always a busy place, with guidebooks and souvenirs for sale, a Bureau de Change, a wealth of free tourist brochures, and computerized information on the Edinburgh Festival in season.

In the station it is easy to find the buffet, Railbar, City Transport Information, Festival Office (for the Edinburgh Festival), GNER's first-class lounge, and the Travel Centre. You also find a "Shopping Parade" of kiosks. Waverley's smooth floors are ideal for suitcases with wheels because you must walk long distances. Look for luggage carts hidden away in the corners.

Above the station, the Balmoral, extravagantly remodeled, is the former North British Hotel. As it was once, it is again considered by some as the best in Edinburgh. The black hands of the clock atop are set two minutes fast so travelers won't miss their trains.

		Weekday Flying Scotsman Service		
1000	dep.	LONDON (Kings Cross)	dep.	1739
1044	dep.	Peterborough	dep.	1641
		Doncaster	dep	1555
1151	dep.	York	dep.	1528
1220	dep.	Darlington	dep	1459
1251	dep.	Newcastle	dep.	1428
1422	dep.	EDINBURGH	dep	1255

The Gutsy Kyle Line
Wild and Romantic

While your Kyle train's ScotRail (*www.scotrail.co.uk*) diesel railcar in its flashy purple, green, red, and white livery, its face painted safety yellow, climbs steeply into the sparsely settled northwest corner of Scotland, your fellow passengers prepare for the wildest and most romantic passage in all of Great Britain. For best results, sit on the right.

The Highlands' wild landscape and sparse population make building difficult and expensive, yet Kyle was ultimately served. Riding the North Highland Kyle line from Inverness to Kyle of Lochalsh reveals the essence of Scotland, exposing tough new images every moment. Your 82-mile run shows peaks, headlands, forlorn islands and skerries, lochs and glens—and yet cries of protest from the local people were needed in 1974 to save from closure this line much admired by train-lovers and adventurers.

When your train pulls in at one of the 14 lonely stations along the

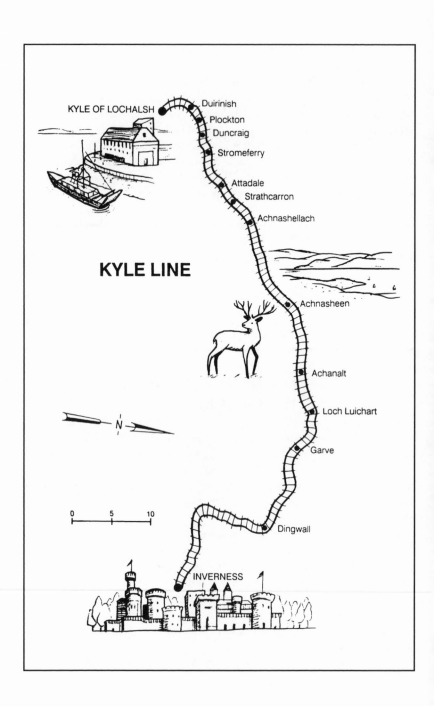

line, villagers climb aboard, marvel at the train, and greet friends. Postal workers collect the mail while passengers board from creaky wooden footstools still used because there are few boarding platforms.

Your Kyle train is designed for longer-distance, cross-country journeys. Five sets of panoramic windows, each with about six feet of antiglare, tinted, and double-glazed glass, show you a changing picture of Scotland's Highlands.

You never lose sight of the views. The line twists so tightly that you see both the driver ahead and the carriages trailing you as you round the many curves.

Kyle line trains run from the brightly remodeled Inverness station. BritRail and Freedom of Scotland Travelpasses are welcome. Be sure to pick up a free Kyle line color brochure at Inverness Travel Centre. Maps and cameras are required equipment on this line.

Passing over the nine arches of the 1990-rebuilt stone viaduct over the river Ness, you travel half an hour to Dingwall. In the green fields past Dingwall, try to picture one of the bloodiest clan battles in history, pitting the Mackenzies against the MacDonalds in 1429. It took place on Knockfarril (579 feet), near the vitrified fort built by King Brude of the Picts.

Now you climb steeply past Raven Rock, hunching 250 feet over the line to your left. At the summit of your first climb you see the dramatic contrast between the quieter green countryside dotted with cattle that stretches back below your train to Dingwall and the harsh Highlands ahead. Over the crest you approach brown, lifeless hills, wild woodlands, and rocky landscapes. Until the beginning of June, snow hugs mountains you see on your right.

Your ScotRail train picks up speed on the downhill slope, crosses the Blackwater, and races beside Loch Garve on your right. Loch Garve, which means "Rough Lake," is mirror-smooth on calm days, and you see the reflection in the lake of pine-covered Little Wyvis (2,497 feet). The greater bulk of Ben Wyvis (3,297 feet) hulks behind it.

Your diesel coasts to a stop at Garve beside the tiny, tan, plaster station house surrounded in summer by cut wheat cropped in the fields. You see the pink Garve Hotel nearby. Garve, in the mountains of Wester Ross, is a camping center during the summer.

From Garve you pass through rolling countryside and past reforesting plantations. Passing over the Corriemoillie Summit (429 feet), you see heather-clad Loch Luichart with birches lined along its shores.

The sky is incandescent with blue. The six miles of Loch Luichart join the weather systems east and west.

Loch Luichart was the first lake in the Highlands used to generate electricity in 1952. The hydroelectric project lifted the water 20 feet and submerged two miles of land, including the former track and station. Your train has been rerouted to the hastily built stone station house replacing the one sitting underwater.

You enter Strath Bran on the south side of Loch a Chuilinn, then cross quickly to the north side of sparkling Loch Achanalt (the two lakes are practically continuous) past marshy fields to Achanalt station.

Continuing along Strath Bran through wet, green grasslands, with desolate mountains in the distance, the scenery hardens, and when you approach the tiny village of Achnasheen, meaning "Field of Rain," you have reached the bleakest bit of the line.

Your train comes to a stop. Post-office workers unload mail. Then your train climbs again. The treeless and rocky hills are especially attractive to a certain breed of mountaineer. Looking westward toward Glen Docherty you see the Torridon Mountains, old even in geologic terms. Liathach is the great barrel peak to the left, banded with hoops of sandstone and rising shear. To its right you see high-ridged Ben Eighe, looking white as snow but really covered with pale quartzite fragments for much of its height.

The summit of the line, Luib summit, lies only 700 feet above sea level between Loch Scaven and Loch Gowen, which drain into different seas. It is not high, but wild. You hear the crying of curlews and the loud, fluting calls of European sandpipers. Sometimes you see herds of deer, and golden eagles soaring on broad wings. In September, you may well hear great stags roaring at one another.

You almost hear your heated diesel sighing with relief as it heads downhill. At the Glencarron halt, some of the passengers with packs, ropes, and pickaxes climb off, planning to scale the cleft peak of Fuar Tholl (2,968 feet) on your right.

You then enter the deer-haunted Achnashellach Forest, thick with spruce, willow, birch, and holly. Watch for the splendid view of Glen Carron on your left before you glide into Achnashellach station.

Out of Achnashellach you pass Loch Dhugaill, surrounded with spruce. This is the country of the oldest rocks in the world, Archean gneiss forming its floor and Cambrian quartzite its walls, so that the predominant colors are pinks and grays.

At Strathcarron, the second double-tracked station, a warm burst of air prompts you to remove your parka. You leave behind cold hills and enter the softer Gulf Stream climate.

Across the lake to your right, you see the whitewashed cottages of Loch Carron village gaily bedecked with roses. Loch Carron had good herring and salmon fishing before fishing failed about 1850, too early for the Kyle line to be of any help. It widens on your right, and the pressing question of the moment, as you look back at Fuar Tholl, is whether you really make out the famous profile of George Washington in the outline of the mountain.

You stop next at Attadale, meaning "Valley of the Fight." Here you try to imagine Vikings dueling and sporting. You run side by side with the highway on dangerously steep slopes between Attadale and Stromeferry through tall spruce forests.

Stromeferry, at the narrowest part of Loch Carron, was a short-lived terminus of ships to the Hebridean Islands, but piracy and shipwrecks abruptly terminated trading.

This last part of the Kyle line, past Duncraig, is the most spectacular. Look sharply, for the scenery dashes by faster than words. On level ground you race below Duncraig Castle past the village of Plockton before finally slowing for Plockton's train station on the western outskirts. Duncraig Castle, dating from 1886, is hardly visible from your train, but in 2001 it became a hostel for 100 youthful backpackers.

Plockton is the gem of the Kyle line. Your train curves along the shore of saltwater Loch Carron, revealing gleaming white cottages across azure water with silver-gray Harbor seals frolicking and playing in the sunny waters. The striking, pink-rock Applecross peaks rise in the background. Plockton owes its size to the days when its schooners traded as far away as the Baltic. It looks like an island from your view but is actually on a thin promontory.

You see it best from across the water, a classic picture with wonderful changeable light and palm trees. You see paintings of this scene, complete with romantic yachts decorating the foreground, hanging in parlors and pubs throughout Britain.

When you run along the lakeside between tall mountains past Plockton, you become more excited than during any other section of the line. You see the western shore. You had not imagined such enchanting colors. Clouds, seaweed, and waterfalls suffuse in a soft, bluish light. Dozens of rivulets dash down. In the water, granite chunks

lie pink, freckled with bright gold algae. Glorious views glow in changing shades of watercolor.

Past Duirinish, you travel inland through the Drumbuie crofting
area. You realize your trip has to end soon when you cross the wild
coast colored with orange lichen-daubed rocks, tide pools alive with
sea creatures, and magnificent vistas of islands with pig-Latin names:
Rassay, Scalpay, Loggay, Pabay, and the Crowlin Islands.

Breathe deeply the salty air when you step off in the Kyle of
Lochalsh station. The terminus, whose site was blasted from solid rock,
is right on water's edge. Fishing boats, cottages, the old hotel, the
ferry, and the incomparable scenery make Kyle one of the best-placed
stations in Britain. Photographers immediately scurry up the hill
behind the Railway Terrace next to the Tourist Information Centre to
capture on film the big, sweeping picture of mountains, islands, and
the houses that look like white miniatures ready to tumble into the sea.

Kyle is Gaelic meaning "strait" or "narrows." It was simply "Kyle,"
population 600, until it took on its elegant new name on that historic
day in November 1897, when dignitaries from all over Scotland came
to declare the railroad officially open.

It is by no means the end of your travels. A Scottish Citylink Coach
will take you across the 1995 balanced-cantilever Skye Bridge, which
was the first link to the island since glacial times, to Kyleakin on the
Isle of Skye. The bridge is a political football because of tolls that the
locals consider exorbitant. The Bank of America owns it. From here,
travel by bus across Skye to Armadale for the frequent Caledonian
MacBrayne ferries to Mallaig (*www.calmac.co.uk/skye-timetable.html*) and
the return West Highland line connection to Fort William (see the following section).

The Lochalsh Hotel, the old-fashioned resort hotel opposite the
train station at water's edge, offers overnighters magnificent views
across the sound of the Isle of Skye, except of course when the famous
Skye mist descends.

Kyle Line Service
Monday-Saturday

0853	1048	1800	dep	INVERNESS	arr.	0949	1423	1950
0906	1106	1818	dep.	Beauly	dep.	0936	1406	1933
0912	1111	1823	dep	Muir of Ord	dep	0930	1400	1927
0921	1120	1832	dep.	Dingwall	dep.	0922	1352	1919
0942	1141	1855	dep.	Garve	dep.	0857	1329	1856
0951	1150	1904	dep.	Lochluichart	dep.	0848	1318	1843
0957	1156	1910	dep.	Achanalt	dep.	0842	1312	1837
1008	1207	1921	dep.	Achnasheen	dep.	0832	1302	1827
1025	1224	1938	dep.	Achnashellach	dep.	0813	1243	1808
1035	1236	1943	dep.	Strathcarron	dep.	0805	1235	1800
1040	1241	1953	dep.	Attadale	dep.	0759	1228	1754
1053	1254	2006	dep.	Stromeferry	dep.	0748	1217	1743
1101	1302	2014	dep.	Duncraig	dep.	0739	1208	1734
1105	1306	2018	dep.	Plockton	dep.	0736	1205	1731
1108	1309	2021	dep.	Duirinish	dep.	0732	1201	1727
1117	1318	2030	arr.	KYLE	dep.	0723	1152	1718

West Highland Line
Bonnie Banks and Bonnie Braes

"Is the gradient very steep?" you wonder as your train pulls away from Glasgow's Queen Street station.

"Steep?" roars the conductor. "It's vertical!"

He does not exaggerate all that much. After Ben Nevis, your view narrows into a rock defile shared with brawling Highland streams. Rock strata line the faces right and left. Then suddenly you face Loch Treig, an intensely dramatic lagoon stretched like a vast silvered pane of glass below the great green hump of Stob Coire Easain, 3,658 feet up.

There is no road. Your train wobbles giddily along a ledge hacked from the mountainside. Reflections shine from below through gaps in the bracken. Details float by in slow motion. A Cheviot sheep stares you in the eye. A tiny scintillation of mica catches the evening sun.

From Corrour summit you descend along Loch Treig and curve westward to Tulloch. Now your one-class, flashy ScotRail (*www.scotrail .co.uk/scotrwhl.htm*) diesel train runs west along Glen Spean into the wild Monessie Gorge. Water rushes and foams through the tortuous, rocky gully. You feel the influence of the great commanding presences

of Nevis, Dorain, Vorlich, and Vain and the breathtaking vistas opening up from among these giants.

Thundering on a narrow ledge along the vertical rock walls, you
suddenly see the valley opening again to Roy Bridge.

Dramatic engineering makes traveling along Scotland's 164-mile
West Highland Line between Glasgow and Mallaig exhilarating. You
make more than a train trip to Mallaig through pretty countryside. It
is a dramatic experience. Your train rumbles through laborious cuttings hewn through rock, crosses 11 tunnels, climbs gradients as high
as 1 in 48, and threads its way atop remarkable bridges and magnificent viaducts mastering the most tortuous terrain in Britain. The West
Highland Line was not meant to be a tourist attraction, but to open up
parts of Scotland nearly impossible to reach and to carry the cargo of
the profitable west coast fish trade.

Departing from Glasgow's Queen Street station, your train purrs
through the steep Cowlairs tunnel also used by Glasgow's electrified
commuter trains and begins the West Highland Line proper at
Helensburgh Central station.

Past Craigendoran you climb through the woods above Gare Loch to
Garelochhead, the first of the stations noted for their wooden shingles
and two-tone green decor. Like a postcard below is the Faslane naval
base, where Winston Churchill departed on his voyage to North Africa
during World War II. The large, amphibious shed anchored above the
waves recently sheltered American Polaris nuclear submarines.

Now you cross to Loch Long and climb above it. At the head, the
bulk of "The Cobbler" mountain (2,891 feet) makes you feel insignif-
icant. While crossing the mile-wide neck of land separating Loch Long
from the fresh water of Loch Lomond, wonderful views of the loch
appear. Then you climb high above the loch through woods and above
waterfalls to Ardlui. On the far side of the loch, Ben Lomond towers
3,192 feet. The lochs disappear while you climb steadily up Glen
Falloch and curve across the Dubh Eas water on Glen Falloch viaduct.

Separate portions to Oban and Mallaig trains are usually connected
together until Crianlarich except when heavy passenger traffic
demands running separate trains. Platform lengths limit train length
to six carriages. So when your Scots conductor announces, "We are
approaching Crianlarich station where the train will 'splat,'" loud guf-
faws resound through your carriage from the Londoners riding in
back. Be sure you are in the right portion.

Mallaig Line

Your train for Mallaig climbs above the Strath Fillan River to the south. Clinging to the hillside, you cross the great watershed of Scotland where the rivers flow to the Atlantic instead of the North Sea.

Ahead appear two large steel viaducts standing on tall masonry piers. This is called the Horseshoe Curve, the most spectacular of the line. The line doubles back on itself in the form of a horseshoe as you round Ben Odhar, crossing the viaduct to the foot of Beinn A Chaistel, and then continuing by the second viaduct to the mighty Ben Dorain.

From Bridge of Orchy, high above Loch Tulla, you swing eastward and enter the wild Rannoch Moor, 20 miles long and 20 miles wide. Sunlight glitters on pools and summer colors blaze from the yellow Scotch broom, purplish-pink heather, and emerald Highland grasses. Railroad engineers defeated this vast, desolate stretch of treacherous peat bogs by piling thousands of tons of ash and earth upon a mattress of tree roots and brushwood.

At the heart of the moor, the remote, chalet-style Rannoch station with Swiss birch shingles is the exodus for hikers with metal-tipped walking sticks, knickers, and heavy woolen sweaters so thick a sheep would sweat.

Then you cross a large viaduct to climb steadily north through the only snowshed in Britain to the 1,350-foot summit at Corrour, another mountaineer haven. Expect to see deer in winter and spring. From this forsaken, windswept station you look down toward Loch Ossian (1,269 feet—the highest in Scotland) at the foot of Beinn na Lap mountain (3,066 feet).

Past Roy Bridge at the mouth of Glen Roy, you see on the left Keppoch House, the ancient seat of the McDonalds. Your last lap to Fort William takes you past Inverlochy Castle and the Lochaber Mountains.

The only substantial town on the Mallaig Line, busy Fort William's station occupies the shore of Loch Linnhe, cutting off the sea from the main street. Ben Nevis mountain, Britain's highest, fills the horizon.

During the summer, the "Jacobite" steam train operated by West Coast Railway Company, Carnforth (Tel. 01463-239026, *www.mallaigheritage.org.uk*), conveys passengers between Fort William and Mallaig, departing Fort William at 10:25 A.M. Rail passes are not honored. Locomotives sometimes include the ex LMSR Class 5 "Black Five" No. 5407 and ex LNER Class K1 No. 2005.

Leaving Fort William, your train reverses direction to cross the River Lochy past the old Inverlochy Castle ruins (the "fort" from which the town takes its name; the "William" is from King William of Orange) and continues along the 1901 stretch of track taking you to Mallaig.

After Banavie, your next stop is Corpach, with its huge paper mill, and then you travel along the shore of Loch Eil. Look back to see a wonderful view of Ben Nevis. You pass through stations overlooking the long stretch of water and then climb steeply through rocks to Glenfinnan. This is probably the most delightful stretch of your entire journey.

The curving, concrete Glenfinnan viaduct is one of the most photographed scenes in Scotland. It was a mighty challenge to build out of concrete, a new engineering material, because it meant carrying the railroad over 416 yards across the valley on 100-foot stilts supporting 21, 50-foot spans. You see on your left a magnificent view of silvery Loch Shiel and the Bonnie Prince Charlie Monument below where the prince rallied the clans and began his ill-fated rebellion. His forlorn, kilted statue faces up the glen, with Loch Shiel shimmering behind him.

Your head swirls as you wind through rock cuttings and above exquisite Loch Eil with delightful islets and tall silver ilex and beech. The hint of lonely, uninhabited country that you have felt from the beginning becomes overwhelming.

Following the rushing river Ailort to Lochailort, you see, on the left again, the delightful view of Loch Ailort feeding toward the Atlantic. Then you pass through a series of short tunnels with Loch Dubh on the right, clatter over Loch Dubh by viaduct, and see another spellbinding view on the left over Loch Nan Uamh.

Now you are on the edge of an exciting stretch. Your train plunges from the viaduct into a tunnel, emerges, and disappears into a second. Borrodale Bridge appears at the end of the 349-yard tunnel as you break into daylight only 86 feet above the glen on a single span of 127.5 feet.

Through more short tunnels to Arisaig, everything now looks westward to the Atlantic. Look over Loch Nan Ceall to see the weird mountain shapes of the islands of Rum and Eigg floating on the sea. You can identify Eigg, the notched island with its flat top and the molar-tooth Scour of Eigg rising 1,289 feet.

Past the sandy bays of the Morar estuary, with Loch Morar (the deepest in Britain, home of the Morag monster) to the east, you run along the Sound of Sleat opposite Skye before descending peacefully toward Mallaig, still looking to the offshore islands.

Pass a miniature blizzard of the wings of white gulls and auks. Scarlet and tawny fishing trawlers crowd the harbor. With seals and glinting sea, Mallaig, one of Europe's major herring ports, is a prosperous place with white houses running up around the bay.

Crowds watch trawlers unloading through the night, bathed in hectic orange from the fish-pier lights. Cranes dip and swing their dangling fish through darkness. Mackerels crunch underfoot; ice crashes, slung by men in grotesque orange overalls.

From Mallaig station, 650 feet away, the pier for Caledonian MacBrayne berths ferries for the 30-minute crossings to Armadale on the Isle of Skye, and for Rum, Muck, and Eigg. Follow the arrow, "Skye Ferry," on your right. Don't hurry; the Caledonian MacBrayne office is locked until shortly before departure.

As you exit the Mallaig train station, the small tourist office (for hotel reservations) is at the end of the street on the right.

Oban Spur

Blooming orange nasturtiums and red roses amongst grass so green it could only be in Scotland surround remote Crianlarich's 1880 stucco station. From here a delightful spur of the West Highland Line, also dating from 1880, takes you through wild scenery to Oban terminus, the old port where you can board Caledonian MacBrayne steamers to Scottish islands. The mountains of Scotland surround you. To the east towers Ben More (3,843 feet). In the west rise Ben Oss (3,374 feet), Ben Dhu Craig (3,024 feet), and Ben Lui (3,708 feet). Look for the remains of the Callendar & Oban eastern branch north of Crianlarich station.

You run northwest along Strath Fillan. Along this stretch you watch the Mallaig Line piercing the flat spread north across the river. Entering woods, you reach Tyndrum Lower station and then swing west through hills into Argyll along beautiful Glen Lochy. You have to be an expert to keep track of the breeds of sheep you see in the Highlands. There are more than 30. The ones you see here each have a black face with a white spot and horns.

You drop through hills overlooked by peaks to the south and then

reach the glazed canopy of the red stone Dalmally station at the southern end of Glen Orchy. The line came to an end here until money
raised in the 1870s allowed construction to Oban.

Sweeping around the head of Loch Awe you see the ruin of Kilchurn
Castle, the ancient stronghold of the Clan Campbell, and the loch
beyond. Loch Awe station has a small pier for steamer trips on the loch.

You curve along the edge of the lake, passing the hydroelectric
power station near Cruachan. When the loch narrows sharply, you
enter the skinny, rock-walled Pass of Brander. This is a memorable
stretch linking Loch Awe and Loch Etive. You skirt mighty Ben
Cruachan (3,689 feet) to the north and landslide-marked slopes to the
south. Note the wire landscape fencing protecting the track.

You cross River Awe on the bridge that was the setting for Sir Walter
Scott's romance, *The Highland Widow*. Past white Inverawe House, you
turn west to Taynuilt, a delightful village on the shores of Loch Etive,
then run through woods and rock cuttings beside the lake through the
region known locally as "Australia" because of its bushlike character.
Look across the water to Benderloch and then ahead to the great 1903
steel cantilever bridge at Connel Ferry. Near Connel Ferry you see the
Falls of Lorc, where the tidal waters flow over a ledge of rock at the
narrow entrance to Loch Etive.

You now climb through Glen Cruitten across hills and around
Oban to descend with splendid views of the town and its harbor.
Ferries berth below its handsome Victorian stone buildings, and the
strange circular coliseum ruin known as McCaig's Folly perches high
above.

Oban is a sheltered, coastal resort, famous for its single-malt Oban
whiskey. The town and its picturesque bay are nearly landlocked.
Hotels lining the promenade cater to thousands of visitors making this
their base.

Oban is the main port for Mull, Ionc, and all the Inner Hebrides
and Outer Hebrides islands via Caledonian MacBrayne ferries. "The
Earth belongs unto the Lord and all that it contains. That is, except
the Western Isles, which are Caledonian MacBrayne's." Rail fans visiting the Isle of Mull will find that their ship is equipped with everything
suitable for the 40-minute crossing. Upon landing at Mull, walk seven
minutes left along the coast rather than along the highway to reach
the MullRail train, which doesn't leave until the last passenger off the
ship has arrived.

MullRail is a delight for five-year-olds and rail fans. This happy train runs on a straight line following the coast on 10¼-inch gauge using Mull-grown timber sleepers over peat bogs through pristine forests alive with pheasants. Fallen trees are covered with lush green moss. Freedom of Scotland Travelpass holders receive a 15 percent discount on tickets.

Mull managed without a railroad for over 150 years. When the 1858 Torosay Castle, a Scots Baronial Mansion, and its beautiful Italian gardens were opened to the public in 1975, visitors were reluctant to walk the best part of over two miles from the pier at Craignure to the castle. Thus, the Mull Railroad, the first island passenger railroad ever to be built in Scotland, was opened in June 1984. MullRail is open at Easter, then from early May to mid-October.

West Highland Line Monday-Saturday Service
Glasgow-Mallaig/Oban

0812	1240	1812	dep.	GLASGOW (Queen St.)	arr.	1121	1545	2117
0827	1255	1827	dep.	Dalmuir	dep.	1057	1523	2054
0837	1305	1837	dep.	Dumbarton Central	dep.	1047	1514	2045
0855	1323	1855	dep.	Helensburgh Upper	dep.	1035	1458	2032
1906	1334	1907	dep.	Garelochhead	dep.	1023	1446	2020
1926	1355	1927	dep.	Arrochar & Tarbet	dep.	1003	1427	2001
0950	1412	1948	dep.	Ardlui	dep.	0949	1413	1947
1006	1427	2003	arr.	CRIANLARICH	dep.	0933	1353	1931

Branch to/from Mallaig

1017	1439	2015	dep.	CRIANLARICH	arr.	0926	1347	1925
1028	1450	2026	dep.	Tyndrum Upper	dep.	0913	1335	1914
1042	1504	2040	dep.	Bridge of Orchy	dep.	0857	1319	1858
1103	1525	2106	dep.	Rannoch	dep.	0837	1300	1838
1115	1537	2118	dep.	Corrour	dep.	0822	1249	1827
1131	1553	2134	dep.	Tulloch	dep.	0805	1232	1811
1141	1603	2144	dep.	Roy Bridge	dep.	0754	1221	1800
1147	1609	2150	dep.	Spean Bridge	dep.	0748	1215	1753
1200	1622	2203	arr.	FORT WILLIAM		0735	1202	1740
1205	1627	2210	dep.	FORT WILLIAM	arr.	0730	1152	1736
1211	1633	2216	dep.	Banavie	dep.	0723	1143	1727
1216	1638	2221	dep.	Corpach	dep.	0719	1139	1723
1222	1644	2227	dep.	Loch Eil (outward)	dep.	0713	1133	1717
1227	1649	2232	dep.	Locheilside	dep.	0707	1127	1711
1237	1700	2242	dep.	Glenfinnan	dep.	0658	1118	1659
1253	1716	2258	dep.	Lochailort	dep.	0641	1101	1639
1302	1725	2307	dep.	Beasdale	dep.	0632	1052	1630
1310	1733	2315	dep.	Arisaig	dep.	0626	1046	1624
1318	1741	2323	dep.	Morar	dep.	0617	1037	1615
1325	1748	2330	arr.	MALLAIG	dep.	0610	1030	1608

Branch to/from Oban

1011	1433	2009	dep.	CRIANLARICH	arr.	0927	1346	1924
1018	1440	2016	dep.	Tyndrum Lower	dep.	0917	1334	1910
1035	1457	2033	dep.	Dalmally	dep.	0859	1316	1852
1040	1502	2038	dep.	Loch Awe	dep.	0854	1311	1846
1054	1516	2052	dep.	Taynuilt	dep.	0840	1257	1832
1105	1527	2103	dep.	Connel Ferry	dep.	0829	1246	1821
1117	1539	2115	arr.	OBAN	dep.	0818	1235	1810

Isle of Man
Train-Lover's Paradise

Your coastal car swings out to Laxey Head. A splendid view opens beneath you of Douglas's Victorian promenade, its pink-and-green horse trams, and the Irish Sea breaking on its strand. When your climb toughens and your frail car tilts upward more steeply to climb one foot in every 24 instead of one in 38, you see the rugged coastline stretching out to far Maughold Head.

Your car labors at its effort. It vibrates, shakes, and rumbles. Wood rubbing on wood sings of excellent maintenance.

Your cautious pace gives you time to appreciate the view as you near Ballaragh, meaning "Place of the Rocks." You could not find a better name. Cliffs rise to more than 600 feet. While you run along the cliff-side more than 500 feet above the frothy breaking waves of Bulgham Bay, you are traveling on one of the most spectacular railroad stretches anywhere in the British Isles.

When you near the end of your dramatic climb beside the cliff, you reach the highest point of Isle of Man's coastline, 588 feet above the crashing surf. Turning inland, your car descends more or less continuously through lush green countryside to Ramsey.

Manx Electric Railroad's (MER) (*www.mers.org.im*) charming electric streetcars trundle through glens and atop cliffs. Aboard its cars you see some of the loveliest and most romantic scenery on the Isle of Man, the 32-mile-long dot in the Irish Sea midway between the coasts of England, Ireland, Scotland, and Wales. It is served by Manx Airways and Irish Sea Ferries' (*www.steam-packet.com*) Seacat ferries to and from Belfast and Heysham and Superseacats to and from Liverpool and Dublin. It is an island of railways and tramways.

MER's three-foot-gauge electric fleet is admired by train-lovers the world around. Their pleasing cars have waged a continual 100-year war against modernization and closure since their delivery and first use in 1893-1906. Now that they earn their keep by attracting visitors, they receive funding adequate to ensure their safe running and meticulous maintenance. During the MER Centenary celebrations in 1999, Manx from the whole island turned out.

The Isle of Man has been heavily hit by changes in vacation patterns. The railroads and the unspoiled environment used to attract

ISLE OF MAN RAILROADS

RAMSEY

Snaefell Summit

Laxey

Derby Castle

DOUGLAS

-N-

PORT ERIN

Ballasalla

Castletown

Port St. Mary

0   2   5   10

MILES

workers from the industrial north of England (Birmingham, Manchester, and Liverpool). Brightly polished steam locomotives, colorful additions to the countryside, took them to deep Manx glens, patchwork quilts of fields, the breathtaking sea—places their friends in smoke-filled cities could hardly contemplate. Now, "sun holidays" on the Mediterranean lure away its visitors with cheap airfares and mass air transportation.

From 500,000 annual visitors after World War II, Isle of Man now welcomes only 200,000. The result is that you can take advantage of tremendous overcapacity and remarkable, well-maintained electric and mountain railroads and steam trains. With the drying up of Man's traditional tourist market, a new breed of visitor has discovered this anachronism. The Isle of Man is known the world over as a vintage transport paradise.

Manx Electric Railroad

You board the MER within reach of the salt spray at the north end of the Douglas promenade and climb to almost 600 feet along a precipitous ledge before returning almost level with the Irish Sea in Ramsey, 17¾ miles and 75 minutes to the north.

Derby Castle station lies at the northern end of Douglas's Victorian promenade. (The unique steam locomotive trip to Port Erin, from the Douglas Bank Hill station, is described later in this section.) Purchase your tickets at the whimsical ticket house designed with lacquered branches to resemble an illustration in a child's fairy-tale book. BritRail Passes are not honored on the Isle of Man.

One glance around the car reveals meticulous attention to preservation and detail. MER still operates its original rolling stock—the newest dating from 1906, and original tramcars 1 and 2 dating back to the opening in 1893. Your lacquered car shines with such a gloss that you can make out your reflection in the walnut paneling. Seats covered with flowery maroon plush have reversible backs for travel in either direction.

Leaving Douglas's promenade, anchored on the opposite end by the bright Gaiety Playhouse, your car crawls and squeaks up the persistent rise. Squealing wheels rounding the curves excite remarks from many of the younger passengers. Passing the ungated level crossings, your motorman sounds his air whistle or gongs loudly to tell automobile drivers that he is insisting on his right-of-way.

Soon after departure comes the spectacular stretch along the cliffs high above Bulgham Bay. When you near the stone-covered Howstrake station, look down at the splendid panorama of Douglas Bay to the east. To the west, the hedge-lined green fields are filled with grazing sturdy Frisian cows standing like plaster statues ignoring the rain. Black-faced sheep cluster together in the fields; none are the curious four-horned Loaghtans native to the island.

Your car levels and the motorman eases back on his brass handle before swinging sharply inland and starting his descent, one foot in 24, along the wooded approach to Groudle, the terminus of the 1893 line. The Victorians created Groudle Glen as a pleasure park complete with waterwheel. Two-foot-gauge tracks linked the glen with a clifftop zoo. After falling into disuse, the line has now been lovingly restored by enthusiasts and, by 1992, extended to its original length. Built in 1896, the line climbs from the seclusion of a wooded glen before bursting onto the clifftops with magnificent views out to sea. Services are normally hauled by the original steam loco "Sea Lion," which is supplemented on occasion by diesel.

The long descent of your MER past Groudle into Laxey opens the lovely panorama of the Laxey bay and beach, the tiny harbor with its neat, white-painted lighthouses, and the headlands beyond.

At Fairy Cottage and South Cape stops you see the signs, "Alight here for the beach." In summer there is a minibus return.

MER shares the brown Laxey station house with the 1895 Snaefell Mountain Railroad, which runs daily during the summer (subject to weather). Their terminus lies in a romantic wooded glen in the center of the village, decorated by nearby Christ Church.

While in Laxey, walk down the convenient, well-marked path through the green, gorse-clad valley of Agneash to visit Lady Isabella. She's not a member of the British aristocracy but the name given to the celebrated Laxey Wheel, the largest waterwheel in the world at 72 feet in diameter. Built in 1854, the red-and-white wheel pumped the Laxey lead and silver mines until the 1920s. Now it is primarily a well-manicured tourist attraction.

Your car scrapes the white paint of the Mines Tavern leaving Laxey. It is a wonderful, old-fashioned British pub with needlepoint-covered chairs, gleaming brass, shining glasses, darts, and an open fire.

You run parallel to the six original tramcars of the Snaefell Mountain Railroad until they turn up the mountain and begin to climb at a gradient of one in 12 feet on their 30-minute journey. In 1996, No. 7 "Maria"—the only freight tram on the railroad—was reinaugurated.

When you climb to the summit of Snaefell (2,036 feet—the highest point on the Isle of Man) in that train, sit on the left side so you can see the rail of the Fell brake mounted on its side between the running rails. From the summit you can see England, Scotland, and Ireland on a good day.

The hardest part of your trip aboard the MER is over. Your MER car seems to fly past farms—sheep, cows, and green- and straw-colored meadows ringed with stone walls harboring scores of cats, not the tailless Manx breed, husbanded in Douglas's cattery, but the common alley variety.

About a mile past the green hut beside the Cornea halt, you pass Ballafayle, the residence of Sir Charles Kerruish. He is the Speaker of the House of Keys, the ancient parliament that celebrated its 1,000th anniversary in 1979. Look for his Manx "Three Legs" flag fluttering in the breeze.

Descending steadily toward Ramsey Bay, you see the Victorian hotels lining the Ramsey waterfront, a smaller echo of Douglas, and you find this symmetry most satisfying. Your car formerly ran out on the 2,000-foot Ramsey Pier but now you complete your electric railroad run not far from the city center. At Ramsey, a small museum recounts the history of the railroad with a fascinating collection of old photographs.

Isle of Man Steam Railroad

The Port Erin line, the longest narrow-gauge steam railroad line in the British Isles, uses historic carriages pulled by one of the 2-4-0 engines—Loch (1874), Maitland (1905), Hutchinson (1908), or Kissock (1910)—from Douglas Bank Hill station in the Isle's capital city, to the southwestern hamlet of Port Erin.

The 15½-mile stretch opened August 1, 1874. It is built now much as it was then. The train's story is one of evolution, with change sometimes for the better, often for the worse, but with a spirit of continuity for over a century.

The four steam locomotives still used are a fraction of the 16 original ones. They are lovingly maintained and professionally cared for. Two are red, one is blue, and one is green, and they are named for original directors of the railroad. They look chubby because of the side tanks holding cold water, and they don't need a tender for supplemental fuel.

Buy your ticket for Port Erin at Douglas's redbrick train station at the head of the harbor. Arched ornamental gates sparkle with domes and pinnacles still glittering with the gold leaf applied in the railroad's more optimistic days.

You depart Douglas with a climb of one foot in 65. You can feel your blue No. 12 engine, the Hutchinson (1908), working hard. Sitting in one of the original wooden carriages, you really know you are traveling by steam. Even the Hutchinson's modest climb produces loud puffing, smoke, soot, and flying cinders, leaving you little doubt that there is a steam engine up front.

You cross the Douglas River on the 1979 girder-span Nunnery Bridge. Past the Nunnery on your left, one of the Isle's "Stately Homes," you enter a narrow rock cutting where engines are prone to lose traction in autumn due to fallen leaves.

After a half-mile, you see spectacular cliff views opening out toward Santon Head in the south, and toward Little Ness in the Douglas direction.

Past Port Soderick station (3⅛ miles, 13 minutes), you run through the wooded Crogga valley—a treat in bluebell time. In season, dazzling displays of rhododendrons open up beside the line. Children reach from windows to catch wild flowers and leaves brushing gently against your train as it passes.

Beyond Santon (5⅝ miles, 24 minutes), the main highway runs below the track on your left but climbs up and passes over the train at the Blackboards. You don't see any black boards now, but when the road traffic was drawn by horse, a wooden screen was erected between the train and the highway to prevent horses from taking flight at smoke-belching monsters.

The airport you see on your left is Ronaldsway, site of the celebrated battle in Manx history. From here, Manx Airlines serves London, Liverpool, and Dublin.

Break your trip at Castletown (9⅞ miles, 42 minutes), the capital of the Isle until the 1860s, to explore Castle Rushen, one of the finest preserved medieval castles in Europe. Its Elizabethan clock with only the hour hand is still in use. You also see the Nautical Museum, the harbor, the beach, and King Williams College, where Bragg, the Nobel-prize-winning physicist, was educated.

When the Hutchinson pulls you past Port St. Mary (15¾ miles, 62 minutes), you see Port Erin in the distance, nestling between ground rising to the south toward the Sound, which separates the Island from the Calf of Man, and the high ground of Bradda Head to the north. Crowned by Milners Tower, Bradda Head makes a popular subject for amateur photographers.

When you arrive at the award-winning redbrick terminus at Port Erin (15⅝ miles, 65 minutes), head for the beach or train museum. You will see there the locomotive that hauled the first train of 1873, a great sampling of historic locomotives, the coaches used by Queen Elizabeth in 1972, and those used by the Duke of Sutherland on opening day, 1873.

After the electric trams, mountain railroads, and steam locomotives, your four-ring entertainment is completed by returning to Douglas and riding one of its 23 famous horse trams along the promenade. After being pulled by one of the 19th-century iron horses, you wonder which is more temperamental, the four-footed white trotters or the red, blue, and green steam locomotives.

Douglas is served by traditional ferry service with four-hour crossings from Belfast, Dublin, Liverpool, Fleetwood, and Heysham and an eight-hour sailing from Ardrossen in Scotland.

BritRail Passes are not honored on the Isle of Man, but you may purchase a one-day Rail Rover, a three-day Rail Rover allowing you unlimited travel within a week on scheduled Steam, Snaefell Mountain, and Manx Electric railroads, or a seven-consecutive-day Island Freedom pass.

MER trains run half-hourly during the summer from 9:40 A.M. to 6:40 P.M. The Steam Railway runs six departures on Mondays to Thursdays beginning at 10:10 A.M. and finishing at 6:20 P.M. On Fridays to Sundays, there are four departures, concluding an hour earlier.

Gwynedd
Sea, Steam, and Slate

Hold on to your tongue. You struggle and stutter on the Welsh consonants of Blaenau Ffestiniog, Tan-y-bwlch, Betws-y-coed, and Llyn Ystradau.

Your adventure in Gwynedd, Wales' north county, is a wild, dramatic trip beside the crashing waves of the Irish Sea, below soaring

13th-century castles, and through green valleys on a narrow-gauge, Victorian steam train.

You first follow the Cambrian Coast of Wales. A classic steam locomotive of the Ffestiniog slate railroad takes you on a volunteer-restored narrow-gauge line. Finally, you sweep down the Conwy Valley line past Conwy Castle.

Cambrian Coast Line

When you enter Wales at Machynlleth station on the Cambrian mainline from Shrewsbury (covered by BritRail Passes) aboard Central Trains (*www.centraltrains.co.uk*), take a second to glance at the classic stone station house. Its restoration was completed in 1996. It looks like a million dollars, and it should, for that was the cost of its restoration. Guards split your train, so be sure you are in the correct segment. Sit on the left.

Once past Machynlleth you have a new feeling—less cultivation and more wilderness. The river pours into the bay. You run past vast tidelands. Waterfowl of all feather are stalking the mud flats for food; boats are aground waiting for the return of the sea. Your train runs along an embankment, through cuttings and tunnels on high ground where the sea thunders against cliffs.

Your train is slow. Welsh claim they have proof that Superman is Welsh. "It is well known," they say, "that Superman can outrun a speeding train, and only in Wales is that possible." The panorama is great—over salt marsh and fine brown sand marked only with the footprints of fowl. Fishing boats have found the deep-water channel close to shore. High stone breakwaters show how violent the sea becomes.

Just short of Tywyn station, you pass the Talyllyn Railroad Museum (*www.talyllyn.co.uk*). The sign reads: "Tywyn for the Talyllyn Railway."

Curving high on the cliff, you swing for a memorable vast panorama of the village of Fairbourne (for the railroad of the same name). Steep rocky hills push the track right to the water's edge; you feel the power and beauty of the sea.

Stone walls, none of them straight, divide the green fields below the mountains into jigsaw pieces filled with sheep of different markings. Rhododendrons bloom profusely.

Cross Barmouth Bridge, which was restored as part of the $25 million, 1996 modernization of the Cambrian Line. Soon you see Harlech Castle, formidable on a crag 200 feet above sea level. Look back after passing Harlech for another view of this mighty 13th-century fortress.

Rheilffordd Ffestiniog Railroad

You alight at the two-level Minffordd station, It is unstaffed and lonesome. It has a locked stone station house with green shutters, lonesome green benches, and that's all. Climb steps up the narrow path to board the world's oldest railroad company, the private, steam-hauled Rheilffordd Ffestiniog Railroad (FR, *www.festrail.co.uk*), the greatest of the "Great Little Trains" (*www.greatlittletrainsofwales.co.uk*) that steam-train-lovers and adventurers use to explore Wales' normally inaccessible rich, green countryside.

When you have time to spare, board at FR's larger Harbor station Porthmadog terminus. This gives you a chance to admire the Welsh Pony, beautifully painted and lined in the style of the 1920s atop a slate plinth, stroll along Porthmadog's sandy beaches, dine or snack in FR's station restaurant, shop in the large souvenir and model store, and enjoy FR's small museum—but the FR station is about a 15-minute walk at the opposite end of the town's main street from the town's Cambrian Coast Line station.

Incorporated in 1832 and operated almost continuously since 1836, the slim-gauge (one foot, 11½ inches) FR stands in the record books as the oldest surviving company in the train transportation business. Now that the volunteers have renewed the operation and restored its antique steam locomotives to their original shine and vigor, FR is a point of pride for everyone of Welsh origin.

BritRail Passes are not accepted on FR, but FR honors the North & Mid-Wales Rover valid for three days in seven, which you can buy in Britain.

You sit in first-class observation cars, with high-backed upholstered seats, or third-class 2+1 seats. FR won't let you be a second-class traveler here. (First-class tickets cost about 25 percent more.)

Your coach is small but your fellow passengers and the friendly staff give it a happy feeling. The best place to sit to see the rugged scenery is on the east, the same side as the platform at Minffordd. Elbow room is tight, but your interest is fun, not transportation.

Your antique locomotive hisses steam and begins its 65-minute trip at Porthmadog's harbor. It runs across the "Cob," an embankment for the toll highway and the railroad across the wide estuary. Its first request stop, Boston Lodge, fenced by original FR ironwork, is the location of the foundry works responsible for maintaining—and in some cases actually building—the rolling stock.

You see the panorama of Snowdonia opening on your left. On the right, you duck your head to see Harlech Castle. Now your rattling carriage begins to tilt upward for a narrow, tottering, almost continuous climb of one foot in every 70 you pass, sheer above the Vale of Ffestiniog and through the green Snowdonia mountain range with the Dwyryd River meandering below. You look for the pointed summit of Mount Snowdon (3,650 feet), the highest in England and Wales, barely visible in the distance. The valley below Snowdon was known as Cum Hetiau (Hat Valley) in the 19th century because so many train passengers lost their hats in the open carriages.

Past Minffordd, your hissing locomotive pauses to take water beside the creeper-covered stationmaster's stone house in Tan-y-bwlch, 7½ miles from Porthmadog. Tracks run around three sides of the parklike bowl in the mountains.

In a few minutes your train puffs through Dduallt and then you begin a spiral—the only one in Britain. A distant nuclear power station appears on your right, on your left, and then on your right again.

Engineers abandoned the original line and built the spiral to gain elevation when the reservoir of the coming Tanygrisiau pumped-storage hydroelectric power station flooded their first tunnel. You pass through a more recent tunnel in a spur of the Moelyn Mountains before you reach the shores of the new manmade lake. Below, you see the former roadbed looking like a grass-topped wall running beside the reservoir (now a gravel highway and perfect for a hiking trail).

From the reservoir, you descend to the Tanygrisiau station, crossing first a road to the parking lot and then Wales' highest road, leading to the top dam of the power station. The automatic traffic lights flash red, the bells clang, and traffic backs up 15 car lengths, more or less. Some of the motorists take their children from the backseats to have a good view of your classic steam engine hissing past.

In Tanygrisiau, look back to a mountain still covered with a shower of chips of slate. It seems more significant to you when you realize this slate is the reason for your train's existence.

It's downhill now. You pass a waterfall and wind between two-story, slate-roof houses built of the same stone as the craggy peaks around you. The calliope-like sound of your train's steam whistle announces your arrival in the joint terminus in Blaenau Ffestiniog, the slate capital of the world. It was opened virtually on FR's 150th anniversary in 1982.

The Ffestiniog steam operation dates from the grimy times when handcrafted blue-gray slates were exported around the world for fancy roofing, paving, and fencing. The Welsh slate industry employed 16,000 workers—a quarter of them in the Llechwedd mines in Blaenau Ffestiniog.

Transporting large loads of finished slates became an acute problem by the 1820s. The roads were so rocky that slate had to be first carried in wicker baskets slung over the backs of mules and then transferred to horse-drawn wagons rented from local farmers at rates the slate entrepreneurs considered exorbitant.

After the horses pulled the slates down the Vale of Ffestiniog, the slate was reloaded into small sailing boats, each manned by two men known as Philistines and dressed in tall felt hats like the gamekeepers of the day.

In 1836, management began a simple rail operation. Tracks were laid and gravity-drawn trams loaded with slate were rolled down from the quarries to a new port facility. Horses hauled the empty cars back up (and then returned by riding down in so-called "dandy cars"). Passenger transportation began in 1865, two years after the horses had been replaced by steam locomotives.

On the FR's celebration of 150 years of service in 1986, a gravity slate train was run for the first time in nearly 50 years—and stole the show.

To save the railroad, in severe disrepair in 1954, most of its shares were transferred to a charitable trust. More than 6,500 dedicated volunteers and an accomplished salaried staff turned it from near ruin into a top pleasure railroad. Any profit is returned for expansion and improvement.

There are six steam locomotives (the "Merddin Emrys" was returned in 1988 to Victorian-style service), including strange-looking "double" engines known as Fairlie Articulated. These pieces of machinery are polished, buffed, and lubricated to peak efficiency and luster. "Prince," one of the original six locomotives, restored again to a vivid recreation of an early FR livery, is again in regular passenger service. Prince's twin locomotive is the highlight of FR's museum in Porthmadog.

Today FR carries only passengers on its 13½-mile route, giving you an excellent way to see the wooded Welsh countryside once ripped apart by the Industrial Revolution. A bus from the train station takes you to the Llechwedd slate caverns, Wales' largest working slate mine.

FR Timetable Details

Porthmadog	dep.	1020	1120	1230	1340	1550	1600
Minffordd	dep.	1030	1130	1240	1350	1500	1610
Penrhyn	dep.	1035	1135	1245	1355	1505	1615
Tan y Bwlch	dep.	1100	1210	1315	1420	1535	1645
Blaenau Ffestiniog	arr.	1130	1235	1340	1455	1600	1710
Blaenau Ffestiniog	dep.	1145	1250	1350	1510	1620	1730
Tan y Bwlch	dep.	1215	1320	1425	1540	1650	1800
Penrhyn	dep.	1230	1335	1440	1555	1795	1815
Minffordd	dep.	1240	1350	1500	1610	1715	1825
Porthmadog	arr.	1250	1400	1510	1620	1725	1835

Conwy Valley Line

At Blaenau Ffestiniog interchange, cross a crooked concrete foot-bridge above the rail lines rather than simply changing platforms. First North Western Trains' (*www.firstnorthwestern.co.uk*) Conwy Valley Line takes you on your final segment through industrial history because of the stone quarries. You travel from the mountainous heart of the country, following the Conwy River to its estuary.

Leaving Blaenau Ffestiniog you travel through a long tunnel through the mountains. Then you follow the twisting route of the River Lledr, winding downward through rocky cuttings and under rough stone bridges.

Be sure to sit up front, behind the driver, for the excellent view down the Conwy Valley. You meet the North Wales scenic line at Llandudno Junction, where you see a splendid view of the magnificent 13th-century Conwy Castle, which England's King Edward I built to subdue the Welsh. With walls and towers almost complete, it is one of the most spectacular examples of medieval military architecture in Britain. It was named a World Heritage Site by UNESCO in 1988.

From Llandudno Junction, diesel InterCity high-speed Arriva and Virgin Trains equipment will whisk you along the beautiful North Wales Coast Mainline west to Holyhead (for ferries to Ireland) or east to Manchester or Chester (for London). Farther up the line, Llandudno was built to become North Wales' premier seaside resort.

Dublin's Electric Odyssey
A Nice Bit of an Outin'

The Irish know that Howth is a seaside place for fishermen, Dun Laoghaire for gentry, Dalkey for artists, Killiney for lovers, and Bray for all of the above.

Visiting adventurers may not be familiar with these distinctions, but the Dublin Area Regional Transit (DART, *www.irishrail.ie/dart*) trains make it convenient for you to explore the area around Dublin for yourself, free on an IrishRail or Eurail product, but it is so inexpensive you will not want to use a Eurail Flexipass box. DART takes you north to Malahide and the picture-book fishing village of Howth and south along one of the most scenic stretches of coastline to Bray and Greystones. You hop on and off to visit pretty coastal towns and yacht harbors, museums, and restaurants.

Dubliners, among the most critical of people, criticized DART when it was proposed in 1984, when 80 carriages carried 35,000 daily users. With the electrified system running flawlessly, they have taken it to their hearts and DART carries 80,000 daily riders. It is much more than a boon to commuters or a vast technological improvement; it is an indispensable part of Dublin's transportation infrastructure and more—it has taken on the character of a leisure pursuit, giving to Dubliners and visitors "a nice bit of an outin'."

Howth (say "Hooth"; the name comes from the Scandinavian "hoved," meaning "head") is a mixture historic village, busy fishing port, and Dublin suburb. The seagulls in Howth are the fattest in the northern hemisphere. One step out from Howth station and you smell the aroma of fresh salmon, which sells extremely reasonably.

From the summit of the Hill of Howth, 567 feet above the station at sea level, you can see Bay of Dublin, the Wicklow Mountains, and, on a clear day, the top of Mount Snowdon in Wales.

Stone buildings line the pier facing the station. Dry-docked green-and-white, blue-and-brown fishing vessels are propped above the pier, workers scraping and repairing their hulls.

Your DART electric railcar, appropriately green, leaves Howth past heather-covered islands to the west, across mud flats busy with seagulls,

and past shacks and fishing craft in dry dock. After you glide smoothly south past the rear of Parson's steel-fabrication works, you see across the main road to the east, on the high ground, the spire of St. Mary's Church of Ireland emerging above the trees, and below, almost in the shadow of the spire, the entrance gate to Howth Castle.

You pass the first of at least three golf courses—just as green as all Ireland in spring. Just south of Howth, Sutton station lies at the narrowest part of the isthmus connecting Howth with the mainland. Your next stop, Howth Junction, is the joining of mainline trains from Dublin to the DART corridor south to Dublin's Connolly Station.

At Killester, you reach the famous "Skew Bridge." Built in 1843, the bridge was regarded as a triumph of engineering at the time. From here you run on the original embankment, which was entirely surrounded by water a century ago but now is all but lost amidst the ever-expanding land reclamation.

From Killester you glide south past row houses and parks. You see red-sweatered men struggling with bad weather on the golf course to the west, and shipping cranes and storage facilities in the distance to the east.

Dublin's Connolly Station, formerly known as Amiens Street Station, is Dublin's major terminus in size but not in number of passengers served. It has been transformed into a bright, functional station, with Oslo restaurant, newsstand, and ATM ("Cash Point") down the escalator. You have access to the Mainline Booking Office, the Information Bureau, the cloakroom, the cafeteria, the central bus station, and a taxi pickup in front.

DART platform 6 takes you north; platform 7 takes you south to Greystones. Enter through the gate to platform 4. Check the departure times on the standard railroad departure sheet in the Connolly ticketing hall.

When your southbound DART leaves Connolly, you glide almost noiselessly out onto the beginning of the Loop Line over Amiens Street. Take a look at the Italianate tower of the mainline terminal building facing Talbot Street and the fine old grimy and faded red-brick Victorian railroad offices with yellow brick window arches and dull-blue brick band. Inside, workers pilot the entire "space-age" computerized Central Control of today's rail system.

You pass through the rooftops past the new Irish Life Assurance building complex with golden windows. In front you see the Chariot of Life sculpture, "Look Ma, no reins!"

You travel on the elevated railroad to the stop at Tara Street Bridge over the Liffey River, but Tara Street station has no exit or entrance on Tara Street. The station opens onto George's Quay.

The stretch of the Loop Line between the Tara Street station and Pearse station (formerly Westland Row) is the shortest distance between any two DART stations, yet for so short a stretch you see much: the notable spire of City Quay Parish Church, the more ponderous roofline of St. Mark's, Hawkins House, the darkly tinted glass of the *Irish Press* newspaper office, and the distinctive 130-foot watchtower of the Tara Street fire station. Finally you pass through Trinity College. Yours may be the only train actually to run through part of a university. The Loop Line viaduct curves gently across the Botany Bay area of the university, giving you a close-up of Trinity's Parade Ground and science buildings.

You arrive on the green ironwork bridge in red-brick Pearse station with antique girders and a glass arch overhead.

From Pearse station you reach the interesting three-span skew bridge over the Grand Canal. To the west is the tall, gaunt Guinness malt store. Originally, in 1834, planners sketched a single bridge here, but engineering problems necessitated building two, the first almost square on, and the second a genuine "skew" bridge of 33 degrees—and both so low that in later years no double-decked streetcar or bus could pass under them.

At Landsdowne Road station, sports fans depart almost beneath a modern two-tier sports stadium straddling the station and the railroad line. This is the mecca of Irish rugby and a regular site for international and European Cup soccer matches.

The annual fair in Donnybrook nearby gave a new word to the English language. Established by King John in 1204, the fair was finally abolished in 1855 because more fistfights broke out outside the bareknuckle prizefighters' rings than within.

The DART station in the pleasant seaside village of Sandymount, one of the line's most attractive stops, stands on the site of stations dating back to 1835.

Just after Sandymount, and before you stop at Sydney Parade, you see a fine view of Gothic St. John's Church across the green grass of Monkstown Rugby Club. On a late summer evening the church's warm sand-colored stones and its ornamental windows catch the last glow of the setting sun.

Past Sydney Parade, the setting for James Joyce's short story "A Painful Case," you spring suddenly into a panoramic scene of the bay. The vista opens across the bay that Dubliners claim is lovelier than the Bay of Naples and your senses dance an Irish jig. Your railcar, like a child dashing eagerly to water's edge, runs along the sands and as close to the seabirds fishing in the waves as prudent.

Past Blackrock, you watch clammers shoveling through the mud flats, filling their red plastic buckets to the limit. The coastline is alive with windsurfers steering their colorful craft and assembling their bright-as-buttons equipment in parking lots from Blackrock to Dun Laoghaire. Yachts dance in the harbor and seawalls protect oceangoing ferries.

Passengers on the *Stena Lynx III* fast ferry service from Holyhead get their first taste of the DART system at Dun Laoghaire (say "Dunleary"). South Eastern Suburban service to and from Dublin's Connolly station is also available.

Dun Laoghaire, which was first called "Dunleary" and then "Kingstown" in honor of the visit of King George IV, is primarily a sea town, the only Irish port directly administered by the government and not by locally elected officials. Between the harbor and the DART station, look for the tiny brick office marked by the green *i*, which combines the tourist information office, the Bureau de Change, and the Stena office. New berthing facilities and passenger terminal building were constructed in 1994-95 for the arrival of the Stena HSS, the world's largest high-speed ferry.

DARTing south from Dun Laoghaire to Sandycove takes you beneath seven overpasses including three major road crossings. To complete DART, these either had to be lifted, rebuilt, and the highway approaches altered, or your train's roadbed had to be lowered by about 20 inches. As a result, you now pass over a one-mile stretch of continuously paved concrete railbed, the first in Ireland.

From your stop at Sandycove you see teams of windsurfers, canoeists, and water-skiers in Scotsman's Bay immediately outside Dun Laoghaire's east pier. Walk 15 minutes from the station to Sandycove's premier attraction, the Martello Tower, built in 1804 to withstand the Napoleonic invasion that never came.

From Dalkey's green cement station house, you, like George Bernard Shaw, see beautiful seascapes. Dogs play in waves. Anglers cast into the surf. The great playwright spent the happiest days of his youth here on Torca Hill, overlooking the splendid sweep of Bay of Dublin.

South of Dalkey, you travel on cliffs overhanging the sea. Mountains rise in the distance. At Killiney you have a chance to walk parallel to the DART line for breathtaking views, or to climb the steep lane opposite the station and in 10 minutes reach a charming district distinguished by early Irish Christian architecture. Past Killiney and Shankhill you journey inland; white row houses separate you from the ocean. You pass through the middle of a golf course. All Ireland looks like a golf course in springtime, but this is probably the only golf course with a commuter hazard.

You now approach Bray, one of Ireland's premier seaside resorts. The welcoming promontory of Bray Head stands high above the sea and Bray crowns the southern shore of Bay of Dublin.

At Bray station you see the original iron pillars bearing the logo, "Irish Engineering Co., Seville Works, 1853." "David's Diner and Market" sells fresh fruit and soft ice cream.

Bray, in County Wicklow, the only city outside County Dublin to be served by DART, is a fishing harbor, a holiday resort, a town of handsome urban architecture, an important shopping area, . . . and the honeymoon capital of Ireland.

DART continues to update and enlarge its train fleet. DART placed in service 26 new carriages in 2003 and is proceeding to lengthen all its platforms, upgrade station accesses, and purchase an additional 36 DART carriages.

Dublin Commuter Tickets are sold for one, four, and seven days, a month, and a year. The one- and four-day tickets do not require a photocard but have various restrictions. Seven-day tickets commence on Sundays; monthly tickets on the first of the month. Short Hop tickets are available for zone *A* and zone *B*. Medium, Long, and Giant Hop tickets extend the Short Hop tickets in three consecutively larger zones.

Benelux

Savvy Traveling on the Trains of the Netherlands, Belgium, and Luxembourg

Dutch trains—Belgian trains—Belgian train stations— Luxembourgois trains—Airport trains—Getting around Amsterdam—Getting around Brussels—Railroad museums— Flower Train circuit—Channel ferry service—Rail-pass travel

The well-developed national railroads of the three Benelux coun- tries make it easy for you to travel from city to city. Over the "Nederlandse Spoorwegen" (NS, *www.ns.nl*) network, 1,760 miles, NS runs some 2,288 coaches (including multiple units) providing more than 135,000 seats on more than 4,300 passenger trains from 360 sta- tions. About 1,300 of these units consist of electric railcar units (or EMUs) made up of two, three, or four carriages. Ninety-five percent are on time.

The "Societe Nationale des Chemins de Fer belge" (SNCB, *b- rail.be*), which is called "Belgische Spoorwegen" in Dutch, and the "Societe Nationale des Chemins de Fer Luxembourgois" (CFL, *www.cfl.lu*) are nearly as busy and punctual.

Nowhere do the trains run so often and so efficiently. When GermanRail officials visited the Netherlands, they said, "It is impossible to run a train system this way." The Dutch turn the trick by running primarily short, busy railcars that combine and split frequently. Their platforms are long to serve two or even three trains one after another on one track.

The Belgian railroads similarly offer frequent services on a dense network. Luxembourg, because of its modest size, offers inexpensive service over a nominal railroad infrastructure supplemented with buses.

Flat countrysides, dense train networks, frequent services, and short distances make it easy for you to see the Benelux nations by train. You can see any of these countries easily from wherever you make your base. You don't have to pack or unpack here.

Dutch Trains: "No Train, No Gain"

NS is an autonomous and financially independent body. However, the Dutch government finances track maintenance and construction, including the Amsterdam-Antwerp high-speed line expected to be completed in 2006-7, and pays subsidies to NS to compensate for reduced fares for certain categories of traveler.

The Dutch railroads' network operates like one efficient rapid-transit area with international services superimposed upon it. NS trains are sets of electric railcars plus a few diesel railcars connected together in twos and threes to provide high capacity, frequent service, and great flexibility. Some trains, particularly double-deckers, have "quiet" areas, where NS prohibits cellular telephones, discourages excessive gregariousness by passengers, and offers books to read. Because of the food and drink available inexpensively in stations, where you often find supermarkets, it is uneconomic for NS to provide food or drink services on their trains. Domestic trains do not require reservations, so don't even try to make them.

You find all kinds of services listed in the NS timetable, which is for sale in the station bookstores, and the "Intercityboekje" (InterCity Summary) available free, although a timetable is scarcely necessary because of the frequent running of trains.

• Intercity trains serve some 30 large and middle-sized cities. For longer stretches they are very comfortable and very fast. They run almost always half-hourly between IC stations.

• Sneltreins are fast trains serving some 80 stations.

• Stoptreins stop at every windmill.

• Night trains carry you during the early-morning hours on the crescent between Utrecht (Centraal station) and Rotterdam (Centraal station) with stops in Amsterdam (Centraal station), Amsterdam Schiphol Airport, Leiden, The Hague (HS), and Delft.

• International trains include Thalys to Brussels and Paris, described in the "International" chapter; the Swiss EC to Basel, Bern, and Interlaken that carries a Swiss panoramic carriage; CityNightLine Pegasus (see "International Night Trains" chapter) to Basel and Zurich and CityNightLine Pollux to Munich and Garmisch-Partenkirchen (on winter Fridays only); three-a-day German InterCity trains to Hanover-Berlin and one to Hanover-Leipzig; and the ICE 3M trains between Amsterdam and Cologne that began service in October 2000 and were extended to Frankfurt/Main in 2002 (see "ICE International" section in "International" chapter).

All bets are off during rush hours, when everyone wants to get home as soon as possible. High-density trains take charge on the busiest commuter corridors. Depending on the region, these trains are called "City Pendel, "Spits Pendel," or "Star Net" and replace stoptreins for this time only. These local trains carry no first class and run eight times an hour instead of four. Passengers are not surprised to have to stand. IC and sneltreins continue business as usual.

You can travel anywhere in the Netherlands speedily by combining trains. The yellow departure timetables posted in the train stations are your key to finding your way about easily and quickly. There are usually four domestic sheets and one international sheet. Find the sheet showing your destination. The simple schematic route diagrams showing you the order of stations on your route make your planning easy.

The departure time and platform number followed by an *a* or *b* are printed beside every train's destination. Pay special attention to these letters, which refer to portions of the platform where your train boards. NS platforms are extraordinarily long in order to accommodate two or more trains at the same time. The train you want will be at the portion indicated on the timetable.

Dutch stations are generally quite easy to navigate, except that some, like Utrecht Centraal station, The Hague Centraal station, and Amsterdam Schiphol Airport station, have attached shopping complexes, which overwhelm you with an array of too many shops and too much fast food. The bright, newer stations, built in a flurry of construction, use an economical but sound construction technique—tinker-toy modern. You always find up escalators. If there are no down escalators, look for the elevator to help you get your luggage to street level. Most stations have a GWK Bank for changing money and an ATM ("Geldautomat") not far away.

Transporting one million Dutch travelers a day, it is no wonder NS prefers double-decked trains, and with good results. The double-deckers have double the comfort of the trains they replaced.

The Dutch used imagination creating a lexicon for their trains:

• The "Buffel" (Buffalo) is a popular diesel railcar with 2+2 seating in first and second class. Its name comes from its distinctive profile.

• The pride of the NS fleet is the air-conditioned "Regiorunner," a 1995 double-decked railcar with a distinctive nose, tapered sides, and striped very attractively in blue and yellow. First-class sections, above and below, are fitted with plush seats, 2+1, which recline grudgingly a few inches. Second-class sections are 2+2 and have uncommonly comfortable vinyl upholstery. You will like the good headroom, even upstairs. Incidental tables are located below the windows. All sections have linoleum flooring.

There is a second, 1980s double-decker fleet, which was refurbished earlier this decade. You can identify them by their flat sides and unimaginative yellow-and-blue markings. They are much less comfortable although air-conditioning was installed. The seats don't recline. You sit in 2+2, worsted-fabric seats, even in first class, or second-class seats that are vinyl but more primitive than the newer double-deckers.

• NS's IC-3 "Koploper" railcar was introduced in 1977. You recognize it miles away by its raised driver's cabin, which allows the driver a better view and ingeniously permits passengers to cross from one independent unit to another when IC-3s are coupled together. It is the 747 of the train world. You ride this 100-mph train between the Randstad (the high-population-density area stretching from Rotterdam to Amsterdam to Utrecht) and the east and north of the country.

• You can tell the three-carriage, 78-mph Sprinter train by its beveled profile. This electric railcar set was introduced in 1975 for fast acceleration and braking so it could decrease the travel time between nearby stations. Many were modernized in 2003 with a white, yellow, and blue livery, plush-covered individual seats, information displays, and the addition of a third door in the center of the middle carriage.

• The 1994 electric "Railhopper" two-carriage stoptrein with hooked nose bulges outward in the center in order to allow five people across in second class (four in first) for short trips, but Dutch travelers, larger than the European average, protested so vigorously that the train was reseated 2+2. It is usually run in multiples connected together.

Round-trip tickets ("Retour") are less than twice the single fare ("Enkele reis") but valid on the day of issue only. Children under four travel free; those four to 11 for about U.S. $1.50 when accompanied by an adult over 19—limit three children per adult. NS ticket machines take euro coins and give change but will not accept euro banknotes. They accept Dutch debit cards but not foreign debit cards nor credit cards of any origin. NS ticket offices take cash but not credit cards.

Your train ticket enables you to hire a taxi in 114 cities for a flat rate. The "Train Taxi" is a clearly marked normal taxi that you share with other passengers. Its driver will transfer you from the train station to anywhere within the city limits. About 230,000 passengers a month use the service, and the subsidized program, begun in 1990, now is self-sufficient. You must buy your ticket at the ticket office in the station you depart. With a rail pass, just show it when buying your Train Taxi ticket. When you arrive at your destination, take your computer-printed Train Taxi ticket to the clearly marked taxi stand. It couldn't be easier, and a bargain, too. Train Taxis operate from 7 A.M. on weekdays and Saturdays and from 8 A.M. on Sundays and holidays until the last train has arrived at the station. This special service is not available in Amsterdam, Rotterdam, or The Hague because of violent hostility from the cab-driver establishment.

With a train ticket or pass, you can rent a bicycle at a discount. You must provide identification and you are usually required to put down a substantial deposit. Not all stations have this service, but you bike well in the Netherlands, where there are more bicyclists than voters, bike lanes are common, and the land is flat.

Belgian Trains

You hardly can turn around in Brussels' refurbished South (Midi/Zuid) station without seeing a high-speed train going somewhere.

Brussels is the capital of Belgium, NATO headquarters, seat of European Union institutions and EU Parliament plenary meetings, and, since the completion of the Belgian high-speed line to France in December 1997, also the heart of the northwest European high-speed network.

Brussels South hosts services of four different high-speed trains. High-speed lines take passengers to London, Paris, Lille, Frankfurt, and Cologne, and a new high-speed line leading to Amsterdam is under construction.

You can ride at amazing speeds Eurostar trains to London, Thalys trains in all directions, and Brussels-France TGV trains via Lille to the Atlantic Ocean and Mediterranean Sea, and after the new German high-speed line opened you traveled from Brussels to Frankfurt in three hours, 20 minutes, compared with five hours, 10 minutes previously.

The four-mile-long, six-track tunnel linking Brussels North (Nord/Noord) and South stations forms the backbone of the almost completely electrified, 2,170-mile, domestic Belgian Railroad network, which is the second densest in Europe (after the Czech Republic).

Belgian trains come in several different liveries, all bearing the network's distinctive *B* logo. You ride four categories of SNCB domestic trains. InterCity and InterRegio (IR) trains usually run hourly. IC lines are designated *A* through *N*. IR lines are labeled *a* through *p*. InterCity trains give you fast connections between major centers of Belgium and foreign termini. IR trains take you to more intermediate stops. Local (L) trains stop everywhere except stations where only peak trains (P-trains) stop. Peak trains are often double-deckers running at busy travel hours.

When you buy an ordinary one-way or round-trip domestic ticket (including those to the airport), remember that both directions must be used on the day you buy your ticket. You may buy a ticket five days in advance, but be sure to say on what date you plan to travel. Train tickets issued to or from the "Brussels Agglomeration" are valid for connecting train travel to or from any of the 28 stations in the Brussels Capital Region. As a rule, tickets are not sold on trains, except to those who board at an unmanned train stop. If you are unable to buy a ticket, you can buy one on board, but be sure to tell the conductor before boarding that you have no ticket. If you fail to do so, a conductor may fine you and a add a fee to a ticket bought on the train.

You ride in the latest in electric InterCity trains and carriages. New 100-mph double-decked carriages run on longer-distance InterCity routes. They are air-conditioned and have individual cloth-covered seats arranged 2+2, even in first class (but there is more leg space in first class), a majority of seats arranged face-to-face with tables, retention toilets, deep windows located beside the seats, baggage space, a carpeted entrance, and curved glass doors to insulate the seats from noise and wind at station stops.

For shorter routes, 100-mph railcars have individual, comfortable seats arranged 2+1 in first class and 2+2 in second. They have air-conditioning, heating, telephones, and retention toilets. SNCB claims these railcars are the quietest in Europe. Derived from the Danish IC3s, they may be recognized by the thick rubber seal around the whole of the front and a driver's area that can be folded sideways when two units are coupled together. The digital passenger information system is displayed both at the corridor ends inside and by doors outside.

Belgian Train Stations

Brussels' South station (Gare du Midi/Zuidstation) consists of one long departure hall with escalators to and from the platforms above. Most passengers enter and leave the station via the connecting Brussels metro station (with both orange and green lines), where they pass the money-exchange (Change/Wissel) office. SNCB's "Travel Centre" (open 6 A.M. to 10 P.M.) begins at the escalator leading to platform 10. Their agents accept bank credit cards for payment.

For tourist and hotel information and reservations, look for the hotel *i* sign. Electronic departure signs above the track entrances ensure that you board the correct train. Be aware that two sets of train arrival and departure sheets are posted. One set provides the times for Monday to Friday departures and arrivals. The second set is valid on Saturdays, Sundays, and holidays (read: "Zaterdag, Zondag/Samedi, Dimanche"). The post office is next door.

The entire Brussels South station has been brightened and better organized over the last few years because of the high-speed train traffic. Eurostar and Thalys customers have their own high-tech terminals. The Eurostar arena stretches off to the right (as you depart). Changing between Eurostar, Thalys, or conventional trains at Brussels' South station is very easy. Platform one is used for Eurostar arrivals from London; platform two for departures. Brussels South has sparkling, improved Thalys platforms, but the domestic platforms can't be renewed until the station redevelopment is complete.

Brussels' Central station is most used as a commuter station serving downtown Brussels and the Grande Place. A statue of a train worker represents the 3,012 workers killed for the fatherland during the wars of 1914-18 and 1940-44. The "Vertrek/Depart" electronic departures board is next to the "Consigne/Bewaring" luggage-check counter.

Brussels' North station (Gare du Nord/Noordstation) is a remodeled and expanded CCN ("Communication Center North") combining train, metro, bus, and airport connections and includes the Belgian Railroad's Train Museum as well. The train information office is located in the departures hall. Nearby is a change bank and pubs where beer flows freely, but the brightest is the "Taverne Edelweiss" in the subway section, where food is presentably served. There is also a waiting room in the underground passage between the entrances to tracks 9 and 10. You also board railcars to Brussels' Zaventem Airport here from various platforms shown on the departure signs.

The construction of new high-speed lines and the increasing numbers of domestic and new international travelers gave Belgian Railways (SNCB, *www.b-rail.be*) the impetus to rebuild three stations: Brussels South, Antwerp Centraal, and Liege Guillemins. The results are astonishing.

Brussels South station was already pleasant to use, but it was nothing compared with what is taking place. Cranes are lifting and crews are pouring cement in a gigantic enlargement of the station into a massive urban-renewal program, which will include a new hotel.

The *Liege Guillemins station,* 500 feet from Liege's old station, is arising to host the 2002 high-speed line from Brussels, which was built to the same engineering standards as the Belgian high-speed line south to the French border and supports trains running at 186 mph. The station will be astonishing, and no wonder: Santiago Calatrava, the preeminent railroad architect of the modern era and the man responsible for the stunning Lyon Airport train station and amazing Lisbon Oriente station, designed it.

Liege's new Guillemins station will have a gigantic steel-and-glass vault arching elegantly over the tracks to connect the district of the Cointe Hill to the Guillemins District. On the city side, the station will open on three levels linked together by escalators and elevators. On the Cointe Hill side, the station will be organized on five levels including three levels of parking and the roof of the passenger building in the form of a pergola.

Perhaps even more astonishing are the modifications being

performed on *Antwerp Centraal station,* which will open its new tracks in 2005 preliminary to the 2006 opening of the Belgian-Dutch high-speed line to Amsterdam. The present station is architecturally one of the most beautiful in Europe. Locals refer to it as the "Railroad Cathedral" because of its impressive exterior. Its historic value is so great that it was unthinkable to replace it with an alternate station.

But Antwerp's existing station is a problem dead-end station, and through trains have to reverse direction in order to continue. This is too time-consuming for high-speed trains, so the solution was to provide through tracks on a level below the existing station's tracks, and this involved extensive tunneling.

Rebuilt Antwerp Centraal station will have four different levels including six dead-end tracks on the top level where the present tracks are located. The street level will be a pedestrian area with shops and station services, the first underground level will have four dead-end tracks, and finally the lowest level will have four high-speed tracks leading to two new single-track tunnels that constitute the actual north-south connection.

Luxembourgois Trains

Luxembourg City, the Grand Duchy of Luxembourg's enchanting capital, is so well connected to the rest of Europe by train that the tourist board is tempted to call it the "Green Heart of Europe." Once there you easily explore Luxembourg's gracious mountains and valleys by CFL's extensive bus network.

Luxembourg City's modest train station is one of the few with leaded-glass windows and a striking, green patina steeple. A modern wing leads to a fourth, functional east platform, completed in 1990, with bright, friendly colors and a weather-resistant Plexiglas cover. Free luggage carts stand on platforms, and elevators are available to take you between platforms.

The modern leaded-glass windows picturing the profile of Luxembourg Castle dominate the interior and cast colored southern lights on the central hall. Train information is in a modern office; money change and a pleasant pub/cafeteria are opposite. Use the coin-operated lockers in the main hall. When they are filled, check your luggage with the "Consigne des Bagages" down the hall. You orient yourself with city and regional maps protected in a glass case in front of the station.

Hotels and banks for changing your money surround the Place de la Gare. Turn to your right as you exit for the bus stands where you board both the Luxair airport bus and the city buses to the airport. Past the bus stands, the Luxair terminus accommodates the information office of the Luxembourg Tourist Board. They give you a hotel brochure with prices, photos, addresses, and a map (most hotels are in a circle around the train station). "We do not make hotel recommendations, but we will telephone for you." They do, at no cost, according to your selection from the brochure, but everything closes tightly from noon to 2 P.M. for lunch.

Make Luxembourg City your base. Like a star, five lines with two electrical systems converge here. Luxembourg lies on the mainline of the Swiss Brussels-Namur-Luxembourg-Metz-Strasbourg-Basel route and it is an easy access to Paris's Est station.

Electrification of the "Ligne du Nord" or "Nord-Streck," the Northern line, was completed in 1993, completing electrification of CFL's 171-mile network (except for two short stretches), and with the completion of the electrification of Belgium's Liege-Luxembourg line in summer 2000, you ride trains formed of CFL electric locomotives and SNCB carriages between Liege and Luxembourg.

As Luxembourg is such a small country, international traffic is of great importance. The most frequent service is to and from Brussels, usually hourly, using new, double-decked, 100-mph trains integrated into the Belgian InterCity network. Travelers to France pass through Thionville to Metz and then onward to Paris's Gare de l'Est or Basel via Strasbourg. InterRegio trains take you along the Wasserbillig route to Trier, Germany, and then Koblenz. In addition, two-carriage Regional Express railcars operate hourly to Trier. While you are in Wasserbillig, note the Mosel River flowing behind the station. You can see German trains on the opposite bank.

Airport Trains

When you arrive by air in Benelux, you have it easy.

Amsterdam Schiphol Airport is one of the two best train airports in Europe because of its mainline connections completed in 1986. Schiphol station was extended from three to six platform tracks in 2000 to cope with traffic growth. InterCity trains take you from Amsterdam's airport without change to Berlin, Germany, and Groningen and Leeuwarden in northern Netherlands. Thalys takes you without change to Brussels and Paris and, with a change to Eurostar in Brussels, all the way to London, thus giving you a way to reach all of northern Europe.

Seven train an hour whiz you north to Amsterdam's Central station, so you won't have to wait over 13 minutes and might need to wait only six. Travel time is 19 minutes. Trains south to Leiden take 19 minutes; to The Hague's Centraal station 29-40 minutes; and 45 minutes to Rotterdam Centraal.

Amsterdam Schiphol Airport has been enlarged and transformed into something of a shopping mall, but follow the signs showing the profile of a train that does not much resemble a train at all. You must use your imagination. These signs lead you to the train station hall. In the large hall (past the Burger King) devoted to railroad functions, you see the NS Reisburo (travel bureau) and clearly marked counters for international and domestic (Netherlands/Belgium) ticketing. "Vertrek/Aankomst Departures/Arrivals" directions are printed on backlit yellow posters and country maps. Current departures are shown on video displays. Moving walkways lead you to the platforms below.

SNCB's three-carriage electric trains with the large red-and-blue "Brussels Airport Express" letters on the sides take you between *Brussels' Zaventem Airport* and Brussels' three downtown train stations. They are covered by rail passes. Between 5:24 A.M. and 11:46 P.M., three or four trains an hour connect the airport with Brussels' North, Central, and South stations and hourly with Schaerbeck station. Allow 10 minutes to reach Schaerbeck, 15 to North, 20 to Central, and 24 to South stations. Hourly trains travel through Brussels to Mons, Ghent, and De Panne.

Riders going to Brussels' Zaventem Airport find departure times and platform numbers on the large departure signs of the Brussels downtown stations. From the Central station, look for the signs "Bruxelles National-Aeroport/Brussel Nationaal-Luchthaven" and an airplane pictograph pointing to Track A, across the subterranean station from all the rest.

The airport train serves level "minus 2" of the airport. Follow the pictographs over the escalators and elevators to level 3 for departures. Use the pushcarts you find on the platforms, but of course not on the escalators.

Air arrivals descend from level 2 to level "minus 1," where you can validate your rail pass, buy tickets to major Belgian cities—as well as Paris—and make international reservations at the Belgian Railroads' ticket office, and then proceed to "minus 2" for the train platforms.

The Brussels Airport Express's stop at South station allows you to make rapid connections for Paris, Amsterdam, and Cologne.

You have two choices for travel between *Luxembourg Findel Airport* and the train station. Most take the blue-and-white Luxair bus leaving every 30 minutes from the front of the airport terminal. Others walk across the airport's small parking lot to the yellow sign marking the bus stop for Luxembourg city bus line 9, which departs every 15 minutes during the week, hourly on Sundays, and costs about one-fifth that of the airport bus. The city bus takes about 10 minutes longer to the train station but you can get off near many hotels and the youth hostel.

Getting around Amsterdam

There are four locations of the Amsterdam Tourist Office ("VVV") to help you with hotel reservations for the day you arrive and coming days, in Amsterdam and for the rest of the Netherlands. They are located:

• on Stationsplein, the square facing Amsterdam Central station (open daily, 9 A.M. to 5 P.M.),

• near Leidseplein, the popular gathering point reached by street-cars 1, 2, and 5 (open daily, 8:30 A.M. to 8 P.M.),

• on Stadionsplein, near the Olympic Stadium in Amsterdam's outskirts (open Mon.-Sat., 9 A.M. to 5 P.M.; Sun., 9 A.M. to noon), and

• in the Central station itself, track two.

The Holland Tourist Information Board has an office at Amsterdam Schiphol Airport (open daily, 9 A.M. to 10 P.M.).

The tourist office personnel also will give you information on every sort of activity, including visiting museums, shopping, dining, making excursions, and attending the theater, opera, or ballet.

You are fortunate that Amsterdam has an excellent public transportation system with modern, Siemens Combino, low-floor streetcars gradually replacing the older blue-and-white streetcars. There are 17 streetcar lines (five originate in front of Central station), 30 bus lines, and four metro lines plus eight night bus lines. The red, white, and blue Sneltrams (fast streetcars) of metro Line 51 run between Central, Amstel, Duivendrecht, RAI, South, and Amstelveen stations, which are equipped with twin-level platforms.

Of special note is Circle Tram 20. It is just what the name indicates. Tram 20 makes a round trip through Amsterdam in both directions, and its route was chosen to take you past almost all tourist attractions. You don't have to change streetcars. You can stay seated until you come to the museum, square, or monument you want to visit, or you can use Circle Tram for a mini sightseeing trip. The streetcar rides every 10 minutes from 9 A.M. to 7 P.M. The last streetcar leaves from Central station at 6 P.M.

Streetcars on most lines require you to enter the back door, where there may or may not be a seated inspector to check your ticket. Strip-tickets are the cheapest and most convenient way to ride streetcars and buses, rather than day or multiday passes, because you can use strip-tickets whenever you need to over a period of days. A strip-ticket is just what it says—a long card divided into horizontal strips. You are permitted to travel on one validation throughout the entire central city—the large zone that includes everywhere you are likely to go—for an hour including transfers between streetcar lines, buses, and the metro. Thus you can make a short trip and return all within an hour using only one validation. If there is an inspector aboard, he or she will stamp your strip-ticket according to your destination. If not, for your first trip, fold the ticket on the line between strips one and two. Stamp strip number two by pushing it (strip side down) into the slot of one of the squat yellow stamping machines inside the streetcar. Wait for the "ping!" sound.

You can buy 15-box tickets (two boxes equal one trip in one zone) at machines in the train stations ("Nationale Strippen Kaart"). The correct code to order strip-tickets is "2-2-2-2." You can also buy them at the white "GVB" transport office opposite Amsterdam's Central station, at a city information (VVV) office, or at any post office. Streetcar drivers are allowed to sell day tickets, one-hour tickets, and two-, three-, and eight-strip strip-tickets, except on Line 5, where there are ticketing machines (with directions in English) located in the middle. You won't have any trouble with these machines so long as you pick your zone before putting in your money.

Unless you plan to spend a day riding public transportation or traveling to and from Amsterdam's suburbs, strip-tickets are cheaper and more flexible than the Circle-Amsterdam ticket, which is valid day and night for up to nine days. Consider strip-tickets as national currency. Use them for transportation not only on Amsterdam's public transportation but for transportation in all of the Netherlands' major cities.

Getting around Brussels

Your best access to Brussels' Old Town is Brussels Central station (Gare Centrale/Centraal Station) located roughly halfway along the *Jonction Nord-Midi* tunnel between North and South stations, but international trains do not stop here because Central's platforms are too short. But Central station is only a few minutes away by local train from North or South train station and trains run about every three minutes.

Remodeled in 1991, Central station is bright and airy with metro connections. Walk five minutes downhill past convenient hotels toward the town hall's spire to the Grande Place. Belgium's tourist information office, for hotel bookings and abundant information, is one block north, at 61, rue du Marche aux Herbes (open 9 A.M. to 8 P.M., June-Sept.; to 6 P.M. in winter), or use the smaller tourist information office located in the city hall (the magnificent building dominating the west side—open 9 A.M. to 6 P.M.; closed Sunday during the winter).

You can get around Brussels using the integrated network of metro, streetcar, and bus lines on a single or 10-journey ticket that allows you an hour's unlimited travel, or you can buy a day card. The transit authority maintains a Web site, *www.stib.be,* for you to plot your route of travel. Enter an address, stop name, or landmark, your time of travel, and some details to find the fastest route. Network maps and schedules are displayed in metro stations and at most stops. Pick up a free pocket map and schedule booklet ("Transports Publics/Openbaar Vervoeror") at one of the transit authority's information offices in the South train station, Rogier, and Porte de Nemur metro stations. The metro's busy main corridor connects the North and South train stations. At the stop "De Brouckere," you change to the red or yellow line (Line 1a or 1b) for the Central and Schuman stations.

Railroad Museums

The Netherlands Railroad Museum in the former station of Utrecht Maliebaan will reopen in 2004 with a new 75,000-square-foot building having a square in front that looks like a roundhouse, including turntable. The museum will present some of the specially refurbished equipment and rolling stock that was stored away, until the museum's reopening, from climatic influences that might cause rusting.

You can reach it by a short walk to the south from the exit of Utrecht's modern, innovative Central station.

SNCB's Railroad Museum is a much smaller version, admission free, that train enthusiasts will enjoy despite explanations in Flemish and French only. It is clearly marked by arrows in the railroad (not the metro) portion of Brussels' Gare du Nord. Its central feature is the astonishing "Land of Wales," built 1842-47 in Brussels, a narrow-gauge steam train that ran between Antwerp and Ghent. Visitors see exhibits of every sort including signaling, types of rail, sleepers, etc.

The Railroad Museum in Schepdaal, Belgium (open 2 to 6 P.M., Sun. and holidays, Apr.-mid-Oct.; Sat., July-Aug.), about 10 miles from Brussels, is housed in an old tram depot, which opened in 1887 for steam trains on the Brussels-Schepdaal route. It features steam locomotives, a fuel tram, two-axle electric trams, and postwar vehicles.

Flower Train Circuit

NS devised a one-day Flower Train itinerary for the many visitors to the Netherlands enchanted with the floral beauty brightening the low country. It begins and ends in Amsterdam's Central station, but you have the freedom to join at any point along NS's dense network.

From Amsterdam Central the stretch to Haarlem takes you over the oldest railroad section of the Netherlands (1839), and you see vivid contrasts between old and new. You pass old warehouses and the 17th-century harbor area; on your right, a bird preserve. Parallel to the track on the left runs the Haarlemmer Trekwaart, a commercial canal dug in the 17th century.

Past the lake to your south, Haarlemmermeer, the railroad, and canal suddenly come close together. The last of a medieval peat polder unfolds on the north. Past the highway you see the Roman church towers of Spaarnwoude, situated on the most easterly part of an old beach wall. A little farther you cross the water of De Liede, and farther on you pass an elegant series of windmills. Entering Haarlem, you see on your left the somber 19th-century prison and the medieval Amsterdamse Poort. Haarlem's 1908 station is a showcase of Art Nouveau. Look at the tile tableaus or visit the first-class restaurant.

The train from Haarlem takes you down the length of the bulb-growing area. The most beautiful time to visit here is April and May, when the view of the bulb fields is absolutely breathtaking with unexpected combinations of bright colors. You enter the bulb-growing area at the village of Vogelenzang, which is situated exactly on the edge of the inner sand dune and the geest (the sandy soil between the dunes and the polder). About three miles farther is the former station of Lisse on the left and the world-famous De Keukenhof, the greatest tulip and bulb show in the world during the spring. You can reach it by bus from Haarlem and Leiden stations. Flower lovers will visit the Hortus Botanicus in Leiden.

As you enter The Hague, capital of the Netherlands, a long strip of private market gardens and sports fields extends along both sides of the track deep into the city. Flower lovers will take a walk to the Clingendael.

After changing trains in Hague Central station (CS) (do not confuse with Hague NS station) you zigzag easterly through the green heart of Holland, where narrow, straight fields lie parallel to silver lines of canals. Just before Zoetermeer you see on your right the site of the Floriade exhibitions. Past Zoetermeer Oost station, you cross the Rotte River, which is high above surrounding land. On your right you see a line of four fine windmills constructed in the 18th century to reclaim a peat bog. The Tweemanspolder is almost 15 feet below sea level.

At Gouda station change to the train taking you through Waddinxveen station and past Boskoop, the nursery center of Dutch trees. Immediately after leaving the station you see a view of the tree nurseries.

At Alphen aan de Rijn change to the train up the Oude Rijn (old Rhine River) to Utrecht, crossing it about a mile past Woerden. Farther on the left the towers of the 19th-century castle "De Haar" rise above the forest.

Returning from Utrecht to Amsterdam you pass through woods, hills, and the forested area of "Het Gooi" southeast of Amsterdam.

Channel Ferry Service

With cross-channel traffic siphoned away by the Eurotunnel, ferry crossings of the English Channel have been decelerated. Still, times are competitive with Eurostar from the Netherlands and if you find yourself near a port, you may avoid the roundabout trip. Look for special, all-inclusive, bargain offers at the train and tourism offices when you visit Amsterdam, Brussels, or London.

Crossing the English Channel by steamship, such as the new *Stena Britannica,* is certainly one of the most pleasant, or miserable, events of your European vacation. You avoid the roundabout train trip and airport termini but face possible boredom or foul weather. It can be great fun or a horror best forgotten.

To reach London quickly from Amsterdam, ride Stena Line's 40-knot high-speed *Stena Discovery* catamaran service via Hook of Holland to Harwich, where you can take the train to London's Liverpool Street station. The transfer at Hook of Holland is easy because moving walkways and luggage carts help you from train to boat. There are four crossings per day that take four hours and carry up to 1,000 passengers. Eurail-product holders receive a 30 percent discount.

The company Speedferries operates cross-channel service between Folkestone and Boulogne, Belgium, with five round trips a day by catamaran.

Rail-Pass Travel

Eurail products consider that Belgium, Netherlands, and Luxembourg are one unit, so that you can travel in this area using up only one "country" of your Eurail Selectpass choices. Eurail-product passes not only cover unlimited train transportation over the three networks, but they are valid on NS's sea-green, cross-country "Interline" buses in the Netherlands and railroad buses in Belgium and Luxembourg. Simply show your pass to the coach driver.

You can make a number of excursions through Luxembourg's delightful countryside into quaint villages aboard CFL's tan coaches striped with burgundy red. Because you use your rail pass, you visit the same sights as the tour buses without cost. Your bus calls at all small villages, enabling you to see the detail of the landscape and get on and off as you wish to explore.

You receive a 30 percent reduction on the full fares of the Stena Line's two daily sailings between Hoek van Holland and Harwich, Britain, taking three hours and 40 minutes.

The railroads of Benelux cooperate on a regional rail pass called the *Benelux Tourrail.* This gives you unlimited travel on the trains of SNCB, NS, CFL, and the bus lines in Luxembourg. You also receive more than a 25 percent discount on Panorama-Tours' city tour in Brussels and at the Antwerp Zoo, which is located next to Antwerp's Central station.

Either a first- or second-class flexipass, the Benelux Tourrail is valid for travel on any five days of your choosing within a month. The Tourrail is a single coupon, computer printed on ticket stock with spaces for five travel days ("Reisdag"). Date the spaces as you travel. Buy them in the U.S. before departure. When two adults travel together, the second person pays only half. Second-class passes are about one-third less expensive than first-class ones. Those between four and 25 buy a second-class Benelux Junior Tourrail for another one-third off.

Holders of a Eurail product valid in Benelux or a Benelux Tourrail receive a discount for Eurostar travel between Brussels and London. Holders pay about 75 percent for first-class Eurostar tickets and about 65 percent for second class but have to validate their passes before the trip. Youthpass holders may buy a first-class Eurostar ticket and first-class pass holders may buy a second-class Eurostar ticket.

You save a lot of green with passes on the mostly yellow NS trains. The *Holland Railpass,* which like the Benelux Tourrail is not sold in the Netherlands, is valid for three or five travel days within a month, either first or second class, for unlimited travel on the entire NS network and on specially marked Interliner buses saving time between stations. An even better deal is the "Zomertoer," but it is available only between July 1 and September 9 and only in the Netherlands. The Zomertoer allows you three days of second-class train travel in Holland within 10 days. Single and two-person tickets are available.

For a single day's unlimited travel you can buy in the Netherlands a "Dagkaart." In conjunction with this pass you do well buying an "OV Dagkaart," Public Transport Link, to give yourself unlimited travel on all the public streetcars and city and regional buses throughout the Netherlands and on the Amsterdam subway—a convenient and economical advantage.

Up to three children aged four to 11 can travel with an adult (19 or older) for only about a dollar. A "Weekendretour" is the same as a Day Return ticket, except that it is valid between 7 P.M. Friday and 4 A.M. the following Monday.

SNCB offers first- and second-class *B-Tourrail passes* similar to Benelux Tourrail but valid for travel five days in one month in Belgium only. You buy these in euros at Belgian train stations for about 60 percent of the cost of a comparable Benelux Tourrail. They are not available in the U.S.

In addition, SNCB offers a great variety of specialized tickets and deals including a Weekend Ticket, a Go Pass, a Fidelity Pass, a Rail Pass, and a Golden Railpass for those over 60. Ask for details.

In Luxembourg you can buy a *Luxembourg Card* for unlimited travel on CFL for one, two, or three days. You can cover the entire CFL network in 12 hours with proper planning. Groups may buy a family ticket for two to five people, including not more than three adults. You receive a free 32-page information brochure and free admission to more than 40 tourist sights. Seniors over 60 receive a 10 percent reduction. The card is available at hotels, campsites, and tourist-information stations as well as Luxembourg train station. Don't forget to validate your tickets using the validating machine on the platform.

Travel through the Benelux countries by boat across the Netherlands' Zuider Zee, aboard Europe's lowest train, and spend a day in the Ardennes.

Around the Zuider Zee
Tamed Sea and Steam

Have you ever wanted to sail across the Netherlands' Zuider Zee (nowadays known as the Ijsselmeer)? Crossing this inland sea is smooth as Dutch peanut butter. When your train arrives in Stavoren, the *Bep Glasius* is unloading passengers and a line of bicyclists is forming to wheel their "feetsers" onto its deck. The full fare is only about $6. Ask for your rail-pass discount.

The *Bep Glasius* is primarily a pleasure boat. Those without bicycles have backpacks.

The Netherlands has no rugged Alps or ragged fjords. Its charm lies in its tamed sea and in the fertile, flat farmlands crisscrossed with canals.

A one-day round trip through the north of the Netherlands, across the Ijsselmeer, and south through West Friesland samples the pleasing scenery of this low country. Plan your departure from Amsterdam for an early hour so you have time to cross the Ijsselmeer and browse leisurely through the open-air Zuider Zee Museum in Enkhuizen.

Tamed Sea

Be sure you board the appropriate segment of your yellow-and-blue InterCity train at Amsterdam's Central station. It divides in Zwolle.

AROUND THE ZUIDER ZEE

NORTH SEA

Leeuwarden

Sneek

Akkrum

STAVOREN

MEDEMBLIK

HOORN

ENKHUIZEN

IJSSELMEER

Zwolle

AMSTERDAM

Nunspeet

Ermelo

Hilversum

Amersfoort

–N–

0   10   20
MILES

One half goes to Groningen. You want to be in the half marked "Leeuwarden."

On its run to Leeuwarden your train makes very few stops. Your first, after 20 minutes, is in the 1992 station in Hilversum, the headquarters for Dutch radio. Your second (after another 12 minutes) is in Amersfoort, the junction for trains coming from Hook of Holland and Rotterdam. By the time you stop in Zwolle, where your train splits, you are entering Friesland, the land of cows, cheese, and tall, blond people.

Your train proceeds as a local. By the time you approach Akkrum, the land is appealing. Broad fields are peppered with black-and-white cows. You pass ribbonlike, calm canals busy with pleasure motor yachts, sailboats, and barges.

After waiting almost a half-hour in the white-brick Leeuwarden station (you can lunch in the station restaurant or hire a bicycle), you board a second-class-only, lime-green-livery "Wadloper" single or two-carriage diesel railcar that has large open areas at the ends marked for bicycles. New plush seats were installed in 1997. On the exterior, units have a dark gray panel around the cab windows and a "cow catcher." The driver revs its motor like an old Ford, and—clickety-clack—off you go down the single-track line, past sheep, cows, and horses, for a 49-minute run to Stavoren. NS does not operate this train. It is operated by NoordNed (meaning Network North, *www.noordned-ov.nl*), one of the regional train-operating companies that assumed money-losing routes of NS in 1999.

Some farms have black, glazed-tile roofs. This is a region of intensive farming. Of course, one of the hazards of traveling by train through farm country is that the windows will be lowered and farmers will be fertilizing.

Herons stand sentry in stagnant, water-filled ditches. Most passengers get off at Sneek. The farmhouses have acre-size red-tile roofs enveloping everything down to the first floor.

The canal running adjacent to your train is packed with small pleasure boats when you reach Workum. You often see curious sights along the tracks. Here you see a stack of bundled thatches for thatching roofs.

From the end of the line at Stavoren, cross the bricked plaza to the VVV office to buy your ticket, and show your rail pass for a discount. The 12-mph *Bep Glasius,* a 300-passenger ship built by Peters'

Scheepsbouw in 1966 (*www.veerboot.info*), crosses the Ijsselmeer only in summer. Aboard, you buy sandwiches and fabulous Dutch fast food such as french-fried potatoes and split pea soup in the luncheon area below deck.

From the deck you see a crazy, kaleidoscopic world of fantasy sails and ships: sailboats, cabin cruisers, schooners, very daring wind-surfers, huge barges, Chinese junks, Singaporean bum boats with eyes painted on them, and dark masted fishing vessels that look as if they might be manned by pirates. About halfway, you are met by a fleet of kayaks.

The afterdeck becomes one huge parking place for fully laden bicycles. After an hour, you finally view the profile of Enkhuizen—the city hall and church.

When you approach one of Rederij V&O's three slips (the others take you to Urk and Medemblik) after your one-and-three-quarter-hour crossing, you are greeted with the rare contrasting scene of the train station with a train and boat unloading passengers at the same time. *Tip:* Have your camera ready.

This area of West Friesland is interesting for its seafaring tradition. West Friesian ships sailed the world's oceans from Enkhuizen, Medemblik, and Hoorn (say "Hoor'n") to trade with faraway countries.

Enkhuizen is lined with the old seawall that used to protect the city from storms on the former Zuider Zee, ending at the Old Harbor, where you see traditional sailing vessels, the fishing fleet, and numerous yachts. Beyond the seawall is the "living" Zuider Zee Museum, showcasing preserved fishing-village homes and giving you a remarkable picture of the life and work of the people of the region, who depended on this inland sea until 1932, when the Barrier Dam sealed the Zuider Zee from the North Sea.

From your landing near the train station, walk five minutes to the boat quay for your boat ride to the Zuider Zee showcase.

Leave the open-air museum on foot, pass through the town proper, and walk back to the train station in order to see the West Church and the South Church and to photograph the old fortified tower named "Drommedaris."

At the brick Enkhuizen station house you can rejoin the electrified lines of NS. It takes you slightly less than an hour to reach Amsterdam Central station by half-hourly double-decker stoptrein—but better, while you're here, travel the Historic Triangle.

Typical Round Trip
Crossing Zuider Zee

1036	dep.	Amsterdam (CS)	arr.	1757
1100	arr.	Amersfoort	arr.	1727
1152	arr.	Zwolle	arr.	1648
1209	arr.	Meppel	arr.	1623
1256	arr.	Leeuwarden	dep.	1536
		Change trains		
1322	dep.	Leeuwarden	arr.	1507
1342	arr.	Sneek	arr.	1443
1411	arr.	Stavoren	dep.	1414
		Change between train and boat		
1415	dep.	Stavoren	arr.	1405
1600	arr.	Enkhuizen	dep.	1245
		Change between train and boat		
1607	dep.	Enkhuizen	arr.	1223
1714	arr.	Amsterdam (CS)	dep.	1119

Daily Rederij V&O Service
May to September

0845	1245	1645	dep.	Enkhuizen	arr.	1200	1600	1935
I	I	I	arr.	Zuider Zee Museum	arr.	1130	I	I
1005	1405	1805	arr.	Stavoren	dep.	1015	1415	1815

Historic Triangle

Steam-enthusiast volunteers come from all over the Netherlands to donate their time freely so you can travel on the 1887 line from Medemblik to Hoorn (the namesake for Africa's Cape Horn). The restored steam locomotive "Bello," built in 1914, and the blue loco "Sluiskil" pull an excursion train comprised of classic Austrian-built coaches (*www.museumstoomtram.nl*). Highlights on the12-mile line include the beautifully restored station buildings at Wognum, Twisk, and Opperdoes.

This is the same Rail Idee as an NS day tour, but with a rail pass you save money because you don't pay for the NS transportation to and from Enkhuizen and Hoorn.

• Begin your excursion in Enkhuizen by boarding the boat for Medemblik at the quay.

• When you would rather begin in Hoorn, take an IC train from Amsterdam to Hoorn's 1991 brick NS station house departing at 19 or 49 past the hour. The trip to Hoorn takes 39 minutes. Immediately cross the metal overpass to the small "Stoom Trein" building. The red-brick station house, with yellow-brick striping and a Spanish tile roof, is a museum in itself—filled with train memorabilia. Beds of flowers (tulips in the spring) surround the "P + R" (park and ride) parking lot. At trackside is the entrance to the museum workshop.

At Medemblik, you can visit the Dutch Steam Engine Museum (*www/stoommachinemuseum.nl*). The museum is housed in a traditional, monumental, steam-driven pumping station, the *Vier Noorder Koggen,* built partly in 1869 and 1907. It is not only unique in the Netherlands but far beyond the Dutch borders. The majority of the large collection of steam engines from shipping and industry is maintained in working order and is usually shown in operation, powered by steam, to the public.

Most of your train trip back to Amsterdam from Hoorn takes you through lovely farmland: lovely because it is flat and fertile; lovely because colorful flowers are grown for sale. Shortly after Zaandam's bright, new station you see the shipping and shipbuilding on Amsterdam Harbor. Your final stop before Amsterdam's Central station, at Amsterdam's futuristic 1986 Sloterdijk station, is interesting because it serves cross traffic in two directions from two levels. The train to Amsterdam Schiphol Airport leaves at right angles from the upper platform.

Amsterdam-Flevoland
Europe's Lowest Train

Weesp is your last chance to admire a traditional Dutch village in the old land. You leave Weesp's needlelike church spires and traditional drawbridge and head into the Netherlands' new land. You have no feeling you are traveling 20 feet below sea level on Europe's lowest open-air train line (the Channel Tunnel, of course, is even lower).

You would be thrilled to look up and see an oceangoing ship passing on the way up the Rhine River, but everything you see is perfectly natural. Fish swim in sub-sea-level canals. Rabbits scamper in negative-elevation fields. Unconcerned cows amble with full udders. And new cities grow larger brick by brick as you travel through the Flevoland, the reclaimed plot of land that once lay below the Zuider Zee.

This is an interesting adventure not because of the scenery, but because it shows you the magnitude of Dutch determination, and success, in reclaiming fertile land from the sea.

Of the 30-mile Flevoline, you travel over 25 miles of land newly reclaimed from the sea and descend from a high point of 50 feet above sea level to 20 feet below. Between Amsterdam and Almere, your first stop in the Flevoland, you cross more than 100 bridges.

The Dutch have been winning battles over the sea for centuries. It is a part of their history and an essential element in their country's security and prosperity. Their story's crowning glory is the Zuider Zee project—the draining of more than 616,730 acres of sea; the creation of land in five polders. Three of these—the North East Polder (the oldest, dry for 58 years), East Flevoland, and South Flevoland (the newest, dry for 33 years)—now make up the new province of Flevoland, northeast of Amsterdam. The provincial capital, Lelystad, is only some 63 miles by train from Amsterdam.

You have a great deal of luxury choosing your train through the Flevoland. From Amsterdam, take a streetcar to Amsterdam's Centraal station, look on the yellow departure billboards for "Lelystad C," and ride an escalator to your correct platform. Sneltreins arriving from Amsterdam Schiphol Airport leave every 30 minutes.

From Amsterdam's CS, your sneltrein first passes Amsterdam's Muiderpoort station, one of the many satellite stations still in Amsterdam city, which in fact you also can reach easily by streetcar. From Muiderpoort, you pass a small part of Amsterdam's harbor sheltering many small Dutch naval vessels, industry, and then a private marina.

You see cows of all colors: brown, black and white, fawn. The fields are broad and green and the superhighways you pass have eight or more lanes and are blacktopped.

Shortly before Weesp, you cross over a canal with heavy shipping. Below, a red Belgian fishing vessel cuts under the bridge. On one side of the train you see the black needlelike church spire of Weesp and modern apartment blocks of brown brick, which are so common in the Netherlands, and on the other, across from the village, grazing land for more cows. Alternate sneltreins stop at Weesp's open-air station for passengers for villages along the line to change to a stoptrein. On departure you pass on your right the only windmills you will see. They aren't large and they aren't rotating, but they are adjoined by several thatched-roof houses.

In Weesp, you also leave the main rail line leading toward Amersfoort and then to Germany. Traveling on the diverging rails you see IC trains and a GermanRail train connecting Amsterdam Schiphol Airport with Berlin.

On May 21, 1993, Queen Beatrix inaugurated Amsterdam's southern ring connection between Amsterdam's RAI convention hall station and Weesp, which created a shortcut between Lelystad and Amsterdam Schiphol Airport and is now served by half-hourly trains. You just as easily board a train to Lelystad at the RAI station as at Amsterdam Centraal, whichever is more convenient.

Your train enters Flevoland when water opens on your left and then your right and you cross a causeway parallel to the main highway. This is part of the ring of water left circling the Flevoland, connected to the Markermeer, the remaining southern body of water from the preexisting Zuider Zee ("meer" means "lake," "zee" means "sea").

Flevoland is very grassy and flat, with farmers furrowing their fields with tractors. Past Almere Muziekwijk station you can read "1987" embedded in the concrete.

While your conductor is announcing Almere Centrum station you see an ultramodern steeple to your right, apartment blocks everywhere, and canals. This is the new land.

Almere Centrum, a stop for both stoptreins and sneltreins, is covered with red tinker-toy struts to support the plastic and plaster covering. You realize the extent to which this is a planned city. Everything you see is modern, blocky, and space saving, but not crowded. From all appearances, it is a comfortable place to live.

You stop at Almere Buiten station, where a city is still abuilding. The station is already in place. Your train skims above the flat furrowed fields and rows of trees acting as windbreaks. You see no windmills. In fact, you travel a long way with no distinctive feature except for green acres and fields checkered with golden cylinders of rolled-up hay and the brown leavings of the wheat harvest.

Past Almere, woods of fast-growing trees have already appeared. At last, you see Lelystad in the distance, not so much as a soaring Oz at the end of a yellow brick road, but as a low accumulation of efficient three- and four-story apartment buildings mixed with industrial buildings of so many Dutch and international companies that it appears there has been a financial incentive to build here.

Lelystad Centrum's surprisingly spacious, spick-and-span, and uncluttered train station has a "Het Station Petit Restaurant." Inside is a brass plaque marking its opening in 1988 by the queen, a GWK bank and ATM machine, ticketing, bookstore, secure bicycle stand, and bright flower shop—all the amenities that the Dutch consider necessary for a full-service station.

End-of-the-line Lelystad Centrum is like all the new NS stations circling Amsterdam. They feature bright blues, reds, greens, and yellows. These flamboyant colors make the architecturally exciting stations fresh.

Sample Sneltrein Timetable
Amsterdam-Flevoland

0936	dep.	Schiphol (Airport)	arr.	1025
0945	dep.	Amsterdam Lelylaan	dep.	1018
0950	dep.	Amsterdam Sloterdijk	dep.	1013
1002	dep.	Amsterdam Centraal	dep.	1006
1023	dep.	Almere Centrum	dep.	0941
1028	dep.	Almere Buiten	dep.	0935
1039	arr.	Lelystad Centrum	dep.	0923

Through sneltreins depart Amsterdam (CS) daily, half-hourly, at the same time past the hour from 6:38 A.M. to 11:08 P.M.; from Lelystad (Centrum), through sneltreins depart daily from 6:23 A.M. to 10:53 P.M.. Regional trains run through the night.

A Day in the Ardennes
Battle of the Bulge

An excursion through the back rails of the Ardennes forest, where the Battle of the Bulge raged, to Bastogne takes you on so many changes of train that it seems like a relay marathon. It is not for those with heavy luggage, just for those seeking pleasure.

Begin your train relay by pushing the button to open the door of the InterCity train on the route Brussels-Liege-Liers. Departures are hourly, calling at Brussels-Central, Brussels-Nord with its outdoors platforms, Brussels-Schuman, and then Brussels-Luxembourg, which corresponds to the district where it is situated.

A woman conductor wearing a bulky blue sweater and meter-maid cap with SNCB insignia checks your train ticket, Benelux or Belgian Tourrail Pass, or Eurail product.

Speeding along the mainline, you reach Namur, known to Flemish speakers as Namen, via Ottignies and Gembloux on the River Orneau. Namur, the largest city of your adventure, is the capital of Wallonia at the confluence of the Rivers Sambre and Meuse. Dominating Namur is the Citadel, which houses a Weapons and a Forest Museum. There are beautiful churches in the center, the famous Rue des Brasseurs pedestrian area, and the museum Felicien Rops.

You have eight minutes to change to the InterCity diesel unit to Dinant. *Tip:* Sit on the right side of the train to admire the coming stretch of idyllic scenery. Your IC takes you alongside the banks of the Meuse to Dinant parallel to the river on the right. Nowhere is the Meuse more beautiful and better suited to visitors than in the Namur region, where numerous rivers and streams join it. Abbeys are almost as commonplace as castles. The old brick-and-stone villages, the rocks, and the fortresses all form a permanent pageant on the banks of a river that continues peacefully and romantically on its way.

You see wonderful luxurious landscapes with views of the Meuse on the right. You see tiled-roof vacation homes mixed with ancient stone buildings that are worn and still sturdy after resisting centuries.

You pass Godinne standing on a meander of the Meuse. Its old center dates from the 17th century, and you see old farms, half-timbered houses, and a Spanish-style castle. The area is soft and amiable. You pass frequent locks on the Meuse, which is channeled and controlled.

Yvoir is perhaps the most charming of all the Meuse region summer resorts, set among woods and rocks, with its island accessible by ferry. The ruins of Poilvache Castle, one of the largest in the county, overlook the Meuse.

Dinant is the prettiest of all the Meuse's daughters according to Victor Hugo. It's the queen of tourism for the region. Its modern train station is happily sited just across the Meuse from the formidable Citadel fortress 325 feet above the river (besieged 17 times) and the riverbank Collegiate Church with an onion dome. The fortress flies a yellow, red, and black Belgian flag at full mast.

You may spend the day along the Meuse or quickly change to the regional train taking you along a recently electrified line to

Libramont. *Tip:* Sit on the left for views of the Meuse and romantic rock formations.

Your regional train leaves the Meuse at Anseremme to follow the smaller, wilder Lesse. The most popular stop is Houyet, which is a busy trailer and camping site. You know you are in wild, vacation country when you see kayakers splashing along the eight-mile segment from Houyet to Anseremme on the River Lesse. The Lesse is tip to toe with blue, yellow, and red plastic kayaks.

Past Houyet your train takes you through quiet farmland toward Beauraing, known to Christians by the frequent appearance of the Virgin Mary between 1932 and 1933. It is now a place of pilgrimage with a museum dedicated to the Virgin.

You reach the River Wimbe and the country becomes hilly and wooded. On the upper plateau of Orchimote, villages become widely scattered and less important. Gedinne is a large, characteristic village with church and nearby ski slopes. After Gedinne the trees thin, the land becomes flatter, farming takes over, and cows become conspicuously fat. Through this remote district, at Paliseul, you cross the major highway with trucks hauling much lumber along the main route south to France. Approaching Bertrix, the houses become stone, two stories tall, and surrounded by fields of corn.

From Bertrix continue by train seven miles to Libramont. Libramont is a larger station lying on the mainline between Luxembourg and Brussels so that international trains come screaming through without stop.

At Libramont, around July 21, the largest agricultural show in Belgium takes place annually with more than 100,000 visitors. It features demonstrations and trials of the last Ardennes carthorses, which are exported worldwide and were used by Julius Caesar's legionnaires and during Napoleon's Russian campaign.

You again change to a regional train from Libramont to Bastogne and the farming country becomes mixed with increasingly dense woods: the Ardennes. Bastogne has two train stations: north and south. Bastogne-Sud is brownstone with red brick piping. Bastogne-Nord is relatively new. Both are about equidistant from the city center, but Sud may be more convenient, and is the first stop for your train.

Bastogne is known to history as the center of the terrible Von Rundstedt offensive in the winter of 1944-45, which marked the start of the Allies' final advance. It was during the Battle of the Bulge that

General McAuliffe pronounced the resounding "Nuts!" to the call for his surrender.

Standing at the crossroads of the Ardennes, Bastogne still bears vivid reminders of this bloody episode. The most moving place is Mardasson Hill and its memorial to the 77,000 American soldiers killed during the battle. Mosaics by Fernand Leger decorate the crypt containing three places of worship (Catholic, Protestant, and Jewish).

Illustrating the battle, the Bastogne Historical Center on the same hill is built in the shape of a five-pointed star. Everywhere in the town and its vicinity are memorials to the terrible winter: a Sherman tank and monument, a bust of McAuliffe on McAuliffe Square (where the tourist office is located), and one of the "freedom milestones" along the way taken by American troops from Normandy.

Because of the constant hustle and bustle (there are 300 shops open every Sunday), Bastogne was nicknamed "Paris in Ardennes" as far back as the 17th century. Other sights worth seeing include St. Peter's Church and Trier's Gate, and the Mathelin House (open Tue.-Sun., 10 A.M. to noon and 1 to 5 P.M., July-Aug.).

From Bastogne, you may return by regional train to Libramont and change to one of the hourly, fast InterCity trains back to Brussels, passing Jemelle, Marloie, and Ciney, or travel east to Luxembourg.

A Day in the Ardennes*

0906	dep.	BRUSSELS (South) arr.		2024
0910	dep.	Brussels (Central)	dep.	2021
0915	dep.	Brussels (North)	dep.	2017
0923	dep.	Brussels (Schuman)	dep.	2008
0927	dep.	Brussels (Luxembourg)	dep.	2005
0945	dep.	Ottignies	dep.	1947
0956	dep.	Gembloux	dep.	1936
1007	arr.	NAMUR	dep.	1923
		Change trains		
1015	dep.	NAMUR	arr.	1921
1019	dep.	Jambes		l
1028	dep.	Lustin		l
1031	dep.	Godinne		l
1036	dep.	Yvoir		l
1042	arr.	DINANT		l
		Change trains		
1051	dep.	DINANT		l
1055	dep.	Anseremme		l
1101	dep.	Gendron-Celles		l
1107	dep.	Houyet		l
1116	dep.	Beauraing		l
1131	dep.	Gedinne		l
1137	dep.	Graide		l
1141	dep.	Carlsbourg		l
1145	dep.	Paliseul		l
1201	dep.	Bertrix		l
1209	arr.	Libramont	dep.	1816
		Change trains		
1230	dep.	Libramont	arr.	1805
1315	dep.	Bastogne (Sud)	dep.	1718
1320	arr.	Bastogne (Nord)	dep.	1713

*Monday to Friday only
l = Does not travel this route

Switzerland

Savvy Traveling on the Trains of Switzerland

Tilting Zurich-Geneva—Airport trains—Zurich S-Bahn—Rail-pass travel—Regional passes

In 1847, the Spanisch-Brotli-Bahn (Spanish bread-roll railroad—Spanish Brotli are an old pastry specialty of Baden) began the history of the Swiss Federal Railroads (SBB) by puffing from Baden to Zurich for the first time. In the four-language confederation, the railroad has Web pages in four languages, *www.rail.ch* in English, although English is not one of the four Swiss languages, *www.sbb.ch* in German, *www.cff.ch* in French, and *www.ffs.ch* in Italian.

In 2000, SBB completed, for the most part, its extensive and expensive commitment to introduce new rolling stock, including tilting and double-decked trains, improve travel time with new track and tunnels, and provide on-time, regular-interval departures as often as quarter-hourly on the most heavily traveled routes.

The Swiss are proud of their train network. Their trains are best, according to travelers' votes. The trains give you unsurpassed views of the Alpine country and take you places automobiles can't. The trains'

217

punctuality, impeccable maintenance, helpful personnel (who often speak English), comfort and cleanliness, and service to the tiniest and most colorful villages make Switzerland come close to being a train travelers' kingdom and certainly Swiss travelers are kings. It's said that you can get anywhere in Switzerland by train. That's quite untrue. Switzerland has 3,600 incorporated communities but only 1,900 train stations. Yet, buses, ships, cable cars, and trams make Switzerland so accessible that half of all Swiss households live within a kilometer (0.6 miles) of a train station, and 97 percent of all Swiss households live within a kilometer of public transportation. Every Swiss makes 48 train trips a year and covers more than 1,100 miles on average over the 9,000 miles of train, boat, and postal bus routes comprising the Swiss Travel System. This high usage is due not only to ecological consider-ations but to the proximity of stations. It makes the Swiss the European leaders in train travel.

Keeping track of the Swiss train companies is like tabulating a can of alphabet soup. The Swiss Federal Railroads has nine initials—three initials for each of the three largest language groups: SBB (Schweizerische Bundesbahnen) for the German-speaking region, CFF (Chemins de Fer Federaux Suisses) for the French, FFS (Ferrovie Federali Svizzere) for the Italian, and Web sites for each, plus English. Coaches carry all three designations but you'll see "SBB" in this book. Nearly a hundred additional companies operating private railroad lines, funiculars, ships, and cable cars with their particular initials in one or more languages are combined into the integrated Swiss Travel System with dovetailed timetables and coordinated connections. All schedules are posted for you to see in every station, posted on the Web, and grouped into a single official timetable ("Indicateur," "Kursbuch," "Orario"), which for your convenience is revised only once a year in two volumes, one for trains and one for buses.

SBB has three kinds of domestic trains: InterCity (IC), InterRegio (IR), and Regio Express (RX). New class 2000 locomotives pull SBB's IC train fleet at the fastest speed on the Swiss network, 143 mph, over the seven-mile stretch between Martigny and Riddes. When you ride them you find they are utilitarian but not flashy. New (1998-2000) double-decked ("bilevel") IC2000 trains with Bistro carriages carry you on the routes between Zurich and Lucerne, Geneva, Interlaken, Basel, Chur, and Bern. Every IC2000 carries a "silent compartment," where cellular telephones and portable stereos are banned.

Some InterCity trains carry sit-down restaurant carriages with white linens, tables for two or four, waiters in white jackets, and excellent cuisine catered by local companies. "Le Buffet Suisse" carriages characterized by a band of violet around the windows and a diagonal swathe across the kitchen area specialize in cafe grills and dishes such as spaghetti. The Glacier Express has a particularly famous dining car, but more of that below. In the "Fromage Express," a dining car made up to look like Gruyere cheese traveling daily on the Basel-Bern-Lotschberg-Brig line, you can enjoy fondue, raclette, or cheese plates in cooperation with the Switzerland Cheese Association. You can shop in a rolling supermarket on the Zurich-Bern route. The supermarket, run in cooperation with the supermarket chain Coop, offers more than 800 products, including fresh milk and meat.

EuroCity trains take you to and across Switzerland, which, because of its location, is a crossroads of Europe and, because of its beauty, is a popular destination. EuroCity trains include SBB air-conditioned salon carriages built in 1990-91 for use on 125-mph routes to Paris, Stuttgart, Milan, Brussels, Ventimiglia, and Amsterdam.

On EuroCity trains to and from Switzerland, SBB runs a number of first-class-only panoramic cars with raised floors and deep windows that curve to shrink the roof to about four feet across. It is possible for you to ride in these "Panoramawagen" between Switzerland and Austria, Italy, France, or the Netherlands on the EC Canaletto between Zurich and Venice, the EC Transalpin between Basel and Vienna, the IC Riviera dei Fiori between Basel and Nice via Milan, and the EC Berner Oberland between Interlaken and Amsterdam. *Tip:* When you travel first class on these routes, be sure to use these trains and specify reservations in the Panoramawagen.

Switzerland is the only country where you see so many kinds of high-speed trains. French TGVs from Paris arrive in Bern, Lausanne, Geneva, and Zurich. Two GermanRail ICE trains from Hamburg via Frankfurt/Main pass through Basel and run right into Zurich's Hauptbahnhof. The ICE Thunersee runs between Kiel and Interlaken's East station. Cisalpino ETR 470 tilting trains connect Geneva, Basel, and Zurich with Milan. Both Cisalpino and GermanRail ICE T trains cruise between Stuttgart and Zurich, and ICE TD trains connect Zurich and Munich. The two night trains, CityNightLine and EuroNight (see "International" chapter), both serve Zurich.

Except for the scenic express trains and international Cisalpino trains to Milan, reservations are not obligatory in Switzerland, but they are available on most Swiss InterCity trains. When you reserve on these trains, one of the first-class carriages may be marked *R* where the reserved seats are located. Unmarked first-class carriages are open to all first-class ticket holders.

When you trace the outline of Switzerland on a map, it's all bulges and squeezed-out extrusions. Vertically, it's even tougher. You find few straightaways because the Swiss network through the Alps is built to circumvent the high Alpine peaks. This makes it ideal terrain for tilting trains. In addition to sampling the five slow train adventures below, you'll enjoy riding the Cisalpino trains described in the International chapter on the Gotthard route between Zurich and Lugano; the narrow-gauge Rhaetian Railroads (RhB, *www.rhb.ch*) connections to Arosa, Scuol, and other mountain resorts; the 1996 Mont Blanc Express between Martigny in Switzerland and Chamonix in France; and the modern blue-and-white electric railcars of the Centovalli line between Locarno and Domodossola, mostly on Italian soil but covered by the Swiss Pass described below.

SBB operates 726 train stations divided into three levels of service. The top, Basel, Zurich, Bern, Geneva, Lausanne, Winterthur, and Lucerne, have the title "RailCity" and encompass shops of every conceivable description, including chocolates and watches. At 11 major stations of RhB in the mountainous canton of Graubunden, you can rent scooters (*Trottinett*), ride them downhill over country paths and quiet roads, and return them at the next RhB station. Cost is $7 per half-day.

Tilting Zurich-Geneva

The InterCity Neigezug ("tilting train") is the best thing to happen to SBB since the opening of the Alpine passes. ICN is better outfitted and more comfortable than the Italian Pendolinos and larger, too (except for the Finnish Pendolino version), and more reliable than the German tilting trains.

Switzerland's 23 ICNs, which curiously are classified as IR (InterRegio) trains, were introduced on May 28, 2000. They are named in honor of famous Swiss citizens. Le Corbusier was an architect, Germaine de Stael was an author, Heinrich Pestalozzi was an educator and founder of the Red Cross, and Albert Einstein was a physicist.

At maximum speed of 137 mph, these trains take the curves very smartly between eastern and western Switzerland, carrying you hourly along the route St. Gallen-Zurich Kloten Airport-Zurich Hauptbahnhof-Biel (called Bienne in French)-Neuchatel-Lausanne-Geneva-Geneva International Airport and making the complete trip in four hours, 38 minutes. Future service between Geneva and Basel awaits delivery of a second order.

Each of the ICNs is composed of seven comfortable carriages equipped with air-conditioning, passenger information systems, wheelchair spaces, and retention toilets. They have 113 seats in first class plus 12 in first-class business, 326 seats in second class, and 23 in the dining carriage. In addition to the restaurant, first-class passengers can enjoy at-seat service. Reservations are not possible except in first-class business.

Airport Trains

You find it very convenient to use SBB's excellent airport trains in Zurich and Geneva. Stations at both airports are integrated into the Swiss railroad network by long-distance IC trains not only to city centers but also directly to international destinations. At Zurich and Geneva airports, first stop by train information *i* to have your Swiss Pass or Eurail product validated. Arriving at Zurich Kloten Airport, proceed via escalators (direction: "Bahn/Railway") using the escalator-friendly luggage carts. At Geneva International Airport, you merely push your cart across to the adjacent train terminus to catch your local, IR, or IC train.

The Zurich Tourist Office in Kloten airport is located in terminal B for tourist information, hotel reservations, and streetcar tickets (open daily, 10 A.M. to 7 P.M.).

Departing Zurich Hauptbahnhof, look for the airplane symbol for the trains serving Kloten. Some are ICs, some are IRs, and some are double-decked S-Bahn (rapid-transit) trains. The through trains make getting to Zurich airport from long distances easy. The S-Bahn trains make getting to Zurich airport from anywhere in canton Zurich as easy as conceivable because you don't have to go through Zurich Hauptbahnhof.

Because of the convenience of the air/train connections, most airlines (excepting U.S. carriers) allow you to check in with your luggage and receive your boarding pass in advance at 24 Swiss railroad stations.

When you reach Zurich or Geneva airport, just go directly to the gate. In reverse, you can send your luggage from the U.S. directly to your Swiss destination's train station so that you don't have to pick it up from the airport carousel and carry it onto the train. Economy-class passengers pay about $17 per piece.

Basel-bound visitors should consider using the Basel/Mulhouse airport (which is in France) served by Air France and Swissair.

Zurich S-Bahn

The entrance to the Zurich Tourist Office is located in the cavernous main train station hall, which after reconstruction is the largest in Switzerland. The tourist office is an excellent place to pick up free tourist information and make hotel reservations. In summer it is open from 8:30 A.M. to 8:30 P.M. on weekdays; to 6:30 P.M. on weekends.

Opposite you find Cybergate, "the Ultimate Internet Bar," open 11:30 A.M.-11 P.M. daily; on the first lower level you find ATMs open 24 hours.

The escalators that you find in the direction of the Limmat River on the east side of Zurich's main train station take you to platforms 20-24, the underground center of Zurich's environmentally friendly S-Bahn system, which opened in May 1990 and accepts Eurail products and Swiss and France 'n Switzerland passes. Use them to travel to every village in canton Zurich and many excellent places in the greater Zurich region in a reasonable time at hourly or half-hourly intervals.

These trains consist of double-decker carriages with first-class sections tucked away on the lower level. They are shorter, so you must use the middle of the platform to board. The S-Bahn's main corridor takes you from Winterthur, through Effretikon (with a branch to the Zurich airport), to Zurich's main station, and along the west bank of Lake Zurich through Thalwil and Wadenswil. On Lake Zurich's east bank, S-Bahn's "Gold Coast Express" runs to Rapperswil.

Some of the other scenic places to visit easily by S-Bahn include Stein am Rhein, Schaffhausen, Bremgarten, Zug, Einsiedeln, Baden, and Brugg. Travelers without rail passes encounter a patchwork of price zones. Single tickets are priced by destination keyed to postal (zip) codes. The color-keyed maps on the automatic ticketing machines give you your destination number, and the machines in the stations do the calculations for you. Twelve-trip strip cards and six-day S-Bahn Flexipasses give travelers a 16 percent discount.

Rail-Pass Travel

Swiss Passes are versatile. You receive free travel on the SBB; most of Switzerland's privately owned railroads (more than Eurail products); lake steamers on the lakes of Geneva, Lucerne, Thun, Brienz, Zurich, Neuchatel, Biel, and Murten; on the Rhine between Schaffhausen and Kreuzlingen; on the Aare River between Biel and Solothurn; and all of the Swiss postal buses. In addition, you may purchase as you please tickets on mountain funiculars and private lines at reductions up to 25 percent. Further, you may ride free public transportation (streetcars and buses) in 30 cities.

You buy Swiss Passes for four, eight, 15, or 21 days' or a month's consecutive travel or a Swiss Flexipass valid for any three up to eight travel days in one month, either for first- or second-class travel. First class costs about 70 percent of a Eurailpass. You save still more because you can buy Swiss Passes for shorter periods and second-class travel, which is still quality travel in Switzerland.

The 2004 France 'n Switzerland Pass covers four days of train travel in both countries within a two-month period. You may use the rail days non-consecutively and purchase up to six additional days.

The Swiss Pass and France 'n Switzerland Pass are also available for youth to age 26 at a 25 percent discount on the full fare. Exactly the same advantages are offered as with the Swiss Pass. The Swiss Youth Pass is not available as a Swiss Flexipass.

Two or more companions traveling together are eligible to buy a sharply reduced price Swiss Saverpass or Swiss Saver Flexipass. This reduces their total cost dramatically but limits their ability to travel separately. The Swiss Youth Pass cannot be bought in conjunction with the Saverpass discount.

When you buy a Swiss Pass or Swiss Card, ask for and fill out the free Swiss Family Card, which allows a parent to take along children under age 16 at no charge. Children six-15 pay half for second-class passes and receive 40 percent off first-class passes. Those under six travel free.

Swiss Passes and Flexipasses are available only to those residing outside Switzerland and Leichtenstein, but they may be purchased in Switzerland and at most European train stations, although of course it is more convenient to purchase them before you leave the U.S. They are valid beginning at 12:01 A.M. on the date you choose and end at 1 A.M. on the day following the last date of validity.

All lines covered are shown on a map supplied with your pass. You pay a supplement for Bernina Expresses, Glacier Expresses, and some touristic postal-coach routes.

You can receive a refund only by returning your pass to the issuing office before the first day of validity or in case of documented illness or accident. It will not be replaced if lost or stolen.

You often see yellow-and-white buses with bold red stripes and posthorns front and side parked in front of train stations. These are the famous Swiss postal buses (*www.postbus.ch*) that you ride free with a Swiss Pass. Of the thousand or so routes you may wish to use, the most exciting include the transit of Italy from Lugano/Menaggio/Chiavenna/St. Moritz and the dazzling routes over the Susten, Furka, Neufenen, and Gotthard passes from Meiringen and Andermatt.

Using only one day of a Swiss Pass, you can ride free over the ingenious combination of postal bus/trains between St. Moritz and Zermatt. Postal buses take you over the Maloja Pass and through the Italian lake region between St. Moritz and Locarno, where you change to the Centovalli train to Domodossola, Italy; transfer to postal bus over the Simplon Pass to Brig; and then ride the Matterhorn-Gotthard Railroad (MGB) to Zermatt. Integrated timetables allow you to leave St. Moritz at 8 A.M., arriving in Zermatt at 7:45 P.M., or depart Zermatt at 8:10 A.M., arriving in St. Moritz at 7:50 P.M. Seat reservations on the postal buses are compulsory but free of charge.

You may also take free cruises on Lakes Geneva, Constance, Zurich, Lucerne, Thun, Brienz, Neuchatel, Biel, and Murten, on the Untersee segment of the Rhine River between Schaffhausen and Kreuzlingen, and on the Aare River between Biel and Solothurn. You will find it very enjoyable to break your travels with restful day outings on these big white steamers. The most beautiful way to enter Geneva is by lake steamer.

A Swiss Pass or Swiss Card allows you a 10 percent discount on the total rental cost of skis, poles, and snowboards in more than 30 Swiss ski resorts. Wherever you see the sign "Swiss Rent-A-Ski" outside a sporting-goods store, you can rent material in perfect condition for downhill or cross-country skiing.

Finally, show your Swiss Pass or Swiss Card for a 35 percent discount to the Transportation Museum in Lucerne (*www.verkehrshaus.ch*), which you can reach by streetcar or ship from the main train station. This is the largest museum of its kind in Europe.

SBB offers the Swiss Card valid for half-fare travel on all public transportation (including city buses and streetcars—simply press the "½" button on the ticket vending machine). One in three Swiss adults owns one. One version combines a rail card with a bank credit card. You buy them, valid for one month, in U.S. dollars. Your children under 16 traveling with you are free.

Although you pay half-fare for many trips that Eurail product or Swiss Pass holders ride free, you frequently come out ahead when:

• Your travel is lighter than it would take for a Swiss Pass to pay for itself, or

• When you travel on routes not fully covered by the Swiss Pass such as to the Jungfraujoch, Schilthorn, and Gornergrat.

When you buy them in the U.S., Swiss Cards include a one-day trip from a Swiss airport or border station to your destination in Switzerland and return. You are allowed to use different Swiss airports or border crossings arriving and departing.

Swiss Cards cannot be purchased in Switzerland, only at border and airport train stations. You buy in Switzerland the "Swiss Half-Fare Card," which costs about two-thirds of the Swiss Card and gives you all the advantages of a Swiss Card except that the transfer is not included. When you plan to fly to Zurich or Geneva and base your first and last days near those cities, you won't need the transfer and can save a few dollars buying a Swiss Half-Fare Card in Switzerland. Normally you save money buying your card in North America and using the transfer ticket to your destination in Switzerland.

You may also buy the Swiss Transfer Ticket separately. It costs nearly 75 percent of the Swiss Card and is valid for your first and last day in Switzerland, but nothing else.

For longer stays or multiple visits to Switzerland, buy a Swiss Half-Fare Card in Switzerland valid for a year. Analyze your itinerary before making a purchase, but it is a good bet that a half-fare card will save you money.

Eurail-product holders receive free travel on the SBB network, lake steamers, and most of the railroads listed for Swiss Pass but with significant exceptions. Not participating in these programs (but in the Swiss Pass arrangement) are Matterhorn-Gotthard Railroad, which you need to use on the Brig-Disentis and the Brig-Zermatt segments of the Glacier Express, and the Goschenen/Andermatt connection with the Gotthard line. You are not allowed to ride free the private railroads of the Jungfrau Region, or the Rigi Railways, but you receive a 25 percent reduction by showing your pass when you buy your tickets. You don't have to validate a day box of a flexipass to receive this discount, which is a major savings. You also don't receive free public transportation, nor are Eurail-product holders eligible to use the Swiss Family Card for their children.

You receive a 30 percent reduction to the top of Mt. Pilatus near Lucerne, so you can ride by funicular from Alpnachstad (which you can reach by included lake ferry) and by aerial gondola from Kriens (30 percent off). You also receive a 35 percent reduction on admission to the Transportation Museum in Lucerne, a must-see for anyone interested in transportation, and a 50 percent reduction on the Burgenstock funicular.

Regional Passes

When you are interested in traveling intensively in only one particular region, you may be able to save money by buying a summer-season-only regional pass that blankets all sorts of transportation within your region of interest. In the Bernese Oberland and Central Switzerland (where it is called the "Tell-Pass") you can buy passes valid for 15 days, of which you choose five for unlimited travel and the remaining days for travel at half-fare. Passes valid for two or three days' free travel in seven (the rest are at half-price) are also available in these regions and for the Lake Geneva, Lausanne/Montreux, and Oberwallis regions, as well. In Graubunden, you can buy passes for three, five, seven, or 10 free days within 10. The Lugano region offers you passes for second-class-only travel in either three or seven days out of seven. The Appenzell card is valid for one, three, or five consecutive days. The Berner Oberland pass is available for three or five free travel days in seven or 15 days including on Lake Thun.

Regional passes vary in price between $45 and $150, and you can choose them for first- or second-class travel except in the Lugano region. You receive a 20 percent discount on their purchase when you already hold a Swiss Pass or Swiss Card. Unmarried children aged 16 to 25 receive half off when traveling with parents. Purchase regional passes at train stations of the regions you are visiting.

Now that you have your travel pass or ticket in hand, discover five great Swiss trips: the Glacier Express from Zermatt, the Bernina Express, the William Tell Express, the railroads of the Jungfrau Region, and the GoldenPass Panoramic from Montreux to Lucerne.

Glacier Express
Alpine Discovery

Glacier Express train service between Zermatt and Chur or St. Moritz has flowered since tourism officials realized, with surprise, that a glamorous trip in a spectacular train 169 miles across the top of the Alps could attract visitors without trampling the landscape or forcing taxpayers to invest additional Swiss francs.

One train a day since 1930 was good enough until visitors discovered the excitement of traveling above the Rhone and Rhine rivers along their valleys to their sources at the Furka Pass. The route atop the Alps that carried 20,000 passengers during 1980 ballooned to 250,000. The newest timetable shows four Glacier Expresses a day in each direction. They feature specially built first-class panoramic dome cars similar to the ones on the Panoramic Express (see section on the GoldenPass Panoramic, below) and famous dining carriages.

This train curiously has always been named "Glacier Express," in English and French, although you pass through three language regions (French, German, and Romansch). When the Furka tunnel was opened in 1982, the Glacier Express moved from summer-only adventure to a year-round delight.

Glacier Express's Swiss-built panorama cars are designed to satisfy the demands of tourists who come from far away to experience Switzerland's Alpine scenery. The panorama cars, with red interiors, are first class only. Passengers sit 2+2, separated by white tables.

The expansive windows measure about 6¼ feet high and almost 4 feet across. They open the carriage to the outdoors so greatly that it seems as if you can pick the wildflowers beside the tracks. They make the carriages seem enormous—as they say, "as big as all outdoors." They turn your trip from an adventure into an unforgettable experience. It hardly seems as though you are aboard a train, which is, of course, most unfortunate for confirmed train-lovers.

The windows of the air-conditioned carriages are crystal clean, but still, you can't open them and lean out. *Tip:* Photographers should avoid Glacier Express trains that convey *only* panorama cars.

Because the top windows are canted to show mountaintops, there are no overhead racks; instead, the seat arrangement allows you to stow your luggage between the seat backs or in the luggage areas at both ends (one end has coat hangers).

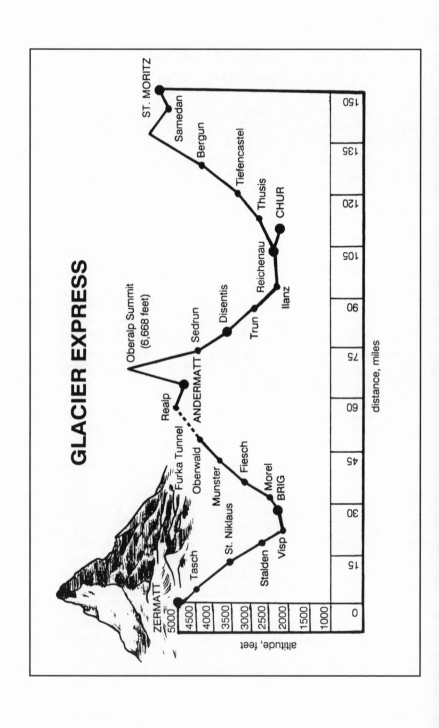

GLACIER EXPRESS

Make reservations in advance unless you only use the segments east of Disentis carried by the Rhaetian Railroads (RhB, *www.rhb.ch*). Obligatory seat reservations cost about $7, second class, and $11, first class. They may be made in most large train stations throughout Europe.

The belle epoque Glacier Express dining carriages are all walnut paneled with heavy brass fixtures and yellow-brown petit-point upholstery (the newest one seats 60). White-jacketed waiters serve lunch. *Tip:* Dining reservations are obligatory. Make them at any train station. There are never enough seats to accommodate all travelers. The conversation piece is the Glacier Express wineglass (for sale) with a stem bent so that, in theory, you face it one way uphill and reverse it downhill. In fact, you worry more about your wine sloshing over when you are traveling horizontally.

When you arrive at the Zermatt train station, you are immediately drawn into that magical square in front of it that bubbles with enchantment and leads to the fairy-tale main street lined with hotels and shops designed in the characteristic architecture made fashionable by the Seilers, the family of hoteliers who established Zermatt in 1855. The Bahnhofplatz is dominated by horse-drawn carts and is filled with charm. You are welcomed by parties of bell captains and drivers in black hotel caps, ready to lead you in a horse-drawn carriage to your nearby hotel. In winter, riding in horse-drawn sleighs gives you the feeling of being in a winter wonderland.

When you clear the sparkle from your eyes, you see that Zermatt's modern Gornergratbahn station stands opposite the train station on one side of the Bahnhofplatz and a Swiss chalet housing the tourist bureau stands on the other. The tourist office is open 8 A.M. to 8 P.M., Monday to Saturday, and 4 to 8 P.M. on Sundays.

While you are in Zermatt, take a journey up the world's first electrified rack railroad, the Gornergratbahn, for one of the most rewarding mountain train adventures in Switzerland. The Matterhorn (and there is no competition) is one of the world's most-photographed natural wonders. It dominates the scene throughout most of your journey and you see increasingly magnificent views of the surrounding peaks as you climb.

From the Gornergrat (10,132 feet), extend your excursion still more by climbing farther to the east on the 2.8-mile cable line to Stockhorn (11,588 feet) on the highest open-air transport in the Swiss Alps.

Leaving Zermatt, the Glacier Express retraces your cogwheel train's ascent, because there is no other way to Zermatt, but you still enjoy revisiting the 1½ hours of smashing scenery. You pass cataracts, rushing waters, and tall, wooden Valais houses and storage barns, or Spychers, protected from rats by stones.

The powerful red railcar required for the steep upward climb on the Matterhorn-Gotthard Railroad (MGB, *www.mgbahn.ch*), formed as a result of merger in 2003, engages the cogwheels and pulls your Glacier Express train out of Zermatt. (The MGB accepts Swiss Passes but not Eurail products.) Red carriages are narrow, because of the slim gauge, but still offer ample space to first-class passengers riding 2+1.

You follow your path on diagrams inserted in the utility table below your window showing altitude relative to distance to St. Moritz. St. Moritz (5,822 feet) and Zermatt (5,261 feet) surmount each end, but on the way you climb to 6,668 feet at the summit, Oberalp Passhohe, cross 291 bridges and viaducts, and pass through 91 tunnels.

When your train stops at the 2003 Tasch terminal, the point closest to Zermatt accessible by car, you look out on the parking lot. It is said that this is the largest parking lot in Europe. Since 1965, the MGB has maintained hourly bus service between St. Niklaus and Visp and even runs a school bus between Stalden and Visp.

The MGB lives in mortal fear of road building. Rail travel is profitable here. The MGB is one of the few narrow-gauge railroads turning a profit. Renewals and reconstructions were undertaken on guarantees from federal and cantonal authorities that no road would be built up the Visp Valley above Stalden, but this promise lapsed in 1952. A highway from Tasch to St. Niklaus was authorized in July 1961.

The cogs reengage at Randa, seven miles down the Glacier Express route, where you see the Dom rising up one side and the Weisshorn up the other. These are the highest peaks in the Alps after Mont Blanc and Monte Rosa. Descending another eight miles, you pass through Brattbach tunnel, 428 feet long, and a series of concrete avalanche shelters. Officials realized these were necessary to maintain Zermatt as a winter sports center when the winter avalanche of 1931-32 buried the line.

In Visp, your MGB train stops in the street in front of the SBB station. Your final 5¼ miles of the meter-gauge MGB parallel the tracks of the SBB. The MGB segment makes it possible for you to travel by meter-gauge lines from the top of the Gornergrat 211 miles to Tirano in Italy, with only two changes, at Zermatt and St. Moritz.

The junction at Brig allows you to connect to or from north-south and east-west trains. Your MGB train runs into the south side of an island platform in front of the main station building with road traffic rushing past on both sides. This is a good point to connect from the narrow-gauge MGB from Zermatt and from Andermatt with the standard-gauge SBB to Lausanne and BLS Lotschbergbahn (BLS stands for Bern-Lotschberg-Simplon, *www.bls.ch*) line to and from Italy.

The main station has both stairs and ramps to the platforms. The higher-numbered platforms refer to the MGB station on the open square in front of the station. Glacier Expresses eastbound usually depart from platform 14, westbound from platform 13.

A new locomotive takes command of the Glacier Express in Brig, but you don't change trains. While it departs over MGB tracks through the scenic and broad upper Rhone Valley at 3,300 to 4,300 feet, you hear the first of the frequent, recorded descriptions in English, French, and German that add so much to the enjoyment of your trip that you are scarcely tempted to doze.

The valley supports farms and farmhouses on both sides of the line. You can always see one snowcapped peak at the end of your line of sight, which in turn dissolves into another when you reach there. Dense pine forests clothe the lower slopes of the mountains. Above, you make out high Alpine pastures and still higher summits covered with snow the year around.

Your train climbs steadily from Brig except for abrupt steps typical of glacial valleys, at Grengiols, above Fiesch, and below Gletsch. Above Grengiols, the valley is known as the Goms. At these steps, the valley also narrows, forcing your train to use loops, spirals, or a rack, or even all three, to overcome the height.

After you pass through the chestnut forests surrounding the village of Morel, you reach Betten, where you feel the cogwheels chattering as you climb. Past Grengiols, you cross the viaduct of the same name (102 feet high, the highest bridge of the MGB) and enter a tunnel looped to correct an altitude difference of 505 feet.

Leaving behind the Rhone Valley's picturesque villages, you reach the reddish-brown Oberwald station (4,480 feet), where your train swings into the all-weather, 9.59-mile Furka tunnel, the longest narrow-gauge train tunnel in the world, which permits the Glacier Express to operate all year round. However, it deprives you of views of the Rhone glacier that awed early travelers. You must now take the postal coach over the Furka Pass to approach this azure glacier.

Special flatcars transport automobiles through the Furka tunnel in winter, when the Furka Pass is closed—a great convenience for skiers—but unfortunately corrosion of the rails in the humid tunnel is proceeding twice as fast as expected. This is partially due to salt-containing snow melting from the automobiles onto the rails. Engineers watch the rails closely, prevent galvanic corrosion, and wash them regularly.

After 17 minutes, you emerge from the tunnel at Realp (5,045 feet). From here you serpentine downward through six U-turns with a view down on Andermatt (4,701 feet), the famous ski resort, which bristles even more in summer with Swiss soldiers on their compulsory annual military service maneuvers. Andermatt's depot and spacious, modern station also connect to MGB's 2.3-mile-long, double-rack railroad, which gives you the option of descending the mountainside in 15 minutes to Goschenen on the north side of the Gotthard tunnel to change to trains of the Gotthard line.

Past Andermatt, you begin climbing sharply to the Oberalp Pass, the highest point on the line (6,670 feet), but you feel the cogwheels under the train chattering, so you know your climb is under total control. When you leave, Andermatt appears almost vertically below your train, first on one side and then on the other. You trace out your train's path ahead by the ribbon of rail zigzagging above you. These curves on the Glacier Express are nearly right-angle turns.

Beyond the Oberalp Pass, you have some fine views over the Outer Rhine Valley as you descend to Sedrun on a ledge high above the river. It is said that Sedrun is where the Rhine spends its vacation.

Nineteen minutes later you come to a stop in Disentis (3,707 feet), but don't look for inspiration in the eye-catching onion-shaped dome of the baroque church on the valley floor. Look up to the left (north) to the imposing Benedictine Abbey on the mountainside, which is the place of prayer for the rich folks. The poorer folk attend the church on the valley floor. Disentis used to be divided into two villages: one by the abbey, one by the river.

Disentis is the geographic center of the Alps. On the north (Germanic culture), the mountains have German and Romansch names; on the south (Italian culture), they have Italian and Romansch names.

In Disentis, your Glacier Express train joins the Rhaetian Railroads (RhB, *www.rhb.ch*) system (which accepts Eurail products). Your first segment, to Ilanz, was laid specifically to connect the RhB with what is now the MGB. This is the least challenging of all the narrow-gauge sections, although you pass over the lofty Val Rusein and Val Lumpegna viaducts shortly out of Disentis.

You descend steadily all the way from Disentis to Ilanz, with good views of the valley in the first four miles as you run high above the left bank of the Outer Rhine on a rock ledge. As you approach Ilanz, the lower slopes of the valley are thickly wooded with conifers. The typical farmhouses you see on the mountainsides, in the Valais style, are quite a change from the Engadine houses you will soon see.

Ilanz (2,289 feet) is the first town on the Rhine and is the beginning of Switzerland's Romansch-speaking region. Yellow and red postal buses stand by ready to take passengers up the twisting Vals Valley to the health resort of Vals, where the mineral water, Valser, is bottled. (You might also see a tanker car labeled "Valser" transporting the water.)

Past Ilanz, on the Ilanz line opened in 1903, you see spectacular limestone scenery. The major obstacle to construction was the deep gorge that the Outer Rhine had carved through prehistoric landslides of rubble more than 2,000 feet deep. A second handicap was that high villages along the route were remote and inaccessible. Steeply graded roads had to be built between the stations and the villages.

In Reichenau, where the Outer Rhine and the Inner Rhine converge right next to the imposing railroad bridge, you meet the Albula line. From here, Glacier Express trains continue north to Chur, before heading south to St. Moritz through the Albula tunnel, and follow the paths in the section below describing the Bernina Express, which departs from Chur.

Connections between Zurich and Chur are convenient, so that you can begin or end your trip in the Swiss metropolis.

Summer Glacier Express Service

A900	B902	C904	D906				F901	G903	H905	K907
0810	0850	0930	1010	dep.	Zermatt	arr.	1143	1643	1702	1802
0821	I	I	I	dep.	Tasch	arr.	1431	I	I	I
0955	1025	1105	1148	dep.	Brig	arr.	1311	1511	1536	1636
1140	1200	1250	1330	dep.	Andermatt	arr.	1122	1322	1400	1500
1253	1308	1357	1435	dep.	Disentis	dep.	1020	1220	1350	1350
1315	1315	1415	1452	dep.	Disentis	arr.	1008	1208	1236	1335
1357	1357	1457	1530	arr.	Ilanz	dep.	0936	1132	I	1259
1432	1432	1533	1607	arr.	Chur	dep.	0857	1057	I	1222
I	1655	1755	I	arr.	St. Moritz	dep.	I	I	0925	1002
					Change trains					
I	I	I	1724	arr.	Klosters	dep.	I	0931	I	I
I	I	I	1749	arr.	Davos Dorf	dep.	I	0906	I	I
I	I	I	1753	arr.	Davos Platz	dep.	I	0902	I	I

I = Does not run on this route or does not stop

Bernina Express
The Impossible Takes a Little Longer

You roar into the cliff of the black Landwasser tunnel, your Bernina Express throttled wide open, soaring high above the stream and over the treetops, riding the summit of an unseen viaduct without guard railings. It is like flying—or falling.

This high point of the 6½-mile section from Tiefencastel to Filisur follows your crossing of two famous viaducts. First you pass the Schmittentobel viaduct, 6.1 miles out of Tiefencastel. Its seven arches rise 118 feet. Then, out of a 164-foot tunnel, you quickly glimpse ahead the five classic arches of the elegant 1903 Landwasser viaduct curving to the right over the river far below. The viaduct's 400-foot span rests on 213-foot piers, and its celebrated southern arch plunges you directly into the Landwasser tunnel.

The Albula line is a triumph of creative railroad engineering. Your powerful, red, electric locomotive climbs through so many extraordinary spirals and tunnels up the Albula Valley that it resembles a model engine racing through every complicated loop, tunnel, bridge, cloverleaf, and dramatic overpass that an ingenious toyshop display can conjure.

Your locomotive's speed of 30 to 35 mph seems heady, given the acrobatics, but your narrow-gauge coach swings around tight corners so smoothly that you don't feel frightened—even at the edges of sheer cliffs. You are too preoccupied watching the extraordinary views.

Classic Bernina Express

The Rhaetian Railroads (RhB, *www.rhb.ch*) introduced the best train on this line, your classic Bernina Express, in 1973, for a one-day excursion through a rarely visited corner of Switzerland. With the introduction of a postal bus connection in 1992, it became possible for you to make a round trip. In 2000, the addition of panoramic carriages made it an irresistible trip.

To sit in a panoramic carriage, it is obligatory that passengers pay a surcharge of seven Swiss francs, which includes a seat reservation and covers the explanation of the scenery and route on the loudspeaker system and the colored Bernina Express certificate you receive. Make your reservation in advance at any train station in Switzerland, Germany, or Austria. Passengers in conventional carriages pay five Swiss francs for the recommended reservation.

Your red carriage departs from track six of Chur's award-winning 1994 train station with a 165-foot, fully glazed arched roof soaring over the high-level postal bus station (RhB trains for Arosa leave from the square in front of the station) down a broad flat valley with forested mountains on both sides. Blauburgender (pinot noir) vineyards flourish. Blauburgender is one of the most prized Swiss wines. You see corn; cows; big, busy factories; and churches with onion-shaped steeples. On the first stretch from the mountain capital of Graubunden canton, you will be traveling on the Albula line. Between Pontresina and the Swiss border across from Tirano, Italy, you will be riding on the Bernina line.

RhB is a private company serving the largest, mountainous canton of eastern Switzerland. It celebrated its 100th birthday in 1989. Your seats in its first-class panoramic carriages give you astonishing views. The spic-and-span 1983 conventional carriages were refurbished in 1992 with maroon plush upholstery and matching carpets. These carriages remind you of SBB's InterCity trains and seem just as spacious, and when you lean out their windows, you hear cowbells. You feel nature and the excitement of historic railroad engineering and nearly miraculous construction.

Hikers push the windows down from the top to admit fresh mountain

TIRANO

Poschiavo

Alp Grum

Samedan — PONTRESINA

ST. MORITZ

Albula Tunnel

BERNINA EXPRESS

Filisur

Heidiland to Landquart

Tiefencastel

Thusis

CHUR

Glacier Express

Reichenau

0   5   10
MILES

air. Photographers lean out, snapping photos nearly the whole length of the trip. In winter, skiers and beautiful people traveling to St. Moritz are warmly dressed. The train passes through the most agreeable summer and winter mountain climate in Europe.

During your 2¼-hour, 55-mile trip from Chur to Pontresina, you pass through 42 well-engineered tunnels or galleries totaling more than 10 miles (well over a quarter of the mountain segment). The line's 108 bridges and towering viaducts of arched rock and stone come to nearly two miles.

You first follow the Rhine Valley to Reichenau, where the Inner Rhine (Hinterrhein) comes from the south to join the Outer Rhine (Vorderrhein) beneath the Castle of Reichenau. The two rapid rivers churn together, mixing their chalky blues and cloudy whites of melted snow and glacier runoff.

You pass steep and thickly wooded slopes with villages and ruins of feudal fortresses secluded in green foliage. Bends are so sharp that you can see both the locomotive and the end of the train.

At 1994's aluminum-and-glass Thusis station house (2,286 feet) you will notice a lady seated on her suitcase, waiting for her train with furled umbrella. She is clearly unprepared for snow swirling at her feet, but she is only one of three bronzes at the station by Robert Indermaur, one of Graubunden's favorite artists. The station's other two whimsical sculptures depict a man waving good-bye to a departing passenger and a man running furiously to board a train.

Past Thusis you travel eight miles through the Schyn gorges to Tiefencastel, one-third in tunnels and one mile over early-20th-century viaducts. The sturdy, hand-built stone bridges complement the wonderful scenery rather than cheapen it.

The view here is very good from the left side, but the back seats of the carriage give a better panorama of the unfolding landscape outside. The murky tints of the blue-white waters of the Albula River run far below your train twisting on the mountainside.

The valley widens again and you see the Tinzerhorn mountain group ahead. Change to the right side for better views of the breathtaking scenes you are approaching. Past Tiefencastel, the Albula River runs fast and the valley becomes more and more wooded with fir trees, larches, and arolla pines. At this point you cross the Schmittentobel viaduct and roar into the Landwasser tunnel, as described at the beginning of this section.

Like many admirers of the Landwasser viaduct, break your journey at Filisur station (boarding a local train later on) to walk down the footpath and inspect the dramatic structure from below.

It is at Filisur (3,556 feet) that the route of the Heidi Express (see below) from Landquart joins the core route and enters the Albula line south into the Engadine region.

The most difficult terrain of your trip is on the 5.8-mile segment from Filisur to Bergun. You climb one foot for every 28 traveled. The Albula Valley becomes narrower and your route becomes more steeply walled in. In this short section, you pass through 14 tunnels and over eight viaducts.

The 1903 section past Bergun to Preda is technically the most interesting and one you will always remember. "Slow but sure" is the watchword you appreciate during this stretch. The direct distance to Preda from Bergun is four miles, but surveyors have bent your line into such extraordinary contortions of loops and spirals that you actually travel 7.6 miles, including 1.7 miles through seven tunnels. If you climbed directly, you would climb one foot for every 16, but the expensive spirals and reversals of direction safely reduce your grade to one in 30.

Plan to change from side to side to watch the elegant contortions. Look back for at least three extraordinary sights of the pleasing village of Bergun while your train climbs higher and higher. The noted "Rail Trail" alongside this segment attracts many hikers. In winter, from your window you see fathers with their kids and their neighbors', too, in tow, renting wooden sleds in Preda to sled the 1,368-foot drop from Preda to Bergun along a five-mile sled route, taking about 20 minutes.

From Preda, your Bernina Express picks up speed through the 3.6-mile Albula tunnel. It seems to go on forever. It is the highest (6,242 feet) principal tunnel through the Alps and the most expensive and difficult engineering work of the RhB.

You enter the Engadine region. Engadine architecture is so unique and bright that it sets the region off from the rest of Switzerland more distinctly than if you had crossed a frontier. The houses you see are white and thick walled, with small, irregularly spaced windows widening outward. Their most distinctive feature is their "sgraffito" (now you know where the word "graffiti" came from). Masons covered rough, gray plaster with coats of white limewash and then artfully scraped away the wash to bring out charming gray scrolls, interesting geometries, and fascinating embroideries.

When you emerge from the Albula tunnel at Spinas, clumps of larch have reappeared and your train is pointed downward. You cross and recross the Beverin River at Bever, where you see beautiful examples of Engadine architecture on your west side. Then you run down the flat floor of the Inn Valley above the Inn River. The colors of the glorious peaks of the Bernina massif ahead through the Pontresina Gap are vivid. The air is electrified with natural radiation.

Both St. Moritz and Pontresina—all the villages of the Engadine region, in fact—welcome tourists. The inhabitants speak Romansch, Switzerland's fourth national language, but the area is so international that English is widely understood.

St. Moritz (*www.stmoritz.ch*) (5,822 feet) likes to think of itself as "Top of the World," not for elevation, but for quality and prestige. The sports calendar is packed with events ranging from bobsledding to tobogganing to international horse racing on frozen Lake St. Moritz.

St. Moritz's five-star hotels attract movie stars, crown princes, and the jet set, but less extravagant accommodations won't crack your budget and still give you the experience of 322 sunny days a year (the most in Switzerland), the 6,000-foot landscapes, and 25 mountain lakes.

Besides more aerial acrobatics, the Bernina line presents you with another distinction: it is a joy to photograph. You are able to focus on the magnificent scenery through pulled-down windows of conventional carriages while traveling along at only a snail's pace. Trains south of Pontresina average only 20.5 mph, including stops, making your train even slower than the Glacier Express.

Beyond Pontresina, the valley becomes wider with every mile. Panoramas open on every side while your train runs high on the mountainside on tracks that were laid to avoid spoiling the beauty of the Taiser Forest. Past the Berninabach Falls bubbling with froth in early summer, you turn your lens to the right for a splendid picture of the magnificent Morteratsch glacier and the most glorious peaks of the Bernina range, especially Piz Bernina itself, a double rocky summit of 13,261 feet.

High above the timberline, you reach the summit at Bernina Hospiz (7,403 feet), where winter lasts seven months. You have climbed 5,973 feet by simple adhesion—even more than any Swiss rack railroad with cogs—and reached the highest station in Switzerland served by adhesion railroad.

Lago Bianco to your right, covered by ice until late May, was originally four lakes but it was dammed to form a reservoir for the Brusio power station, forcing the railroad to be moved some 30 feet higher. Look for the former path running along the edge of the lake. From here you descend through the 630-foot Scala tunnel, the Pozzo del Drago tunnel (the dragon is rumored to lurk in the nearby lake), and an avalanche gallery to reach Alp Grum (6,858 feet).

It is time for lunch. Your Bernina Express carries a refreshments trolley where most passengers buy snacks, but travelers have a chance to disembark at the brownstone Alp Grum station, which is a popular jumping-off place for Alpine hiking and an amazing place for lunch, and then continue on a later train. You enjoy vast views over the Palu glacier and its surrounding peaks. There is also an Alpine garden. Most thrilling of all is the view from above the tracks on the terrace of the Bellavista cafe with a view across to the Palu Glacier and down the Poschiavo Valley to blue Lake Poschiavo, 4,231 feet below and only 6.8 miles away. The trains calling at the toylike Puschlav station below look like those on a scale-model railroad.

Climbing from Pontresina has been relatively easy. Descending follows a route that required surveyors to perform near miracles. To reach Poschiavo, your train has to drop 4,034 feet through larch and spruce forests in a horizontal distance of only 4.7 miles. Engineers solved this problem by designing a series of cautious, cascading cuts, circular tunnels, sharp zigzags, and astonishing loops.

First you descend to the right in a semicircle, your train's wheels screeching, below Alp Grum station to the 833-foot Palu tunnel, in which you make a three-quarter turn and emerge down the mountain. For a second time you pass below the Bellavista terrace into the 948-foot Stabline tunnel, emerging on the back slope of Alp Grum before doubling back through the 745-foot Pila tunnel and returning below the terrace for a third time.

In less than 10 minutes, you look up from Cavaglia (5,553 feet) to see the restaurant at Alp Grum, now 1,305 feet above you. The forests have turned to deciduous trees: hazel, aspen, alder, and birch.

Your final approach to Poschiavo is the most miraculous of all. Your train makes four more zigzags and tunnel turnarounds. You see Poschiavo first on the left and then four more times on the right while your train loops above the towers of the city. Photographers race back and forth across the carriage in order to capture all of the kaleidoscopic scenery, exclaiming, "Why am I always on the wrong side?"

Past Mira Lago (whose name, "Look at the Lake," refers to your view), you again descend steeply. After passing Brusio your train makes one of the world's most amazing loops across a raised, corkscrew stone viaduct having a radius of only 164 feet. Nearby highway traffic comes to a standstill while drivers and passengers watch you descend.

Then your Bernina Express continues effortlessly down the valley past vineyards, fig trees, and former tobacco fields that now yield herbs for healthful teas, across a steel bridge over the pressure pipes of the Brusio power station (which generate electricity powering the line), and past the Renaissance pilgrim's church of the Madonna di Tirano to the Italian frontier at Tirano.

Pick up your free colored Bernina Express certificate by showing your ticket at the Swiss train station before you walk the few feet into Italy and border guards check your passport. Tirano is a pleasant little town of mountain houses and terraced vineyards where you will have time for lunch at one of the outdoor cafes on the city's main street.

Heidi Express

> *You mount a narrow-gauge train and as the small but very powerful engine gets under way, there begins the thrilling part of the journey, a steep and steady climb that seems never to come to an end. For the station of Landquart lies at a relatively low altitude, but now the wild and rocky route pushes grimly onward into the Alps themselves.*   Thomas Mann, *The Magic Mountain*

The Bernina Express's 1995 sibling follows a slightly different route. Named the Heidi Express, this time Heidi isn't leaving her grandfather to travel northward to Klara and Fraulein Rottenmeier, but southward. And what a lot there is for her to see: colorful, flower-dotted meadows, Davos, Engadine, and mountains that grow taller by the moment. The goats and cows look much the same as at home, but the friendly local farmers at the end of her trip greet her in Italian: *"Ciao, Heidi. Come stai?"* Like the classic Bernina Express from Chur, this train is on its way to the Mediterranean-like valley of Veltlin with its olive trees, oleanders, and vineyards.

The children's book *Heidi,* by Johanna Spyri, made the village of

Maienfeld into something of a tourist attraction and gave the region, and the train, its nickname "Heidi."

RhB's new train leaves not from Chur, but Landquart, close to the original Heidi's home, up the Rhine Valley 1,715 feet high. When you board the Heidi Express, you follow the foaming River Landquart upstream through the steep rock walls of the Chlus gorge and reach the luscious green meadows and woodlands of the mountain valley Prattigau with its capital, Klosters (3,870 feet). After you cross the summit of the Wolfgang pass (5,350 feet) using loop tunnels to cope with the rise in altitude, your Heidi Express cruises down the Landwasser Valley beside Davos Lake to Davos-Platz.

Your path from Landquart to Klosters covered the origins of the RhB lines. It was opened on October 9, 1889, and at the time was the highest adhesion line in Europe and one of the steepest. Its extension to Davos was opened on July 20, 1890.

The mountain metropolis of Davos, the highest city in Europe (5,117 feet), is a leading winter sports center with several extensive winter sports areas including Europe's largest natural ice rink. At the coldest time of year, Davos maintains 53 miles of winter walking paths, and many enjoy snowshoe trekking.

Thomas Mann was in Davos for just four weeks, but his novel, *The Magic Mountain,* established Davos in world literature.

The Parsenn funicular, renovated in 2002, is now Switzerland's fastest funicular. It lifts skiers and summer hikers from the valley floor (5,117 feet) to Weissfluhjoch (8,636 feet), where an aerial gondola takes you to Weissfluh (9,328 feet).

Davos' Kirchner Museum, built in 1992, is an architectural gem and houses over 500 of the Expressionist's works, the largest collection of its kind on exhibition to the public. The German artist went to Davos in 1917 and lived and worked there until his suicide in 1938.

From Davos your Heidi Express rolls over the 1909 stretch across bridges and through tunnels to the RhB's longest bridge, the 688-foot-long Wiesner Viaduct, 288 feet above the River Landwasser.

In Filisur (3,556 feet) your Heidi Express merges with the route of the classic Bernina Express from Chur and you begin the Albula line south into the Engadine region.

The introduction of the Heidi Express gives you a choice of premium trains on a thrilling route. Which to take? Take one going down, the other coming back. It's a day not to be missed.

Bernina Express Bus

The Swiss Travel System added a whole new dimension to scenic train experience when they introduced in 1992 postal bus service between Tirano and two stops in Lugano, Via S. Balestre stop in the center of the city and Lugano train station.

The blue-and-white, Italian-plated Giuliani e Laudi Bernina Express buses leave from the square on the Italian side. The buses run during the summer only. It is obligatory that you make advance reservations costing 12 Swiss francs at any Swiss train station or from your travel agent before departure. Diretto trains leave approximately every two hours over the lines of the Italian Railroads to Milan's Centrale station.

Lugano is a satisfying vacation destination because of its mild weather, excellent tourist facilities, and its site on beautiful Lake Lugano with funicular to Monte San Salvatore and cogwheel railroad to Monte Generoso. When you step out of your train at Lugano's hillside train station you are face to face with the funicular to the center of the lovely city. The official language here is Italian, but in season you hear more English and German.

Now you have a great, convenient goal and a sensational way to get there. Just as exciting, you can make your trip aboard the Bernina Express in the opposite direction, by starting at Lugano. All segments—including mainline connections, the narrow-gauge Rhaetian Railroads, and the new postal bus—are covered by Swiss Passes, Swiss Cards, France 'n Switzerland Passes, and Eurail products.

Should you want only to make a day trip from Zurich, you can use the Bernina bus connection to make an early-morning to late-evening round trip through this spectacular route. Every visitor interested in the outdoors, however, will prefer to break his or her trip to stay in one of the charming mountain villages in the spectacular Engadine region of Graubunden and in Lugano beside the lake.

Summer Bernina Express and Heidi Express Trains

Bernina	Heidi			Station		Heidi	Bernina	
|	|	0745	dep.	Landquart	arr.	1916	|	|
|	|	0828	dep.	Klosters	dep.	1828	|	|
|	|	0855	dep.	Davos Platz	dep.	1740	|	|
0848	|	|	dep.	Chur	dep.	|	1849	|
|	|	|	dep.	Thusis	dep.	|	1814	|
0932	|	|	dep.	Tiefencastel	dep.	|	1758	|
|	|	0918	dep.	Filisur	dep.	1715	1740	|
|	0940	|	dep.	St. Moritz	arr.	|	|	1748
1052	0952	1021	dep.	Pontresina	arr.	1620|	1647	1736
1126	1029	1102	dep.	Alp Grum	dep.	|1526	|	1652
1202	1101	1136	dep.	Poschiavo	dep.	1444	1535	1558
1217	1127	1147	dep.	La Prese	dep.	1414	1519	1532
1246	1159	1219	arr.	Tirano	dep.	1402	1450	1511
				Change from train to bus				
1415	1415	1415	dep.	Tirano	arr.	1315	1315	1315
1715	1715	1715	arr.	Lugano	dep.	1030	1030	1030

\| = No stop or different route

The Route of William Tell
The Cradle of Switzerland

*Swear we the oath of our confederacy! We swear we will be free and
sooner die than live in slavery.*   F. Schiller, *William Tell*

With the completed restoration the Lake Lucerne paddle-steamer
fleet (*www.lakeLucerne.ch*) and the Swiss railroad's dedicated panoramic carriages from Fluelen, there seems no more relevant time to
travel the route of the William Tell Express to remind yourself of the
importance of freedom.

One of the great Alpine journeys for tourists of the 1880s was the
William Tell Express, which consisted of paddle-steamer travel from
Lucerne to Fluelen at the distant southeastern corner of Lake
Lucerne, and a steam train, which took them through the St.
Gotthard Tunnel (completed in 1882). The trip through the beauti-
ful cradle of Swiss freedom and independence was revived in 1988,
using meticulously restored, authentic paddle steamers, but with

passengers transferring to panoramic electric train to Lugano or Locarno.

Now, the William Tell Express is a guided, enjoyable adventure to see the birthplace of independence on Lake Lucerne in the core of the Swiss confederation.

In Lucerne you begin the first of two integrated laps of the Swiss Transportation System. "Across lake; over mountains." You can follow the route of William Tell independently with a Eurail product, Swiss Pass, or Central Switzerland's regional "Tell Pass," or trace it with the help of the escorted William Tell Express trip. You relive the birth of independence on Lake Lucerne in the core of the confederation.

While you steam across Lake Lucerne to Fluelen at the southeastern tip of Lake Lucerne in about 3½ hours, romantic Alps of every shape rise about you, and then you climb by train through the heart of the Alps through the high St. Gotthard Pass. Significantly, the route sings of freedom with memories of William Tell, the Swiss folk hero credited with rallying the Forest Cantons from the Hapsburg's grasp and the formation of independent Switzerland.

The red-and-white Swiss flag on the stern waves smartly when, depending on demand, either the 323-passenger paddle steamer *Stadt Luzern,* rebuilt in 1990, the 224-passenger *Uri,* or the 200-passenger *Unterwalden* sets out on one of Switzerland's largest lakes, Lake Lucerne, from the well-marked pier directly across from Lucerne's main train station.

The *Uri* celebrated its hundredth anniversary in 2001. Switzerland's oldest paddle steamer was built by Sulzer Bros., Winterthur, in 1901. Following 2½ years' total revision in the Lake Lucerne Navigation Company's (SVG) own shipyard, the *Uri* made its second maiden voyage in 1994.

Uri's first-class salon is built in the new-baroque style, and its interior floral decorations remind you of a garden hall from the turn of the last century. The etched-glass inserts on the salon doors are particularly valuable, and equally fascinating are the gleaming workings of the *Uri*'s steam engine, recognized in 1998 by the American Society of Mechanical Engineers (ASME) as a "Historic Mechanical Engineering Landmark."

Unterwalden, built in 1902, was returned to service on May 16, 1985, after having been meticulously restored with $1.2 million donated by those listed on a scroll aboard the ship as "Friends of the Steamship Association."

Unterwalden's first-class salons, where the William Tell Express passengers dine, shine with parquet floors, inlaid furniture, wooden scrolls, tables covered with white spreads, and frilly curtains so inconspicuous that they don't hide the delicate carvings surrounding the windows and covering the sills.

While you enjoy your typically Swiss meal in the first-class salons, the Forest Cantons of Central Switzerland spread out before you in all directions. To the east you see Mount Rigi (5,800 feet). Looking to the south you see the Burgenstock (2,700 feet). To the west, Pilatus (6,985 feet), surmounted by the world's steepest cogwheel railroad (which is also an ASME award recipient), is disappearing in the distance. Your meal starts with minestrone soup, followed by roast of veal, pasta, and vegetables in season. It is topped by the ice-cream tart, "William Tell."

Across the lake your paddle steamer coasts to a stop at Weggis, the queen of the resorts on Lake Lucerne. The aerial gondola here leads to the crest of Mount Rigi rising above you. In 1870, some 40,000 travelers (like Mark Twain) visited the summit by foot, horseback, or sedan chair to witness the magical sunrise and hear for themselves authentic Alpine yodeling.

The Vitznau-Rigi Railroad to the mountain's summit, with its terminus at lakeside adjacent to your next landing, at Vitznau, opened the following year, making it the oldest cogwheel railroad in Europe. Together, the Vitznau-Rigi Railroad and the gondola from Weggis meet in Rigi Kaltbad, 3,290 feet above Lake Lucerne.

Your paddle steamer makes its premier stop on Lake Lucerne at the resort of Brunnen in canton Schwyz. The people of Schwyz gave Switzerland its name as well as its flag when, two years before the oath of freedom, as a result of an uprising, they were awarded a banner showing, on a red field, a white cross representing the Lake of Lucerne.

In Brunnen you can visit the "Square of the Swiss Abroad," the end of the new "Swiss Trail," opened May 4, 1991. Sections of the walking trail are allotted to the cantons in the order of their joining the confederation. The lengths of the segments depend on the cantons' populations, so that every Swiss has a millimeter or so of trail dedicated to him or her.

Sailing from Brunnen, your paddle steamer passes the Schiller Stone, the gleaming monolith rising from the lake that is a memorial to the author of Switzerland's national epic. The inscription reads: "To him who sang Tell's glory, Friedrich Schiller—the Original Cantons, 1859," and according to Schiller's play,

> *Right against the Mytenstein, deep-hidden in the wood, a meadow*
> *lies, by shepherds called the Rutli because the wood has been*
> *uprooted there. Tis where your canton boundaries merge.*

The Rutli landing, decorated with hand-carved insignia of the three original cantons, has a very special meaning for respect of freedom. On this almost inaccessible stretch of meadowland every Swiss child knows that 33 representatives of the founding cantons (Schwyz, Uri, and Unterwalden) pledged to defend themselves against all forms of foreign domination.

> *The cantons three are to each other pledged to hunt the tyrants from*
> *the land. The league has been concluded and a sacred oath con-*
> *firms your union.*

The landing at Tellsplatte, where you see the Chapel of William Tell (*Tellskapelle*), commemorates the point where William Tell, a prisoner, leaped to freedom from Viceroy Gessler's ship on hurricane-ripped Lake Uri. It lies at water level accessible only by a narrow path along the shoreline.

> *And when you have descried a shelving crag that jutted, smooth*
> *atop, into the lake, with a bound I swung myself upon the flattened*
> *shelf and thrust off the puny bark into the hell of waters.*

By the time you have finished your three-course meal, Lake Uri has narrowed and the Urirotstock Alp rises vertically from the water in the west while you cruise to your landing in Fluelen below the gilded points of the church's steeples. English-speaking guides take you and your luggage a few hundred feet to the blue-and-white William Tell Express signboard, where the panoramic carriages of the William Tell Express train are already waiting. It couldn't be more convenient.

Almost before you settle into the first-class seat of Europe's most spacious panoramic carriage, your train is speeding through the deep ravines and precipitous cliffs of the Reuss Valley, taking you past Altdorf, the capital of canton Uri and the key to the St. Gotthard Pass.

> *This cap will be set upon a lofty pole in Altdorf, in the market*
> *place, and this is the Lord Governor's good-will and pleasure, the*
> *cap shall have like honor as himself and all shall reverence it with*
> *bended knee and head uncovered.*

In Altdorf's main square, the statue of the storied archer, his hand resting on his son's shoulder against a primitively painted mountainside panorama, stands at the spot where, according to local folklore, vicious Viceroy Gessler of the town of Altdorf ordered a flagpole erected in the year 1291 and directed passers-by to bow in submission. Tell ignored it, enraged Gessler, and was ordered to

Take thy bow and make thee ready to shoot an apple from the stripling's head.

We all know about Tell's marksmanship.

The St. Gotthard line carries your carriage from 1,540 feet to 3,628 feet at the entrance to the 9.3-mile St. Gotthard Tunnel at Goschenen. Engineers required seven years to complete the tunnel. On June 1, 1882, the inaugural train reached Airolo, replacing the stagecoach that had required a whole day between Goschenen and Airolo.

If one thing is certain about the weather, it is that it will be different north and south of the Alps. After 10 minutes, you emerge from the tunnel at Airolo, see palm trees, and feel the milder climate of Ticino, Switzerland's Italian-speaking canton.

From the UNESCO World Heritage site of Bellinzona, your train tunnels below Montebello Castle's crenellated walls and enters the fruitful Lombard plain of Italy, taking another 26 minutes to Lugano. You depart from Lucerne at 11:20 A.M., arrive in Fluelen at 2:57 P.M., and are escorted to your panoramic carriage departing at 3:16 P.M. You arrive in Lugano at 5:23 P.M., or if you change trains in Bellinzona, you arrive in Locarno at 5:30 P.M. From Lugano, you can take a Cisalpino train to Milan, Venice, Florence, or back to Zurich, a EuroCity train to Rome, the Bernina bus to connect with the Bernina Express, or best of all you can remain to enjoy Lugano.

Lugano is a satisfying vacation destination because of its mild weather, its excellent tourist facilities, and its site on beautiful Lake Lugano with funicular to Monte San Salvatore and cogwheel railroad to Monte Generoso. The official language here is Italian, but in season you hear more English and German.

The William Tell Express operates only during the summer. One-way fare, first class, is CHF163 (about $100); with a Swiss Card, you pay CHF105 (about $65). Adults and children holding Swiss Passes or Eurail products valid in Switzerland pay only a supplement of CHF47 (about $30) to cover the meal, commentary aboard the steamer, interesting guide pamphlet in English, a reserved seat, and a small souvenir presented during the train ride.

Railroads of the Jungfrau Region
Scaling the Eiger

The North Face of the Eiger

After burrowing through the solid rock of the Eiger for several miles, Eigerwand station is startling. You hear "ahs" as your train passes portals glowing with reflected white light. Folk music plays on the platform. It gives you an eerie feeling to be at this treacherous location where climber after climber tried and failed to scale the outside wall until finally, in 1938, the sheer face was conquered for the first time.

Passengers surge from your train to a set of 12 plate-glass picture windows—enough for everyone—revealing an amazing view of the Grindelwald Valley, some 6,000 feet below. From the portals you look out onto the very center of the Eiger North Face.

The Railroads of the Jungfrau Region (*www.jungfraubahn.ch*) carry you to lands of snow and ice you cannot possibly reach otherwise unless you are a competent Alpine climber accompanied by guides.

Interlaken Ost (for "east") train station is your stepping-stone to the Jungfrau Region. Narrow-gauge BOB (Bernese Oberland Bahn) trains departing from platform 2 take you to the region famous for the highest train station in Europe, a score of great mountaineering centers, and the spot where James Bond confronted his archenemy in *On Her Majesty's Secret Service.*

When you travel from Interlaken Ost to the Jungfraujoch, BOB's route takes you through Grindelwald to Kleine Scheidegg, where you board the yellow-striped maroon carriages of the Jungfrau Railroads, new in 1992. When you return to Interlaken Ost, take the western arc descending from Kleine Scheidegg on the Wengernalp Railroad (WAB) to Wengen's train station. WAB celebrated its centenary in 1993.

Your second option from Interlaken Ost station takes you to the Schilthorn (of James Bond's Piz Gloria notoriety). It treats you to four spectacular modes of travel. Leave the WAB at Lauterbrunnen, board the BLM funicular to Grutschalp, transfer to the mountain Murren Railroad, and top your ascent with a dramatic gondola ride to the mountaintop restaurant crowning the Schilthorn (9,748 feet).

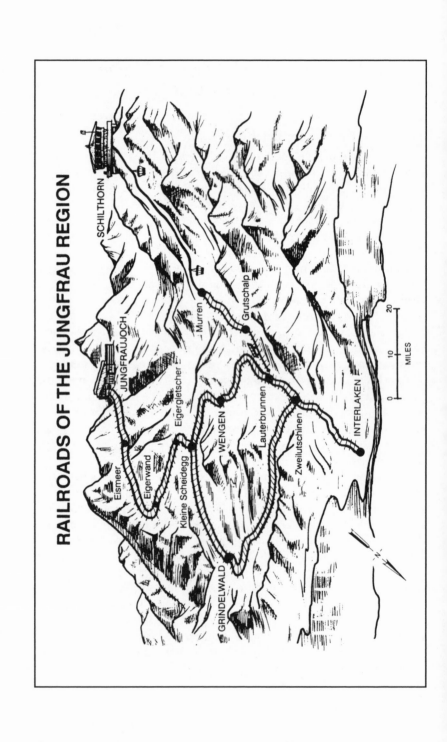

RAILROADS OF THE JUNGFRAU REGION

When you have taken both the Schilthorn and the Jungfraujoch trips, you judge the question: "Which is better?" The Jungfraujoch is more famous and gives you things to do at the top—a museum, ice palace, "Toporama," and more. The Schilthorn gives you a stunning panorama, a thrilling ascent, and Bond's Piz Gloria. Try both.

Your climb to the Jungfraujoch is expensive (the Schilthorn adventure is less expensive). Eurail products get you only a 25 percent reduction, but without using a day of your flexible pass, past Interlaken Ost, and Swiss Passes take you free only as far as Grindelwald and Wengen with a 25 percent discount from Grindelwald/Wengen to Kleine Scheidegg and Jungfraujoch (although the cards come in handy again during the Schilthorn trip). Although trains are second class only, do not invest in this trip when it is cloudy at the summit. The tourist office next to the extravagant Grand Hotel Victoria Jungfrau, a 10-minute walk from Ost station about halfway to the West station, will give you reliable advice before you set out, and your hotel may be connected to the rotating video camera at the summit, so that you can see for yourself. At the same time, check to see if there is an early-morning departure (before the connecting trains from Zurich and Geneva arrive) at reduced prices.

To the Jungfraujoch

Your 1990, brown-and-tan BOB car marked for Grindelwald (those in front marked for "Lauterbrunnen" travel up the Lauterbrunnen valley for Wengen, Lauterbrunnen, and the funicular to Grutschalp) stops first in Wilderswil. Several Swiss with walking boots and Alpine walking sticks get off for the rack-and-pinion railroad to Schynige Platte.

Shortly before making your second stop, you get your first teasing view of the great white Alps in the distance. You feel a surge of anticipation as you cross the first frolicking branch of two Lutschinen torrents, the White Lutschine and the Black Lutschine, and you arrive in Zweilutschinen, where the rivers meet. Railroad workers separate the two sections of your train.

Your car to Grindelwald climbs along the raging Black Lutschine, carefully banked with flagstones on the left. Contrary to its name, it is white with melted glacial runoff.

Through the Grindelwald valley, you see tall chalets scattered on the left. On the right you hear bell-tolling cows. Outside your pulled-down window you can almost pick a dazzling horticultural bouquet of delicate white wild flowers. A river on your right charges down over huge boulders and the waterfall dropping from above makes a rainbow arc from the sun.

Now you come round a bend, revealing a vision. The magnificent Eiger towers like a giant wall, its peak hidden in flying clouds. You look to the left and there is the Schweizerhof Hotel with its red shutters. Now your train coasts to a stop in the brown-shuttered Grindelwald station (3,392 feet).

On an unforgettable site, Grindelwald, the "Glacier Village," is the center of the eastern Jungfrau Region and looks the way a Swiss village should look. Each chalet is neatly arranged and tucked under a tree, balconies are swept, geraniums are in full bloom, and fuchsias flower from every window box. Firewood is corded neatly and stored symmetrically under the eaves. In the fields, hay is carefully stacked.

Grindelwald has changed with the times by adding a few key hotels and a modern indoor swimming pool, but it has not lost its essential mountaineering charm or its good mountain air. The tourist office (open 8 A.M. to noon and 2 to 5 P.M., closed Sun.) is three to four minutes to the right up the main highway from the station.

You quickly change to the waiting, 31-inch-gauge, green-and-yellow-striped, 1993 WAB train carriage, which starts out down the mountainside past gardens filled with fruit and great dahlias of all colors before stopping at Grund station, the WAB train depot. Then you zigzag up the opposite mountain slope for your approach to Kleine Scheidegg.

This is a playground for long camera lenses. You see model farms, summerhouses, hotels, chalets, churches, and cows with bells swinging on their necks.

At the Brandegg stop (4,272 feet), your ears pop. The clang of cowbells wafts through the lowered windows. The animals look uncomfortable on the steep mountainside as they take the last clumps of green grass.

Past Alpiglen (5,252 feet), your train enters a snow shed and then clanks through a double-tracked passing point. The landscape has scattered trees, stubborn shrubs, and a marshy look. You pass through more snow sheds with extruded steel uprights for strength.

Kleine Scheidegg (6,762 feet) comes into view. From a distance, the big hotels look like those found on a game board. A lilting alphorn serenades you as you climb off into a semicircle of hotels and restaurants. On this ledge connecting the Lauterbrunnen and Grindelwald valleys, you can cross to one of several large restaurants facing the station. Crowds of adventurers bask in the sun and enjoy the outdoor service on sunny days. Usually you will see a man in full Swiss folk costume playing an alphorn. You can order a nice lunch, a pair of sausages with potato salad, or just a beer while you listen to the melodious sounds of the alphorn and relish the incredible view of the Eiger, immense before you like a wall.

Kleine Scheidegg's shingled train station faces the waiting carriages of the 39-inch-gauge, Jungfrau Railroads (JB) for your trip to the summit. In addition to their 1993 maroon-and-yellow carriages, new (2002) carriages were added to respond to growing popularity. Of these, two carriages can be hooked together.

So formidable were the difficulties of working at this great altitude that 16 years were required to complete the 5¾ miles upward from Kleine Scheidegg. Even then, the track ended at the Jungfraujoch, 1¼ miles and more than 2,000 feet below the summit of the Jungfrau, its intended goal.

Over the first half-mile, which is flat, your train reaches its maximum speed, 15 mph, but slows perceptibly when you start to climb. Immediately you have wonderful views back on Kleine Scheidegg and the Eiger glacier close on the right glaring brightly at you. When you near the glacier you see its detail, the scalloping and furrows caused by runoff, and you appreciate the vastness of it even more.

Your climb is so steep that those facing forward are thrown against their seat backs and those facing backward brace themselves to keep from sliding out of their seats. Be sure to choose a forward-facing seat on the right side.

Your first stop is the Eigergletscher (Eiger glacier) station (7,612 feet), which was faced with granite in 1990. This is where the construction crew in 1898 established a colony of 150 workers just below the perpendicular North Face. Now you see the repair shop for the Jungfrau Railroad just below the entry to the long tunnel ahead.

Surging ahead, you enter the 4.4-mile tunnel gallery where you will spend some 41 minutes in darkness. Travelers exclaim and push up the windows because of cold air suddenly blasting on them. Heat percolates from under the seats. You sit 2+2 in one-class, fancy seats more spacious than the other narrow-gauge trains of the Jungfrau Region.

You climb so steeply that when you pass the horizontal sign "Open all year round," it appears cocked at an angle. The maximum gradient would be one foot in four on a direct route, so a corkscrew tunnel had to be constructed. The curved course allows you to stop at two intermediate stations with extraordinary views.

A gong sounds. Now you hear yodeling. Then an impersonal, recorded greeting in German and then French and English announces a five-minute stop at Eigerwand, the "Face of the Eiger" (9,400 feet).

From Eigerwand your train curves slightly more than 90 degrees in order to continue its climb. It runs through a tunnel scarcely big enough for one train only. You wouldn't dare walk alongside.

Less than a mile farther, now below the southeastern face of the Eiger and 10,368 feet high (a job that took the tunnelers two years to excavate), you reach the Eismeer (Sea of Ice) station. A hollow has been carved out of the rock big enough to hold a double track, so that ascending and descending trains pass one another. Once again you hear yodel music and an announcement for a five-minute stop. Here you see a view over the ragged surface of the glacier toward the Wetterhorn, the Schreckhorn, the Fiescherhorner, and the great crevasse under the Monchsjoch.

Your final segment lifts you only 970 feet, so the designers flattened the gradient from one in four to one in 16 feet (except for the last 1,640 feet). For many years this stretch was carried by ordinary adhesion, at just more than 11 miles an hour, but now the line is rack and pinion throughout.

The Alpine world of the Jungfraujoch (11,336 feet) is on view at the "Top of Europe" complex, where five levels of modern architecture blend harmoniously with the surroundings. Take the elevator to the Sphinx Terrace overlooking the Aletsch Glacier; see the ice sculptures in the Ice Palace; visit the scientific exhibit. When you get hungry, dine in a restaurant or cafe. This is a wonderful complex of mountain restaurants, panoramas, activities, husky dogs, mountaineering, and the "Toporama" slide show.

Departures are half-hourly during the summer. If you miss one there is always another carriage waiting for you. You will be warm and satisfied after your magnificent day, and you won't be alone dozing on your way down.

To the Schilthorn

For the Schilthorn (*www.Schilthorn.ch*), be sure to board a BOB car at Interlaken Ost station marked for Lauterbrunnen (alternately, you can descend via WAB to Lauterbrunnen from the Jungfraujoch). In Lauterbrunnen, you can either scramble across the tracks or use the underpass to the blue building, the lower terminus of the BLM "Bergbahn Lauterbrunnen-Murren." Your climb in the stepped, 60-passenger funicular will surprise you with its steep incline and length.

When you reach the upper terminus you immediately board the waiting Murren Railroad, a one- to four-car, brown-and-tan electric tram that takes you 2¾ miles horizontally to Murren (5,373 feet).

You will see one of the grandest views of the world here. The magnificent presence of the Jungfrau seems only a stone's throw away across a precipitous chasm. On your return, a casual walk from Murren to Grutschalp will long remain one of your fondest memories.

When your tram reaches Murren, disembark and walk through the village 15 minutes to the Schilthornbahn—there is only one street through Murren so you can't get lost. You pass every shop conceivable for a small village and carefully tended, flower-covered chalets as pleasant as any. Benches along the way offer places to break your walk.

You join the Schilthornbahn at its second stage. The first stage brings riders from the valley floor (free with the Swiss Pass) in 100-passenger gondolas from the Stechelberg Valley terminus at Gimmelwald (4,484 feet), with free parking for 1,500 automobiles and served by postal bus from Lauterbrunnen.

Your second-stage, swinging, 80-passenger red gondola with white "Schilthorn Bahn" lettered in front (25 percent reduction with a Swiss Pass) glides over the spacious Blumental ("Flower Valley") in a cable span of 3,038 yards supported by only two intermediate pylons. You appear simply to glide up a threatening rock face to a stop at the top of a towering bastion. First you look down on unbelievable rock formations sculpted by snow and glaciers. Then you look down on the glaciers.

At Birg, you change gondolas. Birg (8,781 feet) has a restaurant and sun terrace. Your second gondola is a single cabin for 100 persons. Between Birg and the summit, you see the scenery unfolding in all directions until you see Mont Blanc and Germany's Black Forest appearing in the distance and the Jungfrau Alps facing you. This span is 1,931 yards long—the longest unsupported span in the country. You notice even the gondola operators look exposed and weathered and wear dark glasses and sun creams. Finally you see some venturesome, hearty Swiss outside clambering down the snow. Your gondola swings to a final stop and you feel as daring as James Bond himself when he took those last few steps here to meet his archenemy in *On Her Majesty's Secret Service.*

Piz Gloria has been enlarged after that film. It is still a round build-ing but now with a two-level restaurant and an open sun terrace. The solar-powered restaurant revolves in 50-minute cycles past a continu-ous circle of picture windows that show off sectors of the 360-degree panorama. There are revolving restaurants and other revolving restau-rants, but none have prepared you for the sense of the Swiss Alps rotat-ing around you while you enjoy hearty Swiss specialties to the melodies of a mountain accordionist. Below, there is a self-service cafeteria with modest prices.

On the sun terrace, deck chairs are especially valued by travelers who have trouble with the high altitude. The red-and-white Swiss flag fluttering overhead seems planted as a backdrop for your photo-graphs. If you err and come when Piz Gloria is shrouded in clouds, there is a panoramic vision show called "Touristorama."

Railroads of the Jungfrau Region
Typical Service

Interlaken—Grindelwald—Kl. Scheidegg—Jungfraujoch

0905	dep.	INTERLAKEN Ost	arr.	1855
0910	dep.	Wilderswil	dep.	1851
0917	dep.	Zweilutschinen	dep.	1845
0924	dep.	Lutschental	dep.	1836
0930	dep.	Berglauenen	dep.	1829
0933	dep.	Schwendi	dep.	1826
0939	arr.	Grindelwald	dep.	1820
		Change between trains		

0949	dep.	Grindelwald	arr.	1815
0956	dep.	Grund	dep.	1811
1004	dep.	Brandegg	dep.	1755
1009	dep.	Alpiglen	dep.	1750
1024	arr.	Kleine Scheidegg	dep.	1732
		Change between trains		
1030	dep.	Kleine Scheidegg	arr.	1719
1040	dep.	Eigergletscher	dep.	1710
1122	arr.	Jungfraujoch	dep.	1630

Interlaken—Lauterbrunnen—Wengen—Kl. Scheidegg—Jungfraujoch

0935	dep.	INTERLAKEN Ost	arr.	1855
0940	dep.	Wilderswil	dep.	1851
0946	dep.	Zweilutschinen	dep.	1845
0955	arr.	Lauterbrunnen	dep.	1835
		Change between trains		
1010	dep.	Lauterbrunnen	arr.	1820
1021	dep.	Wengwald	dep.	1804
1030	dep.	Wengen	dep.	1802
1037	dep.	Allmend	dep.	1749
1046	dep.	Wengernalp	dep.	1737
1055	arr.	Kleine Scheidegg	dep.	1727
		Change between trains		
1102	dep.	Kleine Scheidegg	arr.	1719
1112	dep.	Eigergletscher	dep.	1710
1153	arr.	Jungfraujoch	dep.	1630

Interlaken—Lauterbrunnen—Murren—Schilthorn

0905	dep.	INTERLAKEN Ost	arr.	1755
0910	dep.	Wilderswil	dep.	1751
0916	dep.	Zweilutschinen	dep.	1745
0925	arr.	Lauterbrunnen	dep.	1735
		Walk three minutes between train and funicular		
0947	dep.	Lauterbrunnen BLM	arr.	1713
0958	dep.	Grutschalp	dep.	1702
1007	dep.	Winteregg	dep.	1651
1015	arr.	Murren BLM	dep.	1645
		Walk 15 minutes between train and aerial gondola		
1040	dep.	Murren LSMS	arr.	1620
1053	dep.	Birg	dep.	1610
1057	arr.	Schilthorn	dep.	1603

New Glitz on the Golden Pass
A Joint Effort

Snowcapped Alps, deep blue lakes, forested Alpine valleys, and cog-wheel-assisted crossings of high mountain passes reward passengers aboard the GoldenPass Panoramic, the newest of Switzerland's panoramic trains.

In the past, two changes of train, gauge, and equipment made breaking the trip into segments more convenient than taking the complete cross-Switzerland Golden Pass route because it sometimes felt more like a trek than a treat.

In a great development for opening the beauty of Switzerland by train, three individual Swiss railroads rolled out dedicated new locomotives and carriages on June 6, 2001, opened a new GoldenPass Center in Montreux on November 9, 2001, and began working closely together to provide a quality panoramic ride, branded the GoldenPass Panoramic (*www.goldenpass.ch*).

You now can reserve seats for the entire route between Montreux and Lucerne to cross Switzerland in panoramic comfort through eye-popping scenery and nursing a neck strained from gawking, and I recommend it.

Previously, each segment had is own individuality and livery. Now the three railroads cooperate to project the image of a single, continuous line. Each upgraded its carriages and adopted a single, distinctive livery of gold-and-white carriages and gold-colored locomotives.

• The Montreux-Oberland Bernois Railroad (MOB, *www.mob.ch*) between Montreux and Zweisimmen bought a new locomotive and rearranged their carriages for more frequent service over their 55-mile segment.

• The BLS Lotchbergbahn, which is the railroad's official new name (BLS, *www.bls.ch*), between Zweisimmen and Interlaken Ost (East) station, renovated carriages into some of the most comfortable in Europe.

• The SBB Brunig's 46-mile segment (*www.breunig.ch*) from Interlaken Ost to Lucerne reliveried their panoramic dome carriages and added a new handicapped-accessible carriage and a new restaurant carriage served by Mitropa Suisse.

Five GoldenPass Panoramic trains take you from Montreux daily. Three are headed by the Pininfarina-designed carriages that drew so

Lenk

To Interlaken

ZWEISIMMEN

Gstaad

Chateau-d'Oex

**GOLDENPASS
PANORAMIC**

Les Avants

N

0   5   10   20
      MILES

MONTREUX

LAKE GENEVA

much attention when they were introduced on the former Crystal Panoramic train, and the other two are hauled by the new locomotive splashed with scenes of western Switzerland and a golden "GoldenPassLine" poster in the center.

Your cream-and-night-blue designer train curls back and forth, up through terrace after terrace of lush vineyards. Your stiff climb takes you up a gradient of one in 15.4 over the six miles between Montreux and Chamby as you zigzag upward from 1,300 feet to 2,500 feet.

You look down on Montreux's freshly whitewashed hotels, patina-green copper roofs, and brown wooden chalets getting smaller and smaller. The little strip of town set upon the only place the Swiss could find for it between the steep Vaudois Alps and the "Vaud Riviera" on the shores of Lake Geneva never loses its charm.

You have powerful views from the GoldenPass Panoramic of the narrow-gauge Montreux-Oberland Bernois Railroad (MOB, *www.mob.ch*).

Eight lucky passengers sit nose to nose with onrushing scenery in the "VIP" seats of the three-times-daily Pininfarina carriages, which are the first two rows in front of and below the driver. You have nothing between you and the view but wraparound glass. The experience is the best of its kind in Europe.

These VIP seats may be reserved for CHF15 (about $9) in advance on a first-come, first-seated basis, so you should secure one early. Reservations are recommended on the remaining seats of both the Pininfarina trains and those pulled by the snazzy new locomotive.

The driver sits above, isolated and locked for his privacy and safety, and you store your luggage in the middle carriage—which is the "Saanen" electric locomotive cunningly tucked away inconspicuously—so that there are not overhead racks to obscure your views through the dome windows above. His raised driver's cabin is cramped, but your train has video cameras on the body sides and above the buffer beam to improve visibility.

The GoldenPass Panoramic is divided into two first-class sections, front and back, each served by a hostess who welcomes you aboard. Catering is by the SSG, the subsidiary of the Swiss Federal Railroads.

Doors open with a tug on the handle and close automatically. Even the very spacious number two, "Grande Vue" carriages excel for their panoramas. The window ledge is lower than usual and the window posts are extremely narrow, so you not only look through the overhead and panoramic windows, but you see down to the railbed below. It gives you a feeling of being outdoors yourself among the spectacular mountain scenery.

Travel is free on a first-class Eurail product or Swiss Pass. All you need is the reservation, which makes this one of the great finds of European train travel.

The end carriages contain a bar and a lounge with divans, which are not reserved, so that you can move around to enjoy the freedom and watch different perspectives unfold of the changing panorama unfold. These glassed wonders show you beautiful scenery in a way no other carriage can.

There is no better place to stay before beginning or after ending your Golden Pass trip than Montreux. The flower-scented promenade here is one of Europe's most beautiful. Montreux occupies a lovely site sheltered from the wind on the eastern end of Lake Geneva and known for the mildest climate north of the Alps. Tourists enjoy excursions, water sports, tennis, and just strolling along the promenade. Snow in winter falls only a few hundred feet above the town.

Montreux's train station, one of the few in Europe with three track gauges, is arranged awkwardly on the side of a mountain but the recently installed escalators and elevator make it easy to get from one level to the other.

The MOB office is next to platform No. 5, where you leave your narrow-gauge GoldenPass Panoramic train. Platform No. 1 is used for the Swiss Federal Railroads' standard-gauge line to Lausanne/Geneva/ Geneva Airport. Swiss International check-in for Geneva Airport is directly below at the street-level entrance.

Montreux's tourist office is beside the lake down the flight of stairs across the street from the train station. Go to the promenade and 1,000 feet to the left (south). Agents at the tourist office will give you a free GoldenPass Panoramic color brochure and map. Of course, they will also make hotel arrangements.

The steamers circling the Lake of Geneva dock nearby before proceeding around Chillon Castle. (They, too, are free on Eurail and Swiss passes—even for landings in France, and an excursion to Yvoire is recommended.) To reach the train station from the lake steamers, walk left and up the steps.

As your GoldenPass Panoramic leaves Montreux and weaves farther up the mountainside, Lake Geneva shrinks and becomes dwarfed by gray, snow-streaked French Alps towering in the background. With a view like a satellite in the sky, you can pick out the casino and the red-and-white Swiss flag over the Montreux Palace Hotel. The tall building you see near the lake was built in 1964, when high-rises were the rage. It is a condominium boasting a 26th-floor restaurant. The Eurotel to its right was built the same year. It is the second tallest in town. You see the lake hamlets Vevey and Lausanne to the north, and the Rhone River valley to the south disappearing toward the Simplon Pass.

The hillside above Montreux is famous for its trees and flowers. You pass through grape arbors to an altitude of nearly 2,000 feet, past walnut trees to 2,300 feet, and among fruit trees to the summit. Fields of wild narcissus sparkle in springtime. Chernex is the site of MOB's workshop, where MOB's dedicated crew is passionate about making the GoldenPass Panoramic the best train running.

On your left you see the first of the charming chalets like those in the Bernese Oberland; they give you a warm first impression of the celebrated Golden Pass route, which rivals the Glacier Express for the most spectacular east-west route in Switzerland. Looking up through the oblique windows reveals the crests of the Alps and gives you great depth of perspective. You feel inspired by the devastating height of the Alps above you. Because about 90 percent of your car is glass, be thankful for the air-conditioning that overcomes the greenhouse heating.

Climbing through the stiffest gradient of the line, you cross the crest. You final memory is your long view down the valley to Chillon Castle, with a white Lake Geneva steamer gliding into dock.

Through the 8,000-foot-long Jaman tunnel you enter the wholly different Sarine valley. Your Panoramic picks up speed through a series of reverse curves on the single, narrow-gauge track. The Saanen locomotive set the MOB's speed record: almost 70 mph. The conductor with a blue-and-white MOB winged emblem pinned to his black cap (patent leather visor) accepts your Eurailpass, Europass, or Swiss Pass with a smile.

Now you are riding through cuts in the limestone mountainsides past Les Scieres. Brown-and-white contented-looking cows graze in the tall, green grass. Families harvesting hay wave at you with green handkerchiefs, glad of an excuse to lean on their wooden rakes. Most passengers wave back. The brown-and-white cows shake their heavy bells and more or less ignore them.

The valley is wild and green, but above, the limestone Vaudois Alps form flat-topped ridges and throw long shadows you see through the oblique windows. You regret that your train seems to rush. You wish it would slow down so you could study the rugged mountain crests, the peaceful valleys, and the randomly scattered, typical houses with broad, graceful eaves, intricate woodwork, and flower boxes overflowing with bright yellow and blue blossoms.

Looking at the homes, the dress, and the work, you form an impression of the way of life of these mountain people who speak French, are generally Protestant, and decorate their farmhouses profusely. They live in tidier versions of those you will see only a half-hour ahead in the Bernese Oberland, the region that gave our language the word "chalet" and made this form of house synonymous with Switzerland the world over. They have low-pitched roofs and wide eaves on four sides.

Your GoldenPass Panoramic departs Switzerland's eastern canton, Vaud, at Chateau-d'Oex (say "Chateau Day," *www.chateau-doex.ch*). You are halfway through your trip and halfway between the Bernese Oberland and the Lake of Geneva.

The mountain village set among towering Alps at 3,083 feet becomes in January the world's colorful capital of hot-air ballooning. In winter, skiers race along the slopes and in summer, mountain bikers in competition tear through the trees.

Chateau-d'Oex's traditional architecture mixes chalets, farmhouses, and hotels. Here you find the typical family resort of the Vaudois Alps, with public pool and skating rink and a high lift to La Braye on the summit above. Guests congregate around the tables of mountain inns to enjoy the local fondue and raclette made from the tart l'Etivaz cheese produced in some 150 chalet dairies. Its flavor makes the regional cheese specialties the most renowned in Switzerland.

The ladies in the tourist office some three minutes down the hillside from the train station are pleased to provide you information and hotel assistance.

You pass through Rougemont station (3,254 feet), remarkable for its carved-wood decorations. The huge sloping roof below the train that catches your eye covers an early Romanesque church built on the site of an 11th-century, Cluniac priory. Swiss from all over the country travel here to visit the church and the adjacent 16th-century castle.

The quaint Saanen station (3,364 feet) marks the point where you leave the French-speaking Sarine valley and enter German-speaking Canton Bern. Some houses here, now adorned with climbing greenery, date from the 17th century. Saanen's old-fashioned character makes a good contrast with that of its booming neighbor, pricey Gstaad, only three minutes ahead.

In Gstaad, buildings get bigger. The hotels do well here in this smart village, one of Switzerland's premier winter resorts and a quiet summer destination.

When your panoramic train winds up the 180-degree Reichenbach curve overlooking Gstaad, the view back is ideal for photographers. Passengers cluster to the windows to take advantage.

You reach the summit of your trip at Saanenmoser's train station, 4,043 feet, with green shutters and cutouts in the shape of hearts. The station must be the most filigreed in the world. The station's dark brown wood sets off the white detailing and lace curtains on the windows.

Picking up speed, you sweep down the Saanenmoser depression. Spike-tipped, 5,000-foot Alpine peaks stand in the distance and farmhouses defy the pull of gravity on both slopes of the valley.

You are ready for the next leg of the GoldenPass Panoramic when you pass through a spiral tunnel to arrive on the valley floor at Zweisimmen (3,090 feet). This is your junction for Spiez and Interlaken. Tracks 1 and 2 (42-inch gauge) are devoted to your narrow-gauge train from Montreux. Tracks 3, 4, 11, and 13 (60 inches) lead BLS trains to Spiez and Interlaken. At Zweisimmen the MOB and BLS GoldenPass Panoramic trains arrive and depart on the same platform.

Almost everyone changes across the platform for the refurbished GoldenPass Panoramic carriages of the BLS for the leisurely 27-mile journey to Spiez through the rural Simmen Valley region. The BLS is the longest standard-gauge private railroad in Switzerland. Its main route is through the Lotschberg Tunnel, but the track from Spiez to Interlaken acquired in 1913 is an added extra. The railroad also accepts Eurail products and Swiss Passes.

BLS's new gold-and-white carriages have sparkling new interiors with bucket seats arranged in several ensembles, all with great space, functional tables, posh carpeting, and attractive blue velvet seats.

You are back on big rails, and it is amazing to find the comfort of BLS's newly appointed carriages. The first-class salon cars have a comfortable "Bernese lounge bar" and an at-seat dining service operated by Mitropa Suisse.

You pass prosperous farms and fortunate Swiss cows. In no time, you arrive above the lakeside harbor at Spiez's station house, where InterCity trains depart quarter-hourly for Bern. Your GoldenPass Panoramic then takes you along the shore of Lake Thun to Interlaken Ost (East) station.

Ost station (1,860 feet) is your junction for the Jungfrau Railroads, no doubt the most scenic collection of private railroads that have gathered together to promote travel in their spectacular region. With its majestically Alpine 13,000-foot mountains, you have the opportunity to change to mountain railroads and cableways leading to the famous "Top of Europe" Jungfraujoch and the Schilthorn of James Bond fame.

At Interlaken Ost you change to the Brunig Line's newly reliveried GoldenPass Panoramic 1994 aluminum-body panoramic carriage. Pulled by a gaily colored locomotive, it features curved windows that soar high and partially wrap above you to reveal dramatic Alpine peaks during your heady trip over the precipitous Brunig Pass between Interlaken and Lucerne.

Your train over the narrow-gauge stretch also carries conventional second-class carriages with pull-down windows, a red "Brunig Bar" dining car, and a weirdly conceived, first-class carriage filled with swivel chairs.

Your GoldenPass Panoramic approaches Brienz (1,856 feet) past lakeside villages lining the road with a picture-book array of typical Bernese Oberland houses their owners beautified with characteristic overhanging eaves and balconies overflowing with flowers. This is your stop for the gingerbread Brienzer Rothorn station higher up the mountain, where steam locomotives are hissing, ready to begin their climb to the summit.

You travel up the Aare Valley, where waterfalls on the opposite walls drop into a fine mist. Past Brienzwiler your second stop is in the big station at Meiringen (1,952 feet), a functional transportation center of stone, brick, and concrete.

In Meiringen, postal buses stand nearby to take you on scenic routes through astonishing mountain passes, to the spectacular Aare Gorge, and to Reichenbach Falls, made famous by the furious battle between Sherlock Holmes and Professor Moriarity.

You nevertheless become nervous when cogwheels underneath slam into place and you begin an ascent and descent to and from a pass so steep that it must be negotiated with the safety of the clattering rack invented by Nicholas Riggenbach (1817-99) in 1863.

Climbing from Meiringen, you feel the cogwheels engage and hear the thump and jangle of engagement of the cogwheel track that takes you securely over and down the north slope of the Brunig Pass. You feel as though your GoldenPass Panoramic is tiptoeing up a spiral staircase.

Soon you are at home with the comforting sounds of cogwheels as you approach Brunig-Hasliberg (3,287 feet) through a short tunnel. A group waiting is eager to climb aboard. The Brunigstube Restaurant at the station house has tables set outdoors where visitors enjoy the mountain sunshine.

You leave snow-covered Alps and pass through dense forest high above the village of Lugern, far below on the lakeside. Its towering church seems to anchor the end of the lake. The grass is short-cropped. Lake Lugern looks slate green.

Although passengers are already charmed by scenery provided by rugged Alps, forests, and serene farmlands, each view of a new, bluer lake elicits more "ahs" than the last.

Approaching Sarnen (1,558 feet), you pass Lake Sarnen's well-groomed promenade on the west and its variety of boats, swans, and swimming sites. Across the lake, you see shoreline chalets arranged below dense forest.

Past Alpnachstad you see the docked lake steamers and the cog-wheel railroad to the summit of Mount Pilatus, but when you want to ride them you'll have to choose a local train stopping here.

Then your GoldenPass Panoramic tunnels away from the lakeshore through a ridge of Mount Pilatus itself and, after 4¾ hours, you complete your GoldenPass Panoramic trip in the modern Lucerne Hauptbahnhof (1,430 feet) with connections on to Zurich and Zurich Kloten Airport.

GoldenPass Panoramic Train Service

0909	1309	dep.	Geneva Airport	arr.	1425	1825
0918	1318	dep.	Geneva	arr.	1416	1816
1019	1419	arr.	Montreux	dep.	1300	1700
			Change trains			
1026*	1426*	dep.	Montreux	arr.	1246*	1646
1215*	1615*	arr.	Zweisimmen	dep.	1050*	1450
			Change trains			
1220	1620	dep.	Zweisimmen	arr.	1039	1439
1324	1724	arr.	Interlaken Ost	dep.	0935	1335
			Change trains			
1530	1730	dep.	Interlaken Ost	arr.	0929	1129
1924	1924	arr.	Lucerne	dep.	0735	0935
			Change trains			
1735	1935	dep.	Lucerne	arr.	0727	0927
1825	2025	arr.	Zurich	dep.	0635	0835
1850	2050	arr.	Zurich Airport	dep.	0613	0813

*VIP front seats

Iberia

Savvy Traveling on the Trains of Spain and Portugal

Spanish trains—Aboard the high-speed Madrid-Barcelona train (at least as far as Lleida)—Madrid-Seville by AVE—Talgo 200 branches—Barcelona-Valencia-Alicant with Euromed—Madrid-Valencia on Alaris—Riding RENFE's domestic overnight trains—Using Madrid's and Barcelona's train stations—Airport connections—Rail lounges—Portuguese railroads—Using Lisbon's public transportation—Rail-pass travel

It's surprising that traveling between the two Iberian countries, Spain and Portugal, is so difficult. No mainline train connection between the two countries is available with rail pass and no through day train, at all, between Madrid and Lisbon. Your best connection between the two capital cities is the Tren Hotel Lusitania, and this uses "Global" pricing, which puts rail-pass holders at a disadvantage. Rail-pass holders' alternate way between Madrid and Lisbon is to take the 7:45 A.M. Spanish Talgo train from Madrid to Badajoz, make a change to a regional train to Abrantes, and change again to a regional train to Lisbon, arriving at 6:37 P.M.

If you want to travel to Portugal from France, and care to bypass Spain, take the TGV connection from Paris for the Sud Express and don't go through Madrid.

The alternatives for crossing between Spain and Portugal are to use the secondary lines in the north of Portugal connecting to Galicia or the DAMAS bus service (or ferry) in Andalusia crossing the Guadiana River to Portugal's Algarve. These options are described in the text below and you may consult the "Spain/Portugal" map offered free by Rail Europe.

Travelers curious about visiting Andorra, Europe's newest republic (1993), should use the French overnight train carrying first- and second-class French couchettes and second-class compartments from Paris (Austerlitz) to L'Hospitalet, France, your bus gateway to the tiny republic. The bus service operated by Societe Franco-Andorrane de Transports makes immediate connections. From Andorra via bus to La Tour-de-Carol you connect with a second-class-only Spanish "Delta" train for Barcelona.

Spanish Trains

If you traveled aboard the trains of Spain just 12 years ago, you would not believe the status of high-speed travel in Spain today. With the European Union pouring in 38 billion euros between 1994 and 2000 to Spain as a "developing country," Spain opened high-speed lines connecting cities at unprecedented speeds. If the EU funding holds up, by 2010 Spain will have leap-frogged France as the European leader for high-speed travel.

RENFE, the acronym for the Spanish Railroads, "Red Nacional de los Ferrocarriles Espanoles" (*www.renfe.es*), is in hot competition with deregulated airfares and automobile traffic. Their trains are innovative and comfortable to ride. AVE is *Alta Velocidad Espanola,* the 186-mph high-speed train between Madrid and Seville. Euromed (Em) indicates the 124-mph trains Barcelona-Alicant. Talgo 200 (T200) are Talgo trains equipped to run on both the high-speed line and the broad-gauge tracks.

Talgo stands for "Tren Articulado Ligero Goicoechea y Oriol." The last two names are those of the inventors of the system and the first three words mean "lightweight articulated train." Because they are articulated units, the string of shorter, connected, low-profile parlors bends around curves like a rubber snake. The generation called the "Pendular" additionally tilts according to ingenious design.

Suspension from above the center of gravity causes the bodies to swing centrifugally and round curves so smoothly you'll see scarcely a ripple in your coffee.

InterCity (IC) and Arco are quality day express trains. "Trenhotel" (hotel) are quality night trains, while "Estrella" (Estr) are night trains with sleeping cars, couchettes, and seated carriages. "Alaris" are 124-mph tilting trains on the Madrid-Albacete-Valencia line. "Diurno" (*D*) trains are ordinary day trains.

On July 10, 2002, a Talgo XXI reached 146 mph, breaking the world speed record for diesel trains with hydraulic transmission, but Spain's remarkable success has been based on the acquisition of electric high-speed TGV Atlantic and ICE 3 trains and rapid-fire gauge changers that facilitate transfer between standard- and broad-gauge rails.

Unfortunately, the Spanish Railroads puts a lump in your travel plans by limiting the use of rail passes on AVEs, Talgo 200s, and posh Trens Hotel. Pass holders do, however, receive discounts. RENFE's point-to-point ticket fares are not based on mileage traveled, but are set to reflect variations in seasonal demand and relative advantage over competing air and road transportation.

You use sparkling stations like Madrid's Puerta de Atocha, Seville's Santa Justa, and Barcelona's Estacio de Franca (Termino); you transit well-managed hubs such as Madrid's Chamartin station; and you relax in first-class lounges open free to all first-class rail-pass holders. You agree that Spain is a great nation to visit by train.

RENFE requires reservations on its long-distance trains, but RENFE's computerized system makes them easy for you to obtain at any RENFE office or train station or even up to two months in advance from the U.S., from Rail Europe (see Appendix A). At Madrid's very convenient, downtown RENFE office at Alcala, 44 (open Mon.-Fri., 9:30 A.M. to 8 P.M.; use the Banco de Espana metro stop), agents can make your reservations for Spain, Italy, and Portugal. They accept bank credit cards for payment but not for reservations. Be sure to flash your credit card in advance to alert the booking agent.

All of RENFE's trains formerly ran on wide-gauge (5 feet, 6 inches) rails, but the government decided to build all new high-speed tracks to the European standard (4 feet, 8½ inches), so that Spain is now a country running on two gauges (three, if you count the meter-gauge FEVE railroad in the north). New gauge-changing operations allow trains to cross between lines of different gauges on the move.

Because of the gauge differences, you change trains or gauge when you cross the frontier between Spain and France. RENFE mechanics change gauge by adjusting the wheelsets on the go so smoothly that you can realize it only by the slowing of the train through the gauge-change station. Talgo trains such as the EN Jean Miro, EN Francisco de Goya, EN Pablo Casals, and EC Catalan Talgo are designed so mechanics in a work pit at the border widen or narrow their wheelsets while at night passengers remain sound asleep and during the day curious passengers open the doors to watch. Similar arrangements allow Talgo 200 trains to enter and exit the standard-gauge high-speed line.

Travelers from northern Europe to Morocco frequently use the overnight Media Luna train between Irun and Algeciras. In Algeciras, they change to ferry, but this overnight service runs during the summer only. A Talgo 200 leaves Madrid Atocha Station in the morning, runs via the high-speed line to Cordoba, where it changes gauge, and reaches Algeciras in early afternoon, averaging about 68 mph over the 400-mile distance. South of Bobadilla you pass through superb mountain scenery and climb some steep gradients, especially the S-shaped rise out of the Guadiaro Valley between La Indiana and Ronda.

Many travelers are surprised to learn about the well-running secondary meter-gauge train network across the north of Spain because they don't see it on the Eurail train map—for the reason that FEVE does not accept Eurail products. FEVE, "Ferrocarriles de Via Estretcha," claims to be the longest continuous narrow-gauge network in Europe, a claim that is echoed by Switzerland's Rhaetian Railroads. Their "Mini-Apolo" diesel units were modernized in 1999 with Volvo engines, air-conditioning, digital passenger information displays, retention toilets, and upholstered 2+2 seating.

Aboard the High-Speed Madrid-Barcelona Train (at Least as Far as Lleida)

After RENFE gives the go-ahead for high-speed running, you will burst from the tunnel in the cliffs on the right bank of the Cinca River, shoot at breakneck speed immediately onto the viaduct over the Cinca Valley, and veer upward onto the lower hills on the east bank to your left.

You board your Siemens S-103 (based on the German ICE 3) or duck-nosed Talgo S-102 in Madrid's Atocha train station and head southeast on the line toward Seville until you branch at a triangular junction onto the new line to Barcelona and cross through the growing residential suburbs of Spain's capital city. You climb gradually through the Henares Valley to the new park-and-ride train station serving the provincial capital of Guadalajara, two and a half miles to the northwest.

Heading northeast, your train will accelerate on the highest high-speed line in Europe, between Gajanejos and Calatayud. Most of the route is above 3,300 feet and reaches about 4,000 feet at Alcolea del Pinar. Past Alcolea you descend through rough, wild, remote, forgotten countryside untouched by human hands. Through several tunnels, you meet the earlier Madrid-Zaragoza line a few miles before Calatayud, in the Jalon Valley.

Your train calls at the new Calatayud station. Notice that the station has platforms for broad-gauge trains in addition to the European-gauge rails that your train is traveling over. Then you continue into the most difficult section of your route. The Jalon River, followed by the old single-track railroad, enters a series of gorges. You cross numerous viaducts and pass through several tunnels, keeping high on the mountainsides above the river.

Past Ricla, the landscape opens and you enter the flourishing Ebro river basin. Leaving the Jalon River, you cut across the low Sierras to Zaragoza. Your train bypasses the city, but you can make it out in the north.

Some trains will serve the 2003 Zaragoza Delicias station and train museum. The station has five tracks of both gauges lying 25 feet below the level of the main concourse. Surprisingly, the new train-bus-car park station is free of commerce, so that you can walk unimpeded by fast-food vendors to your 1,300-foot-long departure platform or from your arrival platform—they are separate.

Past Zaragoza, you cross over the old railroad line to Tarragona and then over the River Ebro on a long viaduct, climbing into the lonely, sparsely populated Los Monegros region, which was once the heart of the Aragon desert. Now you see tall wheat and rye thanks to irrigation.

As your train continues parallel to the Zaragoza-Barcelona highway, hold your breath for the spectacular crossing of the Cinca Valley.

At Raimat, you join the former mainline between Zaragoza and Lleida and tunnel to the former Lleida station, which has tracks of both gauges. At high speed, you cover 289 miles averaging 161 mph, arriving one hour, 50 minutes after leaving Madrid. From here your high-speed train will follow the River Lleida and take you to Barcelona's expanded Sants train station, but not now; that line is expected to open in 2006, when it will take you three hours to travel between Madrid and Barcelona compared with 6½ hours formerly.

The section of the high-speed line between Zaragoza and Lleida was beset by difficulties, not the least of which were geological. Some areas contain caverns, which open into chasms when disturbed, but it was finally opened to passenger service on October 11, 2003.

Madrid-Seville by AVE

After 100 different names were considered, Spain's 186-mph train between Madrid and Seville was dubbed AVE, which stands both for "Alta Velocidad Espanola" (Spanish high speed) and "Ancho de Via Europeo" (European gauge) and also means "bird" in Castilian, which led to the design of the logo. After its debut, it suffered mechanical problems, causing the AVE to soon become known as the "Averias," which is Spanish for breakdowns. After the running in was completed, it became known to tens of thousands of visitors to Seville's Expo as Europe's best train.

The vice-president of the Spanish government opened the high-speed line on April 14, 1992, and then traveled from Madrid to Seville in two hours, 55 minutes, with three publicity stops. Scheduled service began a week later, on April 21, 1992. A Spanish-built AVE established a new Spanish speed record of 221.6 mph on April 23, 1993.

Sadly, Eurail products, Iberia Railpasses, or Spain Railpasses do not cover travel on AVEs, but pass holders do get a price break. AVE has three classes: "Turista," "Preferente," and "Club," which are shown on the exterior of the carriages. The fares are not calculated by distance traveled; the special fare structure depends on the class of travel and the time of day. (The monstrous "yield management" system used by airlines is at work.) Time division No. 1 (early; trains departing at 7 A.M.) has the lowest fares. Division No. 2 (normal) applies to trains departing all day and evening except peak. Division No. 3 (peak) applies to trains departing at 8 A.M., 2 P.M., and 7 P.M.

Reservations are required. In Spain you receive 25 percent off for one-day, round-trip tickets, 20 percent off for round trips within 15 days. The return trips may be made on Talgo 200 trains. Those 65 and over receive a 25 percent discount; children four to 11 pay 60 percent.

AVE's Turista Class with 2+2 seating offers audio-video, a bar/cafeteria, a drink machine, and telephones. Travelers in the open salons of Preferente Class sit 2+1 and also receive newspapers and magazines. Travelers in Club Class sit in the mixed compartment/aisle arrangement of the preferred TGV Atlantique-type (see "France" chapter) carriages. They additionally receive a very fine meal service at their seats. Again, the full-length bar car resembles TGV Atlantique's except for stand-up, wooden-topped islands for passengers to snack.

You depart from the ground level of Puerta de Atocha station. Departures ("salida") are shown on an electronic board in the departures hall and again over the platforms in the departure area. Show your ticket at the gate before entering the platform. South of Getafe, some 13 miles south of the Spanish capital, you follow the track bed of the former Madrid-Badajoz broad-gauge line whose track was torn up and parts of the bed straightened to allow you to reach 186 mph. After you pass Ciudad Real, you run parallel to the still-existing broad-gauge line to Brazatortas. Building the northern segment on the right-of-way of a prior secondary line broke all construction speed records. In one year the infrastructure was completed.

Your introduction to Andalusia is entirely olives. Olive trees, with their twisted trunks and stunted branches pruned to grow no higher than a man on a ladder can reach, define the arid hills and gorges and break into the crusty brick-red soil. They *are* the landscape.

From Brazatortas you enter the challenging Sierra Morena Mountains that provided the second segment of track construction. At Villanueva you slow along the difficult 17-mile section to Adamuz, climbing at a gradient of 1 in 80 and negotiating curves with a minimum radius of 7,500 feet. This segment built through difficult mountainous terrain required construction of 3.7 miles of long bridges and 9.4 miles of tunnel in the 69.6 miles to Cordoba. On two occasions an embankment collapsed on completed stretches of the line.

You arrive on one of Cordoba's station's six AVE tracks. There are three more for broad-gauge trains, and parking for over 1,500 automobiles. During excavation to move underground the station facilities, together with 2½ miles of track, extensive Roman ruins were found and incorporated into the design of the new station, which was eventually inaugurated by King Juan Carlos on September 9, 1994.

From Cordoba south to Seville you hug the existing broad-gauge line very closely. You arrive at the new Santa Justa station in Seville. In all, you have passed through 17 tunnels, 9.8 miles in total length, and crossed 31 viaducts totaling 6.1 miles.

Seville's 860,000-square-foot permanent terminus was inaugurated on May 2, 1991, on Avenida Kansas City (named for Seville's sister city) with both standard- and broad-gauge platforms, and with a new link to the line west to Huelva. If a new train station can be blocky—constructed of brick, concrete, and glass—and grand at the same time, it is due to the long, sweeping "travelators," or moving walkways rising and descending to track level from the mezzanine-level entrance hall. Above you find all the necessary train functions. The timetables are on posts scattered about this level. Luggage carts are available for a coin deposit.

Seville's magnificent, Eiffel-designed, neo-Mudejar Plaza de Armas Station was transformed into an attractive shopping center. *Tip:* You can stop by to imagine the way it used to look and admire the displays of model trains. A modern hotel of the same name is adjacent.

On the average weekday there are 18 Madrid-Seville AVE departures. All stop in Cordoba, taking one hour, 38 minutes from Madrid at 131 mph; except the 8 A.M. departures from the termini, which take two hours, 15 minutes from Madrid to Seville. Formerly, you needed about 6½ hours to reach Seville from Madrid partially because the roundabout route followed by the old rails skirted the mountains.

Each of the 16 AVE trainsets, which can be linked together to form a doubled train, comprises two power cars and eight carriages, and is 656 feet long overall. Weighing 393 tons empty and 421 tons fully booked, it will ordinarily come to a stop in 6.8 miles from 186 mph, but can be braked in 2.2 miles in an emergency. Only one of the two pantographs is used on the high-speed line, but both would be used to travel on broad-gauge lines.

The AVEs have cosmetically changed nose profiles midway between FrenchRail's Atlantique and GermanRail's ICE, designed to withstand a direct impact at 62 mph without collapsing. Their livery was modified to the white, blue, and gray colors adopted by RENFE for all their high-speed trains and high-performance locomotives.

Each AVE provides 329 seats—30 in Club Class, which is laid out with four-person compartments on one side of the aisle and a single file of seats on the other; 78 seated 2+1 in Preferente; and 213 in Turista. There are another eight places in the conference room and 21 seats in the vestibules. Space between seats is very generous and several video screens are fitted in the ceiling of each carriage.

Preferente Class passengers have access to at-seat meal service. Club Class travelers receive airline-style meals. In both classes, you have access to free newspapers, coffee, and soft drinks, included in your fare, but panoramic windows and pleasing counter arrangements make the bar/cafeteria, located between the Turista and Preferente classes, a popular place to visit for snacks and something to drink.

Talgo 200 Branches

The high-speed line for the AVEs brought broad implications for travel throughout Spain. Gauge-changing, high-speed Talgo 200 trains take you over a peninsula-wide high-speed network. These trains, blue and white with yellow striping, leave from the same standard-gauge platforms of Puerta de Atocha as the other high-speed trains.

Simultaneously with the construction of the AVE trainsets, RENFE obtained gauge-changing, 124-mph Pendular sets from the Talgo company for Talgo 200 high-speed service beyond Seville over wide-gauge lines to Malaga, Cadiz, and Huelva, and gauge-changing, dual-electrical-system "Europa" locomotives built in Munich, Germany, by Krauss-Maffei capable of 125 mph (140 mph for short periods). These tall locomotives, painted in AVE livery, use one electrical system on the high-speed line, the second on the broad-gauge lines. Gauge-changing installations in Madrid, Cordoba, and Seville make it possible for the convertible-gauge trains to take you on and off the high-speed line.

Five daily Madrid-Malaga Talgo 200 trains require less than two hours over the 280-mile high-speed line between Madrid and the gauge-change station near Cordoba, while it takes an additional two hours, 10 minutes over the single-track, 118-mile run to Malaga after changing gauge near Cordoba.

Two daily Talgo 200 services between Madrid and Cadiz (one with a portion to Huelva) using the gauge-changing installation near Seville reduce your travel time by two and a half hours. The Torre del Oro train from Barcelona to Cadiz, composed of Talgo Pendular carriages, also takes advantage of the Madrid-Seville high-speed line over part of its route, as does the overnight Antonio Machado hotel train between Barcelona and Seville/Malaga.

Barcelona-Valencia-Alicant with Euromed

At 7:42 A.M. the sun begins to reveal with weak light the rippling waves of the Mediterranean Sea. It is a delightful wake-up. Beside your

Euromed train, white cubic buildings emerge like phantoms from the morning glimmer.

You may have made the trip by train between Barcelona and Valencia several times, but this trip is the speediest, this trip is the earliest (the sun may not come up until you reach Tarragona), and this trip is aboard a Euromed, one of the eight AVE trains converted to wide-gauge with revised interiors and only two classes.

The sunrise over the Mediterranean is the most stunning of all. The scattered clouds glowing red and rose-colored in morning sky over the sea are even more dramatic after the rains left in Barcelona.

This trip has many neckties in the posh Preferente (first class). Early risers also sit there with a rail pass plus substantial reservation fee. Turista class has fewer neckties and more backpacks.

The scrub-covered hills shine in the golden sunrise. They look magnificent, and the low angle of the sun casting long shadows makes them look much higher than they appear at midday.

Upgraded Euromed passenger service between Barcelona and Alicant via Valencia was introduced on June 15, 1997, following extensive rebuilding of the "Mediterranean Corridor," the line that follows the coast from Barcelona via Tarragona to Valencia.

The major upgrade of the infrastructure on the 229-mile line included track renewal and doubling, new cutoffs, and level crossing eliminations. The work cost about U.S. $660 million, including a 0.6-mile-long viaduct over the Ebro delta in order to avoid a dogleg via Tortosa. End-to-end train times were reduced from six hours, 10 minutes in 1992 to four hours, 40 minutes.

A second phase of work costing U.S. $330 million was completed in 1999 between Sagonte and Oropesa del Mar, cutting another half-hour off your travel time.

Confusingly, 186 mph on a new line is know as *alta velocidad*, whereas 124 to 137 mph on an upgraded line is known as *velocidad alta*.

Euromed takes you between Barcelona and Alicant, making stops only in Tarragona, Castellon, and Valencia. Five trains run daily between Barcelona and Valencia, three of which continue on to Alicant.

Each Euromed train consists of three Preferente, four Turista, and a cafeteria/bar carriage. First-class travel includes a food and beverage catering service by Wagons-Lits Spain, as well as access to the Euromed lounges at the train stations in Barcelona, Valencia, and Alicant.

Preferente carriages seat 39 passengers each and feature individual luggage lockers. You travel in grass-green interiors with 2+1 seating. At 7 A.M., Preferente is nearly 100 percent business. First, bright-as-a-button hostesses hand out in-ear earphones. You hear announcements in Spanish, Catalan, and English.

Turista class, with dark-blue 2+2 seating, accommodates 56 passengers, with the exception of the one nearest the power car that contains a baggage compartment and seats only 45.

Carriage 4 is the "cafeteria," a very efficient full-length bar car similar in concept to the French TGV Atlantique but differently arranged. Telephones are available in carriages 4 and 5. Carriage 7 is designated for the use of cellular telephones.

When you descend by elevator in Barcelona's Sants train station, you find your white-and-blue Euromed purring beside a makeshift check-in desk where two English-speaking ladies cancel your ticket and direct you to your carriage ("coche"). A large "Euromed" is marked on the sides of the power cars. Luggage carts are available here.

A video starts with a "Welcome to Euromed" introduction. You receive Spanish and English (sometimes) newspapers. You leave Barcelona's Sants station through a tunnel that seems to go on forever.

This is a good train for working—the ride is the smoothest in Europe (the equal of the TGV Atlantique that I have written postcards upon while traveling 186 mph), the service is uplifting, and the ambience is excellent.

You scan a breakfast menu. One's Spanish may not be good, but you can guess that you will receive scrambled eggs, cubes of potatoes, York ham, fruit of the season, bread, orange juice, butter, marmalade, and infusion coffee. Breakfast appears on a tray designed to neatly fit the fold-down seat-back table, with white tablecloth and napkin.

It is still dark outside, but the lights appearing in the windows of the blocky white buildings tell you that families are breakfasting and getting ready for work. In the harsh glare of afternoon you see that the beachfront cities here have the same washed-out, sun-bleached, and hung-over look of beach cities throughout the world. Why do they all have tile roofs, white walls, and balconies?

Euromed arrives at Tarragona's blocky, modern station on track ("via") 1. More attache cases board. Tarragona is a modern city of wide avenues and busy streets. The sea front rises in tiers up a cliffside brilliant with flowers.

The morning light has become bright enough for you to make out the deep red color of the earth. Artichoke plants are just beginning to make their way. There are olive trees and so many orange trees that one would think one was in the province of Valencia instead of Castellon. Valencia is famous for the export of oranges to England for the manufacture of marmalade.

While sailing through the orange groves you are at Euromed's top speed of 125 mph.

About 10 minutes before you arrive in Valencia you enter a long submerged stretch with occasional cuttings leading you above ground to high-rise buildings and booming construction projects.

Valencia is the capital of the province of the same name and Spain's third-largest city. Valencia's Termino station was formerly known as Estacio del Nord. It is a bright, traditional station—as old-fashioned and pleasant as you can get. It has all services including baggage checking (lockers). The tourist office by track 1 is open 10 A.M. to 6:30 P.M.

Arrival and departure times are displayed on electric signs identified in both Spanish and Catalan: Llegadas/Arribades and Salidas/Eixides. One notes that these Catalan words are closer to English.

First-class ticket and pass holders can well take advantage of Termino station's quaint first-class lounge, called Sala Euromed, beside track 1. It contains antique floral glazed tiles, overstuffed seats, and a refrigerator filled with free soft drinks, mineral water, and orange juice. The coffee machine is working well. The room might remind you of your grandmother's parlor.

Euromed Daily Service
Barcelona—Valencia/Alicant

dep. BARCELONA (Sants)	dep. Tarragona	arr. Castellon de la Plana	dep. Castellon de la Plana	arr. VALENCIA (Nord)	dep. VALENCIA (Nord)	arr. Alicant (Terminal)
0700*	0748	0904	0956	0945	1000	1135
0900	0949	1106	1108	1154	1200	1335
1100	1149	1305	1307	1355	1400	1538
1600	1649	1805	1807	1855	1900	2035
1800	1849	2006	2008	2054	2100	2235
2030	2119	2235	2237	2320	N/A	N/A

N/A = Not available
*Runs Mon.-Sat.

Valencia/Alicant—Barcelona

dep. Alicant (Terminal)	arr. VALENCIA (Nord)	dep. VALENCIA (Nord)	arr. Castellon de la Plana	dep. Castellon de la Plana	dep. Tarragona	arr. BARCELONA (Sants)
N/A	N/A	0640*	0717	0719	0836	0936
0655	0829	0835	0914	0916	1037	1133
0925	1055	1105	1145	1147	1306	1403
1420	1555	1605	1644	1646	1807	1903
1620	1755	1805	1844	1846	2005	2105
1825	1958	2005	2044	2046	2205	2303

N/A = Not available
*Runs Mon.-Sat.
The first departures each direction do not operate Sundays. The last departures each direction do not operate Saturdays.

Madrid-Valencia on Alaris

Madrid-Valencia is the domain of Alaris, the brand name for RENFE's first Italian-style tilting trains. Inaugurated on February 16, 1999, Alaris takes you at up to 134 mph (*velocidad alta*) between Madrid and Valencia, via Albacete, over rebuilt line, taking three and a half hours to travel 306 miles. Once the latest upgrade is complete, you will arrive in less than three hours. Alaris features a buffet/bar car located in the center of the train, plus a child chaperone, and each passenger has access to on-board audio and video entertainment.

Based on the ETR 460 Pendolino, Alaris is unique from other ETR 460 derivatives because up to three of the three-carriage sets can operate in multiple. Tilt operates to a maximum of eight degrees and allows Alaris to take curves 30 percent faster than normal.

Riding RENFE's Domestic Overnight Trains

RENFE's standard domestic overnight trains are called "Estrella" and provide you with adequate accommodations in conventional, second-class, brown-and-white couchette carriages (French Corail equipment), in carriages with seats that do not recline, and in well-worn first- and second-class sleeping cars. Estrella Gibralfaro takes you between Barcelona and Malaga/Cadiz/Granada and the Estrella Bahia de Cadiz takes you between Barcelona and Granada/Almeira/Cadiz. Estrella Atlantico runs Madrid-Ferrol. Estrella Picasso between Bilbao and Malaga and Sun of the Levant between Bilbao/Irun and Alicant each carry a reclining-seat coach.

Using Madrid's and Barcelona's Train Stations

The 1992 Seville World Exposition and the 1992 Summer Olympic Games in Barcelona had a very positive fallout for train travelers. In addition to the new high-speed line between Madrid and Seville (see "AVEs," above) and the new Seville train station, you will be using bright new-from-the-ground-up stations in Madrid and Barcelona.

You will probably use Madrid's large Atocha station, where, at the Puerta de Atocha, AVEs and Talgo 200s for Andalusia and high-speed trains for Barcelona depart on eight ground-level, standard-gauge platforms. This 1989, glass-and-cement station relies extensively upon unpretentious red brick, concrete, and matte-texture cast iron. It is really a transportation hub with three separate departure and arrival areas. Excellent direction sign posting simplifies getting around its confusion of many levels of activity. The direction for AVE departures is well marked as are the metro, the platforms for the Cerciana trains, and other station facilities. There is a dedicated first-class waiting room on the mezzanine, which otherwise struts a long, glass wall fully overlooking the tracks and the waiting high-speed trains. Suburban trains depart on the 10 tracks of the lower level that run across the city to Chamartin station.

Atocha station's magnificent 1892 train shed designed by Alberto del Palacio was transformed by architect Rafael Moneo into a humid tropical garden with water-misted palms, banana trees, and water lilies and with numerous retail outlets. It features an "outdoor" cafe on the same level as train departures. With the birds chirping, it doesn't take too much imagination to feel yourself in deepest Africa or an Amazon rain forest. All this still has every feature of a mainline station, including taxis, luggage checking, ticketing, money changing, LED departure boards, and information counters. Reach the AVE club area on a moving walkway.

Whereas Atocha is the high-speed train terminus, Chamartin is your wide-gauge terminus for Talgo and Alaris trains. You will probably arrive or depart from Chamartin station, one of Europe's brightest, in the northern outskirts of the city. Here you find at least three banks offering to change money, a hotel reservation ("Reserva Hotelera") booth opposite tracks 7/8, a post office opposite tracks 9/10, train information counters between tracks 11 and 12, the Sala Club Intercity between 13 and 14, and a small Internet point opposite track 18. Luggage lockers are across the driveway as is the check-in counter for the Hotel Chamartin.

Reach these stations by Madrid's 143-mile underground metro network. (Ask for a metro map—"Guia del Metro"—upon entering the system.) To reach Puerta de Atocha station use the metro stop called "Atocha RENFE" (do not confuse with "Atocha" stop).

Nuevos Ministerios station is a space-age creation of crisscrossing escalators, elevators, and marble floors serving as a high-tech transportation hub for cercanias (rapid-transit trains), three metro lines, and the airport terminal for metro line 8. It has 26 airline check-in desks with luggage-handling equipment together with underground parking for 130 taxis. It is connected by metro line 10, which has been converted to broad gauge, and cercania directly to Charmartin station, by line 8 directly to Madrid Barajas Airport, and directly by cercania and with one metro change to Atocha RENFE.

The metro trains are for the most part composed of the most modern and comfortable new carriages. Emphasis is on passenger capacity, hence a minimum of fixed seating. You can use Nuevos Ministerios riding escalators (no steps) but in the older stations serious flights of stairs will confront you.

A 10-ride magnetically encoded ticket costing €5.20 gives you a substantial per-ride savings and eliminates the bother of buying separate tickets costing €1.10 each for each metro trip. "Sol" metro stop below the Puerta del Sol, the center of Spain, is the hub of Madrid's metro.

Supporting RENFE's long-distance trains, Cercanias Madrid is an extensive and far-reaching rapid-transit system of 10 lines with fares depending on the distance traveled (a zone concept). Lines form a ring around downtown Madrid, with the principal corridor Atocha-Recoletos-Nuevos Ministerios-Chamartin supporting five lines. From the ring, lines run as far as El Escorial (where the new subterranean station was inaugurated on June 12, 2002), Guadalajara, and Aranjuez. *Tip:* These make worthwhile, interesting excursions. Madrid has 20 six-car double-deck units for use on routes where journey times exceed 30 minutes, where most of the demand is concentrated at the end of the line, and where there is more than 2½ miles between stations. This enables RENFE to put to good use the enormous seating capacity of these units.

Entering through the turnstiles demands a magnetically encoded ticket, so if you are traveling with a rail pass you must alert the guard that you want through so he or she can open the barrier for you. In Atocha station, look for the sign: "Billetes *sin* banda magnetica."

Along the underground train tunnel between Chamartin and Atocha stations, look for "Nuevos Ministerios" and "Recoletos," RENFE's small station resembling a subway stop. Line C-2 rapid-transit cercanias pass through these stops five times an hour from 5:08 A.M. to 11:38 P.M., taking you to El Escorial and Aranjuez (among others). Depending on where you stay in Madrid, it may be more convenient for you to board here than Chamartin or Atocha (check RENFE's timetable and posters on the walls). Automatic ticketing machines reduce the length of lines and congestion. You may find also that RENFE's frequent rapid-transit train service ("cercanias") between Nuevos Ministerios/Recoletos and the big stations gives you more convenient access to long-distance trains originating at Chamartin and/or Atocha than by a long metro ride or surface transportation—and these cercanias are covered by rail pass.

Reach Nuevos Ministerios RENFE station by metro line 6, 8, or 10. Follow the signs: "Accesos RENFE."

In Barcelona, a complex of three train termini and rambling subway lines that were completely rejuvenated for the Olympic Games is guaranteed to get you around town comfortably.

Barcelona's busiest station is the large Sants station (also called "Central"). It has everything. When it was new it was virtually empty. Now they have managed to create chaos out of order. It is a helter-skelter station, a busy transportation hub, handling as it does RENFE's long-distance trains to Madrid and Andalusia, regional trains, single- and double-deck local trains ("Cercanias/Rodalies"), "Delta" trains to La Tour de Carol, and two metro lines. Each has its own separate departures board. Schedules are shown on the information posters. Here you board Talgo 200s to Madrid, Seville, and Cadiz; Diurno trains to Cordoba and Seville over the old tracks; and Estrella trains to Malaga, Seville, and Cadiz. Sants also is the terminus for the Tren Hotel Pablo Casals for Zurich, the Salvador Dali for Milan, and the through Barcelona-Seville/Malaga Antonio Machado gauge-convertible Talgo train that uses the high-speed line between Madrid and Seville.

In the station you find money change, hotel booking counters, an in-station hotel (the Hotel Barcelo-Sants, *http://www.hotelbook.com*), and stairs and elevators to the tracks on subterranean level (choose the latter). Sala Euromed for first-class ticket holders and Tourist Information are both in the same row as the elevators. The Sala Euromed is open well before the first departure to Valencia at 7 A.M. Tourist Information sleeps late. In Sants station it is helpful to study the large, backlighted diagram of Barcelona's complex transportation systems all shown together. It includes RENFE stations, metro and provincial networks, and the "Ferrocarrils de la Generalitat de Catalunya" (FGC), which consists of a standard-gauge railroad from the Placa Catalunya that you can use for visiting Mount Montserrat and a meter-gauge railroad from the Placa Espanya running north and west from Barcelona. Both are accessible by metro and operated by the Catalan government.

The smaller, underground Passeig de Gracia station lies on the same line as Sants. Gracia, with an underground reception hall, is very likely the most convenient place for you to debark because its central location places you adjacent to Barcelona's subway and only four blocks north of the Placa de Catalunya. Be prepared to climb a modest flight of stairs.

Officially named "Estacio de Franca," the former Termino station was reopened in 1992 with marble, gilding, and a good scrubbing after a four-year remodeling project that cost $80 million. The 1929 original ironwork and glass classic facade was retained, including the station's clock, which has seen much turmoil during its history. The ornamental, historical lamps positioned at the head of each track make a distinctive statement.

The totally renovated station includes a huge departures/arrivals hall with restaurant and cafeteria. Franca's platform area gives you a feeling of great spaciousness. Platforms 9 through 12 have been either covered with concrete or permanently covered so that the entire central area gives you a feeling of great spaciousness.

Barcelona's subway network is undergoing massive expansion. All lines are being extended and 230 new stations constructed. The first new station, opening in 2004, will serve the campus of the Catalonian Polytechnic University. On lines L1 and L3 you ride 1992 Mitsubishi equipment, license built in Spain. On lines L4 and L5, you ride refurbished 1970s trains with air-conditioning added. The metro stations require much walking. To reach Sants RENFE station, use Sants-Estacion on lines L3 and L5, not Praca de Sants on lines L1 and L5. Barceloneta (line L4) is the closest metro station to Franca. Look at the area map when you come out of Barceloneta for directions to Franca around the corner. Passeig de Gracia station lies on lines L3 and L4.

The entire metropolitan area of Barcelona has a unified fare system for bus, RENFE's cercanias, and FGC. The area is divided into six zones. If you buy a ticket for zone 1, it is valid throughout Barcelona and into neighboring towns on any operator for 75 minutes. Change from one mode of transportation to another as you please.

The 1929 funicular from Paral-lel metro stop to the top of Mount Montjuic was upgraded into a high-speed system for the Olympics to carry 8,000 travelers an hour at 33 feet per second, making it the world's highest-capacity funicular. You can reach Paral-lel on metro line L2 as well as metro line L3 thanks to the December 1995 extension.

Airport Connections

On June 14, 1999, Madrid Barajas Airport was connected to the city's 1,445-mm-gauge metro system on line 8, so that you may travel to or from nearly any destination in Madrid by boarding at the airport. Follow the signs to "Metro." It's a long walk. There you find line 8, with escalators and comfortable subway carriages specially fitted with luggage racks. From the airport, you can take line 8 to Nuevos Ministerios and trains to other train stations, or you can change after two stops to lines more convenient to your destination. The tourist office in the airport will help you.

In Barcelona, board Cercanias/Rodalie rapid-transit line No. 1 trains for the airport at Barcelona's Sants station. The trip takes 18 minutes.

Rail Lounges

RENFE has taken a page from the airlines' attempts to build upper-class travel. They offer a perk that is not often realized by rail-pass holders: RENFE maintains "Sala Clubs" in all its main stations, which are like are first-class airline lounges. They are oases of quiet and gentility featuring overstuffed furniture, magazines, and television, with coffee and soft drinks, bottles of water, beer, and orange juice free for the helping. For admission, the receptionist checks for a first-class reservation coupon ("Billette + Reserva") on an InterCity (first class), Estrella (sleeping compartment), Talgo (first class or sleeping compartment), or AVE (Club or Preferente Class). You must reserve these trains anyway, so all first-class passengers including rail-pass holders should make a point of enjoying these havens.

For quiet before boarding, look for rail clubs at Madrid-Chamartin station (between the entrances to tracks 13 and 14), on the mezzanine of Madrid's Puerta de Atocha station, at Barcelona's Sants station (in the center island between elevators to tracks 10 and 11), in the Vigo terminal (brightly marked in the center), in Cordoba (up a flight of stairs), Valencia Terminus (by track 1), and Zaragoza.

Portuguese Railroads

The Portuguese Railroads ("Companha dos Caminhos de Ferro Portugueses," or "CP," *www.cp.pt*) suffered for decades from Portuguese economic difficulties and political uncertainties. CP has tried to maintain a comprehensive regional and InterCity network service for the country's citizens on little more than a shoestring budget. Ridership decreased as the Portuguese gained in purchasing power, and road building outpaced rail network improvements, so that Portuguese turn more and more to using the family auto. Realizing this, it is surprising that CP's trains run as efficiently as they do and are as comfortable as they are.

Portuguese trains are classified as Alfa Pendular, Intercidade (IC), Interregional (IR), Regional, and Suburbano, in decreasing order of quality. The first two require reservations costing about $3.50. Best make them at the departure train station minutes before departure. When you want assurance of a seat, tickets and reservations for the Alfa Pendular trains and the IC trains Lisbon-Porto and Lisbon-Algarve can be made electronically 20 days in advance.

CP's international train is the overnight Sud Express that connects from Lisbon and Porto not to Spain but to France at the French/Spanish border. There you change to the connecting TGV Atlantique train to save four hours to Paris. Reservations are required.

CP's trains run on wide-gauge rails, the same as Spanish trains, so you won't be delayed by changing trains at the border. Since 1995, when the Schengen agreement took effect, there are no passport checks or customs formalities.

In addition to the hotel train Lusitania between Lisbon and Madrid and the Sud Express, travelers use two other less-traveled routes for crossing the border between Spain and Portugal on secondary lines. In the north, railcars, with first- and second-class seating, take you between Vigo's 1990 station and Porto's Sao Bento station.

In the far south, the 2,185-foot, 1991 international bridge crosses the Guadiana River at Vila Real de Santo Antonio. Construction of the harp-shaped bridge, which had to be supported by pillars sunk in an artificial island because of marshland, took 15 years for the two governments to agree upon. Take the Algarve train (see section below) to Vila Real de Santo Antonio station, about 5,000 feet from the bus station and ferry landing for the still-operating ferries to Ayamonte. DAMAS buses connect with train arrivals, departing at 11:15 A.M. and 2 P.M. for the 20-minute, 75-cent ride across the bridge to Ayamonte. At Ayamonte, you change to DAMAS buses (*www.damas-sa.es*) to Huelva, which takes 60 to 75 minutes, or to Seville, which takes about two hours, 30 minutes. You can save money with a rail pass by taking the bus to Huelva and then walking about three blocks (15 to 20 minutes) down Italia Street to the Huelva train station, where the 4:15 P.M. Talgo Pendular train departs for Madrid. This is free with rail passes. Similarly, DAMAS buses from Huelva to Ayamonte connect immediately to the DAMAS buses across the bridge to Guadiana station, where you can board an Algarve train.

Using Lisbon's Public Transportation

Lisbon boasts a modern metro system that was extended in 1995-99 to double its track length, increase the number of carriages in its fleet from 245 to 361, and lengthen its trains from four to six carriages. You ride four metro lines, identified by color. These are red, with a compass rose insignia; yellow, with a sunflower ("girasol"); green with a caravel sailing ship ("caravela"); and blue, with a seagull ("gaivota").

Luckily for train travelers, the metro planning commission gave priority to connections to and between Lisbon's dispersed train stations. The April 1998 extension was the green line between Rossio and Cais do Sodre train stations. The red line from Oriente train station to Alameda metro station was opened May 1998. Santa Apolonia and Terreiro do Paco train stations were connected on the blue line in late 1999.

The subway stations are beautifully decorated but rarely offer escalators or elevators, so be prepared to climb stairs. They are remarkable for their originality and ambience. Many are magnificent, elegantly adorned with *azulejos* (glazed, colored tiles). Entrances are indicated from the street by large red "metro" signs with a broken-letter *M*.

Convenient special tourist transportation tickets issued by Lisbon's bus and tram operator, Carris (*www.carris.pt*), allow unlimited travel on all Carris buses, trams, and funiculars for one day (about $2.25) or three days ($5). "Passe Turistico" tickets include travel also on the metro for four days ($8.50) and seven days ($12). They are sold Mondays through Fridays from 8 A.M. to 8 P.M. at Carris kiosks throughout Lisbon and at Alvalade, Areeiro, Campo Grande, Colegio Militar, Entre Campos, Pontinha, Marques de Pombal, and Jardim Zoologico metro stations. You will find them outside the Santa Apolonia station, in the so-called Eiffel elevator, and at the foot of the Park Eduardo VII near the Praca Marques Pombal.

You may also buy the Lisboa Card valid for 24 hours (about $8.75), 48 hours ($14.50), or 72 hours ($18.50), which provides not only free unlimited travel on Carris bus, trams, the Santa Justa elevator, and the metro but also offers free entrance to 25 museums and monuments and discounts on various services. You can purchase the Lisbon Card at the central office, 50 Rua Jardim do Regedor (Tel. 343-36-72/3), the Museu Nacional de Arte Antigua, the Mosteiro dos Jeronimos, and the tourist office in the Lisboa Camping-Parque Municipal.

To use the metro, obtain a pocket map ("Guia do Metro") at a tourist office or subway station or check the posters in any subway station. A normal ticket is valid for one hour after being validated and costs 40 cents. A 10-ticket "cademeta" is $3. You can buy tickets in every station at an automatic ticket vending machine or at a ticket office. You must keep them until the end of your journey. One-day ($1.25) and seven-day ($3.35) tickets are good buys. You board the train in the direction of the last station shown on the branch you wish to use.

Carris acquired 10 articulated trams in 1995. With three air-conditioned bodies in stainless steel, they seat 65 passengers and have space for 145 standing, with entries made through four tilting doors. The low-floor design allows easy entries and exits, even to handicapped passengers.

Carris runs a fleet of 30, 1995, articulated, orange Volvo buses throughout the city. Consult your Carris map for route information. Arriving and departing airline passengers can use the Aerobus between Lisbon Portela Airport and Cais do Sodre train station with stops at Marques Pombal, Avenida Liberdade, Restauradores Square, and Rossio, among others. Buses leave every 20 minutes, from 7 A.M. to 9 P.M.

In an effort to ease commuting traffic congestion in Lisbon, where up to 450,000 vehicles enter every Monday morning, Prime Minister Antonio Guterres himself drove the first train on November 15, 1998, across the new rail line added onto 25 de Abril bridge.

Four-carriage, double-deck 87-mph electric rapid-transit trains built by Alstom/CAF in 1998-99 let you travel in air-conditioned comfort between central Lisbon and the south bank of the Tagus River in 25 minutes.

Safety engineers allow only one train in each direction on the bridge at any one time. You can board at stations in central Lisbon including Entre Campos (with an interchange to the yellow metro line), Sete Rios, Campolide, and Alvita.

Trains operate every 15 minutes, off peak, and every seven minutes during rush hours. Planners figured to reduce gridlock traffic on the bridge by 11 percent from 140,000 vehicles a day. The extension of Lisbon's yellow metro line relieves traffic over a second bottlenecked artery.

Rail-Pass Travel

The two-country France 'n Spain Pass vies with individual Spain and Portugal national rail passes as well as the two-country Iberic Railpass covering both Spain and Portugal and the three-country Eurail

Selectpass that could include Spain, Portugal, and France. Check the prices to see which pass best fits your travel plans.

With an Iberic Railpass you may travel as you please within and between Spain and Portugal. You may purchase one, for three to 10 days according to the exact number of days you plan to use them within two months. Alternately, you may opt for separate Spain or Portugal rail passes when you plan to spend more or less of your time in one or the other nation. The advantage of a rail pass covering both countries is that you will have to validate only a single day box on the day you cross the border. With separate passes you must use up a day box on each pass. The disadvantage is that Iberic Railpasses are priced for first class only, while you can buy Spain Flexipasses for second-class travel and, also, although you can buy them only in multiples of four days, Portuguese Railpasses cost about half as much per day.

Like Iberic Railpasses, Spain Flexipasses for unlimited travel on RENFE are available for three to 10 days of travel within two months. You choose the number of days you will be traveling. The prices for first-class travel are considerably less than those for a Eurail Selectpass and you can buy one for as few as three days. Second-class Spain Flexipasses save you even more.

The France 'n Spain pass covers the national railroads of the two countries for any four days of unlimited travel. Up to six additional days may be added as needed. The pass is available for both first- and second-class travel and has different pricing schedules for adults, two or more traveling together, and youth. Children under four travel free and those between four and 11 pay half the adult fare. You receive a complete list of bonuses when you purchase the pass.

Expressly excluded from all passes are Trens Hotel, the AVE high-speed trains, and Talgos operating on the high-speed lines, and to ride these trains you will be required to pay hefty supplements. Supplements for your use of all other trains, including those normally requiring *A* supplements, are included, but not sleeping or eating surcharges. Neither FEVE nor the Al Andalus tourist train honor these passes. Transmediterranea Line gives 20 percent discounts on all passes for its sailings from Barcelona and Valencia to Palma de Mallorca, Menorca, and Ibiza as well as from Algeciras to Tangiers, Morocco.

The Portuguese Railpass available from Rail Europe in the U.S. allows travel in first class on any four days in 15. The price is very reasonable, but Portugal's small size limits your train-traveling potential.

In Portugal you can buy Tourist Tickets ("Bilhete Turistico") giving you unlimited first- or second-class travel on CP trains and buses for seven, 14, or 21 consecutive days, but you must pay supplements and seat reservation costs to ride on Alfa Pendular and IC trains. Tourist Tickets may be purchased only at major CP stations such as Lisbon Santa Apolonia. The Terreiro do Paco-Barreiro ferry is not covered. Children four to 11 and adults over 65 receive about a 50 percent reduction on the Tourist Tickets. Similarly, CP grants adults over 65 years of age a 50 percent reduction simply by showing proof of age, such as a passport, when you buy a point-to-point ticket. Such tickets are valid only for travel between 9:30 A.M. and 5 P.M. and after 8 P.M.

In conjunction with Spain Railpasses, you can also purchase a Spain Rail 'n Drive Pass. It is a very attractive combination in Iberia, where automobile drivers enjoy staying at Spain's paradors and Portugal's pousadas. The Spain Rail 'n Drive combines three days of train travel in Spain with three days of Avis car rental.

The three train discoveries described in this chapter take you aboard the Talgo Pendular from Madrid to Santiago de Compostela, the terrifying trams through Lisbon's Alfama district, and trains tip to toe through Portugal.

Tilting Train Pilgrimage
Lazy Way to Santiago de Compostela

While you are lounging lazily on Spain's sparkling Talgo Pendular train, waiting for the television to blink on and wondering whether this posh train really tilts around curves as designed, you might consider reading chapter XIII, "Santiago de Compostela," of Michener's *Iberia.*

You are entering the Galicia region from Madrid and are still three hours from Santiago, your destination.

When one traveler made this trip, he came alive with Michener's sentence: "I was fortunate in reaching Compostela at the precise point in the year when I could best witness the significance of the town and its cathedral in Spanish life, for El dia de Santiago (the day of St. James) occurs each year on July 25, and is the occasion for a religious celebration of great dimension." The traveler looked at his day-date watch. It was indeed July 24.

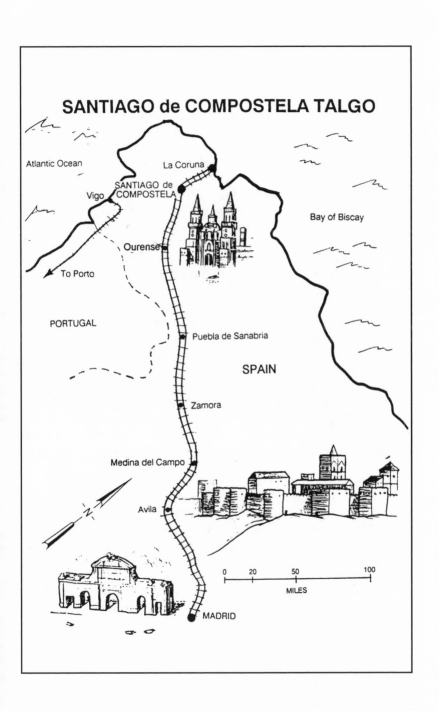

SANTIAGO de COMPOSTELA TALGO

Atlantic Ocean

La Coruna

SANTIAGO de
COMPOSTELA

Vigo

Bay of Biscay

Ourense

To Porto

PORTUGAL

Puebla de Sanabria

SPAIN

Zamora

Medina del Campo

Avila

0   20   50   100
MILES

MADRID

A pilgrimage to Santiago de Compostela is still important not only for the devoted but for casual students of world history. In A.D. 812, a hermit saw in the heavens a bright star hovering over a vacant field where the body of St. James (Sant Iago), uncorrupted by the passage of time, was unearthed. The apostle, who became known as St. James Matamore, the Slayer of the Moors, was later seen riding a white horse and instilled the spirit for the reconquest of Spain from the infidels. Today Santiago de Compostela's cathedral stands where that vacant field presumably lay.

Any pilgrimage aboard the Talgo Pendular, free on a rail pass, is a convenient, but lazy, way to visit Europe's No. 2 (after Rome) holy city and the site of one of Christendom's most venerated cathedrals. Santiago was named one of the "Cultural Capitals of Europe" for 2000.

During the eight-hour, 420-mile run, you are treated to the scenic contrasts of desiccated Old Castile and the twisting adventure of a mountain railroad into green Galicia.

The Virgen del Pilar diesel locomotive pulls away from Madrid's Chamartin station exactly on time, with a rumble like thunder. Your slate-blue-and-white Talgo Pendular is among the most comfortable riding and innovative in Europe. You stretch out in oversize, 2+1, deep bucket seats. They have folding tables in their backs, but when you recline, your seat's cushions slide forward so you don't disturb the person behind you. The 21-inch-wide seats have a 39-inch pitch in first class. Each first-class parlor holds 26 seats; the second-class parlors, four across, hold 36. First class is smoke free. Second class has one parlor allotted to smokers. First-class smokers head to the bar to light up.

You see a long, panoramic, industry-free view open back on the city through a forest of umbrella pines. Spanish children delight in eating the pinenuts, which are similar to chestnuts and almonds. Almost instantly the conductor comes through to check your reservation card and ticket or pass. Staff passes out the food price list and menu, plus earphones for the movie. About halfway to Avila (pop. 40,000), your Talgo enters the summer-parched high plateau known as Old Castile. Outside, the ground is rocky and not very rich, so you are hardly surprised when you come eye to eye with a black bull snorting angrily and pawing the yellow leavings of a wheat harvest.

Entering Avila, watch for Europe's most vivid enduring example of medieval fortification. When the station no longer blocks your view, your eyes rivet to the sight and you can trace out the cathedral and the crenellated walls and battlements not far to the south.

Past Avila, the rocks become more hostile and the live oaks juiceless. Your Talgo climbs relentlessly. It is uncompromising country.

You may have lunch, catered by the Wagons-Lits company, either at your seat or at the counter of the bar car located between first- and second-class sections. Dinner is not served, but the bar car is available for snacks.

When, after nearly two hours, your Talgo reaches Medina del Campo, a busy agricultural market and major railroad junction, and pulls to a stop next to the Eiffel-designed canopy of the brick train station, you can't help but remark how green things are becoming. Sunflowers are tall, pines begin dotting the hills, and farmers are harvesting leafy vegetables.

Your Talgo makes a *V* turn when the Virgen del Pilar shuffles by on an adjacent track and the new Virgen de la Macarena diesel locomotive takes charge of your train and pulls away with passengers facing backward. You rotate your seat to look forward once more.

In about 40 minutes, your Talgo Pendular passes Toro, the fine-looking village with picture-book profiles of the Romanesque Collegiate and San Lorenzo churches. The Duero below, one of Spain's five major rivers, flows slowly but still looks fresh and blue. Wheat flourishes north of the river, grapes to the south. The light blossoms of almond trees dot the landscape in spring.

Irrigation takes hold outside. There is heavy cultivation. Stalks of corn line the fields, peach and pear trees droop with fruit, tractors ready the slopes for vegetables, and, in the distance, sheepherders prod their flocks with crooked staves.

When the Virgen de la Macarena locomotive begins its serious climb into the Leon Mountains, it passes hay deposited in peaked piles. Burros and horses mill about. The land is now dry and soon changes into mountains.

Except for the handsome Romanesque facade of the train station, modernized to look very efficient, historic Zamora—three hours out of Madrid—now seems to be composed entirely of tall red-brick and white-brick apartment structures. The return Talgo arrives on the adjacent track. It left from A Coruna 65 minutes earlier than you started.

With hardly a warning, the video lights up on four television sets suspended from the ceiling so that every passenger can see them easily without craning their necks. The train manager passes down the aisle renting out blue-and-yellow earphones that plug into the outlet in your armrest. If you don't appear to speak Spanish he will pass you by. The audio is all in Spanish. *Jaws* and *Star Wars* are evergreens with RENFE.

About four hours away from Madrid, you first glimpse the mountain lake of Sanabria (3,280 feet), spotted with vacationers kayaking and windsurfers maneuvering their bright sails.

The mountain village of Puebla de Sanabria is a postcard-perfect picture of houses with granite roofs and white walls. It lies at the foot of the Sanabria valley, which is alive with streams rushing through its undergrowth. The black slate-covered station house with white lawn chairs overlooking the lake could be a model for a miniature railroad display.

You see the train is entering different countryside, wet and green and chock-full of granite. This is the isolated, rainy region at the northwestern corner of the Iberian Peninsula called Galicia. There are no seductive Carmens or flamenco dancers here. Myrtles and camellias bloom. Beaches are empty and churches full. General Franco came from here.

Galicia is one of Spain's least affluent regions and also one of its most independent. Its language is half-Portuguese. Its wealth of granite sets it apart from the rest of Spain, as do its culture and Celtic heritage. Bagpipes are the native instrument.

Builders have turned their abundance of the gray-and-white stone into barns, corncribs, garages, homes, terraces, and fences that range across the countryside in elaborate mazes only goats understand.

By the time your Talgo reaches La Gudina, thoughts of dried Old Castile are replaced by the view to the north beckoning with charisma. An occasional flock of sheep meanders to the train line.

The Virgen de la Macarena curves in and out of tunnels. This is the true mark of a mountain railroad. Fields look like patchworks. Ferns flourish on embankments beside the windows. Pastoral fields of corn and vineyards spread below. The majestic Cantabrian Cordillera Mountains rise before you, almost blue in the distance, crisscrossed with brown firebreaks.

This corner of Spain is on the western fringe of the Middle European Time Zone. In summer, the sun is still high. Your carriage for Santiago dawdles at Ourense, while workers split the train.

Passengers lug their suitcases up and down the aisle to get into the correct half. Some continue to the 1990 terminal at Vigo overlooking its busy, beautiful, natural harbor on the Atlantic coast north of Portugal. The segment taking you to Santiago continues farther to A Coruna, Galicia's principal port and city.

It is getting late. You are restless to arrive, but the vistas are some of the most idyllic in Spain. You see tiny, cone-shaped haystacks and grapevines trained on wooden trellises. The hills roll as far as the horizon.

The Virgen pulls steadily on a long climb until finally, a few minutes late, it snakes through the crisscrossing pattern of rails to arrive at track No. 1 in Santiago de Compostela.

The five-track, canopied, through station is across town from the cathedral, but still it is the popular destination for throngs of modern-day pilgrims and students. You find train information (but no tourist information), ticketing, and an ATM machine in the lobby. Orange-and-white "Region Galicia" diesel railcars idle on adjacent tracks. Lockers are located in a stone satellite building. The guardrails are lined with blue-painted, cast-iron cockleshells. This symbol honors those who came, beginning in the 11th century, not by tilting train, but by wearing out countless pairs of stout sandals.

Santiago de Compostela's Praza do Obradoiro, the square before the cathedral, is one of Europe's most magnificent. Across from the cathedral, Santiago's splendid, five-star Hostal de los Reyes Catolicos is part of Spain's National System of Paradors. This national monument, commissioned by the monarchs to house the poor, the sick, and the pilgrims, dates from 1501. It is the most desirable hotel in Galicia.

Talgo Service between Madrid and Santiago de Compostela

Mon.-Sat.				Sun.-Fri
1400	dep.	MADRID (Chamartin)	arr.	2130
1521	dep.	Avila	dep.	2003
1611	dep	Medina del Campo	dep.	1920
1700	dep.	Zamora	dep.	1820
1816	dep.	Puebla de Sanabria	dep.	1708
1955	dep	Ourense-Empalme	dep.	1532
2119	arr.	SANTIAGO DE COMPOSTELA	dep.	1347
2220	arr.	A Coruna-San Cristobal	dep.	1255

Terror Trams of Alfama
Seeing Lisbon Cheaply and Easily

You swoop and rise through hills and drops that measure a good 500 feet. You clutch, white-knuckled, at the grips of the advertisement-pasted cars while rows of pastel houses whiz beside you and glimpses of churches flash at you from cobblestone alleyways.

You look up and see stairways leading toward blue skies. Automobile horns honk on streets above your head. On your elec-trico's grinding struggle to the summit, your trolley wheezes, jerks, creaks, and chatters so loudly that many passengers standing elbow to elbow wonder, "Can this wreck take it one more time or is its axle going to snap and take me with it?"

Circling through Alfama, Lisbon's Moorish neighborhood that sur-vived the murderous earthquake of 1755, you ride the most infamous stretch of rail experience in Europe. Portugal's capital city can easily claim to have the most thrilling streetcar network built. Its tram system is widely held to be the most terrifying in the world.

Riding through Alfama on one of the rickety, two-axle trolley cars is an adventure that ages you prematurely, like a ride on a killer roller coaster. Part of the excitement comes from riding on cars that groan from heavy use and seem to go back to shortly after Ulysses founded Lisbon. They climb the hills with the reckless drive of San Francisco's cable cars, but Lisbon's terror trams, with posters advertising blue jeans, beer, and vacations in Paris, have no strong cables to save them from breaking away and skidding into the Tagus River below.

Most of the little trams are only large enough for 14 sitting on the green leatherette seats and 20 hanging on the cracking leather straps or clutching at the chromium-plated poles. The floors are made of brown, abused wooden slats with dust accumulated in their crevices.

As you ride downward, fascinating side scenes plunge past you and the rows of houses you glimpsed ahead seem to twirl around and fly past you on the opposite side.

Lisboans on the "electricos" (the name began in the early 20th cen-tury when electric-powered trams replaced horse-drawn vehicles) gaze calmly at the passing sights. Mothers cradle their babies and hum lull-abies while young boys stretch and rap the church windows alongside and smudge fingertips against the stuccoed walls sweeping past. Some alleys are so narrow that the streetcars fill the few feet separating houses. Pedestrians dodge nimbly into doorways to avoid the pushy, onrushing trams. Stop-and-go signals are essential on the narrowest curves to regulate traffic and reduce the number of head-on collisions.

Instead of the automatic, electric signal lights you expect to see, you sometimes find casually dressed guards still assigned to blind corners, directing traffic by hand with a signal baton and rickety box to sit on, coping with streetcars plummeting down the wrong direction of one-way streets and mad auto drivers sneaking behind them against oncoming one-way traffic.

So that the trams could maneuver through the claustrophobic maze of streets, engineers laid the tracks narrow gauge (only 23.6 inches) with only one pair of thin rails. Luckily, just when an approaching tram seems ready to crash into another and panicky tourists realize the emergency brakes might not be working, the tracks part at the last instant and the cars veer sideways as if testing the riders' nerves and sanity.

In such a hodgepodge, the safe use of vehicles secured by tracks embedded in cobblestones is essential. Their limited freedom prevents reckless or annoyed tram drivers from nicking or scraping the already peeling whitewash on the house walls (or the advertising on the trams, for that matter).

Find your way using a free map from the tourist office on the Praca dos Restauradores next to the Eden Theater. They also will secure hotel reservations and provide free information. Schedules and maps pinpointing the zigzagging routes of trams and buses throughout Lisbon are posted on the walls of the glassed-in bus stops in the business district and timetables are posted at stops on cylindrical orange tubes. You can buy a thorough guide to the public transportation system of Lisbon and its environs (including an official map of bus and tram lines) in the booth at the foot of the Santa Justa elevator ("Eiffel Elevator").

Running double trolley carriages through the narrow streets is out of the question. It would be indictable to try to pull passive passenger trailers around the curves. They are operated by Carris, the transit authority, using trams with bodies built between 1932 and 1937 in the Carris works at Santo Amaro on chassis built by Brill between 1899 and 1901. The youngest tram is older than the parents of most of today's straphangers. Rather than completely scrapping the antiquated remnants, in 1992 Carris sent number 270 electrico to Nuremberg, Germany, for refurbishment and subsequent return to the streets of

Lisbon. The Germans installed a new chassis with new braking and improved suspension and electrical controls but didn't touch the original body. With this new know-how, the Carris shop in Lisbon modernized 44 more. In all fairness, in a city offering magnificent surprises to walkers, the trams are convenient, if unnerving, and inexpensive. Considering the hilly terrain and capricious nature of the streets, it is surprising the trams do as well as they do.

Starting at Praca do Comercio you can board an electrico and, with an English-speaking guide, travel in one and a half hours through the historic city (Alfama, Graca, Baiza, Estrela, Amoreiras, and Seventh Hill). Departures are on the hour or half-hour between 9 A.M. and 6 P.M. (7 P.M. in summer).

Along your route you will find the excellent Miradouro (meaning "belvedere") Santa Luzia extending from the small church of Santa Luzia and built over the remains of old Arab fortifications. It is one of Lisbon's most attractive lookout points, where you will see a splendid panorama of Lisbon and shipping on the Tagus River. The Belvedere of Santa Luzia is an oasis of trellises, benches, and blue-and-white-tiled murals. Under the vines' shade, local men play cards and checkers. This is the perfect place to begin a walking tour down through Alfama but first to see St. George Castle, where Portugal's first king, Alfonso Henriques, conquered the Moors in 1147. Cross the road and follow the yellow signs pointed uphill to "Castelo S. Jorge."

Line 28 is in danger of becoming a tourist route like San Francisco's cable cars. Even worse, Carris has discontinued many tramlines and is introducing (horrors!) long, articulated Star-Wars-yellow streetcars ("Electrico Articulado") in a city long resistant to fads.

Prime example of 1996's Electrico Articulado is tram line 15 between Praca da Figueira and Alges, which is a relatively level stretch, and therefore unfortunately susceptible to the garish articulados. Riders of the articulated streetcars without a ticket push the button to open the doors and buy the ticket (coins only) using the automatic ticket machine inside the streetcar's center articulated unit. Those with prepurchased tickets punch their tickets at the validation units located at each door.

Leaving tram No. 28, and happy to be back to steady terra firma, you nod to your fellow passengers to say, "Well, we made it—this time at least. There won't be any articulados here."

The 1999 Museu da Carris (open Mon.-Sat., 10 A.M. to 4 P.M., Sun.,

10 A.M. to 1 P.M. and 2 to 4:30 P.M.), located at the Lisbon Santo Amaro
tram depot, displays practically every Lisbon tramcar type and many
other rare and interesting exhibits.

Portugal Tip to Toe
The Porto Alfa Pendular, Algarve,
Castles, Casinos, and Port Wine

"Under no circumstances should you take the train from the
Algarve to Lisbon." Algarvian Senhor Jaoa Lima, graduate of the
University of Wisconsin, was adamant. He waved his arms like a sea-
gull. "If you must, take a bus. They have videos."

"We didn't come all the way from California to the Algarve to watch
a video in Portuguese. We want to see Portugal up close, the people,
and how you live."

Lima looked discouraged. "The videos merely have Portuguese
subtitles.

"We complain continuously to the government for better train service to our region," he confided. "If you want to ride an excellent train,
take the train from Lisbon to Porto."

Contrary to Lima's expectations, the InterCity train taking you from
Portugal's Algarve region is spacious and clean, often arrives in Lisbon
seven minutes early, and is as quiet as a dormitory—except for the rau-
cous noises you hear resounding from the bar two carriages away.

Many Portuguese are critical of their country's facilities, but even
their secondary trains are decent, their food is never bad even in the
bistros, and Lisbon's subway is convenient. On the other hand, when
you say the facade of their magnificent neo-Manuelino Rossio train station is dirty, they say it is "discolored."

Because of the network structure in Portugal, you are virtually
locked into using Lisbon as your base for train travel. There are no
through trains passing through Lisbon. Lisbon has five stations and
five lines.

Santa Apolonia Station

Conveniently near the foot of Alfama is the dark-rose-colored Santa
Apolonia train station, your gateway to the trains of Europe and where
you may have your rail pass first validated at door No. 47.

ATLANTIC OCEAN

ALFA PENDULAR AND ALGARVE

SPAIN

PORTO
Gaia
Aveiro
Coimbra-B
Alfarelos
Entroncamento
LISBON
Barreiro
Pragal
Ermidas-Sado
Vila Real de Santo Antonio
LAGOS
Portimao
Tunes
Faro

-N-

0   50   100
MILES

Santa Apolonia is literally the end of the line for international traffic. It is a tidy station, but small. Santa Apolonia faces out on a taxi loop and a modern sculpture honoring immigrants to Portugal. It is easy to reach by the newest (1999) station of the Lisbon metro system on the blue line, or you walk not far from the city center or take buses 9, 12, 46, or 90. Buses 9 and 12 take you down Avenida Liberdade, the main artery, past the tourist office.

When you enter Santa Apolonia, you find the ticket windows 1 to 11 straight ahead. Although usually a formality, because the trains are rarely totally filled, CP requires you to make seat reservations for all CP's InterCity and Alfa Pendular trains from here to Porto and the Algarve. CP merely recommends reservations for IRs.

Through the middle is the train gallery. Track No. 3, where the "Sud Express" leaves for Paris, is on the north and on the south is track No. 5. You must walk farther down the gallery to find tracks 1, 2, 6, and 7. There are no luggage carts, but porters are available.

Down the tracks on the south side next to track ("Linha") No. 5, you come to doorway No. 47, which is the international terminal office for validating your rail pass, changing money at the bank (open 8:30 A.M. to 1 P.M. and 2 to 5 P.M.), and making sleeping reservations for the Sud Express to France. Next door is the room with luggage lockers. The luggage checking counter is nearby. The currency change machine is next to track No. 5. There's an ATM on the opposite side next to track No. 3.

The train information office is located around the corner on the far left north corridor (look for the *i* sign) together with the waiting room. English-speaking ladies give train information.

Oriente Train Station

Lisbon's stunning new train station, among concrete palm fronds, is Europe's most astonishing. The 1998 Oriente station was designed to serve the Lisbon Expo '98 site, but it is underused, serving as a stop for the Lisbon-Porto service and the double-deck trains on the Cintura line. When electrification of the Algarve line is completed in April 2004, Oriente will also become the Lisbon terminus for the Algarve.

With this work, Barcelona-born Santiago Calatrava secured his reputation as the greatest contemporary railroad architect. Like his imaginative Lyon Airport's TGV station and Liege Guillemins, Oriente is graceful with wide arches and sweeping curves.

The magnificent glass roof is supported by 15 50-foot "palm trees" that make you feel as though you are passing through an Amazonian cathedral. Descend escalators below the train platforms and you find Oriente metro station, beautifully decorated with colorful, contemporary *azulejos* (artistic tiles) at the terminus of the red (compass rose) line.

Lisbon-Porto

The line between Portugal's two main cities deserves to be served by one of Europe's most technically advanced trains. It is. The route that links almost one-third of all Portugal's inhabitants (in a country of 10 million, 2.5 million call Lisbon home, and Porto is home to 800,000) is almost totally double tracked with tight curves served by Portugal's Alfa Pendular train. You ride in one of 10 six-carriage sets derived from the Italian Pendolino design. The introduction of the red, white, and blue tilting trains, a wide-gauge version of the Italian ETR 460 Pendolino, on the Portugal's main north-south line was terribly delayed. The 10 trains were originally expected for the 1996 Lisbon Expo. The units were actually delivered from 1998 to 2000 and were plagued with problems. They operate four daily round-trip services between Lisbon and Porto. You can board the first train from Lisbon in the morning and alight from the last train from Porto at Pragal on the southern side of the Tagus Bridge, but the remainder originates and terminates in Lisbon's Santa Apolonia station. Fiat Ferroviaria designed and largely manufactured the trains in its Savigliano plant near Turin, Italy, but ADtranz Portugal assembled them at Amadore in Lisbon's suburbs.

These trains differ from the Spanish tilting Talgo Pendular trains because these use Italian active tilting technology rather than Spanish passive tilting technology. At first glance, they look like the Italian Pendolino, but Portugal's trains (the work of Italian designer Guigiari, who also worked on Cisalpino's ETR470 liveries) are nearly five inches higher and five inches wider. They also differ from the Italian trains because they use German rather than Italian electrical equipment. Inside, you enjoy TV screens in every carriage.

Shortly out of Santa Apolonia terminal, your train makes a quick stop among the concrete palm fronds of the 1996 Oriente station. You may of course board here, as well, because of the station's convenient subway connection.

Before your second stop, in Coimbra, you pass the city of Caxarias, where an interchange between local trains and buses was opened in 2000 to give connections to the Sanctuary of Fatima, the center of pilgrimage.

Coimbra (say "Queem-bra") is a romantic city with the legendary landmark fountain of the Portuguese Romeo and Juliet. It boasts the oldest and most prestigious university in Portugal. Your Alfa Pendular stops in Coimbra-B station, which was built on the mainline when engineers couldn't figure a way to divert the tracks into the core of the city. In case you wonder, there is a Coimbra-A station still standing on the banks of the Mondego River and still connected to Coimbra-B by heavy-duty local trains, much to the annoyance of the city fathers, who object to the intrusion of large trains into the city center.

At Aveiro stop, look to the west and the station's facade decorated with blue murals. This is one of Portugal's three great *azulejo*-decorated stations. (The others are Porto's Sao Bento and Pinhao in the Douro Valley.) A new station, part of the *Estaceos com Vida* (Stations with Life) program, will be completed in time for the Euro 2004 soccer championships. One of the city's most important avenues is being extended through a new underpass under the tracks to accommodate changes in the surrounding areas.

Before crossing the Douro River into Porto, you stop briefly at Vila Nova de Gaia on the south bank. The city is the home of the port wine companies. You then proceed along the south bank of the "Golden River," perhaps gasping as the best view of your trip comes into view as you cross the 1991 Sao Joao Bridge over the Douro River and the panorama of the old stone city of Porto spreads on the right bank before you. You see the old town, topped by the towers of the cathedral and the Clerigos belfry, rising in tiers from the Douro. Overlapping series of hillside alleys are lined with architecturally dazzling houses decorated with corbels and (occasionally) tiled facades.

Some 186 yards to the west, and built 103 years earlier, you see the original Queen Maria Pia railroad bridge built entirely of steel girders by French engineer Gustav Eiffel while he lived in Porto for several years. The bridge is now a national monument. It had to be abandoned in 1991 because safety engineers imposed a speed restriction of 12.4 mph and created a terrible bottleneck. The new bridge carries a double track and may be crossed at 75 mph, which reduces your Lisbon-Porto travel time by a few minutes.

Sadly, you leave your view of Porto when your train enters the tunnel and comes to a stop in the mainline Campanha station, where there are special Alfa Pendular facilities. This gives you a chance to board one of the many connecting trains and continue to the downtown Sao Bento station just to the see the great display of *azulejos,* which echo the skies and cover the walls of the reception hall. It is the pride of CP. Although in need of a good cleaning, they're a feast for the eyes.

Painted in 1930 by Jorge Colaco, these tile pictures include a full-color frieze of everyday life in Portugal and feature historic panoramas in blue: Joao's entry into Porto (top right) and his capture of Cueta (bottom right).

Across the Douro River from the lodges and showrooms of the wine producers, Porto is a veritable hive of activity and the capital of Portuguese baroque, epitomized in the church of Sao Francisco.

Porto has three train stations. The most important is Campanha. From here you will board the train up the Douro Valley or travel north across the border to Spain's Galicia or settle into a high-speed train racing south to Lisbon, but the Lisbon trains no longer cross the now-unused railroad bridge built in 1877 by Eiffel with a soaring arch span of 530 feet.

Trindade station is used to reach nearby villages, but Sao Bento terminus in the city center is special.

Daily Alfa Pendular Services

0805	1105	1405	1705	dep.	Porto (Campanha)	arr.	1115	1415	1705	2005
0810	1110	1411	1711	dep.	Gaia	dep.	1110	1410	1700	2000
0820	I	I	I	dep.	Espinho	dep.	1050	I	I	I
0848	1148	1445	1745	dep.	Aveiro	dep.	1030	1330	1623	1923
0919	1219	1516	1816	dep.	Coimbra-B	dep.	1004	1304	1557	1857
0943	1243	I	I	dep.	Pombal	dep.	0938	1238	I	I
1019	1319	I	I	dep.	Entroncamento	dep.	0859	1159	I	I
1040	1340	I	I	dep.	Santarem	dep.	0840	1140	I	I
1118	1418	1707	2007	dep.	Lisbon (Oriente)	dep.	0804	1104	1404	1804
1125	1425	1715	2015	arr.	LISBON (Santa Apolonia)	dep.	0755	1055	1355	1655

I = Does not stop

First-class passengers on earliest departures are served breakfast at their seats. First-class passengers on second-earliest departures are served lunch at their seats. All seats must be reserved.

Douro River Train

Your train from Porto, the northern capital of Portugal, running up the parched Douro Valley is not new, and not fast, and clatters somewhat, but it is in good condition and you have room to stretch out.

Just as your train gives you a sense of motion, the gritty landscape gives you a sense of being as you run east following the right bank of the Douro, the *Rio do Ouro,* or River of Gold, below.

When the river rises deep among the summers' infernos of the Urbion Mountains north of Madrid it is called the Duero; in Portugal, the Douro.

Your train's whistle bellows like a conch horn or a call for a fox hunt. Terraced vineyards embrace both banks, but when you look from the north of the river to the south, the orderly rows of grapevines appear more picturesque. Your views are sweeping and you are charmed by the valley's varied Mediterranean appearance.

Romans planted vines here, but the port wine industry traces its history to two sons of an English merchant, who while visiting some remote monastery in about 1678 sipped the sweet wine mixed with brandy to stop its fermentation.

Generations of winemakers labored to tame the wild Douro Valley and turn it into the primary residence of port wine. "God created the earth, man the Douro," say inscriptions on the vineyards. Wine is the valley's pride and virtually its only pursuit.

You may relax knowing that your train into the rugged country beats hours driving down bumpy roads along the winding river into the heart of vineyard country and that Portugal has the highest traffic fatality rate in Europe.

Out of Porto you first pass through the gentle green hills and villages nestling amidst almond and olive groves of the *Baizo Corgo* (lower Douro). This area's accessibility makes it the most productive and most visited zone but its wine is of lower quality than the higher and more difficult river regions.

The mountainside looks like hell to work, so it is surprising that the tenacious vines endure, struggle to survive, and even bear fruit in such a parched environment.

The secret is the stratum of highly permeable schist set in a sea of granite. The schist, rich in minerals, maintains the vines through the long, hot, arid summers and winters so bitter that "even the vines cry with cold," according to poet Maguel Torga.

In 1757 the Marquis of Pombal's bureaucrats turned the area into the world's first controlled appellation zone.

After about two hours your train brings you to Regua, a junction. Unless you happen to be aboard one of the two daily direct trains, you have some 10 minutes to change here. In Regua the wine is stored after harvest. On the riverbanks a few wine barges still depart for the lodges in the city of Vila Nova de Gaia across from Porto.

The transfer to the lodges down the Douro from the vineyards where men once trampled the grapes underfoot to the sound of the accordion, always singing, was formerly accomplished by great barges, with four oarsmen who guided the craft down the rushing river. Now transportation is largely by truck and rail and the wine press has replaced the trampling men.

Though some producers age their ports in their *quintas,* the estates founded by the dynasties of the port trade, they send most barrels from Regua to the merchants' lodges in Vila Nova de Gaia, where, since the 1700s, the sheds have clung to the steep banks of the Douro in a veritable maze of long buildings with the names of the shippers lettered on the roofs.

After the skins and juice ferment together the liquid is spiked with high-proof grape brandy to produce a red wine with 18 or 19 percent alcohol. Over 90 percent of the precious wine is exported. France is the biggest consumer, followed by Belgium, Luxembourg, and the United Kingdom.

You may change at Regua from your wide-gauge train to the narrow-gauge train for Vila Real, which will take you along a jolting but scenic route into the high, austere mountain range of Serra da Estrela. This nature preserve is a landscape of jagged boulders, pine and chestnut forests, and rich pastures that provide the source of Serra cheese.

In the higher elevation of *Cima Corgo,* the middle Douro region, you arrive at the jewel-box train station of Pinhao. It is famous for its *azulejos,* a national craft taken up from the Moors.

The *azulejos* on the Pinhao train station's exterior give you a vivid picture of valley life when producing port wines was not so mechanized. You see scenes of women plucking the blue grapes, laborers' backs bending under 125-pound basketfuls, *rabelo* barques used to transport the pressed fruit to the lodges in Gaia, oxen hauling the oaken casks filled with already fermenting juice, and of course panoramic scenes of the terraces and the Douro Valley and River.

The *Cima Corgo* is the center of the port-producing region where serious ports originate. Hillsides give way to steep slopes, green turns to brown, and terraces must be hewn out of unbaked slopes.

Your train continues farther upstream toward the Spanish frontier. The river becomes crowded between steep mountains and the vines become sparser. Although the schist here is easier to work because it is older, only the brave cultivate the land. For some this is a land rich in promise.

Rail passes valid in Portugal cover the Douro River train, but it's not worth validating a day box of one of the flexible passes because using the train is cheap. Pay $19 one-way first class from Porto to Pinhao; $14 second class.

Six port wine cellars in Vila Nova de Gaia are open daily except Sunday for tours, sampling and selling at various hours, but you can expect reduced hours on Saturdays and during the winter. Ask at the Porto tourist offices at Rua Clube dos Fenianos, 25 (Tel. 312-740) or Rua Infante D. Henrique, 63 (Tel. 200-9770).

Reach the port wine cellars on buses No. 57 and No. 91 from Praca Almeida Garrett next to Sao Bento train station.

Lisbon-Algarve

The best trains to the Algarve, the "Portuguese Riviera" stretching along Portugal's sunny southern shores, are two crack diesel InterCity trains that whisk you in less than four hours from Lisbon's waterfront Terreiro do Paco Station to Faro. The trains were cascaded from Porto duty when Alfa Pendular trains were introduced. Their exteriors were fabricated in Portugal of stainless steel but the interiors duplicate snappy French Corail materials and design. The only difference is the language of the newspapers the passengers read. The bar car features sandwiches, cakes, coffee, and bottles of liquor. Less expensive InterRegional trains take you along the same route in about five hours, 15 minutes, but don't require reservations.

The 1999 extension of the blue metro line to the new Terreiro do Paco metro station allows you easily to reach the spruced-up and now-exquisite Terreiro do Paco train station adjacent to the finest square in Lisbon, the Praca do Comercio, which is known to all as Terreiro do

Paco, the "Palace Terrace." Past the train station decorated with tiles depicting Algarvian city crests, you board, through separate first- and second-class entrances, CP's half-hourly blue-and-white ferries across the Tagus River to the Barreiro station. Rail passes are accepted aboard.

After your ferry crossing to Barreiro, follow the crowd down a ramp past kiosks, shops, and a waiting room through a ticket-checking station onto your waiting train of French Corail design. Your carriage is pleasant and the French-design bar car is available.

There are big improvements happening that will eliminate the ferry crossing. By April 2004, you will be able to board in Lisbon Oriente station and travel via Pinhal Novo to Faro and beyond.

Running 155 miles in three hours, 45 minutes, to Tunes, you may change to the regional trains to Lagos in the western Algarve or remain aboard for your connection in Faro for the regional trains to the eastern Algarve and Vila Real Santo Antonio for your crossing to Spain.

Your InterCity is not fast, but comfortable, and gives you just the right pace to distinguish the harvest years painted on the cork trees. You see sights you never see from the colorless, commercial highway. You absorb the feeling of the region as you observe casual cowherds with staff and cap and brown bulls with wicked-looking horns drinking from streams. You see olive trees, orange groves, pine and eucalyptus forests, and many small farms.

You cross what seems like an invisible line across Portugal. South of the line the villages consist of boxy, flat-roofed houses. North of it, they are all peaked with tile roofs.

Algarve Train Service

0810	1320	1730	dep.	Lisbon (Terreiro do Paco)	arr.	1410	1855	2330
0840	1350	1800	arr.	Barreiro	dep.	1340	1825	2300

Change between ship and train

IR871	**IC581**	**IC571**				**IR870**	**IC582**	**IR872**
0855	1425	1825	dep.	Barreiro	arr.	1330	1805	2211
0925	I	1855	dep.	Setubal	dep.	1302	I	2143
1237	1725	2137	arr.	Tunes*	dep.	0941	1501	1822
1241	1731	2144	dep.	Tunes	arr.	0935	1457	1817
1249	1736	2150	dep.	Albufeira	dep.	0930	1453	1813
1312	1752	2206	dep.	Loule	dep.	0912	1437	1755
1325	1805	2220	arr.	Faro	dep.	0900	1425	1741

Change trains

R5717	**R5727**	**R5733**				**R5706**	**R5714**	**R5722**
1418	1822	2225	dep.	Faro	arr.	0848	1353	1732
1448	1858	2256	dep.	Luz	dep.	0817	1320	1700
1523	1936	2328	arr.	Vila Real Santo Antonio	dep.	0744	1245	1625

*Change trains for Lagos (see table below)
I = Does not stop

Tunes-Lagos Train Service

R5902	**R5908**	**R5912**				**R5905**	**R5805**	**R5913**
1249	1733	2148	dep.	Tunes	arr.	0929	1450	1814
1327	1806	2220	dep.	Portimao	dep.	0839	1417	1736
1343	1827	2236	arr.	Lagos	dep.	0820	1358	1717

Lisbon-Sintra

Your trip to Sintra to see the extravagant Palace of Pena begins at Lisbon's Rossio brightly remodeled (1996) station. Terminus of one of the heaviest trafficked lines in Europe, Rossio station is located in the heart of Lisbon across from the Teatro National (National Theater) and the metro station named Rossio (on the green line) on Rossio Square. You enter the station through one of the most astonishing facades of the European railroads. It is in the neo-Manuelino style of the 19th century (connected to the adjacent hotel so royalty could proceed directly) but discolored by the traffic exhaust from Rossio Square in front.

Its interior is also charming. You see tile pictures of local produce on the east side and saints on the west. Visit the information counter (English spoken) on the ground floor, but follow the stairs and several flights of escalators all the way past various shops to "Gare," where travelers without rail passes buy tickets. When you come via the steps ("calcada") leading down from the crest of the hill above, enter the side door on the top level, where there is also taxi access.

The two-class, red-and-stainless-steel air-conditioned electric railcars built by Sorefame (now ADtranz Portugal) were introduced in 1998, although some 1992 units have been renovated and reintroduced. Four-carriage units, usually doubled, depart quarter-hourly from 5:08 A.M. to 10:08 P.M. through the long tunnel into Campolide station. In 2001, CP began additional service to Sintra from Alverca through the new Oriente station using 12 of the same double-decked trains that cross the Tagus Bridge. This is the first use of double-decked trains on the Sintra Line.

As you travel along the line to Sintra, you pass a disorderly array of suburbs. Finally, you see to the left Ferdinand of Coburg's palace on the highest peak of the Sintra hills above the Portela de Sintra station.

On fast trains your trip takes 45 minutes; nearly 100 trains run on weekdays. Outside the end-of-the-line peeling-paint Sintra station, taxis stand offering to take you to the palace. You can change to or from the cross-Tagus rapid-transit trains at Campolide station or to or from the metro blue line at Sete Rios station.

Lisbon-Cascais

Take one of the frequent, simple, one-class, stainless-steel Sorefame/Budd electric trains from Lisbon to Cascais along the so-called Estoril line departing from Cais do Sodre train station. Your 16-mile excursion along the Tagus River to the coast is covered by rail pass.

The trains date from between 1950 and 1979, although some of the units from 1959 were set on 1924 chassis from wooden-bodied units built in France. In 1999-2000 these units were refurbished—new fiberglass front ends, new doors, reflective window bands, new seating, modernized interiors, and air-conditioning—instead of being replaced, so that the 1924 chassis will continue service well into the millennium. Perhaps some will reach a century of service.

You easily reach (and find) the Cais do Sodre train station because it is the terminus of the green metro line opened on April 19, 1998. With a rail pass you ride up the escalators and walk through the open portals of the presentable, buff-colored station's gates to the boarding area, where video monitors inform you of your track number (according to destination) and departure time.

After the Alcantara station, your Estoril Railroad train passes under the Ponte 25 de Abril suspension bridge—Portugal's "Golden Gate." Note the addition of the new, lower deck to support the electric rapid-transit trains linking the northern and southern portions of Lisbon. The River Tagus has always been a major barrier between the two sides of the river, but the problem became acute after the 1966 opening of the bridge facilitated explosive growth south of the river and automobile traffic became so heavy that 30-minute delays became normal. It took up to two hours to travel nine miles. Construction of the Cross-Tagus line was awarded to the same New York consulting engineering firm that originally designed that bridge and modeled it on San Francisco's famous landmark.

You run a block from the Tagus until you reach the Henry the Navigator Memorial, where you begin to travel alongside the sailboats and Tagus promenade. Your best view of the bridge is looking back immediately before you reach the Belem station—a superb view. The lighting effects at night are particularly spectacular.

The Belem station is a convenient place to debark to view Belem Tower, the great Jeronimos Monastery across the highway, and the Henry the Navigator Memorial.

Past the Alges stop, your train travels closer to the Tagus and you have a better view of the shipping, the breakwaters, and then the beaches. All along the stretch from Alges to Cruz Quebrada to Caxias, looking back toward Lisbon gives you a fine long view of the graceful suspension bridge.

You don't appreciate the splendor of the coast—the blue water and frothy waves breaking on the white sand—until just before your stop at S. Pedro do Estoril station, where you see a nice panorama of things to come.

Estoril is your glamor stop, in front of the Casino. The tourist office is across the street. Past Estoril to Cascais, you pass beaches and luxury hotels. The bay and sandy beach for which Cascais is famous begins just before its unsheltered end-of-the-line train station.

There are departures for Estoril and Cascais about every 12 to 20 minutes from 5:30 A.M. until 2:30 A.M. Departures for stations as far as San Pedro alternately leave Lisbon every 12 to 20 minutes. On weekdays nearly 300 trains run daily in both directions. Your trip to Estoril takes 28 minutes. The faster trains make five stops along the way.

Scandinavia
and Finland

Savvy Traveling on the Trains
of Scandinavia and Finland

*Oresund Fixed Link—Swedish trains—Norwegian trains—
Danish trains—Finnish trains—Airport trains—Copenhagen
airport train—Stockholm airport train—Oslo airport train—
Stations and subways—Your gateway to Russia—Rail-pass
travel—City travel cards*

Hans Christian Andersen traveled by mail coach and sailing ship on
his first trip from his home, Odense, on the island of Funen, to the
Danish royal capital of Copenhagen in September 1819. You can make
that trip now in two hours, 40 minutes by Danish IC3 InterCity train.

The great Scandinavian writer was the consummate adventurer: "To
travel is to live." He realized travel meant meeting new people, visiting
new surroundings, absorbing new impressions, discovering new joys in
nature, and feeling vibrantly alive.

Traveling by train through Scandinavia is easy using the 1,366-mile
network of the Danish State Railroads (DSB), the 2,500 miles of the
Norwegian State Railroads (NSB), and the 7,000 combined miles of
the Swedish State Railroads (SJ) and private train companies. Finnish

State Railroads' (VR) 3,659 miles complete your Nordic adventuring. Ride them from where the storks nest in the chimneys of Denmark to the blue fjords and stark glaciers of Norway to where the Midnight Sun beats down on the land of the Lapps above the Arctic Circle in Sweden and Finland.

Your best way to reach Copenhagen for jumping off to Norway and Sweden/Finland is aboard one of six DSB IC3 EuroCity trains from Hamburg, Germany, taking slightly over five hours via the mainline named for the migratory flight path of birds. *Tip:* These trains can be swamped in summer. Seat reservations are essential. Make them well in advance. One train, the Hamlet, continues across the Fixed Link to Malmo as well. The EC Christian Morgenstern, the EC Thomas Mann, the EC Karen Blixen, and the EC Bertel Thorvaldsen terminate in Copenhagen. To accommodate these high-tech trains (see "Danish Trains" below), GermanRail increased track spacing at three critical locations and DSB modified the leaf doors of their trains to match the height of the German platforms.

Your EC train takes you aboard alternating half-hourly DSB and GermanRail ferries from Puttgarden to Rodby and on to Copenhagen. Remain in your train while it is being shunted aboard the ferry to Rodby, and after it is locked into position, be sure to dine, shop, and return to your seat when it docks. Don't miss your chance to enjoy an open-faced sandwich, Danish pastry (better on a DSB ferry than a German one), and Danish beer in the cafeteria. You buy cigarettes and liquor in the 24-hour duty-free shops aboard the ferries. Even at prices higher than at home, they are bargains here—something obvious by the long lines of Swedish shoppers struggling with fully loaded red plastic shopping baskets. Be sure to do enough duty-free shopping to last throughout your entire stay in Scandinavia.

In addition to Linx's mainline trains up the Swedish West Coast to Oslo (see "International" chapter), you can reach Norway by several ferries from Denmark or by new Trondheim-Ostersund, Sweden, "Nabotager" daily trains taking four hours. The railroads terminated the night train to Oslo as "uneconomical," but DSB arranged night ferries with shipping line DFDS leaving Copenhagen and Oslo at 5 P.M. each day, arriving at 9 A.M. the following morning.

Reach Finland by Silja Line ship from Stockholm or by bus (covered by rail passes) north of the Gulf of Bothnia between Sweden and Finland. The line from Boden to Haparanda between mid-June and mid-August reopened, but VR closed its rail connection from Kemi to the Swedish border in 1988.

Oresund Fixed Link

When Queen Margrethe of Denmark and King Carl Gustaf of Sweden opened the Oresund Fixed Link (*www.oresundskonsortiet.com*) connecting the two countries by tunnel and bridge, road and rail, on July 1, 2000, they changed train travel in the Scandinavian countries. After 10 years' construction work, trains began regular departures from Malmo's Central Station at 6:09 A.M., and from Copenhagen's Central Station at 6:16 A.M., on July 2, cutting the travel time between these two cities to 35 minutes, compared with an hour (in good weather) aboard the ferry that previously took you.

Engineers adapted 11 X2000 train sets to run on both Swedish and Danish electrical power supplies, and scheduled five departures daily on weekdays—every two hours—to take you via the Fixed Link in high style between Copenhagen and Stockholm in about five and a half hours, with stops at Copenhagen Kastrup Airport.

Combined with the Eurotunnel and Denmark's Great Belt bridge, the 10-mile Oresund Fixed Link makes it possible for you to travel without sea ferry from Edinburgh, Scotland, to Narvik, Norway, above the Arctic Circle. It brings closer the island of Zeeland (the eastern part of Denmark) and Scania (the southern part of Sweden with strong ties to Denmark), and their two cities, Copenhagen and Malmo, to form the Oresund Region. With 3.5 million inhabitants, the Oresund Region is the largest domestic market in northern Europe and the eighth richest in Europe in terms of GNP. It is larger than Stockholm and equal in size to Berlin, Hamburg, or Amsterdam.

The $3 billion Oresund Fixed Link is the longest combined rail/road/tunnel crossing in the world. Train traffic is running much higher than forecast. In 2001, 4.3 million passengers used the Oresund shuttle trains, 30 percent more than forecast. An additional 650,000 passengers crossed by X2000, EuroCity, Kuspilen, and InterCity Bornholm trains. Accountants expect the Link to pay off construction costs and become a cash cow for the two governments after 24 years of its operation at an average of 10,000 vehicle crossings per day.

Trains depart every 20 minutes by day and hourly by night between Copenhagen and Malmo. Travel time is 35 minutes with three or four stops en route, including Copenhagen Kastrup Airport. Fare is about $10, and discount tickets are offered for frequent travelers, compared with about $32 charged for automobiles crossing the Link. Charges to the trains are less than true cost because they are cross-subsidized from highway tolls in order to promote environmentally friendly train travel. You can use credit cards for both train and toll.

Via the Oresund Link you can take passenger trains from Helsingor and Copenhagen beyond Malmo; one an hour to Helsingborg and one every second hour to Kristianstad. Six of the Helsingborg trains continue to Gothenburg and one continues to Halmstad. Also you can ride seven trains a day up the Stockholm mainline from Malmo to Alvesta.

The 112-mph, silver-gray Oresund electric units resemble Denmark's InterCity trains in many ways. The three-carriage trains seat 20 first class and 176 second class and have 41 jump seats for those who wish to sit near their luggage. They have the rubber-ring front ends, which allow the driver's position to be folded away when two units are coupled together for multiple service, and up to five may be joined together. However, the new units are not articulated and have wide central doors and smooth rather than ribbed sides. The wide doors and low floor design mean that you can load your luggage on and off easily.

Boarding your train at Copenhagen Kastrup Airport, your train across the Link first runs parallel to cars on the highway onto an artificial peninsula on the Danish coast before you enter the 2.2-mile tunnel, which is the world's largest immersed tunnel based on volume, with four parallel tunnel tubes, including two auto lanes.

The Link was a trade-off between tunnel and bridge. A tunnel below the whole waterway would have been prohibitively expensive. A total bridge would have been cheaper, but it was necessary to build a tunnel at the western side to provide a shipping channel through the Oresund.

Surfacing on Peberholm, the artificial island 2½ miles long, your train takes the lower deck of the 4.8-mile world's strongest cable stay bridge. Automobiles climb on the top deck of the bridge and take 10 minutes to drive across the Fixed Link.

DSB trains run on the right; SJ on the left. To solve this conflict, right-hand running is used on the bridge and into the outskirts of Malmo.

You leave the bridge at Lernacken, just on Swedish soil, and your train changes from Danish power, 25 kV A.C. 50 Hz, to Swedish 15 kV A.C. 16.7 Hz power supply while coasting. The changeover in the westbound direction is made at Kastrup.

You circle through the outskirts of Malmo, with a stop at Malmo Syd Station, which is built in the middle of nowhere but is well used by passengers arriving by car and traveling to and from Kastrup Airport. Your final stop is Malmo Central Station, which is a dead-end station.

The Oresund Fixed Link replaces the most heavily traveled international ferry route in the world. There was a ferry crossing every seven minutes, four train ferries an hour, 400 train carriages a day. Each crossing took 25 minutes.

Swedish Trains

SJ (www.sj.se) operates only some 60 percent of the services in Sweden. The company Connex Sweden operates 1,600 miles of long-distance train in the north of Sweden covering Stockholm-Narvik (Norway), Gothenburg-Gavle, Boden-Lulea, plus Boden-Tornio (Finland) and Vassas-Umea, which had no service (see adventure below). Linx, a company jointly owned by SJ and NSB, operates the line between Stockholm and Oslo (see "International" chapter). Local traffic in Stockholm (SL) is also privatized. The Arlanda Express is run by A-Train AB. As a result, SJ had to take down the SJ signs in stations serving the new railroads.

Swedish trains are designated X2000, InterCity, Nattaget (night trains), plus Oresund trains and the Arlanda Airport Express. Ticket prices are based on relative advantage over competing forms of transportation, not on distance traveled, and thus are relatively arbitrary. Reservations are required on all journeys over 90 miles. Point-to-point fares include seat reservations.

Swedish trains are nonsmoking. This was necessary because Swedish cigarette smokers had been reserving seats in nonsmoking sections and then moving into the smoking section to light up. This meant some nonsmokers had to sit in the smoking section. Now smokers have to search out smoke ghettos in vestibules at each end of the train, spaces nonsmokers do not have to walk through. SJ removed card telephones from its trains because most passengers now use cellular telephones.

X2000 trains are the tilting blue-and-white, four-headlight (required by law in Sweden), stainless-steel bullets you see speeding across the landscape between Stockholm, Gothenburg, and Malmo. They are Scandinavia's fastest (running at 125 mph), sleekest, and most innovative trains. They hold the Swedish speed record at 171 mph.

Lacking a large population base to support massive investment in megaspeed trains, yet threatened by loss of business to domestic air travel, SJ manufactured the X2000 to comfort visitors' rides around curves by tilting like the Italian Pendolino (see the chapter on Italy) except that the power car remains upright in order to simplify transmission of electricity.

Traffic analysts determined that hourly departures for X2000s were essential to attract business travelers. Because of their frequent runnings, X2000s are short trains consisting of single power cars, two first-class and two second-class intermediate passenger coaches (the second-class coach with 2+2 seating was not added until 1996), a bistro carriage, and a driving trailer incorporating second-class seating.

Following X2000's premier running on September 4, 1990, SJ gradually added trainsets and departures to the timetable. Departures from Stockholm complement conventional InterCity trains (which make more stops) between city centers and make the 280-mile trip to Gothenburg in close to three hours. Air passengers need two and three-quarters hours from city center to city center. Motorists take about five hours to drive.

The X2000 is a big, roomy, substantial train. You probably won't feel it tilting on its run between Stockholm and Gothenburg, but if you hear a hiss, it's tilting. You receive a high level of service on board, sitting 2+1 in two different classes named "X2000" and "X2000 budget." First-class passengers receive a cold meal and plug-in earphones that you control by the console at the edge of your chair. The fidelity is good (much better than airlines). Second-class passengers must bring their own earphones (or rent), but they can use the earphone jacks. The Bistro serves sandwiches, hot and cold dishes, and some alcoholic beverages. A gift shop sells chocolates and games, etc.

You need reservations on all X2000 and InterCity trains. ScanRail Pass holders must pay a supplement to ride the X2000. This includes their seat reservation. Eurail-product holders pay no supplement but must make a reservation costing about $5.

SJ's two-class InterCity trains (which sometimes carry Family Carriages with supervised children's playrooms) have some of the widest seats in Europe, and they recline more than those in other European trains. Seat backs and tables are high—to fit the tall Swedes.

Some InterCity trains have a Bistro, serving hot and cold dishes, fresh sandwiches, beer, wine, coffee, tea, and cakes. There is also a shop selling chocolates, sweets, and games. On some trains, refreshments are served at each seat or from a kiosk.

Oresund trains depart for Denmark from Malmo Central station's platforms 5 and 6. Skanetrafiken's Svagertorp is the last train station on the Swedish side.

SJ's overnight trains carry you between Gothenburg and Ostersund/Storlien (the Night Arrow), Stockholm-Ostersund/Storlien, and Malmo-Stockholm. The Northern Arrow has a movie and Bistro carriage. Two films are shown each evening as well as a free short film for children. The Stockholm-Ostersund route also has a Bistro carriage.

The EN Berlin Night Express is a train of another color inside and out because it is a joint operation of the private company GVG together with the Swedish State Railways. The EN train with Swedish sleeping carriages runs along the route Berlin-Malmo-Copenhagen-Gothenburg-Stockholm daily over the Oresund Fixed Link.

The 800-mile Inland Railroad (*Inlandsbanan,* IB) between Mora and Gallivare is a private railroad offering a 25 percent discount to holders of ScanRail Passes but no discount for Eurail-product holders. Trains had been pulled by steam locomotives, but for environmental reasons Inlandsbanan AB now uses three diesel railcars with ethanol-fueled Volvo bus engines for daily tourist departures during two summer months between Mora and Ostersund and between Gallivare and Ostersund, which cost about $20 and $40, respectively. Reservations are required and must be made early at Tel. 498-20-33-80 or *www.inlandsbanan.se* or *www.ief.se*. The line is surrounded with trees, so "wild" is what you see on this scenic railroad—no mountains, which are distant, and few Lapps.

Norwegian Trains

You will appreciate the results of NSB's (*www.nsb.no*) renewal process. There are three trains concepts: Agenda for medium-distance journeys, Signatur for long distance, and Puls for short-haul commuter lines. Service to Sweden has been handed over to Linx AB (see "International" chapter), with the exception of two new Trondheim-Ostersund, Sweden, "Nabotager" daily trains taking four hours.

Three electrified mainline routes run from Oslo: south and west to Stavanger (the Sorland line), due west to Bergen (the Bergen line), and north to Trondheim (the Dovre line). From Trondheim, adventurers continue north to Bodo (the Nordland line) or cross into Sweden by diesel-hauled train (the Meraker line). The diesel-operated route north and east from Oslo (the Roros line) is protected by UNESCO because of its mining history.

During late 1999, NSB began to put into service the first of 16 gray and dark blue Class BM73 130-mph tilting trains with the brand name Signatur on routes between Oslo and Trondheim, Oslo and Stavanger, and Oslo and Bergen, cutting journey times by about one hour. The four-carriage Signatur trains are equipped with undercarriages adapted from the Swedish X2000 tilting train, but with steerable axles.

Signatur trains, which surely must be the ugliest trains in Europe and appear like racing earthworms, have interiors designed for long-distance travelers, with 56 passengers in first class and 151 in second. You can buy meals from the cafe/bistro car located in the center of the train or opt for at-seat service in Signatur Pluss (first) class. Comfortable seats and a table make it easy for business travelers to place their laptop computers and use the power connection. When you want to listen to music, you can buy a set of headphones at the coffee bar. Smokers utilize a separate smoking compartment. Young children use a play area with parents' seats alongside. Point-to-point tickets require paying a supplement that includes a seat reservation. Holders of Eurail products are welcomed in Signatur (second) class and pay the normal reservations fee. For travel in Signatur Pluss, railpass holders must pay a supplement. Holders of first-class rail passes pay half the supplement.

Aboard Express trains on the Bergen and Dovre lines, you ride in NSB's good-looking "B7" carriages, maroon with black detailing. They sparkle with good space, high-quality materials, and unexcelled ambience. Their panoramic windows, almost twice as wide as high, are safer and give you even broader views ahead. They were refurbished in 1995, when they added a stylish bistro car with Scandinavian-modern tables and cafeteria service. Staff in the new bistro cars offers snacks and beverages, a breakfast buffet, lunch, and dinner.

B7 carriages have smooth aerodynamic profiles, making them look different from other European trains. Longitudinal aluminum sections make them five to six tons lighter than steel cars, dynamic undercarriages send them around curves 10 percent faster, and air-filled rubber cushions dampen track noises and vibration.

Express trains have no first-class section. The nine-seat deluxe section is the "Salong," which requires a second-class ticket and a supplement costing about $31. These passengers sit in reclining seats and receive blankets, fresh fruit, coffee or tea, and one meal.

One carriage devoted to "Standard" seating offers coffee or tea and a newspaper. Travelers with first-class rail passes may sit in this preferred section without paying a supplement. Those with second-class tickets or passes pay a supplement of about $8.

"Economy" 2+2 seating makes up the balance of the train. The supplement costs about $3. You can bring your own food and let the scenery entertain you. There is also a "Barnetog" section for children and their parents, plus seats for the handicapped. The smoking section car is half of the last carriage on the train. Without pull-down windows, the smoking ghetto becomes so foul that some smokers are tempted to quit.

The first Agenda diesel tilting train manufactured by Siemens went into service northwest of Oslo on the scenic mountain route between Dombaas and Aandalsnes in October 2000. In the southeast around Oslo the first Agenda was introduced to customers the following month and by 2002 both Skien-Oslo-Lillehammer and Oslo-Halden routes were served every hour by Agenda. Farther north, 11 totally new Agenda trains entered service on the Hamar-Roros-Trondheim, Dombaas-Aandalsnes, and Trondheim-Bodo lines.

• The AgendaOffice compartment is designed to make it easy and convenient to work aboard the train. You find adjustable seats, a socket for your PC, and specially designed tables. Seat reservation is compulsory in AgendaOffice and the fee covers coffee, tea, and the day's Norwegian newspapers.

• The AgendaActive compartment is designed for people traveling together and for those who would like to listen to music or the radio on headphones, read, talk on their cellular telephones, or chat with fellow travelers. No reservations are possible except for adults with children under two and for those with disabilities.

• The AgendaQuiet compartment allows you to sleep or relax in adjustable reclining seats. Cellular telephones must be switched off. No reservations are possible.

• The AgendaCoffeestation has self-service coffee, tea, and hot chocolate in every carriage of the train.

• The AgendaKiosk maintains vending machines for snacks, sweets, and mineral water. You do not have to wait for a food trolley to come through the train, but you do need Norwegian coins.

Danish Trains

You have no trouble getting around Denmark from Copenhagen to hamlet. DSB's (*www.dsb.dk*) modular, 112-mph, IC3 diesel and IR4 electric trains with recessed drivers' cabins racing along DSB's mainlines are already being supplanted by the 2003-4 arrival of streamlined, blue and white IC4 diesel units that do not have the distinctive rubber-ring corridor connections of the earlier designs. The IC3 units are designed for long-distance work and the IR4 units for suburban, local, and middle-distance work. They are the world's most computerized—they sniff the temperature outside and decide how early to turn themselves on in the morning. First-class sections are marked with yellow stripes on the outside. Passengers rely on their seat reservation numbers to find their carriage, which is indicated above the carriage doorway.

The 83 new IC4 125-mph diesel units each consist of four articulated carriages seating 187 arranged 2+2, even in business class, plus 21 jump seats. You can put your cycle and baby buggy in one carriage with a low-floor "Flex Area." The new trains were built in Italy and based on the body shell of the Italian ETR 500 high-speed train, although the IC4s' aluminum bodies are shorter and each has one wide central entrance door.

The interiors are divided in "Salong" (first class), "Hvidepladser" (quiet area), "Familiepladser," and "ICpladser." All seating is in open salons. The seats themselves are arranged facing across tables in IC3s, and mostly airline style in IC4s. Opening the interior doors is tricky because a beam from the ceiling triggers them. Merely touch the center of the door to activate the mechanism. Adapted to the Danish countryside, where there is less than 14 miles on average between cities, these trains accelerate and brake rapidly, slashing journey times and increasing convenience. Both the IC3 and IR4 have the same aluminum bodywork, articulate, and employ the same microprocessor control system. These factors allow DSB to join them together to form a single train for peak-hour service.

Along the great crescent mainline taking you from Copenhagen to the northern tip of Denmark, your train dives beneath Danish waters through the East tunnel of the bridge-and-tunnel Fixed Link across the Great Belt waterway opened on June 1, 1997, to connect the Danish capital on the main island of Zealand with the peninsula of Jutland. From Zealand to the tiny island of Sprogo, you travel for five miles, up to 255 feet beneath sea level, in the two-tube tunnel with 38 miles of new track, including approaches. Passenger traffic across the Great Belt is now 77 percent greater than before the Link opened. Commuter traffic comprises 20 percent.

In contrast to your train's route, which takes you through tunnel and over bridge, the automobile path crosses the waters of the Great Belt entirely on bridges including the East bridge, the world's longest suspension bridge at 4.2 miles, suspended between two pylons, each 833 feet high (about six times the height of the Statue of Liberty) and 5,327 feet apart. Automobile drivers view the waters 213 feet below.

Train tunnel and bridge construction was a mammoth job. They reduce your crossing time from 70 to seven minutes and tie Denmark's capital city with the Jutland peninsula economically, socially, and politically.

Rising to sea level from the Great Belt tube, your train now crosses the western expanse of the Great Belt 1993 from the island of Sprogo to Funen on the 4.1-mile low bridge delivered in 1994. It carries two train lines and the parallel four-lane superhighway.

On Funen, your train calls at Odense, where many passengers disembark to visit the Hans Christian Andersen city. Others continue to Fredericia, the junction for international trains from Hamburg. Past Fredericia, travelers continue on the mainline trains north on the Jutland peninsula to Aarhus, Aalborg, and finally to Hjorring. There, travelers take the connecting second-class-only private train for the 12-mile trip to Hirtshals (20 to 25 minutes), for a Color Line's crossing to Kristiansand, Norway (both offer a 50 percent rail pass discount), or Oslo on the M/S *Color Festival*. They might also continue a half-hour more to Frederikshavn for the Stena Line crossing to Gothenburg, Sweden, or Oslo, Norway, the Larvik Line crossing to Larvik, Norway, or the DA-NO Linjen crossing to Oslo.

DSB and 14 local railroads (with trackage of 324 miles, including the Hirstshals-Hjorring and Skagen-Frederikshavn railroads) make traveling easy in Denmark by covering the country with a dense network of modern services supplemented with buses on quieter sections. Trains are classified InterCity (IC), InterRegional (IR), Regional (Re), and InterCity "Lyn," meaning "lightning." EuroCity (EC) trains run to and from Hamburg and a EuroNight (EN) train runs to Munich, Innsbruck, and Stuttgart. The rapid-transit S-bane (suburban train) network carries you through greater Copenhagen.

IC trains are the backbone of Denmark's national railroad service. They call at most main city stations hourly. Generally, IC trains link Zealand, Funen, and Jutland, starting and ending in Copenhagen or Copenhagen's airport. You can use IC trains for short trips all over Denmark but not for local trips in the greater Copenhagen area. Lyn is a special service that links most Danish provinces during the day, Monday through Friday. This service is designed for business travelers and requires a first-class Eurail product or ScanRail Pass. Re trains link local and rural stations all over Denmark. You cannot reserve seats on Re trains, but you can bring your bicycle, baby carriage, or wheelchair. "S-tog" is the Copenhagen rail service. Trains run every five to 10 minutes during the day and at longer intervals at night. The Copenhagen Card (see below), a 24-hour ticket, or a 10-trip ticket is useful for bus and train throughout greater Copenhagen.

IC trains offer Standard (second) class and Business (first) class. Standard includes only your trip. Business gives you a complimentary buffet with coffee, tea, and soft drinks. Lyn trains carry no standard-class seats but offer Business and Business Plus, which includes a welcome drink and a menu.

DSB provides no-smoking sections on all trains and allows no smoking at all for Business passengers traveling on certain IC trains. Baby carriages are allowed on all trains, but you need to book a space in advance on an IC train. Bicycles are allowed on all trains except Lyn and rush-hour S-trains. On some IC trains you need to make advance reservations for your bicycle. Most Re trains have space for six to eight bicycles. Pets may travel on all trains but are restricted to special areas. Mobile telephones are welcome except in the reservable resting area of IC and Lyn trains. Seats on most IC and Lyn trains have plugs for earphones and 220-volt electrical outlets.

DFDS Scandinavian Seaways offers 20-hour crossings between Harwich, England, and Esbjerg, Denmark.

Finnish Trains

Finnish Railroads (VR, *www.vr.fi*) operates about 260 daily trains traveling in both directions. For differing passenger requirements, the trains include a mix of fast S220 Pendolino trains, double-deck InterCity trains, Express trains, Regional trains, and night trains.

Trains usually depart hourly on the same minute after the hour. Connections are coordinated in Toijala, Tampere, Seinajoki, and Kouvola. Tickets include seat reservations and the extra cost of Pendolino and InterCity trains.

VR took possession of their first S220 Pendolino electric tilting express trains in 1996. Immediately they became the pride of VR. They are so named because of their speed, up to 220 km/hr (137 mph) on conventional track. They were so successful chopping your travel time on the south coastal route between Turku and Helsinki with a 95 percent on-time record that VR put a second series of eight more Pendolino trains into service in 2001, overhauled the original sets, and introduced a new Helsinki-Jyvaskyla Pendolino service. In 2002, VR extended their range, permitting shorter travel times, between Jyvaskyla and Kuopio and between Helsinki and Oulu via Seinaajoki. Compared with the first sets, the latest units have better snow protection for the tilt mechanisms, sanding gear, and low-noise wheels.

S220 is unique as the world's first wide-gauge and the most spacious tilting train. They are Fiat adaptations of Italy's ETR460. While the ETR460 has a luxurious dining car suitable for long travel times, the short travel time between Helsinki and Turku allowed VR to substitute the self-service "Prego" restaurant with 22 seats, four standing tables, and generous menu choices. Two seats are designed for handicapped passengers.

Every weekday you ride the S220 Pendolino round trip between Turku and Helsinki four times, three times on Saturdays and Sundays. It makes intermediate stops at Kupitaa, Salo, Karjaa, Espoo, and Pasila. Overhead monitors display the layouts of the main arrival stations. Giugiaro designed the Pendolino's interior, like Italy's ETR460, while the comfortable blue-gray seats and carpeting were made in Finland.

Each tilting train has six carriages seating 309 passengers, including 27 traveling business class and 13 Business Plus class. The trains can be hooked together to form a doubled train. You have plenty of room because Finland's VR uses nearly the same wide gauge (five feet) as in Russia because the lines were laid before Finland became independent of Russia. It allows these trains to be wider by almost 16 inches, and higher by 10.6 inches, than their counterparts running in Italy (see "Italy" chapter).

Second-class passengers sit 2+2 in seats equipped with radio panels. You also find plug contacts for laptops and mobile phones. The carriages have phone amplifiers. In business class, arranged 2+1, your ticket (or pass) includes the morning and afternoon newspapers, radio earphones, and coffee or tea with pastry from the self-service table. In addition to the papers and earphones, hostesses serve breakfast or a snack to the Business Plus class passengers. In business classes the food trolley also offers alcoholic beverages.

S220 Pendolino trains alternate service between Helsinki and Turku with Intercity 2 (IC2) trains of four to six double-deck, air-conditioned, totally nonsmoking carriages made in 2000. Telephone booths are provided on both levels, and there is a special play area for young children. You can use the Mini-Buffet no matter on which deck you sit. In business class, you can reserve two adjoining seats in order to spread out. There are compartments for travelers with allergies, as well as for families and the handicapped. You can bring your pet along, and there are spaces for three bicycles.

New Sr2 locomotives that set the Nordic speed record for locomotives (141 mph) are painted red and white to match the red-and-white InterCity (IC) trains with flashing LED displays on the outside showing their destinations and times of arrival.

VR times InterCity and Pendolino trains primarily to suit business travelers who want to reach Helsinki in the morning and depart in the afternoon. Business-class reservations cost about $5. You also must reserve second-class seats on IC and Pendolino trains.

InterCity first-class carriages consist of compartments with fixed seats and an end salon with fixed seats at the ends and swivel chairs around red plastic tables.

VR's diesel-hauled trains usually consist of older carriages, sometimes outfitted with video monitors showing American movies with Finnish subtitles. They require no reservations. You usually will ride them on secondary lines.

VR's night trains travel from the south to the north of Finland. In addition to single, double, or three-person sleeping compartments, the night trains also have day carriages with seats and a smoking room. Night trains consist of blue carriages and possibly car-carrier wagons. All night trains have a fully licensed restaurant carriage that is only closed for a few hours during the early morning. The trains also have a luggage van for the transportation of luggage, baby buggies, bicycles, and skis.

Airport Trains

Planners located the new airport train stations in Copenhagen, Stockholm, and Oslo so that mainline, long-distance trains call to discharge and board passengers. In addition, dedicated airport trains to and from the respective city centers serve the airports.

Copenhagen Airport Train

Three times an hour, since September 27, 1998, when DSB began its dedicated Airport-Copenhagen center Air Rail Train, these trains depart from the surprisingly elegant, subterranean terminal beneath the delta-wing-shaped Copenhagen Kastrup Airport for their 10-minute run to downtown Copenhagen. Your ride costs about $2.50.

The distance from Kastrup's train platforms to Terminal Three airport check-in is the shortest in the world, only 200 feet. Free luggage carts await you on the platform. You ride an escalator or elevator to airline check-in counters, ticketing offices, information desks, restaurants, and fast-food outlets. The DSB ticketing office, for travel to Copenhagen, Malmo, Sweden, and even Stockholm, and for rail-pass validation, is on train level.

Passengers not only take the Oresund Link trains and X2000 trains to Sweden, but on weekdays those heading west across the Great Belt bridge can reach destinations such as Odense with no need to change trains at Copenhagen's main train station. This arrangement makes Kastrup one of the most versatile of Europe's many airport train stations. From Kastrup you reach Odense in one hour, 45 minutes, and Aarhus in Eastern Jutland in three hours, two minutes.

The first international hotel to be built in Copenhagen, the Copenhagen Airport Hilton, is adjacent to the new Air Rail Terminal within walking distance of the air terminals, ground transportation, parking, and car rental companies.

Your 11-mile trip to the airport from Copenhagen's main station begins through a one-mile tunnel, completed in 1996 to protect a densely populated urban area with many businesses. You then cross the harbor on a new bridge to flat, very marshy Amager Island.

Past the new station at Orestad, the center of a new town, and Tarnby station, which is 20 feet below ground level, your train dips underground approaching Copenhagen Kastrup Airport, tunnels below a two-story car park, and then heads into the station.

Stockholm Airport Train

Threatening, with dragon eyes, Stockholm's otherworldly Arlanda Express (*www.arlandaexpress.com*) airport train with yellow face and gray livery occupies its own special terminus at platforms 1 and 2 in Stockholm's Central station. It has its own platforms, its own lounge, and its own tickets, although Eurail products, ScanRail Passes, and Sweden Railpasses are valid.

In the reception area you have a private waiting room and a counter for check-in by British Airways, Finnair, and Iberia passengers and SAS passengers with hand luggage only. There is also a Forex money-change counter, but the ATMs are located in Central station's main hall. You will not find any luggage carts, but the platforms are smooth, and everything is on street level, so there are no stairs.

King Carl Gustaf and Queen Silvia officially inaugurated the 124-mph, surface-level Arlanda Express from Stockholm's Central station to Stockholm Arlanda Airport on November 24, 1999. The trains take 20 minutes for the 25-mile trip. You ride seven four-carriage electrical units carrying 190 passengers each. All seats are arranged 2+2 facing the generous luggage storage racks. Announcements are in Swedish and English. It speeds so fast the signs on the SL train platforms seem a blue streak. The train is handicapped accessible. Service is from 4:35 A.M. to 12:35 A.M., every 10 minutes, except half-hourly on Saturdays and Sunday mornings.

Tickets cost about $13.50 for an adult and $6.75 for ages eight to 17. Those under eight ride free. Seniors and students pay $9; full families $27. Taxis charge $39 from Arlanda to Stockholm and $49 from Stockholm to Arlanda.

At Stockholm Arlanda Airport, the high-class, high-speed shuttle dips below the airport, making two stops. Its first stop serves airport Terminals 2, 3, and 4. Its second stop is for Terminal 5 and Skycity. Among the larger airlines, American Airlines, British Airways, Finnair, Iberia, and Swissair serve Terminal 2. SAS (domestic) serves Terminal 3. Air France, KLM, Lufthansa, and SAS (international) are located in Terminal 5. Luggage carts are available at the airport stations, and you will use the elevators ("Hiss"), not the escalators.

In addition to the Arlanda Express train, all SJ mainline trains north of Stockholm detour onto the new branch to call at Arlanda, making it convenient for all passengers two hours north, which at 125 mph is 250 miles. It also is convenient for travelers to and from Uppsala, Gavle, Borlange, and Sundsvall. From the south, trains take

passengers to and from Eskilstuna and Sodertalje to Arlanda, 25 miles
north of Stockholm, via Stockholm Central station.

Oslo Airport Train

The 30-mile-long link connecting Oslo Gardermoen Airport train
station and Sentral station takes you through the Romeriksporten tunnel, Norway's longest, which opened on August 22, 2000. Oslo's rather
ugly, tilting "Flytoget" (Airport Express trains), which officially
debuted on October 8, 1998, depart every 10 minutes between the airport and Oslo like gray bullets, reaching 130 mph and averaging 94
mph. Every second one continues to Asker, southwest of Oslo. The
trains are similar to Signatur units, but the interiors of the air-conditioned, three-car electric units feature flight information displays.
Travel time is 19 minutes. Punctuality has been good. Passenger satis-
faction is excellent. NSB provides in Oslo Sentral station a separate
check-in area for the Flytoget at the head of platform 13/14.

One child up to the age of 15 can ride free for each adult. Rail
passes are not valid on Oslo's Flytoget. Those with rail passes may prefer to ride InterCity trains between Skien in the south and
Lillehammer in the north (via Oslo Sentral station). Also, the day and
night trains to and from Trondheim stop at Gardermoen but at separate platforms from the Airport Express Trains. Your rail pass is valid
on these trains, allowing you to save the Airport Express Train fare.

Stations and Subways

Plan to use the centrally located train stations in all of Scandinavia's
capital cities as your bases. They all contain tourist offices/hotel booking services and are hubs for subways leading throughout their cities.
Their frequently running suburban rapid-transit systems are a convenience for everyone. When you book a hotel room at a hotel reservations counter in or near a station, ask whether your chosen hotel is
near a rapid-transit station. Using these trains saves you time, struggling with luggage, and is free with a rail pass.

Copenhagen's clean and safe "Hovedbanegard," or "head train station,"
comfortable as an old shoe, is a red-brick, busy antique dating from 1911.
Take a glance at the interior. The structure was renovated in 1994 to
expose the original roof beams and the original lamps were duplicated.
It is small, but very charming, accommodating 100,000 passengers a day.
Twenty-five shops and restaurants are housed in the central hall with a

post office at one end. Escalators run parallel to the ramp to the InterCity platform and elevators marked "Spor" (for track) located in the center of the main hall descend to each of the platforms. The "InterRail Center" (open daily, 6:30 to 10:30 A.M. and 4 to 10 P.M., May-Oct.) is a young traveler's haven open to holders of Eurail Youthpasses. It has a room to hang out in, toilets, showers, bulletin board covered with lodging notices and personal messages, and soft-drink machines. It is basic and funky, but perhaps more attractive to those under 26 because of the casual exchange of information with their peers.

Lockers located downstairs with the entrance at the west end of the hall past track 12, where they are electronically monitored, are safer and out of the way to prevent theft, and also provide more commercial space in the main hall.

The large, modern international travel center ("DSB Rejsecenter") is located at the north entrance across from the information center. Here you find free information leaflets for various international destinations and a free timetable for international connections. You can validate your Eurail product or ScanRail Pass, and Danish residents may buy the various passes available to them (take a number for service).

Copenhagen has a bank inside the station. After 8 P.M. closing, you may still use the ATMs ("KontantService" or "Kontantnen") on the wall. Outside, in the same block as the station, facing the Tourist Office is also a full-service bank with ATMs on the street.

The Tourist Information Office (open daily 9 A.M. to 8 P.M. during the summer) and accommodations service/hotel reservations bureau (open daily 9 A.M. to midnight during the summer) are located across the street from the station's east entrance at Bernstoffsgade 1, next to the Tivoli Gardens. There are several good hotels in front of the station and many cheaper hotels to the left of the station in a seedier area.

You may use "City Bike" bicycles free within the Copenhagen city area by depositing a coin at any City Bike stand. Your coin is returned when you return the bike to any stand. There is one stand on Tietgensgade on the street bridge over the back of the station platforms, and two on Vesterbrogade, the main street across the train plaza in front of the station—one near the 7-11 Market and one near Hotel Astoria. If all bikes are in use, there are maps showing other City Bike stands. Failing this, visit the Cycling Center rent-a-bike with entrance outside Copenhagen H station. Use the left station exit.

InterCity platforms are divided into sectors with video monitors to advise you at which sector to find your carriage ("Vogn") according to your destination. The kiosk at the center of the platform between InterCity tracks 5 and 6 selling optional InterCity seat reservations opens 30 minutes before train departures (and you are asked to be in your seat two minutes before departure). Oresund trains leave from a special terminal at the end of platform 5/6.

The electric S-tog (trains) depart from nearby platforms along corridors through Copenhagen with stops at Vesterport, Norreport, and Osterport. The 1996 fleet differs substantially from the former S-tog trains. The trains are comprised of six short cars that are two feet wider than the old ones to allow a 30 percent increase in seating capacity to 330. All stations on the S-tog network have an elevator or ramp access to the platform.

When you arrive on an international ticket marked "Kobenhavn," and not for any particular station, your ticket is valid on an S-bane train to wherever you choose. When you book a room at the tourist office across the street from Copenhagen station, ask whether your hotel is convenient to an S-bane train station.

Odense train station is surprisingly large. It has everything for you: fast-food restaurants, shopping, a library, lockers, and center for reservations and train information. Luggage carts are available for a 10 or 20 DKK deposit. The escalators taking you to and from the platforms help make the station passenger friendly, and you may exit to the "Centrum" or to the regional bus station.

Odense is Hans Christian Andersen's "Fairy Tale City," home to the Danish Railroad Museum and the Viking Ship Museum, and well worth an excursion.

Oslo Sentral station, christened by King Olav V in February 1987, underwent a complete rebuilding of the main hall completed in 2001. You find everything you need—bank, post office, tourist office in the station (open 8 A.M. to 11 P.M.), fast food and not-so-fast food, and more—because part of the complex is a virtual shopping mall as well as supermarket. Luggage carts are available on mainline platforms for a deposit. Ramps and moving walkways take you throughout the complex station.

In Oslo, twice-an-hour local train-service tunnels from the outdoor platforms take you through the heart of the city. Use stops such as "National Theater" to get around. An entrance to the subway ("T-Bane") taking you throughout the Oslo area is within Sentral station. Connected by walkway/overpass is the "Bussterminalen" for regional buses and also the airport buses, "Flybussen."

You may arrive from Sweden on platforms 14-19 in the Ostbanehalle, the former Oslo East station remodeled in 1994 into a light and airy annex adjoining the Sentral station. The Ostbanehalle contains lockers, kiosks, cafes, flower shops, a grocery for travelers' provisions, and a fast-food outlet.

The Oslo Transport Museum in Vognhall 5 (open Sun.-Mon., noon to 3 P.M.), built in 1913 on Majorstuen, contains a horse-drawn tram from 1875, streetcars, and Oslo's last trolleybus.

Trondheim Sentral station sports a shining 1999 annex with ATM ("Minibank") and ticketing for train, boat, and bus. The international reservation office is separate, in the earlier structure. Luggage carts are available with a deposit; ramps connect the platforms.

The famous Hell station is within walking distance of Vaernes, the Trondheim airport stop on the mainline, but you can reach Hell by the TronderBanen network of rapid-transit trains from Trondheim Sentral station, if you like.

Stockholm Central station is an expanded multilevel complex with all services and many entrances. Look in the elegant Orient Express Restaurant on the street level, south end, next to McDonald's, or enter from the street. As you would hope by its name, the Orient Express is decorated with original Wagons-Lits memorabilia. The Central Hotel Booking Service is on the street level (open daily, 9 A.M. to 6 P.M.). The Forex money-change counter is at the main entrance. Hosts in the "Citysalong" first-class lounge (open weekdays, 7 A.M. to 9 P.M.) invite those holding first-class reservations on X2000 trains to wait for their train in comfort.

Stockholm's Central station is well connected to the region with regional trains (SL) and subways. SL accepts rail passes; show them to the guard at the entrance gate. The subway is marked by a *T* ("Tunnelbana") in Stockholm.

Malmo Central station is a bright, cheerful station with a central hall brightened by sunlight through the glass skylight cascading onto comfortable wooden benches. The station is dominated by Forex money change (open daily, 7 A.M. to 9 P.M.) and Malmo City Tourist Office (open Mon.-Fri., 9 A.M. to 8 P.M.; Sat.-Sun., 10 A.M. to 5 P.M.) at one end, and a fast-food outlet at the other. A single ATM faces Forex in the central hall. Malmo C is an easy station because it is on one level with no stairs to climb. Luggage carts are available on the platform for a deposit of a 5 or 10 SEK coin. Oresund trains depart from platform 5/6.

Gothenburg Central station, remodeled in 1993, impresses with extensive wooden paneling and judicious use of glass to make it bright and comfortable. Hosts at the "Citysalong" lounge opposite platform 2 welcome first-class ticket and pass holders. Free coffee and cookies are available.

Helsinki's 1919 art nouveau train station is a wonder. On both sides of the handsome building's main entrance you see massive granite sentinels holding large glass-and-copper globes that illuminate the front of the red-granite building at night. The 156-foot-tall clock tower above is still one of the highest in Helsinki. The restaurant was refurbished in 2002 as near to its original state as possible. It has been renamed "Asemaravintola," meaning "station restaurant."

The Helsinki ticketing/reservations room chimes with bells calling customers to the windows. Take a number: green button for Finnish trains; white for international trains including trains to Russia, which agents handle in the back of the hall. For information, visit the small office to the right at the entrance to save time.

When you arrive by train seeking a hotel, do not go into the arrivals hall. Pass directly to the entrance next to track 11 for "Hotelcentralen" (open Mon.-Sat., 9 A.M. to 7 P.M.; Sun., 10 A.M. to 6 P.M.). Agents make reservations for you and give you all information about Helsinki as well as other Finnish towns you may want to visit. There is also a hotel console for you to make reservations by telephone. The post office/Postal Museum (free admission) faces the station. Look for the subway entrance, an *M* for "Metroon/Metron," down an escalator in a busy shopping center.

The small *Turku* station has a restaurant upstairs, ticketing, and tourist kiosk where you can buy your Turku Card (see below) and receive information, but not make hotel reservations—just telephone numbers. The electronic departures board shows trains for Helsinki, IC departures for Kuopio, and *P* train departures for Pieksamaki and Tampere. There is also a Turku satama station to convey passengers arriving and departing on the great Baltic ferries.

Your Gateway to Russia

Your Eurail product, ScanRail Pass, or Finnrail Pass is valid to Finland's Russian border, so you save nearly half on your ticket from

Helsinki to St. Petersburg by showing your pass at the international ticketing section in Helsinki's station. *Tip:* If you don't plan to return to Helsinki, time your trip to coincide with the expiration of your consecutive-day rail pass. Pass holders entering Finland from Russia may have their passes validated by the Finnish train conductor on board.

Sibelius is the second-class-only Finnish morning train to St. Petersburg using dual-voltage Pendolinos. Repin is the Russian afternoon train to St. Petersburg, and Tolstoi is the Russian night train to Moscow. All trains stop at Vyborg and call at St. Petersburg Ladoga station, opened on May 16, 2003, as part of the city's 300th anniversary celebrations. The Repin and Tolstoi trains and their crews are Russian. All coaches have their own coach attendants. First-class passengers (two passengers per compartment suitable for sleeping) on the Repin receive a soft drink with sweet snack served at their seat. Second-class passengers on the Repin sit six per compartment. The Tolstoi night train is air-conditioned with a closed WC system and electronic data displays. You will enjoy the longer couchette berths. Second-class ticket holders sleep in four-person compartments. First-class passengers sleep in compartments for two persons.

All trains have a restaurant carriage. You may pay your bills aboard the Sibelius with euros, Swedish crowns, British pounds, or U.S. dollars, or you may use a credit card. In Finland, you pay the restaurant bills in the Tolstoi with euros; in Russia, with Russian rubles.

The Russian Connection from Helsinki

Sibelius	Repin	Tolstoi				Tolstoi	Repin	Sibelius
0742	1542	1742	dep.	HELSINKI	arr.	1118	1218	2118
0831	1632	1834	dep.	Riihimaki	dep.	I	1132	2032
0903	1705	1912	dep.	Lahti	dep.	I	1057	1957
0937	1739	1954	dep.	Kouvola	dep.	I	1024	1924
1046	1848	2128	dep.	Vainikkala*	dep.	I	0924	1834
1245	2027	2346	dep.	Vyborg	dep.	0801	0934	1834
1426	2227	0130	arr.	ST. PETERSBURG (Ladoga Station)	dep.	0541	0731	1631
I	I	0825	arr.	MOSCOW (October Station)	dep.	2250	I	I

*Note time change
I = Does not travel this route

Rail-Pass Travel

Eurail products are valid on the national railroads of all four Nordic countries, on the railroad buses in Finland, and on the railroad ferries in Denmark. Eurail products can be used on all the networks as well or can be combined with travel in other adjoining countries, such as Germany. Eurail products allow holders a slight discount aboard Silja Line between Stockholm and Helsinki, Turku and Mariehamn, but the pass must be valid in Finland and Sweden. Superfast Ferries provides free transportation between Hanko, Finland, and Rostock, Germany, when the pass is valid in both countries. Finnjet, between Helsinki and Rostock, gives a 50 percent reduction in Budget or Tourist Class when booked within seven days before departure.

The Rodby-Puttgarden ferry is free when the pass is valid in both Germany and Denmark. The free ferry between Helsingborg, Sweden, and Helsingor, Denmark, is available when the pass is valid in both countries.

You receive 50 percent off on the Hjorring-Hirtshals and Frederikshavn-Skagen railroads in Denmark, as well as 25 percent off admission to the Danish Railway Museum in Odense.

Reduced boat-travel bonuses include 30 percent off Stena Line Frederikshavn-Gothenburg and 50 percent off Hirtshals-Kristiansand, Frederikshavn-Larvik, Trelleborg-Travemunde, Trelleborg-Rostock, and ANS Flaggruter Bergen-Haugesund-Stavanger.

The railroads of Denmark, Norway, Sweden, and Finland together offer second-class *ScanRail Passes* for unlimited travel on either a flexipass or consecutive-day basis on northern Europe's four networks and include the buses connecting the networks of Sweden and Finland north of the Gulf of Bothnia. Buy them for five or 10 travel days in two months or 21 days of consecutive travel. They save big compared to Eurail products of the same durations. Adults over 60 receive an 11 percent discount buying a ScanRail 60 Pass. Children four-11 pay half the adult fare. Youth passes cost about 30 percent less than adult passes.

ScanRail Passes are available from agents in North America and Britain; in North America through Rail Europe, Destination Europe Resources, CIT Travel, and ACP Rail International. They are also available in Scandinavia with the restrictions that the five-day Flexipass is limited to 15 days' validity, the 10-day Flexipass is not available, and only three days travel are allowed in the country of purchase. ScanRail

Passes issued in North America consist of a single ticket for your name, signature, and validity limits that the agent inks in when you present it for validation and stamping in Scandinavia or Finland. You also see a network of day boxes for you to complete sequentially when you travel.

With a ScanRail Pass, you receive more than the bonuses listed for Eurail products, including discounts on youth hostels and Oslo cards.

Not included are supplements for the Flam railroad (about $6), DSB IC trains, SJ X2000 trains, Linx, VR IC and S220 Pendolino trains, seating in NSB's Signatur trains' premium sections, and reservation fees.

A ScanRail Pass gives you 25-50 percent discounts on Silja Line and Viking Line ferries between Stockholm and Helsinki and Stockholm and Turku.

A ScanRail Pass also gives you 50 percent discounts on
• Stena Line ferries between Frederikshavn and Gothenburg, Frederikshavn and Oslo, and Varberg and Grena (you must make seat reservations),
• Bornholmstrafikken between Copenhagen and Ronne and between Ystad and Ronne,
• Color Line ferries between Hirtshals and Kristiansand, Frederikshavn and Larvik, Hirtshals and Oslo, and Hirtshals and Larvik,
• TT Line ferries between Travemunde and Trelleborg and between Trelleborg and Rostock,
• High-speed catamarans ("Flaggruten") between Stavanger and Bergen,
• Hjorring Railroad between Hjorring and Hirtshals,
• Skagen Railroad between Frederikshavn and Skagen, and
• Bus routes operated by Nordtrafikk AS, A/S TIRB-rutene, FFR, Ofotens Bilruter, Saltens Bilruter, Nordtrafikk Harstad, Nordfjordekspressen, Moreekspressen, Morelinjen, Sogn og Fjordane Ekspressen, Vestlandsbussen, Fjordekspressen, and Ekspressbussen Bergen-Trondheim.

Your ScanRail Pass entitles you to free entrance to the Gavle Railroad Museum, where SJ 4-6-2 steam loco is SJ's "parade loco" and is resplendent on the Gavle roundhouse; Hamar and Hyvinge railroad museums; plus a 50 percent discount at the Odense Railroad Museum.

It allows a discount in more than 160 Nordic hotels of the Best Western chain.

Norway Rail Passes allow for unlimited travel on NSB only. They are available for either three, four, or five days' second-class travel within one month. Passengers 60 and over receive a 25 percent discount. Children under 16 pay half the adult fare. The four- and five-day versions are only available outside Scandinavia. Within Norway, you can purchase the pass also for seven or 14 consecutive days. NSB automatically gives half off to travelers over 67 for train tickets. Buy passes and tickets at any train station in Norway. Norwegian students receive discounts, but foreign students with foreign student cards are out of luck.

The Norway Rail Pass is not valid on the Flam railroad, but pass holders receive a 30 percent discount. A supplement is required for Signatur Express trains.

On "green departures" (off-peak departures are marked with a green point in the timetable), students can purchase for 60 percent off a special one-way ticket for point-to-point travel with no stopovers allowed, and adults can take two children up to 12 years of age free. You must purchase these tickets one day in advance at any train station in Norway.

A *Sweden Railpass* is available for three to eight travel days in one month, either first or second class. Up to two children travel free with each adult. In Sweden, travelers over 65 receive a 50 percent discount on train tickets. Just show your passport.

Finnrail Passes are available for unlimited first- or second-class travel for three, five, or 10 travel days within a month. They are distributed in the U.S. by Rail Europe, Destination Europe Resources, Scantours (Tel. 800-223-7226), and Sea'N Air Travel (Tel. 800-848-6444), or you can buy them (or Senior Passes) in euros at VR's major stations or when you step off the Silja Line ferries in the Silja Line terminals.

Travelers 65 and over receive half off on tickets for trips covering at least 48 miles one way. Just present your passport. All trains in Finland give a 20 percent discount for three or more adults traveling together. When you travel with a group of 10 or more, you are eligible for a 25-50 percent discount. These discounts are only available at train stations in Finland. VR designates "green departures," giving a 15 percent reduction on nonpeak trains, even on already reduced fares such as those for seniors, students, and children under 16.

The Holiday Pass is your travel bargain for summer (June 1-Aug. 31) travel in Finland. It is valid for three days within a month, second class. VR charges a supplement for Pendolino trains, but you receive discounts from major Finnish hotel chains. Juniors under 16 travel free with a regular-price ticket. The price is about 25 percent less than an equivalent Finnrail Pass.

Over 700 clean and modern express buses leave Helsinki every day for all parts of the country. Traveling by bus is especially practical in Lapland, where buses are the main form of public transportation. You can buy a Coach Holiday Ticket, which allows you to travel up to 525 miles during any two-week period, at any bus station or travel agency in Finland.

In Denmark you can buy a "Pendlerskort" for 30 days unlimited travel on all DSB services. It costs about $480, first class; $330, second. Second-class seat reservations cost about $2; business-class reservations are included in the price. A photo card is required.

DSB discounts fares for groups of eight adults traveling together and offers half-price tickets to those over 65, but you need to ask. You can buy 10-ride passes for about a 20 percent discount. Children under nine travel free. Those aged 10 to 15 pay about half the adult fare.

City Travel Cards

In larger cities in the Nordic countries you can usually buy city travel cards to save money on local trains, buses, subways, and sometimes ferries. Buy them valid for one, two, or three days at train stations, tourist offices, hotels, and kiosks in their areas. These cards are especially economical for local transportation when you are traveling with a flexi Eurail product or ScanRail Flexipass, so that you can save your day-box validations for long trips.

The Copenhagen Card, with half-price for children aged five to 11, inclusive, gives you free transportation on the S-train network and buses in the entire metropolitan region including all of North Zealand, Roskilde, and Koge; discounts to Sweden; and free admission to more than 70 surprisingly varied museums and castles, such as the Tivoli Gardens, HT Museum for streetcars and buses in Rodovre, and the Classic Automobile Museum. When you show the card, more than 20 restaurants offer two drinks for the price of one. The helpful booklet that comes with the card lists admission prices for adults and children, open hours, and buses and trains and includes a reference map. The booklet alone is worth the card price. You can buy it valid for 24 (about $24), 48 (about $39), or 72 (about $49) hours. For information, access *www.visitcopenhagen.dk.*

All trains and buses in the greater Copenhagen area are part of a common fare and ticket system. You use the same tickets on trains and buses and fares are calculated the same way. Greater Copenhagen is divided into 95 zones and you pay to enter every one. It's a bewildering system. If you have trouble programming your VCR, a glance at the color-coded maps in stations and at bus stops will show you that it is hopeless. Luckily, downtown Copenhagen is all in one zone and the minimum fare covers two zones, which is just about anywhere a typical traveler will go. The Copenhagen transit authority (HT) sells a 24-hour ticket for unlimited bus or train travel in the greater Copenhagen area. All you have to do is validate it in the bus or at the station before starting. Then you can get on and off as you please. You don't have to worry about zones.

Oslo Cards provide free admission to most Oslo museums and sights plus you receive unlimited free travel by streetcar, bus, train, boat, and subway within Oslo, including NSB commuter trains within Oslo, free car parking, and more. The seven-day card gives you 30 percent off round trips from Oslo to anywhere in Norway. The Oslo Package consists of discounted hotel accommodations, breakfast, and the Oslo Card. Apply at the tourist office in Oslo's Sentral train station.

In Norway you can buy similar Stavanger and Bergen cards and packages. In addition to the perks included in the Oslo Card, the Stavanger card provides a 50 percent discount on the catamarans between Stavanger and Lysebotn and a 25 percent discount on the catamaran to Bergen. The Bergen Card provides free bus transportation within the city limits and free admission to most museums and attractions, including the Mount Floien funicular. You can buy it at the train station, Tourist Information at Vagsallmenningen, some hotels, and the express bus terminal, valid for 24 or 48 hours.

Stockholm Cards include unlimited free travel by bus, metro, and local trains (except airport buses), free parking, free sightseeing by boat with Stockholm Sightseeing, free one-hour bus sightseeing with City Sightseeing, free admission at 70 attractions and museums, a round trip by boat to Drottningholm for the price of a one-way ticket, and many more discounts on cruises, shopping, and dining.

When you need only a discount card to get around Stockholm, buy an "SL Tourist Card" at subway station entrances for one-third the price of a Stockholm Card. It is valid for a day (choose between either the inner city only or the whole network) or three days on the networks of suburban trains, subways, and buses in the county of Stockholm (except the SAS airport bus), on Djurgarden ferries, and at the Tram Museum. A three-day card also includes admission to Skansen, Grona Lund, and Kaknas Tower. When you stay longer, a monthly (or yearly) card is your most cost-efficient way to get around. A 15-trip strip card saves you 30 percent. Buy all tickets at kiosks called "Pressbyran" and at the central station, "T-Centralen."

Gothenburg, the capital of Sweden's West Coast, promotes the Goteborg Card covering free travel on buses, trams, Paddan Canal sightseeing, and free entry to Liseberg amusement park (Sweden's most popular visitor attraction) plus dozens of other places of interest, museums, and sports and recreation facilities. It includes a free day's excursion on the Stena Line to Frederikshavn in Denmark that alone would cost more than the card. Be sure to ride the vintage tram to Liseberg that is covered by the card. The Goteborg Card is included free in the "Goteborg Package" for hotels during the summer—one of the cheapest ways of staying in Gothenburg. The Gothenburg tourist office is located a short walk from the train station in the Nordstan shopping center (open Mon.-Fri., 9:30 A.M. to 6 P.M.; Sat. to 3 P.M.).

Helsinki Cards give you an 80 percent reduction on Helsinki sightseeing, unlimited free travel on public transportation, ferry and waterbus to Suomenlinna and Korkeasaari, a guided city walk, admission to nearly 50 museums, discounts on guided tours out of Helsinki, and opera, theater, and concerts. You also get a 100-page guidebook. You can buy the card for 24, 48, or 72 hours at the Hotel Book Center in the train station before you book a hotel, at travel agencies, ferry terminals, and the Helsinki City Tourist Office (*www.hol.fi*) located at Pohjoisesplanadi 19 (open Mon.-Fri., 9 A.M. to 7 P.M.; Sat. to 3 P.M.).

For one-third off, you can buy a Helsinki-region "Tourist Ticket," a pass for one, three, or five days limited to subway trains, trams, and buses, or you can buy a 10-trip ticket giving one-sixth off the single-fare price. Buy them in the subway station below the train terminus or you can buy the "Tourist Ticket" before you leave (contact the Finnish Tourist Board, Appendix A).

The Turku Card for 24 or 48 hours is valid for free entrance to most museums in Turku, discounts in many shops and restaurants, free bus within the city limits, and telephone calls up to FIM 5. A similar card is available in Tampere, Finland's second city.

Ready yourself for fresh clean air and sparkling fjords as you travel through Lapland and the land of the Midnight Sun on the following adventures: Norway in a nutshell, a trip across the Arctic Circle, Norway's Rauma Train, a crossing by deluxe ferry from Stockholm to Finland, and a circle trip through Finland's natural lakelands.

Norway in a Nutshell
Complete Travel with the Trolls

The plateau is a vast stretch of mountaintop, uninhabited, treeless, flat. You see no spiked Matterhorns here, just featureless mountains with tops swept away by glaciers—a frozen, crystalline surface, polished by howling wind. It is Arctic, remote, lonely, and only your powerful train keeps you from feeling stranded at the top of the world.

You are well above the timberline so far north, running along the stark, clear-aired, snow-pocked edge of the Hardanger Plateau. It is so white that any speck of color seems to be out of place. Just before you stop at Myrdal, you look to your right and see the browns and greens of the mountain walls of a grand canyon of a rift. You gasp at the sight so many hundred feet down of the temperate Flam valley. The Oslo-Bergen route is NSB's important flagship route. Without it, Bergen would be isolated by land from the rest of the country, because behind Bergen, the wall of the Hardanger Plateau forms a dead end.

When you look at a topographic map of Norway, you can appreciate that this route is an engineering triumph. Engineers successfully designed the line to climb and descend safely from sea level to 4,267 feet in inaccessible, hostile Arctic country.

Your early-morning departure hurried punctually out of Oslo Sentral station through built-up Oslo and past the suburbs. Climbing alongside a broad river, you first pass flowery meadows, placid lakes, and foliage brightened by red rowanberries. Then you hear the whine of sawmills at work and see tractors idling beside red farmhouses in patchwork fields close by the rails.

You cross through meager and noticeably thinning farmland, past natural, untouched emerald valleys, and finally out of pine groves and woods of ringed silver birch trees, away from the temperate environment of the Oslo Fjord and up into the mountains.

Thirty minutes past Drammen, dramatic scenery unfolds. You see the waters run faster. The trees thin. Patches of snow appear. The country is mantled in white by the time you arrive in Geilo. At 2,650 feet, you are only miles short of the timberline.

Geilo, known as the St. Moritz of Norway for its excellent skiing, is also a good base for mountaineering in summer. The small yellow station house is comfortable, with heated waiting room and lockers outside. The post office and modern tourist office with helpful ladies are just below the station and below that is the "Geilojordet," which is an interesting assembly of seven preserved wooden, historic houses moved from farms in Hol and arranged on the site to create a farm-yard typical for the period and the district.

In Geilo you can hire bicycles to follow northern Europe's most popular biking route, the Rallarvegen (Raller Road), the Bergen line's construction road, which is now closed to automobiles for most of its length, and return your bicycle in Flam or even Voss.

As you continue to climb, the scenery changes from ski resort to glacier. You leave the last of the trees at Ustaoset.

At Storodi, about six miles east of Finse, your train accelerates to nearly 105 mph. A nine-mile segment of new line, built on a low embankment to ease snow clearance problems, was put into service in 1999. The landscape glares whitely. It is dominated by the frigid Hardanger glacier looming in the south higher by 2,000 feet than Finse (4,010 feet). George Lucas filmed here the bitterly cold opening sequences of *The Empire Strikes Back.*

Finse is the highest stop on the line—the entire NSB network, in fact. The train station was closed in 2000, although train tickets are sold in Finse Hotel, when it is open during the summer. You might like to tramp into the snowbanks to take spectacular photos of the glacier and visit the Finse Rallarmuseum (open daily during summer, 10 A.M. to 10 P.M.), which shows the history of the Bergen Railroad, from the early preparation starting in 1871 until it was officially opened in 1909. It shows how it was kept open during the winter, and you see different snowplow equipment. The museum is situated in the locomotive stable, with the Documentation Center for the Bergen Railroad. See *www.rallarmuseet.no.*

West of Finse you enter the 1993, 6.4-mile Finse tunnel, which prevents line closings due to avalanches. The tunnel to Myrdal, which cut 2.7 miles from the length of your trip, is unfortunate from a scenic point of view, but no tragedy, because views from this section were obscured by snow sheds. Curiously, the highest point of the line, 4,123 feet, is in this tunnel. Before the tunnel was built, the highest point was at 4,267 feet.

Flam Railroad

At Myrdal station, dominated by a mountain with icy whiskers of frozen waterfalls, you don your parka and bundle into the coaches of the waiting apple-green Flam train. You leave behind a high, bleak, and contrary glacial plateau for the green and serene beauty of one of Norway's sweetest valleys. Your trip doesn't take long, but minute by minute, as your train inches down Europe's steepest adhesion route and turns surprising corners, you are rewarded by one of the most breathtaking of Norway's adventurous trains. The conductors also make it Norway's friendliest.

The Flam valley you see is an immense opening through the mountains, similar to the Grand Canyon in the sheer inclination of its mountain walls. Its upper railhead, Myrdal, is 2,845 feet above sea level. The lower terminus, Flam, near the ferry landing on the Aurlandsfjord, is an hour and 12 miles down the valley. This section is the steepest of any NSB line. In one stretch you drop one foot for every 18 you travel, quite brave for an adhesion train without cog-wheels. The five braking systems give your cautious engineer more sureness than a Norwegian mountain goat. Any one system is enough to halt the train safely.

This line was not built for passenger traffic. Perhaps that is why it is so unspoiled. It was built in the wilds, connecting fjord and glacier, to carry construction materials and heavy machinery for completing the central section of the Bergen line. They were ferried up the fjord to Flam and then carted by horses up to Myrdal. You see the surviving horse trail of 1895-96 still paralleling the line. The line was originally designed to carry 24,000 a year. In 1999, it carried around 370,000, mostly tourists.

You follow a tortuous path of 21 hairpin curves, in and out of tunnels. On the most scenic sections, your engineer thoughtfully slows or stops, so you can linger and absorb the impact of views more dazzling than you have imagined. You see sturdy wild mountain goats peering curiously at the train from granite boulders only a few feet from your window.

At first descent, your Flam train moves roughly parallel to the

Bergen line, between snow fences, but after Vatnahalsen, splendid panoramas quickly begin to unfold. You soon reach the highlight of your trip. Your train trudges across a sturdy embankment and the engineer brakes politely.

Beside the line, so close you can feel the pressure of the roaring action filling cameras' viewfinders, a fury of foam plunges over a cliff, raging down at you in a smoking torrent. It is not so much a waterfall as rapids out of nowhere. At your feet it vanishes safely into a natural channel beneath the trestle supporting your train. This is Kjosfoss, "foss" meaning "waterfall."

You appreciate the announcements, in English, over the loudspeaker by the conductor. These men take a sincere interest in the well-being and pleasure of travelers who come to visit their proud little valley.

If they feel a certain affinity for Americans, it is because more than a third of the population left this valley during the hard years of 1845-65 to settle in the New World, mostly in the Midwest. More than 1,000 emigrated. More than a century later, 2,000 live here, mostly making their living from farming, and English is widely spoken.

The conductors actually encourage passengers to scatter off the train onto the wooden-plank platform and soggy turf at Kjosfoss, to gawk and admire and pose for photographs before the powerful, raging waterfall/rapids less than a stone's toss away. Its fury easily drowns out the accumulated sounds of shutters clicking.

Farther down, you cross lesser wild rivers without benefit of bridges. (There are no bridges on this line.) Here again, the viaducts were blasted out of the mountains just as the construction engineers blasted the looping tunnels. When you enter the longest tunnel, Nali (1,476 yards), you look back and see the extraordinary sight of the rail bed cutting four ledges of the mountainside, one almost above the other.

When you leave the tunnel, you have a brief glimpse of the highest Flam valley farm, where 3,000 goats are kept to produce orange-colored Norwegian goat cheese. Another waterfall, Fjoandfoss, drops 400 feet down the mountainside in the afternoon shade.

At Hareina (158 feet), a timid village beside the prospering Flam River, where anglers make their catches at the break of day, your views from between tunnels and cuttings disappear, the valley widens, and you see the panorama of the highest toylike farms below. The fields here seem more vividly green than possible because your eyes are still adjusting from the white glare above. Looking ahead, you see the 300-year-old Flam Church, flowering fruit orchards, the blue of the fjord coming near, and the brown of the mountains behind.

The formerly remote village of Flam has blossomed into a significant tourist minihub. The lonesome station house, Fretheim Hotel catering to proper English ladies, and camping grounds have been supplemented by a larger station house, a sweater "factory," restaurants (one in historic railroad carriages), a cafeteria, the Flam Line Museum, a vast car and tour bus parking lot, souvenir shops, and a supermarket.

Norway's newest craze is bicycling the Flam line. Since a feature appeared on Norwegian television and was then picked up by the *New York Times,* the number of visitors renting a bicycle in Geilo or Myrdal (no deposit required), bicycling to Flam, and returning to Myrdal by train has doubled and redoubled to 800 bicycles a day.

With cafeteria open until 8 P.M., Flam's Hotel Fretheim Touristhotell is white with wooden lace and seems more like a romantic summer cottage or guesthouse than a dignified vacation hotel with mostly British visitors. You know before you enter that everything will be spotless, the waitresses will wear dirndls, and all guests will be snoring by 10:30 P.M. but will be up at the crow of the cock and the glimmer of dawn—except that in summer, day breaks at 2 A.M. and roosters crow all night.

Norway in a Nutshell Program

Your descent along the Flam line is your first leg of "Norway in a Nutshell," the three-stage excursion to reveal the essence of this beautiful country. For the second leg, board Kaptain Lid Kjell's *Skagastol* at Flam's pier, located at the end of the rail line, to begin a tranquil cruise of both the Aurlandsfjord and the Naeroyfjord, which are branches of the larger Sognefjord.

Kaptain Kjell is proud of his vessel and of his country's beauty. He is proud that so many foreigners come such long distances to admire the loveliness of his surroundings and he does his best to make their visit a happy one.

"But," he says, "the *Skagastol* is a boat. In our country, a ferry carries automobiles." Try to tell him that it is a passenger ferry. He shrugs.

In fact, the *Skagastol,* named for the tallest mountain on the Sognefjord, is a ferry converted with the extensive addition of glass to make it convenient from most of the boat to see high to the crests of the steep walls surrounding the fjords. It cruises at 12 knots and carries up to 500 passengers (during bad weather it carries 300 inside).

After 20 minutes, you make your first landing at Aurland (pop. 1,900), the county seat. Farther along the fjord you pass Undredal (pop. 100) on your left. Undredal boasts Scandinavia's smallest stave church still in use. It dates from 1147.

On the steep and rugged mountainside you see the two farms of Stigen (980 feet). Stigen was settled continuously until 1949, but now it is farmed only during the summer.

As you approach the mouth of the Naeroyfjord at Beitelen, Kaptain Kjell swings your boat left and you enter the narrowest and wildest arm of the Sognefjord. Snowcapped peaks reach to 4,500 feet. Small and peaceful farms and villages nestle beside the fjord.

Norway's fjords look and feel like mountain lakes rather than labyrinthine arms of the sea. The water is calm, slightly saline, and cold from the melting snow.

Passengers constantly exclaim about the filmy waterfalls cascading down those steep walls. There are no beaches, swimmers, sailboats, or water skiers. It is just you and nature together. On a good day you may see a seal diving to avoid the boat.

As the color of the fjord lightens and the fjord becomes shallower, Kaptain Kjell orders the motor stopped and you cruise the final stretch up the Naeroyfjord to the landing at Gudvangen.

Gudvangen grew into a small tourist center at the end of the 19th century. It is your assembly point for the low-gear, one-hour bus climb up the steep Stalheimskleivane road to Voss through the narrow Naeroy Valley.

Here is a "Kafeteria-Souvenirs" shop and a small green space below birch trees to relax. More importantly, in the parking area passengers are already boarding a fleet of blue-and-white Volvo and Mercedes buses ready to take you up the mountainside through Stalheim to Voss.

The drivers shift into low gear and the several buses crawl in caravan up the narrow, corkscrew highway. Your windows expose views of valleys, rivers, and farmhouses far below and bring you face to face with many a roaring waterfall.

You are rolling merrily along when a sign demands: "Change to Low Gear." Obediently, your driver complies as his bus crosses a stretch of road cantilevered over a precipice. Swinging wide on a hairpin turn, you look back on the waterfall you just passed.

Finally, the driver slips his bus into second gear and your bus seems to dart along a level stretch and pulls into the parking lot of the Stalheim Hotel.

"Ten minutes," says the driver.

Most buses stop in Stalheim—lunch is included in the itinerary of some tour groups. It has a grand and spectacular outdoor veranda and glassed indoor lounge for rainy days.

The ice-cream-cone peak of Mount Jondal is the centerpiece of the marvelous panorama from the veranda and you realize, tossing a pebble from the stone balcony, what a long, long way it is down to the floor of the Naeroy Valley.

Your bus's final stretch carries you past a high mountain lake with rowboats at the ready. Yellow fields of hay stretch down to the water's edge.

When your bus pulls up in front of the Voss train station, you have completed the third and final leg of "Norway in a Nutshell." You can join a train to Bergen or Oslo or use Voss as your base for further exploration of Norway's rugged mountains.

NSB offers Norway in a Nutshell day tickets from Bergen or Oslo and one way between Oslo and Bergen. Those holding a Eurail product, ScanRail Pass, or Norwegian rail pass pay only for the boat and bus tickets plus the small supplement to ride the Flam railroad because the Flam railroad grants only a 30 percent reduction to holders of these passes.

Two options are available. You must depart Oslo aboard the 6:11 A.M. express train if you are to return to Oslo the same day. If you choose to end your journey in Bergen, you may opt for the 8:11 A.M. more comfortable Signatur train. Reservations are required on all NSB trains from Oslo to Myrdal and Voss to Oslo or Bergen.

Norway in a Nutshell				
dep.	Oslo Sentral	0611	0811	Reserve Train
arr.	Myrdal	1114	1258	
dep.	Myrdal	1203	1316	Flam Line
arr.	Flam	1300	1415	
dep.	Flam	1315	1500	Boat
arr.	Gudvangen	1515	1500	
dep.	Gudvangen	1520	1715	Bus
arr.	Voss	1645	1830	
dep.	Voss	1711	2130	Reserve Train
arr.	Oslo Sentral	2230		
arr.	Bergen		2235	

Bergen Railroad

Returning to the Bergen line at Myrdal or Voss, you continue westward toward Bergen. Leaden-looking, chilling, and forbidding lakes surround you. Reindeer race between boulders and leap over patches of snow. Afternoon sun on granite boulders seems to shiver against icy, rushing rivers. Tattered tunnels burrow like snow snakes. You catch glimpses of brown, purple, and flaky yellow mosses through gapes in the drifts.

Then you suddenly realize the snow is melting and the water is running west instead of east, and you know your train is descending to Bergen and the North Sea's warm Gulf Stream.

You pass giant waterfalls, leaving bleak and wind-scoured snowland and entering valleys with dazzling, purple rhododendrons blooming all around you. No sooner do you clear your ears from the increasing air pressure than you are rolling along the shores of Sorfjorden and then through the five-mile Ulriken tunnel into Bergen's end-of-the-line train terminal, where the glass arches were restored in 1992 to the classical style of the 1930s, when steam locomotives were used.

Bergen's end-of-the-line graystone train station is small—only four platforms—but convenient. The tourist office (*i*) (open daily, 7:15 A.M. to 11 P.M.) is well marked at your left as you arrive. You can arrange accommodations and change money as well as pick up useful literature. An extensive array of lockers ("Oppbevaring") stands opposite.

You still see evidence of Bergen's former isolation. Hansa merchants came to Bergen in the Middle Ages, making it their trade center for dried fish. Even now new buildings are patterned after Hanseatic architecture. Houses have a red- and black-brick look similar to northern Germany's Hansa cities. But this architecture is deceiving, because the Bergenese soon reveal the city is fiercely Norwegian.

The Bergenese are particularly friendly to Americans, sophisticated, and many speak English. Named a "Cultural Capital of Europe" for 2000, Bergen is a vital city, a major gateway opening on the West, the former home of Edvard Grieg, and the center of an international music festival. It has reputedly the finest youth hostel in the North.

For a fine overview and orientation of Bergen and its harbor setting, make your first project the six-minute funicular ride to the top of 1,050-foot-high Mount Floien. The funicular in 2003 had its most extensive refurbishment in its 84-year history. To increase capacity, the operating company purchased new carriages holding up to 100 and

featuring glass ceilings and panoramic windows. The track, equipment, three intermediate stations, lower landmark station, and ticketing system were also upgraded. On weekdays, Scandinavia's runs daily
from 7:30 A.M. to midnight during the summer and until 11 P.M. in winter. Opening hours are 8 A.M. on Saturdays and 9 A.M. on Sundays.

Daily Bergen Railroad Service

EX609	St61	EX601	St63				St62	EX602	EX608	St64
0611	0811	1043	1611	dep.	Oslo S	arr.	1452	1752	2149	2230
0747	0942	1226	1742	dep.	Hoenefoss	dep.	1310	1606	2022	2059
0906	1103	1358	1901	dep.	Gol	dep.	1143	1430	1859	1939
0926	1124	1424	1922	dep.	Aal	dep.	1122	1405	1833	1920
0946	1145	1445	1943	dep.	Geilo	dep.	1100	1344	1812	1859
1039	1225	1528	2021	dep.	Finse	dep.	1017	1257	1725	1819
1114	1258	1557	2047	dep.	MYRDAL	dep.	0951	1225	1650	1753
1211	1342	1642	2130	dep.	Voss	dep.	0908	1139	1555	1711
1334	1452	1752	2235	arr.	Bergen	dep.	0758	1028	1428	1558

Express trains carry first- and second-class carriages and Bistro Car. Reservations required.
Signatur trains (St) carry first- and second-class carriages, restaurant, and children's carriage and have handicapped access. Reservations required.

Midnight Sun to Narvik

Your steep descent into Narvik on the northernmost train in
Western Europe is heady stuff. Each bend of your Ofot train opens up
the quintessence of Norwegian travel. You see new vistas of unspoiled
mountain, sea, and sky. While your Iron-Ore Railroad train passes
through stands of spruce, wild reindeer leap between snowbanks. You
lean forward to better watch—on your right—your climactic, precipitous descent down to the Ofot Fjord.

The direct descent from the summit is 27 miles, but your zigzagging
descent on this stretch of the Lapland train takes nearly a full hour.

As you descend, surroundings change from bleak, icy lakes and the
snow remnants of winter. You feel the green embrace of the warming
Gulf Stream. Looking down 350 feet you see the silvery surface of the
Romsdalfjord creeping in an arc under the distant Skjombrua
(bridge) from the Norwegian Sea, and you begin to make out the

waves of the Norwegian Sea breaking on the shores. Then you see Narvik's wooden houses. Brick shops form a patchwork pattern of color against black conveyor belts and iron-ore loading facilities.

Setting off in Stockholm or Gothenburg, your train takes you through the remote top of the Scandinavian Peninsula, across the Arctic Circle, and finally to Norway's end-of-the-line train station on the Ofot Fjord. You see it all while it is light in the domain of the Midnight Sun.

You travel north toward the Arctic Circle through fir forests. Blue placid lakes mirror the serene beauty of the sturdy, rounded mountains. Puffy clouds are made golden from the sun deep on the horizon at midnight. The lonesome clickety-clack of your train tattoos over and over because of spaces between the northern rails. You see sights unlike anywhere. It makes you never want to close your eyes to sleep. Northern Swedes tell you not to set your sleep by the sun, but by the clock.

In the eerie midnight glow, you inhale the sweet scent of pine in the air and gaze at foggy mists in the rocky terrain and in the birches, leafless until early summer. Clouds in the silvery sky reflect in the remote, silent lakes. And then the shimmering orange globe rises in the northeast. It seems as if it should be on the eastern horizon, but it is the wee hours and your train is entering the domain of the Midnight Sun. Birds chirp at this unlikely hour. Then the red of sunrise spreads across the peaceful lakes and creates a fragile, glassy pink, beginning your second day north.

It is an experience for the intrepid, romantic adventurer who admires the green and blue (and white) outdoors. Sweden has the most lakes of all nations. When you travel by train beyond the Arctic Circle, there is only you, your chugging, solitary diesel locomotive, moonlit freshwater lakes, wild moose, reindeer, cackling birds, and the rich, sweet smells of pine forest and mossy brook.

In Boden you find a pristine frontier city set along a blue lake. From Boden you can take the train service that was reopened to Haparanda on June 13, 2000 (until mid-August), and from there walk about 2,500 feet to the Finnish bus station.

Carriages are detached in Boden, and your section for Narvik rolls on. About 1¼ hours out of Boden, your train slows for photographs. Have your camera ready for the large, neat sign on your left: "Arctic Circle." Even the Swedes admit that while they were children, they

Svolvaer

NARVIK

Kiruna

Bodo Fauske

Arctic Circle

Lulea

Boden

SWEDEN

Vannas

Trondheim

Ange

NORWAY

MIDNIGHT TRAINS

OSLO

Orebro

STOCKHOLM

NORTH SEA

Gothenburg

Nassjo

-N-

DENMARK

Helsing-
borg

Hassle-
holm

0   100   200

COPENHAGEN

Malmo

MILES

Oresund
fixed link

visualized the Arctic Circle as a green line running around the earth. You are in the land of the Midnight Sun.

From here you pass through barren and remote tundra, climb past scraggly trees and then scrubby bushes, until you reach Kiruna (pop. 27,000), the preeminent iron-ore-mining city and most northerly commune in Sweden. You see on the hill the colorful wooden houses painted rust-red, green, brown, and yellow with copper and tile roofs, but you can only imagine the huge, labyrinthine tunnels of the world's largest underground mine, where work is done by gigantic machines that could be out of a George Lucas movie.

You thread your way northwest from the mines of Kiruna through green spruce and clean earth damp with melting snow. White stripes of birch trunks pattern the blanket of deep, green grass. Lovers of the outdoors and mountaineers leave your train at primitive outposts. This is one big national park north of the Arctic Circle.

From Kiruna, you are traveling along the route of the Iron-Ore Railroad built specifically to carry ore from Kiruna in Sweden to Narvik, Norway, the all-year port kept free of ice by the Gulf Stream. Swedish politicians would have preferred to use a port in Sweden for export of their ore, but the freezing of the Gulf of Bothnia in winter left them no choice.

Swedish train experts insist the so-called Ofotbanen, carrying 20 million tons of ore annually through Norway, is the most exciting piece of track in the Swedish system. Iron-ore trains run frequently, except from mid-June to mid-July, when everyone in Sweden is on vacation. The line was electrified in 1923, just 20 years after being opened. For years, this was the world's most northerly railroad, but the line reaching Murmansk in Russia has now taken this distinction. When conditions allow, you can see the complete disk of the sun at midnight from May 26 to July 19.

You cross the border into Norway at Riksgransen. Over the crest, you enter Norway slowly, through steel-and-wood snowsheds. You descend along the 68-mile segment from 1,700 feet to 20 feet at the port of Narvik. The gradient is one in 59.

The Goteborg/Stockholm-Umea-Kiruna/Narvik route was considered unprofitable by SJ and put out for bid. Connex Sweden (*www.connex.se*) assumed operation on June 15, 2003.

The former SJ carriages are comfortable, and the doors open with a nudge on a bar. The brown second-class seats in the nonsleeping carriages are comfortable, arranged 2+2 or 3+1 with seats facing. This curious arrangement allows passengers to fold the arm rests into the seat backs and to lie, and sleep, across three seats if the train is not crowded. Alternately, passengers may recline facing seats by pulling cushions forward and stretch out parallel to the direction of travel.

Connex accepts Eurail products valid in Sweden, ScanRail Passes, and Sweden Rail Passes. Reservations are required, but you must telephone 46-771-26-00-00 or fax 46-771-28-00-00 in Sweden or email kundtjanst@tag.connex.se.

Narvik (pop. 20,000) is a pup among cities. In 1880, there were but one or two isolated farms and a few not-so-contented-cows grazing here. Narvik grew out of the railway construction town of Rombaksbotn, which burned to the ground in 1903. It was here that the "rallarne" lived—the migrant construction workers who built the Ofoten Line. The "rallar," with his broad-brimmed hat, became a symbol of the town and the railway. At the train station, look for the statue of the workers' cook, known as "Svarta Bjorn" (Black Bear).

The low but constant angle of the sun on the horizon causes very little temperature change between day and night. It is already warm when you awake and still pleasant late into the evening.

The Narvik train station is cozy, with attached cafeteria. Up the hill from the station on the corner of Kongens Gt. ("Kings' Street"), you find a small shopping mall, which includes an ATM ("MiniBank"). Across from the prizewinning city hall, a small, thought-provoking museum (open Mon.-Sat., 10 A.M. to 10 P.M.; Sun., 11 A.M. to 5 P.M., during the summer) records Narvik's place in history. In May 1940, the British sank 10 Nazi destroyers in Narvik Fjord and temporarily recaptured the city, the first Allied victory of World War II.

The Narvik Tourist Office (*www.Narvikinfo.no*, open 9 A.M. to 4:30 P.M.) is about a 20-minute walk from the train station down Kongens Gt. to 26, past the museum. The cableway 10 minutes from the city center, at the head of Kongens Gt., lifts you 2,000 feet to the very top of Mount Fagernesfjell in only 13 minutes. When you rise in the aerial gondola above the city, your perspective adjusts. First you see the iron-ore loading facilities open up and then the fjords gradually surrounding and then dwarfing the village while snow-covered mountains appear to rise in the distance.

From the top of the lift, the sun warms the terrace of the restaurant and you see the "Sleeping Queen," a panorama resembling Queen Victoria reposed, 5,191 feet high. The official name of Narvik at the turn of the 20th century was "Victoriahamn," meaning "Victoria's Harbor."

Midnight Sun Trains to Narvik

I	I	1700	dep.	Gothenburg	arr.	1050	I	I
1727	2028	I	dep.	STOCKHOLM C.	arr.	I	0730	1202
1752	2054	I	dep.	Arlanda	arr.	I	0705	1137
1817	2121	I	dep.	Uppsala	arr.	I	0644	1113
2343	0133	0150	dep.	Ange	dep.	0255	0227	0619
0419	0617	0651	arr.	Vannas	dep.	2222	2143	0136
0734	1045	1120	arr.	Boden C.	dep.	1753	1720	2225
1002	1323	1323	dep.	Gallivare	dep.	1445	1445	1956
1107	1433	1433	arr.	Kiruna C.	dep.	1334	1334	1851
1400	1740	1740	arr.	NARVIK	dep.	1025	1025	1605

You can return by train directly to Stockholm, take the buses north to Kirkenes near the Russian border, or take the nearly five-hour, red, white, and blue NOR-WAY bus trip (*www.nor-way.no*) south across fjords to Fauske to join NSB's network south to Trondheim. You may purchase tickets in the Narvik train station or on the bus (about $30, no reduction for Eurail products, 50 percent for ScanRail Pass holders and seniors).

From Fauske or Bodo, you ride NSB's Nordland line, the longest line in Norway. The "journey that's worth every penny" takes nine hours to Trondheim. Your 2002 red-and-silver "Agenda" tilting diesel train with panoramic windows, the day train, starts at sea level and ends at sea level, but you wend your way between fjords and hills, cross two mountain ranges, and pass the Arctic Circle at 67.2 degrees north. The summer stop at the Arctic Circle delights the groups of children enjoying the special children's carriage playroom. Have your cameras ready for the pyramid on the west side of the train. This is the highest point of the Nordland line, at 1,620 feet.

The night trains are diesel locomotive hauled, second class only, with reclining seats with curtains to close or you can reserve sleeping compartments with one, two, or three berths. Smokers use a special, glassed-in smoking room next to the wooden-panel Bistro carriage.

Breakfast is included for those in one- or two-berth compartments. The Bistro carriage serves the others. All trains on this run must be reserved in advance.

Instead of the NOR-WAY bus, a more adventurous way south from Narvik to Bodo, and worth the additional cost, are the steamers operated by the Ofotens S.S. Co. to connect with coastal steamers north and south. You can sit snugly in the cafeteria of the 30-knot m.v. *Skogoy*, built in 1985, or go on deck to watch the landings and deliveries of cargo at the tiny hamlets along the way. You reach the codfish city of Svolvaer for a change to the much larger cruise ships of the Coastal Express Service. This gives you a few hours in Svolvaer to explore the interesting codfishing harbor.

Train and NOR-WAY Bus Service between Narvik and Trondheim

1610	0700	dep.	NARVIK	arr.	1420	2300
2120	1150	arr.	FAUSKE	dep.	0920	1825
			Change between bus and train			
2145	1302	dep.	FAUSKE	arr.	0828	1714
N/A	1418	dep.	Arctic Circle*	dep.	N/A	1601
0706	I	arr.	Vaernes	dep.	2251	1815
0750	2215	arr.	TRONDHEIM	dep.	2220	0742

*Mid-June to mid-August only

The Rauma Train Marvels per Minute

You look down the valley and see three railroad lines. You are twisting along one, there's another farther on, on the edge of a cliff, and still farther, below a cascading waterfall on the other side of the valley, you see a third. All three belong to the Rauma Railroad, carrying you in a huge double spiral to reach the valley floor through two circular tunnels in the Norwegian mountainsides.

Halfway down the 71-mile Rauma Railroad to Aandalsnes, you are still nearly 1,700 feet above sea level, the best scenery is yet to come, and you have to get down somehow. Your train must circle to lose altitude. You pass wild mountains, soaring peaks, and crashing

TRONDHEIM

ANDALSNES

Lesjaskog

Lesja

Dombas

**NORWAY'S RAUMA
AND DOVRE LINES**

Lillehammer

Hamar

NORWAY

Eidsvoll

Lillestrom

OSLO

SWEDEN

-N-

```
0      20      50           100
|------|-------|-------------|
         MILES
```

Oslo Fjord

waterfalls and then you enter mountains cored by internal twists and spirals.

The first tunnel you enter, the Stavem, is 4,650 feet long. In the heart of the mountain, you retrace your path. When you return to daylight, you are running on the second segment, opposite to your direction a few minutes ago. You are several levels farther down the valley and see the Vermafoss falls straight ahead plummeting in misty cascades about 1,250 feet down the mountain ridge opposite.

The mint-green Rauma River below you dashes with all the gusto of a Norwegian hare, tumbling down over steep precipices and slabs of rock.

Entering the Kylling Tunnel, you sweep through the mountain and under the highway in a long shallow curve, 1,500 feet long and so gentle you don't feel it. Back into daylight, you cross Kylling Bridge over a narrow gorge and see again the Rauma River, now frothing and foaming untamed only 200 feet below. As though to make itself most beautiful, the river snakes around pebbly white islets and sandbars of white granite powder and jumps across rapids, trailing glorious white bubbly wakes.

You have reached the third and lowest track and finally you can look back on this ingeniously engineered line from below. The complex double curve made the Rauma Railroad about five miles longer, but allowed you to descend 330 feet safely.

While the Rauma River gradually tires and meanders more calmly through wide gentle bends, the mountain scenery by contrast turns starker and more rugged and you are entering a new episode in the adventure of the Rauma Railroad. You are now traveling at the foot of towering rocky precipices and looking up at triple-tongued, monstrous waterfalls crashing down at you.

This is what makes train travel exciting. You have passed from one spectacular phase into still another differently wondrous. Passengers run from side to side of your tilting Agenda InterCity diesel unit pointing and shouting to each other with delight. One rider shouts, "This is the most beautiful ride in the world!"

This one-hour, 17-minute descent, unfolding rich detail and color, justifies you making a single memorable trip to Norway and is, happily, completely covered by Eurail, Norwegian, and ScanRail passes, like most NSB travel. Agenda's amenities are described under the heading "Norwegian Trains."

The morning departure of your Signatur tilting train northward

Rauma Line InterCity Service

#2341	#2343	#2345	#2347				#2340	#2342	#2344	#2346
1120	1230	1856	2030	dep.	Dombass	arr.	0859	1100	1651	1730
1132	1242	1908	2042	dep.	Lesja	dep.	0844	1045	1636	I
1142	1252	1918	2052	dep.	Lesjaverk	dep.	0832	1032	1624	I
1154	1304	1930	2104	dep.	Bjorli	dep.	0822	1022	1614	1814
1237	1347	2013	2147	arr.	Aandalsnes	dep.	0738	0938	1530	1730

from Oslo Sentral first passes through severe architecture, Star-Wars designs, and the tunnel under 1998 Oslo Gardermoen Airport before continuing through rich farmlands and then up the eastern shore of Lake Mjosa, Norway's largest and deeper than the North Sea. On the lake you see the one-funnel steamship, the P. S. *Skibladner* (say "Shebladner"), the world's oldest paddle steamer still in regular service, built in 1854, in Sweden. You pass red-and-brown wooden summer cottages and wild flowers dancing like yellow fire—dandelions, buttercups, mustard, and rapeseed (Canola) for monounsaturated oil.

Your first stop on Lake Mjosa is in the important hub of Hamar, at the widest point. Inhale deeply here. The air is fresh and pure, reputedly the most healthful in Scandinavia. The 1896 Norwegian State Railroad Museum in Hamar (*www.jernbaneverket.no*, open daily, 10 A.M. to 4 P.M., during the summer) is one of the oldest train museums in the world. Visit the outdoor museum park with tracks, signals, and engine sheds. A narrow-gauge steam train operates during the summer.

At your second stop on Lake Mjosa, the vacation center of Lillehammer, you see the improvements the Norwegian government invested ($370 million) for the 1994 Winter Olympic Games. Past Lillehammer, you enter Gudbrandsdal, the "Valley of Valleys" ("dal" means "valley"). Farmers here still maintain the old building styles. You pass lined-up farmhouses climbing the mountainsides like soldiers.

At Dombaas' brown plaster station house with warm interior, you change to the Rauma Railroad down the Romsdal. Now, looking forward as you wind down toward Aandalsnes on the Ice Fjord, the sheer face of unscalable Trollveggen, meaning Troll Wall, stands in front of you. You must crane your neck to see the summits of the huge mountains soaring heavenward on either side, one after another. From a terrible height, famous waterfalls drop from the mountainside like countless silver fingers.

When you approach Marstein, where the mountains stand so high the stationmaster only sees the sun seven months of the year, your ride has settled down to merely splendid. You watch capricious mists of cloud dancing midway up sturdy cliffs nearly barren of trees.

You wind around the wedge-shaped, 4,250-foot high Mongegjura Mountain and the weird range of peaks resembling a row of trolls squatting menacingly over the valley. Its gray walls, scarred and stained, rise sheer from the valley floor to 6,000 feet.

Trolls reputedly set up camp here to gain an advantage over their enemies, gnomes on the valley floor. In one battle, they hid until the gnomes appeared at the foot of the mountains and then hurled down a terrible avalanche to bury them in rock and stone. But the gnomes triumphed in the end, for they had tricked the trolls, who are permitted to roam only at night. For their foolish midday attack, the trolls fossilized into these jagged blue-gray mountain massifs, so steep the snow will not lie on their slopes and no vegetation will grow.

The valley is almost entirely surrounded by the peaks above you. You cannot see the top of the Romsdalshorn. Finally, you look up at the 6,300-foot Trollveggen, the highest vertical rock face in northern Europe.

Now you descend. You have always been dropping, of course, following a course above the mint-green river, but now you sense it by the multiplication of the flowering wild plants and the passing of the terrible, high mountains.

You see the river joining the fjord and rows of pleasant homes along ordered streets. This is the tidy township of Aandalsnes, where you come to a halt beside the modern, 1991 station house with cafe.

Aandalsnes (pop. 2,500) is one of the loveliest settings along the coast of Norway. Situated on the Ice Fjord, the head of the Romsdalsfjord, at the foot of the Romsdal, it is framed by the Setnefjell mountain on the west and Mount Nesaksla on the east.

You won't find much to do in Aandalsnes but admire the scenery and hike the mountains. That is more than enough. Buses (not covered by rail pass) stand by the train station to take you to Alesund and Molde, which is a stopping place for the coastal steamers, a superb 2½-hour mail-boat trip across the fjord.

You can return up the mountainside to connect with Signatur from Oslo to continue from Dombaas to Trondheim, Norway's third city, with a population of 145,000. About 25 minutes north of Dombaas, you pass the highest point of the line, about 3,360 feet, and see the snow-capped, highest mountain in Norway (7,500 feet) to the west.

Trondheim, under its former name of Nidaros, was Norway's first capital. There is much for you to see here, including numerous colorful wharf houses and Nidaros Cathedral, where Norway's kings are crowned. It is the largest medieval building in Scandinavia. Since Trondheim's Sentral station was redeveloped with a stunning 1999 annex, with ATM ("MiniBank"), taxi stand, bus station, and sales counters for train, bus, and express-boat tickets, there has been a large increase in suburban traffic, attracting many away from their autos. Luggage carts are available for a deposit and ramps connect the platforms. The InterRail Center in the train station is open 7 A.M. to 11 P.M. during July and August.

When you wish to go to Hell simply to have your photograph taken below the famous ochre Hell train station's signboard, you can reach Hell by the TronderBanen network of rapid-transit trains.

Dovre Line Train Service
Oslo to Trondheim

St41	St43	EX45	St47				St40	EX42	St44	St46
0719	0817	1457	1619	dep.	OSLO Sentral	arr.	1313	1513	2113	2313
0731	0830	1510	1631	dep.	Lillestroem		I	I	I	I
0746	0845	1525	1646	dep.	Oslo Airport		I	I	I	I
0838	0939	1619	1738	dep.	Hamar	dep.	1146	1350	1944	2154
0923	1028	1703	1824	dep.	Lillehammer	dep.	1103	1302	1817	2111
1004	1114	1744	1911	dep.	Ringebu	dep.	1020	1219	1817	2029
1021	1130	1801	1928	dep.	Vinstra	dep.	0958	1201	1800	2013
1042	1157	1823	1950	dep.	Otta	dep.	0937	1140	1736	1952
1113	1227	1854	2022	dep.	DOMBAAS	dep.	0907	1110	1706	1921
1137	1328	1951	2123	dep.	Oppdal	dep.	0809	1009	1605	1816
1240	1354	2017	2149	dep.	Berkaak	dep.	0741	0941	1536	1748
1335	1500	2125	2255	arr.	TRONDHEIM	dep.	0630	0830	1425	1640

Crossing the Bothnia
Free Deck to Finland

"Tervetuloa. Welcome aboard the Silja Line." The veteran captain speaks from the bridge of your ship crossing from Stockholm to Finland—Turku or Helsinki—a vantage point some 100 feet and 12 stories above the water.

You watch fir trees gliding by your window. Your entry to Finland across the Gulf of Bothnia is not as absent of scenery as you might

CROSSING
THE BOTHNIA

Umea

OULU

Langsele

Seinajoki

-N-

FINLAND

GULF OF BOTHNIA

Tampere

Toljala

Gavle

TURKU

Salo

HELSINKI

Aland
Islands

MARIEHAMN

Karyaa

SWEDEN

Tallinn

STOCKHOLM

ESTONIA

0   50   100

expect. You sail through an endless archipelago of 80,000 islands, rocks, and skerries. Some are tree covered. All are remnants of the glacier era and the geologic rising of the earth's crust under the gulf.

Almost everything is fresh aboard ship—and well kept up. Passengers are doing whatever pleases them. Their natural mobility aboard ship allows them to mingle, or not, as they please. Everyone seems friendly. You hear that Finnish is the predominant language on board, but everyone speaks English to you. All announcements are in Swedish, Finnish, and English.

Most of the travelers seem to be in their 20s, but Nordic children seem to be having the best of it. Northern parents know how to look after their offspring. Children frolic in a glassed playroom filled with colored plastic bubbles. You can see that they are returning from a family excursion to the "big city" of Stockholm.

The Silja Line (*www.Silja.com*) is the premier line carrying passengers across the Gulf of Bothnia from Stockholm to Turku or Helsinki. You depart from Silja Line's Stockholm pier in the port of Vartan—in the northeastern part of town. Silja Line's information and ticketing offices are located there and you can also make use of a self-service cafe, children's playroom, souvenir kiosk, tourist information (for arrivals), waiting room, telephones, rest rooms, lockers, and check-in counter, which opens two hours before sailing. A mailbox is outside.

To reach Vartan, you may ride, with surcharge, the white Silja Line bus from City Terminalen, the bus terminal on the bottom floor of the 1990 World Trade Center attached to Stockholm's Central train station. You can also take a Tunnelbana (subway) train to Gardet station, next to the end of the line. From Gardet you walk—a relatively easy, 10-minute hike. Signs to Vartahamnen, Silja Line's port, are posted in the subway.

The attraction is irresistible on Silja Line ships offering a tropical Sunflower Oasis with water slides, swimming pools, steam bath and bars; a play area for children; a promenade, teak-covered atrium, lined with reasonably priced restaurants and shops and overlooked by cabins above; a casino with Las Vegas-style slot machines; the Neon Disco and a romantic dance floor; duty-free shopping; gourmet restaurants sprinkled throughout the ship. . . .

Silja Line's 1993, 55,000-ton, M.S. *Europa,* the world's biggest cruise liner with 3,000 berths, provides morning departures from Stockholm and evening departures from Turku during the summer. Her 765,000 square feet of glass opens up vast seascapes to travelers. Enormous windows cover the prow, giving you unobstructed views from the buffet restaurant and nightclub. Below, a 90-seat McDonald's restaurant is open late for Big Mac attacks and the 500-seat Moulin Rouge theater mounts musicals such as Rodgers and Hammerstein's *Oklahoma!*

All year round, the *Silja Festival* provides evening departures from Stockholm and morning departures from Turku.

The 1991 M.S. *Silja Symphony*, Silja Line's 23-knot, 58,400-ton luxury liner, carries up to 2,500 passengers and incorporates cruise-vessel luxuries never before seen in the industry. It is paired with her identical sister ship, the 1990 M.S. *Silja Serenade*, for daily service all year round from Helsinki and Stockholm with departures from each port in the evening and arrivals the next morning.

Silja Line's ships were designed for service between Finland and Sweden, but they also comply with rules of construction for long international voyages and meet the requirements for ice navigation without the help of icebreakers. Due to dense traffic and narrow routes in the archipelagoes, the bottoms of the hulls are designed for minimal wave generation and minimal response to heavy seas.

The fare structure for Silja Line makes little sense. Between Helsinki and Stockholm, the new ships have no available deck space. Between Stockholm and Turku, Silja has seven classes of cabins and the fares vary by season, day of the week, number of persons in the cabin, and time of departure. Eurail-product holders receive discounts that vary from zero to 10 percent. ScanRail Pass holders pay 25-50 percent less than full-fare travelers. Cheapest fare available is about $9, deck passage.

On the Helsinki-Stockholm ships, you find eight classes of cabin, and the same range of discounts apply.

If you choose deck passage Stockholm-Turku ("Sittsalong"), you will find that the Pullman chairs are surprisingly comfortable with spacious washrooms nearby. You stow your small bags in nearby lockers. Leave your large luggage in the luggage room. The ships' cabins give you many comforts: shower, bunk beds, mirror, toilet, washbasin, and open closet.

When the captain announces your ship will be docking in Helsinki in half an hour, look to your left entering Helsinki's harbor. Your ship's only possible navigable channel takes you through

Suomenlinna, Finland's Seafortress, a complex of six islands fortified in 1748. Once the greatest fortress of the Swedish empire, it was surrendered to the Russians in 1808 and then bombarded by the British fleet in 1855 during the Crimean War. It finally became Finnish in 1917, when it was renamed "Finland's Seafortress."

The first building you spot in Helsinki will probably be the white capitol-like dome of the 1852 Uspensky Lutheran Cathedral. On debarking, pass through the customs hall and you will see an office to change money and a Tourist Office where you can buy Helsinki Cards for transportation or book a hotel room in the city for a small service charge. Tram 3T goes to Market Square a few blocks away and Tram 3B (which runs the opposite direction of Tram 3T) takes you to the train station.

Travelers sailing into Turku see an unmatched view of high Turku Castle, a medieval bastion (but now a museum) guarding the harbor. Turku Harbor's Olympic Terminal is about three-quarters of a mile from the main Turku train station. Trams 3B and 3T take you to the center of Turku from the stop next to the terminal. From Turku train station, hourly trains take you to Helsinki in less than two hours, or you may board trains to Tampere and Joensuu.

Silja Line Service
between Stockholm and Turku or Helsinki

Symphony/ Serenade	Festival	Europa				Europa	Festival	Symphony/ Serenade
1700	2015	0800	dep.	STOCKHOLM	arr.	0700	1915	0930
2355	0345	1445	dep.	Aaland	dep.	0135	1445	0425
I	0800	2010	arr.	TURKU	dep.	2115	0910	I
1700	I	I	arr.	HELSINKI	dep.	I	I	1700

Silja Europa sailings summer only
I = Does not travel this route

Round Lapland in Three Laps

You suddenly come within inches of a granite sculpture. The powerful figure sitting on the ground cradles its head with one arm and peers steadily down upon you at the window of your train. Then you enter a black tunnel, and when you emerge, on your left, the medieval towers and ramparts of Olavinlinna castle, the best-preserved in the Nordic countries, unravel doubly, one vision straight ahead, and one image dancing in the calm waters of Kyronsalmi Straits.

Nature becomes redefined: quiet waters, towering firs, singing birds, pine needles on forest floor filtered by magical light. About 180 endangered Saimaa fresh-water seals frolic in the lake, their last refuge. It is said that trout fight among themselves to be the first to take anglers' lures in Kyronsalmi Straits.

The lakeside village of Savonlinna is your heart of Finland's Saimaa Lakeland. The community grew around Olavinlinna castle, and together with the captivating countryside has become Finland's most magnetic place. The granite sculpture that greeted you marked the entrance to the Retretti Art Center at Punkaharju, the largest art center in the Nordic countries. Curators fill its subterranean grottoes with outstanding exhibits of modern and traditional international art.

The diesel train or bus that brought you to Savonlinna's Olavinlinna castle connected with the electric IC train from Helsinki at Parikkala. Visitors flock throughout July to attend the Savonlinna Opera Festival, which is held on the stage magnificently located within the walls of Olavinlinna. Unfortunately, VR threatens to replace trains on the Parikkala-Savonlinna line with buses, which nevertheless will honor rail passes.

Finland does not end with Helsinki. The beauty and serenity of Finland lies in the lake districts. Luckily for visitors, the geography of Finland dictates that rail lines originally built for lumber transport must link lakeside villages and reveal Finland's secrets to train travelers.

Like the limbs of a pear tree, with Helsinki at its root, VR's Ostrobothnian line shoots to the north beside the Gulf of Bothnia, VR's Karelian line branches north beside the Russian border, and the Savo line shoots straight north between lakes. At Joensuu a regional train takes you to Nurmes for a connection to the Ostrobothnian line at Oulu and thus completes a pear-shaped ring around Finland's two magnificent lakelands and makes a circle trip not only feasible, but essential to absorb the grandness, greatness, and captivation of the enchanting Finnish lakeland.

Ten percent of Europe's fifth-largest country is water—lakes and rapids. In Finland, the rivers flow garnet, tinted with soluble iron ores. The Saimaa Lakeland runs from Lappeenranta in the south to

Nurmes in the north. The Western Lakeland is bounded by Tampere on the west and Hameenlinna on the south.

Varieties of trees commingle on the flat Finnish countryside as happily and thickly as birds on their limbs. Pines prefer dryer land and make up more than half of Finland's forests. Spruce make up about one-third; birch about one-tenth. In the south, occasional oak, lime, ash, and maple join the forests.

Leg one begins in Helsinki's startling, red-granite Central train station, where you ask for the free pocket timetable, "Taskuaikataulu" (English is the first foreign language in Finland). You leave from a central train yard with all departures marked by electronic signs.

The preserved wooden station houses you come upon in the Finnish countryside are kept in mint condition. Count on them being painted either ochre or rust red and trimmed with white. And almost always, you see an ancient, black steam locomotive standing nearby on a pedestal.

When your train branches onto the Karelian line north toward Lappeenranta, away from the route leading into Russia, the land by the tracks looks marshy but the trees look sturdy. Looking north, you see your first lake. Now your adventure begins.

Reaching Parikkala, only two miles from the present border of Russia, birders pull out their color booklets. Parikkala is a lure for birders. Siberian birds nest and fly over the Siikalahti Conservation Area, as far west as they venture.

After your respite in lovely Savonlinna, leg two continues north to Joensuu, the provincial capital meaning "river mouth," where the branches of Finnish State Railroads thin. Out of Joensuu, you pass through rolling hills with stands primarily of spruce. You see lakes everywhere, but no one using the waters. Occasionally you see an abandoned canoe pulled up onto turf or a quiet outboard motorboat with its motor lying beside it.

At Lieksa station the black steam locomotive that usually stands on display outside every Finnish train station is not present. Instead you see a tiny railroad cart loaded with a single, cut commemorative segment of tree trunk, honoring the origins of this railroad as a lumber-hauling operation.

You travel up the east shore of 60-mile-long Lake Pielinen, the biggest lake in Karelia, until you halt on the northern tip of the lake at Nurmes, center of ski and hiking trails. Nearby is the touristy

Karelian settlement of Bomba. You recognize Karelian architecture by its log houses with wide balconies, pillars, balustrades, overhanging eaves, and ornate "pretty" window frames giving them a cutesy charm.

VR buses from Nurmes have replaced trains to Kajaani. At Nurmes, you have reached the top branch of the tree of electrified lines. Your bus takes slightly over two hours to Kajaani, where you could choose to return south to Helsinki via the Savo line, but adventurers making the great loop north continue aboard the bus to Oulu on the Gulf of Bothnia.

After passing through solitude, you are surprised by Oulu. Dynamic and progressive, happy and prosperous, 100,000-population Oulu claims to be the Silicon Valley of northern Scandinavia. You find astonishingly modern hotels such as the Rivoli and the Eden at half the price of Helsinki hotels on weekends and in June and July, a university town, a marvelous Science Museum, a magnificent Lutheran cathedral, and preserved neo-Renaissance architecture. Oulu is your natural jumping-off point to see Lapland or travel by bus north of the Gulf of Bothnia to Sweden and Norway.

Leg three takes you south from Oulu aboard the fully electrified Ostrobothnian line. South to Helsinki, your train runs faster. IC trains are the fastest way to return to Helsinki. As your InterCity approaches Tampere, you see that you are entering the Western Lakeland—and welcome it is to see—as Lake Nasijarvi opens to your east. Crossing the long bridge across Tampere's Tammerkoski Rapids, you stop in the city center.

One glance at Tampere's brick stacks and you see that Tampere is industrialized—in fact it is the most heavily industrialized city in Finland, but here industry does not look like the dirty word that adventurers fear. Tampere charms you as you walk wide boulevards past quiet green parks and see the plentiful hotels, art nouveau architecture from which Finland adopted its national Romantic style, rolling hills, and blissful lakes. Those quiet stacks give vertical thrusts to Tampere's beautiful setting like exclamation points.

Situated as Tampere is, the hub of the electrified Ostrobothnian line and the east-west spoke from Puri to Pieksamaki and Joensuu, Tampere is your natural home for the Western Lakeland. To reach Tampere's Tourist Office, head four blocks straight down

Hameenkatu from in front of the station and then turn left at Verkatehtaankatu, 2.

As your train continues south, approaching Hameenlinna, look for one of the most impressive sights you can see from a mainline train. While you feel your train braking for the station house, look across the narrow lake to the brick Hameenlinna ("linna" means "castle"), dating from the 1260s. It was built by the Swedes to link the Hame region with the mother country and—you guessed it—to collect taxes from the relatively wealthy area.

Hameenlinna was the northern terminus of Finland's first railroad line from Helsinki in 1862, when goods were transloaded between railroad and lake steamer for further shipment along the lake system to and from the north. Rapid progress soon connected Hameenlinna station to St. Petersburg before it was named Leningrad. The present station building was erected in 1920 following the old one's demolition during the Finnish revolution when Germans, who were supporting "White" Finns in their battles with the "Red" Finns, exploded a railroad carriage filled with gunpowder.

Leg One—Helsinki to Savonlinna

IC1	IC3				IC6	IC8
0634	0934	dep.	HELSINKI	arr.	1428	1720
0640	0940	dep.	Pasila	dep.	1422	1710
0650	0950	dep.	Tikkurila	dep.	1412	1638
0724	1024	dep.	Riihimaki	dep.	1340	1604
0757	1057	dep.	Lahti	dep.	1306	1530
0832	1135	dep.	Kouvola	dep.	1232	1500
0916	1224	dep.	Lappeenranta	dep.	1145	1438
0932	1242	dep.	Joutseno	dep.	1125	1417
0947	1301	dep.	Imatra	dep.	1112	1404
1016	1334	dep.	Simpele	dep.	1034	1334
1029	1347	arr.	Parikkala	dep.	1030	1321
		Change between trains and bus				
R743	**Bus**				**Bus**	**Bus**
1038	1355	dep.	Parikkala	arr.	1020	1245
1057	1420	dep.	Punkaharju	dep.	0950	1215
1104	1435	dep.	Retretti	dep.	0930	1205
1130	1510	arr.	SAVONLINNA (Nyslott)	dep.	0850	1135

Leg Two—Savonlinna to Oulu via Karelian Railroad

Bus					R747
0850	dep.		SAVONLINNA (Nyslott)	arr.	1745
0930	dep.		Retretti	dep.	1719
0950	dep.		Punkaharju	dep.	1712
1020	arr.		Parikkala	dep.	1653
		Change between trains and bus			
IC1					**R10**
1032	dep.		Parikkala	arr.	1609
1056	dep.		Kesalahti	dep.	1543
1115	dep.		Kitee	dep.	1523
1147	arr.		Joensuu	dep.	1443
		Change between trains and bus			
R861					**Bus**
1200	dep.		Joensuu	arr.	1430
1225	dep.		Eno	dep.	I
1236	dep.		Uimaharju	dep.	I
1258	dep.		Vuonislahti	dep.	I
1318	dep.		Lieksa	dep.	I
1328	dep.		Kylanlahti	dep.	I
1344	dep.		Holjakka	dep.	I
1351	dep.		Kohtavaara	dep.	I
1400	arr.		Nurmes	dep.	1235
		Change between trains and bus			
Bus					**Bus**
1615	dep.		Nurmes	arr.	1230
1640	dep.		Valtimo	dep.	1205
1735	dep.		Vuokatti	dep.	1105
1820	dep.		Kajaani	dep.	1040
1858	dep.		Paltamo	dep.	0950
1930	dep.		Vaala	dep.	0910
2000	dep.		Utajarvi	dep.	0840
2020	dep.		Muhos	dep.	0825
2055	arr.		OULU	dep.	0750

Leg Three—Oulu to Helsinki via Ostrobothnian Line

IC50	IC52				IC491	IC51
0710	0953	dep.	OULU	arr.	1357	1657
0753	1037	dep.	Vihanti	dep.	1321	1619
0809	1053	dep.	Oulainen	dep.	1302	1602
0828	1112	dep.	Ylivieska	dep.	1246	1545
0851	1135	dep.	Kannus	dep.	1222	1521
0917	1201	dep.	Kokkola	dep.	1158	1456
0936	1221	dep.	Pannaien	dep.	1135	1433
1008	1253	dep.	Kauhava	dep.	1102	1400
1040	1340	dep.	Seinajoki	dep.	1033	1334
1120	1420	dep.	Parkano	dep.	0941	1244
1207	1507	dep.	TAMPERE	dep.	0902	1202
1250	1550	dep.	Hameenlinna	dep.	0811	1116
1309	1609	dep.	Riihimaki	dep.	0752	1054
1340	1640	dep.	Tikkurila	dep.	0720	1020
1350	1650	dep.	Pasila	dep.	0710	1010
1356	1656	arr.	HELSINKI	dep.	0704	1004

Germany

Savvy Traveling on the Trains of Germany

Germany on ICE—ICE 3—ICE 2—ICE T—ICE TD—InterCity trains—Domestic night trains—S-Bahn trains—Metropolitan trains Cologne-Hamburg—Airport trains—Rail-pass travel

Germany's Deutsche Bahn prefers to be known as "Die Bahn" (DB, "The Railroad," *www.bahn.de*). It is the combination of the former Deutsche Bundesbahn (DB) of West Germany and Deutsche Reichsbahn (DR) of the East. DB takes you everywhere you want to go. Overall, DB spans 24,800 miles, of which 10,500 miles are electrified. More than 30,500 trains, including 1,200 long-distance trains, transport 4.7 million passengers per day and serve nearly 8,000 cities and villages in unified Germany. Trains take you to the Alps, North Sea beaches, along the Rhine River, and through the Black Forest. Many conductors and staff speak English.

DB has made massive investments in the speediest trains in Europe, the high-speed tracks to carry them, and in tilting trains, but their investments in regional and suburban trains mean that you will ride fewer and fewer of the traditional locomotive-hauled trains and

375

more and more electric and diesel motorized units and double-decked trains.

GermanRail EC (EuroCity) and ICE (InterCity Express) trains link practically all of the major cities in Europe, e.g., Paris, Prague, Budapest, Vienna, Amsterdam, Zurich, Innsbruck, and Copenhagen. ICE trains connect with Cisalpino trains in Stuttgart and Zurich for services to Milan and Venice, and they connect with the Thalys network at Cologne for Paris. You receive an on-board timetable called "Ihr Reiseplan" ("Your Travel Schedule") on every ICE, IC (InterCity), EC, and even many slower trains, showing not only your time of arrival and departure at every stop along your way but—more useful—telling you where to change for your ultimate destination.

DB's ICE, EC, and IC trains run punctually at least every other hour, usually hourly, and depart at the same minute after the hour. If you miss a train, it is usually wiser to wait for the next train of the same class than to take a local train that departs sooner. Even then, check the yellow departure sheets to make sure the train stops where you want to go.

DB has three basic fare levels for point-to-point ticketing. Rail-pass holders ride free regardless of the fare category. The highest point-to-point ticket price is for ICE services, the medium for IC and night services, and the lowest for regional trains. You may receive a discount of 25 or 50 percent if you book your trip in advance on restricted trains. When you reserve three days in advance, you save 25 percent but must make a round-trip purchase. For 50 percent discount you must make a Saturday-night stay or travel on Saturday or Sunday.

If you miss your prebooked train, you will have to pay the difference between the discounted and full fare, plus a substantial penalty. *Tip:* To take advantage of these fares before you leave for Germany, log onto *www.bahn.de,* click "International Guests," check the timetables and prices, purchase, and print out your tickets.

Children under 14 travel free with their parent and you can save an additional 50 percent for up to four individuals traveling with a primary passenger. Also see "Rail-Pass Travel" below.

Reservations are not required on German trains, but if you desire, it is easy to make reservations in Germany (and you save money by not making them from the U.S.). You pay a lower reservations fee when you buy a ticket and reserve at the same time, but a higher fee if you first buy a ticket and then come back later for a reservation.

DB accepts MasterCard (Eurocard), Visa, Diners Club, and traveler's checks in U.S. dollars, euros, and British pounds sterling.

Larger GermanRail stations have escalators to the platforms (Berlin's Zoo, Friedrichstasse, and Alexanderplatz, Dusseldorf, Koblenz, Hamburg, Hanover, Heidelberg, Mainz, Mannheim, etc.), and some 130 smaller ones such as Freiburg have automatic conveyer belts to lift your luggage. In most DB platforms you find racks of luggage carts ("Kofferkulis") so that you can unlock one for a deposit. You get your coin back if you return your cart, but you won't find abandoned carts because DB employees are instructed to round up stray carts to prevent them from rolling onto the tracks.

DB offers porter service at some 18 larger train stations, including Berlin Zoo and Hamburg, Freiburg, Leipzig, Dresden, Frankfurt/Main, Stuttgart, and Munich main stations. The charge is about $3.50 for the first two pieces of luggage and $1.75 for each additional piece. DB encourages bicycle rentals, and you can find "Bahn & Bike" programs in most German states. Almost 60 percent of all long-distance trains allow you to take along your bike.

Nearly all DB stations have lockers for you to store your luggage in a safe place. There are four sizes of lockers, with rentals ranging from about $1 to $3 for 24 hours, depending on size. Maximum storage time is 72 hours. If you do not remove your luggage on time, attendants remove your belongings and charge you a $7.50 service charge. Long-term rentals are also available for $30 to $60 a month, depending on locker size.

DB maintains first-class lounges (open daily, 6:30 A.M. to 11 P.M., and some later) in Cologne Hbf , Frankfurt/Main International Airport train station, Leipzig Hbf, Hanover Hbf, Bremen Hbf, Mannheim Hbf, Stuttgart Hbf, Nuremberg Hbf, Munich Hbf, and Frankfurt/Main Hbf, which was enlarged in 2003. Hamburg Hbf, Berlin Zoo, Dusseldorf Hbf, and Dortmund open in 2004. Show your first-class pass or ticket and enjoy a quiet atmosphere, comfortable seats, free drinks and snacks, functional laptop workplaces, and access to a conference room. Those without first-class passes or tickets can pay €7.60 for admission.

Germany on ICE

DB's primary claim to greatness comes from its magnificent network of ICE trains running hourly and even half-hourly along long high-speed lines through the West.

Since the first InterCity Express train was introduced in 1991, DB's enormous, well-synchronized, integrated ICE network takes you from Kiel and Hamburg and Berlin to Munich, Interlaken, Zurich, Vienna, Brussels, Copenhagen, and Amsterdam and throughout the entire transportation infrastructure of most of Germany. It is thus the world's largest, most complex, and most expensive high-speed network. ICE trains surpass everything running in travel comfort and service. They are environmentally friendly, fast, and safe. All conform to the color codes of the GermanRail: red and pink with a gray-white background. Lavender horizontal striping below the noses of the power cars at each end makes them appear more streamlined. Prominent gray *ICE* letters identify each side.

Around 50 of the 216 ICE train sets bear the names of cities. Look for the name of the city and its coat of arms on both sides of the train near the ends of the set. The first set named was an ICE T, named "Berlin." Few train services bear names.

Germany on ICE

	ICE 1	ICE 2	ICE 3	ICE T	ICE TD
Year	1991	1996	2000-2001	1999-2000	2001
Number of Trains	59	44	50	32+28	20
Carriages	12	7	8	5-7	4
Power Cars	2 Electric	1 Electric	0* Electric	0* Electric	0* Diesel
Length, Feet	1,174	672	656	436-607	351
Seats	673	391	404/415	250-381	195
Top Speed	174 mph	174 mph	205 mph	143 mph	125 mph
Power	9,600 kW	4,800 kW	8,000 kW	3,000-4,000 kW	1,700 kW
Other			13 Multivoltage	Tilting	Tilting
Routes	Hanover-Wurzburg; Mannheim-Stuttgart	Berlin-Hanover	Cologne-Frankfurt/Main	Munich-Leipzig-Berlin-Hamburg, Dresden-Leipzig-Frankfurt/Main	Dresden-Nuremberg, Zurich-Munich, Zurich-Stuttgart, Ruhr-Weimar

*Power distributed below carriages

ICE 3

While the first-generation ICE 1 was designed for the Hanover-Wurzburg and Mannheim-Stuttgart high-speed lines and the second-generation ICE 2 for the Berlin-Hanover line, the third-generation ICE 3 was introduced for the 2002 Frankfurt/Main-Cologne 186-mph line.

Your roller-coaster ride begins when your 186-mph ICE 3 speed burner passes Siegburg's new train station on the 2002 Cologne-Frankfurt/Main high-speed line about 31 miles south of Cologne. The station acts as a hub for the populous area southeast of Cologne and is important for its light-rail trains running every 10 minutes to Bonn.

Past Siegburg your train climbs almost continuously from about 200 feet above sea level to nearly 1,000 feet as you cross from Nordrhein-Westfalen to Rheinland-Pfalz. From the summit, you head downhill, speeding at 186 mph, nose down, steeper and steeper, until you are descending at 4 percent (one foot in every 25 feet crossed) across the 1,128-foot Fischerhaus Viaduct and plunging into the 3,600-foot Gunterscheid Tunnel, still on a 4 percent slide.

This hilly section of DB's new high-speed line between Cologne and Frankfurt/Main gives you an exciting ride through the Siebengebirge (mountains) with occasional glimpses of the cars on the Autobahn that appear to be going backward. The highest peak of the Siebengebirge is at 1,500 feet, where from the summit you can admire the panorama of the Rhine Valley on the west and Europe's speediest train racing through the mountains on your east. But the scenery does not stop racing past your window in the Siebengebirge as you continue through the Westerwald (forest) and then the Taunus mountainous region.

The August 1 opening of the ICE 3 on the high-speed line between Cologne and Frankfurt/Main and its December 15 integration with the international network comprised Europe's biggest rail event of 2002. DB publicized it with a big, red, numeral one, indicating one hour saved on the line.

DB's 2002 line takes you over 136 miles of dedicated high-speed track, through 30 tunnels and across 18 major viaducts at 186 mph. You pass through the extensive new Montabaur station, only 12 miles from Koblenz, and the new park-and-ride Limburg Sud station, which is served by shuttle buses to and from the Limburg Hbf. The new direct track between Frankfurt and Cologne is 30 miles shorter than the former Rhine River route.

This new route is an integral part of the central north-south axis of European train travel. You travel it between Amsterdam and Switzerland and continuing into Italy. You even save time from Wiesbaden Hbf and Mainz Hbf via a branch past Limburg that takes you beside the Wiesbaden U.S. Air Force base.

ICE 3 is the latest, and crown, of the evolution of high-speed and comfortable ICE trains DB offers visitors. It is rated at 205 mph maximum speed, but running at line speeds up to 186 mph, it isn't permitted to go full throttle. It is a complete break from the design of the ICE 1 and ICE 2 trains described below because the power equipment is distributed throughout train. The driving cars are powered but do not have pantographs, which are placed on intermediate carriages to accommodate the roller-coaster running of the high-speed line through the Taunus hills with steep gradients. ICE 3's exterior appears similar to the other third-generation ICE trains, the ICE TD and ICE T described below, but longer and with a sharper front end.

The lounge in the ICE 3 is an eye-opener because the oncoming scenery and tracks rush past you over the driver's shoulder through the cockpit window. The lounges front and back are the most startling interior innovation of the ICE 3 as well as other third-generation ICEs, but the reclining black leather bucket seats in first class and dark blue moquette seats in second will catch your eye. They give you the impression that you are racing in an expensive sports car and make your speed seem even faster than 186 mph. Light woods and brushed metal fittings add to the ambience.

You can use the standard-equipment laptop and audio connections at the 342 second-class seats as well as at the 98 first-class seats. Seats in first class have video screens and individual reading lights.

You may choose to order meals at your seat from an extensive menu in either first or second class, or visit the BordBistro cafe. The catering concept of serving food and drinks at your seat is more popular than the traditional restaurant services on earlier ICE trains.

The high-speed line, which took six years to build, was built to follow the busy A3 motorway for much of its length with an eye to preserving open space and minimizing environmental impact.

Plans to build a high-speed line through the Westerwald go back to

1969, but building the Hanover-Wurzburg and Mannheim-Stuttgart high-speed lines took precedence, and when Germany was reunified, DB's management rushed to build the Hanover-Berlin high-speed connection.

IC services to and from Dusseldorf use Cologne-Deutz's low-level station on the opposite bank of the Rhine River from the Cologne Hauptbahnhof to save some 15 minutes crossing the Rhine into the main station, and it is also the terminus for Thalys trains to and from Brussels.

Past your stop at Frankfurt/Main International Airport, you arrive at Frankfurt/Main Hbf. It is the largest train station in Europe but well laid out, with mainline trains arriving on the surface level but most S-Bahn trains arriving and departing on the lower level "Tiefbahnhof." It is a nonsmoking station, but certain areas are indicated where smoking is permitted. The Tourist Office is the first thing you find when you come in the front entrance, and the DB first-class lounge is nearby. The InterCity Hotel Frankfurt (*www.intercityhotel.de*), which you can reserve at any DB station or through Steigenburger reservations, is convenient. You exit through the train station's north exit and you see it across the street. *Tip:* Ask for the free public-transportation pass. The "Touring" kiosk for the Romantic Road Europabuses (see section below) is in front of the station.

ICE 1

German children behave like such lambs with their earphones plugged in, watching the video, that their parents leave them to themselves and repair to the bar car. The American teenager is glued to the German-language-dubbed video although he can't understand a word of German. "I've already seen it."

The business traveler has spread his papers across the table and is tapping his analysis into his laptop. You are in the vestibule watching the digital speedometer readout inch toward 280 km/hr (174 mph) as you head south from Hanover toward Wurzburg aboard GermanRail's spacious ICE 1 train, which first ran on June 1, 1991.

While ICE high-speed lines were being financed and laboriously constructed, GermanRail engineers approached the design of their first-generation high-speed trains with admirable scientific method. First, engineers built a full-size "InterCity Experimental" train, a research and demonstration tool; loaded it with sensors and recorders;

tested it under various conditions of speed, track condition, weather, and loading; and evaluated every significant variable.

These tests led to two important developments in train design technology and provided a firm basis for ICE 1's final design and cosmetic appearance.

• Depressurization caused by high speeds in tunnels had to be considered unacceptable.

Depressurization of the InterCity Experimental train while racing through tunnels caused riders to complain. (Engineers recognize the Bernoulli effect at work.) GermanRail's new trains had to be made pressure tight. It was a blow, especially because the Landrucken tunnel lies on the line chosen for ICE 1's inaugural run. It meant not only sealing ICE 1's windows, doors, and ventilation, but also redesigning its closed toilet systems.

• A wider train would ride more efficiently.

Serendipitously, engineers found they could increase ICE 1's width.

• Cosmetic changes would increase the marketing appeal of the train.

The rounding of the nose of the power car was given a sharper radius to reduce its drag coefficient and improve its appearance. A grille was introduced between the headlights to ventilate the drivers' compartment.

The drivers' cabin is celebrated as a haven for rail fans and government ministers making publicity trips. It was redesigned to make it more photogenic and functional.

Sensationalism fell from the ICE 1 when FrenchRail's TGV Atlantique began setting new world speed records one after another (the last was 320 mph on May 18, 1990), surpassing the earlier ICE speed record of 253 mph. It became apparent that first running of a 155-mph ICE 1 (later 174 mph) in Germany two years after implementation of 186-mph TGV Atlantique service in France would no longer be considered by the world as a breakthrough, but rather the heart of Europe catching up.

ICE 1's 12 aluminum-body middle carriages include four first- and six second-class cars, a specially fitted carriage, and a dual-service dining car called a "BordRestaurant." Riding first class reminds you of riding in a modern, five-star hotel, because of the spaciousness and deluxe furnishings, but riding second class is a significant step down because the carriages are so popular that you lose the chance to wander about, admiring this and that, such as the vacuum-emptied WCs; the elaborate telephone booths with portable telephones designed to work without interruption even in the many tunnels punctuating the lines; 30 seats featuring small, flat, LCD color screens; individual jacks and controls for earphones; the computer readouts in the vestibules alternately announcing your route, carriage and train number, coming stop, current speed in kilometers per hour, and time of day; the free private lockers for purses, briefcases, cameras, and day packs (take the key with you); the coat closets breaking the potential monotony of large interiors; and above all the marvelous BordRestaurant.

Push the buttons to enter. The doors close automatically behind you. The LCD display shows you whether you are in second or first class. The tinted windows give a cool appearance, but you see that what appears to be a continuous, mirrored window line from the outside is merely a clever cosmetic touch. In reality, the extraordinarily long windows corresponding to two rows of seats are indeed separated and provide spaces to hang coats. It strikes you immediately that you are in a *big* train. As you walk through the wide aisle, the doors open and close automatically and crossing between the carriages is as safe as a baby's crib.

ICE 1's BordRestaurant is a revelation. Waiters from a central kitchen crammed with stainless-steel, high-tech equipment and microwave ovens serve a selection of German and European meals, with wine selection, to the travelers in the sit-down, white-tablecloth dining room on the end adjacent to the first-class carriage. In the other dining room, adjacent to the second-class carriage, travelers gather in the "BordTreff" at Formica tables, bunching around a German Stehbar. Draft beer is the product of choice (as you can tell by the laughter), but snacks are also available to eat at benches around the side in the casual, self-service, bistro-style cafe. Bright modern pink, blue, and white interiors with beech-wood fittings and large semi-panoramic windows have recessed lighting and—almost like an atrium—raised ceilings with futuristic latticework to shield direct sunlight. With rooflines higher than the rest of the train, ICE's BordRestaurants recall the panorama of the former TEE Rheingold observation cars and give you an airy, spacious feeling. You cannot smoke in either the dining room or "BordTreff." More than 77 percent of those surveyed preferred no smoking.

By making the ICE 1 slightly wider than conventional trains, GermanRail could allow travelers to ride more comfortably. Instead of 111.2 inches, the width of GermanRail's early 1990s InterCity carriages, GermanRail made the ICE 1 118.9 inches wide. Couple that with a more generous salon seat area than in a French TGV (12.9 square feet versus 9.7 square feet in first class; 9.7 square feet compared to 6.5 square feet in second class), and passengers are elated. Also, dining cars, toilets, and compartments are larger and more comfortable.

Ironically, this widening and lengthening subjected GermanRail to great criticism within Germany when the German public realized that their expensive ($30 million each) new domestic ICE 1s were just that: domestic. The trains were too wide, too long, and not equipped to cope with differing electrical power supplies in neighboring countries. ICE 1's range beyond Germany was limited to Switzerland and Austria.

ICE 2

Therefore 368-seat, 1996 second-generation ICE 2 trains were made shorter and lighter, but remained limited to domestic electrical supplies. ICE 2s consist of one locomotive and seven carriages instead of ICE 1's two locomotives and up to 14 carriages. When DB needs high capacity, it couples two ICE 2s together with an automatic coupler but can separate the two halves quickly at a station and send them to different destinations. They were designed primarily to make DB's timetable more flexible. ICE 2 first went into service in September 1996, on the line between Hamburg and Frankfurt/Main.

Riding ICE 2s, you realize they are an efficient, swift way to get you from place to place at the fastest-feasible speed. ICE 2 is clearly the more cost-effective train that accountants prefer but not nearly as comfortable to ride.

Except for the couplers, ICE 2's power cars are otherwise interchangeable with the ICE 1's so as to give DB complete fleet flexibility. Their length (67.5 feet), operating power (4,800 kW), and maximum speed (174 mph) are the same, while the weight is slightly less (86 tons). Most mechanical and electrical components are also the same.

You probably won't realize you have boarded one of GermanRail's ICE 2 trains instead of an ICE 1 until you take your seat. Both ICE 1 and second-generation ICE 2 have the same red-striped white livery and the same distinctive semi-continuous line of reflective windows.

In addition to the ICE 2 being shorter, a careful observer will see that the new generation's front headlights rise much higher, changing the appearance noticeably. Under covers in the nose you can detect the automatic couplers that make ICE 2 special.

You won't need a seat reservation ticket, so when you board, be sure to check the electronic destination indicators outside. These indicators are essential for a train that splits. You don't want to suddenly find you are on the train to Dusseldorf when your friends are waiting in Cologne.

Once you find your seat (reserved seats are indicated by electronic displays, which replace the paper reservation slips in most trains—railpass holders don't need reservations, but you don't want to sit in someone's reserved seat), you are disappointed when the first thing you notice is that DB figured out a diabolical way to arrange seats more closely together without crimping your leg- or elbowroom. This way they can pack more paying passengers into an ICE 2.

Although the seats are clearly less substantial, DB's spin doctors explain eight ways the new seats are more comfortable, including the fact that you can manually recline the first-class seats (but not the second). Console yourself that at least you have a footrest.

ICE 2's designers squeezed out even more places to sit by minimizing ICE 1's gracious wardrobe/luggage locker spaces and eliminating the popular six-person compartments. Both first- and second-class ICE 2 sections are arranged around a wide central aisle, partly in rows, partly around tables.

Some carriages are divided into smoking and nonsmoking sections, with the smoking sections located at the end. In the smoking sections only, you may use cellular telephones. The nonsmoking sections are quiet zones.

There are two restaurants in two ICE 2s coupled together, and your walk to a restaurant is shorter, so you won't object to their smaller size.

Seating is limited in the restaurant section. Eight tables seat 23, but the gray, polka-dot decor is quite pleasant and the ceiling, although lacking the striking atrium roof of the ICE 1, is attractively contoured.

The Bistro sections are separated from the restaurants by a kitchen. They will disappoint you. You have no place to sit and only two stand-up counters at which to snack. DB expects second-class passengers to take their food to their seats. The space went to the relocated conductor's compartment and a toilet for the disabled.

ICE T

The 1999-2000 member of the ICE family, the ICE T uses tilting technology to gain higher speeds over the old tracks, which have frequent curves. This technical innovation allowed DB to offer faster speed and greater comfort where laying entirely new tracks was not economic. Taking charge of the IC routes, these tilting trains take you along the slower lines that the DB has no funds to upgrade. You ride seven-carriage IC Ts Berlin-Leipzig-Munich and Frankfurt/Main-Dresden. They are able to maintain their speed around curves by using the same Fiat tilting system as the Italian Pendolino trains ETR 460 and ETR 470 (see "Italy" and "International" chapters).

When your ICE T Helene Weigel begins to snake with tender tilts through the curves and hilly terrain of Germany's Frankenwald (forest), you will begin to fully appreciate the advantages of ICE T's active tilt system and the comforts of its deluxe interior. Your trip through the hilly Frankenwald is an eye-opener. As you pass from Lichtenfels to Saalfeld, tilting among gracious spruce and pine forests at 61 mph, you realize you are riding one heck of a good train.

Thirty-two, 143-mph, first-series ICE T trains assumed former InterCity (IC) duties from locomotive-pulled IC trains on electrified routes throughout Germany, and you are reaping the benefits. ICE T's first series was so well received that DB added 28 second-series ICE Ts costing nearly $400 million.

Since the introduction of ICE Ts between Munich and Berlin via Nuremberg and Leipzig, your travel time decreased from seven hours, 34 minutes over the 442-mile route at 58 mph average to six hours, 55 minutes (64 mph average). The same route would have taken you eight hours, 48 minutes by IC train in summer 1992.

ICE T's active tilt system is not the only thing that makes it radically different from earlier ICE trains. Like the ICE 3, DB's engineers distributed the power equipment below the passenger carriages instead of using separate locomotive/power cars to pull or push like conventional trains. The lack of a power car makes it possible for six first-class passengers to sit in front and look over the shoulder of the driver, who is separated only by a glass panel. From these seats you see the scenery not only to the sides but also straight ahead through the wraparound driver's window, and you also see the driver sitting in the center of his cockpit.

First-class passengers sit in seats arranged two opposite one, but the rows are staggered and have little symmetry. Some seats are aligned in conventional airline style with seatback video screens showing German-language movies, some are clustered around handsome wood-veneer tables with folding flaps that make getting in and out easy, and some, in the centers of the carriages, are enclosed in three semiprivate four-person compartments with glass doors that may be closed.

Second-class seating is more conventional. Seats are dark blue moquette arranged two opposite two, the flooring is carpeted, and several tables are scattered to relieve the monotony.

The large windows make the train seem airy. Sunscreens pull down manually. The doors fly open on your approach, triggered by sensors in the carpet. Smoking is not allowed except in the second carriage, which is mixed first and second class, and in the dining carriage only.

The high-tech design extends to replacing paper-slip reservations markers with electronic indicators above the seats. You can read real-time messages overhead at the ends of the carriages, including actual speed. In the vestibule, LCD screens display not only the next stop but also indicate on which side to exit. A separate touch-screen computer provides timetable planning information.

Electrical outlets for notebook computers are located at every seat. Some designated carriages in the ICE T have been fitted with repeaters to enhance cellular telephone connections. Use of cellular telephones in the other, quiet carriages is *verboten*.

In both classes you have no trouble finding a place for your luggage. In addition to the usual above-seat shelves, at the ends of carriages you find coin-operated lockers requiring a €2 deposit. In one carriage you can use an open luggage rack with cables to attach to your luggage to prevent its theft.

ICE T has a children's play area as well. It is not large, but it is large enough for children to romp and do what children do. Other passengers appreciate that it has a glass door that closes to shield them from the inevitable screams and shouts.

The simulated blond-wood restaurant car is disappointing, with two-opposite-one seating on red Naugahyde seats, and the menu is sparse and expensive.

To comply with international restrictions, the shorter carriages are narrower than ICE 1 by 2.8 inches, which is still wider than the early 1990s InterCity carriages. Like the ICE 2, two trains can be coupled together.

ICE TD

The ICE TD, DB's third-generation tilting ICE train, made a highly successful debut over the curving tracks between Zurich and Stuttgart on May 30, 1999. ICE TD lines now take you over non-electrified lines Hamburg-Copenhagen-Malmo and Munich-Zurich in addition to Stuttgart-Zurich.

The Zurich-Stuttgart ICE TD consists of five carriages, one first class with lounge, three second class, and one with a cafe plus second-class seating. The ICE TD is exciting to ride because lounges in front for first-class passengers and in back for second-class passengers allow you to look over the driver's shoulder at the views he sees ahead. This new perspective is possible because there is no locomotive.

The driver's location in the center of the cockpit is especially auspicious on the Zurich-Stuttgart route because in Switzerland the trains run on the left, while in Germany they run on the right.

You have no trouble finding a place for your luggage. In addition to the usual above-seat shelves, there are coin-operated lockers at the ends of carriages. In one carriage you can use an open luggage rack with devices to attach to your luggage to prevent its theft.

Every ICE TD has either a cafe (*BordBistro*) or restaurant (*BordRestaurant*), and where the five-carriage ICE TD fails is the quality of the dining facility. Whereas Cisalpino on the same Zurich-Stuttgart route devotes a full carriage to the best and most tasteful dining area to be found on the trains of Europe, the five-carriage ICE TD has only a token cafe with no seats. It provides only places to lean while using four oval stand-alone tables.

Some carriages in the ICE TD have been fitted with repeaters to enhance cellular telephone communication. Use of cellular telephones in the other carriages is discouraged. The cellular-friendly carriages are No. 28 (first class) and Nos. 21 and 23 (second class).

Certain ICE TDs have a bicycle room, but because of limited space, bicycle take-along should be reserved in advance.

InterCity Trains

DB has no central hub, such as FrenchRail's Paris or SpanishRail's Madrid, but rather a spread of key cities with equal commercial status. DB has cunningly interlaced hourly IC service with ICE timetables so that it is possible for you to board at any of the IC- or ICE-network cities and, by following the on-board timetable, arrive with all speed in any other station you might choose by making only one split-second across-the-platform change or two at most. GermanRail's trains and platforms are designed to simplify connections. First-class carriages are in the front of the train; second-class ones in the rear. Travelers need only cross the platform to find equivalent accommodation on the connecting train. Travelers boarding for the first time know where to stand by consulting the "Wagenstandanzeiger" train composition boards on the platforms or the digital signs overhead, which in addition to the usual departure information also show you where the first- and second-class sections come to rest.

GermanRail's IC carriages were refurbished in 1999-2000 with a second-generation interior refurbishment known as "Redesign 2," with new seats, extensive light wood and brushed aluminum trim, family compartments, and an improved catering area. The exteriors more recently were repainted white with red stripe, identical to the ICE livery.

Most of GermanRail's IC and EC trains carry one or two salon carriages while the rest of the train consists of compartment carriages. Dining cars are located between the first- and second-class sections.

Domestic Night Trains

GermanRail's Nachtzuge trains (NZ) are excellent. On four routes they actually consist of Spanish-designed Tren Hotel tilting carriages painted in GermanRail's night-blue livery with GermanRail embellishments. New 2003 sleeping carriages have improved suspension, potable water, and a compartment with shower and toilet.

The routes of these tilting NZ are
• Berlin (Lichtenberg)-Berlin (Zoo)-Berlin (Wannsee)-Halle-Augsburg-Munich,
• Berlin (Lichtenberg)-Berlin (Zoo)-Berlin (Wannsee)-Dortmund-Essen-Duisburg-Dusseldorf-Cologne-Bonn,
  • Hamburg-Bremen-Hanover-Augsburg-Munich,
  • Hamburg-Bremen-Frankfurt/Main-Heidelberg-Stuttgart, and
  • Stuttgart-Munich-Leipzig-Dresden.
These Talgo night trains are so low-slung that GermanRail's standard locomotives rise high above them. The trains tilt rounding curves and include a lavish dining room for first-class passengers and a Bistro for those less affluent, with the exception of the Berlin-Bonn train, which provides only the Bistro.

The first-class, air-conditioned cabins contain their own private shower, washbasin, and toilet. You can book them either as a single or a double. The beds are aligned in the direction of travel. You lock your compartment with your key card.

In addition to carriages, which each contain five deluxe single and double sleeping compartments, you can ride in second-class carriages fitted with 1996-designed couchettes, which, on the Berlin-Bonn train, are aligned in the direction of travel and separated by curtains. Traditional DB couchette carriages sleep 60, the new ones, 48. In the middle are 12, two-person compartments with curtains. In addition there are two compartments with sliding doors designed for four adults and a child and two compartments designed for two adults and two children.

The GermanRail sleeperette seats, which recline deeply, are the equivalent of business class in air travel. Caterers provide food service from a trolley. The luggage car also carries bicycles for a nominal charge.

When you hold a rail pass, you pay less than half for cabins, and the equivalent of $3 for a sleeperette seat or couchette when you make your reservation in Germany.

In addition to the tilting NZ you can ride traditional NZ on the routes between Binz and Munich, Binz and Stuttgart, and Munich and Dortmund. These carry couchettes, sleeping cars, and second-class compartments for six and provide a Bistro.

S-Bahn Trains

Use GermanRail's rapid-transit, frequent-service "S-Bahn" trains in seven independent regions of intense train travel in and around Berlin, Frankfurt/Main, Hamburg, Munich, Nuremberg, the Ruhr, Cologne, Stuttgart, and Leipzig. You will especially appreciate them in Berlin, where they take you to Potsdam for Sanssouci and are a vital link between East and West, and in Munich, where S-Bahn trains parallel Munich's subways and use the same underground station entrances along the Hauptbahnhof-Marienplatz-Ostbahnhof corridor. Look for the green-and-white *S* signs marking station entrances. *Tip:* Rail passes are valid on S-Bahn trains but not U-Bahn trains.

Metropolitan Trains Cologne-Hamburg

Silver-livery "Metropolitan" business trains between Cologne and Hamburg began running on August 1, 1999, with stops only in

Dusseldorf and Essen. The Metropolitan is an elite train, operated by Metropolitan Express Train GmbH, Hewlett-Packard Strasse 4, 61352 Bad Homburg (*www.met.de*), which is 63 percent owned by DB and 37 percent by the company's employees. Rail passes are not honored. Trains have 350 seats, all upholstered in black leather. Interior finish is largely of light wood. Business travelers can sit in three areas: "Office," which is like working in an office; "Silence," where they find blankets, pillows, and earphones, and cellular phones are banned; and "Club," where they find a choice of films or DVDs. Metropolitan introduced a new "Traveller" class in 2001, which is a third cheaper than the high normal fares aimed at businesspeople. You can make a reservation costing DM 30 (about $15) through the usual DB channels. Although you receive a discount with a rail pass, you need a first-class, full-fare DB ticket.

Metropolitan Train Service

0618	1118	1518	1918	dep.	Cologne (Hbf)	arr.	0941	1441	1841	2241
0639	1129	1539	1939	dep.	Dusseldorf	arr.	0917	1417	1817	2217
0703	1203	1603	2003	dep.	Essen	arr.	0853	1353	1753	2153
0949	1444	1844	2244	arr.	Hamburg (Hbf)	dep.	0615	1115	1515	1915

Airport Trains

The $220 million *Frankfurt/Main International Airport* high-speed train station ("Fernbahnhof") opened on May 31, 1999. At the underground station, which is 2,300 feet long and 200 feet wide, you can board 84 daily mainline ICE and IC trains (from 5:30 A.M. to midnight) on four tracks to take you directly to and from the airport on ICE and IC lines using the new high-speed Cologne-Frankfurt/Main line that was integrated into the regular interval timetable on December 15, 2002.

The Fernbahnhof is magnificent, with escalators connecting the levels and platforms. The DB first-class lounge is spacious and the light-wood paneling is attractive. Like in an airline lounge, a receptionist greets you, checks your first-class train ticket, and helps you with arrangements. Two levels above the station you can buy train tickets and validate your rail pass at the Reisezentrum, you can relax in the DB first-class lounge, and departing passengers can check in for some flights. On the roof level, agents will give you hotel and other service information, and you can patronize restaurants.

Frankfurt/Main International Airport already was served (and still is) by rapid-transit S-Bahn trains from the many Frankfurt city stations to the airport and to and from Mainz. This station is now called the Frankfurt Airport Regionalbahnhof. S-Bahn line S8 trains leave the Regionalbahnhof four or five times per hour for the 11-minute, six-mile trip to Frankfurt/Main's Hauptbahnhof with three intermediate city stops. Rail passes cover all of these trains.

To board your train, simply follow the signs "Fernbahnhof" and "Regionalbahnhof." Push your luggage on the airport's escalator-friendly carts right to the doors of your selected train.

Similarly, American Airlines has a code-share arrangement with DB from Frankfurt Airport to Dusseldorf, Hamburg, Cologne, Munich, Stuttgart, and other German cities.

In 2000, *Dusseldorf Airport* became the third German airport (after Frankfurt/Main International Airport and Berlin Schonefeld Airport) to provide ICE connections. German Chancellor Gerhard Schroeder, President Wolfgang Clement, and the head of DB opened the station, which will be served by 270 ICE, IC, IR, local, and S-Bahn trains daily. You transfer between the airport and ICE station by a modern people-mover.

The separate S-Bahn terminal remains directly under the airport and is now named "Dusseldorf Flughafen Terminal." Since 1990, you have been able to use regular-interval S-Bahn trains to Dortmund and Duisberg as well as to Cologne and Dusseldorf's main train station. Passengers on the line to Ohligs will ride in 2000 trains. Use the escalator right from the airport's main hall. Line S7 S-Bahn trains run every 20 minutes to the Dusseldorf Hbf, 13 minutes away.

Munich Franz-Josef Strauss Airport in Erding, Germany's second-largest airport, opened their new Terminal 2 on June 29, 2003, for Lufthansa and its Star Alliance partners, to facilitate transfers in just 30 minutes. The airport is locked into the Munich S-Bahn system by line two lines, S-1 and S-8. By different routes, the S-Bahn lines stagger 20-minute departures, taking you from the 1992 underground station below the airport terminal to Munich's Old Town and the Hauptbahnhof. Rail passes are accepted.

Line S-1's 13-mile S-Bahn stretch was connected with the airport in 1998. It takes 45 minutes to approach the Hauptbahnhof from the west. Trains run every 20 minutes, beginning at 4:35 A.M. until 12:15 A.M.

Line S-8's three-carriage S-Bahn trains run every 20 minutes starting at 4:05 A.M. from the airport and finishing with their 1:05 A.M. departure. Traveling the 23 miles from the airport terminal to Munich's Hauptbahnhof takes 40 minutes.

Berlin Schonefeld Airport, in the East, opened on October 6, 1960, with a 2.1-mile runway. It is so far in the outskirts of Berlin that it adds another unwanted leg to your long journey. Luckily, few travelers from the West will have occasion to use it, unless after visiting Berlin they continue to the East. Mainline trains, including the ICE, stop here on their long runs between Berlin and Dresden, and it also is served by GermanRail's frequent regional "Airport Express" line RB24 trains, which will carry you with few stops to the center of Berlin—Ostbahnhof, Friedrichstrasse, Alexanderplatz, and Zoo train stations. S-Bahn trains serve additional stops along the way and therefore take longer. Tickets for both regional and S-Bahn trains are sold at the airport. Rail passes are valid on both. Alternately, you may take bus 171 from the airport to U-Bhf Rudow to join the U-Bahn network—and this will be your fastest way to the southern part of Berlin, Kreuzberg, and Tempelhof. Your Berlin Transit Authority bus ticket will also put you aboard Berlin's U-Bahn system.

Berlin Tegel Airport is not a mega-airport like Frankfurt/Main's. It is constructed like a hexagonal doughnut. International pictographs are used (the same as in the train stations), so finding your way around is not difficult. At the main entrance, a bank, transportation office for ticketing, and post office are grouped. Hotel information and booking is opposite Gate 8. Several cafes and a fast-food outlet are scattered through the doughnut. Several bus lines, both express and local, have stops in front of the station at the curb. You have a choice of express bus to the city centers. One takes you to East Berlin, one to West Berlin. You may consult the posted route maps. The buses require normal bus tickets, which are available from the machines facing the curb.

The *Stuttgart Airport* is connected to Stuttgart Hauptbahnhof by 1993 S-Bahn lines S2 and S3 on the lower level of the train station. S-Bahn departures every 10 minutes carry you the 13 miles in 25 minutes. Rail passes cover the S-Bahn.

From *Hamburg Fuhlsbuttel Airport,* the "Airport Express" bus shuttle waits by the Kirchenallee/Hachmannplatz exit. Running every 10 minutes, they take you to the main train station in 30 minutes. Or you may take bus line 110 to Ohlsdorf rapid-transit station, where you cross the highway and board S-Bahn train line 1 or U-Bahn train line 1. Both lines take you to the Hauptbahnhof in 30 minutes, but via different routes. Some of the trains are from 2002. Only the S-Bahn line is covered by rail pass.

The new two-mile rail link from the Hamburg Airport (to Ohlsdorf) will open in 2005.

Dresden Airport's 2001, two-mile rail link from the underground airport terminus to Dresden's Hbf runs hourly, while the service to Dresden Neustadt runs every half-hour. When the line was electrified in 2003, the Airport-Dresden Hbf-Heidenau S-Bahn service was inaugurated.

A 10-mile loop serving the *Cologne/Bonn Airport* is ancillary to the main Frankfurt/Main-Cologne high-speed route. ICE trains will begin serving the midsize airport (and connecting it with the Frankfurt and Dusseldorf airports) on June 8, 2004, for both ICE and S-Bahn trains.

The *Leipzig/Halle Airport* on June 30, 2003, began being served over a new 15-mile rail segment by both hourly IC trains and half-hourly RE trains with services to both Leipzig Hbf and Halle.

Rail-Pass Travel

Eurail products and the German Railpass take you over the entire network of GermanRail, both East and West Germany. They also give you the famous Rhine Cruise from Cologne to Mainz, absolutely free. In addition, you receive free Moselle River cruises provided by the KD German Rhine Line between Koblenz and Cochem. Rail-pass holders must pay extra to travel by hydrofoil ("Tragflugelboot") on the Rhine River. Specifically excluded are the tourist cruise ships making multiple stops between Basel and Rotterdam and between Trier and Koblenz.

Travelers to Sweden travel free on Scandlines between Sassnitz and Trelleborg and receive half off from TT-Line's Travemunde Skandinavienkai pier to Trelleborg and half off the full fare of TR-Line's ferries between Rostock and Trelleborg. Rostock to Hanko, Finland, is free on Superfast Ferries. A group/student rate is applicable for the ferry crossing Rostock-Helsinki on Finnjet (earliest reservations seven days before departure).

Fringe benefits allow half off the fares of the regular steamer services on Lake Constance; a reduced fare on the Freiburg im Breisgau's Schauinsland rack railroad; half off Wurm & Kock Danube cruises from Passau to Linz, Austria; and one-quarter off the Zugspitze rack railroad from Garmish-Partenkirchen.

The crossing between Puttgarden and Rodby is free only if your pass is valid in both Germany and Denmark.

Buy German Railpasses in one-day increments from four to 10 days of travel within one month, either first or second class. DB gives an additional bargain to two adults traveling together, either first or second class. The second person pays about 50 percent less than the first German Railpass for what GermanRail calls a "Twinpass."

The German Rail 'n Drive Pass gives travelers two days of unlimited train travel and two days of an unlimited-mileage Avis rental car within a one-month period, using either first- or second-class train and a choice of economy, compact, intermediate, or compact automatic vehicles. You may add additional rail days (up to three) and additional auto days.

In Germany you can buy a GermanRail BahnCard valid for a 25, 50, or 100 percent discount on all regularly scheduled GermanRail trains throughout Germany. It is highly recommended for anyone visiting Germany more than once a year, especially seniors over 60. It is valid for one year from date of validation at prices varying from €50 (second class) to €5,000 (first class), depending on the level of discount chosen.

Many states ("Lander") offer one-day Landertickets for unlimited travel for up to five people traveling together with any number of their children under 18, second class, on weekdays between 9 A.M. and 3 A.M. of the following day or the entire day on weekends. Costing about $21-25, depending on region, they are valid on all local trains.

Discoverers in Germany cruise aboard laid-back steamers on the Rhine, tramp through the Black Forest, uncover well-preserved medieval towns by Europabuses, and discover Germany's new metropolis.

Rollin' on the Rhine
Lured by a Siren's Song

The Rhine River is squeezed down to one-third its normal width. The Lorelei towers 430 feet above you. You feel the rock's magnetism and almost hear the beautiful Lorelei's singing to lure fishermen and cause their deaths on those rocks and cliffs close to the prow of your white steamer.

The quiet of your waterway's west bank is occasionally pierced by

RHINE CRUISE

To Cologne

KOBLENZ

Ehrenbreitstein

Moselle

Schloss Stolzenfels

Burg Lahneck

Lahn

Marksburg

Boppard

Feindliche Brude

Burg Maus

Burg Katz

Burg Rheinfels

St. Goar

Lorelei

Schonburg

Oberwesel

Kaub

Pfalz

Stahleck

Bacharach

Assmannshausen

Burg Ehrenfels

Niederwalddenkmal

Mauseturm

RUDESHEIM

Bingen

To Mainz

Nahe

N

0   5   10

MILES

shrieks of trains racing along GermanRail's west bank line below castles and above barges. On the east bank, freight trains and passenger trains rumble between the wine villages that dot the shore.

Traveling by train along the west bank of the Rhine, studying the scenery from above the river, epitomizes relaxing train travel at its finest. Every once in a while a hilltop jewel sparkles into view, but Germans generally prefer the faster ICE 3s on the high-speed line between Cologne and Frankfurt/Main opened in 2002.

Luckily for you, your cruise from Koblenz to Mainz is even better. It gives you time to savor the beauty of this river. Vater Rhein, Europe's busiest waterway, carries a constant stream of barges and passenger ships, including the KD German Rhine Line steamer you are riding.

You are participating in a beloved trip for holders of Eurail products and GermanRail Passes. Rail-pass holders ride free on the KD German Rhine Line (Koln-Dusseldorfer Deutsche Rheinschiffahrt, *www.koeln-duesseldorfer.com*) making regular runs between Cologne and Mainz. Just show your pass when boarding. No boarding pass is required.

The complete run upstream takes 17 hours, so it not possible to do it in one day, but you see the most scenic parts making a six-hour trip upstream (or four hours downstream) from Koblenz to Rudesheim. You sail past the Lorelei, the Rhine gorge and dozens of world-famous castles and through the Rhine's most scenic region. You have little trouble making train connections on either end.

It is best to make the cruise on a sunny day. In the morning the west bank presents portraits for your camera and in the afternoon the east bank puts its historic castles in the right light.

When you commence this stretch filled with castles, it is useful to remember that the English word "castle" has two equivalents in the German language. You pass both "Burg," a fortified castle built for defensive purposes, and "Schloss," a palace that may or may not have been fortified and was usually the seat of royalty.

A good place to begin a trip upstream is in Koblenz, where the Moselle (Mosel) River flows into the Rhine. In front of the Koblenz Hauptbahnhof is a signboard/map illustrating the location of the various bus stops. You want to take bus line No. 1 to "Rheinfahre" stop, which shows an outline of a ferry. The bus runs every 20 minutes from across the street in front of the station (the round Tourist Office side) to the Deutsches Eck monument. The ferry dock is on Konrad

Adenauer Ufer ("river bank") on the river below. Only when you are sailing upstream ("Rheinaufwarts"), walk 10 to 15 minutes directly east down the Markenbildchenweg to the "Rheinanlagen," KD's second landing on the Rhine. Ships sailing upstream call here five minutes after casting off from KD's main Koblenz landing.

Seamen release the ropes and your ship bound upstream steams against the current of the Rhine. Passengers scramble for chairs. The paddle-wheel steamship *Goethe* carries the 9 A.M. departure.

Huge Festung Ehrenbreitstein, atop the hill overlooking your vessel, is one of the strongest fortresses in Europe. The French captured it in 1799 only by starving out its defenders. The neoclassical architecture that you see today was added between 1817 and 1828.

Below the railroad bridge, you see orange-brown Schloss Stolzenfels with crenellated turrets and walls high on the west bank. Once a customs point for the city of Trier, Friedrich Wilhelm IV of Prussia had it reconstructed in 1825-45 for a summer residence.

At the confluence of the Lahn and the Rhine, you dock in Oberlahnstein, formerly a rich and important center because of its toll station and local silver mining. Burg Lahneck was built to protect it. Over the centuries this castle has collapsed into ruin, thus becoming an inspiration for Rhine Romanticists.

The best-kept castle on the Rhine, high above Oberlahnstein, is the Marksburg, on a steep slate cliff 490 feet over the Rhine. It contains cannons, weapons, chastity belts, and a good castle inn. Nowhere else on the Rhine are the Middle Ages so well preserved as in the Marksburg. Now it is the seat of the German Castles Association and houses the largest collection of castle-related literature in Europe.

All high castles have one aspect in common: a lovely view. Long sight lines on the river were necessary to supervise the collection of tolls from passing ships, and an overview of the surrounding lands and forests was necessary for protection from enemies.

A big curve in the Rhine takes you past Osterspay, which is famous due to Schloss Liebeneck, high above on the east bank, erected around 1700 as a hunting and summer castle. You still see the original baroque forms despite the numerous subsequent alterations.

Lovely Boppard, a popular stop-off, interrupts the barren hills. Shortly, you see on top of the hills the castles of the Feindliche Brude. Legend has it that two arguing brothers erected ramparts between their castles. Since then the castles have been referred to as "The Hostile Brothers."

Passing Bad Salzig on the west bank in springtime is unforgettable because of its flowering cherry orchards. You sail back to the west bank below Burg Maus ("Mouse Castle"), one of the technically outstanding structures of its time. The archbishop of Trier built it in 1356. In 1806, it was partially destroyed and rebuilt between 1900 and 1909.

St. Goarshausen, with partly intact city walls, on the east bank, is hemmed tightly below Burg Katz on a jutting cliff. The counts of Katzeneinbogen, one of the richest families in medieval Germany, built the castle in 1393.

St. Goar back on the west bank is a pilgrim's center for the grave of St. Goar, who died in 611, below the Rheinfels ruins.

Burg Rheinfels is so close it seems you could reach up and rub the dust off the walls of its rambling terraces. This mighty ruin used to be the greatest castle on the Rhine. The French destroyed it in 1797.

Now you are below the Lorelei rock. When you pass the cliff, your captain plays a tape of Heinrich Heine's poem about the Lorelei virgin combing her golden hair and singing to lure sailors to the rocks. Now the song of the beautiful Lorelei is the best-known folk song of the Rhine. This is the narrowest spot of the river. In the water you see the rocks of the "Sieben Jungfrauen" (Seven Virgins) turned to stone.

In Oberwesel, on the west bank, you pass the homes of fishermen and Rhine sailors. It is a tiny and romantic place dominated by its 14th-century, red-brick Gothic Liebfrauenkirche (church), narrow and steep like a ship.

Schonburg castle is situated above Oberwesel. It was built in the 12th century. At one time it served as an imperial castle. Today parts of it are used as an international youth hostel.

The five-sided customs fortress in the center of the Rhine upstream from Kaub, the "Pfalz," was completed in its current form in the 17th and 18th centuries. Its many pinnacles and little towers contain a naval museum. From water level it looks like a stone barge on the swirling Rhine. Following its restoration it was repainted in the old Gothic colors.

Above Kaub on the east bank, a friendly city profiting from slate quarrying, you see Burg Gutenfels (1200), one of the most important examples of defensive and living structures in the period of the Hohenstaufen. It is now used as a hotel.

Crossing again to the west bank you arrive in Bacharach, a village with 16 watchtowers and black-slate-roofed Burg Stahleck above. Burg Stahleck, built in 1134, was destroyed in 1689. Beautifully rebuilt between 1925 and 1967, it serves as a youth hostel.

Eleventh-century Burg Nollig was erected upstream of Lorch as part of Lorchhausen's main fortifications. Ships, which had to avoid the Bingerloch, the whirlpool on the Rhine, docked here for reloading of their cargoes onto smaller ships or for transportation overland.

You sail past the Mauseturm ("Mice Tower") on an island near the west bank. Since the rise of Rhine Romanticism, Mice Tower on a rock in the Rhine has become Bingen's emblem although it actually once was a customs house belonging to Burg Ehrenfels, the magnificent tower on the opposite bank. Later Mice Tower served as a signal tower for this once perilous stretch of the Rhine. Now that the danger of the Bingerloch, the whirlpool, has been alleviated, the tower merely serves to remind you of the story that Bishop Hatto, who fled here after burning starving farmers' barns, was eaten alive by thousands of rats who swam the Rhine and scaled the tower's walls to reach him. Since its renovation in 1972, you again see the Mauseturm in its medieval hues.

Where the Nahe River flows from the west into the Rhine, you stop in the wine village of Bingen, below Burg Klopp. The large KD Rhine Line landing at Bingen lies a quarter-mile downstream from the Bingen Stadt train station and 0.6 miles upstream from the Bingen Hauptbahnhof/Bingerbruck train station. InterCity trains skim right past these stations but local trains take you leisurely to Mainz and Koblenz. Do not confuse Bingen Hauptbahnhof and Bingen Stadt stations. Use the latter.

Famous Rudesheim is an excellent village to stop over or to conclude your trip on the Rhine with a glass of wine on the famous Drosselgasse, a street only about 10 feet wide and 200 yards long but resounding with the constant percussion of bands playing traditional oompah to modern music. Enjoy a free wine-tasting session at a celebrated winery. You will feel the Rhineland's "Frohsinn," gaiety, everywhere.

Be sure to top off your trip with a gondola ride up over Rudesheim's vineyards to the colossal Niederwalddenkmal, the neoclassical memorial on an outlook plateau 980 feet above the city, commemorating the unification of the German Empire after the 1870 defeat of the French. Born of national enthusiasm in an era fond of monuments, the proportions of the lady are equally optimistic. She is about 125 feet tall and weighs some 700 pounds. From her feet you see one of the top 10 panoramas in Germany.

Rudesheim's train station is well situated below the village near the east bank of the Rhine. From here the KD Rhine Line's landing is a 12-minute walk upstream on the path between the railroad tracks and the Rhine. You make train connections on the secondary line running along the east bank of the Rhine and into Mainz.

Mainz is an excellent place to stay overnight. It is only 18 minutes by train to Frankfurt/Main International Airport and is connected to the new high-speed line to Cologne. You push your luggage carts to the hotels across the Bahnhofplatz from the station with no stairs to climb.

KD German Rhine Line sails frequently during July and August, less often in the spring and fall, and not at all between late October and late March.

Daily KD German Rhine Line Summer Service

0900*	1100	1400	dep.	KOBLENZ	arr.	I		1810	2010
0930	1125	1425	dep.	Niederlahnstein	dep.	I		1750	1950
0940	1135	1435	dep.	Oberlahnstein	dep.	I		1740	1940
0950	1145	1445	dep.	Rhens	dep.	I		1730	1930
1005	1200	1500	dep.	Braubach	dep.	I		1720	1920
1100	1300	1600	dep.	Boppard	dep.	1250		1650	1850
1115	1310	1610	dep.	Kamp-Bornhofen	dep.	1340		1640	1840
I	1320	1620	dep.	Bad Salzig	dep.	1330		1630	1830
1210	1405	1705	dep.	St. Gorshausen	dep.	1305		1605	1805
1220	1415	1715	dep.	St. Goar	dep.	1255		1555	1755
1250	1445	1745	dep.	Oberwesel	dep.	1235		1535	1735
1305	1500	1800	dep.	Kaub	dep.	1225		1525	1725
1335	1525	1825	dep.	Bacharach	dep.	1215		1515	1715
I	1530	1830	dep.	Lorch	dep.	1205		1505	1705
1430	1620	1920	dep.	Assmannshausen	dep.	1145		1445	1645
1505	1650	1950	dep.	Bingen	dep.	1130		1430	1630
1513	1700	2000	dep.	RUDESHEIM	dep.	1115		1415	1615*
I	1810	I	dep.	Eltville	dep.	1025	I		I
I	1850	I	dep.	Wiesbaden-Bieb.	dep.	1005	I		I
I	1920	I	arr.	MAINZ	dep.	0945	I		I

*Paddle-wheel steamship *Goethe*
I = Does not serve these landings

Through the Valley of Hell
Cuckoo Clocks and Black Forest Character

Your ride through Hell's Valley ("Hollental") is romantic enough for an archduchess on her way to her wedding. Marie Antoinette's advisors planned her carriage trip through this scenic valley in 1770, on her way from Vienna to Paris to marry the future King Louis XVI. She was 14½ years old at the time. She was beheaded 23 years later.

When you travel on the Black Forest Railroad and you see the famous "mighty roof" Black Forest houses, onion-dome churches, and even occasional cuckoo clocks, you know you are in the Black Forest. The railroad's length of 62 miles from Offenburg to Donaueschingen takes you over the crest of the Black Forest in an unusual series of loops. From Donaueschingen, you have a second view of a quieter Black Forest by changing to your connecting Hell's Valley ("Hollental") train, which justifies its name in only a few spots. Rail passes cover both trains.

When German railroad construction from Paris reached Freiburg, now the western terminus of the Hell's Valley train, dreamers talked of linking Paris to Vienna by train through Hell's Valley. On May 23, 1887, the Hell's Valley Railroad was opened—the first German State railroad with mixed cogwheel and adhesion traction.

It remained that way until 1933, when the cogwheels were taken out and special locomotives put into service on the steep stretch. The line was electrified in 1936 on a trial basis and patched into GermanRail's grid in 1960. Now you ride in GermanRail's comfortable regional trains, but the landscape remains more romantic than on most other stretches.

Beginning south from the mainline at Offenburg (522 feet) in one of GermanRail's electrified InterRegio Express (IRE) or Regional Express (RE) trains, the first stretch of the Black Forest Railroad takes you past vineyards, fruit trees, wheat, hops, and corn and below a dramatic Romanesque hilltop castle on your left.

While you pass along a pretty stream with fishermen in green jackets and hats on the right of your train, the hillsides grow steeper and more wooded and the first houses with red geraniums in window boxes appear. This is a sure sign the Black Forest is not far away.

The eye-catching gilded minute and hour hands and numerals on the brown-and-tan clock tower give Gengenbach (564 feet) a Black

BLACK FOREST RAILROADS

Strasbourg

GERMANY

FRANCE

OFFENBURG

Hausach

Triberg

Villingen

FREIBURG

Hinterzarten

DONAUESCHINGEN

Titisee

Neustadt

To Konstanz

Basel

SWITZERLAND

0   10   20

MILES

Forest gateway feeling. The newer houses tend to have long sloping roofs.

When you stop at Hausach (790 feet), the Black Forest store across from the station is decorated with multicolored baskets on a rope. From Hausach, you begin one of the most rugged and picturesque stretches in Germany.

The valley is more romantic with black-and-white cows in the fields and houses with gigantic roofs. They have eaves on four sides and balconies of hand-carved wood, front and back, but not the sides, where the canted roofs overhang nearly to the ground.

Soon you see thatched, wooden Black Forest houses to your right— just like in the tourist literature—and an onion-shaped church belfry, also on your right. The mighty-roof houses are landmarked and subsidized by the government. Some houses offer rooms to let; look for "Zimmer Frei."

The farms get bigger, the trees get bigger, and your climb gets steeper. You are traveling across the pages of a picture book of the Black Forest. It is pleasant to see all these textbook examples from the comfort of your train.

At Hornberg (1,260 feet), you come to a stop at a site overlooking the village and below a castle amazingly perched atop a hill. A small black, red, and yellow German flag flies from its tower.

Across the valley you see a cuckoo-clock factory. Hikers wearing leather shorts and green knee socks and carrying walking sticks tramp through forests down the mountainsides.

Now it gets wilder suddenly. You pass through tunnel after tunnel— every one punctuated by screeches from the train's whistle. Read their conveniently placed names as you enter. Between tunnels, you have picture-postcard views of farms and forests.

Triberg's modern train station (2,020 feet) centers this watch- and clock-making hub, which is the highlight of this stretch, smack in the heart of the Black Forest, and this is a good place to break your trip. Walk directly to the Black Forest Museum to enjoy quietly (except for the blasting mechanical organ) old local costumes, watch- and clock-making exhibits, and a working model of your Black Forest Railroad.

Back on your train, you continue to climb. You emerge from a long tunnel into thick forest.

The Black Forest is more attractive than other woods not because the trees grow close together, but because they are evenly spaced, not wild. They are uniform, almost tailored, so they don't allow much light to fall except for a few spots of sunlight on the flooring of pine needles.

After you cross the summit you pick up speed. Although you aren't rushing, your pace seems breakneck compared to your slow ascent.

Past Sommerau (2,729 feet), the hills below you still have their wild look. Exiting the tunnel before St. Georgen brings a whole new experience. The surroundings are mundane, more developed, and modestly industrialized. The excitement and enchantment is over. By the time you descend to the large brown-brick, tile-roofed Villingen station house (2,309 feet), industry has sadly triumphed over the Black Forest.

In Donaueschingen (2,221 feet), change from your Black Forest train, which continues to Lake Constance, for the Hell's Valley train, beginning with GermanRail's red Regional Express diesel (direction: Neustadt), which takes you west again. You reenter the Black Forest. The trees grow stronger and stronger and surround your slick railcar as you glide downhill toward Hufingen (2,220 feet) in Hell's Valley. You are making a charming if not spectacular journey through forests, fields, and meadows to give you a second impression of a quieter Black Forest.

At Neustadt you join once more an electrified line to Freiburg im Breisgau and change from your diesel to a red, electrified, double-deck Regional Bahn (RB) train to Freiburg. Your next stop, Titisee (2,814 feet), is your major stop on the Hell's Valley line. Titisee ("See" means "lake," although it's not visible from here) is the premier resort of the Black Forest. It is a hiker and vacationer's paradise. On your right stand vacation homes; on your left forests trail down to the valley.

The segment between Hollsteig and Hinterzarten takes you up at a gradient of one foot for every 18 you pass. This is the third-steepest segment in Germany using adhesion traction.

Hinterzarten (2,903 feet), a stylish mountain resort, is the highest point of the Hell's Valley Railroad, higher even than the summit of the Black Forest Railroad. Hiking trails, timbered houses, and trees of every sort, leaves rustling in the breezes, surround you. The air feels woodsy.

Downhill you travel through the thick of the Black Forest. It must be idyllic if Marie Antoinette passed here. You see trees, mountains, and many autos. Then you see nothing. You are passing through a tunnel. The conductor checks your pass. You enter two tunnels and pass Posthalde station without stopping. Then you reach another tunnel.

There are supposed to be nine tunnels between Posthalde and Freiburg, but it seems you pass at least a dozen. Many are very short and are possibly counted as underpasses. In GermanRail's list the shortest tunnel, Ravenna Tunnel, is 157 feet long, third from the crest. Maybe 150 or 125 feet is too short for DB's tunnel census takers.

By the time you reach Himmelreich (1,493 feet), you have left behind most of the heavy forest.

When you stop in Kirchzarten (1,286 feet), across from Gasthaus Alte Post, the kilometer markers show you have 11 km (6.8 miles) left to travel.

You travel through a broad valley; mountains surround you, rye and corn flourish, and you near Freiburg-Littenweller stop (1,040 feet) on the outskirts of Freiburg. Still in the Black Forest, you see red-tile roofs, gardens for pensioners, picnic grounds, and a sports stadium on your right.

Now you have 5.6 km to the main train station. But that didn't used to be true because the train ran through the middle of Freiburg. In 1934, the track was moved and the line rerouted in a loop around the city, thus adding another 1.4 kilometers to your trip. This meant all kilometer markers had to be changed, but the administration of the time skimped. It changed only the markers near its offices in Freiburg. When you reach Freiburg-Wiehre's green station house (918 feet), you come to kilometer marker "0." By the time you arrive in Freiburg's Hauptbahnhof you have entered the "Twilight Zone." You have traveled on a line with a negative length. Look for the enameled, black-on-white kilometer marker: "-1.4," with numbers arranged vertically.

The Freiburg im Breisgau train station, located just outside the former city walls, was finally built in 2000-2001 after officials agonized over the rebuilding for 35 years. The adjacent high-rise is filled with business offices. The station has hotel information, ATMs, a McDonald's, and an attached InterCity Hotel.

Freiburg (pop. 200,000) is a jewel of southern Germany and the capital of the Black Forest in an economic and cultural sense only, not governmental, but it is the seat of regional administration of the south Black Forest. The dukes of Zahringer founded it in the 12th century and its architecture was formed under Austrian Hapsburg rule. At the Kaufhaus you see four statues of Austrian emperors and the streets have Hapsburg names. Its Gothic cathedral, with its most wonderful octagonal tower, and dazzling market square make your visit here unforgettable. The cathedral was the only cathedral that was *completed* during the Gothic period.

For the tourist office (Schwarzwald-und-Freiburg-Informationen) at Rotteneckring 14, walk straight ahead from the station down Eisenbahnstrasse five minutes, but first look at the Hotel Victoria at #54. The owners are ardent environmentalists. The roof is covered with solar panels that supply 7 percent of the hotel's electricity. The remaining electricity comes from a windmill in a windmill park. They supply their heating needs by burning compacted pellets of waste sawdust. The tourist office is open Monday through Friday 9:30 A.M. to 8 P.M., Saturday to 5 P.M., and Sunday 10 A.M. to noon. Go inside; there is also hotel information outside. You find Freiburg online at *www.Freiburg.de* and *www.Freiburg-online.com.*

It was in Freiburg on May 4 or 5, 1770, that Archduchess Marie Antoinette said goodbye to Austria and entered France at Strasbourg.

Regular Interval Black Forest Railroad Schedule

IRE	RE				IRE	RE
0759	0859	dep.	OFFENBURG	arr.	0958	09858
I	0906	dep.	Gengenbach	arr.	I	0852
I	0916	dep.	Haslach	arr.	I	0842
0818	0922	dep.	Hausach	dep.	0940	0836
0826	0930	dep.	Hornberg	dep.	0928	0829
0839	0944	dep.	TRIBERG	dep.	0918	0815
0854	0959	dep.	St. Georgen	dep.	0903	0801
0904	1009	dep.	Villingen	arr.	0854	0752
0912	1017	arr.	DONAUESCHINGEN	dep.	0845	0742

I = Does not stop

IRE trains and RE trains alternate departures every two hours approximately on the minute. RE trains run between 6:xx A.M. and 9:xx P.M.; IRE trains run between 6:xx A.M. and 6:xx P.M. IC trains substitute for IRE trains twice daily.

Hourly Hell's Valley Train Service

0750	dep.	DONAUESCHINGEN	arr.	0910
I	dep.	Hufingen	dep.	0907
0800	dep.	Doggingen	dep.	0859
0811	dep.	Loffingen	dep.	0846
0816	dep.	Rotehbach	dep.	0841
0827	arr.	Neustadt (Schwarzwald)	dep.	0831
		Change between RB and RE trains		
0831	dep.	Neustadt (Schwarzwald)	arr.	0825
0838	dep.	TITISEE	dep.	0819
0845	dep.	Hinterzarten	dep.	0814
0900	dep.	Himmelreich	dep.	0801
0904	dep.	Kirchzarten	dep.	0757
0909	dep.	Freiburg-Littenweiler	dep.	0752
0913	dep.	Freiburg-Wiehre	dep.	0748
0918	arr.	FREIBURG Hbf.	dep.	0743

I = Does not stop

Trains depart hourly approximately on the minute from 6:xx A.M. until 7:xx P.M.

Medieval Germany by Europabus
Castles, Romance, and Rococo

You can take a local train to the small branch station outside the city walls of Rothenburg ob der Tauber (*www.Rothenburg.de*), which means "Red castle above the Tauber (River)." The castle is long gone and the Tauber is little better than a mud puddle, but Rothenburg's Old Town is the jewel of Bavaria. But I have a better idea than the local train—use your rail pass to travel to Rothenburg aboard a deluxe sea-green Europabus from Munich showing you the Romantic Highway (*www.romantischestrasse.de*) or along the Castle Road from Mannheim or Heidelberg.

You ride 60 percent off with a Eurail product or GermanRail Pass. Seniors over 60 get 50 percent off and students under 26 receive 10 percent off.

In the 1890s the city fathers decided never to build a train station. They expected iron horses to corrupt the ambience of their fair city. They wanted Rothenburg ob der Tauber to remain the finest surviving medieval town.

This city, by law, remains as it was in the 17th century, after the Thirty Years War. The city council regulates progress so carefully that even house colors are set out in official government rulebooks. The householder with the prettiest window-box flower display wins a cash prize.

Romantic Highway and Castle Road Europabuses converge on Rothenburg after passing along the most scenic coach routes in Germany. Europabus is the network of long-distance motor coaches throughout most of Europe operated in association with the national railroad administrations. Their vehicles are Mercedes coaches with continuous windows and ample luggage space below. Passengers on the scenic routes are guided by an exemplary recorded commentary in English, German, and Japanese and by English-speaking hosts giving personal directions.

Travelers with even the slightest curiosity in seeing old gabled houses, Gothic roofs, oriel windows, fortress walls, fairy-tale watchtowers, cobbled streets, and graceful, flowing fountains make discovering Rothenburg top priority.

Sorry, "Romantic" does not necessarily refer to boy meets girl.

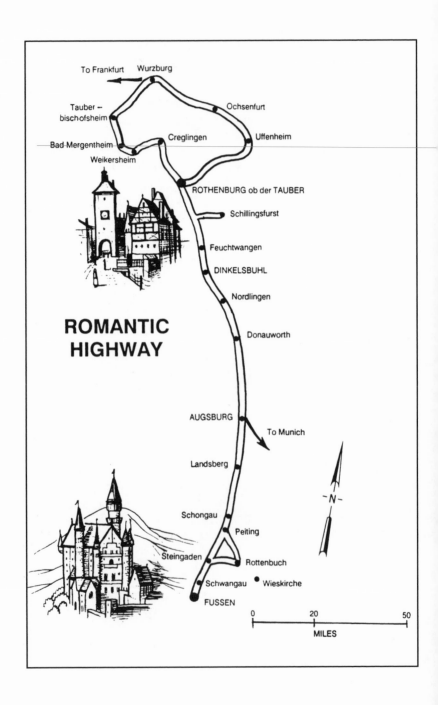

Instead, you feel a special romance—a nostalgic pleasure in half-timbered houses, restored ramparts, town gates, baroque cherubs, palace gardens, arching stone bridges over rivers, and royal castles implanted on steep, rocky slopes.

Your big, smooth-riding coach takes you through one charming village after another with their carefully preserved and colorfully painted Romantic structures. Leaving the Autobahn at Augsburg, capital of the Schwabian region, you wind along the slower road to Donauworth (*www.donauwoerth.de*), where the Reichstrasse, one of South Germany's most attractive streets lined with imposing patrician houses with its Minster (cathedral), forms a lovely picture.

In Nordlingen (*www.noerdlingen.de*) you pass through the almost fully preserved medieval city center dominated by "Daniel," the 300-foot-high bell tower of the late Gothic church. You can walk atop the town walls and battlements circling the whole town, which make it the only example of its kind in Germany.

Discovering Dinkelsbuhl (*www.dinkelsbuehl.de*) makes the whole trip memorable. Nearly to Rothenburg, your bus gives you a 50-minute break in Dinkelsbuhl, where renovators are multiplying the number of preserved medieval gems faster than a Pentium processor. Eighteen towers and the fully preserved town walls recall the glories of the past. Ask your guide for directions to the Deutsches Haus, which will remind you of Dinkelsbuhl's prosperity in the 15th and 16th centuries. You do not want to miss photographing this admired 15th-century gabled building, which you see on the "Visit Germany" travel posters.

When your Europabus lets you off outside Rothenburg's train station, don't be tempted to jump aboard the first departing train like most of the Asian tourists, who have their noses buried in their guidebooks. It is a shame because they could take some wonderful photos in the old city itself. If they stayed overnight, they could walk with the Night Watchman through the city, but it is doubtful that the Night Watchman speaks an Asian language as well as English.

Those staying in Rothenburg rather than continuing by train or Europabus to Frankfurt or Mannheim/Heidelberg (which is an excellent option when they depart) will have time to visit the important art treasures in the churches and museums, stay in historic hotels, and visit fascinating museums and modern facilities that guarantee a delightful stay.

If you decide not to stay in Rothenburg, you have 70-85 minutes in

Rothenburg before your chosen Europabus departs. Climb the Town Hall belfry, dating from the 14th century, and walk along the wide city wall, but first head directly down the Schmiedgasse to see the Plonlein, the most photographed scene in Germany (and every photo is a gem).

Rothenburg's pleasures include the Imperial City Museum located in the former Dominican monastery of 1258, the jewel-box Doll and Toy Museum, Historical Vaults, and the fascinating Medieval Crime Museum.

The driver of the second Europabus from Rothenburg continues southwest through Bavaria to Fussen with distant views of King Ludwig's fantasy Neuschwanstein Castle. You pass the astonishing church in the Wies going south, but stop there northbound. Its breathtaking rococo interior makes it often mentioned as Germany's finest church. From Fussen, there are hourly Regional Express train departures to Augsburg or Munich until 11:05 P.M. Fussen's principal welcome is a nearby youth hostel.

The Castle Road between Rothenburg and Heidelberg is so called because it connects red-sandstone Heidelberg Castle, heart of Romanticism, on one end, with the gray-granite Neuschwanstein Castle on the other, and features castles, large and small, around every curve of the Neckar Valley (Heidelberg to Rothenburg). Board either in Mannheim or the "Student-Prince" university town, spend your lunch hours in Rothenburg, explore Dinkelsbuhl, and then join a Romantic Highway bus to Fussen or Munich.

When you want to tempt the rage of Rothenburg's city fathers, use the small, local railroad that is, in fact, outside of Rothenburg's city walls. Thirteen trains a day on weekdays (fewer on weekends) connect to Steinach, seven miles away, where you change for Wurzburg to join the ICE network. Bus service is sometimes substituted (covered by rail passes), especially on weekends. Be sure you check the timetable for the day you will be traveling, because bus connections are usually a few minutes different from train connections.

Make reservations at a Europabus office in Germany or by postcard or fax (to arrive at least three days before departure) to Deutsche Touring GmbH, Am Romerhof 17, D-60486 Frankfurt/Main (Tel. 069-79-03-50, Fax 069-79-03-2-19, www.deutsche-touring.de). Indicate date, route, and number of seats you require. Seat reservations are free of charge, but you must pay a nominal fee for registration and checking of your luggage. It includes insurance up to about $1,200.

Romantic Highway Summer Europabus Service between Frankfurt/Main and Wurzburg and Augsburg, Munich, and Fussen

0800	I	dep.	FRANKFURT/M (Hbf./bus 9)	arr.	I	1955
1000	I	dep.	WURZBURG (Busbf.)	arr.	I	1810
1035	I	dep.	Tauberbischofsheim	dep.	I	1735
1045	I	dep.	Lauda-Konigshofen (Rat.)	arr.	I	1725
1100	I	dep.	Bad Mergentheim (Bf.)	dep.	I	1710
1130	I	dep.	Weikersheim (Marktpl.)	dep.	I	1657
1140	I	dep.	Rottingen (Marktpl.)	dep.	I	1645
1245	I	arr.	ROTHENBURG o.d.T. (Bf.)	dep.	I	1600
			Change buses			
1430	1430	dep.	ROTHENBURG o.d.T. (Bf.)	arr.	1450	1450
1448	1448	dep.	Schillingfurst (Hotel Post)	dep.	1425	1425
1510	1510	dep.	Feuchtwangen (Omnibusbf.)	dep.	1415	1415
1525	1525	arr.	DINKELSBUHL (Schweine.)	dep.	1400	1400
1615	1530	dep.	DINKELSBUHL (Schweine.)	arr.	1245	1245
1657	1615	dep.	Nordlingen (Rathaus)	dep.	1215	1215
1730	1645	dep.	Donauworth (Kirche)	dep.	1130	1115
1835	1750	dep.	AUGSBURG (Hbf.)	dep.	1050	1035
1950	I	arr.	MUNICH (Starnberger Bf.)	dep.	I	0900
I	1852	dep.	Schongau (Bf.)	arr.	0925	I
I	I		WIESKIRCHE	dep.	0855	I
I	1920	dep.	Steingaden (Ammergau Str.)	dep.	0835	I
I	1940	arr.	Schwangau (Tourist Office)	dep.	0810	I
I	1945	arr.	Hohenschwangau	dep.	0807	I
I	1955	arr.	FUSSEN (Bf.)	dep.	0800	I

I = Does not travel this route or does not stop

Castle Road Summer Europabus Service Mannheim-Heidelberg–Rothenburg

0730	dep.	MANNHEIM (Hbf.)	arr.	2055
0800	dep.	HEIDELBERG (Bf.)	arr.	2035
0822	dep.	Neckargemund (Bf.)	dep.	2013
0845	dep.	Eberbach (Neckaranlagen)	dep.	1950
1045	dep.	Heilbrunn (Behind Harmonie)	dep.	1855
1145	dep.	Schwabisch Hall (Busbf.)	dep.	1725
1330	arr.	ROTHENBURG o.d.T. (Bf.)	dep.	1615

Berlin
High-speed Metropolis

You get to and from Berlin (*www.berlin.germany.com*) easily using either a regular train ticket or a rail pass. *Tip:* Your pass or train ticket is also valid for travel on Berlin's S-Bahn (but not on the U-Bahn). You won't find it economic to validate a day box for inexpensive S-Bahn trips but you can use the S-Bahn to and from a residential quarter on the days of your arrival and departure.

The fastest way to Berlin is from Hanover, over DB's high-speed line opened in May 1997. Don't be disappointed at first in this key link in the European high-speed rail superhighway London/Paris-Brussels-Cologne-Hanover-Berlin-Warsaw-Moscow. Leaving Hanover's Hauptbahnhof, you're not yet on the high-speed line. Your ICE first travels 48 miles to Wolfsburg over merely upgraded line. Leaving urban Hanover at Hanover Berliner Allee, your ICE reaches 100 mph over the 10-mile stretch to the outskirts of Lehrte, but then cuts back to 75 mph to traverse a complicated junction. From Lehrte through Gifhorn to the outskirts of Wolfsburg, you peak at 124 mph. At last you enter the flat, 98-mile stretch across marshy country about 180 feet above sea level. You feel the acceleration as your ICE bursts to 155 mph. At Stendal you cross the new Elbe River bridge, the longest of the series of bridges over canals and rivers parallel to the nearby, old line that you see about two miles away on your left.

You stop only once before reaching downtown Berlin, at the Spandau station that DB opened to full service on December 14, 1998.

About 12 minutes before you arrive in Spandau (check your watch and your on-board timetable), now east of Rathenow, be sure to take note of the expensive, high, weed-covered embankments squeezing your line through a flat, particularly marshy area.

This marks the Buckow Conservation Area and the habitat of a colony of great bustards, one of the rarest birds in Europe. They are so rare you will be hard-pressed to see one, and the embankments mean you seldom see birds of any kind.

Great bustards (Otis tarda) are one of the largest land birds in Europe, over three feet long. They are related to cranes and vaguely resemble skinny, flying turkeys. Citizens were concerned that 155-mph trains straight through the last breeding grounds of the bustards might offend the flying creatures and cause them some danger; in particular, environmentalists feared that bustards might be tempted to fly smack in front of speedy ICEs.

To shield the rare birds, DB and the Brandenburg state government agreed to build 10-foot-high earthen banks alongside the three-mile critical path in question with the idea that the banks would divert the birds' flight trajectory and induce them to fly over, not in front of, the ICEs.

Construction of the banks was suspended from May to October, during the bashful birds' breeding season, to avoid disturbing the love habits of the endangered species. The German government picked up the additional cost, $45 million, or about $1.3 million per bird. DB pointed out that it could fly the birds out one by one to save taxpayers' money.

In a 2000 announcement, DB reported that the population of the large birds had increased from 16 to 37 since the beginning of work on the line. Evidently, bustards are prevailing over the multiplying foxes in the area, which have been vaccinated against rabies and pose a threat to the bustard population.

By Dallgow you feel Berlin growing close, as you gradually slow and enter the greater Berlin metropolitan complex. After stopping at Spandau's station, you cruise through Westend at 62 mph and sight Berlin's S-Bahn trains running beside you. Now you wind your way along Berlin's Stadtbahn at 37 mph through Charlottenburg, Zoo, Friedrichstrasse, and Alexanderplatz stations to Ostbahnhof.

You complete your trip in one hour, 45 minutes, which is considerably better than the four hours that former InterCity trains required with stops along the way.

The upgraded line between Hamburg and Berlin was the second project of the transport infrastructure program for Germany dubbed "German unity." Conversion of the line to twin track and full electrification began in 1991 following the reunification of Germany even while the line continued to carry passengers. Engineers installed a modern signaling system to guarantee traffic safety at 100 mph. In 2003, it was further upgraded for 143-mph operation via Wittenberge.

German rail fans anticipated at last beating the 1934 timing achieved by the legendary Fliegender Hamburger streamlined diesel train. The original Flying Hamburger was powered by Maybeck diesel engines that took it between cities in two hours, 18 minutes, which was the fastest service in the world in 1933. It is supposed that the Flying

HIGH-SPEED BERLIN

BERLIN
Friedrichstrasse
Spandau
ZOO
Wannsee
To Hamburg
Potsdam
IC/EC
(1993)
Rathenow
Stendal
InterCity Express
(1997)
Magdeburg
Marienborn
Helmstedt
Wolfsburg
Braunschweig
Gifhorn
Lehrte
HANOVER

0   10   20   50
MILES

Hamburger's development at that time was used to subversively make and test engines for submarines despite the armaments prohibition of the Versailles Treaty at the end of the First World War.

Berlin Train Stations

The first railroad company in Berlin (to Potsdam, in 1838) built Berlin's first terminal, the Potsdamer Bahnhof. Until 1877 each new railroad company entering Berlin built its separate terminus. In 1882, the Kaiser ordered 11 stations connected by an east-west line across the city center on a still-standing, elevated brick viaduct and this was known as the Stadtbahn. From west to east, these stations were Charlottenburg, Savignyplatz, Zoologischer Garten, Tiergarten, Bellevue, Lehrter, Friedrichstrasse, Borse (renamed Marx-Engels-Platz and now Hackescher Markt), Alexanderplatz, Jannowitzbrucke, and Schlesischer Bahnhof (renamed Hauptbahnhof in 1882, then Ostbahnhof, then again Hauptbahnhof under the communists, and now again Ostbahnhof).

As one of the federal government's reunification projects following the "Wende," Berlin's major trains stations were rebuilt and regional and mainline train traffic was reorganized. Mainline trains call at Zoo, Ostbahnhof, and Spandau mainline stations, while regional trains call additionally at Alexanderplatz and Friedrichstrasse regional train stations.

The Berlin Transit Authority called it "rejuvenation." Commuters used harder words. GermanRail and the Berlin Transit Authority spent about one billion U.S. dollars to modernize the 5.5-mile, two-track S-Bahn and parallel mainline stretches. Workers installed escalators. Stations Friedrichstrasse and Alexanderplatz were realigned into regional train hubs despite delays caused by the unexploded World War II bomb embedded in the brick Stadtbahn foundation and specialists from the bomb squad searching the whole length for more.

Bahnhof Zoo, which handles both mainline and S-Bahn trains, and U-Bahn trains in an underneath annex, was remodeled with DM 40 million. The structure was cleaned, relighted, and modernized stage by stage. Escalators and a travel center were installed.

Because Zoo station is the center of the Zoo complex, you can't fail to find any possible service or shop in the station itself or nearby. In the station itself you find a bookstore, a restaurant, and snack opportunities of every sort. On the mezzanine there is a private hotel booking service, and look for the hotel reservations display of some 42 hotels with an accompanying map showing their locations. Inserts show pictures of the hotels, their prices for single and double rooms, what services they offer, and other details. Adjacent is a cluster of buttons that are either red or green depending on whether they are full or have rooms available. Using this information you can choose one suiting your location and financial requirements and call the telephone number shown in the insert rather than walk over to the tourist office and stand in line and pay their service fee.

You find lockers in back of the station and luggage carts standing on the platforms. The elevators in back that you will have to search for assist getting your luggage to street level.

The DB agent in the service center in the middle of the hall is available to answer quick questions only. The Reisezentrum is the place to go for reservations and ticket purchases, where you stand in lines, which move *very* slowly. For first-class ticket holders, including holders of first-class Eurail products and GermanRail Passes, a special counter is open.

The toilets are called "McClean" and the troop of ladies responsible for the cleaning tries to live up to its reputation. Children relieve themselves without charge but sooner or later in Berlin, probably sooner, you will be confronted by one of Berlin's take-no-prisoners Toilettenfrauen ("toilet women") who will demand small change. Grin and bear it. It's their profession and they should be paid handsomely for working in such disgusting surroundings. It's also cheaper than in some neighboring countries.

EurAide, an American-run operation, has a neat office in the rear of Zoo train station. Look for the EurAide Office down the corridor past the stairs to McClean toilets. Not only will they book your reservations and issue you train tickets in colloquial English, they will give you free information on getting where you want to go by train in Germany and guide you through the rail-pass jungle (German Railpass and Eurail products as well as InterRailpass). Further they will help you with low-cost accommodations in Berlin and steer you onto the right "Berlin Walks" tours in English. They are open daily during the summer 8 A.M. to noon and 1 to 6 P.M.

A five-minute walk out of the front of Zoo station leads you across the Kurfurstendamm to the Berlin Tourist Office in the Europa Center on Budapesterstrasse (open Mon.-Sat., 8 A.M. to 11:30 P.M.;

Sun., 9 A.M. to 9 P.M.). Branches are located at the Brandenburg Gate and on Alexanderplatz. The post office is across the street.

Mainline station *Ostbahnhof* lacks charm despite extensive reconstruction, which was begun by the East German Railways before unification and not completed until 1992. It is the terminus of the high-speed line to the west. Most westbound long-distance trains originate here and call at Bahnhof Zoo and Bahnhof Spandau before branching to their destination. Trains arriving from the south or east all call here before stopping at Zoo train station. The station contains all facilities, elevators and escalators, an InterCity Hotel, and an Internet Cafe on the mezzanine. S-Bahn trains use platforms 8, 9, and 10.

Mainline train station *Bahnhof Spandau* was inaugurated in September 1998, when the great, long ICE trains began make their first Berlin stops before approaching the center of the city. Bahnhof Spandau platforms were lengthened to accommodate the long trains and covered with glass arches to protect arriving and departing passengers from the weather. Inside you find all the functions you expect in a mainline train station—new ticketing counters and an information center. Regional trains supplement the high-speed trains and S-Bahn connections to Berlin neighborhoods.

Regional *Bahnhof Alexanderplatz* was built in 1880-82 out of glazed yellow-brown brick as a station for the new Stadtbahn ("City Railroad"), but you are hard put to see the early structure because of its 1994-98 reconstruction. After nearly four years of reconstruction from the ground up, politicians finally got their opportunity to make their speeches at the reopening of Berlin's historic Alexanderplatz train station on March 12, 1998.

Berlin mayor Eberhard Diepgen said, "Alexanderplatz is the pulsating heart of Berlin. The new station is a symbol of the growing together of the city." The reconstruction was such a success that the station is easy and comfortable to use. Automatic doors fly open so wide that they seem to know you are towing a fully packed suitcase. The arch-covered through station is used by both S-Bahn and regional trains on elevated tracks. From this level you have interesting views through the windows on the south side of the close-by Television Tower and the activities on Alexanderplatz.

Underground, far removed from the elevated Alexanderplatz train station, U-Bhf Alexanderplatz is a junction of three S-Bahn lines. It is a complete, sprawling complex below Alex S-Bahn station.

Regional *Bahnhof Friedrichstrasse* was completely rebuilt from the ground up into a regional train station. Opened May 1999, it shines. Alive with trains rumbling, it is a hub of huge activity. Passengers scamper freely back and forth, jumping aboard elevated regional trains and east-west S-Bahn lines, or up and down escalators to north-south S-Bahn and U-Bahn trains below ground. On the ground level, autos and streetcars on busy Friedrichstrasse bisect the station.

Now that it's a beautiful station with every modern convenience, you have to use your imagination to visualize what it was like before the unification and Friedrichstrasse station was the only possible rail crossing point between East and West. Visitors from the West had to pass a solid iron wall right in the station and undergo heavy scrutiny and painstaking security inspections to visit East Berlin. You got out of the train, clutching your passport, climbed down into an underground cavern, and took a number to await clearance by the Grepo, who manned the barrier. If you didn't understand German when your number was called, you were out of luck. You sat on a bench for a half-hour or more. You had to pass gray-faced border guards sitting behind bulletproof glass at several observation posts and surrender your passport to a succession of guards who studied it as if they were learning to read. They looked at it, looked at you, looked at the mirror in back of you, consulted a computer, took some mysterious notes, and eventually waved you on, always expressionless, without exchanging any talk. You had to have your film-loaded camera X-rayed. If you had a suitcase, guards passed it through a curtain to a back room for inspection. If you carried any Western books or newspapers, you had to leave them behind. You also had to exchange DM 25 at the official rate of one to one when you could get five times more on Alexanderplatz, but you could never find anything worthwhile to buy with them, so it didn't matter. And just when at last you thought you were finished with the inspecting and registering, you might be pulled out of line and taken to a small room for further interrogation.

Now you can't figure out where the labyrinth of guard posts and interrogation rooms might have existed. Everything is pastel.

Regional *Bahnhof Lichtenberg*'s brick station building with glass front has been enlarged. You can transfer between S- and U-Bahn trains, but it is not convenient. The station has a bright interior and is large enough and well enough organized that right in the station you can make reservations and buy tickets to foreign countries and within

Germany in the efficient "Reisezentrum." There are telephones ("Fernsprecher"), lockers, a drugstore, a McDonald's, and a traveler's shop. Lichtenberg's upstairs Bistro cafe is nicely located in the "Galerie" mezzanine.

Lehrter-Hauptbahnhof has been rebuilt into the largest train station in Europe. New platforms rising 30 feet over the street carry traditional mainline, regional, and S-Bahn trains in the usual east-west direction. Lehrter's new tracks opened on June 21, 2002. S-Bahn trains began calling there on July 4, 2002. New exits lead to the new chancellor's offices and Invalidenstrasse.

When trains start rolling in 2006 through the north-south tunnel below Berlin's center, the name will change to simply Hauptbahnhof, and trains will also call at Potsdamer Platz Bahnhof (where you can see the marked entrance on the street level) and the new Sudkreuz station near the present Papestrasse S-Bahn station. Platforms 50 feet below ground will be crowded with 240,000 travelers daily crossing through the new two-mile-long north-south tunnel below the Spree River, the new federal chancellor's office, the Tiergarten Park, and the new city quarter at Potsdamer Platz ending south of the Landwehr Canal. While the tunnel was being built, a 660-foot stretch of the Spree River had to be moved 230 feet north because the riverbed was only three feet above the new tunnel, making it too difficult to dig from below. The new tunnel will allow passengers to get on and off at stations along a nearly five-and-a-half-mile travel corridor.

Getting around Berlin

In Berlin you are able to ride an extensive, integrated system of U-Bahn ("Subway") trains, S-Bahn trains in their historic livery of blood and custard, single- and double-decker buses, and streetcars reaching from the East into the West. One ticket, valid for two hours, covers all.

Most of the U- and S-Bahn stops have escalators and/or elevators. Too many visitors tote heavy suitcases up flights of stairs because they don't take the time to look for the signs indicating the location of the escalator or elevator. There are usually local street maps in stations to help you find your way in the neighborhood. Look at the information (*i*) bulletin board.

The transportation authority, BVG, operates the largest public transportation system in Germany. Anyone who has mastered getting around London or Paris will have no trouble in Berlin. By referring to the charts posted in all U- and S-Bahn stations, pasted to the walls of the trains themselves, available free from the BVG kiosk in front of Zoo station, and included in dozens of kinds of advertising material, you can move seamlessly from one line to another.

Berlin's public transportation has an amazingly simple ticketing system. There are three zones: *A, B,* and *C.* Forget all this and buy a Day Card, a Welcome (three-day) Card, or a 7-Day Ticket. They are remarkably cheap compared to single tickets.

Zone *A* covers everything you probably want to see and includes all of the main train stations. Zone *B* gets you to Berlin Tegel Airport and Schonefeld. You can get as far as Potsdam in zone *C.*

With any ticket, you can take, without extra charge, up to three children under seven years with you. Bicycles are allowed on S-Bahn trains from 9 A.M. to 2 P.M., after 5:30 P.M., and all day Saturdays, Sundays, and holidays. There is a fare for dogs, but buyers of some of the multiday cards below take their dogs without additional charge.

A "Kurzstrecke" ("short-distance") ticket covers only three stations by U- or S-Bahn or six stops with bus or streetcar. A "Langstrecke" ("long-distance") ticket is valid for up to two hours in two zones so that you can change trains or buses in any direction, even run an errand and return to your starting point. A "Ganzstrecke" ("network") ticket is valid for two hours in all three zones.

A "Tageskarte" ("Day Card"), valid until 3 A.M. the following day, is a bargain. With your three children you can also take along a baby buggy and a dog. You can add a third zone for an additional charge.

The so-called Berlin Potsdam Welcome Card is valid for 72 hours and covers all zones, three children, a baby buggy, happy pooch, and museum discounts. Included with your Welcome Card is a booklet allowing you sightseeing discounts. Note that these discounts duplicate some of those granted by the Culture Card, so you may not want to have both cards at the same time.

The best transportation value of all is the "7-Tage-Karte" ("7-Day Ticket") valid up to midnight on the seventh calendar day. Lend it to your companion when you aren't using it.

The Welcome Card is available at U- and S-Bahn ticket counters, the Service Office at Berlin Tegel Airport, and many hotels. The rest are dispensed by the blue machines at the entrances of all stations and bus stops, including that at the Tegel Airport. A single two-hour ticket ("Fahrschein") is delivered already time stamped. Insert all others for time stamping into one of the orange automatic date/time/location validators at platform entrances.

The Berlin U-Bahn network is one of the longest in the world. The first lines were opened in 1902 and included an elevated line on viaduct (now part of Line U1). The initial system was completed in 1930, and construction did not start again until 1953. Since then, several lines have been newly built or extended. For visitors, the S-Bahn network in the West is centered on Zoo station, but you may change between S-Bahn trains at any of the many hubs throughout the city. Use the maps posted in the trains. In the East, Alexanderplatz and Friedrichstrasse are often used for changing.

The term S-Bahn used for Berlin's suburban electric railroad system is an abbreviation of "Schnellbahn" and not of "Stadtbahn." It's not true that all S-Bahn trains are old and rickety and run on square wheels. There are beautiful new trains that coast into the stations with doors that open with a press of the button instead of having to tear them apart like Hercules breaking chains.

Regional trains supplementing the S-Bahn trains take you into Berlin's suburbs. A transportation ticket or pass covering zone *C* will cover the entire local network, although only zone *B* coverage is required to Potsdam's Hauptbahnhof, which opened on May 28, 2000. Regional train departure times from Zoo station are shown on the mechanical departures board in the main hall. They provide fast, limited-stop regional services with space for bicycles. Traveling in a regional train, although far short of riding in an ICE, is faster and more comfortable than traveling aboard an S-Bahn, but the trains call at far fewer stations.

Berliners take their far-reaching, on-time, and reliable bus network for granted. West Berlin is one of the few places in the world outside the British Isles where a large number of the buses are double-decked.

Given the time, you see more while traveling by bus than S-Bahn, and in fact many routes save you time by not requiring you to make S-Bahn changes. On glassed-in bus-stop walls and in most S-Bahn stations you find large Berlin maps showing the bus routes. Streetcars complete the transportation network in the East the same way that buses do in the West. They are an effective way of getting to places located between U- and S-Bahn stations.

Most subway and regular streetcar and bus lines stop running about 1-1:30 A.M. and don't start again until 4-5 A.M. (except Lines U12 and

U9, which run 24 hours during the weekends). During this downtime the night bus system in the West and the night streetcar system in the East provide excellent half-hourly service from about 1 A.M. to 4 A.M.

Great Train Attractions

Through Anhalter Bahnhof, Europe's largest covered train-station building, Sally Bowles made her grand entry into Berlin in Isherwood's *Goodbye to Berlin*. Built from 1875 to 1880, it could have contained Berlin's mammoth Congress Center with room to spare. The rail yards stretched for three miles through Kreuzberg. Each day saw 120 trains speeding to destinations like Constantinople, Brindisi, and Nice.

The station was severely damaged during World War II, but despite gaping holes in the roof, the walls remained sound and it was thought at the time that it would make an excellent museum. Despite the damage, trains continued running until May 18, 1952, when a surprise terrorist bombing for unknown reasons destroyed the surviving remains.

Except for the portico, which luckily survived the explosion, the station was razed in 1960-61. From Anhalter S-Bahn station you can see merely the preserved brown-brick facade consisting of four columns and four circular windows, but it is worth seeing because decoration and detail such as Corinthian columns allow you to try to imagine the station.

After you have seen the demolished Anhalter train station, visit the delightful jewel-box Wittenbergplatz U-Bahn station, Germany's first and finest. It has been brightly restored in Jugendstil as a historical monument.

The Deutsches Technikmuseum Berlin ("German Technical Museum in Berlin") sports a new wing. You will spot it by the eye-catching airplane mounted on its exterior. It was one of the "raisin bombers" that, during the Berlin Airlift, brought supplies to Berlin during the Berlin Blockade.

Partially set in the converted, overgrown freight yard of the former Anhalter Bahnhof, in the courtyard you see an original round table and a steam-driven snowplow locomotive. Included is an original arch salvaged from the Anhalter Bahnhof after its destruction. Filling the old hall is the greatest steam locomotive display of Prussian locomotives of various kinds, small and large, in the world. Side-by-side examples include a mammoth freight steam locomotive of the Austrian

Sudbahn built in 1860, small 1903 colonial field locomotives, and an enormous ("gigantic" is not too tame a word) 1914 Prussian traffic locomotive P-8. All show years of hard usage. A Prussian S-10 Schnellzug ("Fast Train") has been arc-torch-separated away to display the steam-driven inner workings, with each part marked in German explaining its function. You can walk in a clean trench below one train to study the undercarriage to get a feeling for the oil and grease that accumulates during service.

The Museum fur Gegenwart Berlin ("Museum for Contemporary Art"), Invalidenstrasse 50-51, Tel. 39-78-34-0, Fax 39-78-34-13 (open Tue.-Fri., 10 A.M. to 5 P.M.; Sat.-Sun., from 11 A.M.), was opened on November 3, 1996, north of the Spree River and beside the Schifffahrtskanal ("Shipping Canal") in the Hamburger Bahnhof ("Hamburg Train Station"). The building, the oldest existing train station in Berlin, had been the terminus of the 180-mile (300-kilometer) stretch connecting industrial Berlin with port-city Hamburg. When traffic dwindled at the end of the 19th century, a new Traffic and Building Museum moved in. Hamburger Bahnhof was restored for Berlin's 750th anniversary in 1987 after it had come to the West as part of the DM 3 million package that the West Berlin transport authority paid to take over the rundown S-Bahn system in 1984. The Hamburger Bahnhof, like the S-Bahn, had been owned by the East German railroads despite being situated in the West's Tiergarten District. The original purpose of the building is quickly revealed when you enter and see the high, glassed roof designed for steam engines and the slightly elevated areas that were boarding platforms.

Austria, Hungary, Slovenia, and Croatia

Savvy Traveling on the Trains of Austria, Hungary, Slovenia, and Croatia

Austrian trains—Hungarian trains—Slovenian trains— Croatian trains—Vienna to Budapest—Austria's private lines and steam trains—Vienna's train stations—Getting around Vienna—Vienna's City Airport Train (CAT)—Budapest's train stations—Steam Railroad Museum—Rail-pass travel

Austria, Hungary, and Slovenia were partners during the Hapsburg Austro-Hungarian Empire that expired after the First World War, and Vienna is the logical railroad hub of the area. Rail Europe (see Appendix A) has a free rail map, "Central Europe," that shows the networks of these countries.

On May 1, 2004, Hungary and Slovenia will join Austria as European Union (EU) member states, and in anticipation of that event, Austria Railroads has improved local passenger services to its neighboring countries with the introduction of reduced-fare EURegio (ER) trains.

Many of the trains serving Budapest and Vienna reflect the musical heritage of the Hungarian and Austrian capitals. When you board one of the five trains named after a Hungarian or Austrian composer, you hear a musical accompaniment in stations and on the trains themselves. While you watch the Bela Bartok arriving, you hear the charming "Evening in the Village." The Franz Lehar is greeted with the more up-tempo "Gold and Silver." The Franz Liszt leaves Budapest and Vienna to the strains of the "Hungarian Fantasy" and the Kalman Imre elicits music from the composer's "Gypsy Princess."

You reach Austria, one of the world's most beautiful countries, with a vast choice of EuroCity and EuroNight trains from Austria's neighboring countries, plus Benelux. However, some EuroCity trains call only in Innsbruck, not in the heart of the Austrian Federal Railroads (Osterreichischen Bundesbahnen, OBB, www.oebb.at), and several travel between Munich and Switzerland, picking up passengers only in Bregenz en route. OBB's flagship EC Transalpin with the first-class Swiss panoramic carriage takes you between Vienna, Linz, Salzburg, Innsbruck, Zurich, and Basel. It has been the fastest connection between Switzerland and Austria since 1958. Transalpin's carriage with the Teddy bear drawing is the children's play carriage.

Most travelers discover Vienna before Budapest, but you can reach Budapest directly along the Berlin-Dresden-Prague-Bratislava-Budapest main line as well as through trains that continue through Vienna en route.

Austrian Trains

The most sweeping change and massive investment program that OBB has experienced since its 1923-24 creation is gathering momentum year by year. The Vienna-Salzburg route, the "Westbahn," has been quadrupled and upgraded to 125 mph. You speed across new bridges, through new tunnels, and over newly electrified stretches, stop in new stations in new air-conditioned carriages with at-seat drinks and snacks from a restaurant car, and sleep in the most modern trains.

On June 15, 2003, OBB released seven superfast IC and EC trains over the Westbahn and the Sudbahn, cutting 33 minutes off the connections between Vienna, Linz, Salzburg, Graz, and Klagenfurt, and offered a real alternative to autos and domestic flights.

The 27-mile stretch of the Sudbahn between Gloggnitz in Lower Austria and Murzzuschlag in Styria ranks as a classic example of railroad construction. It was Europe's first railroad to traverse a mountain chain and was constructed between 1848 and 1854. The Semmering Railroad (*www.noe.co.at*) contains 16 viaducts, some of which are multilevel, and 15 tunnels.

This stretch of track was laid by some 20,000 workers, more than 750 of whom died of cholera and typhus. Opened on July 17, 1854, this railroad was electrified in 1959. In 1998, it became the first property belonging to OBB to be honored as a UNESCO World Heritage Site.

You may notice hikers along the Semmering Trail leading from beside the railroad line at Semmering one mile to Wolfsbergkogel station. After passing the turn-of-the-20th-century hotel, the Kurhaus Semmering, the hikers continue to the observation tower at the Doppelreiterkogel. At a marvelous panoramic viewpoint they watch your train from Klamm and follow it wriggling through the landscape, passing the gallery of the Weinzettlwand-Krauselklause-Tunnel, the Krauselklause viaduct, and the viaduct across the Kalte Rinne.

OBB's gray-and-red InterCity and OBB EuroCity trains are the heart of fast and comfortable travel in Austria. First-class salon carriages have facing 2+1 seating, plush upholstery, air-conditioning, curtains, matting on floor, and four "business class" compartments with four seats only that must be reserved in advance with a surcharge of about $15. Waiters serve meals at the seats of the business-class passengers, who have a choice between two menus. Others can patronize the restaurant carriage.

You may ride InterCity trains on seven lines: 1) Vienna-Salzburg-Bregenz (via Rosenheim, Germany); 2) Vienna-Salzburg (via Bischofshofen); 3) Vienna-Graz; 4) Vienna-Villach-(Salzburg); 5) Bruck an der Mer-Villach; 6) Linz-Selzthal-(Graz); and 7) Graz-Salzburg/Innsbruck.

Further, OBB provides excellent, punctual service with a full complement of express trains (*D*), semifast trains (*E*), and Schnellbahen (rapid-transit suburban trains) on a regular-interval timetable with departures either hourly or two-hourly on all main routes.

Hungarian Trains

Hungary is very proud of its railroads ("Magyar Allamvasutak," known as MAV, *www.mav.hu*). The year 1996 marked the 150th anniversary of railroads in Hungary. MAV's gray-blue and white fleet of modern carriages is the cornerstone of the EC network serving eastern Europe. The Gyor-Sopron line is operated by Gyor-Sopron-Edbenfurthi

Vasut (GySEV). MAV plays a central role in the nation's economy, carrying a far higher percentage of travelers than do most other European railroads; even so, MAV has suffered drastic passenger losses since the beginning of the free-market economy.

Budapest, with three large train stations, is the hub. Diesel and electric local, fast, express, InterCity, and EuroCity trains serve the country well. Most of the main network is electrified. MAV's domestic trains are reliable and travel is very cheap. Yellow stripes mark first class. MAV's international carriages travel far, to Frankfurt/Main and Berlin. The carriages are fine, but with fewer comforts than their Western counterparts. The gauge throughout Hungary is the same as in western Europe. At Zahony, on the Ukraine frontier, a change from European to wide gauge takes place.

Hungarian train stations are all well posted with arrival and departure signs, but you cannot trust printed timetables or schedules available on Web sites. Trains to the countryside are pulled by red diesel locomotives.

MAV has no fewer than 19 types of train. InterCity Rapid (ICR) are higher-quality domestic trains developed from InterCity trains and run between Budapest and major county seats. The trains are fully air-conditioned, with compulsory seat reservations. ICR trains can run up to 125 mph without intermediate stops on the Budapest-Debrecen-Nyiregyhaza and Budapest-Pecs lines.

InterCity (IC) trains with obligatory seat reservation are engaged in direct traffic between cities. They stop at county seats, major tourist centers, and stations with high passenger traffic. There are five InterCity (IC) lines.

Fast trains are engaged in direct interregional traffic. Semifast trains serve interregional traffic. Inter Pici (IP) trains with compulsory seat reservation are used primarily for connections to IC trains. Cross-border traffic trains are slow trains covering about 60 miles within Hungary. Suburban trains are slow trains operating within 60 miles of a village or town. Interregional trains are slow trains operating on main and branch lines.

Although train fares are cheap in Hungary, a Eurail product, European East Pass, or Hungarian Railpass really pays for itself in the time and hassle you save trying to buy a correct ticket. You thank your lucky stars for a rail pass that allows you to escape the incredible confusion of the complex and unmarked ticketing windows;

nevertheless, the Hungarian Railpass, which contains a full page of information in Hungarian, may be scrutinized before you are allowed to buy the required seat reservation.

Budapest is as dazzling a city as you will find in Europe, but sightseeing in the flat Hungarian countryside is disappointing. Hungary is a breadbasket. You imagine Batu Khan's Mongol army sweeping south of the Carpathian Mountains across the plain, horsemen with no barriers to hinder them, the run of the country by horseback—yet from the train you see no horses.

Do not expect the same comfort as you find aboard western European trains. The Hungarian language barrier is difficult to break. Some of those with connections to tourism speak English; more speak German, so go prepared. Excursions into the countryside are not as scenic as those in the West. Each little train station in the countryside is alive with flowers and boasts a showpiece black steam locomotive on a pedestal in front, but you don't see charming villages or church spires, no thatched roofs or typical architecture.

Slovenian Trains

Following a 10-day war after the proclamation of independence from Yugoslavia, on June 26, 1991, the nation of two million people became independent and, in 1992, a new railroad company appeared. Slovenia's national railroad, Slovenske Zeleznice (SZ, *www.slozeleznice.si*), is not affiliated with any of the rail-pass programs.

The best way to Slovenia is aboard the EC Mimara day train, which runs Zagreb-Ljubljana-Salzburg-Munich, or aboard EuroCity 151 from Vienna via Graz. Train D411 runs south to Zagreb and overnight to Belgrade and Thessaloniki. Domestically, SZ operates IC, ICS, Zeleni vlak, and Regional trains.

The sky-blue and white, 124-mph Slovenian tilting train, the ETR 310, which is based on the Italian ETR 470, is known as ICS (Inter City Special, or sometimes Inter City Slovenia). It began operation on September 24, 2000, between Ljubljana and Maribor, Slovenia's two largest cities, with only two intermediate stops, cutting half an hour off previous schedules. In 2004, you will be able to ride it to and from Venice, Italy. Passengers in all three levels of seating (second class, second class plus, and first class plus) are offered free parking in Ljubljana or the option of a taxi for a flat fee. Future dual-voltage sets will allow operation into Croatia and Hungary.

Zeleni vlak ("Green Train," for the livery) are InterCity diesel rail-cars purchased in 1970 from Germany. Vivid, sun-colored (red, orange, and yellow) SZ electric railcars serve domestic routes. International carriages are brightly repainted carriages of Austrian origin. Those inherited from the Yugoslavian Railroads are drab green with repainted logos.

The IC Kras runs to Trieste, and the IC Drava to Venice. You may arrive or depart on the overnight Lisinski to Munich or Venezia Express to Venice. Visas are issued aboard trains at the border without fees, forms, or photos. Slovenian conductors generally speak English.

The best crossing from the West to Slovenia is via Jesenice on the Austrian border because it is the closest to Ljubljana and thus holders of rail passes, valid in Austria but not Slovenia, only pay extra for the shorter distance.

Although Slovenia has 36 miles of Adriatic coastline, it is essentially an Alpine country "on the sunny side of the Alps," and solicits visitors in cooperation with the Alpine Tourist Commission.

Ljubljana (meaning "my loved one") is known as the Salzburg of the Slovenes, with river, castle, and baroque architecture. In its thrown-together train station, currently being remodeled, all functions are conveniently located in one room—International Ticketing, Money Change, Train Information, and Tourist Information—making it as easy as possible for you first to request your ticket to the border at the International Ticketing counter, ask the price, change the right number of dollars or other hard currency into Slovenian tolar at the Change counter, and return to International Ticketing to pay for your ticket. It is very smooth. All signs have English-language subtitles. An underground passage connects platforms.

Traditionally, however, Ljubljana has been primarily an important stop for the mainline trains along the Balkan mainline from Switzerland and Germany to Zagreb, which is now across a second border to Croatia.

The timetable "Vozni Red" is helpful. It costs about $4 at main train stations. "Zahod" means departures, and "Vzhod" means arrivals. "Cas" means time and "tir" refers to track number. A word of caution is appropriate: be very careful when boarding. Many of the international trains split departing Ljubljana so that you must double-check to board the correct section of the poorly marked trains.

Within Slovenia, you can take the train to Lesce-Bled station, but it is about three miles from Bled, the exquisite Julian Alps resort on glacial Lake Bled, so you'll need to take a bus into the city itself. Most prefer the hourly 90-minute bus trip directly to Bled from the bus terminal in front of the Ljubljana train station.

Trains between Ljubljana and Postojna, taking about an hour, bring you a half-hour's walk from the entrance to one of the world's great natural wonders, the Postojna Caves. Again, a bus may be more convenient because it cuts about 10 minutes from your walking time. A narrow-gauge train takes you about a mile into the cave.

The Slovenian Railroad Museum at Parmova 35, Ljubljana (open Mon.-Thur., 9 A.M. to 1 P.M., Tel. 01-29-12-641), housed in low buildings beside the Ljubljana-Villach mainline, has a remarkable collection, including an 1861 Sudbahn locomotive.

Croatian Trains

Zagreb, Croatia's capital city, formerly the Austrian Empire city of Agram, has become the dead end of the Balkan mainline. Zagreb's through station, where all trains stopped, was used by suffering merrymakers complaining about their crowded trains as they flocked from Germany and Scandinavia through Zagreb to Athens, Istanbul, and sunny Aegean beaches. Former Yugoslavia's defunct finest train, an InterCity, used to run between Zagreb and Belgrade. At the height of the Yugoslav War, traffic had to be withdrawn from 35 percent of the new Croatian Railroads' ("HZ," for "Hrvatske Zeljeznice") 1,809-mile network. Bridges were destroyed or damaged, stations were in shambles, and locomotives and carriages were stolen, destroyed, and seized. As a result, HZ is truncated—travel south of Zagreb is difficult although Zagreb-Sarajevo, Bosnia, service was restored in 2001. Travel is better north of Zagreb. In 2003, HZ put into service rebuilt 100-mph carriages in HZ's 2003 livery—white with gray and red stripes—and began introducing tilting, air-conditioned railcars based on the German RegioSwinger for use on the lines from Zagreb to the coastal resorts of Split, Sibenik, and Zadar, cutting for example the time for the trip from Zagreb to Split from seven and a half hours to five hours. Zagreb is connected via Ljubljana to western Europe's EuroCity network by the EC Mimara to Munich and Berlin.

A "vozna karta" is a ticket; "potvrda" is reservation; "kola" is carriage; and "sjedalo" is seat.

Life is normal in Zagreb, but prices are very high. The city was last bombed in May 1995. Zagreb's Glavni Kolodvor station is long, poor, and mostly in need of refurbishing, but with some modern touches such as its snappy electronic departure signs. It provides all the normal services, including money changing, but note that first- and second-class ticketing windows are in separate rooms. You won't have trouble finding your way around because international pictographs are used throughout. If you look sufficiently lost, a friendly conductor will point your way. Although staff have undergone special training to be proficient in German, someone will speak English. Nevertheless, save time and error by writing out your ticketing requests beforehand. Arrivals are listed on white-paper posters; departures on yellow.

"Croatia Express" is the name of the ticketing and train reservations service. They also have an office facing the green square in front of the station at Trg Tomislava 17.

Worth noting is the short funicular from Tomiceva Street in the lower city to Gradec in the upper town. It is very inexpensive, with departures every 15 minutes, but hardly worth waiting long for because the walk down the stairs is easy.

In addition to the trunk line through Ljubljana to western European capitals, there are international lines that serve as back doors to Budapest and Vienna. Buy your tickets at the "international" ticket counter, even if you have a rail pass valid in Austria, Hungary, or Italy and only need a domestic ticket to the border. The segment of Croatia connecting at the border is subject to international rates, which are astronomically higher than internal Croatian ones. The line to Budapest runs for a long distance along Hungary's Lake Balaton, the mass-tourism vacation area, but there is an interminable wait at the border crossing for customs inspections on board the train and while the locomotive is changed to a Hungarian one. Your 219-mile trip to Budapest takes some six hours, about the same as the 286-mile trip to Vienna. You need not leave the train to have a Eurail product or European East Pass validated. Austrian or Hungarian conductors are responsible for this task.

Vienna to Budapest

You may choose between four excellent day trains along the 156-mile Vienna-Budapest train corridor. The EC 41 Lehar leaves Vienna's Sudbahnhof at 7:15 A.M. IC 345 departs Vienna's Westbahnhof at 10:17 A.M. The EC63 Bela Bartok from Munich leaves the Westbahnhof at

2:15 P.M. The German EC 25 Franz Liszt from Cologne and Frankfurt Airport leaves the Westbahnhof at 3:45 P.M.

The ECs take you between Vienna and Budapest in two hours, 45 minutes. For the first time since 1932 (when the legendary Hungarian train "Arpad" raced along this route), you can travel between Budapest and Vienna in less than three hours, in part due to MAV's recent upgrade of the Hegyeshalom-Budapest line. This fast turn-around makes it possible for you to make a quick one-day excursion from Vienna to Budapest and back.

The flagship EuroCity Lehar consists of a first-class 1993 blue-and-gray MAV salon-type car (with yellow first-class stripes), one similar-livery restaurant car, and six bright red-and-black OBB cars for passengers with standard compartments in second-class coaches. The gray-and-white MAV restaurant car features Magyar specialties. On your seat you find the timetable, "Ihr Zug/Your Train/Az on Vonata." Austrian and Hungarian newspapers are offered en route.

Your border crossing at Hegyeshalom is shortened to three minutes, barely enough time for Hungarian border guards to scramble aboard. Border passport, visa, and customs inspections are performed aboard the Lehar.

Austria's Private Lines and Steam Trains

Step off your OBB mainline train at its first stop traveling east, 18 minutes from Innsbruck, and you step into a special railroading world—a world where you see steam rising from locomotives warming up, well-greased cogwheel tracks leading up sharp inclines, and the promise of secluded Alpine lakes crisscrossed by steamers. Groups of Germans are singing drinking songs on this bright morning.

In Jenbach, the Achensee (Lake Achen) Railroad (*www.tiscover.com/ achensee*), the Zillertal (Ziller Valley) Railroad, and the OBB share the same station and present their departure times on the same yellow timetable sheets, but they leave from different tracks with different gauges.

Over a century ago, engineers opened the meter-gauge, 4.2-mile Achensee Railroad that carries you up an incline reaching 160 o/oo with the help of Riggenbach-system cogwheels. From Jenbach these cogwheels help you ascend over the summit to the high Achensee, rightly known as "Tyrol's fjord." The Achensee Railroad runs May to October.

Find your place in one of the 55-seat, antique carriages. During the first part of your ascent you pass stretches of wildflowers beside the track plus berry bushes, forests of beech, spruce, and fir, and sights of green valleys and grazing cows.

Motorists standing in the woods hiding the railroad have parked their cars and crossed to shoot photos of your passing train. Climbing at only five to six mph gives you the chance to relax and savor the mountains and valleys.

Pushing from the rear of your train to prevent possible breakaway, the world's oldest cogwheel steam locomotive in regular service was built in the Vienna Locomotive factory in Floridasdorf. It is nose down into the earth. This odd-looking design keeps the boiler tubes horizontal to maintain heat transfer and holds the firebox level to prevent firebrands from tumbling onto the footplate. For each round trip, workers load 770 pounds of hard coal and pump 800 gallons of water into the 18-foot-long machine.

When your train slows to a crawl, you see Eben's pilgrim church, the restaurant, and clusters of houses. The church, a jewel of baroque architecture, contains the chalice of St. Notburga, whom locals in the Tyrol and Bavaria venerate as the patroness of servants. Make a visit to the church to be astonished by the remarkable legend. At the summit (3,182 feet) at Eben, you have a 10-minute break as workers exchange the steam locomotive pushing you from behind for another in front to pull you downhill, without cogs, into the valley and to the ships' landing at Seespitz.

During your stop at Maurach, a few mountaineers in hiking boots disembark to walk to the valley station of the white Rofan aerial gondolas (Seilbahnen). In five minutes the aerial gondolas lift them from the valley floor at 3,215 feet to the mountain station, 6,037 feet high in the Rofan Alpine range. They can hike along 90 miles of carefully tended and well-marked walking trails among rare Alpine flowers, chamois, and marmots. Ascent costs about $12; round trip costs about $15.

Your train steams to a final halt at the lakeside terminus of Seespitz (3,117 feet). The steam swirling about you, the merriment at the snack bar created by schnapps sippers, the pier beckoning you aboard the Achensee steamers, and, above all, the serene turquoise lake nestling between the Karwendel and Rofan Alpine mountain ranges give new meaning to the word "idyllic."

The Achensee is the largest lake in Tyrol, with an altitude of 3,025 feet, almost 1,300 feet above the Inn Valley. Schedulers coordinated the railroad timetable with the ship's timetable. The well-outfitted passenger ships crisscrossing the Achensee vary in capacity from 40 to 400 persons. Sooner or later you will pass the historic St. Josef, the St. Benedikt, and the Stadt Innsbruck. The flagship of the Achensee fleet, the 15-mph, 600-passenger ship *Tirol*, was built in 1994 by Oswag Werft Linz under contract to Innsbruck's Tiroler Wasserkraftwerke (Power Station), owner of the lake(!).

The Tyrolean power station itself is in Jenbach. Against all geologic theory, the Achensee empties toward the north through the Achenbach River, which carries the water out of Austria into a tributary of the German river, Isar. Nevertheless, when Austrians laid out the hydroelectric scheme, they directed the water for Tyrol's benefit by cascading it to the Austrian power station about 350 yards below.

Visitors have been navigating Lake Achen since 1887. It is every bit as exciting today as it was then. The lake is 5.5 miles long and 0.6 mile wide. At night, brightly lighted ships cruising the serene waters provide a beautiful spectacle.

You can't help but enjoy yourself on a round trip on the magic Achensee. Get on and off as you please. Join the 15-mile path around the lake, hike, or just sit yourself down for a beverage in a lakeside village and rejoin a later ferry.

Past Buchau your ship calls at the lakeside resort of Pertisau on the only flat ground surrounding the lake. It was created by convergence of the valleys coming down from the Karwendel limestone massif. Your next landing is Gaisalm. An "Alm" is an Alpine pasture. Gaisalm is famous as Europe's only one that is accessible by lake.

Leave your ship at Scholastika landing for the mandatory 10-minute walk through the village of Achenkirch to visit the "Sixenhof," a preserved Tyrolean residence. It stands today on its original site, which goes back to 1361. After a fire it was rebuilt in 1810. A preservation society has maintained the farmhouse as accurately as possible in its original state, except for modern sanitation. Visiting it gives you an insight into how these mountain residents once lived and worked. With forests so close at hand, you won't be surprised to see that most of the working equipment was made of wood.

Austria, filled with high Alps and rolling countryside dotted with spectacularly beautiful lakes, offers you many chances to leave mainline trains for very special local and private lines. Steam locomotives still operate on a scheduled basis, steam rack railroads climb steep inclines to lofty mountaintops, trains on standard- and narrow-gauge short lines make frequent steam excursions, and numerous museum trains welcome rail fans.

The Achensee Railroad is only one of the truly enjoyable private lines in Austria. Others you will long remember visiting include the following:

• The nearby narrow-gauge (30 inches) Zillertal Railroad travels from Jenbach 20 miles into the Ziller Valley (*www.tiscover.com/zillertal*) at speeds up to 22 mph. The Zillertal Railroad's historic locomotives are not tilted because the Ziller Valley route is flatter than the Achensee Railroad's. It is one of Austria's broadest and richest north-south valleys. You see grazing cows. Their milk yields famous cheese. The very popular Zillertal beer is made in Zell am Ziller. The valley terminates at a glacier and the train goes three-fourths of that distance.

• The 11.3-mile Stubaital (*www.tiscover.com/stubai*) Railroad running hourly to Fulpmes is the most amazing city tram in Europe. Once your No. 6 tram leaves Innsbruck's city limits it climbs into the mountains and follows the slope of the green and fertile Stubai Valley. Along the route you cross above Innsbruck's Olympic ice rink, Ambras castle, and the Europa bridge, Europe's highest highway bridge on pillars.

• The eight-mile Montafon Railroad (MBS) opened December 18, 1905, as Austria's westernmost private railroad and the first standard-gauge local electric railroad in the Austro-Hungarian empire. It now is carried by red-and-yellow 2000 electric railcars between Bludenz and Schruns connecting villages in the Montafon mountain valley and serving as a lifeline to the areas of Aussermontafon and Ausserfratte.

• Linz' Postlingberg Railroad is proud to be in the Guinness Book of Records as the world's steepest adhesion railroad. It runs every 20 minutes from its lower terminus along an 18-minute route to the lovely pilgrim's church crowning the Postlingberg summit. The railroad was laid out by Emile Zola's father to allow convenient access for the devout.

One of Austria's provinces is a railroad operator in its own right. Styria runs both standard and 2½-foot gauge lines under the banner of the Steiermarkische Landesbahnen with headquarters in Graz. Its longest line, the 48-mile Murtalbahn, runs from Unzmarkt to Mauterndorf. On Tuesdays and Wednesdays during the summer you ride steam along half of this line.

You are welcome to call numerous train enthusiast groups in Austria. For more details, contact the Austrian National Tourist Office (see Appendix A).

Vienna's Train Stations

The heart of Austria—and the OBB—is Vienna. Vienna has three train stations with high-speed train service. You usually arrive at the West train station, the "Westbahnhof." Vienna's West station handles most traffic from Switzerland and Germany. Vienna's South train station, the "Sudbahnhof," connects with Italy, Slovenia, and the eastern countries.

Travelers arriving from the west or south must use surface transportation to change from the Westbahnhof to the Sudbahnhof or vice versa. This inconvenience makes Vienna an obvious place to break your journey. *Tip:* You can shave at least an hour off your travel time by getting off your train from the west in Vienna-Hutteldorf station, where all international trains stop, before it reaches Vienna-Westbahnhof. In Hutteldorf, change to S-Bahn Line 3, where you make direct connections to the Sudbahnhof.

The highly glassed Westbahnhof is a big, well-organized structure rebuilt in 1953 to handle all electrified train traffic in the direction of Western Europe. It was renovated in 1990 to provide access to the new Line 6 U-Bahn facilities. Information for hotels and trains is available in one office in the middle of the hall. The tourist information office opens early (6:15 A.M.) to accommodate travelers arriving on the first international trains, and remains open late (11 P.M.). Luggage carts fitted for the escalators are available.

The South train station ("Sudbahnhof") is a graceful station because of the moving walkways leading to two upper levels, which make it easy for you to convey carts and luggage with wheels. One flight up takes you to the second floor ("Ostbahn") for departures to Hungary, Slovakia, the Czech Republic, and Poland; two flights up takes you to the "Sudbahn" for Italy, Slovenia, and Croatia. There are separate smoking and nonsmoking waiting rooms and kiosks selling travel provisions ("Reiseproviant"), as well as sit-down coffee shops on these levels.

On the expansive ground floor, you find nearly every service you need, including money changing (open 6:30 A.M. to 10 P.M., during the summer), tourist information (open daily, 6:30 A.M. to 10 P.M.), train information, reservations and ticketing, lockers, a barbershop, and shower. Escalators take you down to the S-Bahn station out the south face. Platform numbers are shown on the electric departure boards.

Vienna's third station is the striking glass-fronted Franz-Josefs-Bahnhof, a model for the modern trend toward integrating train facilities with commercial shopping centers. Most of its traffic is the commuter service along the southern bank of the Danube and north of the Danube, including double-decked trains to Krems, which you use to connect to the Danube River steamers. Electrification of the final 50-mile stretch of the Franz-Josefs line to Gmund, in Lower Austria on the Czech Republic's border, means that OBB no longer has to change locomotives en route and permits faster, through running of the Waldviertel-Kurier and the Waldvietel Express.

Vienna's small Nord train station serves the small area north of the Danube, and Slovakia. Vienna Mitte train station is a sprawling non-mainline hub consisting of four S-Bahn platforms (which also accommodate E trains), a U-Bahn connection of several lines, check-in platforms for the Vienna City Airport Train, buses stopping in front, and a streetcar stop on the corner (line 0 to the Sudbahnhof).

Getting around Vienna

Plan to use Vienna's public transportation from the train stations, including the surface streetcar and bus network, S-Bahn, and U-Bahn. They interchange at Karlsplatz on the Ring. A ticket for one is good for unlimited transfers to all. You can change from metro to tram to bus without having to buy another ticket. Tickets are valid in one direction only for 1½ hours.

Franz Josef I of Austria-Hungary, the dour emperor with mutton-chop whiskers, disapproved of citizens traveling underground like moles and lower animals. He refused to allow engineers to cover the first sunken railroads of Vienna and went to great pains to avoid officially opening the new stations.

The master of Vienna's art nouveau movement, Otto Wagner, created the splendid Hofpavilon Hietzing train station close by Schonbrunn Palace, the emperor's summer residence, specifically for the emperor's use. However, the emperor traveled only twice in his beautifully appointed personal carriage along Vienna's newfangled Stadtbahn, or "city rail system"—once on June 16, 1899, to open the Vienna River Line, and once on April 12, 1902, for the Danube Canal Line.

Steam-hauled trains of the Stadtbahn, working with a frequency of three minutes, are gone now, the historic segments of the Viennese present subway (U-Bahn) network are uncovered still, and futuristic silver subway trains race past Schonbrunn Palace, but you still see the gilded traces of the 19th-century Stadtbahn preserved as museums in the heart of Vienna.

Vienna's integrated city transportation system is arguably the most convenient in Europe (and improvements are still continuing), but you still see a few of Otto Wagner's 40 art nouveau stations from Vienna's glamorous heyday at the turn of the century (1895-1902) like tiny jewel boxes along the routes of the old Stadtbahn.

After 1969, the former Danube Canal and Vienna Valley Stadtbahn lines were converted into subway Line U-4. In the process, old station buildings at Schonbrunn, Kettenbruckgasse, Stadtpark, and Rossauer Lande were restored. The centerpiece intersection at Karlsplatz was so extensively enlarged in 1978 that the two Stadtbahn pavilions, particularly elegant with their gilded marble, had to be dismantled, rebuilt, and restored.

One of them now serves as one of the entrances to the Karlsplatz subway station and as the home of small exhibitions on specialized themes; the other as a summer cafe.

South of Vienna's present Hietzing U-4 subway station, look for the Otto Wagner Hofpavilon Hietzing, "Kaiser Franz Josef I Stadtbahnstation." This emperor's train station was never intended for use by the public—it was reserved for the use of Franz Josef, members of his court, and distinguished guests. Now you view a precious museum that is open daily except Mondays, 9 A.M. to 12:15 P.M. and 1 to 4:30 P.M. (except Jan. 1, May 1, and Dec. 25). Inside you see a mural of old Vienna, gilding, flocked wallpaper, and lush carpeting.

Unlimited-mileage rail passes such as Austrian Railpasses, Eurail products, and European East Passes cover the blue-and-cream S-Bahn trains of the Austrian Railroads as well as the railroad's more familiar long-distance trains. The futuristic silver U-Bahn trains, however, are covered only by city passes and not rail passes.

Children under the age of six travel free on Vienna's public transportation network all year round. Youth under the age of 16 may travel free on Sundays and holidays, including the Christmas holidays from December 23 to January 6 and school holidays during the second week of February. Carry a photo I.D. at all times.

For adults, the Viennese city transport system has just the pass, card, or ticket for you to ride U-Bahn trains, S-Bahn trains, streetcars, and buses. Select one to best fit your itinerary at the kiosk below Vienna Schwechat Airport or visit the Transit Authority's information office in the subway station below St. Stephans' Square (Stephansplatz). You can buy single city transportation tickets (€1.30 for adults, €.65 for children) in any U-Bahn station by automat or from any of the tobacco kiosks around the city or aboard a tram or bus for slightly more. Unlimited 24-hour (€4.30) and 72-hour (€10.90) tickets are designed so you can let a friend or spouse use them when you are not. The eight-day network ticket is a bargain (€21.80) for those spending any eight days in Vienna because it can be used on nonconsecutive days even years apart and never expires. Buy your tickets at Vienna Transport Authority ticket offices such as the one at the airport. Validate them in the automatic canceling machines.

The Vienna Card, costing €15.25, offers you 72 hours unrestricted travel on Vienna's underground, streetcar, and bus network as well as various benefits at around 60 museums, shops, and restaurants. It is available from most hotels, Vienna's Tourist Office, Karntner Strasse 38 (open 9 A.M. to 7 P.M., daily), and the major Transport Authority ticket offices.

Reach the Sudbahnhof from Vienna's West station by U-Bahn Line 6 to Meidling station, changing to S-Bahn Line 1, 2, or 3. From Franz-Josefs-Bahnhof to the Westbahnhof, it is easiest to walk a block toward the Danube Canal to the Friedensbrucke U-Bahn station, where U6 takes you to the Westbahnhof.

Vienna City Airport Train (CAT)

In December 2003, the Vienna Airport Express authority, jointly owned by OBB and Vienna Schwechat Airport, inaugurated CAT service between Vienna Schwechat Airport and downtown Vienna. The white, gray, and green, three-carriage, double-decker trains were specially modified with luggage racks and run on half-hourly express service and half-hourly fast service between the airport and Vienna's Mitte station, where you may check in your luggage on the new platform. Vienna Mitte is accessible from S-Bahn lines 1, 2, 3, and 15 and U-Bahn lines U1, U3, and U4, making any place in Vienna within reach. Vienna Mitte has been issued an airport code so that you can ticket your flight right into the center of Vienna.

The new line, mostly completed in 2002, takes you through Rennweg station, which was completely rebuilt with a central platform replacing side platforms, new Geiselbergstrasse station with connections to tram line 6, the rebuilt Zentralfreidhof station, Oberlaa, and the airport. The project cost €350 million, due in part to the 1½ miles of tunnel.

Visitors arriving by plane at Schwechat should follow the pictographs illustrating a train to the station below. At the ticket office on the platform below you can buy a €9 ticket (€16 round trip) for downtown Vienna, or validate your European East Pass, Eurail product, or Austrian Railpass, or buy a city transportation pass.

Alternately, it may be more convenient for you to use one of OBB's "Vienna Airport Lines" bus services, which serve Vienna Airport from the West train station, with a pick-up at the South train station daily between 5:30 A.M. and 12:15 A.M. They take 35 minutes to the airport from the West station.

Budapest's Train Stations

Budapest has four mainline termini, three of which ("Nyugati" or West; "Deli" or South; and "Delete" or East) are named after directions and the other (Jozsefvaros) is named for the district in which it lies. The first three train stations are connected with each other and within the city with three ("yellow," "blue," and "red") no-graffiti subway lines that are the world's second oldest (after London's). The subways and subway stations are excellent. You travel directly between Deli station and Keleti station on the "red" line (M2), but to reach Nyugati (West) train station you change at Deak subway station to board Line M3's (blue) former Hanover, Germany, trams. Be sure to go to the correct station for departure. You can also use blue line M3 to reach Budapest Ferihegy Airport by traveling south to the end of the line, Kobanya Kispest, and transferring there to bus No. 93, which stops at both airport terminals. Reaching the airport takes about an hour and requires two metro tickets (70 cents). Single metro tickets costing about 35 cents are valid for 30 minutes. Validate them in the punching machines. Guards are especially zealous checking foreigners for valid tickets.

The most convenient place for you to buy train tickets in Hungary is at Hungarian Travel Bureau offices. Someone there usually speaks English. There is an office of the Budapest Tourist Information Office in Nyugati station, but the main office,

Hungarian Tourism Service at Margit korut 85 (Tel. 36-1-155-1691; Fax 36-1-175-3819), provides a wide range of tourist information about Budapest's sights and accommodations and sells sightseeing tours, tourist guides, and maps. MAV requires that you reserve express trains ("gyorsvonat") a day in advance, but local trains ("szemelyvonat") need no booking.

You can buy a subway/streetcar/bus map at a metro station ticket office, but the metro stations are so well posted you will not need one when you confine yourself to metro travel.

The three train stations of Budapest have much in common. They are large, sprawling, and bewildering. All have electronic departure signboards in the departure hall and at the heads of platforms. The escalators all work and all have attached, well-marked metro (*M*) stations. Signing is by international pictographs that you may be hard-pressed to find because they are not displayed prominently, and the agents will never speak English. Moreover they all give you a hard time and can be extremely difficult to deal with.

Only Hungarians read Hungarian ("the devil's tongue") so the written signs ring no bells for you. Follow arrows. Search for pictographs. And trust to common sense.

Keleti (East train station), loosely modeled on Berlin's former Lehrter train station, as the main international terminal, is usually the terminus for two lines you will be most likely to travel, the link to Vienna and the Bratislava-Prague-Berlin route. In addition, here you board trains to Venice, Belgrade, Ljubljana, Bucharest, and Warsaw. Keleti is a large, ranging station on the Pest side of Budapest. Statues of George Stephenson, inventor of the locomotive, and James Watt, creator of the steam engine, grace the front of the eclectic, charming exterior of the tremendous 19th-century structure.

Keleti's arrival hall has 13 tracks, but only 6 through 9 stretch to the front. The front entrance is closed, but it is not necessary to descend the stairs. Exit on the side next to platform 6, where you find a wing containing three or four accommodations offices, an Ibusz agency (open Mon.-Sat., 8 A.M. to 7 P.M.), an "Express" youth travel office (open Mon.-Sat., 8 A.M. to 6 P.M.), 24-hour luggage storage, train information (English not spoken), and a couchette and sleeping-car reservations counter. Find ticketing at Window 20, which is not identified in English. Currency change (look for the German-language "Geld Wechsel" sign) is everywhere.

Keleti's metro station below is crowded with shops, more ticketing windows, vending machines, and a hot dog/pizza/pretzel kiosk. You can purchase a cup of espresso coffee on the terrace. Frequent metro service takes you to the city center and under the Danube to Deli station.

Nyugati (West) train station, which was designed and built by the French Eiffel company, is usually the terminus for the InterCity trains. This Pest-side, sprawling, but spic-and-span station at the head of Lenin Street just before it reaches Marx Square is quite handsome with its Victorian-looking red- and brown-brick facade and blue-gray latticework.

You find all the facilities, luggage check, water, barber, traveler's sleeping facilities, Budapest Tourist Information Office (open Mon.-Sat., 8 A.M. to 7 P.M.; Sun., to 6 P.M.), money change, etc., beside platform 10, so walk alongside platform 10 for the escalator exit to this complex.

A car park above the station connects with a massive shopping center next to the station. Below is a complex subterranean metro station on the blue line.

McDonald's has refurbished the former restaurant building, beautifully recalling Belle Epoque railroading. Take a look at the shining furnishings. It was voted the best McDonald's in the world. Enter on street level.

The outdated wooden hall of Deli (South station) in the west (!) was completely destroyed during World War II, and the current modern station was built in stages. Most of the traffic departs on the lines for the Lake Balaton region and nonstop InterCity trains to Pecs. Deli is Budapest's most modern station, with an exterior of aluminum, glass, and concrete. Inside you find a post office, Ibusz agency (open Mon.-Sat., 8 A.M. to 7 P.M.), money change, souvenirs (hard currency only), shops of every nature, coin-operated lockers, and sweeping staircases. The station is also the farthest from the center of town, lying in the Buda side of the Danube (Duna) at the terminus of line M2. You find various foods in the stalls scattered about. Deli's platforms have pushcarts and drinking water from fountains with spigots.

Steam Railroad Museum

Hungary's national railroad preservation site, opened on July 14, 2000, in the northern suburbs of Budapest, is located in the former

Eszaki roundhouse, also known as the Tatai ut shed. The museum is also given the nickname "Fusti," which means "Steamy." A 2002 addition is a fascinating 1937 streamlined train. Giant 1951 steam engines on the museum roundhouse were the last of Hungarian steam-engine production.

Rail-Pass Travel

Eurail products are valid in both Austria and Hungary, including the small GySEV network (but not in Slovenia or Croatia), and because Austria and Hungary are Eurail countries, you may choose to select them for a Eurail Selectpass, e.g., Switzerland-Austria-Hungary. When you enter Austria or Hungary via train from a country that doesn't honor Eurail products (such as Slovenia or Poland), you need not prevalidate your pass at a train station; the Austrian or Hungarian conductor assumes the responsibility.

European East Passes are valid in Austria and Hungary. They let you travel as you please over five countries including the OBB and MAV networks as well as through Poland, the Czech Republic, and Slovakia. These passes are your most convenient way to travel about these Eastern nations, which, like Hungary, present language difficulties. Good international train connections take you from Vienna and Budapest to Bratislava, Prague, and Warsaw.

You buy them for any five to 10 days travel in a month, for first-class or second-class travel. Their price is based on the one-way Salzburg/Vienna/Budapest/Prague/Warsaw Eurail Tariff price, so when you travel more than this stretch, you save money, especially when you make Vienna your gateway to Eastern Europe.

Austrian Railpasses are flexipasses valid for three to eight travel days in 15 of first- or second-class unlimited travel on the OBB network (except between the Austrian border and Hegyeshalom, Hungary). You may choose the exact number of days you wish to use your flexipass. Minimum is three; maximum is eight.

The Puchberg am Schneeberg-Hochschneeberg Rack Railroad described below gives a 10 percent discount to pass holders and the ships of Wurm & Kock give a special price for trips on the Danube between Linz and Passau, while the ships of the DDSG Blue Danube Line allow a 20 percent discount on trips Melk to Krems and Vienna to Durnstein on Sundays. The same company offers 20 percent off sightseeing trips in Vienna.

Use the Austrian port of Bregenz (site of the summer lake festival) to begin journeys on Lake Constance, for which rail passes allow you a 50 percent reduction. You also receive special rates on bicycle rentals at 40 railroad stations.

In Austria you can buy the "VORTEILSCard" (Advantage Card) introduced in 1996 by producing a photo at any train station. This credit-card-size piece of plastic allowing you to travel for half-price over the OBB network for one year is available in 12 variations ranging from Classic to Senior (men over 65, women over 60), Family, and Students. You also receive discounts on bicycle rentals at train stations, the Schneeberg Rck Railroad, and the Austrian timetable. Further, you receive half off automobile rentals with Europcar, Hertz, ARAC, and Avis plus discounts on Best Western and Steigenberger hotels in Austria, Germany, Switzerland, the Netherlands, and Spain. Seniors also get half off buses and Lake Constance steamers.

Buses operated by the Austrian Railroads, the post office, private companies, and the Innsbruck transit authority are united under a common flag and a standard fare structure. Visitors now buying one single ticket are able to use all the "Verkehrsverbund" routes. Prices for a day ticket increase according to increasing distance, with a maximum at about 60 miles. The maximum applies to any distance over 60 miles regardless of actual distance.

Vorarlberg was Austria's first federal state to introduce a grid system for its entire public transportation network covering both bus and train. The Grid Ticket gets you where you want to go at reduced prices. At least 12 regions now provide such regional bus and train passes. Area passes are available as well. Be sure to check at your local train station.

Hungarian Railpasses are first-class flexible rail passes valid for five days in 15 or 10 in one month available from travel agents through Rail Europe. Because travel in Hungary is covered by Eurail products and the European East Pass, few travelers will have occasion to take advantage of their cheap price, but for those not purchasing any of these, buying a Hungarian Railpass will give them a tremendous convenience skirting the language problem.

In Hungary you buy a MAV "Turistaberlet," which is a rail pass giving unlimited travel on domestic MAV trains for seven or 10 consecutive days, first or second class. The pass is not valid on international trains except on MAV carriages attached for domestic service. It also does not cover the much smaller GySEV network, which sells its separate GySEV Turistaberlet, but if you buy either rail pass, you receive a 20 percent discount on tickets for the alternate railroad.

Public transportation fares are very inexpensive in Budapest and you can buy tickets in your hotel, but day passes give you the convenience of unlimited travel on the trams, electric buses, metro, and the four suburban train lines called HEV. For an additional charge, buy one including city bus travel as well.

The great cruise ships on the Austrian Danube and the great train described in this chapter, Austria's Schneeberg Rack Railroad, make your traveling exciting in Austria.

Cruising the Mellow Danube
Off with Your Shoes

Passengers pull their deck chairs closer to the railings. Their maps, guidebooks, camcorders, and digital cameras threaten to fall into the Danube. They read their texts aloud, compare notes, chatter excitedly, and pan their cameras over the sights in front of them.

You see the castle where his enemy, Leopold V, duke of Austria, imprisoned Richard the Lionhearted, king of England.

The sights of castles, abbeys, and picture-book villages and the warmth of the wine- and fruit-bearing slopes make experiencing the Wachau district in Austria from the deck of a Danube River steamer one of the great river adventures. To show it off, proud Austrian hosts take their foreign visitors on the deck of a river steamer for that "special occasion."

Europe's second-longest river (after the Volga) flows through Austria only 224 miles, but this one-eighth segment of the river is wholly navigable. You see commercial vessels, even Russian ones, all along its length, some traveling all the way from West Germany to the Black Sea. Your principal landings are at Linz, Melk, Krems, and of course Vienna.

Commerce pays your freight, so to speak. It keeps the river navigable so you can see the most picturesque sections of the Danube Valley right from the surface of the river itself.

Two Danube River cruise lines make it all possible, and they give discounts to holders of rail passes. You can make a trip in either direction, but there is something more rhythmic and restful about the

throbbing of your ship going downstream from Passau to Linz to Krems to Vienna. Their Danube ships are all one class and shipshape in every respect. You could spend an excellent week exploring the length of the Austrian Danube by river steamer and visiting such highlights as Passau, Linz, Melk, and Durnstein. Only one summer day a week can you cram it all into a getaway: depart Passau Friday, enjoy the night in Linz' Old Town, depart Saturday, cruise through the Wachau, and arrive Vienna at 8:30 P.M. You won't need reservations.

Along the way, you may see signs pointing to "DDSG." Follow those signs. DDSG was the Austrian-government-owned forerunner of today's cruise-ship system. When DDSG collapsed—Austrians blame their politicians—all nine of their ships were sold to private enterprise. Many of the currently active shipping companies bought eight of them. The ninth, a steam-powered paddle wheeler, was sold to OGEG, the Austrian Railroad Preservation Society headquartered in Linz, for one Schilling (about 10 cents) plus tax because the ship had been deemed a national treasure. OGEG shows it off by scheduling occasional excursions.

The Danube is a good river. Its color is always changing, depending on the time of day, weather conditions, time of year, whether the sun is rising and lightening it, whether it is overcast and gloomy, and whether it is carrying the spring glacier runoff or sediment. It is lined by castles, sparkles like an emerald in bright sunlight, and remains joyful for you to travel by ship.

Passau to Linz

Passau, the German port at the very head of the stretch of the Austrian Danube, occupies a beautiful site on the peninsula formed by the Inn and Danube rivers. Passau's Wurm + Kock Danube cruise ships (*www.donauschiffahrt.de*) depart from piers 11 and 12 at the Untere Donaulande at the Hotel Konig. Wurm + Kock gives holders of Eurail products, European East Passes, and Austrian Railpasses deep discounts over their full fares between Passau and Linz.

Wurm + Kock operates two ships based in Linz, the M.S. *Johanna* and the M.S. *Anton Bruckner*. The latter vessel was formerly named the M.S. *Germania,* but it was rechristened in 1996 to honor the noted composer who was born in Linz and now is buried there beneath an organ, as was his wish. The name *Germania* did not appeal to Austrians. The *Johanna* seats 146 on the upper deck and 228 on the lower in bright, restrained ambience. The five- to 13-knot *Bruckner* seats 141 above and 154 on the entrance deck.

After the junction of the Inn River with the Danube below Passau (the Inn is the larger at this point), the Danube is wide and majestic and bordered with wooded, rocky slopes. Gravel plains along the valley were formed when glaciers receded. You sail past green meadows, marshes, and evergreen forests now covering the hills.

After your ship stops at Engelhartszell, you see the river open out into a magnificent lake. This is the reservoir of the Jochenstein Dam. The rocky island in the river was supposedly the dwelling of a water fairy called Isa, the sister of the more infamous Lorelei of Rhine River notoriety.

Past Wesenufer, a pretty village with flowers on the balconies, you reach the highlight of this segment, which is an amazing quirk of nature, a wide, sunken loop called the "Schloegener Schlinge," meaning "Sling of Schloegen." At the outermost point of your great U-turn, a Roman castle of the second century has been excavated. It guarded communications between Castra Batava (Passau) and Lentia (Linz).

After stopping at Aschach, where you see the surprising brown, blue, and orange colors used to decorate the villages in this area, you continue to Linz for a stopover in "The Excursion Center on the Danube."

Linz

Before you sail from Linz (*www.linz.au*) in the morning, visit Linz's showpiece main square, the Hauptplatz, which was renovated in 1990. The staffed Linz tourist office is located on the Hauptplatz. Note particularly the Old Town Hall, which was finally restored in spring 1997. From the Hauptplatz, it is only a block to the Nibelungen Bridge over the Danube, from where you see the embarkation station for the cruise ships. It is an easy walk.

You see a striking ensemble of diverse buildings on the Hauptplatz. The fascinating baroque Trinity column dominates the center of the square. Emperor Charles VI directed that it be erected in 1723 to celebrate the escape of the city from the plague, fire, and Turkish invasion. You see baroque columns of this type in many towns of Austria and Bavaria, but this is the best example. Nearby is the Old Town with narrow, cobbled streets and lined with preserved facades. This is Linz's

"Bermuda Triangle" nightlife section. (Young Austrians go in to have fun. They have so much fun that they *never* come out.)

Linz to Krems

You board your Wurm + Kock vessel at Linz' Nibelungen Bridge. Immediately downstream, you sail past the largest steel mill in Austria and a booming chemical industry, but when you see the hills grow green and wooded and the houses and barns become picturesque and when you find yourself peeping into the lives of dwellers by the river, washing and boating and threshing and piling hay into yellow haystacks, your cruise begins to unroll like a continuous reel of trave-logue color adventure. You have well begun the singing, guitar-strum-ming, cooling swing down the Danube.

Your cruise is a marvelously soothing change from the helter-skel-ter madness of rush-around sightseeing, cathedrals that all look alike after a while, fortresses perched at the ends of dusty climbs, endless museums, crowded palaces, and bumpy cobblestone streets in the summer sun that finally make you believe your feet will burst into flames any minute. Your Danube cruise is fun.

Shortly after you leave Linz at 9 A.M., the youthful aboard shed their shirts, shoes, and socks and gather to play guitars. Even more reserved passengers take this opportunity to slip off their shoes and socks and wriggle their toes from the ship's deck in the fresh, cooling breezes above the river.

Passengers scrape their deck chairs to the railings and compare their geography texts with the highlights of the passing countryside. You overhear no English. You are adventuring off the common tourist path, but all the deck personnel cheerfully answer your questions in English.

Downstream, about noon, you are hemmed between rocky, wooded slopes. Your approach to Grein is beautiful. This pleasant little town, guarded by its castle, lies ideally at the foot of a wooded bluff watching over the entrance to the Strudengau gorges.

Below Grein begins the most dramatic section of the Austrian Danube. At one time river passengers feared the infamous rapids of Strudel and Wirbel. Now with the dangerous rocks blasted away, you pass around willow-covered islands, past the ruins of the castles of Struden and Sarmingstein, and soon find yourself on a placid lake nearing the Ybbs-Persenbeug Dam, a major power station.

The crew members are excited and rushed. They scurry passengers below and rope off the upper deck while the locks of the power station loom larger and larger. When the Danube is high, the clearance between your steamer and the locks is so slim that anyone poking his head above the ship's railings will be seriously injured.

When you pass Persenbeug, look for the castle where the Austrian emperor Charles I was born. From Persenbeug, at the head of a well-tilled plain where the river bends to Melk, you pass through the valley you know from episodes in The Nibelungenlied. You may hear echoes of Brunhild and Kriemhild, Gunther and Siegfried.

Pochlarn, on the right bank, was settled in the 10th century by the Babenbergs, who began the vigorous growth of the Austrian monarchy. When you next land at Melk, with its spectacular Benedictine abbey perched above you, you enter the Wachau.

The Wachau

Competition is keen through the Wachau. In addition to Wurm + Kock service, DDSG Blue Danube Shipping (*www.ddsg-blue-danube.at*) offers three round trips a day during the summer and gives discounts for rail-pass holders aboard the M.S. *Prinz Eugen* and M.S. *Wachau.*

The stretch of the Danube from Melk to Krems, the Wachau, is considered the most interesting stretch of river landscape in Europe. You see charming villages lining the river, the ruins of fortified castles crowning the crests, and onion-shaped belfries adding notes of fantasy to the countryside.

The Wachau is a beautiful sight regardless of whether the trees are in blossom, apricots are bright on trees, or grapes are heavy on vines and every wine village is celebrating the harvest.

You are making one of the premier excursions from Vienna. Frau Vera Kreisky, wife of the president of Austria at the time, took Rosalynn Carter on this trip on June 16, 1979, while the Austrian and American heads of state were in Vienna attending to business.

The Wachau makes a splendid debut at Melk, where the buff-and-gold, 1726 Benedictine abbey rises like a vision above fine middle-class houses. You pass below the abbey's south wall, nearly a quarter-mile long, overlooking the Danube from a 150-foot rocky bluff.

Melk's Donauarm landing is directly below the abbey, a 15- to 20-minute walk from the Melk train station. As you cruise out to the main Danube current, the chords of the "Blue Danube" waltz strike a romantic and unforgettable note. Soon you see Schonbuhel Castle, which has guarded entry to the Wachau since the ninth century.

After passing the yellow-painted village of Aggsbach, your steamer proceeds five minutes past Aggstein, precipitously below the castle, one of the largest and most formidable of the towers high on the mountain. This castle is notorious as a robber baron's haunt where prisoners were forced to jump to their deaths.

Passing Willendorf is especially interesting because the famous "Venus of Willendorf" prehistoric limestone statuette found here proved that man lived in the hills surrounding you since the dawn of civilization.

Spitz is almost the center of the Wachau, and its largest village. You see houses clustering below a hill, graceless but prosperous. The rows after rows of vines flowing over the rocky hillsides make it famous as "Thousand Pail Hill," known for the staggering amount of wine it produces in a good year. There are only 3,580 acres planted in the Wachau and yet it is Austria's premier white-wine region.

Past Spitz on the left, 15th-century St. Michael appears—the oldest church in the Wachau. Thriving vineyards continue to cover the hillsides with spectacular Riesling and gruner veltliner plantings terraced in parallel rows. This region has the mildest climate in Austria.

The next picturesque stop is the village, marked by the fortified steep red-tiled roof, of Weissenkirchen, the center of the region known as "Wahowa" that gave its name to the entire Wachau.

Then, after sweeping past a broad bend in the Danube, you see the most famous scene in the Wachau—Durnstein—a historical, fortified town. *Tip:* Have your camera ready. As you near, you can feel its almost completely preserved medieval and baroque character.

Richard the Lionhearted in disguise was seized on his way back to his native England at the end of the Third Crusade. His faithful troubadour/detective, Blondel, discovered his master here in Durnstein by strumming his mandolin and singing Richard's favorite ballad while searching through the castle.

Your next landing marks the end of the Wachau. You pass under a 500-year-old bridge at Krems, the historic city (not village) on the left bank. At the foot of loam hills covered with prominent, terraced vineyards rivaling those upstream, you cross the famous "Iron Route," an ancient trade artery. Now a simple city, Krems was once an imperial fortress, more important than Vienna because of Danube trade.

Krems-Vienna

You have completed the exciting part of your trip. Wachau steamers debark in Krems, where you can take OBB's hourly, second-class-only double-decked electric train into Vienna's Franz-Josefs-Bahnhof (trains run every two hours). The Krems station is far from your ship's landing. On Sundays, you can sail all the way to Vienna aboard DDSG Blue Danube Shipping's M.S. *Admiral Tegetthoff.*

From Krems, the Danube spreads broadly over a wide plain. It does not narrow until just above Vienna, where you pass solid, stone embankments. It will be darkening as your ship from Krems nears the Vienna Woods at Greifenstein.

Your ship docks first in Vienna at the Nussdorf landing, but you continue to the Schiffahrtszentrum, sailing beneath the reinforced-concrete Reichsbrucke, meaning "empire bridge" (the former one suddenly collapsed one morning in 1971 and fell into the river). At Vienna/Reichsbrucke landing you find taxi stops, but you have only an eight-minute walk to the Vorgartenstrasse U-1 subway station.

Passau-Linz Danube River Service

(1)	(1)				(1)	(1)
0900	1310	dep.	Passau	arr.	2040	1510
0945	1415*	arr.	Obernzell	arr.	1950	1415*
1100	1540	arr.	Schlogen	arr.	1750	1200
1220	1730	arr.	Aschach	arr.	1605	0955
1400	1400	arr.	Linz	dep.	1415	0800

*Change in Obernzell
(1) Wurm + Koch, daily except Monday, summer only

Linz-Vienna Danube River Service

(2)	(3)				(2)	(3)
0900	I	dep.	Linz (Nibelungenbrucke)	arr.	2220	I
1020	I	dep.	Mauthausen	dep.	2025	I
1200	I	dep.	Grein	dep.	1820	I
1440	I	dep.	Melk, Island	dep.	1515	I
1530	I	dep.	Spitz	dep.	1345	I
1600	1630	dep.	Durnstein	dep.	1250	1430
1620	1650	dep.	Krems	dep.	1220	1355
1820	1845	dep.	Tulln	dep.	0950	1120
2030	2045	arr.	VIENNA (Reichsbrucke)	dep.	0730	0845

(2) Wurm + Kock, summer Wednesdays only Linz-Krems, summer Saturdays only Linz-Vienna
(3) DDSG, summer Sundays only, reservations required
I = Does not land

Daily DDSG Wachau Cruise Danube River Summer Service

1015	1300	1546	dep.	Krems	arr.	1240	1530	1800
1050	1330	1620	dep.	Durnstein	dep.	1210	1510	1740
1145	1420	1725*	dep.	Spitz	dep.	1150	1440	1720*
1315	1540	1840	arr.	Melk	dep.	1100	1350	1615

*Change in Spitz

Puffing up the Schneeberg
Wieder Kaputt!

The first thing you feel is the chattering of the cogwheels. While your comic steam train pulls you slowly out of the Austrian village of Puchberg, your glimpse ahead does not promise as much as your creaky train finally delivers. The Schneeberg Rack Railroad may be your slowest, steamiest, jerkiest discovery, but it may be the most fun. This diverting day's excursion through 21 tunnels and across 15 long viaducts takes you to Austria's highest train station (5,888 feet).

Then you hear the nasty hissing of the tough steam engine and see the black clouds swirling behind you. The Schneeberg Railroad has enough antique and functional features to turn a rail fan's heart into Apfel Strudel.

What the Austrians call a "schmalspurige dampfbetriebene Zahnradbahn" is a narrow-gauge, steam-driven, cogwheel railroad. It is fired by coal from Poland and belches fumes as black as a loan manager's heart.

When you leave Puchberg am Schneeberg, south of Vienna, each chug of the steam-driven pistons shoves your little engine inches more across the highway and up onto the mountain. Chagrined, you have no doubt you can walk faster than the train can climb, but as your train tilts upward through wild ground, the engine seems to leap ahead and virtually races past the perspiring mountaineers struggling up the nearby trails.

To reach Puchberg from Vienna, you use the Sudbahnhof (South train station). An hourly IC service—covered by rail pass—runs to the city of Wiener Neustadt. Puchberg is a local stop bypassed by express trains, so change in the city of Wiener Neustadt unless you start your trip on a local. It takes just over 1½ hours for the complete journey to Puchberg.

When your OBB train from Wiener Neustadt reaches Puchberg, you file down the platform a few feet to the carved wooden sign: "Zahnradbahn." The Puchberg terminal of the narrow-gauge Schneeberg (meaning "Snow Mountain") cogwheel railroad lies about 50 miles southwest of Vienna.

Your best deal is a "Wanderticket" valid for OBB transportation to Puchberg and the rack railroad's climb to the summit. Attached is a coupon ("Gutschein") for a luncheon meal at any one of the station restaurants. Buy these tickets at the "Inland" ticket counters in Vienna's South train station or stops en route. At Puchberg, show your Wanderticket at the counter and take a "Zahlkarte," a number for boarding one of the little wooden cars to the summit of the Schneeberg.

Try to sit on the left going up. Your car is crammed five abreast with

HOCHSCHNEEBERG

Baumgartner
Haus

PUCHBERG am SCHNEEBERG

RACK RAILROAD

Ternitzer Hutte

Hengsthutte

Hauslitzsattel

Schneeberg Dorf

PUCHBERG

To Vienna

N

0   0.2   1.0

MILES

so many passengers the interior seems like Noah's ark. The Viennese consider Schneeberg their home in the mountains. The fascination of your trip is the little, black steam locomotive with tilted fireboxes.

Passengers complain about the hard seats and crowded conditions. They give thanks for small favors: at least the north wind is blowing the steam locomotive's noxious fumes away from them.

Pushing from the rear of your train to prevent possible breakaway, the four steam locos built by Krauss and Company in Linz in 1896-97 (plus an even older one, built in 1893) are nose-down into the earth like Viennese professors peering over their spectacles. They look as though their front axles have collapsed and they are grubbing for worms. The Schneeberg railroad was offered new oil-burning locomotives but it declined, saying their beloved antiques were good enough. Further, the Schneeberg is the aquifer for Vienna's drinking water. Three large pipelines carry fresh water to Austria's capital and pollution restrictions are severe. Authorities feared oil spillage from oil-burning locomotives might contaminate the precious water supply.

While your train scales the steep mountainsides, this odd-looking design keeps the boiler tubes horizontal to maintain heat transfer and holds the firebox level to prevent firebrands from tumbling onto the footplate.

You climb immediately from the station and curve around the village of Schneebergdorfl (2,007 feet). After about 25 minutes you reach Hauslitzsattel (2,717 feet); your engine brakes. You see blue cornflowers, red poppies, and a dozen delicate Alpine blooms—and, for the first time, smell forest odors. This is the first of a vast system of mountain huts constructed throughout the Austrian Alps for the benefit of mountaineers.

Eleven minutes later you are high enough to see the majesty of the green valley floor below when you reach Hengsthutte (3,323 feet), the halfway point, surrounded by pines. Hikers are stepping downhill with bouquets of wild flowers, sweaters tied around their waists.

You make a stop at Ternitzer Hutte. It is considerably cooler here. Your angle of ascent is so steep, and because you perceive the interior of the carriage as being horizontal, the fir trees outside appear to be growing diagonally out of the mountainside. Passengers disembark but watch their seats so as not to lose them. They are restless.

This is an escapist trip. Few carry a camera to burden them. They are ready for the freedom of the hiking trails above.

A 10-minute halt is scheduled at Baumgartner's station house (4,582 feet). Your locomotive is watered and recoaled while you go inside for refreshment or a snack. Try the prune bread loaf for a pleasant treat.

Now comes your real climb! For a short while, at least, you drive uphill on the cog-tracks through forests, wild valleys, mountain huts, and brooks gurgling down the mountainside. Then you make another unexplained stop. "Wieder kaputt!" ("Broken again!") maintains a stout Bavarian visitor wearing Lederhosen.

Suddenly, the person in front of you sees wild chamois ("Gemse") near your train. As one, 50 passengers stand, point to these small antelope, and shout, "Gemse!" The Gemse are near the first patches of snow and fleeing uphill.

Now you enter a 390-foot tunnel. Passengers sitting next to the windows hurry to shut them tightly to prevent steam locomotive fumes and soot from flooding the carriage. Smoke billows between carriages. When you exit the tunnel, soot has covered the train windows. Passengers lower them immediately.

Shortly you enter a second, 500-foot tunnel. People close the windows once again, but the train stops and sits and they reopen them. "Wieder kaputt!" shouts the Bavarian.

Finally under way, the train's lights come on in the tunnel. Emerging, you are above the timberline. You see swathes of tightly bunched, gold and blue wildflowers blooming through the snow. A pinelike shrub grows in patches. To your right is the green-copper-topped stone chapel, the Elizabeth Kirche. Down the rail line to your left is the Berghaus Hochschneeberg (5,889 feet)—but eager hikers are already well on the winding way up the path in the opposite direction. The summit is Enzian paradise. This tiny, much-admired, blue flower (the gentian) is used for Alpine schnapps. Go immediately into the station house to select your "Zahlkarte" for your choice of return times.

You can cash in the "Wanderticket" coupon for a meal at the Berghaus Hochschneeberg, where they also serve a "Kaisermenu" duplicating that of the Kaiser when he visited in 1901—or use your coupon at other locations. The mountain hotel contains a sauna and solarium.

In addition to experiencing the novel train, this excursion gives you a choice opportunity to hike high in the northern limestone spur of the Austrian Alps. Trails take you around the Waxriegel peak (6,193 feet) to the Dambockhaus, where serious hikers buy inexpensive meals and sleeping accommodations. The Schneeberg retains a covering of snow throughout the summer.

Top off your excursion by walking (2½ hours round trip) up to the Kaiserstein peak (6,762 feet) for the Alpine panorama north as far as the Vienna Woods. Or climb to the Klosterwappen summit (6,808 feet) for the view south across the ravine called "Hell's Valley" (Hollental) to the Rex Plateau, the geologic twin of the Schneeberg.

Your ride down is rocking, swaying, and squeaking like a rusty spring. It takes less time going down, about an hour, but it is more subdued because passengers are tired.

Across the street from the Puchberg train station, an idyllic lakefront promenade is perfect for picnicking. The Puchberg station has a buffet serving meals.

Steam service varies with season and demand. In 1997, OBB and the provincial government of Lower Austria formed the Niederosterreichische Schneebergbahn (NOeSBB, Lower Austria Schneeberg Railroad) and introduced diesel units with the very odd livery of dark green with orange spots. The design is named "Feuersalamander" (spotted salamander) because it resembles the small amphibian abiding on the slopes of the Schneeberg. The shape of the coaches is rounded to pass through the tunnel at the top of the line, which is located on a curve. The Salamanders are narrower than the passenger carriages to allow passengers to leave easily in case of an emergency inside one of the tunnels.

Italy
and Greece

Savvy Traveling on the Trains
of Italy and Greece

Italian trains—Crossing between Italy and Greece—Greek trains—Athens train stations—Getting around Athens—Airport trains—Intercity Night trains—Traveling in Sicily—Compelling Sardinia—Rail-pass travel

Italy is a flashy and artistic country. Expect no less of the showpiece Italian State Railroads, "Ferrovie dello Stado" (FS, *www.fs-on-line.com*). FS's 10,000-mile network has touches of a maestro.

Greece is a country of great history. It's curious how trains mirror the nature of the countries. Don't expect the trains of "Organismos Siderodromon Ellados" (OSE), the Greek Railroads Organization, to provide you with great comfort, speed, or convenience. Greek trains are timeless—without regard to time (so always have a backup plan ready). The best travel experience in Greece is on the Aegean ferries.

Italian Trains

The trains of Italy are as long as a Roman's nose and just as full of character. A full complement of Eurostar Italia (ES★), EuroCity (EC), and Intercity (IC) trains blankets the country. You ride one of Europe's most modern and speediest fleets from the Italian Alps to the newly electrified stretch to Palermo on the tip of Sicily. The rest of FS's fleet takes you to villages and the seaside in an eclectic set of less speed and desirability. Under construction are new high-speed lines between Naples and Rome (opening 2005), Turin and Milan (opening 2006 for the winter Olympic Games), Florence-Bologna (2004), and Bologna-Milan (2007). Contact Rail Europe (Appendix A) for an excellent, free rail map of Italy.

Your fastest ride is the ETR 500, 186-mph train running along the Milan-Florence-Rome-Naples corridor, Milan-Venice, Milan-Lecce, Turin-Lecce, and Rome-Venice. Next speediest are the 155-mph Pendolino ETR 450 and ETR 460 trains, which tilt. FS offers a 50 percent discount on Eurostar Italia if your train is more than 25 minutes delayed, or if the air-conditioning is not working.

New 2000 InterCity trains serve Venice-Milan, Milan-Genoa, and Genoa-Livorno (Leghorn). Open seating in second class is 2 + 2 arranged around 10 small tables. The smaller smoking section is divided from the larger nonsmoking area by a glass panel.

EC trains include the Carlo Goldoni between Venice and Vienna, Garda between Verona and Munich, Leonardo da Vinci between Milan and Munich, Michelangelo between Rome and Munich, Paganini between Verona and Dortmund, and Tiepolo between Venice and Munich.

Reservation requirements are strictly enforced in Italy (except when the computer people are on strike and making reservations is impossible). With few exceptions, all Eurostar Italia trains must be reserved in advance. Eurostar Italia passengers must pay a fee that covers both reservation and supplement, which varies according to destination and type of train. Check the timetables. An *R* in a box indicates that a reservation is obligatory. A *PG* in a box shows that you may make seat reservations, but they are not required. If you board and find an unreserved seat in a train requiring reservations, the conductor will charge you for the seat, plus a penalty!

FS maintains "Club Eurostar" lounges open 8 A.M. to 8 P.M. for holders of first-class tickets in Rome Termini, Milan Centrale, Venice Santa Lucia, Venice Mestre, Padova Centrales, Verona Porta Nuova, Turin Porta Nuova, Florence S.M.N., and Bologna Centrale stations.

Connecting Milan and northern Europe you can ride Cisalpino's trains to/from Geneva, Basel, and Zurich; Artesia's high-speed trains to/from Paris; and conventional FS Eurocity trains. FS's EuroCity trains to northern Europe are gray livery with blue piping. Some use the same deluxe coaches dating from 1975-90 that comprised former Trans Europ Express trains. They retain their superior ambience and convenience with features such as behind-the-seats coat closets. The first-class open salons with 2+1 seating are especially comfortable. The trains carry white-linen "Chef Express" restaurant carriages or "Self Service" cafeteria cars.

At smaller stops in Italy, trackside vendors with fully loaded push-carts are eager to sell you cold drinks, sandwiches, and candy, but they are increasingly discouraged by FS's conversion to sealed-window, air-conditioned carriages. Listen for their persistently tinkling bells. If you can, open your window and make your orders from the train; other-wise, join the clusters at the steps to the train.

In addition to FS, there are numerous private railroads in Italy such as the Transvesuviano between Naples and Sorrento (for Pompeii) and the Circumetna in Sicily. Some provide commuter service and some serve rural districts and reach villages not connected to FS. None honor rail passes.

For travel in Italy, the yellow "Pozzorario Generale" timetable is much more valuable than others are. It gives you such useful additional information as the type of Italian Eurostar train being used on a specific route and departure time, which overnight trains carry sleeperettes in addition to couchettes, and the schedules of private lines. The Pozzorario Generale is for sale in station bookstores and magazine stalls. It also gives you the correct FS timetable in a country where you get three different answers to the same question asked at three different information desks.

Signboards on the trains use Italian shorthand, so for Naples Centrale, expect to read "Napoli C.le," and for Rome Termini station, read "Roma T.ni." The trains are clean inside and out. Train and window washing is performed in Rome Termini, Florence Santa Maria Novella, and Venice Santa Lucia stations by motorized machines that are steered past the trains.

Crossing between Italy and Greece

Greece is a magnet to Eurail-product holders with validity in Greece because of the promise of free deck-class ferry transportation and the carefree stopover on Corfu's beaches. A three-country Eurail Selectpass will bring you from France or Switzerland, and a four-country pass will bring you from Germany. You may sail between Brindisi, Italy, and Patras, Igoumenitsa, or Corfu, Greece, aboard the Greek Hellenic Mediterranean Lines (HML, *www.hml.gr*) and the Blue Star Ferries. The large, white Superfast Ferries of Attika Superfast (*www.attika.com*), a German company, offer free passage between Ancona and Bari to Igoumenitsa and Patras. You pay a €20 surcharge during July and August for all sailings.

In addition you must pay port taxes in euros. Sleeping accommodations such as cabins or airline-type seats cost extra. Before boarding, you must check in at the shipping line's office at the pier. If you wish to stop over in Corfu (Kerkyra) or Igoumenitsa, you must so state when you receive your ferry ticket. When you ticket only to Corfu, you cannot change your mind and continue to Patras. Clearly, there is much bureaucracy involved.

You can easily reach Brindisi by ETR 500 train from Milan via Bologna and Bari. To reach Brindisi harbor from the train station, walk straight downhill past the white fountain (it's about a half-hour all the way to the harbor).

Sailings are scrambled from Brindisi to Patras and vice versa. Some stop in Corfu en route and some take you without stop. Others take you between Brindisi and Corfu and the northern Greek port of Igoumenitsa but don't continue to Patras. Igoumenitsa has no train service, but you can take a bus from Igoumenitsa through the rugged mountains of the Epirus Region to Kalambaka with a second-class-only, narrow-gauge train connection to Karditsa, where you can take a standard-gauge IC train via Paleofarsalos to Athens.

At Patras' landing you board either a train or bus. Buses park near the ship's landing. Trains are a short walk away. From your ferry, you will generally walk to your right, staying within the port fence to gate 3 entrance. The train station, with snack bar and open-air snack restaurant attached, is across the tracks. A Citibank with ATM is across the street. Eurail products do not cover buses, only trains of the Peloponnesian Line.

When you talk with others about this crossing, you hear horror stories. This is the least comfortable of European ferry crossings. The ships are crowded; backpackers cover the deck entirely with their mats; the seating room is stuffy and smells like those sleeping; the cabins are primitive; the crews are hostile. It is sensible to approach this journey with careful planning.

• Make train reservations to Brindisi and also from Brindisi if you know in advance when you will return. Allow extra time for possible train delays en route. Trains run to Brindisi down Italy's Adriatic coast from Rome and Bologna. Station timetables indicate these trains are for "Lecce." Brindisi's Centrale station is the stop before the end station, Lecce.

• Dress coolly. It is sometimes stiflingly hot waiting for the ferry.

• Take your own food aboard the ships. Food served on the ships is unreliable.

• Take a cabin for the crossing. Although Eurail products do not cover it, you will avoid inconveniences. Make your arrangements when you board.

• Allow extra days. When you lay out your overall itinerary, allow several days for unexpected developments.

• Make hotel arrangements in Athens in advance. There is no hotel service at the station in Athens. Especially when you arrive late at night in Athens, the unfamiliar alphabet and the remote location of Athens' train station can cause difficulties for the unprepared.

• You arrive in Athens' Peloponnesia station. Follow the directions below ("Athens Train Stations") to reach the Athens metro rather than being hassled by gouging taxi drivers.

• Stop over in Corfu. Anyone who has read about Corfu or is interested in casual beach life will not miss this opportunity.

• Allow extra time in Brindisi before boarding. You must pass through customs, passport, port tax, ticketing, and boarding bureaucracies.

Greek Trains

Considering that Greece is a country with a population of just 10.5 million and almost half live in greater Athens and two million live in Thessaloniki, it won't surprise you that OSE has one of the sparsest networks of any European country.

Greece has two train networks. The 550-mile long, meter-gauge line circles the Peloponnesian Peninsula through Patras and Athens, while the 970-mile-long, standard-gauge northern network connects Athens to Thessaloniki (Salonika) and supports the trains to the Balkans and central Europe. All OSE trains honor rail passes. There are reduced rates for travelers under 26 and for foreign students presenting an I.D. card.

Traveling with a top-speed capability of 100 mph (which set speed records in Greece), OSE's flagship nonstop InterCity trains began in 1996 connections between Athens and Thessaloniki, cutting 20 minutes from the timetable. They take five hours, 50 minutes, averaging 54 mph over the 318 miles between Athens and Thessaloniki. OSE's 12 air-conditioned red-and-white railcars of East German origin carry 180 passengers without standing in four carriages including driver's cars. Second-class salons are front and back of two middle carriages. The 36-seat first-class middle carriage includes a bar and kitchen.

Local lines are served by the 2003-4 generation of blue-and-white, 70-mph, low-floor articulated railcars built by Bombardier but assembled at Hellenic Shipyards. They consist of two passenger cars plus the short central motor unit. Each unit has 94 seats and space for 106 standing. Variations will run on both Greek networks.

The Peloponnesian trains are modern InterCity red-and-white railcars or falling-apart traditional trains with a diesel locomotive that appears Neolithic. OSE's 1992 InterCity, German-built diesel railcars between Patras and Athens, have a maximum speed of 75 mph. In trials it achieved a speed record on the meter-gauge line of 83.3 mph. You will be lucky to catch it in Patras, so don't delay boarding, because Europe's only meter-gauge InterCity train allows you to reach Athens at a decent hour. If your ferry is late, you will take a local train getting you to the Hellenic capital two hours later. Those holding Eurail products valid in Greece don't have to stand in a long line to buy a ticket and can board before the crowd and before the train pulls away, leaving others angry on the platform.

OSE's Kalavryta Railroad in the Peloponnesus, originally built for mining by an Italian company between 1885 and 1895, is usually considered Greece's most scenic train ride. Rail passes are accepted. Travelers leave from Diakofto, near Patras on the line from Athens, so it is possible to make the excursion as a 14-hour day trip from Athens. The lines of the 14-mile-long, 750-mm-gauge, cogwheel railroad begin across the plaza adjacent to the OSE tracks where a little black steam locomotive retired in the late 1950s stands proudly as the centerpiece. A two-carriage diesel-electric unit was joined on August 31, 1996, by the line's first steam locomotive (1891) that was restored to working order at the OSE workshops in Piraeus. The line climbs 2,300 feet in one and a half hours, taking you through tunnels and along rocky ledges through the mouth of the granite Vouraikos River gorge that has never been pierced by more than your little railroad, to Kalavryta with a stop at Zahlorou, at 2,086 feet, about halfway to the southern terminus at Kalavryta, 14 miles from the Gulf of Corinth. Three-quarters of an hour by foot or on donkey from Zahlorou, the 362 A.D., Orthodox Byzantine monastery of Mega Spileon on the side of a vertical granite peak attracts many pilgrims, but only men may overnight there. The pleasant mountain resort of Kalavryta contains the graveyard of over 1,500 males murdered by the Nazis on December 13, 1943. You may visit the Holocaust Museum, graveyard, and village church.

The port of Athens is Piraeus, just five miles south of the Hellenic capital. This is your gateway for the ferries to Greece's Aegean islands. Although OSE's Peloponnesus trains originate here, and you can take a train from Athens' Peloponnesia station, it is easier to take the subway from Athens' Omonia Square.

The Athens Train Museum at 4 Siokou St., opposite 301 Liossion Ave. (open Fri.-Sun., 9 A.M. to 1 P.M.; Wed., 5 to 8 P.M., admission free), contains actual carriages from an 1884 train as well as preserved fixtures.

Athens Train Stations

Because of OSE's two gauges, Athens—which is the hub of both networks—has two train stations in the city's northwest section. There are no through trains. When you take the train from Patras, you arrive in Peloponnesia station. When you arrive via the Balkans or from Thessaloniki, you arrive in Larissa station.

Small Larissa station has a waiting room, ticketing, an information window, baggage checking, an adjoining snack bar, and potted trees on the platforms. You won't find luggage carts or hotel assistance. The timetables on the walls are last year's, updated with changes in felt pen. There is an ATM ("Telebank") inside and outside. The Larissa subway entrance to Red No. 2 line is directly in front of the station. The elevator access is across the street.

Peloponnesia station is nearly useless except for ticketing and the snack bars. To reach Peloponnesia station from Larissa station, exit, turn right, cross the steel bridge, and walk about 350 feet left. It takes about five minutes. From Peloponnesia station, you need to go to Larissa to access the subway. Cross the street from Peloponnesia station, walk left past the bus station, three minutes to the steel steps, and cross the bridge to Larissa.

Tourist information is unavailable in either train station. The Greek National Tourist Office personnel provide information and free maps plus money conversion at their Infodesk at 2 Amerikis St., on the ground floor next to the Aliki Theater (open Mon.-Fri., 9 A.M. to 7 P.M., Tel. 331-0561). An Internet cafe is nearby, at 5 Stadiou St.

Athens' OSE office is located at Filleilion 18, which is short blocks (five minutes) from Syntagma Square. Pick up a timetable and ask the agent to translate the Greek names for you. Here you can make the required train reservations for international trains to the north and validate rail passes.

Getting Around Athens

Athens metro system, opened with much publicity on January 28, 2000, is an ultramodern, $2.5 billion network, with two additional lines, new stations, new rolling stock, and the latest technology. The largest, most complex project ever undertaken in Greece, the new metro makes getting around Athens remarkably efficient and pleasant. Some stations display replicas and photos of archaeological artifacts uncovered during construction.

Athens' enlarged metro system is perhaps the cleanest and spiffiest in all Europe. Look for the new stations marked by the stylized blue *M* on an illuminated white background, which is the distinctive metro sign. Designed and built by a Greek, French, and German consortium, the new system increased capacity to 780,000 from 330,000 passengers daily, with 168 new subway carriages and a policeman around every corner. The two new red (No. 2) and blue (No. 3) lines added more than 12 miles and 21 new stations to the existing green line (No. 1) that runs between the port of Piraeus in southwest Athens to Kifissia in the northeast. The east-west blue line connects Monastiraki in Plaka, the old town, to Ethniki Amyna, where an extension (*www.ametro.gr*) in time for the 2004 Olympic Games will provide easy access to the 2001 Athens International Airport (*www.aia.gr*) using dual-voltage, air-conditioned, 75-mph metro trains with luggage space. The red line extension in October 2000 connects the southwest suburb of Daphni with Athens' northwest reaches. Both lines intersect at the new two-level station on Constitution (Syntagma) Square, or you can transfer at Monastiraki (green and blue lines), Omonia, or Attiki (red and green lines).

The graffiti-free, six-carriage trains, although criticized as being out of date, unattractive, and not air-conditioned, run every three minutes at rush hours and five to 10 minutes apart at nonpeak hours and cost roughly $0.70 per ride. A day card costs about $2.80. Car floors are level with platforms. Special lighting and signs in Greek and Roman letters make getting around easy. Persons with special needs find ramps, escalators, and elevators. Exits have escalators, but going down long stairways can be a problem with luggage. Always look for the elevator.

The new metro is not only Greece's largest construction project to date, it is also the country's largest archaeological dig. More than 750,000 square feet were excavated at a cost of $20-$30 million. Because five of the new stations lie in ancient Athens within the shadow of the Acropolis, the project intrudes on one of the world's richest classical sites. Archaeologists took care to remove all significant finds and avoid damage to existing monuments. Tunnel-boring machines dug 7½ miles through solid rock to avoid cultural treasures. Underground tunneling techniques, used in preference to surface excavation, were also used at several stations near know archaeological sites. Discoveries included a bathhouse, metalworking shops, aqueducts, cisterns, drains, ancient roads, city walls, and cemeteries. One intriguing discovery turned up a room filled with oil lamps and decorated with erotic scenes. Other surprises included a sarcophagus at Ethniki Amyna station, and large Roman drains at Larissa station. Photos and replicas of the most interesting finds decorate several stations in the area of the dig. The Syntagma station is like a mini-museum. When the Acropolis metro station opened in November 2000, it was more phenomenal than the one in Syntagma Square. In addition, they discovered Aristotle's ancient Lyceum while digging for the metro in Athens' outskirts. If it were not for the subway, this fantastic find might have remained buried forever.

Larissa station stop is your gateway to OSE trains. At the Akropoli station stands the Acropolis itself, the Temple of Olympian Zeus, and Hadrian's Arch, which marked the city limits in 132 A.D. At Thissio station you can view the ancient Agora and the Temple of Hephaestus, the best-preserved temple in Greece.

Airport Trains

Arriving by air in Rome Leonardo da Vinci Airport at Fiumicino, you start out saving money with your rail pass, because the airport train, which FS decided in 2000 to name the Leonardo Express, to Rome's Termini station is fully covered, although one-way fare is about $8, so you might not want to use up a day box of a flexipass. The Fiumicino-Rome Termini airport bus was discontinued when the train service began.

Take the escalator or elevator up from the Arrivals level on the ground floor to the second-floor "Stazione FS," shown by international train pictographs. Air arrivals validate their pass at the airport train station and then use it for the 20-mile run to Rome's Termini station in the center of the Eternal City, or they can purchase their tickets at the entrance to the platforms. The machines accept credit cards. Validate your ticket in an orange validating machine before boarding.

Rome's Leonardo Express connects Fiumicino Airport with Rome Termini station every half-hour from 6:51 A.M. to 9:51 P.M., taking a half-hour, nonstop. The trains are comprised of a loco and four refurbished one-class carriages. Three Leonardos operate on this line, and one is kept on stand-by.

The Leonardo drops you in 2000 reconstructed Terminal Giubileo track ("binario") 25, which falls short of extending into the large Termini station complex. Terminal Giubileo's impressive spaces, brightly colored and precious marbles, a towering roof, big arches, and brick vaults contain a travel agency for train, ferry, and air tickets; Alitalia check-in (for those with hand luggage only); tourist information; and money exchange. Lockers for luggage storage are adjacent to track 24. Taxis await outside Terminal Giubileo.

A second airport service using electric double-decked IR trains leaves from platforms parallel to the Leonardo's at the airport train station. They take you every 15-30 minutes to Orte, with intermediate stops at Rome's Tiburtina, Tuscolana, Ostiense, and Trastevere stations (but not Termini).

It is a 40-minute ride to Rome Tiburtina station, where an island platform on the important north-south bypass of Rome allows you to change to some IR and overnight trains running the Milan-Florence-Naples-Sicily service. When the Rome-Naples high-speed line opens in 2004, Tiburtina will be the high-speed through station for the capital.

Milan's double-decked Malpensa Express trains, in Malpensa

Express livery, white with Bordeaux-red front ends, debuted on May 30, 1999, connecting Milan's Malpensa International Airport with Milan Cadorna station in the center of Milan every 30 minutes. Travel time is 40 minutes over the 6.92-mile double track at 87 mph peak speed with stops at the following stations of Ferrovie Nord Milano (FNM, Northern Railroads): Bovisa Politechnico and Saronno Central. Bus services are substituted for the first two morning runs and the last three night runs. They have no intermediate stops.

Board the Malpensa Express on the lower ground floor in Malpensa Airport Terminal One or at the Cadorna FNM station, platforms one and two. The trains carry 415 passengers, who enjoy air-conditioning, electronic display boards, a public announcement system, low entry platforms, and access for the disabled.

You can buy tickets in every Malpensa Express station—Cadorna, Bovisa Politechnico, Saronno, Malpensa—and in all FNM stations. A single ticket costs about $7.50 for adults, $4 for children 4-15. If you purchase the ticket aboard the train, the charge is $10, $6.50 for children. Day return, monthly, and year tickets are also available. Rail passes are not valid. Your ticket is valid for the Milan Railroad Link ("Passante Ferroviaria"), so you may begin or end your journey at any Milan railroad station, whether it belongs to FNM or FS, and use your ticket on bus 82 or trolley bus 92.

At Cadorna you can connect to metro lines MR1 and MG2, bus, trolley, and taxis at the exit. Or you can change trains departing from Cadorna for Meda-Canzo-Asso, Saronno-Novara, and Saronno-Lake Como.

Cadorna station is the heart of the city's historic center and very close to many of its most important monuments, including Milan Cathedral, Castello Sforzesco, Leonardo's *Last Supper,* and the Scala Opera.

Half-hourly Air Pullman buses from bus platforms 3-4 (use exit 6) take you to the piazza beside the Centrale station. Air Pullman buses also run to Milan's Linate Airport from bus platforms 19-20 (use exit 4). To reach Linate Airport from Milan, take metro line MR1 (see "Milan Centrale" below) to San Babila, then bus No. 73.

Pisa San Giusto Airport, served by both national and international airlines such as Lufthansa, Air France, Alitalia, and British Airways, is about 50 miles from Florence. It is served 10 times daily by the train between Florence S.M.N. station and Livorno (Leghorn). With check-in at S.M.N.'s dedicated Air Terminal at the head of tracks 3 and 4 (open 7:30 A.M. to 3:30 P.M.), travel time is slightly more than an hour.

On October 6, 2001, the Trinacria Express began carrying passengers between a new underground station at Palermo Falcone-Borsellino Airport, which was named after two judges killed by the Mafia, and Palermo Centrale station. The air-conditioned trains taking 45 minutes operate hourly from 5 A.M. to midnight.

The 19-mile line connecting Athens city center with the new Athens Spata Airport includes six miles within the city limits as well as the newly built section to the airport. The $375 million line, built by a consortium under contract from OSE, is expected in time for the summer 2004 Olympic Games.

Intercity Night Trains

Because of the long travel distances within Italy between Milan or Rome and Sicily or Brindisi, FS cascaded air-conditioned InterCity day trains to night duty as Eurostar Italia trains replaced the ICs. Nevertheless, FS's overnight trains are frequently crowded. Rather than hoping for space to stretch out in sitting compartments, first-class rail-pass holders are more comfortable booking FS's domestic first-class couchettes between Rome and Sicily. These contain only four bunks instead of the six you find in second class, and must be reserved in advance. When you don't have time for an advance reservation, you can go directly to the couchette cars and ask the porter. Italian couchette cars have an illuminated sign in three languages (Italian, French, and German) indicating couchette availability. In case of delays of more than 60 minutes on ICN and Express trains, you are entitled to a 30 percent ticket refund.

FS's blue, orange, and white "Sleeperette" carriages contain deeply reclining seats arranged in a salon, so you will avoid paying for a sleeping car. Look for the reclined-seat symbol in FS's timetable and departure billboards in the train station.

For upscale comfort (as discussed in the "International" chapter) you ride the EN Pablo Casals between Milan and Barcelona in unprecedented luxury. This is your best connection between Italy and Spain. From Paris, take Artesia's Galilei to Florence, Palatino to Rome, Rialto to Venice, or Stendhal to Milan. FS EuroNight trains include the Capri between Naples and Munich, Gottardo and Remus between Milan and Zurich, and Roma between Rome, Basel, and Geneva.

Traveling in Sicily

A circuit of Sicily by train gives you a perspective of the sun-toasted island that has been ruled for centuries by foreigners from abroad (meaning Rome in the present case). You see magisterial mountains and farming regulated by water and sun. For 25 centuries Sicilians have accepted Byzantine tax gatherers, Berber emirs, Spanish viceroys, and, since Garibaldi set foot on shore in 1860, the Italian kings and the Italian Republic's governments.

Sicily is by and large a beautiful island but not well laid-out for an adventurer by train, even though renovation of many Sicilian train stations was completed in 1996. The sights are in the countryside. Local trains are second string. There are few tourist offices for finding hotels and these are seldom located near the train stations.

This means that to get the best from Sicily you should
• arrange your sleeping accommodations in advance, and
• use a Rail 'n Drive Pass or car-rental arrangement.

Mainline connections to Sicily are to Palermo on the north coast and Siracusa on the east. Stops along the east coast include Messina, Taormina, and Catania (for the city and Mount Etna). Agrigento lies on the south coast. You can take day trains to/from Rome or Naples or overnight trains to/from Milan, Rome, or Naples (but be sure to check because some of the Rome trains bypass Rome's Termini station and instead use the suburban Ostiense or Tiburtina stations). For those trains that don't serve Naples Centrale, Naples Piazza Garibaldi station is underground and connected to Centrale with escalators.

You cross the Strait of Messina in 15 minutes on 2002 "Bluvia" service featuring 12 modern and comfortable ships with frequent service between Villa San Giovanni and Messina.

Messina Centrale is where the trains from the peninsula split. Half of the carriages go through a 2000 tunnel under Peloritani Mountains to Palermo (saving 20 minutes), half to Siracusa. The opposite is true in reverse. The segments are joined together and travel as one up to Naples, Rome, and Milan.

Messina Centrale is good sized, the threshold for all Sicily. It has a very pleasant bar (in the Italian sense, meaning sandwiches, limited hot plates, and of course espresso) but no restaurant. The tourist information office is across the street. In the brown-marble waiting room you can see the arrivals and departures information on color monitors. "Ritardo" means minutes late.

You will be disappointed in Palermo Centrale station. The entrance hall has a shiny marble floor and looks splendid, but train departures' posting is hard to find. You find them in the entrance hall and on the platforms. The direction pictographs are well organized and easy to see.

There is no restaurant, but the bar has a "Tavalo Caldo" (hot table) with fine pasta and some of the biggest sandwiches you will find. If you happen to find someone in the tourist office, the agent will give you an excellent map of Palermo and the region. Good hotels are in the city center, about a mile away, but there is a clutter of two-star hotels straight across Piazza Giulio Cesare down Via Roma.

The limited subway (Metropolitana) connects Centrale station to the port for sailings to Genoa, Leghorn, Naples, Cagliari (Sardinia), Ustica, and Tunis.

Directly to the right as you enter the station from Piazza Giulio Cesare is the train information office. There is an English-/French-language window that is also the Eurail Aid office for Sicily (see Appendix B). Nearby are a small chapel and a day hotel for a shower or haircut. Reservations and ticketing windows line the ticket hall. The waiting room is next to platform 4.

The first thing you see upon arrival in Agrigento is the chapel, but Agrigento Centrale is built on a hillside and is a split-level station. It was renovated in 1996. Departures are on the lower level. Escalators are up only and it is a long way down the steps with bulky luggage. Outside the station, where the city buses stop, is a large map of the Commune of Agrigento and the addresses of the tourist offices. Unfortunately the Greek treasures of the Agrigento region are too far from town to be seen by the use of train. You will need to rent a car or take a sightseeing tour to the Valley of the Temples and the National Archaeological Museum of San Nicola.

Catania Centrale station sits in a beautiful setting, facing the sea. Foaming breakers crash on the black lava rocks below. Most of the facilities line platform 1, including first- and second-class waiting rooms, but you have to use an underground passage ("Sottopassagio") with no escalator to reach the platforms. There is no cafeteria, but there is the usual bar. The (almost) English-speaking ladies in the tourist office beside the track will supply you with maps and tourist information, but there is a dearth of hotels near the train station.

The Circumetna (FCE) train circles the foot of Mount Etna and does not climb it. You board the diesel railcars of the FCE's 68-mile, narrow-gauge line in Catania's FCE terminal and curve around the crater of Mount Etna in four hours, except that you change to FS for your last leg back to Catania Centrale FS station. Rail passes are not accepted.

Taormina Giardini station, which was renovated in 1996, doesn't live up to its beautiful reputation, although taxis waiting in front are ready to take you to dozens of villas and resorts. The small station is cramped on a level above the sea and below the mountain ridges. There is no cafeteria or tourist office.

Siracusa station, renovated in 1996, is arranged along platform 1 with an underpass connecting platforms. There are first- and second-class waiting rooms. There is no cafeteria but an average bar. On platform 1 you find a large map of Siracusa with red spots indicating the locations of tourist offices within walking distance.

Compelling Sardinia

Italy's green and rocky island of Sardinia is 112 miles from the Italian mainland smack in the center of the western Mediterranean. Getting there by train: very difficult.

Neither Romans nor Phoenicians, Greeks nor Arabs ever subdued Sardinia, the second-largest island in the Mediterranean after Sicily. The uncompromised integrity of the Sardo way of life makes travel through the island personal and compelling.

Nevertheless, rail passes make it possible for you to use without extra charge the fleet of ferries of the Italian State Railroads (FS), which takes you to Golfo Aranci, a town at the foot of Capo Figari and gateway to the stupendous Emerald Coast.

Depart from Civitavecchia, 50 minutes by train from Rome. At the FS pier, board one of five FS ferries ready to take you directly to Golfo Aranci in eight hours. FS's newest ferry, the *Logudoro,* was put into service in 1990.

Golfo Aranci is midway between Olbia and the Costa Smeralda. Connecting FS trains take you to Olbia and, via Ozieri Chilirani, to Sassari and Cagliari.

You can also reach Sardinia by Tirrenia Lines ferries from Genoa (Genova), Leghorn (Livorno), La Spezia, Naples (Napoli), and Palermo, Sicily, but your rail pass does not cover these routes free.

Your rail pass entitles you to free passage aboard the FS ferries using the deck spaces on the verandas, in the salons, and in the bars. For a small supplement you may book reclining chairs for overnight sailings departing both ports at 9:30 P.M. For a greater supplement, you can reserve single or double cabins. Cabin reservations are obligatory. Make them at any Italian train station with a reservations terminal.

The FS network honoring your rail pass connects major cities. Decent, cheap private trains and buses take you past sweeping, high-altitude panoramas and surprising stone outcroppings and through countryside known to harbor notorious sheep-nappers. Rome's Forestation Bureau keeps planting fast-growing Canadian pines; shepherds keep burning them down.

You see rocks sculpted like elephants and bears, visit prehistoric nuraghe structures, walk through jewel-box Argonese Alghero, and relax on beaches named for the unique color of their waters. No one can do "dolce farniente," sweet nothingness, with more elegance than Italians.

Sardinia's most distinctive finds are the 7,000 nuraghi, which are Bronze Age temples, dwellings, and tombs. They remind you of bee-hive-shaped cones with large stones laid one over another without the use of mortar. Openings in the domes let in light.

The nuraghe center is at Barumini, where the ruins are grouped around a central three-story nuraghe. But several are within easy touring distance of the Costa Smeralda.

Sardinia's extensive bus system connects the island's towns and villages, and buses run frequently among the coastal tourist centers. They give the lie to the notion that getting around Sardinia is difficult or dull.

Diesel Pendolino trains scamper through Sardinia's easy central valley. They skirt the wilds that make Sardinia so special. Stop-and-go local trains take you to out-of-the-way, wonderful corners and backwoods. You may miss convenience and luxury, but there is no finer way for you to discover the gracious, proud feel of Sardinia.

Railcars take you from Sassari's busy train station, which is seemingly lost in the center of Sassari's sea of red roofs rolling over graceful hills. But looks are deceiving, for Sassari is a bustling commercial city, the second town in Sardinia, and its train station is crowded.

Sassari's faded, Roman, gold-colored terminus serves both FS (some visitors come by train the whole length of the island from Sardinia's capital city, Cagliari) and the private railroad to Alghero, which has its headquarters here.

Alghero lies on a small peninsula surrounded by Aragonese fortifications. Until 1848 the town was locked tightly at night. The former
entrance, at the stubby tower of the Porta Terra, is still a good place to
begin your walking tour through the narrow streets. The tourist office
is nearby, so pick up free color maps for your explorations.

In a sense, Alghero isn't a Sardinian town at all. It started as one, in
the early Middle Ages, but Spaniards from Aragon began their
Sardinian conquest by annexing Alghero in 1355. The Algherese did
not prove to be docile subjects; after two fierce rebellions the Aragonese
solved their problem by deporting the entire population to the interior
and replacing them with Catalans from the Iberian peninsula.

Everyone enjoys the friendly Catalan atmosphere here—Alghero is
now known as "Little Barcelona." Strolling through the narrow streets
of the old town gives you a sense of quiet adventure and colorful
leisure protected by Aragonese fortifications. You soon discover the
busy quay. Photograph scenes along the dock showing a way of life you
don't find at home. Green and blue fishing boats tie up to unload
crawling, creeping, and leaping Mediterranean marine-life catches.
Fishermen mend orange-colored nets on the beaches. You admire the
raw pink coral destined for the exquisite cameos.

In 1962, the Aga Khan and his well-heeled friends comprising the
Consorzio Costa Smeralda shoveled into Sardinia's northeast coast
more than $35 million 1960s dollars to convert the 35-mile strip into a
jet-set heaven. They named it Costa Smeralda, the Emerald Coast, for
the unparalleled clarity of its waters.

When the Aga Khan arrived, the pastures on the cliffs by the sea
were almost uninhabited. The shepherds considered them less valuable than other pieces of land. Think of the Costa Smeralda as an ecological development before ecology became trendy. The consorzio
designed and built its dwellings resolving not to impose construction
on the environment. The hotels were built to blend into the wild landscape. Tall buildings were forbidden. Construction followed the natural contours of the land. Buildings were earth-colored.

Rail-Pass Travel

Eurail products, Italy Flexi Railcards, and France 'n Italy passes are
valid over the entire FS 10,000-mile network, including the train ferries between Reggio Calabria and Messina, and include the ferry crossings between Civitavecchia and Golfo Aranci, Sardinia, and Villa S.

Giovanni and Messina, Sicily. They include all supplements usually payable for use of high-speed trains except Eurostar Italia.

Eurail products are valid in Greece, but because Italy is Greece's only adjoining Eurail country, you will also need to include Italy as one of your selections for a Eurail Selectpass.

The deck-class crossing to Greece discussed above that is covered free with Eurail products is a great bargain; otherwise, deck passage would cost about $162, first class; $138, second (plus the charges discussed below). Consecutive-day Eurailpasses in Greece are a great waste, however, because the Greek network is so limited and you will watch your Eurailpass days flitting away unused if you head to the Aegean Islands. With a flexipass, you can enjoy your days on sunny beaches without fretting over lost paid-in-advance Eurailpass days.

Italy Flexi Railcards in both first and second class are available for four to 10 travel days in one month. Youth under 26 may buy the less expensive version for second-class travel and small groups of up to five people traveling together qualify for the Saverpass, either first or second class. With a France 'n Italy Pass, you receive four days (total) for travel in France and Italy within two months. An Italy Rail 'n Drive Pass gives you any three days unlimited train travel in either first or second class with one month to complete your travel, plus two days Hertz car rental in a choice of four car categories.

You may buy your Italy Flexi Railcards before you leave or at 13 main train stations in Italy (including Rome Leonardo da Vinci Airport), where you ask for a "Trenitalia Pass." You validate rail passes at an FS ticket counter before you begin your travel. Make sure the agent enters the first date and last date of validity at the same time. You are not permitted to enter the validity dates yourself. Italy Flexi Railcards issued in Europe must be validated within two months after the date of issue; all others must be validated within six months. Before starting your journey with a flexipass, enter your date of travel in an appropriate box on your flexipass. Your flexipass is then valid from midnight to midnight. If you are traveling at midnight, your validation is good until the next scheduled stop. When your journey begins after 7 P.M. on an overnight train, enter the following day's date. When using your flexipass on a sea section (Civitavecchia-Sardinia), enter either the date of departure or the date of arrival. Passes are nonrefundable and you don't receive a refund in case of a railroad strike.

With an Italy Flexi Railcard you receive a 30 percent discount on

HML (see "Crossing between Italy and Greece") before July 15 and after September 1. You receive a 15 percent discount during the summer. In Italy your receive discounts on Starhotels (*www.starhotels.com/dpass.asp*), Notturno Italiano Hotels (*www.partners.notterno.it*), Bed & Breakfast Italiano (*www.bbitalia.it/trenitaliapass*), Volaviamare shipping line for Capri (*www.volaviamare.it*), and the Venice Card (*www.venicecard.it*).

Travelers 60 and older can purchase in Italy a Silver Card allowing a 30 percent reduction on first- and second-class tickets. It is available for one year, five years, and for life. Travelers between 12 and 26 can buy a $20 Green Card valid for one year giving them 30 percent discounts on all first- and second-class tickets (20 percent in high season). A Carta Prima, costing about $20, gives you a 30 percent discount on first-class tickets. For $40 to $75 you can join Club Eurostar to also give yourself access to FS's first-class Eurostar lounges. These cards must be purchased in Italy.

For travel in Greece, you may purchase an adult or youth Greek Flexipass Rail 'n Fly, which gives you two flight coupons for selected Olympic Airlines travel with Ionian Travel and three days travel within a month.

Only at the international ticketing window in Thessaloniki or at the main OSE office at 1 Karolou St., Athens (open 8 A.M. to 3 P.M., about a five-minute walk from Athens Larissa station, near Omonia Square, Tel. 529-7001), can you buy very inexpensive Hellenic Tourpasses valid for 10, 20, or 30 consecutive days travel for one to five people. The 10-day card costs about $40. It does not include supplements payable for travel on IC trains. Senior cards allowing five single trips free (dates restricted) and 50 percent reduction thereafter are granted to travelers over 60.

The Balkan Flexipass is also valid in Greece (see "Eastern Europe and Russia" chapter).

Traveling in Italy takes you aboard sleek Eurostar Italia trains and gives you five great train stations to serve as your bases.

Eurostar Italian Style
Will the Real Eurostar Please Stand Up?

Try to imagine the looks on the faces of the Eurostar executives in London, Paris, and Brussels when they first heard that FS was going to label their ETR services "Eurostar."

ROUTE OF EUROSTAR ITALIA

MILAN

to Venice

Bologna

Florence

N

0 10   50
MILES

ROME

to Naples

Despite their howls, FS did adopt the name Eurostar for its domestic network of high-speed trains. The use of the Eurostar name was agony to operators of the cross-Channel services, but Fiat, the builder of the train, had "protected" the name before cross-Channel Eurostar services were inaugurated and thus was entitled to use it to promote its new, high-quality ETR 460 and ETR 500 services and to solve the marketing problem created when the nontilt ETR 500 went into commercial service. Previously, FS had designated its high-speed services *P*, for its tilting trains, Pendolinos. To encompass also their super-high-speed, nontilting train, they had to find a snappy, new designation and the cross-Channel services had created name recognition. The bright, new, right-raked-star logo that FS has emblazoned on its ETRs does not infringe on the "real" Eurostar symbol.

The ETR Eurostar Italia
Success Story

1988 ETR 450	1st generation Pendolino	155 mph/Tilting Italy
1995 ETR 460	2nd generation Pendolino	155 mph/Tilting Italy
1996 ETR 470	Cisalpino	124 mph/Tilting to Switzerland
1996 ETR 480	Dual-voltage ETR	460 155 mph/Tilting to France
1996 ETR 500	High-speed train	186 mph/No tilt Italy
2000 ETR 500	Second generation	186 mph/Dual voltage

Italy's modern, high-speed trains are known as ETRs, for "Elettro Treni Rapidi," or rapid electric trains.

Board one of the hourly Eurostar Italia ETR 500 trains from Milan. You pick up speed and streak across the flat Po Valley along the 58-mile Milano-Bologna line, which is one of the most congested in Italy, also carrying IC trains. A new high-speed line, costing about $5.7 million, will open in 2006. On the straightaway, the fertile, green Po Valley's fields of grain, corn, and produce whiz past your graceful train, following the first chord of the Milan-Rome ("MI-RO") segment of the Milan-Bologna-Florence-Rome-Naples-Reggio de Calabria spinal chord, which carries about one-third of all FS traffic.

After your four-minute stop in Bologna Centrale station, you run at 125 mph about 45 percent of the time along the sinuous route to Florence. The Bologna-Florence chord of the new high-speed line will open in 2004.

After an eight-minute halt at Florence S.M.N. station, you negotiate the main ranges of the Apennines over the already completed double-tracked direttissima high-speed line to Rome through tunnels one after another built in the 1920s, rebuilt to 186-mph capability in the 1990s, and accelerate along an almost straight swath across Latium, Umbria, and Tuscany. Tunnels, including the 8.7-mile Adriana tunnel, eliminate all road-level crossings and connect FS's older, more wandering route to the new direttissima at various points. On May 30, 2001, a second-generation ETR 500 set a new Italian speed record of 198 mph on this stretch. In effect, FS created a four-track system between Florence and Rome that successfully handles mixed ETRs, ICs, and freight, each traveling at a different speed.

Check your watch: Your trip between Italy's two largest cities, 393 miles, takes you four hours, 30 minutes, at an average speed of over 87 mph, with hourly departures. Compare these times to flying between Rome and Milan. You would spend an hour and five minutes in the air, but by the time you add an hour and a half at each end to get to and from the airports and then allow time to check in before your flight and collect your luggage afterward, the time you spend traveling from city center to city center is about the same. Yet, you spend it more restfully on your luxurious Eurostar Italia, and you can do your work, socialize aboard, and arrive more relaxed.

Perhaps you would rather drive a Lamborghini and pay the tolls on the Autostrada, but you will arrive earlier with the Eurostar Italia at a fraction of the cost. Eurostar Italia gives you more comfort than flying and more speed than a red Lamborghini racing down the Autostrada. ETR 500 competes with the speed of French TGVs, takes you in great luxury, and gives you more time to study the details of the Vatican, the Uffizi, and the Brera museums.

Tilting ETR Pendolino trains have been a success ever since the bullet-nosed, first-generation ETR 450 hit the rails in May 1988. "Si, si," the captain of your train says, nodding to the conductor beside him when you ask about his Pendolino. He volunteers that indeed Pendolino means "little pendulum," because its body tilts gently whenever it rounds a curve, thus minimizing the forces of gravity, but he laughs when he compares the train to a banana, calling the first generation "bananalino" to describe its long and thin profile. Pendolinos' crews are congenial. They are not direct employees of the Italian State Railroads but handpicked employees of FS's subsidiary, "Ristofer," hired to staff these beautiful trains.

As ETR 500 units were delivered to FS from the manufacturer, they displaced ETR 460 trains. The ETR 460s then displaced ETR 450 trains, with the result that FS continually cascaded modern equipment from prime routes onto less busy routes, such as to and from Ancona, Palermo, and Taranto.

Like French TGVs (although the concept was not original with them), sleek integral power cars front and back propel the Eurostar Italia trains. The fabrics, materials, and designs remind you so much of airplane interiors that you can't help comparing them to first-class travel on an airplane.

ETR 500

The ETR 500 is a beefy train of two locomotives plus 11 carriages in striking green-and-white livery by Pininfarina. Its first production units began regular service on June 2, 1996. A second-generation, dual-voltage ETR went into service on May 28, 2000, traveling the Milan-Rome route. Three carriages are first class with 2+1 seating, and six are second class with 2+2 seating.

The first-generation ETR 500's power cars are somewhat ominous looking and vaguely recall a hooded cobra, with a two-piece windshield, but the Pininfarina Company, better known for its design of flashy sports cars, designed them also. The dual-voltage ETRs appear more benign because the front end has been completely redesigned with a central windshield. The second-generation power cars can operate off 25,000 volts A.C. on the high-speed line and off 3,000 volts D.C. on the older Italian systems. It can also operate under reduced power off 1,500 volts D.C, and Artesia hopes to run an eight-carriage ETR 500 between Milan and Paris over the French high-speed lines.

When you board you see the carriage number displayed on the digital display. "FUM" stands for "fumatori," or smoking. "NFM" is nonsmoking. Your first reaction is surprise. It is not like any train you have seen. Perhaps your emotions are heightened by the red color. Flashy red upholstery covers the bucket seats and headrests and extends up the walls to the roofline. It appears big and the carriages long. FS didn't skimp on the furnishings in first class. It's a snazzy train.

The first-class carriages are broken into 2+1 units with facing seats separated by a magazine-rack/trash-receptacle/foldout-lap-table console. The table is ideal for laptop computers. These console dividers add a degree of privacy. It is a tie-and-briefcase train. You are startled occasionally by the sounds of cellular telephones ringing. The seats recline electrically by the press of a button; pushbuttons in the armrest control your reading light intensity; and sunscreens, which you electrically raise and lower between double-paned windows, filter the sun's rays to your comfort level. The corridor connections are pressure sealed, which is a help, because there are many tunnels on the Italian high-speed lines.

Make your way to the art deco cafe with 30 yellow-tablecloth restaurant seats arranged 2+1, a stainless-steel galley with hot plates and microwave ovens. The stand-up bar of the kind that is familiar on high-speed trains is equipped with an overwhelming coffee machine. Finally, there is a "special-service" carriage with 23 first-class seats, facilities for the handicapped, and two four-passenger business compartments.

Although ETR 500s do not tilt, the manufacturers claim that the 500 can corner 10-15 percent faster than conventional trains because of its low center of gravity. Even so, you will observe that the ETR 500's ride is not as smooth as a Pendolino at 125 mph over the Milan-Florence stretch, and over the 186-mph Florence-Rome stretch it is not as smooth as a French TGV at the same speed.

ETR 450

FS's ETR 450 train with the Buck Rogers bullet nose and the "FIAT" nameplate was the leader of the Pendolino generation. It is long and lean and was at first all first class. Racing like an antelope, it gives you a taste of speed, service, and extravagance. These tilting maroon-and-red Pendolino trains that took you between Rome and Milan with unprecedented speed still provide you quality accommodations, ride, and speed over FS's branch lines.

The 450's luxurious interiors allow you to fold down tables and stretch out in the 22-inch-wide, fresh-smelling aquamarine and slate-green plush seats, which are lined up 2+1, with a 39-inch pitch. Wall-to-wall carpeting is blue; cooling and heating originates at baseboards.

Coach bodies are tapered from the waist up so that when the 450 tilts it does not protrude beyond the travel envelope. The windows are streamlined, longer, but not nearly so high as on older trains. You pass through fearless gangways between carriages so you don't feel terrified crossing from car to car while purring along up to 155 mph. Leave your luggage in the luggage racks near the door when you enter.

The environmentally correct closed-cycle toilets in front are also similar to those on airlines, except the Pendolino's are larger and have a rubber-mat flooring.

ETR 460

FS's 40 second-generation ETR 460 trains (there are 15 ETR 450s), which entered service in May 1995 and served as the workhorses of FS, have been largely replaced by popular ETR 500 trains, but ETR 460s still serve routes to and from Genoa, Venice, Bari, Lecce, and Sicily.

You look ahead and see you are approaching a considerable curve: watch to see how your Eurostar Italia ETR 460 Pendolino performs. You are seriously startled to observe one side of your carriage physically rising. Pendolinos overcome curves magnificently. They tilt positively, hold their stance through the arc, and return you comfortably to horizontal without delay.

This second-generation Pendolino differs from the ETR 450 in several significant features.

• The exterior design by Giugiaro replaces the ETR 450's bullet nose, which was considered old-fashioned but which made a statement. The ETR 460's more functional and less dramatic profile gives better vision and more room in the driver's cabin.

• Wider body width makes it less of a "bananalino" and allows second-class seats to be positioned 2+2 without crowding.

• Higher-powered motors allow the number of individual carriages that are powered to be reduced from eight to six.

• Full pressure sealing permits maximum-speed transit through the many tunnels on the direttissima high-speed line between Florence and Rome and the other associated lines served by Pendolinos.

• The tilt system is located entirely beneath the carriages instead of taking up passenger space.

• Improved interiors are equipped with earphone jacks for taped music at every seat.

You find the 460's ride excellent, like gliding on velvet. The interiors are respectable, but not extravagant. The 460s have the same short windows as the 450s and some interior design similarities to the ETR 500s of the same age. The 460's seats recline mechanically. Consoles separate facing seats, which happens seldom in first class, but occurs at every second set of rows in second class. These smaller consoles accommodate foldout tables only.

Grand Train Stations
Islands of Order

Italian train stations are islands of order in seas of confusion. Travelers in Italy find sustenance in five of Europe's best stations. Use Milan's, Rome's, and Florence's centrally located stations as your bases for luxuries and good cafeterias. Venice's remarkably located Santa Lucia station is a scenic vaporetto ride away from the Piazza San Marco. You'll pass through Naples Centrale on your way to the beautiful Amalfi coast aboard the private, narrow-gauge Circumvesuviana train.

Milan Centrale

This is the grand station of Europe, a cyclopean complex opened in 1931. The station itself is a tourist sight. Its grandiose, eclectic style has been characterized as "Assyrian-Babylonian," or "Mussolini Modern." Over the arriving trains a set of five glassed arches ascending in size make this a magnificent construction. Its waiting room is enormous, and its staircases between street and train levels—humanely equipped with up and down escalators—sweeping. If you pause on one of the beautiful landings midway on the stairs, take a long look at the expanse of the lower hall.

When you enter the upper hall you see a feature so gracious it is unique. A bubbling water fountain—its sounds fighting the cacophony of the trains—shoots above a polished rose-colored marble floor surrounded by wire-web jump seats and warm pastel mosaics.

The long hall itself is highlighted by the creatively positioned "Gran Bar" at one end and "Informazioni" (for train information) at the other. FS's Informazioni is where you validate your rail passes. It also contains a money-change counter. In fact, you find three places to change your money in Milan Centrale: in the bank located on the long wall next to the "APT Tourist Information" sign indicating the city information office on the train level (open Mon.-Sat., 8 A.M. to 7 P.M.; Sun., 9:30 A.M. to 12:30 P.M. and 1:30 to 6 P.M.), in the FS Informazioni office, and a glitzy money-change operation right next to the tracks. The bank gives the best rate, the change operator the poorest. There is an ATM machine between the bar in the center and track entrance numbered 3. Outside the bank is a bank-note change machine

ISLANDS OF ORDER

ITALY

MILAN

VENICE

FLORENCE

Mediterranean Sea

-N-

ROME

0   20   100
         MILES

working (hopefully) 24 hours. Instructions are in four languages—press "English." You simply slip in American greenbacks, pounds sterling, and Swiss francs and out come paper euros. Exchange rates are superior to the money-change office in the platform area.

The tourist information office has a back room filled with free brochures and booklets to answer your questions. Be sure to pick up a monthly "What's on in Milan," a good map, and (in English) a comprehensive "Museums in Milan."

Luggage checking is deviously located down a hall near the information office. Look for the illuminated suitcase sign. Also along the corridor you won't miss the "Free Shop." This name must be some kind of a Milanese joke considering the substantial prices, but it is a highlight walk-through to see the most devastatingly complete "travelers' provisions" store in Europe. You find everything that you considered packing but left behind because you didn't have space. Get items ranging from take-out pizza to alarm clocks and blank videotapes. Use it as your source of take-along liter bottles of water.

Near the center of the long wall upstairs is the entrance to the waiting room, "Sala Attesa." The classic second-class room is filled with banks of antique, varnished wooden benches. You would hear echoes from its marble walls except that modernization has introduced an emergency fire exit, a children's play area, and a false ceiling with indirect lighting.

The architectural counterpoint to the Free Shop is the glass and chrome stand-up bar next to the "Gran Bar" at the end of the station. Here you can enjoy coffee, cakes, and sandwiches.

In a station so enormous, it is lucky that ticketing and reservations, domestic and foreign, have been organized on street level into four sections in three halls ("Biglietteria") with towering ceilings. To give it some kind of order, the windows are all numbered. Biglietteria Est (east) windows 49-60 (open 7 A.M. to 8:30 P.M.) are available for seat reservations and couchettes. Take a waiting number from the machine as you enter. Credit cards are not accepted here. In Biglietteria Ovest (west), window 14 is for local lines, window 16 is for resident rail passes, and windows 20 and 22 are for international tickets. In the center you buy domestic tickets at windows 27-46 (credit cards accepted).

The "Self Service" is a dimly lit cafeteria next to the "Gran Bar," down from a place for freshening up called the "Hour Hotel." Food is relatively good, and the lighting fixture looks as though it hopped right out of a 1930s movie.

The entrance to the post office is outside on the ground level, conveniently tucked into the same edifice.

You must produce a ticket or rail pass to enter the train area, a good idea that keeps the platform relatively negotiable. Luggage carts that fit the escalators to street level do not return your deposit.

You can't have much respect for a metro system when the ticketing machines are broken and you must buy your ticket from a newsstand, but Milan has three metro lines. Line 1 (red line) with its sober Italian design dates from the 1960s; Line 2 (green line) was opened second; and Line 3 (yellow line) was opened in 1990. Shorthand designations for the lines are MR1, MG2, and MY3.

Milan's transportation network includes surface lines as well as the three underground lines. A single ticket is valid for 75 minutes in any combination of surface and metro but for only one metro stretch (up to the limits of Cascina Gobba and Sesto Marelli), so be sure to save your ticket when you leave the subway for the free transfers. You may also buy one- or two-day tickets. A booklet of 11 tickets is sold for the price of 10, and more than one person may use them provided one of the group holds the serial number of the ticket booklet. This is a good deal for groups or families visiting Milan for more than one or two days. A day or two-day ticket is better for single travelers zipping back and forth on public transportation. Write your name and passport number on the ticket.

Enter the subway stations at signs with the white letter *M* (Metropolitana) in a red field. Surface stops for streetcars, etc., are marked by orange signposts bearing the emblem of the transit authority (ATM) and showing the stops on the route. Milan's two subway lines from the outlying areas in the western and northeastern sections of the city intersect near the Sforza Castle and Piazzale Loreto. One of Milan's great pleasures is rising on the escalator from the subway and seeing Milan's wedding-cake Duomo (cathedral) revealed before you.

Obtain a free system map and helpful guide (in English) at the office of the transit authority in the Duomo station, the Provincial Tourist Authority in Cathedral Square, or the Municipal Information Office in the nearby Galleria.

Line MY3 takes you from in front of Centrale station to the Duomo, the center of town with adjacent arcade and nearby opera house. The subway corridors are serpentine but decently signed. For the Duomo on Line 3 use direction "S. Donato" from Centrale. To return, use direction "Zara."

Milan's train stations include Porta Garibaldi, which is slightly closer to the center than Centrale, on metro Line MG2, for suburban train service; Porta Genova, on the southwest edge of the city; Lambrate, for trains not intended to serve Milan; Rogoredo; and Porta Romana, mainly used for freight. Cadorna Northern Railroads station at the junction of MR1 and MG2 lines (near Sforza Castle, and only two subway stops from the Duomo) is the terminus for the Malpensa Express airport train and Northern Railroads' connection to Como, Erba, Varese, etc. Porta Genova on Line MG2 connects Milan to the west. Line MG2 connects Lambrate with Centrale, Cadorna, and Piazza Genova train stations.

Rome Termini

On January 29, 2000, the Italian prime minister inaugurated the refurbished Rome Termini station, which after a long and thorough restyling became the largest train station in Europe, according to the prime minister, but he didn't give any basis. In fact, it is 2.37 million square feet large.

Architects designed the enlarged complex to serve not only as a transit point for visitors but also to be a service complex for Romans. Pathways were cleared for access to trains, including the Fiumicino Airport train, buses, taxis, and the Metropolitano subway. New elevators, escalators, a main staircase, and a moving walkway make it easier for you to get around the expanded station and to the Metropolitano below.

The electric signs are the most modern, and a closed-circuit surveillance system connects with a control room to alert police. You find 40 automatic ticketing machines, 240 electronic information points, and 100 shops. Free luggage carts, with no deposit, are aligned in front of the station, but you will be lucky to find one on a platform when you arrive.

On the street level, in the so-called "Dinosaur," the famous glassed-over outer hall built in the 1950s by architect Montouri, you find ticketing for the day of travel, an enormous bookstore, and office for making your reservations and advance ticketing. Take a number, and be prepared for a long wait. If you know your train and date of travel, it is easier to use one of the ticketing machines, which accept debit cards but not credit cards, but rail-pass holders seeking a reservation have no choice but to wait in the reservations/ticketing office.

In the expanded inner hall, adjacent to the train platforms, you find the Eurail Aid office (take a number), Club Eurostar (open only to members), the fine cafeteria "Self Serve," a storefront McDonald's so you can carry food onto the trains, money change, "Bancomat" ATMs, and a tourist information office with friendly interns. Adjacent to track 1 are lockers costing about $1.50 or $2, depending on size (press the "English" button), a pleasant waiting room, and a WC costing about 50 cents. Adjacent to track 24 you find more lockers, the terminal for the Leonardo Express to Rome Leonardo da Vinci Airport, a second information office, and a taxi row.

Termini's "Self Serve" cafeteria is now the best train station cafeteria in Europe and recommendable anywhere. Management has taken a formerly very good cafeteria, added a live piano player at mealtimes, and beautified it with marble, flowers, and modular service centers to make it a pleasure to use. It even has a mezzanine and an outdoor patio with umbrella-shaded tables. Service is good. Selection is excellent.

On the underground level, you find a new 130,000-square-foot center containing Rome's largest bookshop, with many travel titles, an Internet Cafe, a second, sit-down McDonald's, and "Drug Store," which is really a supermarket. Follow the signs *M* to the Metropolitano. Rome has two subway lines: *A* (red) and *B* (blue). One wonders what color the subway trains were originally, because they are so completely covered by graffiti it is impossible to tell. Fares are about $1.25 within Rome, valid for 75 minutes, and about $4 to Rome Leonardo da Vinci Airport by subway.

Metro line *A*'s cars take you between Anagnina station and Ottaviano station near the Vatican City with stops at Roma Nord train station, Spagna for the Spanish Steps, Vittorio E, and Barberini. Metro line *B*'s cars run south to the EUR Center, where some hotels are located. Deposit the correct change in the ticket-vending machines on the walls of the entrance hall or buy metro tickets individually or in booklets of 10 for a 14 percent discount in one of the station's several tobacco shops.

Rome has five train stations. When you ride a through train scheduled to connect two cities other than Rome, the trains stop at Rome's

Tiburtina or Ostiense station in Rome's outskirts. Some 12 FS trains a day depart from Termini via Ostiense, but it is easier to reach Ostiense via subway. Tuscolana and Trastevere serve trains in the direction of Pisa. But your prime destination is Rome's Termini, in the throbbing heart of the Eternal City.

Florence S.M.N.

There is no question that by far the best way to visit the tile-roofed Tuscan town on the Arno River is by train. The whole area between Florence S.M.N. (Santa Maria Novella) station and the Pitti Palace across the Arno is crowded year round with European tourists. Congregation areas include in front of the Duomo (cathedral), Piazza della Signorina, Piazza della Republica, and the Ponte Vecchio.

Florence's station is similar to Rome's Termini. Probably the same architectural firm was employed. It is one of the most pleasing Italian train stations because of its long architectural lines and modern lay-out, and it is airy with its inner and outer halls and shopping mall below. Because there is no metro to complicate getting around, it is easy to find your way, and luggage carts are available.

Facing the spacious track area are the hotel-booking service, money-change counters, and waiting rooms ("Sala di Attesa") opposite track 5. Next to the waiting rooms go to "Informazioni Treni," open 7 A.M. to 9 P.M., for train information. As you exit the platform area into the enclosed hall you pass "Composizione Treni Principali" boards. In the enclosed hall you probably won't use windows 9-20 for domestic ticketing, but enter the side room to find international ticketing ("Biglietti Internazionali") and reservations ("prenotazioni") counters open 7 A.M. to 9 P.M. and window 7 for boat tickets to Sardinia. Take a number from the machine on the wall for your turn to be announced.

S.M.N.'s "Self Service" restaurant is the equal of those in other grand Italian stations. It is managed well and offers excellent selections. In the back you find hot plates with every sort of pasta, including lasagna, and dozens of salads and sweets for you to load on your tray, but Florence Self Service has also a separate pizza counter and, in front, a traditional Italian "Bar" with sandwiches. It is a four-star restaurant at a two-star price.

Below S.M.N. there is a commercial shopping gallery that includes an Internet point. Enter by escalator next to the bus stops on the side of S.M.N. or by corridor on the opposite side.

Florence S.M.N. is conveniently located near the center of Florence. Hotels surround it, and more hotels are located in the direction of the Arno River, the Duomo, and the Piazza della Signorina, but the city nearly cracks at the seams with travelers during the summer so it is best to get there early and to rely on arrangements by the Tourist Office.

Other train stations in Florence include Castello, Rifredi (where FS's Eurostar Italia trains call), Fiesole Caldine, and Campo di Marte, but S.M.N. is your base. Train calls are made in Italian and English.

Venice's Santa Lucia

Leaving Santa Lucia is like stepping into a dream. The Grand Canal stretches right before you, crammed with gondolas and busy with vaporetti (water buses) ready to take you through a wondrous world.

Travelers lured to the City of the Doges will be pleased with their welcome at Venice's beautifully situated Santa Lucia station. Although not a hub like the other grand stations, it provides an appropriate terminal for excellent trains such as Eurostar Italias and InterCities.

At the head of the tracks you find palm trees and blooming red flowers. Facing the platforms is a restaurant, a sweet shop for take-out items, and a self-service cafeteria area extending to an open-air awning-covered veranda facing the canal, where you enjoy dining in one of the most gracious train terminal surroundings. Inside you find a Tourist Office, FS change office, bank, reservations counter open until 10 P.M., ticketing, luggage storage, and post office.

Venice has two stations. Mestre is the stop for your express trains between Italy and Slovenia and Croatia. Santa Lucia is your stop to meet the vaporetti to St. Marks Square. In style it recalls Florence S.M.N. with long marble steps covered with young and old idlers. Across the Grand Canal, visitors lounge on the steps of green-domed Fondamente S. Simeon Piccolo and on the Ponte degli Scalzi soaring over the canal in picture-book Venetian style. Gondoliere mooring their black gondolas across the canal do a brisk business.

Vaporetti require two floating termini. On the left as you exit Santa Lucia, line 2 (Diretto) takes a shortcut through a side canal to reach San Marco. Line 34 (Tourist) takes the scenic route.

Naples Centrale

Naples is a teeming, busy, littered city—Europe's most densely populated. There are almost no green or parks in the center. But it is not threatening either, as you may have heard. Naples is not a tourist destination, but it is a jumping-off point for the beautiful Amalfi coast and Capri, which are some of your best holiday choices. You can visit Sorrento, Pompeii, Herculaneum, and Mount Vesuvius by use of the private Circumvesuviana railroad with a station below the Centrale station. It does not accept Eurail products or Italian Railpasses, but fares are inexpensive.

Naples Centrale train terminus is complex. It consists of four train stations. On the surface you see the glass and steel shell of Naples Centrale, a dead-end station. Sharing the level below are FS's Naples Piazza Garibaldi station (which is a through station), the Metropolitana, and the second station of the Circumvesuviana, the private commuter-cum-tourist mininetwork between Naples and Sorrento. The first Circumvesuviana station is Stazioni Termine. In the bowels of the earth, down a second set of escalators, the trains themselves burrow their separate ways like moles determined to reach the Amalfi coast (with a stop at Pompeii).

Naples Centrale has all the facilities of the great Italian stations. In particular, the snack bar serves the best pizza from a wood-fired pizza oven. Pizza is one of the few things less expensive in Italy than the U.S.

The ticketing windows in the main entry, "Biglietteria," are marked electronically from 1 to 24. Window 17 is for rail passes. Window 18 is for automobile and ship transportation and sleeping-car reservations. Windows 19-23 are for couchette and seat reservations. The tourist office opposite window 1 ("Ente Provinciale per il Turismo di Napoli") is small, with limited brochures. Train information and money change are by window 24.

Naples Centrale is the major station of Naples, but the line through Piazza Garibaldi station also connects Naples Piazza Cavour, Naples Montesanto, Naples Mergellina, and Naples Campi Flegrei stations, east to west.

Eastern Europe and Russia

Most train travelers prefer to travel no farther east than the limits of the EuroCity network, i.e., the guarantee of decent service (which is Warsaw, Prague, Bratislava, Budapest, and Zagreb). Traveling farther east into Russia requires that you be as hardy as a bear. Travel in Russia is an endless exercise in problem solving. When you enjoy this exercise, you'll be at home. For relaxation, travel the trains in the West. As you travel east, trains become slow and dirty, service is rude, reservations are difficult or impossible, and getting as far as Moscow or St. Petersburg from central Europe takes days. The farther you travel from your jumping-off place, Berlin, Prague, or Vienna, the more difficult trains become. Take with you a deck of cards, map(s), pages photocopied from the Thomas Cook European Timetable, meals to eat, and liquids to drink. When you travel with determination and a hide of steel, you'll get to your destination knowing you got a good price.

Trains are improving as the Eastern countries get their economic noses above water. You can buy Polrailpasses, Czech Flexipasses and Prague Excursion Passes, Hungarian Flexipasses, Bulgarian Flexipasses, Romanian Railpasses, European East Passes, and Balkan Flexipasses for excellent prices.

One of the woes of traveling in the East is the non- or partial convertibility of the national currencies. Polish and Czech currencies are accepted nowhere else, but they may be reconverted to hard currency (at a substantial penalty) before you leave. If you have Russian rubles, you are stuck. No one will change rubles into hard currency.

Take as many dollar notes as you feel you may need, and then take 50 percent more. Take lots of $1, $5, and $20 bank notes, crisp from your bank, and you will be surprised how much difficulty this saves you. In Russia, you can get a taxi ride when you say "dollars." Dollar notes are accepted—and given priority—everywhere.

Savvy Traveling on the Trains of Poland, the Czech Republic, and Slovakia

Trains of Poland—Trains of the Czech Republic—Trains of Slovakia—Rail-pass travel

Poland, the Czech Republic, and Slovakia will join the European Union on May 1, 2004, continuing their alignment with Western Europe. Trains of these countries look Western, run on standard European gauge, and boast nearly Western standards. They do, however, share a concession from the Russian Railways—they are the only national railroads that are allowed to run carriages into Russia.

You can get around quite easily provided you don't mind waiting in line for reservations, which makes a rail pass, issued before you leave, even more attractive. Reservations are required on many of the better trains, but when you carry a first-class rail pass, you will find the first-class sections relatively empty, compared with the often-crowded second-class sections. Travelers who enjoy leaning out windows and cursing air-conditioning will love these trains. The windows can be lowered after you locate the pushbutton in the stainless-steel grip at the top.

When you plan to travel in Poland, the Czech Republic, and Slovakia plus Austria and Hungary, a European East Pass (valid for unlimited travel in these countries) works wonders. The European East Pass is available for first- or second-class travel for five days plus optional additional days bringing your total to 10 days travel within a month. Children four-11 pay half the adult fare; those under four travel free. A rail map of Central Europe is available free from Rail Europe (see Appendix A).

Trains of Poland

The Polish Railroads (PKP, for Polskie Koleje Panstwowe, *www.pkp.pl* and click "Europe Online") runs a full complement of first- and second-class trains over its 14,438-mile network. The Polish-built carriages are Western in nature, with compartments on the long-distance trains. Trains are classified

• Pociag osobowy (local), which are uncomfortable and slow, characterized by crowding and generally poor standards of maintenance and cleaning,

• Pociag pospieszny (fast), which stop at moderately sized stations and usually have a first-class carriage,

• Pociag expresowy (express), which run between major cities, charge a higher fare, carry a buffet car, and require seat reservations except for pass holders, and

• Pociag InterCity/Eurocity, which are top-quality expresses, with full-service restaurant car, and require a higher supplement. Seat reservations are advisable even for pass holders and may be easier to make at Orbis offices than train stations. You may receive a complimentary snack at your seat. There are 14 domestic InterCity lines and four international InterCity lines linking Berlin and Hamburg with Wroclaw and Krakow using the reopened border crossing at Forst. The Polish IC Wawel serves Berlin, while the service from Hamburg to Krakow is able to bypass Berlin via Stendal, Potsdam, and Cottbus. Six EuroCity trains take you between Warsaw and Berlin, Vienna, Bratislava, and Budapest in addition to Krakow-Vienna and Poznan-Berlin IC services.

• The light-blue Night Express trains feature two types of carriage and three classes of accommodations. Couchettes provide six bunks per compartment. Sleeping carriages provide two bunks per room in first class, three in second class. *Tip:* The doors between carriages will be locked, so do not explore the train and be locked out. The Night Express on the Krakow-Kiev run provides modern, 125-mph sleeping carriages. Each air-conditioned carriage has eight standard three-berth compartments and two two-berth business-class compartments equipped with small refrigerators, TVs, and DVD players as well as private toilets. Connections to Minsk and Moscow use Polish carriages attached to Russian trains.

Tickets are sold at most stations. Credit cards are usually accepted, but be sure to use a counter displaying a credit-card logo. If you board from a station without an open ticket counter, go immediately upon boarding to the conductor's office in the first carriage to buy one. An *R* inside a box means that reservations are mandatory, an *R* without a box means that seat reservations are required on part of the train, and an *RF* means that you can make reservations if you desire. They are free.

First-class carriages are red and white, seat 3+3, and have carpeting. Green-and-white second-class carriages seat 4+4 and have linoleum on the floor. Couchettes, with six bunks per compartment, are blue and white. The red WARS ("Przedsiebiorstwa Wagonow Sypialnych i Restauracyjnych," *www.wars.pl*) restaurant cars have kitchen and white-tablecloth-covered tables. For short domestic routes, PKP hooks together three-unit, second-class-only, yellow-and-blue electric railcars to form nine-car trains. The domestic timetable shows departures for 20 destinations. ECs, ICs, IRs, and Expresses (Ex) comprise about two-thirds of the total.

Warsaw is the hub of the Polish Railroads' domestic network. PKP radiates from Warsaw along a 201-mile mainline to the Baltic coast at Gdansk; east through Brest to Moscow; south to Krakow; southwest to Vienna with connections to Prague; northeast to St. Petersburg via Vilnius; and west to Berlin via Poznan.

Leave your train at Centraina station on Al. Jerozolimskie for your visit to Warsaw. Trains continue underground until approximately three long blocks west of the Vistula and cross the Vistula rail bridge to Wschodnia station at Ul. Kijowska, but Wschodnia features platforms with little else. Warsaw-Gdanska station (located at ul. M. Buczka) lies on the north side of the Polish capital for service to Gdansk. The Warsaw Railroad Museum is located at the Warsaw Glowna train station near Zawiszy Square, where you see dozens of model trains from around the world, and its outdoor yard has steam locomotives of all types and sizes.

Your train approaches Centraina on ground level and passes into a large, dark platform area with the four-level station building constructed over the tracks. The aluminum-and-glass structure is spattered with posters and grit to make it appear as unattractive as possible, yet it is located in the midst of a new generation of modern hotels with many of the internationally known names represented. It's a convenient arrangement for you, although it is a good mile from Warsaw's beautiful Old City.

The centerpiece of Centraina is the soaring main hall with domestic reservations windows consuming an entire wall. On the opposite side, you find money change ("Kasa Walutowa," open 8 A.M. to 10 P.M.) located in the domestic information ("Informacja") side room. The tourist information office (open 9 A.M. to 7 P.M.) provides information in English, including information on train connections, public transportation in Warsaw, hotel prices, and sightseeing in Warsaw. Sandwich/pizza/snack counters, open 24 hours, are located on the facing side of the hall. Make your international reservations at counters 1-11 on the mezzanine level upstairs (open 24 hours, with breaks). The mezzanine level also contains waiting rooms.

In the main hall, clacking arrivals ("Przyjazdy") and departures ("Odjazdy") signboards direct you to the correct platform ("Peron") below. Train composition charts are posted in the center of the departure platforms.

Much of Warsaw Centraina business is located in the labyrinth of corridors midway between the main hall and the platforms. You find shops of every description, including Polish fast food and at least three Internet Cafes. The Srodmiescie station for local trains is adjacent.

The best train south from Warsaw is the Polish EuroCity Sobieski to Vienna. The Sobieski runs along the Polish CMK (Central Main Line) line through quiet farm country. The line, which is an inverted *Y* with Warsaw at the top, Krakow at the southeast, and Katowice at the southwest, also hosted French TGV-R trains, where they ran at 100 mph, and provided a venue for testing Italian ETR 460 trains, where they established the Polish speed record of 155 mph. The direct Warsaw-Krakow InterCity and Express trains rip right along the CMK reaching Krakow (178 miles) at 69 mph in two hours, 35 minutes.

The new platforms at Krakow's Glowny station are very good and well arranged and PKP has brightly touched up the station house to make it very pleasant and efficient. The station is orderly. Without difficulty you find a money-change office (no ATM), ticketing, information, a bright waiting room with blond wooden benches, and taxis and streetcars outside. There's a pizzeria and a very nice WARS cafeteria ("Restauracja"). The train compositions ("Plan Zestawienia Wagonow") are given in the tunnel beneath the tracks. Departure posters include the departure platform number ("Peron").

Before you go, write the Polish National Tourist Office. They will send you a fine packet containing a good road map of Poland, a good

Poland brochure, as well as Warsaw and Krakow brochures, Orbis and American Travel Abroad brochures, a LOT brochure of nonstop flights to Warsaw from New York and Chicago, a hotel list, and—if you ask—a list of domestic trains.

To Berlin, you will ride one of the Berlin-Warszawa-Express trains jointly operated by DB and PKP with "Berlin-Warszawa-Express" branded on the sides. Each train consists of one first-class, much-used carriage of DB IC heritage reliveried white, a dining carriage, and four second-class carriages. You must make reservations costing €3 in Germany with a valid Eurail product plus Eastern European Pass. The WARS dining carriage is better than adequate and pleasantly inexpensive for filling meals. The menu is in Polish, German, and English.

Berlin-Warszawa-Express Trains

Varsovia	Pader-ewski	Berolina				Berolina	Pader-ewski	Varsovia
0631	1231	1631	dep.	BERLIN (Zoo)	arr.	1330	1730	2235
0644	1244	1644	dep.	Berlin (Ostbahnhof)	arr.	1317	1717	2222
0752	1352	1752	dep.	Frankfurt/Oder	dep.	1211	1611	2111
0824	1424	1824	dep.	Rzepin	dep.	1141	1541	2041
0945	1545	1945	dep.	Poznan (Glowny)	dep.	1014	1414	1914
1032	1632	2032	dep.	Konin	dep.	0922	1322	1822
1114	1714	2114	dep.	Kutno	dep.	0843	1243	1743
1230	1830	2230	arr.	WARSAW (Centraina)	dep.	0730	1130	1630

Trains of the Czech Republic

Americans don't need a visa to visit the Czech Republic for up to 30 days, and British and Irish citizens can stay for up to 180 days, but Canadians, New Zealanders, and Australians must obtain a visa for a stay of up to 30 days. Immigration checks and customs inspections take place aboard your train without its having to stop at the border.

CD (Ceske Drahy, *www.cd.cz*) operates 7,238 passenger trains daily, classified EuroCity (EC), SuperCity (SC), InterCity (IC), Expres (Ex), fast trains (R = Rychlik), semifast trains (Sp = Spesny vlak), and local trains (Os = Osobni vlak). First class costs 50 percent more than second. Visa and MasterCard are accepted.

The premium SuperCity Manazer between Prague and Ostrava provides free at-seat refreshment, daily newspapers, or a free reserved parking space.

CD speeded up operation on the mainline between Prague and Brno, permitting 100-mph operation for the first time in history. Seven pairs of EC trains run via Pardubice and Ceska Trebova, including the EC Johann Gregor Mendel to Vienna, which runs in July and August only, covering the 160-mile line in two hours, 42 minutes, 19 minutes faster than before, at an average speed of 59 mph, the fastest-ever train connection between Prague and Brno. You will see further savings of time with the full completion of the corridor.

On the northern corridor Prague-Berlin, six EC trains run daily, with departures every two hours during most of the day. EC Jan Hus runs between Prague and Dresden. EC Alois Negrelli runs between Prague and Hamburg. An overnight train takes you Prague-Amsterdam via Dresden.

In April 2003, CD began commissioning the first of their 143-mph trivoltage tilting trains based on the Italian ETR 480 Pendolino for running on the Berlin-Dresden-Prague-Vienna corridor. Production took place in the Fiat Ferrovaria plant in Savigliano, Italy. Each seven-carriage set, with two first-class carriages, four second-class carriages, and a bar carriage, offers 102 first-class and 220 second-class seats. The whole fleet will be complete in January 2004 and regular service will commence in June 2004. The colors, air-conditioned compartments, and bar car were designed by Czech designer Patrik Kotas. The sets are equipped for the D.C. and A.C. systems used in the Czech Republic and the power supplies in Germany and Austria.

The green-and-white Czech EC and IC train carriages are of good quality and stop only at major stations. Some have dining cars. Overnight trains have couchettes and sleeping compartments. You can reserve your seat; reservations are obligatory on some fast trains. Semifast trains run over longer routes and stop only at stations judged to be significant. They bypass smaller stations most of the time but may stop at every station in a mountain region. They carry both first- and second-class carriages. Local trains generally stop at every station and provide second-class service only.

Two EuroCity trains provide service from Berlin. The Hungarian EC Hungaria then continues through to Bratislava and Budapest, while the other actually originated in Denmark, calling first in Hamburg. The EC Antonin Dvorak connects Vienna and Prague. The Russian train Vltava leaves Prague's Hlavni station with three CD sleeping cars for a two-day, two-night trip through Poland and Belarus for Moscow.

JLV (Jidelni a Luzkove Vozy), the Czech Restaurant and Sleeping Car company, caters service in sleeping cars, couchettes, restaurant cars, and station facilities. You can ride blue Czech sleeping cars and couchettes arranged the same as those of the Western European railroads and travel over many routes, including the Dukla between Prague and Moscow, and to and from destinations as far away as Malmo, Berlin, Paris, Venice, Athens, and Bucharest. Their restaurant cars travel as far as Zurich, Vienna, Warnemunde, and Budapest. The restaurant cars on these trains are valiantly fighting decay, but it is a losing battle. Nevertheless the meals are very good. The menu is in Czech, German, and English. Although prices are quoted in Czech crowns, Swiss Francs and euros are equally welcome. The price level is about the same as in Germany.

Prague has four train stations, but only Hlavni nadrazi (Main station) and Nadrazi Holesovice handle mainline and international traffic. Trains terminating in the Czech capital favor Hlavni, while Holesovice, north of Prague's center, is preferred by trains en route between north and south.

Hlavni is a through station beneath two glass arches. It is large, modern, dirty, busy, rambling, poorly organized, and puzzling, with dozens of money-change ("Wechselstuben," in German) and accommodations counters and kiosks. Signs are in Czech, sometimes Cyrillic, often German, and only occasionally English, but boarding announcements are given in Czech, German, and English with such a strong British accent that they sound as though a computer generates them. Allow extra time to make your way around. Also be careful of your wallet or purse. Departures ("Odjezo," which you see also in German: "Abfahrt") are grouped by destinations. Compositions of trains ("Rodeni") are meticulously shown in stainless-steel showcases adjacent to complete timetables mounted on turntables. On your way to your train's platform ("Nastupiste"), take a look up at the interior of Hlavni's marvelous cupola.

The CD Centrum contains a hotel-reservations and money-change office (open 6 A.M. to 7:30 P.M.), an ATM, and train information. Also, the Prague Tourist Office has a location at Na Prikope 20, Staromestska radnice (Old City Hall), and Malostranska Mostecka Vez (the Charles Bridge).

For international tickets, go to the small "CD Travel Office" located with an outside door on the south face of Hlavni between the entrance marked "Metro" and the "Cargo" office. Tickets may be issued just as easily by Cedok's downtown office at Na Prikope 18 (Tel. 42-2-212-7359). Domestic tickets for distances up to 60 miles are sold in ticket machines as well as at the cash desks. If you arrive late for your train, you can buy your ticket from the conductor for a surcharge of about 35 cents, but be sure to report to him because if he finds you without a ticket, the surcharge is about $3.50.

Hlavni is served by one of Prague's three interconnecting metro lines with carriages dating from 2001, allowing you to move around the city easily. The Prague metro is simple. Lines *A, B,* and *C* (red, yellow, and green) interconnect at strategic points. The best way to get around town is by metro. It is fast, cheap, and reliable. Tickets are available at hotels, newsstands, and travel agencies as well as from machines perched just outside the ticket-validating machines. Directions are in English. The machines take correct change only in multiples of ticket prices. All Czech coins are accepted. Tickets are valid for one hour and are spot-checked by plain-clothes inspectors who seem to think that foreigners are likely "black travelers," but tickets valid for one, three, seven, or 15 days are more economical and convenient for frequent riders. The bus and clacking, busy streetcar system are some of the best existing in Europe. In Prague, buses and trams run from 4:30 A.M. to 11:30 P.M. Hlavni and Holesovice station are connected on metro Line *C.* Holesovice station is the end of the red line.

Prague's second international station, Holesovice, is in need of a good scrubbing, inside and out, yet the large number of change and hotel-reservations counters will dazzle you. It is a smaller, more approachable station than Hlavni. In Holesovice, EC trains arrive and depart to avoid the dead-end downtown station.

Seat and sleeping reservations counters are clearly marked by international pictographs. Near the display case you can find the composition of express and fast trains ("Radeni Expresnich") and the display of arrival and departure times. Holesovice reminds you of a small airport terminus partly because of its arrangement and partly because of the clacking departure signs.

Accommodations and money-changing agencies abound as well as food kiosks and a Czech Railroads' restaurant above. Access to the trains (in German: "Zu der Zuge") is through a tunnel with both stairs and ramps (which are good for luggage with wheels) to the Holesovice's three platforms. Like those at Hlavni, departure announcements are in three languages.

The connections between Prague and Vienna shave nearly an hour and a half off your trip by using the longer, but faster, fully electrified "Nordbahn" via Brno and Breclav into Vienna's South train station instead of the shorter route from Prague's main train station (Hlavni) via Tabor and Gmund to Vienna's Franz-Josefs-Bahnhof. Austrians strongly criticized this change because of the nine-mile additional length (and increased ticket price, which is based on distance) to Prague's less centrally located Holesovice station. You save 85 minutes traveling north and 88 minutes traveling south and have the advantage of using better Austrian carriages.

Pilsen's (the Czech Republic's second city) repainted Hlavni station looks beautifully baroque outside and conventionally modern inside. The city celebrated its 750th anniversary in 1995.

Trains of Slovakia

The Slovakian Republic Railroads, Zeleznice Slovenskej Republiky (ZSSK, *www.zsr.sk/English/index/zsr.html*), is responsible for the trains running on the 2,276-mile network of the republic. Trains follow rivers, run through mountain valleys, and in some places reach the base of high mountains. The highest train station, at 4,330 feet, is the Strbske Pleso station in the High Tatras. The lowest-altitude station, at 330 feet, is the Streda nad Bodrogom station. The main long-distance service within Slovakia runs Bratislava-Zilina-Kosice.

Express train (Expres) are red, run faster, and make fewer stops than the green (Osobny vlak) trains, which are slower and have open salon seating but no compartments. ZSSK has on order for commercial service in 2005 additional Pendolino trains similar to those in operation in the Czech Republic for operation on the Bratislava-Kosice route (reducing the current journey time from five hours to four hours, 18 minutes), Warsaw-Bratislava-Budapest, and Vienna-Bratislava-Poprad.

Bratislava's nicely remodeled and well-kept Hlavna (Main) train station is modest. It gives you a favorable first impression of Slovakia's capital. Directions are in Slovakian, but well-placed international pictographs make it easy for you to make your way around. Track numbers are marked "K Nastupistiam." Train compositions are given in the "Radenie Expresnych Vlakova Rychlikov" displays. Departures ("Odchod") are shown on the usual European yellow-paper departure posters and arrivals ("Prichod") on white. In the mezzanine you find a currency-exchange office, ATM, café, and the Bratislava Tourist Office. A back hall contains lockers, luggage checking, and WCs.

The new station at Bratislava Petrzalka is the most modern in Slovakia and was rebuilt for the reopening of the cross-border line to Vienna, but it also improves links with urban transport. Of the station's 13 tracks, two are designed for passenger trains to Vienna via Kittsee, Austria. The electrified Vienna-Bratislava line opened on December 15, 1998, allows 100-mph running, but joint customs authorities and border police demand 15 minutes at Petrzalka because they are unable to provide checks en route.

The best train to Bratislava is the ZSSK's flagship, first-class-only, EC Slovenska Strela, one of the four EC trains from Prague. The Slovenska Strela runs up to 100 mph over upgraded portions of the line in the Czech Republic. You can also reach Bratislava in one hour by Danube cruise ships from Vienna.

ZSSK's best domestic train is the first-class-only IC Dunaj between Bratislava and Kosice. It carries a refurbished dining carriage and covers the route in four hours, 48 minutes at an average speed of almost 59 mph, calling only at Zilina and Poprad.

The Tatra Electric Railroad (TEZ) operates the most scenic lines in Slovakia. Meter-gauge, electric mountain railcars climb into the High Tatra Mountains, the most beautiful part of Slovakia, on the 1908 line from Poprad Tatry to Stary Smokovec. The eight-mile climb takes some 40 minutes. You ride a 1970 Swiss-built electric cogwheel train between Strba and Strbske Pleso in the Tatras that takes 13 minutes to climb three miles, where you may change to a narrow-gauge adhesion railcar built in 2001 as a Swiss-Slovak cooperative venture.

Unfortunately, the frequent departures from Bratislava's Hlavna station take about five hours to Poprad Tatry, so it isn't feasible for you to plan a day excursion to the mountains.

Rail-Pass Travel

With a *Polrailpass,* at a moment's notice, you can hop on a train and be on your way. A Polrailpass is available from Orbis in North America (see Appendix A, *www.orbis-usa.com*), Europe, or Poland and at PKP stations within Poland. It may not be readily recognized, but it allows unlimited travel on most trains (including expresses) without prior seat reservation (subject to availability). It is advisable to make reservations for seats on EC and IC trains, and these reservations are free. Reserved sleepers and couchettes require an extra charge. To order a Polrailpass in the U.S., send to Orbis your passport number and date of travel. If you are unsure of your date of travel, Orbis can issue an open pass for you to validate at any railway station in Poland before your trip. On the other hand, if you are entering Poland by train, it will be wise to have a pre-validated pass so that you merely show it to the Polish conductor when he checks.

Adult passes are available, first and second class, for eight, 15, and 21 days' and one month's consecutive travel. Juniors under 26, having the same choices, receive 30 percent off. Children four to 10 pay half. You can refund unused fixed-date passes, less a $10 service charge, provided they are returned before you depart. Open (undated) passes can be refunded, less $10, within six months after date of issue. No refunds are granted for lost or stolen passes.

The *European East Pass* described in the Austria chapter is valid in the Czech Republic and Slovakia but not Poland, and Rail Europe also sells a *Czech Flexipass* valid on the trains of the republic only. The Czech Flexipass is available for three to eight days of travel in 15, first or second class. Children four-11 pay half; those under four travel free.

Since Prague has become so popular with German and foreign visitors, it may be convenient for you to buy a *Prague Excursion Pass*, valid for seven days, which allows round-trip travel (including all supplements) to Prague from Czech Republic borders with Germany, Austria, Poland, and Slovakia. You don't have to use the same border crossing when departing the Czech Republic, which means you can use the Excursion Pass to travel the full length of the republic from Germany to Slovakia.

Prague Excursion Passes are available in first and second classes for adults, youths, and children. You can buy them in Europe at the offices of EurAide in the Munich Hauptbahnhof (room 3, along track 11) and Berlin Zoo stations. In the U.S., Rail Europe and Destination Europe Resources sell the Prague Excursion Pass, so when you plan to buy an Excursion Pass, it is convenient to buy it at the same time you buy a GermanRail Pass or Eurail product. Note that the Czech Republic is not included in the Eurail system.

Savvy Traveling on the Trains of the Balkans

Trains of Romania—Trains of Bulgaria—Trains of former Yugoslavia—Rail-pass travel—Trains of Albania

Adventurers like to ride international trains from Western Europe through the Balkans for the experience. They get an experience to forget. They encounter shoddy trains, broken seats, disgusting toilets, failed heating, and unspeakably awful experiences without a bite to eat.

Through the Balkans by Train

Vienna-Budapest-Belgrade IC Avala

1007	dep.	Vienna (West)	arr.	1850
1335	dep.	Budapest (Keleti)	dep.	1555
2015	arr.	Belgrade	dep.	0820

Belgrade-Sofia-Istanbul Balkan Express

0800	dep.	Belgrade	arr.	2010
1723	dep.	Sofia	dep.	1009
0827	arr.	Istanbul (Sirkeci)	dep.	2300

Make sure your visas are in place before departure. Pack plenty of water and lots to eat. There are no signs, no announcements, and no coach destination boards, and you can get no information from guards who check tickets. Travel is slow, long, time-consuming, and crowded, but you can book from the U.S. or Western Europe. The Balkan Express is as grubby and seedy a piece of rolling stock as you'd ever want to see. It rattles at night along the rails between Belgrade and Istanbul. The bathrooms are filthy and the odor of stale cigarette smoke hangs over everything. There are no sleeping compartments for the long trip and poor security, but six-person couchette compartments are available. There is no dining car. On each side of the borders you cross, police check your passport, transit visas, and other identification.

Be aware that once you settle into your bed or bunk, you should never leave your carriage. The porters lock the doors between carriages, disappear into their compartments, and under no circumstance will allow you back into your paid-for berth or bunk.

Even the much better domestic trains, primarily used by locals, are daunting because of the language difficulties and crowding. Yet it is possible to get around by train and, once aboard, you have a good chance to meet and talk with residents, for trains are the most popularly used form of transportation.

Trains of Romania

Radiating from Bucharest (Bucuresti), CFR (Caile Ferate Romane, www.cfr.ro), the Romanian Railroads, provides a 6,210-mile network serving all parts of this Latin-language land. Although the British built Romania's 37-mile, first railroad in the late 1860s from Bucharest to the Danube, you can see the French influence on later construction.

The diesel railcars that CFR calls "Blue Arrows," marked as RM "Tren Rapid autoMotor," are the best way to see Romania's countryside. Eleven trains a day on the popular, 140-mile line from Bucharest to Constanza, on the Black Sea, cross the 1890-95 Saligny Bridge and causeway system. On three of them, you can remain aboard for the Black Sea resorts of Eforie and Mangalia.

Birders can travel by four trains a day 143 miles northeastward to Galati, where they can take boats downstream through the Danube delta, famous for its bird life. Dracula freaks will take the tourist line into the Transylvanian Mountains, which is also the mainline to Budapest.

Electric, locomotive-hauled day trains arrive from Budapest and you can ride overnight trains to and from Bucharest, including the Pannonia Express from Prague, Munich, and Budapest; the Dacia Express from Vienna; and the EuroNight Ister from Budapest. The night trains carry various combinations of first- and second-class sleeping cars and compartments, couchettes, and dining cars.

Try to buy a CFR timetable ("Mersul Trenurillor"). The keyed map will make it simple for you to get around. Many cities and towns have two stations. Bucharest Nord is the main station for the capital although it is at least a mile distant from the heart of Bucharest. Buses and streetcars serve the station.

CFR's best trains are InterCity and "rapid" ("accelerat") because they make the fewest stops. Train schedules are posted in CFR stations. "Sosire" means "arrival" and "Plecare" means "departure." Book your reservations for seats on long-distance trains and couchettes at a CFR Agentia or in Carpati's central office (generally open Mon.-Fri., 7:30 A.M. to 3:30 P.M.; Sat., 8:30 A.M. to 1:30 P.M.), where you will usually find someone who speaks English.

Trains of Bulgaria

The 2,696-mile Bulgarian State Railroads (Bulgarski Durzhavni Zheleznitsi, or "BDZ," *www.bg400.bg/bdz*) network fans eastward from the capital, Sofia (Sofija), to the Black Sea at Varna and through European Turkey to Istanbul. The line to Belgrade passes through Dimitovgrad, the border station, and you cross through to the wild and dramatic Dragoman Pass. Trains from the Eastern countries and Russia pass through Bucharest, entering at Ruse, before reaching Sofia.

The president of the premier Bulgarian tour operator has been quoted as saying, "Nothing works in Bulgaria. There is the normal mess that comes from destroying an old system and not having enough time to build a new system. We are in a transition period, and even this doesn't work."

BDZ's fastest trains are not the international trains but the domestic ones (average express-train speeds in Bulgaria reach 50-55 mph) between Sofia and Varna, Bulgaria's leading port and recreation area.

Sofia's main station has complete information (if you can speak Bulgarian or German—train information on the station boards is almost always shown in the Cyrillic script). There are cafes and restaurants, and hotels nearby. Contact the Bulgarian Tourist Information Center (Balkan Holidays, Appendix A) in advance for Bulgarian tourist information, and insist on train information.

Trains of Former Yugoslavia

When you visit this corner of the Balkans, you find the trains operated by no fewer than five independent railroad companies: Serbian Railways (ZS, Zeleznice Srbije), Railways of Montenegro (ZCG, Zeleznice Crne Gore), Macedonian Railways (MZ), Bosnian Serb Railways (ZRS), and Bosnian Croat-Muslim Railways (ZHB), as well the Railroads of Kosovo named Kekurudhat e Kosoves/Kosovske Zeleznice (HeK/KZ) in Albanian and Serb respectively, which are under the control of the United Nations. Your train stops at every border crossing to change locomotives.

Amidst the political turmoil, some railroads are making a slow recovery. Notably, international service between Zagreb and Sarajevo was restored in 2001 (taking over nine hours because of border checks and locomotive change) and the railroad bridge over the Danube was replaced, allowing train services to resume between Belgrade and Budapest.

Europe's most spectacular line, with Eastern Europe's finest scenery, reopened in November 1999 between Belgrade and the seaport of Bar on the Adriatic coast. Due to political tensions between Serbia and Montenegro, trains change locomotives at the border station of Vrbnica, as the respective railroads are unwilling to let their locos leave their administrative areas. A first-class-only Express train makes the eight-hour trip over breathtaking viaducts but arrives in Bar after darkness falls, except during the longest days of June. *Tip:* It is worth it.

Train connections from Serbia into Kosovo remain closed as Serbia is not interested in repairing the bridges at present, although Britain, France, and Germany have each supplied diesel locomotives to Kosovo.

Rail-Pass Travel

Unlike other Eurail products, starting in 2004, Eurail Selectpasses are valid in Romania, so that you may select Romania-Hungary-Austria for your three-country Eurail Selectpass.

Valid on the national networks of Romania and Bulgaria, the Romanian Railpass and the Bulgarian Flexipass, respectively, are valid each for first class for any three days within 15 days and one month.

The Balkan Flexipass covers both countries plus Greece, Macedonia, Turkey, and Serbia and Montenegro. It is available for five, 10, or 15 days of travel within one month, either as an adult first-class flexipass or special discounted flexipass for those under 26 or over 60. Children four to 11 pay half the adult fare; those under four travel free.

These passes offer you the freedom of the trains and an excellent way of escaping the bureaucracies of the train stations. The Balkan Flexipass also includes special prices on Superfast Ferries/Blue Star Ferries between Patras and Ancona or Bari. They allow you a 25 percent discount on a day cruise from Athens to Egina, Hydra, and Poros and a reduction of 30 percent on Attica Enterprises/Blue Star Ferries services to Aegean islands. Hotel Oscar in Athens, Hotel Beograd in Belgrade, Hotel Zeleznicar in Vrnjacka Banja, and Hotel Astoria in Bucharest also offer special prices.

Trains of Albania

Albania was a latecomer to the European railroad system. All of Albanian Railroads' (Hekurudhae e Shqiperise, HSH) passenger system was built by "volunteer" labor gangs after the Second World War, with Chinese help. Tirana (Tirane) is the capital, but the port of Durres is the focal point of HSH's 234-mile system.

During the past decade, vandalism and open thievery paralyzed most of HSH's system, but 1.1 million passengers traveled by train over the first six months of 2000, which was an increase of 8.4 percent over 1999. The increasing number of riders is due to service improvements as well as the use of "new" Austrian and Italian carriages. In 2000, the Japanese government provided $1.9 million to buy spare parts for Czech-built locomotives and to help rebuild the system. The lines from Durres to Tirana and Pogradec are operational and the line connecting Fier and Ballsh was restored in 2000. The 22-mile line to Tirana carries six one-class trains a day, taking nearly an hour.

The 1984 line from Shkoder to Podgorica (formerly Titograd, in Montenegro) was reopened in 2002, for freight only. The only known passenger-carrying train was the line's inaugural one, which only took passengers from Podgorica as far as the Albanian border at Hani-Hotit. The Bajza international freight train station, which connects Albania's railroad system to Europe through Montenegro, has reopened.

Italy's Adriatica Line ferries serve Durres, with sailings from Trieste and Bari (rail passes not valid); you also can cross from Corfu. These boats from Italy are the easiest route to Albania, but shipping was greatly dislocated by the Kosovo War and the financial insolvency of the Adriatica Line. The longest, but most spectacular, way to Tirana is by the winding, nine-hour bus ride from Skopje, Macedonia, along sheer mountain roads and past Lake Ohrid.

Savvy Traveling on the Trains of the C.I.S. and Baltic States

Russian Railroads—Moscow—St. Petersburg—Trains of the Ukraine—Trains of the Baltic States—Trains of Belarus—Trains of Moldova

Russian Railroads

Russian Railroads (Rossiyskie Zeleznue Dorogi, RZhD, *www.express-2.ru*) is the most important mode of transportation in the country. RZhD carries some 1.5 trillion passengers a year. For over four decades, former Soviet Railroads (SZhD) and now Russian Railroads have operated the world's most extensive network. Electrified trains take you through areas where temperatures range from -76 degrees in winter to 104 degrees in summer, with winds up to 100 mph.

When you arrive in Moscow's Kiev train station and there is not one sign that you can read or understand—don't worry. If you could read them and understand them they wouldn't help you. There is no place to make hotel arrangements and no place to change money (not that you would want to), and it is very difficult to make train reservations or legally buy train tickets in Russia.

A Russian timetable is not available—it would be too expensive to produce. The clerks at the windows speak no foreign language, and reservations are completely sold out 45 days in advance anyway.

The director of the Russian Ministry of Transportation noted that Russia's trains are often crowded because train travel is much less expensive than flying, but it is not cheap when booked by a foreigner. For example, the one-way fare between Moscow and St. Petersburg is $146 for soft class and $82 for hard class (plus a hefty booking fee), but foreigners are expected to pay more than Russians do. Prices of Aeroflot tickets increased five- to sevenfold when Aeroflot began to compete internationally. Passengers who formerly traveled by air now can't afford it, and take trains. Only business and emergency travelers fly—or those going to places where it is possible only to fly. "It's practically impossible for an American to go up and buy a train ticket" in the C.I.S., the director said.

It's also difficult for a Russian to buy a ticket. A line forms when tickets go on sale, and the tickets are sold out in two or three days except for the quota set aside for foreign tourists, VIPs, and essential business travelers. This special allocation is released an hour before train departure.

There is a black market for railroad tickets. You can find scalpers outside most train stations asking you (in Russian) whether you need a ticket. Don't worry about finding a scalper—he will find you. Most of them are probably reliable, but you can never be sure.

Visitors to Moscow will look in vain for a Russian Railroads' office. They have no staff that can speak English. If you wish to brave long lines and take a gamble, you can visit the Central Railway Agency at Griboedova Str. 6. There you can wait two to three hours and still not be certain of getting tickets, even when you pay in dollars. "Buying a ticket in the U.S. is the only proper way to make a trip in my country," the spokesman said. Tickets and reservations for Russian carriages from Western European cities to Russia and return can also be made at the International Ticketing Office of major European train stations, although reservations must be made before 9 A.M. on the day of departure. For tickets within Russia, agents in Western European train stations can also telex Russia, but they need a four-day minimum lead time.

There are 17 independent divisions in Russia. They include:

• The Moscow Railroad, which spreads over the territory of almost all European Central Russia, from Moscow in the north to Kursk in the south.

• The October Railroad, which links St. Petersburg with Moscow, Novgorod, Pskov, Petrozavodsk, Helsinki, and Murmansk in the north and is the largest division, with a 9,000-mile network. Its headquarters is in St. Petersburg. This was the first Russian passenger railroad. Its construction began in 1836, and the first segment from St. Petersburg to the czar's residence (now Pushkin) was completed in 1837.

• The Northern Railroad, including the Yaroslav Division with more than 39 pairs of daily commuter trains, the Moscow-Aleksandrov Division, the Kostroma Division, and the Vologda Division.

The most interesting and important lines include Moscow to St. Petersburg ($146, soft class), to the Baltic States (about $200), to Kiev ($185), to Minsk ($172), to Warsaw ($306), to Prague ($363), and to Helsinki ($240), plus the Trans-Siberian. It is convenient to ride these routes because you can reserve them in advance and not have to struggle for tickets and reservations.

The secret is to make your reservation as early as possible. Tickets are only sold with reservations for a carriage ("vagon") and seat ("mesto"). Dealing with the Russians takes time. Try to make reservations 45 days in advance if possible; seven to 10 days is dicey.

The prestige/name trains are the most comfortable. The Red Arrow is Russia's most famous, but all prestige trains are quality trains and are almost the same. They run to practically every major city of the former Soviet Union, 160 trains a day.

When you first see them, the intimidating Russian cars look straight from *Dr. Zhivago:* high, formidable, and military green. Except for the prestige cars, they all look the same, with no markings on the outside. The only difference is the number of layers of paint covering the rust of the Russian winters. The prestige trains to Kiev, named the Kiev and the Ukrania, are blue. The six Red Arrow trains to St. Petersburg are red. The prestige trains to the Volga region and to the north are dark yellow. The Trans-Siberian is Bordeaux red.

Russian trains are different from those in the West. When you board you see how difficult the large size of the Russian carriages makes it to hoist luggage aboard. Russian trains generally carry bunks instead of seats. In the West, the sleeping cars have one, two, or three bunks on one wall within about a four-foot-by-six-foot space with washbasin and hangers on the facing wall. Russian compartments have four bunks (two on each side, one above another) per compartment in second class ("hard") and two bunks (one on each side, with no empty bunk hanging above) per compartment in first class ("soft"). Neither has a washbasin within a five-foot-by-six-foot space, and therefore they offer more room.

Attendants ("provodnik," if male; "provodnitsa," if female) provide each bunk with a pillow; a thin, but sufficient, mattress pad; linen consisting of a bottom sheet, clean pillowcase, and either a fresh blanket cover (better) in which you insert your blanket, or a top sheet, plus the blanket; and towel (sometimes there is a small charge for linen). Berths are sold without sex distinction. WCs are at the end of every car. An attendant for every car furnishes tea and hot water from an iron samovar (if you want coffee, take instant with you) but has absolutely no other snack or refreshment.

When the smaller Western European Czech and Polish sleeping carriages are hooked together with Russian ones, their unequal heights make crossing/jumping between them at 40 mph something out of an action movie.

Russian trains carry very basic restaurant cars ("Pectopah") located somewhere in the middle, but the menus are limited. The waiter won't speak English. Don't expect breakfast, lunch, and dinner. Don't expect breakfast at all. Breakfast is the same as dinner. Eggs are available mid-afternoon when a waiter pulls an aluminum basket of hard-boiled eggs through the train. The menus you receive (in Russian) are the same for any and every meal: an excellent soup, a salad, a meat you may or may not be able to identify, lots of potatoes, Coca-Cola (not water), and tea or instant coffee from Israel. Beer is the most readily available item.

You should do what the Russians do: bring with you all the food and drink (except beer, which you buy aboard) you may need—salami, cheese, fruit, bread, etc. At mealtimes you will offer your spread to your neighbors. Don't count on finding food in the stations or from vendors along the track.

Why RZhD runs on wider gauge (five feet) than the rest of Europe, which is four feet, 8½ inches (except in Iberia, which is five feet, 6 inches), is not clear, but the notion that it was built differently to protect Russia from military invasion has been discredited. It is possible that, as in England, engineers determined the width between wheels from the horse-drawn postal coaches of the time, which were wider spaced in Russia than in England. Alternately, the English—where the first locomotive was ordered—measured the width between the inside of the rails and the Russians from the outside. Many historians prefer the report that when the czar received the news that the English had built the first railroad, the czar replied, "Why then, we must have one—but ours will be bigger."

All other things being equal, wide gauge is safer than standard gauge, but all other things are never equal, and in fact maintenance of the rail bed is usually considered the most important safety factor.

For travelers, the wider gauge is a major disadvantage. You must suffer the time wasted entering and leaving the C.I.S. in order to adjust the wheel spacing to the different gauge. It's interesting to watch—but it makes for almost three hours of lost time. First your carriage, with you in it, is hauled to a special facility beside mechanical screw jacks; your carriage is lifted with much banging, great bumping, and violent slamming; the old bogies are rolled away; new ones are rolled below; and your carriage is lowered onto them and pinned through a hole in the floor of the WC. The mechanics are generally pleased with their work when your carriage finally rolls successfully away.

There's real interest in traveling by train into Russia, but a train of paperwork follows you, starting with the visa problem (*www.intourist.com*). When you book hotels or tours through a travel agency, the agency will obtain your visa for you, for an additional fee, and this is the most practical way to go.

The best way to Moscow by train from the West is via St. Petersburg from Helsinki. From Central Europe, it is easier to travel from Berlin via Warsaw so that you pass through Belarus rather than the Ukraine and do not need to buy a Ukrainian visa in addition to your Russian one.

Moscow

On the preferred route from the West to Moscow via Belarus you will travel two days and two nights. The Jan Kiepura carries first- and second-class carriages between Cologne and Moscow, and a dining carriage between Brest and Moscow. The Chopin carries first- and second-class carriages between Vienna and Moscow. The Moskva Express carries first- and second-class sleeping cars between Berlin and Moscow, and the Vltava carries first- and second-class sleeping cars between Prague and Moscow. There are also second-class sleeping cars between Moscow and Budapest and first- and second-class sleeping cars between Moscow and Venice (journey of three nights).

In Moscow you will find nine train stations (called "Vokzal," from London's Vauxhall Gardens, where the czar first saw a train in the 1830s), but Westerners usually use only four or five. Trains from Byelorusski station, which is also known as Smolenski station, serve the line to Belarus and Warsaw; trains from Kiev station ("Kievskiy Vokzal") serve Kiev, the Ukraine, and the Balkans; Oktyabrskaya station serves St. Petersburg; and Yaroslavl station ("Yaroslavskiy Vokzal") is the terminus for the Trans-Siberian train. The others are named Kazanskiy, Kursk, Paveletskiy, Rizhski, and Savelovskiy.

The Oktyabrskaya station, next to the Yaroslavl station, has remarkable, arching eaves and almost whimsical architecture of grand design and magnificent presence. Its interior is Moscow's best kept. It is accessible, with clean lines, counters selling magazines, etc., and windows for ticketing in the outer hall. There is a striking alabaster bust of Lenin dominating the center. The spaces leading to the platforms, which are outside in back of the station, are filled with a wonderful mingling of life. Kiosks and glassed stalls stand in irregular, makeshift rows, their occupants selling anything and everything at very low ruble prices. Passersby crowd to see what is for sale and at what price.

At adjacent Yaroslavl some platforms are covered with galvanized iron; the rest are open. Boarding occurs outdoors. Inside Yaroslavl is a large railroad map of the stations of the former Soviet Union served by Yaroslavl, which extend to Vladivostok and Murmansk. Above the ticket counters, a long schematic drawing divides the Trans-Siberian route into eight different time zones. The hall is marked with columns and an escalator, shops, chairs for waiting, and a bank of telephones. Across the street is the gingerbready configuration of Kazanskiy station with trains to Rostov-on-Don, Kazan, Volgograd, and Central Asian republics.

If Oktyabrskaya station is Moscow's best, Kiev station is the worst. It is crowded, cheap, and stifling.

Between Yaroslavl and Oktyabrskaya stations is a gray building that reminds you of an Orthodox church. It is the Komsomolskaya metro station, which you can use to get there. Smolenski train station is beside the metro stop of the same name. Kiev station is by Kievskaya metro. All three metro stations are on the Circle Line (Koltsevaya Linia), but you will need time to master the Cyrillic complexity of the highly acclaimed and highly bewildering Moscow metro system.

Despite rumor to the contrary, taxis are available at the train stations, usually from in front, but not necessarily where the station signs indicate, and they don't all have yellow lights on the roof. The sign to look for is a double row of checkered squares. In Moscow and St. Petersburg, the taxi drivers seem to be more decent than in many large cities—which is something you can't say for the condition of their cabs or their driving safety. Just tell them you are paying in dollars and they become lambs. Then you can agree on the fare before you put your luggage in the trunk.

St. Petersburg

When you arrive from Moscow in St. Petersburg's Moscow ("Moskovskiy Vokzal") station, you will be stunned. Deja vu. Could you have taken the wrong train and returned to where you started? The interior of St. Petersburg's Moscow station is identical to the interior of Moscow's Oktyabrskaya station, where you departed. Lenin's alabaster bust stands in St. Petersburg just as it did in Moscow. The rectangular hall and the high ceiling of geometric shapes came from the same workshop.

St. Petersburg has five mainline stations. Three of them, Warsaw, Vitebsk, and Finland, share the same metro line. Small Varshavskiy Vokzal (meaning Warsaw station) is peeling yellow plaster with an enormous statue of Lenin facing the highway. Ticket scalpers gathered on the side will approach you in Russian as you pass. Arrivals see the sign that reads, not "St. Petersburg," but "Leningrad," in large Roman letters. Most people, especially in Moscow, by habit often refer to the city by its former name. At No. 2 window you will find someone for international traffic. It will save you trouble if you have your train ticket validated here. St. Petersburg's peeling and run-down Baltic ("Baltiskiy Vokzal") train station is a 10-minute walk from the Warsaw station, but only local trains leave from here in the direction of the Baltic States. The adjacent Baltic metro station is the closest one to Warsaw station as well.

Vitebsk ("Vitebskiy Vokzal") station, with a green patina roof and tile floors, is named for the Belarussian city of the same name. It is the terminus for trains due south to Kiev and Odessa. Follow the signs showing an old-fashioned locomotive to the platforms. A metro station is adjacent.

On the platform of the Finland station ("Finlyandskiy Vokzal") you see the train preserved under glass in which Lenin arrived in Petrograd, as it was known then, on October 7, 1917 (the October revolution was on October 25, but a change in calendar makes it now November 7). The train was a gift of the Finnish people to the Russian people. Finland station's large hall contains a marble floor that is broken in many places.

As part of St. Petersburg's 300th anniversary celebrations, Ladoga station (Ladozhski Vokzal) opened on May 16, 2003, farther east of the city center, near the Neva River crossing. You can use Ladozhskaya metro station.

Ladoga station is the terminus for the Sibelius and Repin trains from Helsinki, Finland, and a stop for the Tolstoi, which runs Helsinki-St. Petersburg-Moscow. Each year 150,000 Finns visit Russia. You won't have trouble paying with euros.

From the West, trains to St. Petersburg via Warsaw, a segment of Belarus, and then Vilnius (Lithuania) leave Cologne (Hbf.) at 7:16 P.M. twice a week and Berlin at 11:02 P.M. nightly, but clearly the easiest way to St. Petersburg is to take a Finnish day train or Russian night train from Helsinki (see "Scandinavia and Finland" chapter).

Trains of the Ukraine

A Russian visa is not sufficient to enter the Ukraine, but you may buy a Ukrainian visa at the border. There are no photos required, but the procedure is not as simple as it might be.

When you reach the Ukraine, literally a small army of customs officers and border guards is waiting for the train. You fill out a Cyrillic-script customs declaration form. Two uniformed border guards march you into a dingy back room. You fill out a second form (with directions in English and Ukrainian) and eventually receive an odd strip of paper, which you take to an obscurely located bank in a back building and pay their fee—only crisp notes are accepted. When you return, guards take your bank receipt, give back your passport, now with an "emergency" Ukrainian visa stamp, and your Russian visa, and you rush to rejoin your train.

Your train isn't there.

It is early in the morning. As well as you can make out, the Cyrillic departure board says a train to Moscow leaves at 10:30 A.M. You are stranded, without breakfast, in a station with no restaurant and nothing to eat. Finally your train pulls in. Your porters are genuinely happy to see you. They were wondering what to do with your possessions.

The Ukrainian Railroads (Ukrainska Zaliznitsa, UZ, *www.uz.gov.ua/index_eng.html*) is gradually moving away from its Russian heritage, with a blue livery replacing military green and by purchasing new trains with open seating instead of compartments for long-distance and local service. Upgrading the 375-mile line between Kiev and Kharkov in 2003 meant that passenger trains could travel up to 80 mph and cover the distance in five hours, 30 minutes instead of the former journey time of 12 hours.

Kiev (Kyiv) is the capital of the Ukraine. People like to walk below the gleaming domes of ancient churches in Kiev. To stroll along Khreshchatyk, the main street, past buildings painted in pastels and shaded by chestnuts, is to feel an Old World softness that Moscow seldom matches.

The Ukraine has a well-developed transportation network. With a total length of 14,500 miles, UZ is divided into six regions: Donetsk Railroads (Donetsk), L'vov Railroads (L'vov), Odessa Railroads (Odessa), By-Dnieper Railroads (Dniepropetrovsk), South Railroads (Kharkov), and Southwest Railroads (Kiev).

Trains of the Baltic States

With the admission of the three Baltic States into the European Union (EU) on May 1, 2004, one hopes that the railroad infrastructure between the nations will improve. Getting between Latvia and Estonia by train is impossible because of the disconnect on the Estonian side. On local routes, served by the Estonian (EVR, Eesti Raudtee, *www.evr.ee*), Latvian (LVD, Latvijas dzelzcels, *www.lvd.lv*), and Lithuanian railroads (LG, Valstybine Imone Lietuvos Gelezinkeliai, *www.randberg.com/li/lithrailways.html*), which are under separate managements, you will find yourself sitting on benches, three across on both sides of the aisle.

To avoid having to get a Belarus or Russian visa, enter the Baltic States via Sestokai, which is the only border crossing point between Poland and Lithuania. The Balti Ekspress departs Warsaw's Centraina station early in the morning. The train carries first- and second-class carriages and an odd dining carriage that closes at noon. You pass through the Polish border station at Trakiszki, with a long wait for Polish customs, and continue on standard-gauge rails to Mackawa, where Lithuanian border checks are made, to Sestokai, which is the end of the line for standard gauge. You walk across the border to a standing, second-class-only train that reaches Vilnius in the evening after an 11-hour trip. With the Balti, you must change trains at the border, but this eliminates waiting for the time-consuming change-of-gauge ritual required for entering Belarus or the Ukraine.

Since the end of October 2000, the night train between Warsaw and Vilnius consists of sleeper cars fitted with Polish adjustable-gauge wheel sets allowing the vehicles to move directly from European gauge to broad gauge. This was the first time passengers had a direct connection between the two neighboring countries, avoiding the need to transit Belarus and eliminating several border checks and the need for visa applications. The crossing at the Mackawa-Trakiszki border point is cut from two hours to a few minutes.

All other travel to the Baltic States by train from Western Europe or Finland takes you through Russia or Belarus. In this case you will need also a one- or two-entry Russian transit visa, which you should obtain before you leave. Trains run St. Petersburg-Tallinn and to Moscow-Riga and Vilnius.

Lithuania. Vilnius's train station is quite acceptable by Western standards. Signs are written in English. Change your money in the office in the waiting hall on the left or at the 24-hour change counter to the left as you exit. Leave your luggage at the storage in the basement (open 24 hours). Find its entrance on the right as you face the station. Electric bus lines 2, 5, and 7 take you from in front of the station to the center of town. Buy your bus tickets at the newsstand in the main hall.

U.S. and U.K. citizens require no visa to enter any of the Baltic States; a 90-day stay is permitted. For multiple-entry visas or longer stays, contact the consulate or embassy of the state in question (Appendix A). Canadian citizens require a visa for any one of the Baltic States to enter the others at will.

Latvia. Day and night second-class-only trains run between Vilnius and Riga taking seven hours by night and five and a half hours by day. *Tip:* These do not run daily; check the calendar. On alternate days, you can take a bus to Riga. Vilnius bus station is next to the Vilnius train station.

You may buy tickets for immediate departures in Riga's Central station ("Centrala Stacija") in the main departure hall on the right of the entrance, counters 3 to 9. Buy tickets for the electric commuter trains in the smaller departure hall on the right of the station. For advance bookings, go into the smaller local-train departure hall, on your right.

Modernized electric trains have been reliveried from greenish gray to bluish yellow. Passenger carriages contain upholstered seats. Station arrivals are announced by voice in displays. Heating in the walls of the train maintain a comfortable temperature. Avoid the so-called "obshti" and "platzkart" carriages, which are very crowded. For overnight trips choose the "coupe," four-bunk compartments, or, on the Latvijas Ekspresis to Moscow, the first-class "SV," two-bunk compartments with video.

Estonia. The Tallinn train station supports local trains to many cities in Estonia and the Tallinna Ekspress to and from Moscow. The station is small but with a busy shopping annex for fresh, take-away nourishment.

The best way to visit Estonia is by ferry. After all, Tallinn was a Hansa port, and it still shows, thanks to careful preservation and restoration. Ferries cross frequently from Helsinki, and during the summer you can arrive by ship from Rostock, Germany.

Trains of Belarus

Political ties are very close between Belarus (*www.Belarus.net*) and Russia. There are no customs checks at their common border. The trains of the Belarussian Railroads (Bielorusse Zeleznue Dorogi, BCZ) are generally a legacy of Soviet rule. Minsk, the capital of Belarus, is located on the Moscow-Warsaw mainline, so many passengers will pass through Minsk in the middle of the night, except for the Moskva Express, which arrives at 12:28 P.M., having left Berlin Lichtenberg station at 6:12 P.M., and the Jan Kiepura, which arrives at 9:28 P.M. Day and night prestige trains connect Minsk with Moscow.

Buy your tickets for C.I.S. and Western European destinations in the main international ticket hall on the first floor of Minsk train station and tickets for local trains in the smaller ticket hall on the ground floor. Only Russian is spoken. An "obshchy" is a single seat and a "mezhoblastnoy" is one that reclines. "Platskartny" carriages are divided into six-bunk compartments with no doors. "Coupes" are four-bunk compartments with doors.

Trains of Moldova

Since Moldova's independence from the former U.S.S.R., Caile Ferate Moldova (SFM, Moldovan Railroads) has had to cope with many problems. Latin script has replaced Cyrillic letters. A major problem is the broad-gauge network, which requires a change of gauge for trains coming from Romania. The trains of the Russian Railroads serve Kishinev (Chisinau) from Kiev or Odessa. The overnight Prietenia, which uses Russian-style sleeping carriages, and Romania Express trains serve Kishinev from Bucharest.

Visas for Moldova are issued only upon authorization by the Moldovan Foreign Ministry. A Moldovan visa is valid for transit through Russia.

Appendix A

Train Information, Tourist Offices, Consulates, and Embassies

U.S.

Alpine Tourist Commission
P.O. Box 5513
New York, NY 10185-5513
Tel. 212-757-5944, Ext. 223
Fax 212-262-6116
www.alpseurope.com

Austrian Tourist Office
P.O. Box 1142
New York, NY 10108-1142
Tel. 212-944-6880
Fax 212-730-4568
www.Austria-tourism.at

Austrian Tourist Office
6520 Platt Avenue, Suite 561
West Hills, CA 91307-3218
Tel. 818-999-4030
Fax 818-999-3910
www.Austria-tourism.at

Balkan Holidays (for Bulgaria)
41 E. 42nd Street
New York, NY 10017
Tel. 212-573-5530

Belarus Embassy
1619 New Hampshire Avenue, N.W.
Washington, DC 20009
Tel. 202-986-1815
www.belarusembassy.org

Belgian Tourist Office
780 Third Avenue, #1501
New York, NY 10017
Tel. 212-758-8130
Fax 212-355-7675
www.visitbelgium.com

Berlin Convention & Visitors Bureau
P.O. Box 46507
Los Angeles, CA 90046
Tel. 323-658-5040
Fax 323-658-8472
www.berlin-tourism.de

British Tourist Authority
(Visit Britain)
551 Fifth Avenue, Suite 701
New York, NY 10176-0799
Tel. 800-GO2-BRIT
Fax 212-986-1188
www.visitbritain.com/usa

British Tourist Authority
625 N. Michigan Avenue, Suite 1001
Chicago, IL 60611
Tel. 800-462-2748
Fax 312-787-9641
www.visitbritain.com/usa

British Tourist Authority
10880 Wilshire Boulevard., Suite 570
Los Angeles, CA 90024
Tel. 310-470-2782
Fax 310-470-8549
www.visitbritain.com/usa

BritRail
Tel. 877-677-1066
Fax 877-477-1066
www.britrail.net

Bulgarian Ministry of Economy
(no U.S. office)
4, Lege Str.
1000 Sofia, Bulgaria
www.mi.government.bg

CIE Tours International
100 Hanover Avenue
P.O. Box 501
Cedar Knolls, NJ 07927-0501
Fax 800-338-3964
www.cietours.com

CIT Rail
15 W. 44th Street, 10th Floor
New York, NY 10036
www.cit-rail.com

Croatian National Tourist Office
350 Fifth Avenue, Suite 4003
New York, NY 10118
Tel. 800-829-4416
Fax 212-279-8683
www.htz.hr

Czech Tourist Authority
1109 Madison Avenue
New York, NY 10028
Tel. 212-288-0830
Fax 212-288-0971
www.czechcenter.com

Danish Tourist Board
655 Third Avenue, Suite 1810
New York, NY 10017
Tel. 212-885-9700
Fax 212-885-9726
www.visitdenmark.com

Destination Europe Resources
9501 W. Devon Avenue
Rosemont, IL 60018-4832
Tel. 888-337-7350
Fax 800-282-7474
www.dertravel.com

Estonian Tourist Board
(no U.S. office)
Roosikrantsi 11
10119 Tallinn, Estonia
visitestonia.com

EurAide, Inc.
P.O. Box 2375
Naperville, IL 60567
Tel. 708-420-2343
Fax 708-420-2369
www.euraide.de

European Travel Commission
One Rockefeller Plaza, Suite 214
New York, NY 10020
www.visiteurope.com

Finnish Tourist Board
655 Third Avenue, Suite 1810
New York, NY 10017
Tel. 212-885-9700
Fax 212-885-9710
www.gofinland.org

French Government Tourist Office
444 Madison Avenue, 16th Floor
New York, NY 10022-6903
Tel. 410-286-8310
Fax 212-838-7855
www.franceguide.com

French Government Tourist Office
9454 Wilshire Boulevard, Suite 210
Beverly Hills, CA 90212-2967
Tel. 410-286-8310
Fax 310-276-2835
www.franceguide.com

French Government Tourist Office
875 N. Michigan Avenue, Suite 3214
Chicago, IL 60611-2819
Tel. 410-286-8310
Fax 312-337-6339
www.franceguide.com

FrenchRail. *See* Rail Europe

German National Tourist Office
122 E. 42nd Street, 52nd Floor
New York, NY 10168-0072
Tel. 212-661-7200
Fax 212-661-7174
www.germany-tourism.de

German National Tourist Office
401 N. Michigan Avenue
Chicago, IL 60611-4212
Tel. 312-644-4212
Fax 312-644-0724
www.germany-tourism.de

German National Tourist Office
P.O. Box 641009
Los Angeles, CA 90064
Tel. 310-234-0250
Fax 310-474-1604
www.germany-tourism.de

Greek National Tourist Organization
645 Fifth Avenue, 5th floor
New York, NY 10022
Tel. 212-421-5777
Fax 212-826-6940
www.gnto.gr

Hungarian National Tourist Office
150 E. 58th Street, 33rd Floor
New York, NY 10155-3398
Tel. 212-355-0240
Fax 212-207-4103
www.gotohungary.com

Irish Railroads. *See* CIE Tours
    International

Irish Tourist Board
(Tourism Ireland)
345 Park Avenue
New York, NY 10154
Tel. 212-418-0800
Fax 212-751-4758
www.tourismireland.com

Italian Government Tourist Board
630 Fifth Avenue
New York, NY 10111
Tel. 212-245-4822
Fax 212-586-9249
www.italiantourism.com

Italian Government Tourist Board
500 N. Michigan Avenue, Suite 2240
Chicago, IL 60611
Tel. 312-644-0996
Fax 312-644-3019
www.italiantourism.com

Italian Government Tourist Board
12400 Wilshire Boulevard, Suite 550
Los Angeles, CA 90025
Tel. 310-820-1898
Fax 310-820-6357
www.italiantourism.com

Italian State Railroads. *See* CIT Rail

Latvian Tourism Development Agency
(no U.S. office)
Pils Laukums 4
Riga, LV-1050, Latvia
www.latviatourism.lv

Lithuanian State Department of
   Tourism
(no U.S. office)
Vilnius Str. 4/35
LT-2600 Vilnius, Lithuania

Luxembourg National Tourist Office
17 Beekman Place
New York, NY 10022
Tel. 212-935-8888
Fax 212-935-5896
www.visitluxembourg.com

Monaco Government Tourist Office
565 Fifth Avenue, 23rd Floor
New York, NY 10017
Tel. 800-753-9697
Fax 212-286-9890
www.Monaco-tourism.com

Netherlands Board of Tourism
355 Lexington Avenue, 19th Floor
New York, NY 10017
Tel. 888-GO-HOLLAND
www.goholland.com

Netherlands Board of Tourism
11101 Aviation Boulevard, Suite 200
Los Angeles, CA 90045
Tel. 310-348-9339
Fax 310-348-9344
Tel. 800-GO-HOLLAND
www.goholland.com

Northern Ireland Tourist Board
551 Fifth Avenue, Suite 701
New York, NY 10176-0799
Tel. 212-922-0101
www.discovernothernireland.com

Norwegian Tourist Board
www.norway.org

Orbis Polish Travel Bureau
342 Madison Avenue, Suite 1512
New York, NY 10173
Tel. 800-223-6037
Fax 212-682-4715
www.orbis-usa.com

Polish National Tourist Office
5 Marineview Plaza
Hoboken, NJ 07030
Tel. 201-420-9910
Fax 201-584-9153
www.polandtour.org

Portuguese National Tourist Office
590 Fifth Avenue
New York, NY 10036
Tel. 800-PORTUGAL
Fax 212-764-6137

Rail Europe (French/SwissRail)
500 Mamaronech Avenue, Suite 314
Harrison, NY 10528
Tel. 888-382-7245
Fax 800-432-1329
www.raileurope.com

Romanian National Tourist Office
14 E. 38th Street, 12th Floor
New York, NY 10016
Tel. 212-545-8484
Fax 212-251-0429
www.Romaniatourism.com

Russian Federation Embassy
1825 Phelps Place, N.W.
Washington, DC 20008
Tel. 202-939-8907
Fax 202-483-7579

Russian National Tourist Office
13 W. 42nd Street, Suite 412
New York, NY 10036
Tel. 877-221-7120
Fax 212-575-3434
www.Russia-travel.com

Slovak Republic Embassy
10 E. 40th Street
New York, NY 10016
Tel. 212-679-7044
Fax 212-679-7045
www.slovakiatourism.sk

Slovenia Tourist Office
345 E. 12th Street (mail only)
New York, NY 10003
www.slovenia-tourism.si

Spain, Tourist Office of
666 Fifth Avenue, 35th Floor
New York, NY 10103
Tel. 212-759-8822
Fax 212-265-8864
www.okspain.org

Spain, Tourist Office of
San Vicente Plaza Building
8383 Wilshire Boulevard, Suite 956
Beverly Hills, CA 90211
Tel. 323-658-7188
Fax 323-658-1061
www.okspain.org

Spain, Tourist Office of
845 N. Michigan Avenue, Suite 915-E
Chicago, IL 60611
Tel. 312-642-1992
Fax 312-642-9817
www.okspain.org

Spain, Tourist Office of
1221 Brickell Avenue, Suite 1850
Miami, FL 33131
Tel. 305-358-1992
Fax 305-358-8223
www.okspain.org

Swedish Travel & Tourism Council
655 Third Avenue, Suite 1810
New York, NY 10017
Tel. 212-885-9700
Fax 212-885-9710
www.visit-sweden.com

Swiss Federal Railroads. *See* Rail
    Europe

Switzerland Tourism
608 Fifth Avenue
New York, NY 10020
Tel. 011-800-100-200-30
Fax 877-794-8037
www.myswitzerland.com

Switzerland Tourism
501 Santa Monica Boulevard, Suite
    607
Santa Monica, CA 90401
Tel. 310-260-2421
Fax 310-260-2923
www.myswitzerland.com

Ukrainian Consulate
240 E. 49th Street
New York, NY 10017
www.Ukraine.org

Yugoslavian Embassy
2410 California Street, N.W.
Washington, DC 20008
www.mfa.gov.yu
www.visitmontenegro.com

CANADA

Austrian National Tourist Office
2 Bloor Street, E., Suite 3330
Toronto, Ont M4W 1A8
Tel. 416-967-3381
Fax 416-967-4101
www.anto.com

Belgian Tourist Office
P.O. Box 760
Succursale N.D.G.
Montreal, P.Q. H4A 3S2
Tel. 514-484-3594
Fax 514-489-8965
visitbelgium.com

British Tourist Authority
111 Avenue Road, Suite 450
Toronto, Ont M5R 3J8
Tel. 416-925-6326
Fax 416-961-2175
www.visitbritain.com

BritRail
Tel. 877-677-1066
Fax 877-477-1066
www.britrail.net

CIT Tours
80 Tiverton Court, Suite 401
Markham, Ont L3R0G4
Tel. 800-387-0711
www.cittours-canada.com

CIT Tours
666 Sherbrooke St., O., Suite 901
Montreal, P.Q. H3A 1E7
Tel. 800-361-7799
www.cittours-canada.com

Czech Republic
P.O. Box 198
Exchange Tower
2 First Canadian Place, 14th Floor
Toronto, Ont M5X 1A6

DER Rail
904 The East Mall
Etobicoke, Ont M9B 6K2
Tel. 416-695-1211
Fax 416-695-4700

Estonian Consulate
958 Broadview Avenue
Toronto, Ont M4K 2R6
Tel. 416-461-0764

French Government Tourist Office
30 St. Patrick Street, Suite 700
Toronto, Ont M5T 3A3
Tel. 416-593-6427

GermanRail. *See* DER Rail

Greek National Tourist Organization
Main Level, 1300 Bay Street
Toronto, Ont M5R 3K8
Tel. 416-968-2220
Fax 416-968-6533
www.gnto.gr

Irish Tourist Board
160 Bloor Street, E., Suite 1150
Toronto, Ont M4W 1B9
Tel. 416-929-2777
Fax 416-929-6783

Italian Government Tourist Board
1 Place Ville Marie, Suite 1914
Montreal, P.Q. H3B 3M9
Tel. 514-866-7667

Italian State Railroads. *See* CIT Tours

Latvian Embassy
112 Kont Street
Place de Ville, Tower B, Suite 208
Ottawa, Ont
Tel. 613-238-6868

Northern Ireland Tourist Board
2 Bloor Street, W., Suite 1501
Toronto, Ont M4W 3E2
Tel. 416-925-6368/800-576-8174
www.discovernorthernireland.com

Portuguese Trade and Tourism
    Commission
60 Bloor Street, W., Suite 1005
Toronto, Ont M4W 3B8
Tel. 416-921-7376
Fax 416-921-1353

Rail Europe
Tel. 800-361-RAIL

Spain, Tourist Office of
2 Bloor Street, W., Suite 3402
Toronto, Ont M6W 1A1
Tel. 416-961-3131
Fax 416-961-1992
www.okspain.org

Switzerland Tourism
926 The East Mall
Etobicoke, Toronto, Ont M9B 6K1
Tel. 011-800-100-200-30
(Mon.-Fri., 9 A.M. to 9 P.M. EST, international toll free)
www.myswitzerland.com

AUSTRALIA

Angas Travel
303 Angas Street
Adelaide South, SA 5000
Tel. 61 8 8223-1690
Fax 61 8 82244-0984

British Tourist Authority
Level 16, Gateway
1 Macquarie Place
Sydney, NSW 2000
Tel. 61 2 9377-4400
Fax 61 2 9377-4499
www.visitbritain.com/au

CIT World Travel
227 Collins Street
Level 4
Melbourne, VIC 3000
Tel. 61 3 9650-5510
Fax 61 3 9654-2490
www.cittravel.com.au

CIT World Travel
263 Clarence Street
Sydney, NSW 2000
Tel. 61 2 9267-1255
Fax 61 2 9261-4664
www.cittravel.com.au

Concorde International Travel
Level 9, 510 King Street
Melbourne, VIC 3000
Tel. 61 3 9920-3833
Fax 61 3 9920-3822
www.concorde.com.au

Dunsborough Travel
Shop 2, Naturalliste Forum
Dunsborough, WA 6281
Tel. 61 8 9755-3122
Fax 61 9 9756-8009

Eden Travel
Shop 626, Royal Arcade
255 Pitt Street
Sydney, NSW 2000
Tel. 61 2 9264-8302
Fax 61 2 9261-3274

Mid City Travel
Level 4, 541 George Street
Sydney, NSW 2000
Tel. 61 2 9283-5818
Fax 61 2 9284-5898

Plain Flying
495 Collins Street
Melbourne, VIC 3000
Tel. 61 3 9629-5302
Fax 61 3 9629-1047

Rail Plus
Level 3, 459 Little Collins Street
Melbourne, VIC 3000
Tel. 61 9 9642-8644
Fax 61 9 9642-8403
www.railplus.com.au

Raine Square Travel
Shop 30B, Raine Square
Perth, WA 6000
Tel. 61 8 9322-5155
Fax 61 8 9322-1310

Travel Talk
11 Blucher Avenue
The Gap, QLD 4061
Tel. 61 7 3300-6000
Fax 61 7 3300-4068
tvltalk@bigpond.net.au

World Wide Travel
15 Toorak Road
South Yarra, VIC 3181
Tel. 61 3 9510-6077
Fax 61 3 9510-6145

NEW ZEALAND

Gullivers Holidays Rep: Budget
   Travel
66 Wyndham Street, Fifth Floor
Auckland
Tel. 0800 80-84-80
budgettravel.co.nz

Gullivers Holidays Rep: Holiday
   Shoppe
66 Wyndham Street, Fifth Floor
Auckland
Tel. 0800 80-84-80
holidayshoppe.co.nz

Gullivers Holidays Rep: United
   Travel
66 Wyndham Street, Fifth Floor
Auckland
Tel. 0800 80-84-80
unitedtravel.co.nz

UNITED KINGDOM

Anglia Railways
Tel. 0870-040-9090
www.angliarailways.co.uk

Deutsche Bahn
Tel. 0870-243-5363
www.deutsche-bahn.co.uk

Eurostar
Tel. 0870-518-6186

Ffestiniog Travel
Portmadog, Gwynedd
Tel. 01766 512400

Rail Europe
178/9 Piccadilly
London WI
Tel. 08705-848-848

Stephen Walker Travel
Market Place, Boston, Lincs.
Tel. 1205-310-000

Switzerland Travel Center
10 Wardour Street
London W1D 6QF
www.sbb.ch

Trainseurope
4 Station Apporach
March, Cambs. PE15 8SJ
Tel. 0900-195-0101
www.trainseurope.co.uk

Appendix B

European Eurail Aid Offices

Austria
Innsbruck Hauptbahnhof
Sudtiroler Platz 7
Tel. (0512) 503-5460
Open Mon.-Sun. 6 A.M. to 9 P.M.

Salzburg Hauptbahnhof
Sudtiroler Platz 1
Tel. (0662) 8887-5428
Open Mon.-Sun. 8. A.M. to 8 P.M.

Vienna Westbahnhof
Europaplatz 1
Tel. (01) 93000-33594
Open Mon.-Fri. 9 A.M. to 4 P.M.

Belgium

Brussels South (Midi/Sud) Train
    Station
Travel Center/Service International
Tel. (02) 528 28 28
Open Mon.-Fri. 9 A.M. to 7:30 P.M.;
    Sat. 9 A.M. to 5 P.M.

Denmark

Copenhagen Central Station
DSB Travel Office
Tel. (033) 54 54 42
Open Mon.-Sun. 8 A.M. to 7 P.M.

Finland

Helsinki Central Train Station
Ticket Office/International Services
Tel. 030 723 706
Open Mon.-Fri. 8:30 A.M. to 5:15 P.M.;
    Sat.-Sun. 10 A.M. to 5:15 P.M.

France

Marseille St. Charles Train Station
Tel. (04) 95-04-14-03
Open Mon.-Sun. 6 A.M. to 10 P.M.

Nice Ville (SNCF) Train Station
Bureau Information/Reservation
Tel. (04) 92-14-82-65
Open Mon.-Sat. 8 to 11 A.M. and 2 to
   6:30 P.M.

Paris Charles de Gaulle Airport
   SNCF Station
Terminal 1—Arrivals Floor/Gate 22
Tel. (01) 4879-91184/6139
Open Mon.-Sun. 8 A.M. to 8 P.M.
Terminal 2
Tel. (01) 48-79-61-39
Open Mon.-Sun. 8 A.M. to 7 P.M.

Paris Lyon Station
International Window
Galerie des Fresques
Tel. (01) 53-33-11-67
Open Mon.-Fri. 6 A.M. to 10 P.M.

Paris Nord Station
Bureau Information
Espace Grandes Lignes
Tel. (01) 55-31-8739
Open Mon.-Sat. 9 A.M. to 8 P.M.

Paris Orly Airport SNCF Office
Tel. (01) 49-75-74-75
Open Mon.-Sat. 8 A.M. to 8 P.M.; Sun.
   9:45 A.M. to 1 P.M. and 2:45 to
   6:30 P.M.

Paris St. Lazare Station
Service International
Tel. (01) 53-42-27-62
Open Mon.-Fri. 10 A.M. to 7 P.M.; Sat.
   9:30 A.M. to noon and 1 to 6 P.M.

Germany

Berlin Zoo Train Station
EurAide Office
Down the hall from Western Union
Hardenburgplatz 11
Tel. (030) 2974-9277
Open Mon.-Sun. 4:45 A.M. to 11 P.M.

Cologne Hauptbahnhof
ReiseZentrum
Trankgasse 11
Tel. (0221)-141-2818
Open Mon.-Fri. 5:30 A.M. to 11 P.M.;
   Sat.-Sun. 5:30 A.M. to 10:30 P.M.

Dresden Hauptbahnhof
ReiseZentrum
Am Hauptbahnhof 4
Tel. (0351) 461-22780
Open Mon.-Sun. 7 A.M. to 10 P.M.

Frankfurt/Main Airport
ReiseZentrum
Hugo-Ecker-Ring
Tel. (069) 691-844
Open Mon.-Sun. 6 A.M. to 10:30 P.M.

Frankfurt/Main Hauptbahnhof
ReiseZentrum
Tel. (069) 265-34581
Open Mon.-Sun. 6 A.M. to 10:30 P.M.

Hamburg Hauptbahnhof
ReiseZentrum
Hochmannplatz 10
Tel. (040) 39-18-43-13
Open Mon.-Fri. 7:30 A.M. to 8 P.M.;
   Sat.-Sun. 10 A.M. to 1 P.M. and 2 to
   5 P.M.

Hanover Hauptbahnhof
ReiseZentrum
Tel. (0511) 286-5004
Open Mon.-Sun. 6 A.M. to 10 P.M.

Heidelberg Hauptbahnhof
ReiseZentrum
Tel. (06221) 525-341
Open Mon.-Fri. 5:45 A.M. to 8:45 P.M.;
   Sat.-Sun. 6:30 A.M. to 8:45 P.M.

Leipzig Hauptbahnhof
ReiseZentrum
Willy-Brandt-Platz 5
Tel. (0341) 968-11661
Open Mon.-Sun. 5:30 A.M. to 10 P.M.

Munich Airport Train Station
DB Counter
Open Mon.-Sun. 7:30 A.M. to 10 P.M.

Munich EurAide Office
Munich Hauptbahnhof
Along track 11, Room 2
Open May-Oct. Mon.-Fri. 7:30 A.M. to
noon and 1 to 5 P.M.; Nov.-Apr.
Mon.-Fri. 8 A.M. to noon and 1 to
4 P.M.

Munich Hauptbahnhof
ReiseZentrum, Windows 19/20
Bahnhofplatz 2
Tel. (089) 130-85-890
Open Mon.-Fri. 7 A.M. to 8 P.M.; Sat.-
Sun. 8 A.M. to 5 P.M.

Stuttgart Hauptbahnhof
ReiseZentrum/Bahn Touristik
Arnulf-Klett-Platz 2
Tel. (0711)-2092-3240
Open Mon.-Fri. 7:30 A.M. to 8 P.M.; Sat.
7:30 A.M. to 1:30 P.M.; Sun. closed

Great Britain

German Rail UK
18 Conduit Street
London
Tel. (0870) 243-5363
Open Mon.-Fri. 9 A.M. to 5 P.M.; Sat.
9:30 A.M. to 1 P.M.

Rail Europe Ltd.
10 Leake Street
London
Tel. (08705) 848-848
Open Mon.-Fri. 8 A.M. to 8 P.M.; Sat.
9 A.M. to 4 P.M.

Rail Europe Travel Shop
179 Picadilly
London
Tel. (08705) 848-848
Open Mon.-Fri. 10 A.M. to 6 P.M.; Sat.
10 A.M. to 5 P.M.

Greece

Athens Hellenic Railway Travel
Agency No. 2
Tel. (01) 529-7005

Patras Central Station
Tel. (061) 639-110
Open summer Mon.-Sun. 8 A.M. to 8
P.M.; winter 8 A.M. to 2 P.M.

Thessaloniki Central Station
Tel. (031) 599-033
Open Mon.-Sun. 5:30 A.M. to 1 P.M.
and 2 to 8 P.M.

Hungary

Menetjegyuiroda
(Customer Service Office)
Andrassy Ut 35
Budapest
Tel. (1) 322-9082
Open Apr.-Sept. Mon.-Fri. 9 A.M. to 6
P.M.; Oct.-Mar. Mon.-Fri. 9 A.M. to
5 P.M.

Ireland

Dublin International Rail
Travel Center
35 Lower Abbey Street
Tel. (01) 703-4127
Open Mon.-Fri. 9 A.M. to 5 P.M.

Italy

Bari Centrale Station
Ticket Office
Tel. (080) 573-2003/521-2202
Open Mon.-Sat. 9 A.M. to 1 P.M. and 4
to 8 P.M.

Florence Santa Maria Novella Station
Information Office
Tel. 284201-40
Open Mon.-Sat. 9 to 11 A.M.

Milan Centrale Station
Information Office
Tel. (02) 669-0351
Open Mon.-Sun. 7:30 A.M. to 9:40 P.M.

Naples Centrale Station
Information Office
Tel. (081) 567-4700
Open Mon.-Sun. 7 A.M. to 9 P.M.

Palermo Centrale Station
Information Office
Tel. (091) 603-3558
Open Mon.-Sun. 8 A.M. to 8 P.M.

Rome Fiumicino Airport
Tel. 06) 6501-1989

Rome Termini Station
Information Office
Tel. (06) 4730-6385
Open Mon.-Sun. 7 A.M. to 9 P.M.

Torino Porta Nuova Station
Tel. (011) 534-663

Venice Santa Lucia Station
Ticket Office
Tel. (041) 715-555
Open Mon.-Sun. 8 A.M. to 8 P.M.

Luxembourg

Luxembourg Train Station
Information and Sales Center
Tel. 4990 4990
Open Mon.-Fri. 8 A.M. to noon and 1
to 5 P.M.

Netherlands

Amsterdam Central Station
International Ticket Counter
Tel. 0900-9296
Open Mon.-Sun. 8 A.M. to 8 P.M.

Amsterdam Schiphol Airport
International Ticket Office
Schiphol Plaza
Tel. 0900-9296
Fax (020) 601-9424
Open Mon.-Sun. 8 A.M. to 9 P.M.

Rotterdam Central Station
International Ticket Office
Tel. 0900-9296
Open Mon.-Fri. 8 A.M. to 7 pm.

Utrecht Central Station
International Ticket Office
Tel. 0900-9296
Open Mon.-Fri. 8:30 A.M. to 9 P.M.

Norway

Oslo Sentral Station
International Ticket Office
Tel. 1 2 315-2448
Open Mon.-Sun. 7 A.M. to 11 P.M.

Portugal

Faro Train Station
Largo de estacao
Tel. (289) 801726
Open Mon.-Sun. 10 A.M. to 6 P.M.

Lisbon Santa Apolonia Station
International Ticket Office
Avenida Infante D. Henrique
Tel. (21) 881 6242
Open Mon.-Sun. 9 A.M. to 6 P.M.

Porto Sao Bento Station
Praca Almeida Garret
Tel. (22) 200 2723
Open Mon.-Sun. 6:30 A.M. to 4 P.M.
   (July-Aug. weekdays to 6 P.M.)

Spain

Barcelona Franca Train Station
Avda. Marques de Argentera s/n
Tel. (093) 496-3008
Open Mon.-Fri. 9 A.M. to 2 P.M. and 4
to 6:30 P.M.

Barcelona Sants Train Station
Tel. (093) 495-6236
Open Mon.-Sun. 9 A.M. to 8 P.M.

Madrid Bajaras Airport
RENFE office
Tel. (091)-305-8544
Open Mon.-Sun. 8 A.M. to 9 P.M.

Madrid Chamartin Station
Travel Office
Tel. (91) 300-6953
Open Mon.-Sun. 9 A.M. to 10 P.M.

Madrid RENFE Downtown Office
Alcala, 44
Tel. (091) 531-4707
Open Mon.-Sat. 9:30 A.M. to 8 P.M.

Seville Santa Justa Station
Tel. (95) 4485-635
Open Mon.-Fri. 9 A.M. to 1 P.M. and 4
to 7 P.M.; Sat. 9 A.M. to 12:30 P.M.

Valencia North Station
Tel. 96-3537-184

Sweden

Stockholm Central Station
Ticket Office
Tel. (08) 762-4858
Open Mon.-Fri. 8 A.M. to 6 P.M.; Sat.
9 A.M. to 5 P.M.; Sun. 9 A.M. to
4 P.M.

Switzerland

Basel SBB Station
Tel. (0512) 292-484
Open Mon.-Fri. 7 A.M. to 8 P.M.; Sat. 7
A.M. to 5 P.M.; Sun. 8 A.M. to 5 P.M.

Bern Main Train Station
Train Information Office
Tel. (0512) 201-451
Open Mon.-Fri. 8 A.M. to 7 P.M.; Sat.
8 A.M. to 5 P.M.

Geneva Airport Train Station
Train Information Office
Tel. (022) 7910-250
Open Mon.-Fri. 9:15 A.M. to 5:45 P.M.;
Sat. 9 A.M. to 5:45 P.M.

Geneva Train Station
Train Information Office
Tel. (0512) 251-410
Open Mon.-Fri. 8 A.M. to 7 P.M.; Sat.
9 A.M. to 5:30 P.M.

Interlaken West Train Station
Tel. (033) 826-4750
Open Mon.-Sun. 8 A.M. to noon and
2 to 6 P.M.

Lucerne Train Station
Train Travel Office
Tel. (0512) 271-350
Open Mon.-Fri. 8 A.M. to 7:45 P.M.;
Sat. 8 A.M. to 6 P.M.; Sun. 9 A.M. to
6 P.M.

Zurich Airport Train Station
Train Travel Center
Tel. (0512) 227-376
Open Mon.-Sun. 7 A.M. to 7 P.M.

Zurich Hauptbahnhof
Train Information Office
Tel. (0512) 223-364
Open Mon.-Fri. 6:45 A.M. to 8:30 P.M.;
Sat.-Sun. 6:45 A.M. to 7:30 P.M.

Index